VOLUNTARY EUTHANASIA
AND THE COMMON LAW

Voluntary Euthanasia and the Common Law

MARGARET OTLOWSKI

OXFORD
UNIVERSITY PRESS

This book has been printed digitally and produced in a standard specification
in order to ensure its continuing availability

OXFORD
UNIVERSITY PRESS

Great Clarendon Street, Oxford OX2 6DP

Oxford University Press is a department of the University of Oxford.
It furthers the University's objective of excellence in research, scholarship,
and education by publishing worldwide in

Oxford New York

Auckland Bangkok Buenos Aires Cape Town Chennai
Dar es Salaam Delhi Hong Kong Istanbul Karachi Kolkata
Kuala Lumpur Madrid Melbourne Mexico City Mumbai Nairobi
São Paulo Shanghai Taipei Tokyo Toronto

Oxford is a registered trade mark of Oxford University Press
in the UK and in certain other countries

Published in the United States
by Oxford University Press Inc., New York

© Margaret Otlowski 1997

The moral rights of the author have been asserted

Database right Oxford University Press (maker)

Reprinted 2004

ISBN 0-19-829868-4

Preface to the Paperback Edition

There have been quite a number of significant developments since the first publication of this work in 1997, including the demise of the Rights of the Terminally Ill Act 1995 which had been enacted in the Northern Territory of Australia. In the course of this work, detailed attention is given to this Act which represents the first occasion that a legislature, anywhere in the world, has passed a law legalizing active voluntary euthanasia and doctor-assisted suicide.[1] The Rights of the Terminally Ill Act was passed on 25 May 1995 and was due to come into force on 1 July 1996. However, within days of the Act's commencement, a case was brought in the Northern Territory Supreme Court by representatives from a coalition of doctors, churches and right to life groups (the 'Coalition Against Euthanasia'), challenging the validity of the legislation on the grounds that it was beyond the Northern Territory's legislative power. The matter was heard early in 1996 by the Full Court of the Supreme Court[2] and the court's decision was reserved. However, the Supreme Court refused an application for an injunction to prevent the legislation from commencing operation on 1 July 1996.

At about the same time, a member of the Federal Parliament of Australia, Liberal back-bencher Mr Kevin Andrews, announced his intention to introduce a Private Member's Bill to overturn the Northern Territory Rights of the Terminally Ill Act. By virtue of the Northern Territory's status as a Territory of Australia (as distinct from a State), this is constitutionally possible as the Federal Parliament has the power, pursuant to s 122 of the Commonwealth Constitution of Australia 1900, to make laws in respect of the Territories.[3]

In late July 1996, the Supreme Court of the Northern Territory handed

---

[1] An Act legalizing doctor-assisted suicide had been passed in the State of Oregon in the US in November 1994 by means of citizen initiated referendum, however, the commencement of this legislation had for some time been held in abeyance as a result of a constitutional challenge to its validity. The Oregon Death with Dignity Act finally commenced operation on 27 October 1997. This development is discussed in more detail below.

[2] Chief Justice Martin of the Supreme Court had referred the matter to the Full Court pursuant to s 21 of the Supreme Court Act 1979 (NT) on the grounds that any decision given by a single judge would inevitably be appealed to the Full Court.

[3] It should be noted that the Commonwealth Parliament would have no clear power to intervene if such legislation were to be enacted by one of the Australian States: the only potential basis for intervention would be in reliance upon the external affairs power in section 51(xxix) of the Constitution of Australia 1900 (Cth) and would involve reading into the phrase a 'right to life' which appears in various international human rights instruments, a 'right' not to be killed, even at one's request—an interpretation which would be debatable, to say the least. The implications of international human rights instruments are discussed in more detail in the body of this work.

down its decision in the case of *Wake and Gondarra v Northern Territory of Australia and Others*, rejecting the challenge to the legislation by a majority of 2: 1.[4] The main argument before the court concerned the recognition of an inalienable right to life as a principle or value underlying the common law—the plaintiffs relying on this proposition to substantiate their assertion that the Act was *ultra vires* the Northern Territory Legislative Assembly. The majority, comprising Chief Justice Martin and Justice Mildren, rejected the plaintiffs' assertion that the 'right to life' is a right 'deeply rooted in our democratic system of government and the common law' such that it places constraints on the exercise of legislative power. Whilst noting that the High Court in the case of *Union Steamship Co of Australia Pty Ltd v The King*[5] had raised the question of whether the exercise of legislative powers may be subject to some constraints by reference to 'rights deeply rooted in our domestic system of government and the common law', Martin CJ and Mildren J were of the view that in the absence of authoritative guidance from the High Court on this issue, no such constraint could be implied. Without deciding whether 'deeply rooted' rights are the same as 'fundamental rights', they also drew attention to established High Court authority which allows the abrogation by a State Parliament of fundamental rights, freedoms and immunities, provided that the intention of the parliament is clearly manifested by unmistakable and unambiguous language.[6] Their Honours found it unnecessary to decide whether the Rights of the Terminally Ill Act 1995 (NT) infringes any fundamental right, although they indicated their view that the true nature of this question is ethical, moral or political, rather than legal. They went on to hold that in so far as the Act affects any abrogation of fundamental rights, its language is clear and unambiguous, and they saw no basis for differentiating between the powers of a State Parliament to abrogate such rights and the powers of a Legislative Assembly (i.e. a Territory) to do so.

The plaintiffs' second ground for challenging that the Administrator could not validly assent to the Act, was also dismissed. In particular, the majority of the court rejected the assertion that the Act did not come within any of the matters specified in the Regulations made under the Northern Territory (Self Government) Act 1978 as matters over which Ministers were to have executive authority. In their joint judgment, Martin CJ and Mildren J indicated their view that the Act relates to a number of matters in reg. 4(1) of the Self Government Regulations, namely, 'maintenance of law and order and the administration of justice', 'private law' and the 'regulation of businesses and professions,' and they disputed the plaintiffs' assertion that various heads of executive authority set out in this regulation

---

[4] (1996) 124 FLR 298; (1996) 109 NTR 1.   [5] (1988–89) 166 CLR 1 at 10.
[6] *Coco v The Queen* (1993–94) 179 CLR 427 at 437.

should be given a narrow meaning. In their Honours' opinion, the Act has a substantial connection with the relevant heads of power and the law was, accordingly, validly assented to by the Administrator.

In his dissenting judgment, Justice Angel upheld the argument that assent of the Administrator was not effectual and that, therefore, the Act had not been lawfully assented to and had not passed into law. This conclusion was based on his view that reg. 4 of the Self Government Regulations gave no warrant to the legislative establishment of institutional termination of human life other than as punishment. Having upheld the plaintiffs' argument on this ground, it was unnecessary for Angel J to decide whether the Act was *ultra vires* the legislative power of the Northern Territory. His Honour did, nevertheless, go on to express some comments on what he described as the far-reaching and complex nature of the questions raised by the plaintiffs' submission. He expressed the view that in addressing the legal question, one cannot ignore the philosophical questions involved, both moral and political, and the values at stake. In clear disagreement with the majority, he went on to state that the plaintiffs' submission involves much deeper and broader questions than whether parliament by clear words can abrogate a 'fundamental right', in particular, resolution of the question raised in *Union Steamship Co of Australia Pty Ltd v The King* as to what constraints may exist on the sovereignty of parliament.

An application for special leave to appeal the majority's decision subsequently came before the High Court, but the Court declined to hear the application on the grounds that the matter was at that stage before the Commonwealth Parliament.[7]

In September 1996 Mr Kevin Andrews introduced his Private Member's Bill, the Euthanasia Laws Bill 1996 (Cth), to override the Northern Territory legislation. This Bill sought to amend the grant of legislative power given by the Commonwealth to the Australian Territories under the Self-Government Acts[8] by stating that 'the Legislative Assemblies in the Territories do not have the power to make laws permitting or having the effect of permitting (whether subject to conditions or not) the form of intentional killing of another called euthanasia (which includes mercy killing) or the assisting of a person to terminate his or her life.' With particular reference to the Northern Territory, the Bill went on to state that for the avoidance of doubt, the enactment of the Legislative Assembly called the Rights of the Terminally Ill Act 1995 has no force or effect as a law of the Territory. It did, however, go on to make clear that the Euthanasia Laws Bill would not operate retrospectively: i.e. it would not affect the lawfulness or validity of

---

[7] *Wake v Northern Territory*, High Court of Australia No D10 of 1996, transcript of proceedings, 15 November 1996.

[8] Northern Territory (Self-Government) Act 1978 and the Australian Capital Territory (Self-Government) Act 1988.

anything done in accordance with the Rights of the Terminally Ill Act 1995 prior to its commencement. Further, the Bill proposed the inclusion of additional provisions in the Self-Government Acts making it clear that the Legislative Assemblies in the Territories do have the power to make laws with respect to the withdrawal or withholding of medical or surgical measures for prolonging the life of a patient and with regard to medical treatment in the provision of palliative care to a dying patient, but not so as to permit the intentional killing of the patient. This proposal gave rise to concerns about the implications of the legislation upon other medical laws, in particular, certain statutory protections conferred on doctors under the Northern Territory's Natural Death Act 1988.[9]

The Euthanasia Laws Bill 1996 had the support of the Prime Minister, John Howard, the then Deputy Prime Minister, Tim Fisher and the Leader of the Opposition, Kim Beazley. The Bill was debated on non-party lines and passed by the House of Representatives (88 votes to 35) in the first major conscience vote in the Australian Federal Parliament for more than a decade.

From the outset, it had been anticipated that the Bill's passage through the Senate (the 'States House'[10]) would be more difficult. The Bill had been considered by the Senate Scrutiny of Bills Committee which had found that it may infringe the Northern Territory's right of self government.[11] The Bill was subsequently referred by the Senate to the Legal and Constitutional Legislation Committee for inquiry and report. In particular, the committee was asked to provide advice to the Senate in relation to the desirability of the enactment of the provisions; the constitutional implications for the Territories of the enactment of the provisions, the impact of the enactment of the provisions on the Northern Territory Criminal Code and the impact on, and attitudes of, the Aboriginal community.[12] In its report to the Senate,[13] the Legal and Constitutional Legislation Committee expressed the view that the Commonwealth Parliament had the power to pass the Bill

---

[9] *The Weekend Australian* 28–29 Sept. 1996.

[10] Under s 7 of the Constitution of Australia 1900 (Cth), the Senate, which was intended to represent the interests of the various States, is composed of Senators for each State (which, since 1975, includes also Senators for the Territories) with each State to have equal representation, but not less than six Senators.

[11] Senate Standing Committee for the Scrutiny of Bills, *Alert Digest*, No 7/96, 18 September 1996.

[12] For many traditional aboriginal communities, voluntary euthanasia constitutes sorcery and is contrary to customary law. The concern was raised that widespread fear of these legislative developments amongst the large aboriginal community in the Northern Territory may result in a reluctance on the part of aborigines to see doctors or attend hospitals and may thereby exacerbate existing difficulties in providing adequate health care for aboriginal communities: *The Australian* 1 July 1996.

[13] Senate Legal and Constitutional Legislation Committee, *Consideration of Legislation Referred to the Committee: Euthanasia Laws Bill 1996*, March 1997.

under s 122 of the Constitution. On the issue of whether it was appropriate for the Commonwealth Parliament to pass the Bill, the committee chose to make no recommendation because of the private member status of the Bill and the fact that it was to be subject to a conscience vote. However, included with the report were comments and statements from members of the committee, setting out their views on whether or not the Senate should pass the Bill. In one such document entitled 'Advice to the Senate', a majority of the members of the committee endorsed the enactment of the Euthanasia Laws Bill 1996 advising that there would be no constitutional implications for the Territories and no adverse impact on the provisions of the Northern Territory Criminal Code. Further, the Committee supported passage of the legislation on the grounds that it would, by overriding the Rights of the Terminally Ill Act 1995, relieve the Aboriginal community of its overwhelming and deeply felt concern about this Act.

Much was made in the report and the associated public debate of the unprecedented number of submissions received by the committee, the over-whelming majority of which had supported the Bill and/or were opposed to euthanasia.[14] However, in view of the strong support for voluntary euthana-sia as reflected in public opinion polls, this was seen by many as evidence of a well organized campaign of opposition to the legislation waged by reli-gious and right to life organizations rather than a true reflection of the views of the public as a whole.

It should be noted that aside from the question of the merits of a volun-tary euthanasia law, there were other matters at issue, including the right of the Northern Territory to enact its own laws without Commonwealth intervention.[15] At a meeting in late September 1996, the leaders of the Australian State and Territories unanimously declared their opposition to the Andrews Bill on 'States' rights' grounds, (here used to encompass also the Territories) without debating the issue of voluntary euthanasia itself. There was also considerable criticism of the process of the Bill's passage, which had proceeded with almost indecent haste and with unprecedented government backing, especially having regard to its status as a Private Member's Bill.[16] Notwithstanding considerable support for the Rights of

---

[14] A total of 12,577 submissions were received, statistical analysis of which appears in Appendix 1 of the Committee Report. According to this information 93.3% of those who made submission to the Committee were for the Bill and/or opposed to euthanasia; 6.4% were against the Bill and/or in favour of euthanasia and 0.3% undecided.

[15] *Weekend Australian* 29–30 June 1996.

[16] One move which attracted particular criticism was the transfer of the debate from the main chamber of the Commonwealth Parliament into the main committee usually reserved for non-controversial matters. This was, ostensibly, to ensure that the debate on the Bill did not interfere with the government's legislative program, but critics of the move claimed that it was a deliberate misuse of the main committee aimed at minimizing the political exposure of an issue that was causing deep divisions in the government.

the Terminally Ill Act 1995 (NT) and the Northern Territory's right to enact this legislation, on 25 March 1997 the Senate voted to pass the Euthanasia Laws Bill 1996 (Cth), albeit only by a narrow margin (38 votes to 33). Following its passage, an appeal was made to the Governor General on behalf of two patients who had fulfilled the requirements under the Rights of the Terminally Ill Act 1995 (NT) to delay formal assent to the legislation in the hope that these patients could still avail themselves of legalized euthanasia without undue time pressure. However, this request was declined and the Governor General's assent was given on 27 March 1997.

The effect of the Euthanasia Laws Act 1997 (Cth) is to overturn the Rights of the Terminally Ill Act 1995 (NT), rendering it inoperative. Notably, however, the Rights of the Terminally Ill Act has not been repealed by the Northern Territory Legislative Assembly.[17] Although now defunct, this legislation represented a significant milestone in the history of voluntary euthanasia reform and remains a useful model for consideration when contemplating law reform in this area. Regrettably, the short period of operation of the Rights of the Terminally Ill Act 1995 (NT) does not permit meaningful evaluation of its effectiveness in practice. Although active voluntary euthanasia and doctor-assisted suicide were technically legal in the Northern Territory from 1 July 1996 to 27 March 1997, from the time the Act came into force it was under legal challenge. Because of speculation about possible retrospective invalidity of the Rights of the Terminally Ill Act, as a result of either the courts striking down the legislation, or the federal parliament overriding it with retrospective effect,[18] doctors in the Northern Territory had been warned by the Territory's Chief Medical Officer not to assist patients to die in reliance on the Rights of the Terminally Ill Act 1995 (NT) because the Act might be later found to be invalid. This undoubtedly deterred some doctors from providing assistance under the Act as was highlighted by the case of Max Bell, a terminally ill 66-year-old man, whose wish to make use of the legislation was thwarted because of the unwillingness of doctors to become involved. Bell had travelled to the Northern Territory to seek active voluntary euthanasia.

---

[17] In the wake of the Euthanasia Laws Act 1997 (Cth) there had been speculation that the Rights of the Terminally Ill Act 1995 (NT) could be reactivated in the event that the Northern Territory of Australia achieved unconditional Statehood. However, this has since been put to rest, at least for the time being, in view of the rejection of statehood by Northern Territory residents at the referendum held on 3 October 1998.

[18] When the architect of the repeal Bill, Mr Kevin Andrews, first announced his proposal, he indicated his intention to frame the legislation in such a way that it would have retrospective effect, rendering the legislation invalid from its commencement: *The Weekend Australian* 29–30 June 1996. This announcement was apparently made with the aim of putting doctors in the Northern Territory on notice of potential criminal liability if they were to assist patients to die under the Act, in the hope of dissuading doctors from using the legislation. However, as noted above, the Bill which was subsequently passed specified that it does not have retrospective effect.

Although he had found a doctor who was willing to assist him to die, the requirements under the Act with regard to the involvement of specialists could not be fulfilled due to the specialists' concerns about possible criminal charges resulting in the event that the legislation was subsequently struck down.[19] Viewed in this light, the legal uncertainties surrounding the Act during its period of operation from 1 July 1996 to 27 March 1997 undoubtedly interfered with the effectiveness of the legislation and the willingness of doctors to perform active voluntary euthanasia or assisted suicide under its provisions. Notwithstanding these constraints, seven patients made formal use of the Rights of the Terminally Ill Act 1995 (NT) four of which died under the Act.[20]

Whilst these developments in the Commonwealth Parliament of Australia invalidating the legislative authority of the Northern Territory Assembly to legislate on the matter came as a great disappointment to proponents of voluntary euthanasia reform, and were subject to sustained criticism also on constitutional grounds,[21] it is not surprising, in all the circumstances, that this legislation has attracted fierce opposition from some quarters. Active voluntary euthanasia is by its nature a controversial and potentially divisive issue, and has traditionally met with opposition from the churches and the medical profession. It is no coincidence that those spearheading the challenge to the legislation included Dr Christopher Wake, President of the Northern Territory branch of the Australian Medical Association, and Mr Kevin Andrews, member of the socially conservative and religiously zealous Lyons Forum (the so called 'God Squad'),[22] and that their cause received financial support from the churches.[23]

Aside from these dramatic Australian developments regarding the overturning of the Northern Territory Rights of the Rights of the Terminally Ill Act 1995, there have also been a number of other noteworthy developments internationally. Significantly, a number of these developments are of particular relevance to the so called 'slippery slope' argument which has featured so prominently in the euthanasia debate. At the time of writing this

---

[19] *The Australian* 5 July 1996.

[20] Kissane, D., Street, A. and Nitschke, P., 'Seven Deaths in Darwin: Case Studies under the Rights of the Terminally Ill Act, Northern Territory, Australia' (1998) 352 *The Lancet* 1097. As noted at 1098 of this article, two of the seven patients had sought euthanasia but had died before the Act became law and one patient had died after the legislation was invalidated by the Euthanasia Laws Act 1997 (Cth).

[21] See for example, Williams, G. and Darke, M., 'Euthanasia Laws and the Australian Constitution' (1997) 20 *University of New South Wales Law Journal* 647. One of the concerns raised is that by expressly removing from the Territories the power to allow the intentional killing of a patient, the Euthanasia Laws Act 1997 (Cth) may have removed legal protection that doctors in the Northern Territory have had the benefit of under the Natural Death Act 1988 (NT) in circumstances where they increase doses of pain-relieving drugs, knowing that their action may hasten death.

[22] *The Australian Financial Review* 16 Sept. 1996.   [23] *The Australian* 4 July 1996.

book, I deliberately avoided overstating the advantages of legalization and duly acknowledged that there are risks involved. The thrust of this work was to argue that there are powerful reasons why the law must be reformed, including arguments based on autonomy and self-determination of patients as well as the protection and support of the medical profession. It is true to say that it was not an argument principally premised on the need for legalization of active voluntary euthanasia as a means of minimizing the risk of abuse as there was no firm evidence at the time, empirical or otherwise, on which such a claim could justifiably be made. The book does, however, make the claim that there is no evidence to indicate that legalization would *increase* the incidence of unacceptable conduct, and suggests that there are good grounds for believing that the risk of abuse would in fact be reduced.

Notably, in the years since first publication, evidence has been mounting to support the view that legalization of active voluntary euthanasia would probably diminish the risk of abuse. This view finds support in the outcomes of two comparable studies which were carried out in the Netherlands and Australia which permit some empirical evaluation of the 'slippery slope' argument. On the strength of the 'slippery slope' reasoning, one would expect that a country with a policy of legalization (or quasi legalization as is the case in the Netherlands) would have a higher incidence of non-voluntary euthanasia as compared with a country such as Australia where active voluntary euthanasia remains illegal. However, analysis of the surveys from these respective jurisdictions suggests that the reverse is in fact the case.

On the basis of a major Dutch study undertaken in 1995 as a follow-up to the 1990 Remmelink study (which is discussed in this work) it seems that there has been no increase in the percentage of cases in which life was ended without the patient's explicit and concurrent request (the study found a statistically non-significant decline from 0.8% in 1990 to 0.7% of all deaths in 1995).[24] This was consistent with expectations of commentators in the Netherlands expressed in the wake of the earlier study, that the figure would decrease because of the growing openness with which end-of-life decisions are discussed with patients.[25] Moreover, this 1995 study found no evidence of a diminution of standards in the practice of active voluntary euthanasia or of decline in the severity of illnesses for which euthanasia was performed.[26] Indeed, the evidence is to the contrary—that there is more

[24] van der Maas, P., *et al.*, 'Euthanasia, Physician Assisted Suicide and Other Medical Practices Involving the End of Life in the Netherlands, 1990–1995' (1996) 335 *New England Journal of Medicine* 1699. As noted by the study authors (at 1707), in the Netherlands, the term euthanasia is not used for these cases.

[25] Pijnenborg, L., *et al.*, 'Life Terminating Acts Without Explicit Request of Patient' (1993) 341 *The Lancet* 1198–1199.

[26] van der Maas, P., *et al.*, 'Euthanasia, Physician Assisted Suicide and Other Medical Practices Involving the End of Life in the Netherlands, 1990–1995' (above) at 1705.

frequent and open consultation between doctors and patients, improved recording of the process and much more regular notification of deaths from euthanasia to the authorities (an increase from 18% in 1990 to 41% in 1995). Further, whilst there had been some increase in the incidence of voluntary euthanasia, a number of factors have been put forward to explain this trend, including increased mortality rates as a consequence of the ageing of the population; an increase in the proportion of deaths from cancer; and the increasing availability of life-prolonging techniques. This study found that a large majority of Dutch physicians consider euthanasia an exceptional but accepted part of medical practice in the Netherlands. As a leading group of Dutch researchers have observed in the light of the 1995 study, there is simply no empirical basis for the assertion that the Dutch have already slid down the slippery slope because there is no evidence that they have moved at all in the direction of unacceptable practices (let alone, that the policy of quasi-legalization of euthanasia was responsible for the slide).[27]

The outcomes of the Dutch research are usefully compared with the results of empirical research in Australia based on the Remmelink study.[28] The Australian study, involving a sample of 3,000 doctors from all Australian States and Territories, revealed a much higher incidence in Australia of unrequested active euthanasia than for active voluntary euthanasia (3.5% of all deaths compared with 1.8% for active voluntary euthanasia) and far in excess of the figure for the same category in the Netherlands (0.7% according to the 1995 study).[29] This appears to be largely

[27] Griffiths, J., Bood, A. and Weyers, H., *Euthanasia and Law in the Netherlands* (1998) Amsterdam University Press, 301–2. It should be noted that the research into the Dutch position is ongoing—a major collaborative research program led by Professor John Griffiths of the Faculty of Law at the University of Groningen and funded, in part, by the Dutch National Science Foundation is underway involving an interdisciplinary and comparative study of questions concerning the regulation of medical behaviour that potentially shortens life including euthanasia and assisted suicide.

[28] Kuhse, H., *et al.*, 'End of Life Decisions in Australian Medical Practice' (1997) 166 *Medical Journal of Australia* 191.

[29] Also of relevance in this regard is the recent data emerging from Belgium (where euthanasia remains a criminal offence) indicating a higher incidence of unrequested termination of life than voluntary euthanasia: according to the findings of empirical research led by Professor Luc Deliens which has investigated end-of-life decisions in Belgium, the incidence of euthanasia in Belgium is comparable with the Netherlands (of a total of 56,000 deaths, there were 600 cases of euthanasia and less than 100 cases of assisted suicide) but there is a significantly higher rate of termination without a request (1000 cases): *De Standaard* 24 January 2000, reporting on research data in respect of Flanders (the Dutch speaking part of Belgium). The Belgian position, and recent moves in that jurisdiction to introduce legislative reform, are discussed further below.

Note also the outcomes of a national study undertaken in the United States in relation to the practices of specialist physicians with regard to physician-assisted suicide and euthanasia which found that more than half (54%) of patients receiving a lethal injection did not make the request themselves: Meir, D., *et al.*, 'A National Survey of Physician-Assisted Suicide and Euthanasia in the United States' (1998) 338 *New England Journal of Medicine* 1193.

attributable to the illegality of the practice and the lack of openness on the issue with the consequence that doctors are often taking this decision upon themselves.[30]

Comparison of these major studies undertaken in the Netherlands and Australia indicates that the practice of bringing about death without explicit request is much more widespread in Australia—a country where the practice of active voluntary euthanasia is prohibited—than it is in the Netherlands where the practice has been quasi-legalized and regulated.[31] The substantially higher incidence of non-requested euthanasia in Australia strongly suggests that there are greater risks inherent in the current laws which hold active euthanasia to be illegal, but which are in practice flouted, than exist when genuine attempts are made to control and regulate the practice as has occurred in the Netherlands. As a number of leading Dutch commentators have pointed out, it is a mistake to assume that criminal prohibition entails effective legal control: indeed, the Dutch experience has shown the reverse to be true—by easing the criminal law prohibition (or at least its enforcement in practice), they have achieved more effective legal control over the practice of euthanasia.[32] Not only do the survey results tend to refute claims of a slippery slope, they provide validation for the view that legalization and regulation of active voluntary euthanasia would be likely to *reduce* the risks of abuse and ultimately protect the interests of patients.[33] This body of evidence certainly bears out the more qualified claims I have made in this book and adds cogent support to what is submitted already to be a compelling case for reform.

Significantly, in the Netherlands the ambivalent legal status of active voluntary euthanasia (technically an offence but not prosecuted in practice if strict guidelines have been adhered to) is widely regarded as the main impediment to achieving complete openness: although rates of reporting have increased significantly in recent years, many doctors are still unwilling

[30] This accords also with the view of the study authors: Kuhse, H., *et al.*, 'End of Life Decisions in Australian Medical Practice' (above) at 196. The Australian study also found a significantly higher incidence of withdrawing or withholding of treatment without the patient's explicit request with the explicit intention of ending life than in the Netherlands: 22.5% of all Australian deaths compared with 5.3% in the Netherlands based on the 1991 study. (There was no comparable figure from the 1995 Dutch study but the 1995 figure for *all* decisions to forgo treatment with an explicit intention of hastening death or not prolonging life in the Netherlands was 13.3%.) See Kuhse, H., *et al.*, 'End of Life Decisions in Australian Medical Practice' (above) at 195.

[31] This also holds true for Belgium in the light of the research emanating from that jurisdiction—see the n. 29 above.

[32] Griffiths, J., Bood, A. and Weyers, H., *Euthanasia and Law in the Netherlands* (above) 302.

[33] See also Ryan, C., 'Pulling Up the Runaway: The Effect of New Evidence of Euthanasia's Slippery Slope' (1998) 24 *Journal of Medical Ethics* 341 and Oddie, G., 'The Moral Case for the Legalisation of Voluntary Euthanasia' (1998) 28 *Victoria University of Wellington Law Review* 207.

to act openly and to report cases through the official channels whilst the practice remains illegal.[34] Legislation has recently been introduced into the Dutch Parliament to give clearer statutory protection to doctors adhering to the established guidelines.[35] Pursuant to this proposal, the provisions in the Penal Code relating to these practices (Articles 293 and 294 respectively) will not apply to doctors who satisfy the carefulness requirements and fulfil the duty to report. Importantly, the Bill proposes changes to the reporting procedures, making reporting euthanasia mandatory (at present it is only an offence to report it as a 'natural death') and it gives the regional assessment committees a formal legislative basis so that prosecution would only be possible if a committee so recommends.

Also of international significance are the developments presently underway in Belgium. In the wake of a long term investigation into all aspects of end-of-life decision-making by the Belgian Advisory Committee on Bioethics in 1997,[36] which had supported active euthanasia under certain circumstances, the representatives of the political parties represented in the new Coalition Government (July 1999) comprising Liberals, Socialists and Greens, introduced a number of legislative proposals for the legalization of euthanasia. The Christian Democrats, in opposition for the first time since the war, although supportive of legalization under certain conditions[37] are opposed to the proposed legislation which seeks to effect legalization through changes to the Criminal Code. They are critical of the liberal content of the proposed reforms and also of the Coalition's handling of this reform initiative, claiming amongst other things, that there was

[34] It should be noted that since 1 November 1998, a new notification procedure has been in force pursuant to which much of the assessment of cases is done outside of the legal system: 5 regional multidisciplinary committees (each composed of a doctor, a jurist and an ethicist) make a preliminary judgement in relation to cases of voluntary euthanasia and assisted suicide and report to the Committee of Procurators-General (end-of-life decisions without a specific request are still assessed directly by the Committee of Procurators-General). The Committee of Procurators-General decides in both cases whether or not to institute criminal proceedings, subject to the approval of the Minister of Justice.

The first annual report of the assessment committees (covering the period 1 November 1998–1 January 2000) indicates, according to reports in the press, that of some 2565 cases of euthanasia and assisted suicide reported by doctors, none was recommended for prosecution; in almost all cases the Committee of Procurators-General has accepted the recommendation, and in 3 cases no final decision has yet been made. (See Trouw, 10 May 2000; NRC HANDELSBLAD, 9 May 2000.)

[35] Second Chamber of Parliament 1998–1999, 26691.

[36] Advies nr. 1, d.d. 12 mei 1997, betreffende de wenselijkheid van een wettelijke regeling van euthanasie. (Advise on the desirability of the legalization of euthanasia). For discussion see Nys, H. 'Advice of the Federal Advisory Committee on Bioethics Concerning Legalisation of Euthanasia' (1997) 4 *European Journal of Health Law* 389 and Schotsmans, P., 'Debating Euthanasia in Belgium' (1997) *Hastings Center Report*, Sep–Oct, 46. Note also Advies nr. 9, d.d. 22 februari 1999, betreffende het levensbeëindigend handelen bij wilsonbekwamen. (Advise on ending of life of incompetent patients.)

[37] The two Christian-Democrat parties have each introduced their own legislative proposals for legalization of euthanasia.

insufficient debate before the proposal was put forward. Belgian doctors are also reported to have been angered by the lack of proper consultation.[38]

At the time of writing, there were a number of different proposals on euthanasia in discussion before the Senate, the most important of which is a proposal introduced on 20 December 1999 signed by six members of parliament of the majority parties which combines a number of the earlier legislative proposals.[39] This latter proposal is reported to be very liberal, allowing euthanasia not only for adults with an incurable illness causing them unbearable and constant suffering (physical or mental) and who are of sound mind and have clearly asked to die, but also for anyone in a coma with no prospect of recovering consciousness and who had requested, before two witnesses, to have their life ended in such circumstances within the previous five years.

At the same time as the proposal of the majority parties was introduced, two bills were introduced for a package of reforms covering euthanasia, palliative care and the establishment of a national evaluation committee for the new euthanasia law. The Commission of the Senate has sought advice from experts in relation to the appropriate direction of the reforms. At this stage, there is a real possibility that the legislative proposals for the legalization of euthanasia may be debated and passed, probably with some changes, by the Senate later this parliamentary year.[40] However, it would still then need to go before the Chamber of Deputies (the lower house of parliament) so inevitably it will still be some time before a Belgian euthanasia law might be accepted and implemented.[41] Passage of this legislation would be very significant as there are presently no other jurisdictions which have legalized euthanasia.[42] The precise content of such legislation is uncertain at this stage but given the range of proposals being considered, it could, potentially, be significantly more liberal than the position in the Netherlands.

Turning to the United States, whilst two important cases have recently come before the United States Supreme Court, the potential for a constitutionally protected right to assisted suicide has not materialized. At the time

[38] Sheldon, T., 'Belgium Considers Legalising Euthanasia' (2000) 320 *British Medical Journal* 137.

[39] Proposal nr.2-244/1 of the Belgian Senate 1999–2000, Law Proposal on Euthanasia, by Mr. Philippe Mahoux, Mrs. Jeannine Leduc, Mr. Philippe Monfils, Mrs. Myriam Vanlerberghe, Mrs. Marie Nagy and Mrs. Jacinta De Roeck.

[40] The Belgian Parliamentary year runs till July 2000.

[41] The timing will depend on whether the Chamber of Deputies accepts the proposal or not. If it accepts the proposal, the legislation may be in place by the end of the year. If, however, the Chamber of Deputies proposes amendments to the Bill, those amendments will have to be debated and approved by the Senate which will delay passage of the legislation.

[42] As explained above, the Northern Territory Rights of the Terminally Ill Act 1995, which had legalized active voluntary euthanasia, has been overturned by the Euthanasia Law Act 1997 (Cth). There is currently also a Dutch proposal for legalization of active voluntary euthanasia, discussed above.

the original manuscript was being finalized, groundbreaking decisions were handed down by the Ninth Circuit Court in Washington and the Second Circuit Court in New York in the cases of *Compassion in Dying v State of Washington*[43] and *Quill v Vacco*[44] respectively, in relation to a constitutionally recognized right to assisted suicide for competent terminally ill patients. In each of these cases, although relying on different grounds, the two respective Federal Courts had struck down as invalid State legislation prohibiting assistance in suicide in so far that it applied to physicians complying with requests for suicide assistance from terminally ill competent patients. (Both of these cases are discussed in some detail in this work.) Appeals were subsequently lodged with the United States Supreme Court and by the time that the original Preface for the book was being finalized (November 1996) it had recently been announced that the Supreme Court had decided to accept review in respect of both cases.

On 26 June 1997, the Supreme Court handed down its long-awaited decisions in respect of the two cases, unanimously ruling that there is no constitutionally protected right to assisted suicide.[45] The prohibition on assisted suicide in the legislation of the States of New York and Washington was accordingly upheld. The Supreme Court rejected the Due Process argument that had been central to the decision of the Ninth Circuit Court as well as the Equal Protection argument upon which the Second Circuit Court had based its decision. Judgment for the Supreme Court was delivered by Chief Justice Rehnquist with whom Justices O'Connor, Scalia, Kennedy and Thomas expressly concurred. Justices Breyer, Ginsburg, Stevens and Souter gave separate concurring opinions.

With regard to the Due Process argument, the liberty interest at issue before the court was broadly framed: whether there is a right to commit suicide which itself includes a right to assistance in doing so. Moreover, the court made clear its position that the Fourteenth Amendment would only be construed as encompassing fundamental rights and liberties that are deeply rooted in the Nation's history and tradition. In the earlier case of *Cruzan*[46] the Supreme Court had been prepared to assume that the right to liberty guaranteed by the US Constitution includes the right to refuse medical treatment. On this occasion, however, when expressly called upon to consider whether a constitutionally protected right to assisted suicide exists, at least for competent, terminally ill patients, the Supreme Court sought to distinguish the protection of the right to refuse life-sustaining

---

[43] No. 94-35534 (9th Cir. March 6 1996 *en banc*).   [44] No. 60 (2nd Cir. April 2 1996).

[45] *Washington v Glucksberg* 96-110 US (1997); *Vacco v Quill* 95-1858 US (1997). For useful analysis of these cases see Pratt, C., 'Efforts to Legalize Physician-Assisted Suicide in New York, Washington and Oregon: A Contrast Between Judicial and Initiative Approaches—Who Should Decide?' (1998) 77 *Oregon Law Review* 1027, at 1043–1080.

[46] 760 SW2d 408 (1988).

treatment from assisted suicide which their Honours held has never enjoyed similar legal protection. Indeed, the court found that the practice has been consistently disapproved for over 700 years by the Anglo-American common law tradition. It was accordingly held that the asserted right was not fundamental which meant that the court only had to be satisfied on the rational basis standard, that the Washington statute banning assisted suicide served legitimate government interests.[47] This was easily established on the grounds that the Washington law was related to a number of State interests that were unquestionably important and legitimate: the State's interests in the preservation of human life, prevention of suicide, protecting the integrity and ethics of the medical profession, protecting vulnerable groups from being pressured to seek physician-assisted suicide and avoiding the slide down the slippery slope to voluntary and perhaps even involuntary euthanasia.

In the appeal from *Quill v Vacco*, the Equal Protection argument was almost summarily dismissed, Chief Justice Rehnquist apparently doubting that the Equal Protection Clause of the Constitution was seriously at issue in this case. It was concluded that New York's laws which ban assisted suicide yet allow withdrawal of life-saving treatment did not infringe fundamental rights nor involve suspect classifications. Rehnquist CJ highlighted the factual neutrality of the laws to support the conclusion that the statutes do not violate the Equal Protection Clause: 'everyone, regardless of physical condition, is entitled, if competent, to refuse unwanted life-saving medical treatment; no one is permitted to assist a suicide'. Further, it was held that the distinctions drawn by the statute between withdrawing of life-sustaining treatment which was permitted, and the act of assisting suicide which was prohibited, were rationally related to legitimate State interests (the same interests that were upheld in the *Washington v Gluckberg* case).

Undoubtedly, those who had been hopeful of a legal breakthrough on the question of a constitutionally protected right to physician-assisted suicide were disappointed with the Supreme Court's decision. However, in assessing the impact of the decision, it is important to be clear on what, exactly, the Supreme Court decided. Whilst the court has, at least for the time being, rejected a federal constitutional right to assisted suicide (which would have meant that States would be compelled to permit physician-assisted suicide for the competent terminally ill), it did not purport to decide whether or not assisted suicide should be illegal. To the contrary, the Supreme Court has emphasized that this is a matter within the jurisdiction of State legislatures and it has in fact encouraged the States to continue with their efforts in

---

[47] According to *Reno v Flores* 113 S.Ct. 1439 (1993), liberty interests and rights that are considered fundamental cannot be infringed by State action unless that action is narrowly tailored to serve a compelling State interest.

exploring this issue. Indeed, there are passages in the judgment of Rehnquist CJ as well in the judgments of O'Connor and Souter JJ to the effect that the States, through their democratic processes, are better placed to deal with the issue, and one suspects that this may have been an influential factor encouraging the court to stay its hand to allow reasonable legislative consideration of the matter.[48] Significantly, the Supreme Court decision expressly leaves it open to States to pass laws legalising physician-assisted suicide.

Linked with this analysis, account should be taken of the commencement of the Oregon Death With Dignity Act which has legalized physician-assisted suicide in the State of Oregon. This legislation was first introduced in November 1994 by means of citizen initiated referendum; however, its commencement was delayed until 27 October 1997 as a result of a constitutional challenge to its validity.[49] In June 1997, the Oregon Legislature voted to place a referendum before the Oregon voters to repeal the Oregon Act. The initiative was accordingly put to the Oregon voters again on 4 November 1997 and was, perhaps unexpectedly,[50] reaffirmed by a significantly greater margin than under the 1994 vote (60% chose not to the repeal the law, compared with the initial vote of 51% in favour.)[51] Now that the legislation has come into effect, the Oregon experience provides a valuable insight into the practical operation of laws legalizing physician-assisted suicide.

The evidence emerging from the Oregon experience based upon a study of the deaths occurring during the first year of the Act's operation as reported in the *New England Journal of Medicine*,[52] should allay many of the concerns that have been raised against such legislation. Many people had feared that if physician-assisted suicide was legalized, it would be disproportionately chosen by or forced on terminally ill patients who were poor, uneducated, uninsured, or fearful of the financial consequences of

[48] In the words of Rehnquist CJ, 'throughout the Nation, Americans are engaged in an earnest and profound debate about the morality, legality, and practicality of physician-assisted suicide. Our holding permits this debate to continue, as it should in a democratic society.'

[49] It was on this date that the US Ninth Circuit Court ordered the removal of the injunction restraining commencement of the legislation that had been imposed in 1994 by Oregon District Court Judge Michael Hogan.

[50] There was only modest funding available to support the campaign for the retention of the Oregon Death with Dignity Act in comparison with the campaign funds of opponents to the legislation (Oregon Catholic Conference and Oregon Right to Life).

[51] For analysis of the legal processes involved see Pratt, C., 'Efforts to Legalize Physician-Assisted Suicide in New York, Washington and Oregon: A Contrast Between Judicial and Initiative Approaches—Who Should Decide?' (above) at 1038–1039 and 1096–1100.

[52] Chin, A., *et al.*, 'Legalized Physician-Assisted Suicide in Oregon—The First Year's Experience' (1999) 340 *New England Journal of Medicine* 577. This research involved a comparison of patients who had secured physician-assisted suicide under the Oregon Death with Dignity Act with those who had died from similar illnesses but did not receive prescriptions for lethal medications.

their illness. In the first year of legalized physician-assisted suicide in Oregon, there was a total of fifteen deaths induced by ingestion of lethal medication accounting for only 5 out of every 10,000 deaths in Oregon in 1998. Moreover, the decision to request and use a prescription for lethal medication was associated with concern about loss of autonomy or control of bodily functions, not with fear of intractable pain or concern about financial loss. Nor was there any evidence to support the hypothesis that patients request lethal prescriptions because of inadequate care at the end of life. Further, it was found that the choice of physician-assisted suicide was not associated with level of education or health insurance coverage. All of the reports submitted by the physicians who prescribed lethal medications to the Oregon Health Division as required under the legislation were in full compliance with the law. These early results show that many of the fears associated with the legalization of physician-assisted suicide have simply proved unfounded.

Whilst the experience under the Oregon Death With Dignity Act ought to have dispelled many of the concerns associated with such measures, there have, nevertheless, been ongoing attempts to override the legislation at the federal level. In this regard, direct parallels can be drawn between these developments in the United States aimed at defeating Oregon's physician-assisted suicide legislation, and events in Australia leading to the demise of the Northern Territory's Rights of the Terminally Ill Act 1995 as outlined above. However, unlike in Australia, (where in respect of the Northern Territory, the Commonwealth Parliament could rely on s 122 of the Constitution of Australia 1900 (Cth) to overturn the Rights of the Terminally Ill Act 1995 (NT)), there is no direct power in Congress to invalidate the Oregon Death With Dignity Act. Following the announcement by the federal Attorney General, Janet Reno that federal drugs agents would have no recourse against doctors who help terminally ill patients to die under Oregon's Death with Dignity Act, efforts have instead focused on amending federal legislation dealing with controlled substances (drugs such as barbiturates) so that it would be illegal under federal law to use scheduled drugs to assist in hastening a death.[53] Pursuant to the proposed legislative amendments, doctors in breach would be at risk of losing their registrations to dispense controlled substances from the Drug Enforcement Administration as well as possibly facing federal prosecution for committing an offence.

A Bill in these terms has been introduced by Illinois Representative Henry Hyde and Oklahoma Senator Don Nickles, the 'Pain Relief Promotion Act of 1999', and was passed by the House of Representatives on 27 October 1999. The Bill is currently before the Congress following an unsuc-

---

[53] To date, each of the 15 reported deaths under the Oregon legislation have been brought about using 'controlled substances' within the federal Controlled Substances legislation.

cessful attempt to introduce such legislation in 1998.[54] The fate of the current Bill remains uncertain at this stage, especially in view of concerns about its implications for palliative care generally and the real potential for under-treatment of pain out of fear of infringing the terms of this legislation. However, it is likely to attract more support than did the previous Bill as this Bill now spells out that using controlled substances to alleviate pain and discomfort is permitted, even if such medications increase the risk of death. Moreover, the Bill, if enacted, authorizes 5 million dollars (US) for more training and education to improve end-of-life care. Even if passed, this legislation would not overturn the Oregon Death With Dignity Act, although it would clearly significantly hamper its operation. In this uncertain climate, there has already been some speculation that ways might be found to allow patients to end their own lives with non-federally controlled drugs such as potassium chloride although such measures are less likely to have the support of doctors and patients.[55]

Elsewhere in the United States and in other common law jurisdictions, attempts to secure legislative reform have continued.[56] There have also been a number of further government inquiries into voluntary euthanasia, including two separate inquiries undertaken in the Australian States of Tasmania[57] and South Australia[58] following the intense interest in the issue generated by the Northern Territory reforms. In each case, however, the respective committees of inquiry have rejected the legalization option, relying in large part on the dangers of a 'slippery slope' and risk of abuse if active voluntary euthanasia is legalized. This, it is submitted, ignores the growing body of evidence which points to potentially greater problems and risk of abuse if the strict criminal prohibition of the practice is maintained. Regrettably, these bodies of inquiry have not taken the opportunity to gain meaningful insight into the practice of active voluntary euthanasia in a controlled and regulated setting as occurs in the Netherlands and, consequently, have foregone the opportunity to benefit from this experience.

[54] The earlier Bill was entitled the 'Lethal Drug Abuse and Prevention Act of 1998'.

[55] 'Oregon's PAS Law Threatened' *VE News* Sept. 1999, 11.

[56] Private Member's Bills for the legalization of active voluntary euthanasia have been introduced in the States of South Australia and Western Australia (Voluntary Euthanasia Bill 1996 (SA) and the Voluntary Euthanasia Bill 1997 (WA) respectively) and in the United Kingdom (Joe Ashton MP's Doctor Assisted Dying Bill 1997). In the United States, Bills for the legalization of physician-assisted suicide have been introduced in a number of States and in others, efforts to secure reform measures have continued pursuant to the citizen initiative process.

[57] *Community Development Committee Report on the Need for Legalisation of Voluntary Euthanasia* (1998) Report No. 6 of the Community Development Committee, House of Assembly.

[58] Parliament of South Australia, *Inquiry into the Voluntary Euthanasia Bill 1996* 20 October 1999.

In South Africa, debate on euthanasia has been firmly put on the agenda. In a recent inquiry into end-of-life decisions, the South African Law Commission chose not to make specific recommendations with regard to euthanasia in view of the array of competing interests and the diversity of social, moral and ethical views. However, on the basis of consultation and responses received from discussion papers which had earlier been circulated, the commission has canvassed a number of options which it has put forward for further public debate and discussion.[59]

In the United Kingdom, a major study conducted by Glasgow's University's Institute of Law and Ethics in Medicine, headed by Professor Sheila Mclean, has been released which supports legislative reform.[60] The Report, *Sometimes a Small Victory*, disagrees with the 1994 Report of the House of Lords Select Committee which had recommended against legalization of active voluntary euthanasia or doctor-assisted suicide. It concludes that the arguments against legalization are not of sufficient weight to tip the scales against the argument in favour, but must be accorded consideration in the drafting of any legislation which would produce change. The Report recommends the introduction of legislation legalizing doctor-assisted suicide and contains a draft Bill intended as a legislative template for reform.

There have also been some encouraging signs from within the medical profession. Articles in the medical journals show signs of growing introspection with regard to the issue. In a progressive move, the British Medical Association has initiated debate on the subject of physician-assisted suicide. It has established a website[61] as part of a wide ranging consultation process in preparation for a conference to promote the development of a consensus on physician-assisted suicide which is planned for the European Spring 2000. The outcome of this process is uncertain—on previous occasions, the British Medical Association's handling of reform initiatives in relation to euthanasia has been disappointing, leaving the Association open to criticism.[62] It is hoped that on this occasion, there will be a genuine attempt to have regard to the views of its membership and the wider community.

In many respects, we remain at the crossroads. With some limited exceptions, the prohibition on active voluntary euthanasia and doctor-assisted suicide remains in place. These laws are, on occasion, tested to their limits as was shown in the United States with the activities of Dr Jack Kevorkian who in defiance of the law, openly assisted dozens of patients to die. After numerous unsuccessful prosecutions of this seasoned euthanasia cam-

[59] South African Law Commission, *Report on Euthanasia and the Artificial Preservation of Life* (1999).

[60] McLean, S. and Britton, A., *Sometimes a Small Victory* (1996) Institute of Law and Ethics in Medicine, Glasgow University.

[61] web.bma.org.uk/public/bmapas.nsf

[62] The earlier reform initiatives are detailed in Chapter 5 of this book.

paigner, Dr Kevorkian was finally convicted of second degree murder by a Michigan court, in respect of the nationally televized death of a 52-year-old terminally ill man to whom Kervorkian had administered a lethal injection.[63] Dr Kevorkian is currently serving a 10–25 year jail sentence. In the United Kingdom, the prosecution of Dr Moor in 1998 in respect of the death of one of his patients certainly added fuel to the euthanasia debate, as did his subsequent acquittal after a jury found him not guilty of murder in May 1999.[64] Whilst Dr Moor had consistently denied the murder charge, claiming that all he had done was to administer pain-relieving drugs to relieve the patient's pain and distress, the case nevertheless galvanized support for the euthanasia cause, with hundreds of supporters joining to form a group named 'Friends of Dr Moor'.[65] In Australia, Dr Philip Nitschke, the only doctor who is reported to have administered active voluntary euthanasia under the Northern Territory Rights of the Terminally Ill Act 1995,[66] has become that country's most prominent euthanasia campaigner. Following the overturn of the Northern Territory legislation by the Euthanasia Laws Act 1997 (Cth), Dr Nitschke has focused his efforts on setting up euthanasia advice clinics in various capital cities in Australia. These clinics, which are funded from donations, offer a free service to patients attending. The clinics provide information about lethal drugs and how to obtain them but no prescriptions will be written out. Dr Nitschke is also reported to have been working on the development of a suicide pill.[67] Dr Nitschke has openly admitted that he has helped patients to die. It has also been reported that he has taken videotapes of each patient he has assisted before they have died to protect himself or the patient's family members in the event of legal action.[68] Dr Nitschke's activities are being closely monitored by police and medical authorities and he is already facing investigation by two medical boards in Australia.[69]

Inevitably, while active voluntary euthanasia and doctor-assisted suicide remain illegal, there will be pressure from various quarters for reform of the law. Whilst there has been important progress, more concerted efforts are needed to secure meaningful reform which will better serve and protect the rights and interests of patients and at the same time afford doctors some

---

[63] Kervorkian had videotaped the death and sent it to CBS's 60 minutes which had broadcast it to more than 15 million viewers on 22 November 1998.

[64] For a detailed discussion of the case see Arlidge, A., 'The Trial of Doctor Moor' (2000) *Criminal Law Review* 31.

[65] The 'Friends of Dr Moor' had gathered 30,000 signatures calling for the charges against Dr Moor to be dropped: 'Cleared: Dr Moor's Delight at Not Guilty Verdict' *VENews* No. 66 May 1999, 4.

[66] Kissane, D., Street, A. and Nitschke, P., 'Seven Deaths in Darwin: Case Studies under the Rights of the Terminally Ill Act, Northern Territory, Australia' (above).

[67] *The Bulletin* 25 May 1999, 35.

[68] *The Age* 27 November 1998.   [69] *The Weekend Australian* 1–2 May 1999.

measure of protection by creating scope for them to perform active voluntary euthanasia lawfully subject to specified conditions. Given the shared nature of the problem, across jurisdictions, and in the light of the benefit that can be gained from the Netherlands experience, the time is ripe for internationalization of the euthanasia debate,[70] particularly with regard to its human rights dimension which is often neglected in the literature. Now, with the very real possibility of legalization of voluntary active euthanasia in Belgium, the outcome of this reform initiative is keenly awaited. If passed, its implementation will no doubt come under intense scrutiny internationally. Importantly, the opportunity would then present itself to examine, over time, the impact of laws legalizing active voluntary euthanasia—an opportunity which was denied in relation to the Northern Territory Rights of the Terminally Ill Act 1995 due to it being overridden by Commonwealth legislation soon after its commencement. Evaluation of the impact of legalization would be of particular significance in the Belgium context in view of the wide ranging research that has been undertaken in that jurisdiction examining end-of life practices[71] which would provide a useful reference point for future post-legalization research.

April 2000

---

[70] van den Akker, B., Janssens R. and Ten Have, H., 'Euthanasia and International Human Rights Law: Prolegomena for an International Debate' (1997) 37 *Med. Sci. Law* 289. For analysis of important legal developments in Europe see Nys, H., 'Physician Involvement in a Patient's Death: A Continental European Perspective' (1999) 7 *Medical Law Review* 208.
[71] See n. 29 and n. 36 above.

Acknowledgements

There are many people to whom I am greatly indebted for their assistance during the course of my preparation of this work—indeed, too numerous to name all individually: they include scholars in law, medicine and related fields, medical practitioners, senior government officials, and representatives from the voluntary euthanasia organisation in the various jurisdictions under consideration. To all those who so generously assisted me, I would like to express my heartfelt thanks.

I also wish to acknowledge the financial assistance I have received from the University of Tasmania, School of Commerce and Law, by way of a research grant, for the completion of this work.

This work has been a long time in the making. I would like to acknowledge the love and support of my family, especially my husband, Justin, for his patience and understanding and my father, for his untiring interest and encouragement throughout the course of its preparation.

November 1996

Contents

Table of Cases

Table of Statutes

AUSTRALIA

Queensland

South Australia

Tasmania

GERMANY

NETHERLANDS

UNITED STATES OF AMERICA

INTERNATIONAL INSTRUMENTS

Introduction

While the problem of euthanasia is an ancient one,[1] it has, in recent years, acquired a new relevance and urgency and has increasingly been the subject of public debate, government inquiries, and legislative reform activity. The current prominence of the euthanasia issue can be attributed to a number of interrelated factors. One of the most significant has been the institutionalization of the process of dying. Developments in medical technology have significantly increased the capacity to sustain life beyond any possible hope of recovery. Patients, who would in the past have died from natural causes can now be sustained almost indefinitely as a result of the intervention of artificial life-support equipment or other medical or surgical procedures. Modern medical technology clearly brings many benefits, but it has also created new legal and ethical problems in determining when to use medical interventions to attempt to save or prolong a patient's life, and when a patient should be permitted to die. One negative consequence of the tremendous advances in sustaining human life is that, in some instances, the dying process is unnecessarily prolonged. In fact, for many people, it is not death that they fear, but the possibility of dying in a painful and undignified manner. Thus, concern about the quality of life for the dying has prompted renewed interest in euthanasia.

Another factor which has contributed to the prominence of the euthanasia issue has been the growing proportion of elderly people in western society, as a result of the general improvement in nutrition and health. Although the issue of euthanasia is not limited to the elderly, clearly those who are approaching the end of life are more likely to be concerned about the manner of their dying and to contemplate euthanasia. There has also been growing community awareness about patients' rights in the health care context, and voluntary euthanasia is regarded by many as providing the ultimate control over dying.

The emergence of the AIDS epidemic has also played a role in drawing attention to the issue. With many of its victims being young and assertive, well informed of the unpleasant death they will face, the demand for control

---

[1] According to a number of commentators, euthanasia was widely endorsed in the ancient world in cases of incurable disease by well-known figures such as Plato and the Stoic, Seneca. For an historical overview, see, for example, Wilson, J., *Death by Decision: The Medical Moral and Legal Dilemmas of Euthanasia* (Philadelphia, 1975) 17–45; Fye, B., 'Active Euthanasia: An Historical Survey of its Conceptual Origins and Introduction into Medical Thought' (1978) 52 *Bull. of the History of Med.* 492; Gruman, G., 'An Historical Introduction to Ideas About Voluntary Euthanasia' (1973) 4 *Omega* 87.

over the time and manner of one's dying has intensified,[2] and there is growing evidence that many AIDS patients are in fact receiving medical assistance to die.[3] There has also been recognition from some official quarters as to the relevance of the euthanasia issue for individuals who are in the terminal stages of AIDS.[4]

The declining influence of religion has also contributed to the current prominence of the euthanasia issue. Whilst various religious denominations, most particularly the Catholic Church, have always been opposed to the concept of euthanasia, there has, as a result of the increasing secularization of society, been less opposition to the idea. Also of significance have been the gradually changing attitudes to death. For a long time, death has been regarded as a taboo subject, but there now appears to be greater appreciation of the issue and a growing demand for a 'good and dignified death'.[5] According to public opinion polls, an overwhelming majority of people believe that doctors should be legally allowed to comply with a patient's request for assistance in dying in certain circumstances.

A further factor which has fuelled the current debate has been the influence of the media. In recent years, there has been increased media coverage on euthanasia reflecting, to a large extent, the growing community interest in the subject. Through its extensive coverage, the media has also played a role in promoting debate and community awareness of the issue. As a result of these interrelated developments, the issue of euthanasia has come into prominence, and the movement for the legalization of active voluntary euthanasia has gained momentum.

In May 1995, groundbreaking legislation was enacted in the Northern Territory of Australia with the passage of the Rights of the Terminally Ill Act 1995 which legalizes medical assistance in dying in certain circumstances. The effect of this historic development has been to further concentrate attention on the subject of active voluntary euthanasia and possible models for reform. However, the position in the Northern Territory remains an exception; elsewhere in Australia and in all common law jurisdictions active voluntary euthanasia constitutes a most serious criminal offence. Under existing criminal law principles, although passive euthanasia

---

[2] e.g. Tindall, B. et al., 'Attitudes to Euthanasia and Assisted Suicide in a Group of Homosexual Men with Advanced HIV Disease' (1993) 6 *J Acquired Immune Deficiency Syndrome* 1069.

[3] See for example, the study by Russel Ogden of AIDS deaths in British Columbia, Canada: Ogden, R., *Euthanasia, Assisted Suicide and AIDS* (British Columbia, 1994).

[4] For example, in Australia, the Australian Federation of AIDS organizations has swung its support behind the legalization of active voluntary euthanasia: *Weekend Australian*, 5–6 Nov. 1994.

[5] For a discussion of the changing attitudes to death, see Steinfels, P. and Veatch, R., (eds.) *Death Inside Out: The Hastings Centre Report* (New York, 1974).

is lawful in certain circumstances, active voluntary euthanasia is treated as murder and no account is taken of the special circumstances existing in such cases. Similarly, doctors who assist their patients to commit suicide face serious criminal liability under legislation prohibiting aiding and abetting suicide. There are, however, major discrepancies between law and practice in this area. There is evidence that active voluntary euthanasia occurs quite frequently (albeit largely as a hidden practice), yet doctors are virtually never prosecuted, or if prosecuted, have almost always escaped conviction. There is also considerable evidence of participation by doctors in assisting their patients to commit suicide, yet here too, there is a dearth of prosecutions, and doctors are very rarely convicted. In addition to these discrepancies, there are a number of inconsistencies and anomalies in the application of the law with regard to certain medical acts which may hasten death, in particular, switching off life-support and the administration of drugs for the relief of pain and other symptoms.

The legal implications of doctors' participation in active voluntary euthanasia have been starkly brought into focus by the conviction of Dr Cox in the United Kingdom. In September 1992, Dr Cox, a consultant rheumatologist at a Winchester hospital, was convicted of the attempted murder of one of his patients and was given a 12-month suspended prison sentence.[6] Dr Cox's crime had been deliberately to hasten the death of an elderly patient, who was in excruciating and unrelievable agony and who had begged him to relieve her of her suffering, by administering a lethal dose of potassium chloride. What came as a surprise to many was not that this doctor had responded to a patient's request for active euthanasia: indeed, this is well known to be a fairly common practice; but the fact that he was actually prosecuted and convicted of attempted murder. Prior to this case, it has been widely assumed that a doctor, acting *bona fide* at the patient's request, would be immune from liability. The *Cox* case has dispelled any such belief and has highlighted the potential criminal liability of doctors who fulfil a patient's request for active euthanasia. Whilst many people have, in the past, been content to tolerate the inconsistencies which exist between medical practice and the strict letter of the law, the conviction of Dr Cox, a well-respected and compassionate doctor, has forced a re-evaluation of the situation. The overwhelming reaction from the public has been one of sympathy and support for Dr Cox,[7] and even the General Medical Council's professional conduct committee has effectively condoned his conduct by

---

[6] This case is discussed in detail at pp. 143–5 below. See also pp. 303–4 below.

[7] In a telephone poll conducted by *News of the World* to gauge community reaction to the verdict, nearly 10,000 readers phoned in to register their response to the question: 'Should doctors be allowed to put patients out of their misery?' Of the respondents, 9,468, nearly 97%, called in to say 'yes'. Only 326, just over 3%, voted 'no'.

permitting him to continue working as a consultant and refraining from taking any serious disciplinary action against him.[8] Not surprisingly, the case has been hailed as something of a watershed in the history of active voluntary euthanasia.[9]

The reality is that, with the exception of the Northern Territory of Australia, the law does not presently distinguish the *bona fide* act of a doctor hastening the death of a patient at the patient's request from an act of murder. The aim of this work is to examine the current legal prohibition of active voluntary euthanasia in a number of common law jurisdictions, and to consider whether there is a need for reform. In particular, attention will be given to the position in the United Kingdom, the USA, Canada, Australia and New Zealand.[10] This work is primarily a legal analysis, but in view of the nature of the subject matter, the study necessarily involves consideration of wider issues, including social change, as reflected in opinion polls and community agitation for reform, the practice and attitudes of the medical profession, as well as consideration of religious, moral, and ethical arguments. In drawing attention to deficiencies in the present law with regard to active voluntary euthanasia, this work is intended to assist both doctors and patients; to protect doctors from the inappropriate imposition of criminal liability, and to protect the interests of patients and promote their right of self-determination.

It is important from the outset to clarify the terminology which is used in this book, particularly in light of the variable meanings which are often attributed to the word 'euthanasia'. This lack of consensus in defining euthanasia is largely due to the emotive and controversial nature of the subject, and the fact that the definitions of euthanasia which are advanced, often reflect a particular moral viewpoint.[11] Etymologically, the word euthanasia means 'good death' from the Greek *eu* for good, and *thanatos* for death. In common usage, however, it is rarely used in this literal sense which emphasizes the type of death experienced, and is more usually employed to refer to the act of deliberately inducing the death of a patient who is in severe pain and distress as a result of a terminal or incurable illness. For example, euthanasia is defined in the Oxford Dictionary as 'a gentle and easy death, the bringing about of this, especially in the case of incurable and painful disease'.[12] Although this definition makes no reference to the person

---

[8] Dr Cox was admonished and given a reprimand by the General Medical Council, but was not struck off the medical register; see further, pp. 303–4 below.

[9] e.g. *The Independent*, 21 Sept. 1992; Smith, R., 'Euthanasia: Time for a Royal Commission' (1992) 305 BMJ 728.

[10] For the purposes of this work, the term 'common law jurisdiction' is used to define those countries which apply the common, as distinct from civil law, irrespective of whether the law is found in case law or has been codified.

[11] For a detailed analysis of the definition of euthanasia, see Beauchamp, T. and Davidson, A., 'The Definition of Euthanasia' (1979) 4 *JMed. & Phil.* 294.

[12] *The Concise Oxford Dictionary of Current English*, 7th edn. (Oxford, 1987).

who brings about such a death, the contemporary understanding of euthanasia upon which this work will focus, envisages a clinical situation where a
doctor assists a terminal or incurable patient to die. This is to be distinguished from the more general concept of 'mercy killing', which can be
defined as an intentional killing, often by a member of the family or a friend
of the victim, for reasons of mercy or pity for the suffering person.[13] In the
interests of clarity, it is also necessary to dispense with the 'death with
dignity' and the 'right to die' terminology. Whilst not wanting to detract
from the importance of a dignified death and the right of a patient to be
treated with dignity, there is widespread agreement that these are ambiguous or meaningless phrases which do not assist in advancing reasoned
analysis of the subject of euthanasia.[14]

In defining euthanasia, a distinction which in law is of utmost importance
is the distinction between active and passive euthanasia. Although there is
by no means universal agreement on the matter, the following definitions
are proposed which are in accordance with the prevailing understanding of
these terms. 'Active euthanasia' can be defined as a deliberate act to end
the life of a terminal or incurable patient, which in fact results in the
patient's death.[15] An example of active euthanasia would be the deliberate
administration of drugs with the object of causing the death of the patient
and which does in fact result in the patient's death. 'Passive euthanasia'[16]
can be defined as the deliberate withholding or withdrawing of life-
prolonging medical treatment in respect of a terminal or incurable patient,
with the object of hastening the patient's death, and as a result of which the
patient dies at an earlier time than he or she would have died, had the
treatment been carried out.[17] An example of passive euthanasia would be
the discontinuation of drugs, for instance, antibiotics in respect of a terminal or incurable patient who has an underlying infection.

It should be noted, however, that there has been considerable resistance
from certain quarters to describing the practice of withholding or withdraw-

[13] For other definitions of 'mercy killing' see, for example, Law Reform Commissioner
Victoria, Working Paper No. 8, *Murder: Mental Element and Punishment* (Melbourne, 1984)
24; *The Concise Oxford Dictionary of Current English*, above n. 12.

[14] e.g. President's Commission for the Study of Ethical Problems in Medicine and Biomedi-
cal and Behavioural Research, *Deciding to Forgo Life-Sustaining Treatment: A Report on the
Ethical, Medical and Legal Issues in Treatment Decisions* (Washington, 1983) 24; Parliament of
Victoria Social Development Committee, Second and Final Report, *Inquiry into Options for
Dying with Dignity* (Melbourne, 1987) 139.

[15] See, for example, British Medical Association (BMA) Working Party Report, *Euthanasia: Report of a Working Party to Review the British Medical Association's Guidance on
Euthanasia* (London, 1988) 3 where 'active euthanasia' is described as 'an active intervention
by a doctor to end life'.

[16] Also sometimes referred to as 'antidysthanasia'; i.e. 'the failure to take positive action to
prolong the life of an incurable patient'; see, for example, Cannon, W., 'The Right to Die'
(1970) 7 *Hous.LRev.* 654, 657.

[17] e.g. BMA Working Party Report, *Euthanasia*, above n. 15, at 3.

ing life-prolonging medical treatment as a form of euthanasia. According to one view which has frequently been expressed in medical circles, the discontinuation of medical treatment in appropriate circumstances is proper medical practice, and to describe it as 'passive euthanasia' is misleading and creates unnecessary confusion.[18] Thus, it has been argued, there is a distinction between intentional killing on the one hand, and appropriate treatment for the dying or terminally ill on the other.[19] Strong objections to the prevailing usage of the term 'passive' euthanasia have also come from various religious denominations, particularly the Catholic Church which has unequivocally condemned the practice of any form of euthanasia. According to traditional principles of Catholic teaching, there is a fundamental distinction between 'ordinary' and 'extraordinary' means of prolonging life.[20] This distinction has its origins in moral theology and is used to distinguish between forms of care which are obligatory (ordinary means), and non-obligatory care (extraordinary means). On the basis of this distinction, the Catholic view is that the term 'passive' euthanasia does not apply in respect of the withholding or withdrawing of *'extra-ordinary'* treatment,[21] whereas the omission of an *'ordinary'* means of prolonging life would be regarded as euthanasia.[22] Apart from the Catholic Church, other religious denominations have also sanctioned non-intervention in appropriate circumstances, claiming that this does not amount to euthanasia.[23] Apart from these sources of opposition, other commentators have argued that passive euthanasia is an inappropriate label for the withholding or withdrawing of treatment.[24] Despite this opposition, the term 'passive euthanasia' is now quite commonly used in this context,[25] and is not an inappropriate label in circumstances where the withholding or withdrawing was done with the object of hastening the death of the patient, and did in fact bring about the patient's death.

[18] e.g. Pollard, B., 'Killing the Dying—Not the Easy Way Out' (1988) 149 MJA 312.

[19] Reichenbach, B., 'Euthanasia and the Active Passive Distinction' (1987) 1 *Bioethics* 51, 72; Twycross, R., 'Debate: Euthanasia—A Physician's Viewpoint' (1982) 8 *J Med. Ethics* 86, 87. The view has also been expressed that stopping treatment out of respect for a patient's wishes is not euthanasia at all; see Potts, S., 'Looking for the Exit Door: Killing and Caring in Modern Medicine' (1988) 25 *Hous. L Rev.* 493, 500.

[20] For discussion of the historical background of this distinction, see the President's Commission Report, *Deciding to Forgo Life-Sustaining Treatment,* above n. 14, at 82–3.

[21] O'Donnell, T., 'Review of "The Physician's Responsibility Toward Hopelessly Ill Patients"' (1984) 51 *Linacre Q* 351; Louisell, D., 'Euthanasia and Biathanasia: On Dying and Killing' 22 (1973) *Catholic UL Rev.* 723, 730.

[22] Smith, W., 'Judeo-Christian Teaching on Euthanasia: Definitions, Distinctions and Decisions' (1987) 54 *Linacre Q* 33.

[23] e.g. Rayner, K., 'Euthanasia—A Church Perspective', proceedings from the 5th Biennial National Aged Care Conference of the Uniting Church of Australia (1986) 43.

[24] e.g. Weir, R., *Abating Treatment with Critically Ill Patients* (New York, 1989) 302; Keyserlingk, E., *Sanctity of Life or Quality of Life in the Context of Ethics, Medicine and Law* (Ottawa, 1979) 120–3. In fact, both these commentators argue that the distinction between active and passive euthanasia should be dispensed with altogether.

[25] e.g. BMA Working Party Report, *Euthanasia,* above n. 15, at 3.

Whilst acknowledging the limitations of this terminology, it is proposed, for the purposes of this work, to use the terms 'active' and 'passive' euthanasia. Apart from the fact that these terms have gained widespread usage and understanding, this approach can be justified on the basis that the distinction between 'active' and 'passive' euthanasia is closely paralleled by the acts/omissions doctrine which underlies the criminal law and which is of central relevance in determining criminal liability. Thus, the position taken in this work is that whilst it may, in the future, be necessary to revise the nomenclature,[26] it would not, for present purposes, advance the analysis of this subject if an attempt was made to depart from this terminology. Attention will, however, be drawn to some of the problems in the application of the acts/omissions distinction.

A critical feature of this work is its focus on *voluntary* euthanasia. Although the criminal law does not presently differentiate between euthanasia which is performed with or without the request of a patient, or indeed, against the patient's express wishes, the differences between 'voluntary' euthanasia on the one hand, and 'involuntary' and 'non-voluntary' euthanasia on the other, are of paramount significance. It is therefore necessary to define these terms and to spell out the precise scope of this work. Euthanasia is 'involuntary' where it is performed without the consent or against the will of a competent patient. Euthanasia is 'non-voluntary' where it is performed on persons who are incompetent and therefore not capable of giving a consent.[27] The aim of this work is to deal solely with 'voluntary euthanasia'; that is, euthanasia which is performed at the request of the patient. This, in turn, involves an assumption about patient competence and decision-making capacity. Competence is not a legal status except when determined by a court of law,[28] and until such time as a formal judicial determination of incompetence is made, individuals are legally presumed competent to manage their own affairs.[29] In recent years, attention has moved away from the rather inflexible notion of competence to the concept of 'decision-making capacity'.[30] Decision-making capacity is now generally understood to refer to an individual's functional ability to make informed health care decisions in accordance with personal val-

[26] See, for example, the analytical framework adopted by the Special Senate Committee on Euthanasia and Assisted Suicide, *Of Life and Death: Report of the Special Senate Committee on Euthanasia and Assisted Suicide* (Ottawa, 1995) 11–15.

[27] e.g. Kohl, M. (ed.), *Beneficent Euthanasia* (Buffalo, New York, 1975); Rachels, J., *The End of Life: The Morality of Euthanasia* (Oxford, 1986); Singer, P., *Practical Ethics* (Cambridge, 1979) 127–57; Young, R., 'Voluntary and Non-Voluntary Euthanasia' (1976) 59 *The Monist* 264.

[28] Dickens, B., 'Terminal Care, Incompetent Persons and Donation' (1986) 3 *Transplantation Today* 54.

[29] Hastings Center Report, *Guidelines on the Termination of Life-Sustaining Treatment and Care for the Dying* (Bloomington, 1987) 131.

[30] Ibid. at 131–3. See also President's Commission for the Study of Ethical Problems in Medicine and Biomedical and Behavioural Research, *Making Health Care Decisions* (Washington, 1982) 55–68.

ues.[31] However, the determination of patient capacity is extremely complex. As a minimum, decision-making capacity requires the ability to communi-cate and understand information relevant to the decision, and the ability to reason and deliberate about the choices in accordance with personal values and goals.[32] Capacity is not an all or nothing matter; there is a spectrum of abilities.[33] The more serious the consequences of a particular decision, the higher the level of decision-making capacity required, and the greater need for certainty on the part of health care professionals in their assessment of that capacity.[34] In view of the gravity of the decision and the finality of the outcome, a request for active voluntary euthanasia would require a high degree of decision-making capacity in order to ensure that the request reflects the truly voluntary and autonomous choice of the patient.

Another distinction which is sometimes made is that between direct and indirect euthanasia:[35] direct euthanasia implies that the intended effect of an act, such as the administration of a dose of narcotic, is to cause the patient's death; in the case of indirect euthanasia, the same dose may be administered with the same effect, but the intention is to relieve the pa-tient's suffering rather than to kill the patient.[36]

At the heart of the euthanasia issue is the question whether individuals should be entitled to exercise control over the time and manner of their death. This raises the issue of an individual's right of autonomy and self-determination—the principle that competent individuals should be free to determine their own life choices. This principle underlies this work, and it is proposed to explore its interrelationship with other important ethical principles and social values, prominent amongst which is the 'sanctity of life' doctrine; the notion that human life has intrinsic value and is worthy of respect and protection. To the extent that the exercise of an individual's self-determination is in conflict with society's interest in the preservation of life, this work will also need to examine the relationship between private and public values, and whether these interests can be reconciled.

It is important to acknowledge the close relationship between doctor-assisted suicide and active voluntary euthanasia. Because of the similarity of the issues involved, the issue of active voluntary euthanasia cannot be fully explored without also examining the issues in relation to doctor-

---

[31] e.g. Hastings Center Report, *Guidelines on the Termination of Life-Sustaining Treatment and Care for the Dying*, above n. 29, at 132.

[32] Ibid. at 131; President's Commission Report, *Making Health Care Decisions,* above n. 30, at 57.

[33] Hastings Center Report, *Guidelines on the Termination of Life-Sustaining Treatment and Care for the Dying*, above n. 29, at 133.

[34] Ibid.; President's Commission Report, *Making Health Care Decisions,* above n. 30, at 60.

[35] Sawyer, D. et al., 'Canadian Physicians and Euthanasia; 2 Definitions and Distinctions' (1993) 148 CMAJ 1463, 1464.

[36] The legal implications of administering drugs for the relief of pain and other symptoms but which are known to be likely to hasten death are examined in detail at pp. 170–84 below.

assisted suicide. Moreover, it would not be logical or feasible to legalize active voluntary euthanasia without also making doctor-assisted suicide legal. Significantly, in the Northern Territory of Australia, both active voluntary euthanasia and doctor-assisted suicide have been legalized under the Rights of the Terminally Ill Act 1995. This is not to say, however, that active voluntary euthanasia and doctor-assisted suicide are entirely equivalent. The most obvious and important difference is that, unlike in the case of doctor-assisted suicide, where the death inducing agent is ultimately self-administered, active voluntary euthanasia requires the direct participation of another in bringing about the patient's death. Although most efforts to secure reform have been directed to active voluntary euthanasia, with legalization of doctor-assisted suicide as a logical corollary to the legalization of active voluntary euthanasia, there have been important developments in the USA relating specifically to doctor-assisted suicide. A number of the legislative reform measures which have been proposed in various states have focused exclusively on 'physician-assisted' suicide, including Measure 16 in the State of Oregon (the Death with Dignity Act) which was passed by a majority of voters in November 1994 in a citizen-initiated referendum, although at the time of writing it was still under constitutional challenge. In a separate development, there have also been some significant judicial moves in the USA towards recognition of a constitutionally recognized interest in physician-assisted suicide for terminally ill, competent patients, as a result of decisions of the Ninth and Second Circuit Courts in *Compassion in Dying* v. *State of Washington*[37] and *Quill* v. *Vacco*[38] respectively. However, the United States Supreme Court is yet to rule on the matter.[39] These developments with regard to physician-assisted suicide in the USA will be examined in some detail, including consideration of their wider ramifications for the issue of active voluntary euthanasia.

This book is divided into eight chapters. In the first chapter, consideration is given to the legal status of medically administered euthanasia under the criminal law, focusing on the law's differential treatment of active and passive euthanasia. Chapter 2 contains an analysis of the law in relation to assisted suicide and the implications for doctors who assist the suicide of their patients. It also examines a number of important case law developments in Canada and the USA, in particular, the case of *Rodriguez* v. *British Columbia (Attorney General)*,[40] involving a challenge to the prohibition on assisted suicide under the Canadian Criminal Code on the basis of the Canadian Charter of Rights and Freedoms, and the US cases involving constitutional challenge to similar legislation on the basis of an alleged

[37] No. 94-35534 (9th Cir. March 6 1996) (*en banc*).
[38] No. 60 (2nd Cir. April 2 1996).
[39] For discussion of these cases see pp. 100–24 below.
[40] [1993] 3 SCR 519.

violation of the Due Process Clause and the Equal Protection Clause of the Fourteenth Amendment of the United States Constitution. Against this legal background, the position in practice with regard to active voluntary euthanasia and doctor-assisted suicide is then explored in Chapter 3. Evidence of doctors' involvement in the practice of active voluntary euthanasia and assisted suicide is analysed, and consideration is given to the treatment of such cases in the criminal justice system. Building on this analysis, attention is then drawn to the various problems which stem from the discrepancies which exist between law and practice in this area. In developing this argument, the discussion extends to a consideration of the legal characterization of a number of other medical practices which bear some similarity to active voluntary euthanasia, yet which are typically characterized in such a way as to avoid the imposition of criminal liability.

Chapter 4 is devoted to an analysis of the euthanasia debate. This involves an examination of the arguments for and against the legalization of active voluntary euthanasia, including analysis of the human rights dimension of the debate. This chapter also canvasses jurisprudential arguments regarding the role of the criminal law. In Chapter 5, changes in society are discussed which have contributed to a more receptive climate for reform. Particular attention is given to the evidence of growing support for the legalization of active voluntary euthanasia amongst the medical profession, and in the community generally. Consideration is then given in Chapter 6 to the reform developments which have occurred in common law jurisdictions, including law reform commission and parliamentary inquiries dealing with the subject and efforts to secure legislative reform. Detailed consideration is given in this chapter to the important legislative developments which have occurred in the Northern Territory of Australia as well as the successful initiative for the legalization of doctor-assisted suicide in the State of Oregon. In Chapter 7 attention is turned to the Netherlands where, although not actually legalized, active voluntary euthanasia has for some years been openly practised by the medical profession with very few legal repercussions. Since the Netherlands has come to be widely regarded as a possible reform model, an attempt is made carefully to evaluate the situation in that country and to ascertain whether it is in fact a suitable model for other jurisdictions to adopt.

The final chapter deals with options for reform. The suitability of a legislative response is examined and criteria are considered for the legalization of active voluntary euthanasia. The conclusion of this work is that, notwithstanding the limitations of legislation, on balance, legislative reform is both necessary and appropriate. A recommendation is accordingly made for the introduction of a very limited exception to the homicide laws that would confer on doctors an immunity from liability, provided active voluntary euthanasia is performed in accordance with strict criteria and safeguards. As already noted, this would also necessarily entail legalization of doctor-assisted suicide, subject to the same conditions and safeguards.

There can be little dispute that the question whether active voluntary euthanasia should be permitted by law raises issues of fundamental importance, considerable difficulty, and enormous controversy. It is hoped that this work will assist in clarifying the issues and advancing the debate so as to pave the way for reform.

1

Euthanasia Under the Criminal Law

INTRODUCTION

The object of this chapter is to examine the present state of the criminal law in the United Kingdom and other common law jurisdictions regarding the practice of active and passive euthanasia with the aim of ascertaining the potential liability of doctors for participation in these practices. Particular attention will be focused on the differential treatment of the law in respect of active and passive euthanasia. Despite the similarities between active and passive euthanasia in terms of intention and outcome, there are significant legal differences between the two, which, it is argued, give rise to questionable distinctions.

The distinction between active and passive euthanasia essentially rests upon the more general distinction between acts and omissions; active interventions as distinct from non-action or refraining from acting. The criminal law maintains a fairly rigid distinction between liability for acts which cause death on the one hand, and liability for omissions which cause death on the other. This has significant implications for the law regarding active and passive euthanasia. In analysing the criminal law in relation to euthanasia, it will therefore be necessary to examine criminal liability for both acts and omissions which cause death. This will be dealt with in parts I and II of this chapter respectively.

It should, however, be noted from the outset that the distinction between active and passive euthanasia and the underlying acts/omissions doctrine is most problematic and unsatisfactory. It will be argued in a later chapter that this distinction is of debatable moral and philosophical significance. Further, it will be shown that it is often difficult to maintain in practice. The practical difficulties in drawing the distinction in particular cases has been compounded by the widespread reluctance to characterize as criminal certain conduct regularly performed in medical practice. Two aspects of medical practice which are highlighted in this study are the switching off of artificial life-support and the administration of drugs for the relief of pain and other symptoms, which are known to be likely to hasten death. It will be demonstrated in a later chapter that this tendency to avoid labelling medical conduct as criminal, whilst readily understandable, has resulted in serious distortions in the interpretation and application of the law.[1] However, notwithstanding the difficulties with the acts/omissions distinction, for the purposes of the present discussion regarding the criminal law it is nevertheless necessary to adhere to this distinction as it continues to have overriding legal significance.

Although there are some variations in the criminal law as between the various jurisdictions under consideration,[2] the law applicable to euthanasia performed by a doctor at the request of a patient is (with the exception of the Northern Territory of Australia[3]) fairly uniform throughout the common law world. The criminal law does not recognize euthanasia as a special category of homicide. Liability in respect of such conduct is determined on the basis of the ordinary criminal law principles. As outlined in the Introduction, euthanasia, as defined for the purposes of this work, involves the deliberate and intentional causing of death either by active or passive means. We are therefore dealing with *intentional* killing as distinct from death caused as a result of *negligent* acts and omissions. Accordingly, the relevant law is principally that pertaining to murder.[4]

In order to establish liability for murder, both the *actus reus* and the *mens rea* for the crime of murder must be made out. The necessary *mens rea* or mental element for the crime of murder includes an intention to kill. The *actus reus* of a crime has been described as the external ingredients of the crime[5] or alternatively, as all the elements in the definition of the crime, except the defendant's mental element.[6] The *actus reus* for the crime of murder requires proof of particular conduct and that, as a matter of causation, the defendant's conduct *caused* the death in question. The requisite conduct of the defendant can be either an act, in the sense of a willed bodily

---

[1] For discussion, see pp. 152–84 below.

[2] In some jurisdictions, such as the UK (Scotland, although politically part of the UK has an independent legal system) and in some US and Australian states, the common law applies with little legislative interference. In others, the criminal law has been codified: Canada has a federal Code (Criminal Code RSC 1985, c. C-46), and a number of the states and territories in Australia also have Criminal Codes (NT Criminal Code 1983; Qld. Criminal Code 1995; Tas. Criminal Code 1924; WA Criminal Code 1913. Note also the Crimes Act 1900 (NSW) which also applies in the ACT.) In New Zealand, the relevant legislation is the Crimes Act 1961. The criminal law has also been codified in most US states: see LaFave, W. and Scott, A., *Criminal Law*, 2nd edn. (Minnesota, 1986) 4.

[3] In 1995 legislation was passed in the Northern Territory permitting doctors to assist patients to die by means of either active voluntary euthanasia or assisted suicide in certain carefully defined circumstances: Rights of the Terminally Ill Act 1995. The legal effect of this legislation has been to create an immunity from criminal liability provided doctors adhere strictly to the requirements of the legislation. For detailed discussion, see pp. 344–55 below.

[4] It is acknowledged that a deliberate failure to act could potentially be analysed in terms of liability for manslaughter and/or criminal negligence causing death depending on the circumstances of the *actus reus* and causation of death. Similarly, with regard to the *mens rea*, an attempt may be made to draw a distinction between a doctor intending to cause death and intending death to result from natural causes the effect of which could have been postponed.

[5] Williams, G., *Textbook of Criminal Law*, 2nd edn. (London, 1983) 146.

[6] Smith J. C. and Hogan, B., *Criminal Law*, 6th edn. (London, 1988) 33.

movement, or an omission; that is, non-action or failure to act. Omissions have a different status under the criminal law than do acts. Whilst the duty not actively to cause harm is virtually absolute, there is no general principle of liability for failure to act and prevent the occurrence of harm. An omission to act which causes death will only give rise to criminal liability in circumstances where the criminal law imposes a *legal duty* to act. The common law has traditionally been very circumspect in imposing a legal duty to prevent harm. Under the criminal law in all common law jurisdictions, a duty to act only arises in certain specified circumstances. One of the special relationships which gives rise to a legally recognized duty to act is the relationship of doctor and patient, although the extent of this duty will depend on the circumstances of the case.[7] The omission by a doctor of his or her legal duty towards a patient may give rise to criminal liability for murder, provided that it can be established, as a matter of causation, that the relevant omission was the cause of death and that the doctor intended to bring about the death of the patient.[8]

I. DOCTORS' CRIMINAL LIABILITY
FOR ACTS WHICH CAUSE DEATH

A. Introduction

In this part of the analysis, it is proposed to examine the criminal liability of a doctor in respect of a deliberate act of euthanasia performed at the request of the patient which results in the patient's death. This area of the law, involving euthanasia by affirmative conduct performed at the patient's request, can be stated with some certainty. In order to establish criminal liability it must be shown that there was some act committed by the doctor which was intended to cause death and which did in fact cause the patient to die at that time and in that manner. The fact that the doctor committed the acts which caused death at the patient's request does not exculpate a doctor from criminal liability since a person cannot validly consent to his or her own death. For the purposes of establishing criminal liability for murder, the law takes no account of the motive of the doctor or the fact that the act was performed in the context of the doctor/patient relationship. Furthermore, it is irrelevant that the death may in any event have been imminent by virtue of the patient's terminal condition. There are

[7] The extent of the doctor's duty and in particular, the legal effect of a patient's right to refuse treatment on a doctor's duty to treat is dealt with later in this chapter.

[8] In some circumstances, *mens rea* short of intention will suffice to establish liability for murder. See below.

no special defences which would apply to protect doctors from incurring criminal liability in these circumstances.

B. The Acts

Although the distinction between acts and omissions is fundamental in the law of homicide, there are no universally accepted criteria for distinguishing between them.[9] Indeed, there is considerable confusion and uncertainty even in defining what is meant by 'an act'.[10] Professor Glanville Williams is of the view that the most acceptable language is to describe an act as a 'willed bodily movement'.[11] This description is in accordance with Justice Holmes' classic definition of an act as a 'voluntary muscular contraction'.[12] If one proceeds on the basis that an act involves some willed bodily or muscular movement,[13] it is possible to identify certain conduct as clearly coming within this definition. In the context of medically-administered active euthanasia, the most obvious example of an act causing death is for the doctor to administer to the patient a lethal injection.

C. The Intention Requirement

In order to establish liability for the crime of murder, the relevant *actus reus*, (here the act causing death), must be accompanied by the necessary *mens rea*. The mental element for murder at common law is traditionally referred to as 'malice aforethought'.[14] This term has acquired a highly technical meaning quite different from the ordinary popular usage of the words themselves. The reference to 'malice' is particularly misleading when considered in the context of active voluntary euthanasia where the relevant conduct causing death is performed out of compassionate and benevolent motives. The term 'malice aforethought' simply describes a number of

[9] Skegg, P., 'The Termination of Life-Support Measures and the Law of Murder' (1978) 41 *Mod.L Rev.* 423, 427.

[10] See Hughes, G., 'Criminal Omissions' (1957–8) 67 *Yale LJ* 590, 597 where he notes that no agreed juristic concept of an act exists and then goes on to discuss some of the suggested definitions.

[11] Williams, *Textbook of Criminal Law*, above n. 5, at 147–8.

[12] Holmes, O. W., *The Common Law* (Boston, 1881) 91. This description has, however, been subject to criticism; see Hughes, 'Criminal Omissions', above n. 10, at 597 where he argues that this definition is not very helpful for the purposes of the criminal law since the criminal law has never prohibited mere muscular contractions; what is needed is reference to muscular contractions, in certain circumstances, and with certain consequences. Note also the concept of 'act' in the Austinian sense, of a movement of the body consequent upon the exercise of the will; Austin, J., *Lectures on Jurisprudence or the Philosophy of Positive Law* (London, 1920) 174.

[13] Note, however, the view of some commentators, e.g. Fletcher, G., 'Prolonging Life' (1967) 42 *Wash.L Rev.* 999, that certain conduct should be classified as an omission, notwithstanding that it involves bodily movement. For further discussion, see pp. 153–7 below.

[14] See the definition of murder at common law by Sir Edward Coke, *Institutes of the Laws of England*, 3rd Part (London, 1641) 47.

different states of mind which will satisfy the *mens rea* requirement for the crime of murder. Neither malice (in the sense of ill will) nor premeditation need in fact be established. Malice aforethought at common law clearly encompasses an *intention to kill* any person. It also includes an intention to inflict grievous bodily harm.

Similarly, for those jurisdictions where the criminal law has been codified, the *mens rea* for murder includes an intention to cause death or grievous bodily harm.[15]

Thus, in circumstances where a doctor deliberately responds to a request from a patient that he or she take active steps to bring about the patient's death, the necessary intention requirement for the crime of murder in all common law jurisdictions will be established, since the doctor clearly intends to bring about the death of the patient.[16]

D. The Causation Requirement

A fundamental component of the *actus reus* for the crime of murder is that the conduct of the defendant *caused* the death of the deceased.[17] There are two distinct aspects to the legal principle of causation at common law; the *sine qua non* test and the issue of imputability.[18]

First of all, it is necessary to establish that the defendant's conduct (whether an act or an omission) is a *sine qua non* of the event; that is, one must be able to say that 'but for' the occurrence of the antecedent factor the event would not have happened. This will be a question of fact in each case, and must be established by the prosecution beyond reasonable doubt. In addition to this 'but for' requirement, it will also be necessary to show that the defendant's conduct is an imputable or legal cause of the consequence;

---

[15] Section 229(i) and (ii) Canadian Criminal Code 1985 (but note that the Criminal Code refers to 'bodily harm' as distinct from 'grievous bodily harm' and there is a further requirement that the person knows that the conduct is likely to cause death and is reckless whether death ensues or not); Australia—NT Criminal Code 1983 s. 162, Qld. Criminal Code 1995 s. 94, Tas. Criminal Code 1924 s. 157(1)(b) and (d), WA Criminal Code 1913 ss. 278 and 279 (note also NSW Crimes Act 1900 s. 18(1)(a)); New Zealand Crimes Act 1961 s. 167. In the USA, homicide statutes take different forms in different states but most modern statutes provide for at least two degrees of murder which include 'intent to kill' murder and 'intent to do serious bodily injury' murder: LaFave and Scott, *Criminal Law*, above n. 2, at 605.

[16] The only exception is the Northern Territory of Australia: see above.

[17] This is subject to the rule at common law that a charge of criminal homicide will not lie unless the death occurred within a year and a day from the act whereby the accused inflicted the injury. This rule also applies under legislation in a number of the jurisdictions where the criminal law has been codified: Canada—Criminal Code 1985 s. 227; New Zealand—Crimes Act 1961 s. 162. The rule also applies in many US states: LaFave and Scott, *Criminal Law*, above n. 2, at 611. Although the rule had originally been codified in a number of the Australian states, following amendments in the early 1990s it has now been abolished in most Australian jurisdictions.

[18] Williams, *Textbook of Criminal Law*, above n. 5, at 379–84.

in other words, that the defendant's conduct is sufficiently connected with the consequences as to attribute to him or her legal responsibility for those consequences. This aspect of the causation test has been variously described as the direct, proximate, substantial, or effective cause. According to Williams, these terms can be misleading and the real question is essentially a value judgement, whether the result can fairly be said to be imputable to the defendant. Whether there is sufficient evidence to support a finding of imputable cause is a question of law for the determination of the court. If the court is of the opinion that there is sufficient evidence to support such a finding, the question of the defendant's guilt or innocence will be left to the jury.[19] However, there are, as yet, no clear principles regarding the appropriate direction to the jury on this aspect of causation. Various formulations have been used, including that the defendant's act or omission must have 'contributed significantly to the death',[20] or alternatively, that it must have been a 'substantial cause of the death'.[21] Whatever the formulation used, it is at least clear that the conduct of the defendant must not be so minute or trivial that it will be ignored under the *de minimis* principle.[22]

The common law principles in respect of causation have been incorporated into the Canadian Criminal Code, the Criminal Codes in the various Australian jurisdictions and the New Zealand Crimes Act.[23]

On the basis of the foregoing principles, in circumstances where a doctor performs certain acts which are intended to bring about the patient's death, and the patient's death ensues some short time thereafter as a direct result of those acts, the legal requirements of causation are clearly made out. The doctor's conduct is a *sine qua non* of the patient's death in that 'but for' the occurrence of the act the patient would not have died at that time. The doctor's conduct would also appear to be an imputable or legal cause of the patient's death since it is sufficiently connected with the death so as to attribute to him or her legal responsibility for that consequence.

The act of the doctor need not be the *sole* or indeed the *main* cause of death of the patient.[24] It is enough if, as a matter of law, it is *a* cause

---

[19] Fisse, B., *Howard's Criminal Law*, 5th edn. (Sydney, 1990) 33.

[20] *Smithers* v. *R* (1977) 34 CCC (2d) 427.

[21] *R* v. *Evans and Gardiner (No. 2)* [1976] VR 523; *Hallet* v. *R* [1969] SASR 141, 150; *R* v. *Bingapore* (1975) 11 SASR 469, 480.

[22] See Smith and Hogan, *Criminal Law*, above n. 6, at 316, referring to the case of *R* v. *Cato* [1976] 1 All ER 260, 265. For a discussion of the defence of minimal causation, see Williams, *Textbook of Criminal Law*, above n. 5, at 385.

[23] Canada—Criminal Code 1985 s. 222; Australia—NT Criminal Code 1983 s. 157, Qld. Criminal Code 1995 s. 97, Tas. Criminal Code 1924 s. 153(1), WA Criminal Code 1913 s. 270 (note also Crimes Act 1900 (NSW) s. 18); New Zealand—Crimes Act 1961 s. 158. For the position in the USA, see LaFave and Scott, *Criminal Law*, above n. 2, at 277–83.

[24] Smith and Hogan, *Criminal Law,* above n. 6, at 314.

which has the effect of accelerating the moment of the patient's death.[25] Circumstances may arise where the acts committed by the doctor which caused the death of the patient would not have resulted in the death of a healthy person. For example, the administration of certain drugs may have greater effect upon someone who is sick and in a debilitated state than they would upon an ordinary person. A doctor committing such acts would nevertheless be liable (provided the necessary *mens rea* is also established) since the doctor's conduct was sufficiently connected with the patient's death so as to hold the doctor legally responsible for that consequence.[26] However, the doctor's contribution to the death of the patient must not be so insignificant that it would be ignored under the *de minimis* principle.

E. Irrelevance of Patient's Terminal Condition

It may be that active euthanasia is performed in respect of a terminally ill patient whose death is impending from natural causes. It is, however, no defence to a charge of murder that the death was in any event imminent by virtue of the patient's terminal condition. This is the position both at common law and in those jurisdictions where the criminal law has been codified.

Position at common law

As Devlin stated in his work *Samples of Lawmaking:*[27] 'The deliberate acceleration of death must prima facie be murder and I do not see how under any system of law it can logically be otherwise. The certainty of death in the immediate future cannot of itself be a defence any more than the certainty in the remote future'.[28] Indeed, since death is, sooner or later, inevitable for all of mankind, *every* killing can be regarded as being simply an acceleration of an inevitable death. Consequently it will make no difference to the liability of the defendant that the victim was suffering from a terminal condition. Accordingly, in *R* v. *Dyson*,[29] the defendant was indicted for the manslaughter of a young boy who had died from injuries the defendant had inflicted, despite the fact that the child was at the time suffering from meningitis from which he would have died in any event. Lord Alverston CJ stated that: 'The proper question to have been submitted to

---

[25] *R* v. *Cato*, above n. 22, at 265.

[26] The separate question of the administration of palliative drugs which may hasten death is dealt with below, pp. 170–184.

[27] (London, 1962).   [28] Ibid. at 94–5.   [29] [1908] 2 KB 454.

the jury was whether the prisoner accelerated the child's death by the injuries which he inflicted. For if he did the fact that the child was already suffering from meningitis from which it would in any event have died before long, would afford no answer to the charge of causing its death'.[30]

The same principle has been formulated by courts in the USA in the following terms: that if any life at all is left in a human body, even the least spark, the extinguishment of it is as much homicide as the killing of the most vital being.[31]

The strictness of the criminal law with respect to active euthanasia is only explicable in the context of the common law philosophy regarding the value of human life. Strongly influenced by ecclesiastical teaching, the attitude of the common law has been to uphold life as sacred and inalienable.[32] The strength of the common law belief in the sacredness of life is demonstrated by the fact that protection of the criminal law extends to all persons, even those who are already dying. Thus, the fact that an act of euthanasia was performed in respect of a terminally ill patient, whose death was in any event imminent, does not prevent liability from arising. All that needs to be shown is that as a result of the doctor's act, death occurred at the time and in the manner in which it did.[33] It should be noted, however, that the condition of the patient may still be relevant, in so far that it must be established that the alleged criminal act and not the terminal illness from which the patient was suffering was, as a matter of causation, the proximate or substantial cause of death.[34] Whilst the mere acceleration of death will suffice to establish criminal liability, as noted earlier, it must not be so minimal or trivial that it will be disregarded under the *de minimis* principle.

Position under statute

The statutory position in Canada, the USA, Australia and New Zealand regarding the condition of the patient, and the acceleration of an imminent death is the same as at common law.[35] The effect of these provisions is to restate the common law rule that the causing of death of a person will constitute murder regardless of that person's condition and the fact that death may in any event have been imminent. Although these various provi-

---

[30] Ibid. at 457. See also *R* v. *Pankotai* [1961] Crim.LR 546; *R* v. *Morby* (1882) 8 QBD 571, 575.

[31] *State* v. *Francis* 152 SC 17 (1929).

[32] *State* v. *Moore* 25 Iowa 128, 135–6 (1868).

[33] Fisse, *Howard's Criminal Law*, above n. 19, at 33.

[34] MacKinnon, P., 'Euthanasia and Homicide' (1983–4) 26 Crim.LQ 483, 493.

[35] Canada—Criminal Code 1985 s. 226; Australia—Tas. Criminal Code 1924 s. 154(d), WA Criminal Code 1913 s. 273; New Zealand—Crimes Act 1961 s. 164. For the position in the USA see LaFave and Scott, *Criminal Law*, above n. 2, at 280.

sions were not drafted specifically with active euthanasia in mind they clearly cover cases where the death of a person has been accelerated as a result of an act of euthanasia. Thus, a doctor who commits such an act is, by virtue of these provisions, deemed to have killed the patient for the purposes of the law of murder.

F. Irrelevance of Patient's Consent

Generally speaking, the consent of the victim is not a defence for the purposes of the criminal law. In *R* v. *Donovan*[36] it was held that: 'If an act is unlawful in the sense of being in itself a criminal act, it is plain that it cannot be rendered lawful because the person to whose detriment it is done consents to it. No person can license another to commit a crime'.[37] Thus, the common law position regarding the effect of consent upon the question of criminal liability for murder is abundantly clear; a person cannot lawfully consent to his or her own death.[38] As was stated in the Scottish case of *HM Advocate* v. *Rutherford*[39] by the High Court of Justiciary in Scotland: 'If life is taken under circumstances which would otherwise infer guilt of murder, the crime does not cease to be murder merely because the victim consented to be murdered, or even urged the assailant to strike the fatal blow'.[40] It is clear from this passage that it makes no difference if the consent of the victim is mere consent, in the sense of acquiescence in what another proposes, or, at the other extreme, a positive direction or request from a person that he or she be assisted to die.[41]

Similarly, for the purposes of the common law in the USA it has long been established that 'murder is no less murder because the homicide is committed at the desire of the victim. He who kills another upon his desire or command is, in the judgment of the law, as much a murderer as if he had done it merely of his own head'.[42]

[36] [1934] 2 KB 498.

[37] Ibid. at 507. See also *R* v. *Brown* [1993] 2 WLR 556; *R* v. *McLeod* (1915) 34 NZLR 430, 433–4.

[38] *R* v. *Cato*, see above n. 22. The common law prohibition on consent applies not only to death, but also to the infliction of bodily harm; see *R* v. *Donovan* [1934] 2 KB 498; *Attorney-General's Reference (No. 6 of 1980)* [1981] 1 QB 715. The law in relation to suicide (as distinct from assisted suicide) is an obvious exception to the principle that one cannot consent to one's own death. For discussion, see pp. 56–7 below.

It should be noted that in some civil law jurisdictions including Germany, Norway, and Switzerland, homicide performed at the request of the victim is treated as a lesser offence. For discussion, see pp. 460–1 below.

[39] 1947 JC 1.   [40] Ibid.

[41] See also the comments of Lord Mustill in the House of Lords decision *Airedale NHS Trust* v. *Bland* [1993] 1 All ER 821 (non-criminal case, discussed further at pp. 39–41, 48–9 below) at 890. For a discussion of the definitions and meaning of consent see Castel, J. G., 'Nature and Effects of Consent with Respect to the Right to Life and the Right to Physical and Mental Integrity in the Medical Field: Criminal and Private Law Aspects' (1978) 16 *Alta.LRev.* 293, 294.

[42] *Turner* v. *State* 119 Tenn. 663, 671 (1908).

Likewise, under the criminal statutes in Canada, the USA, Australia and New Zealand, it is irrelevant for the purposes of determining criminal responsibility, that the person killed requested or consented to his or her own death.[43]

Rationale behind the criminal law prohibition on consent to death

In order to evaluate the status of this criminal law principle it is important to understand the rationale which underlies it. The authoritarian stance of the criminal law regarding consent to death is based upon the belief that the taking of life is a wrong, not only to the person killed, but also to the entire society.[44] In the words of Devlin: 'The reason why a man may not consent to the commission of an offence against himself beforehand or forgive it afterwards is because it is an offence against society'.[45]

As noted previously, the common law tradition has always been to uphold human life as sacred and inalienable, thereby securing the general protection of human life, as well as maintaining social order and promoting the wider interests of society as a whole. The preservation of life has consequently been accorded priority over the autonomy of the individual and consequently, as a matter of public policy, the consent of the victim has never been recognized as a defence to a criminal homicide.[46]

Thus, the fact that the patient consented to his or her own death or even instigated the request does not exculpate the doctor from criminal liability. Although under common law principles, a patient has the right to accept or reject medical treatment,[47] a patient cannot validly consent to or authorize a doctor to perform an act which brings about that patient's death. The special nature of the doctor/patient relationship does not affect the general principles regarding the irrelevance of the victim's consent.

G. *Irrelevance of Motive*

A doctor who responds to a patient's request that he or she take active steps to bring about the patient's death would almost invariably be acting out of

---

[43] Canada—Criminal Code 1985 s. 14; Australia—NT Criminal Code 1983 s. 26(3), Qld. Criminal Code 1995 s. 101, Tas. Criminal Code 1924 s. 53(a), WA Criminal Code 1913 s. 261; New Zealand—Crimes Act 1961 s. 63. For the position in the USA see LaFave and Scott, *Criminal Law*, above n. 2, at 477.

[44] See the President's Commission for the Study of Ethical Problems in Medicine and Biomedical and Behavioural Research, *Deciding to Forgo Life-Sustaining Treatment: A Report on the Ethical, Medical and Legal Issues in Treatment Decisions* (Washington, 1983) 33.

[45] Devlin, P., *The Enforcement of Morals* (London, 1965) 6.

[46] Williams, *Textbook of Criminal Law*, above n. 5, 576–7.

[47] In some jurisdictions patients also have a statutory right to refuse treatment in some circumstances. For discussion, see p. 36, n. 113 below.

humanitarian motives. Indeed, the motivation of the doctor is one of the distinguishing features of active voluntary euthanasia which, in the popular mind, clearly sets it apart from more reprehensible forms of killing.[48] Notwithstanding this seemingly obvious difference between active voluntary euthanasia and other forms of killing, the compassionate motive of a doctor does not protect him or her from criminal liability for murder.[49] Furthermore, irrespective of the special nature of the doctor/patient relationship, it would be irrelevant that the acts causing death were performed by a doctor in the course of medical practice.[50] Nor could a doctor validly claim that he or she acted out of necessity to prevent further pain and suffering: the defence of necessity is not available in cases of murder.

Under general criminal law principles, a sharp distinction is made between motive and intention. Whilst the issue of intention is clearly central to the requirement of *mens rea*, both at common law[51] and in those jurisdictions where the law has been codified, motive is quite irrelevant for the purposes of establishing criminal liability.[52] It should, however, be noted that motive may be relevant with respect to sentencing once liability is found to be established, provided there is some sentencing discretion vested in the court.

II. DOCTORS' CRIMINAL LIABILITY
FOR OMISSIONS WHICH CAUSE DEATH

A. Introduction

It is widely believed that there is an important moral and practical difference between active and passive euthanasia; between 'killing' and 'letting die',[53] and it is often assumed that this distinction has legal significance as well. The word 'killing' clearly implies some active involvement with the

---

[48] Baugham, W. *et al.*, 'Euthanasia: Criminal, Tort, Constitutional and Legislative Considerations' (1973) 48 *Notre Dame Law* 1202, 1205.

[49] See the comments made in the House of Lords decision *Airedale NHS Trust* v. *Bland*, above n. 41, at 867 per Lord Goff and at 890 per Lord Mustill.

[50] Skegg, P., *Law, Ethics and Medicine* (Oxford, 1984) 130 where he refers to the judgments of Devlin J in *R* v. *Adams* (unreported) (1957). See Palmer, H., 'Dr Adams' Trial for Murder' (1957) *Crim.L.Rev.* 365; Farquharson J in *R* v. *Arthur* (unreported) *The Times*, 6 Nov. 1981.

[51] See Lord Hailsham in *Hyam* v. *Director of Public Prosecutions* [1975] AC 55, 73 for a discussion of the distinction between intention and motive. The common law position, as outlined above, also applies in NSW (and the ACT) since the Crimes Act 1900 (NSW) is silent on this matter.

[52] Australia—Qld. Criminal Code 1995 s. 50(5), Tas. Criminal Code 1924 s. 13(4), WA Criminal Code 1913 s. 23. For the position in the USA see LaFave and Scott, *Criminal Law*, above n. 2, at 227–8. Note, however, the position in some civil law jurisdictions where the motive of the accused is taken into account in determining criminal liability: see Silving, H., 'Euthanasia: A Study in Comparative Criminal Law' (1954) 103 UPa.L.Rev. 350.

[53] For consideration of the contrary view, see pp. 163–4, 191–3 below.

death of the patient, whilst 'letting die' is regarded as simply letting nature take its course without any involvement of the medical profession in the death of the patient. Although this distinction between killing and letting die has gained widespread usage and appears to have had a significant influence on medical practice, it is not necessarily a valid distinction for legal purposes. The reality of the matter is that cases of 'letting die' by withholding or withdrawing treatment may well give rise to criminal liability. However, in contrast to the area of euthanasia by affirmative acts (active euthanasia), the law regarding euthanasia by omission (passive euthanasia) is shrouded in unnecessary confusion and uncertainty.

In this part of the analysis, it is proposed to examine the criminal law principles with respect to murder as they apply to the deliberate omission of medical treatment by a doctor which results in the death of a patient. The object of this analysis is to demonstrate that most of the ingredients for criminal liability for murder can be made out in circumstances where a doctor performs passive euthanasia; that is, where a doctor deliberately omits life-sustaining treatment which he or she is under a legal duty to provide, with the object of facilitating the death of the patient, and the patient dies as a result. In turn, the fact that the conduct of doctors in withholding or withdrawing treatment could, potentially at least, be subject to criminal liability for murder highlights the necessity of closely examining the precise *scope* of the doctor's duty towards his or her patient and the legal effect of a patient's right to refuse treatment on the doctor's duty to treat.

B. The Omission

As noted earlier, the *actus reus* for the crime of murder can be either an act or an omission. As generally understood, an 'omission' involves non-performance or inaction in circumstances in which a person knows he or she has the ability and opportunity to act so as to prevent a particular result, but refrains from doing so.[54] In the medical context, this would involve the deliberate omission of medically-indicated treatment which is reasonably available, and the administration of which would have prevented the patient from dying at that time and in that manner.[55]

---

[54] President's Commission Report, *Deciding to Forgo Life-Sustaining Treatment*, above n. 44, at 65. It should be noted that even where there is no knowledge of the ability to act, a person may be guilty of an omission in circumstances where the omission was negligent.

[55] As previously noted, there is an ongoing debate as to whether some forms of discontinuation of treatment (such as the removal of artificial life-support) which involve active intervention should be classified as an 'act' or an 'omission'. This fundamental question is dealt with later in this work; see pp. 152–69 below.

C. *Attitude of the Law to Omissions and the Duty Requirement*

Under criminal law principles, a fairly strict distinction has been drawn between liability for *acts* which cause death, and liability for *omissions* which cause death. Acts which cause death are almost always wrongful, and will attract criminal liability for murder if they are accompanied by the necessary *mens rea* for the crime of murder. However, liability for omissions is exceptional. An omission to act which results in death, and accompanied by the necessary *mens rea* will only give rise to criminal liability in those specified circumstances where the criminal law imposes a legal duty to act.

In contrast to the common law's expansive approach to positive acts of harm, there has traditionally been a reluctance to impose criminal liability for omissions to prevent harm.[56] The basis of this distinction between acts and omissions is to be found in the belief that the function of the criminal law was the prevention of positive harm, and that encouragement of good deeds should be left to public opinion, morality, and religion.[57] In addition, a number of practical reasons have been put forward to explain the differential approach of the common law to acts and omissions. First of all, there are very real difficulties in attributing blame for omissions as distinct from acts. If there is an act, someone acts, but if there is an omission, everyone (in a sense) omits.[58] The difficulty is that in the case of omissions, there are too many potential candidates for liability.[59] Consequently, there has been a tendency to accord criminal responsibility only in circumstances where there is some special relationship or situation of control which is seen as giving rise to a legal obligation to act to prevent harm. Secondly, as Williams points out, it is harder for the general public to learn and remember a law about harmful omissions than it is to learn and remember a law about harmful acts.[60] Whilst ordinary persons can readily understand that they are required not to cause harm to others, they will rarely properly comprehend the circumstances in which they must aid others.

Another, more substantive, explanation for the reluctance of the common law to impose liability for an omission to act is that the imposition of a duty to act is an interference with the liberty of a person who wishes only to mind his or her own business and let others get on with minding theirs.[61] Whilst most people are capable of *refraining* from causing harm, the *prevention* of harm is likely to be more demanding. This point is well made by Williams, when he expresses the view that: 'You can refrain from doing

---

[56] For a critical analysis of the conventional view with respect to liability for omissions, see Ashworth, A., 'The Scope of Criminal Liability for Omissions' (1989) 105 *Law Q Rev.* 424.

[57] Smith J. C. and Hogan, B., *Criminal Law*, 5th edn. (London, 1983) 43.

[58] Williams, *Textbook of Criminal Law*, above n. 5, at 148.

[59] Fletcher, 'Prolonging Life', above n. 13, at 1009–10.

[60] Williams, G., 'What Should the Code do About Omissions?' (1987) 7 *Legal Stud.* 92, 93.

[61] Smith, J. C., 'Liability for Omissions in the Criminal Law' (1984) 4 *Legal Stud.* 88.

something simply by refraining; but you cannot perform a duty to act without, often, going to considerable trouble, inconvenience, expense and perhaps even danger'.[62]

It has also been argued that omissions do not *cause* evil results in the same obvious sense that acts do.[63] The reasoning employed here is that since the defendant does nothing, the evil result would necessarily occur in precisely the same way if, at the moment of the alleged omission, the defendant did not exist.[64] This causation issue, and the attitude of the common law regarding omissions generally, is well illustrated in the oft cited example found in *Stephen's Digest of the Criminal Law*[65] of the passer-by who sees a child drowning in a shallow pool. The passer-by could easily save the child without risk to himself, but allows the child to drown. At common law he commits no offence since he did not drown the child. If he had not come along the child would have drowned in just the same way.

Thus, because of the special nature of omissions to prevent harm, the common law has rarely imposed criminal liability in respect of such conduct, and a duty to act will only arise in certain defined circumstances. A similar position has been adopted in those jurisdictions where the criminal law has been codified. It is clear from the statutory scheme under the Criminal Codes in Canada and Australia that criminal liability for an omission to act will not be established in the absence of a legal *duty* to act. Each of the Codes specifies the duties of care to which one must conform in the preservation of human life[66] and imposes criminal liability for the consequences to life or health of an omission to perform those duties.[67] At both common law and under the Codes, where a duty to act can be established, the omission of that duty by a person obligated to act has the same effect in law as an act that produced the same result.

From the foregoing discussion it is clear that in all common law jurisdictions, criminal liability for omissions will only be established in circumstances where there is a pre-existing legal duty to act. It is therefore necessary to examine the circumstances in which a legal duty to act can be established.

[62] Williams, 'What Should the Code do About Omissions?', above n. 60, at 93.

[63] Hogan, B., 'Omissions and the Duty Myth' in Smith, P. (ed.), *Criminal Law: Essays in Honour of J. C. Smith* (London, 1987) 85.

[64] Smith, 'Liability for Omissions in the Criminal Law', above n. 61, at 88.

[65] 4th edn. (London, 1887) Articles 212, 154.

[66] Canada—Criminal Code 1985 ss. 215–218; Australia—NT Criminal Code 1983 ss. 149–53, Qld. Criminal Code 1995 ss. 87–92, Tas. Criminal Code 1924 ss. 144–51, 156(2)(b), WA Criminal Code 1913 ss. 262–267.

[67] Canada—Criminal Code 1985 ss. 215–18; Australia—NT Criminal Code 1983 s. 153, Qld. Criminal Code 1995 s. 86, Tas. Criminal Code 1924 s. 152, WA Criminal Code 1913 ss. 262–7. New Zealand—Crimes Act 1961 ss. 151–157. For the position in the USA see LaFave and Scott, *Criminal Law,* above n. 2, 204–6.

D. The Imposition of a Legal Duty to Act

As we have seen, as result of the law's cautious attitude to omissions there has been a marked reluctance to impose legal duties, breach of which give rise to criminal liability, and the law has generally required the existence of some kind of special relationship between the parties before a duty to act arises.[68] One such special relationship which has been held to give rise to a legally recognized duty to act is that of doctor and patient. The relationship between doctor and patient is basically contractual, arising from an offer and acceptance.[69] The contract may arise as a result of an express agreement, or, more usually, it may be implied from the conduct or circumstances of the parties. A prospective patient may come to the doctor, seeking to obtain the doctor's services. The doctor is then free to either accept or reject the patient's offer.[70] If the offer is accepted, a contract comes into existence and the law imposes a duty on the doctor to continue treatment as long as the case requires, in the absence of an agreement to the contrary.[71] A doctor cannot abandon his or her patient by purporting to terminate the contractual relationship without allowing the patient to make alternative arrangements.[72] Even in the absence of a contractual duty to provide medical care, a duty may yet arise if it can be established that the doctor has voluntarily assumed or undertaken the care of a patient.[73] Once a duty situation is found to be in existence as in the case of the doctor/patient relationship, the various legal duties which exist at common law and under legislation come into play. In the jurisdictions under consideration, there are two legal duties which may be of particular relevance to the liability of a doctor for withholding or withdrawing treatment; the duty to provide the 'necessaries of life', and the duty to do acts undertaken, the omission of which would be dangerous to human life.

[68] Williams, *Textbook of Criminal Law*, above n. 5, 150.

[69] Kennedy, I. and Grubb, A., *Medical Law: Text and Materials*, 2nd edn. (London, 1994) 69. Note, however, their view (at 52) that the relationship between doctor and patient within the National Health Service in the UK is probably not contractual in nature because there is a statutory duty to provide services.

In circumstances where a patient enters a hospital, the patient contracts with both the hospital and the treating doctor. In countries which have a national health care scheme and the patient does not actually have to pay for health care, questions may arise regarding the legal requirement of consideration. It is arguable, however, that simply submitting to treatment is a sufficient detriment which could serve as consideration; see Picard, E., *Legal Liability of Doctors and Hospitals in Canada*, 2nd edn. (Toronto, 1984) 32.

[70] A doctor will only be under a duty to provide treatment to a patient in circumstances where he or she has given an undertaking to do so: Kennedy and Grubb, *Medical Law*, above, n. 69, at 64.

[71] Baugham, et al., 'Euthanasia: Criminal, Tort, Constitutional and Legislative Considerations', above n. 48, at 1207 referring to the case of *Ricks* v. *Budge* 64 P2d 208, 211 (1937).

[72] Ibid. at 1208 citing *Murray* v. *United States* 329 F2d 270, 272 (1964).

[73] e.g. *R* v. *Instan* [1893] 1 QB 450; *R* v. *Stone* [1977] 1 QB 354. Note, however, the view of Beynon, H., 'Doctors as Murderers' (1982) *Crim.LRev.* 17, 24–5 that this category does not encompass doctors since the cases in support of it either concerned relatives or persons having some financial incentive for providing services.

The duty to provide the necessaries of life

The duty to provide the necessaries of life exists both at common law and the law as codified in Canada, Australia, New Zealand and some US states.[74] The law imposes a duty to provide necessaries in circumstances where a person has charge of another who is unable to provide him or herself with the necessaries of life by reason of some infirmity or condition, for example, due to age, sickness or unsoundness of mind. 'Necessaries of life' have been interpreted by the courts to include medical aid and treatment.[75] There has, however, been no exhaustive statement, either at common law or for the purposes of the Codes, of the meaning of the phrase 'necessaries of life' and the kinds of medical treatment that it covers. It is, for example, not clear whether the duty to provide the necessaries of life would automatically extend to all forms of artificial life-support such as respirators, dialysis, and artificial nutrition and hydration. One view, which has considerable merit, is that the scope of the doctor's duty would depend on the circumstances of the case and on the question whether the failure to provide medical treatment was reasonable in the circumstances.[76] This was the view taken in the New Zealand case *Auckland Area Health Board* v. *Attorney General*[77] which involved a male patient suffering from Guillian-Barre syndrome, with virtually no brain function (although not actually brain-dead) and who was ventilator dependent. Justice Thomas of the Auckland High Court, in interpreting section 151 of the New Zealand Crimes Act 1961, said that the question whether a ventilator should be regarded as a necessary of life must depend on the facts of each case. Thus, it may be regarded as a necessary of life where it is required to prevent, cure, or alleviate a disease that endangers the health or life of the patient. If, however, the patient is surviving only by virtue of the mechanical means which induces heartbeat and breathing and is beyond recovery, the provision of a ventilator cannot properly be construed as a necessary of life.[78] In Mr L's case there was no prospect of improvement and Thomas J held that in these circumstances, it served no purpose, and could not properly be regarded as a necessary of life.[79]

---

[74] Canada—Criminal Code 1985 s. 215; Australia—NT Criminal Code 1983 s. 149, Qld. Criminal Code 1995 s. 87, Tas. Criminal Code 1924 s. 144, WA Criminal Code 1913 s. 262; New Zealand—Crimes Act 1961 s. 151. For the position in the USA see LaFave and Scott, *Criminal Law*, above n. 2, at 205.

[75] *R v. Brooks* (1902) 5 CCC 372; *Oakey v. Jackson* [1914] 1 KB 216; *R v. McDonald* [1904] StR Qd. 151.

[76] Dickens, B., 'The Right to Natural Death' (1981) 26 *McGill LJ* 847, 871.

[77] [1993] 1 NZLR 235. For detailed discussion of this case see Skegg, P., 'Omissions to Provide Life-Prolonging Treatment' (1994) 8 *Otago LRev.* 205.

[78] Ibid.

[79] Some indirect support for this view can also be gleaned from the Canadian case of *Nancy B v. Hôtel-Dieu de Québec* 69 CCC (3d) (1992) 450, 458. Although a civil case concerning the right of a competent patient to direct that a life-sustaining respirator be removed, the Quebec Superior Court also examined the criminal law implications of a doctor's compliance with the

Before the duty to provide a patient with medical treatment and other necessaries of life can arise, the doctor must 'have charge' of the patient. Whether a person has charge of another is a question of fact. A patient may be under a doctor's charge as a result of a contract or some other relationship. Thus, doctors, who have contracted to care for someone who is helpless by reason of age or illness, have a duty to provide that person with necessary medical treatment. Alternatively, in the absence of contract, if a doctor has otherwise undertaken the care of a patient, the law imposes an obligation to provide that patient with necessary medical treatment.

Where a doctor is under a legal duty to provide a patient with the necessaries of life including medical treatment, the doctor will be held criminally liable for any consequences which result to the life or health of the patient by reason of the doctor's omission to perform that duty, provided the requisite *mens rea* is established.[80] If a patient dies as a result of the doctor's deliberate breach of that duty, the doctor could be charged with murder at common law and in Code jurisdictions.

The duty to do acts undertaken

Both at common law and under the Codes, a duty is imposed to do acts undertaken, the omission of which may be dangerous to human life.[81] The duty to do acts undertaken clearly applies to a medical practitioner who has undertaken to provide treatment, (for example, artificial life-support) the omission of which would be dangerous to the life of the patient.[82] In the event of the doctor failing to perform that duty, the doctor will be held criminally liable for the death of the patient by reason of that omission, provided the requisite *mens rea* is established.

E. The Causation Requirement

As we have seen, a doctor may be liable under the criminal law not only for his or her acts which result in death, but also for omissions, in circumstances

---

patient's request. In examining the relevant sections of the Canadian Criminal Code the court was of the view that s. 217 (dealing with the duty of persons undertaking acts) potentially applied. No reference was made to s. 215 dealing with the duty to provide necessaries of life. This could be taken to suggest that the court did not think that the provision of artificial life-support was a 'necessary of life'. For further discussion see pp. 51–2 below.

[80] For the position under the Codes, see Canada—Criminal Code 1985 s. 215; Australia—NT Criminal Code 1983 s. 153, Qld. Criminal Code 1995 s. 86, Tas. Criminal Code 1924 s. 152, WA Criminal Code 1913 s. 262; New Zealand—Crimes Act 1961 s. 151.

[81] For the position under the Codes, see Canada—Criminal Code 1985 s. 215 ; Australia—NT Criminal Code 1983 s. 152, Qld. Criminal Code 1995 s. 90, Tas. Criminal Code 1924 ss. 151 and 152, WA Criminal Code 1913 s. 267; New Zealand—Crimes Act 1961 s. 157. For the position in the USA see LaFave and Scott, *Criminal Law,* above n. 2, at 205–6.

[82] This proposition is supported by the Canadian case of *Nancy B* v. *Hôtel-Dieu de Québec,* above n. 79.

where there was a duty to act. For the purposes of the present discussion it will be assumed that the doctor was under a duty to provide treatment to the patient, and his or her failure to do so was accompanied by the requisite *mens rea* for the crime of murder. In addition to these elements, in order for criminal liability for murder to be established against the doctor, it will also be necessary to prove that the failure to provide treatment was causally connected with the death of the patient. In the majority of homicide cases, there is little doubt as to the cause of death of the victim, and consequently, the issue of causation does not specifically arise.[83] Occasionally, however, difficult problems of causation do occur and one particular area where difficulties may arise is in the context of omissions.

Omissions as a cause of death

An initial objection may be raised that an omission cannot in any real sense be a cause of death.[84] Since the person has simply omitted to act, the death would have occurred in precisely the same way if, at the moment of the alleged omission, he or she did not exist.[85] On this view, the death can readily be attributed to factors other than the non-intervention of the person omitting to act. Thus, in the medical context, where certain treatment or procedures have been withheld or withdrawn from a terminally ill patient, it is easy to attribute the cause of death to the underlying condition or disease of the patient rather than the failure of the doctor to intervene.[86] However, as Williams observes, whatever the philosophical view may be, the courts certainly assume and must assume that an omission can be a cause of death. Whilst it may be easier to find the causation requirement established in a situation where a doctor has taken active steps to kill his or her patient, circumstances can be readily envisaged where the death of the patient was clearly caused by the omission of the doctor to provide necessary treatment. Take, for instance, a situation where an otherwise healthy patient, who desired treatment, dies from untreated pneumonia. In these circumstances, the doctor's failure to provide the necessary treatment could fairly be taken to have caused the death of the patient.

---

[83] Williams, *Textbook of Criminal Law,* above n. 5, 379–80.

[84] e.g. Fletcher, 'Prolonging Life', above n. 13, where he develops the argument that in certain circumstances, an omission which involves the interruption of life-sustaining therapy, such as turning off a mechanical respirator, is not a cause of death.

[85] Smith, 'Liability for Omissions in the Criminal Law', above n. 61, at 88.

[86] See the discussion in the President's Commission Report, *Deciding to Forgo Life-Sustaining Treatment,* above n. 44, at 68–70 where it is pointed out that the identification of the cause of death inevitably involves a normative question of attributing responsibility. In circumstances where a patient dies following non-treatment, the designation of the patient's underlying disease as the cause of death indicates not only that a fatal disease process was present, but also communicates acceptance of the doctor's conduct in forgoing treatment.

Omissions to provide treatment resulting in the death of the patient

As was noted earlier, both at common law and under the Codes, there are two distinct aspects to the legal principle of causation; the *sine qua non* test and the issue of imputability. Under the *sine qua non* or 'but for' test, it is necessary to establish that, as a matter of fact, the doctor's conduct caused the death of the patient although it need not be the sole or the main cause of death. This will be a question of fact in each case, and must be established by the prosecution beyond reasonable doubt. As Williams comments, the application of the usual burden of proof to the issue of causation is of considerable practical importance in the case of omissions[87] and often results in unsuccessful prosecutions.[88] Thus, it would have to be shown beyond reasonable doubt that, had the doctor not withheld or withdrawn treatment, the patient would not have died at that time and in that way. From a practical point of view, it may be difficult to determine the factual cause of the patient's death with any accuracy. In some instances, it will be relatively easy to establish that the cause of the patient dying, at that time and in that manner, was due to the withholding or withdrawing of treatment; for example, a diabetic patient requiring insulin or an accident victim requiring a blood transfusion. However, in the context of terminally ill patients who are in any event close to death, difficulties may arise in establishing beyond reasonable doubt that the death was due to the omission and not the patient's underlying condition.[89]

In addition to the *sine qua non* test it will also be necessary to show that the doctor's conduct was an imputable or legal cause of the patient's death. The imputable cause component of the causation test is, by its nature, incapable of strictly objective assessment. Essentially it involves determination of whether the doctor's conduct is sufficiently connected with the death of the patient so as to attribute to him or her legal responsibility for that death. In circumstances where a patient has died following non-treatment, the court will need to weigh up the factors leading to the death of the patient to determine the significance of the doctor's contribution in withdrawing treatment, and whether legal responsibility for the death should, as a matter of law, be attributed to the doctor. Whilst the involvement in the cause of death need not be substantial to render a defendant guilty of murder,[90] a very minimal or trivial contribution to the cause of death may be

---

[87] *Textbook of Criminal Law,* above n. 5, at 380.

[88] See Hughes, 'Criminal Omissions', above n. 10, at 627–31 for criticism of this rule on the ground that it is inappropriate in the case of homicide by omission, because it allows too easy a let-out for the accused.

[89] Williams, 'What Should the Code do About Omissions?', above n. 60, at 106 where he notes that doctors will often testify that their ministrations would probably have saved the sufferer, but are unlikely to swear that they could, beyond reasonable doubt, have saved him. For a case law example of difficulties which may be encountered in establishing causation, see *R* v. *Arthur,* above, n. 50.

[90] *R* v. *Cato,* above, n. 22, at 265–6.

ignored under the *de minimis* principle: the court may find that although the withholding or withdrawal of treatment contributed to the patient dying at that time and in that manner, the contribution was so minimal or negligible in light of the patient's terminal condition that it should be disregarded. As was noted earlier, the court must decide, as a matter of law, whether there is sufficient evidence to support a finding of imputable cause which could be left to the jury, although in reality this determination involves a value judgement whether the result can fairly be said to be imputable to the defendant.

A number of criminal law cases involving the withdrawal of treatment from victims of assault suggest that the courts may be reluctant to attribute the death of a patient to the conduct of the doctor.[91] In these cases the courts have held that the discontinuance of life-support from a brain-damaged assault victim does not break the chain of causation between the initial injury and the death and therefore did not constitute the relevant cause of death. These cases, although involving different circumstances, lend support to the view that withholding treatment is sometimes a sound medical decision and in some circumstances will not constitute a cause of death.[92]

F. Mens Rea *for the Crime of Murder*

In order to establish criminal liability for murder by omission, the *actus reus* for that crime (the failure to perform a legal duty which causes the death of the victim), must be accompanied by the requisite *mens rea* for the crime of murder. It is therefore necessary to consider the *mens rea* for the crime of murder and its application in circumstances in which a doctor omits to provide medical treatment and the patient dies as a result.[93] As a result of certain differences in the law regarding the *mens rea* for murder as between common law and Code jurisdictions, separate consideration will be given to the law in these respective jurisdictions.

Common law position

As was noted earlier, the mental element for murder at common law is 'malice aforethought' which clearly encompasses an intention to kill or an intention to inflict grievous bodily harm. Under the common law in England as laid down by the House of Lords, foresight of consequences resulting in death as probable may result in a finding by a jury that the defendant

[91] e.g. *R* v. *Malcherek* [1981] 1 WLR 690; *R* v. *Kinash* [1982] QdR 648.
[92] See also *Airedale NHS Trust* v. *Bland*, above n. 41, and the discussion below.
[93] As was noted earlier, even if the necessary intention for the crime of murder cannot be established, a doctor may still face charges of manslaughter or criminal negligence.

intended those consequences.[94] Even in the absence of actual intention, in those Australian states where the common law still applies, the requisite mental element can be established by evidence of knowledge that death or grievous bodily harm was the probable or likely consequence of that conduct.[95]

In the medical context, it is not difficult to accept the possibility that a doctor may omit certain treatment with the intention of causing the death of the patient so as to relieve the patient of prolonged suffering. However, it may appear incongruous to suggest that a doctor could *bona fide* intend to cause a patient grievous bodily harm by his or her omission. As unlikely as it may seem, this possibility cannot be ruled out. It is conceivable that certain treatment may be withheld or withdrawn with the intention of not actually causing the death of the patient, but of diminishing the patient's defences, and thereby leaving the patient more susceptible to the process of death.

On the basis of the foregoing principles it would appear that the prosecution would have little difficulty in establishing the necessary mental element for murder in respect of a doctor who has deliberately withheld or withdrawn life-sustaining medical treatment from a patient. The acceleration of the patient's death would generally be the intended result.[96] Alternatively, for the purposes of the common law in Australia, even where death was not actually intended, death or grievous bodily harm would be within the knowledge of the doctor as the *probable* or *likely* result of the withholding or withdrawing of life-sustaining medical treatment, which would be sufficient to establish liability for murder.

It should be noted, however, that the courts have acknowledged that not every fatal act or omission done with the knowledge that death or grievous bodily harm will probably result is murder. The conduct may be lawful, that is justified or excused by law.[97] The example has been given of a surgeon who competently performs a hazardous but necessary operation and who would not be criminally liable if the patient dies even if the surgeon foresaw that the patient's death was probable.[98] The question thus becomes (as explored later in this chapter) whether the conduct of the doctor can, in some way, be justified or excused by law.

---

[94] *R* v. *Moloney* [1985] AC 905; *R* v. *Hancock and Shankland* [1986] 1 AC 455.

[95] *R* v. *Crabbe* (1985) 58 ALR 417 (High Court of Australia). This category, which is sometimes referred to as 'murder by recklessness', does not form part of the law in England. For the position in Scotland, where 'wicked recklessness' is sufficient to establish *mens rea* for murder, see Gordon, G., *Criminal Law of Scotland*, 2nd edn. (Edinburgh, 1978) 737.

[96] Including, for the purposes of the law in England, circumstances where there was a sufficiently high probability of death or grievous bodily harm resulting from that conduct that the doctor would be found to have intended that result.

[97] *R* v. *Crabbe* (1985), above n. 95, at 421.

[98] Ibid. See also *R* v. *Brown*, above n. 37, at 593.

Position under the codes

As was outlined above, in those jurisdictions where the criminal law has been codified, the mental element for murder includes an intention to cause death or grievous bodily harm. Accordingly, if there is evidence that the doctor actually *intended* to cause the death of the patient or cause the patient grievous bodily harm by the withholding or withdrawing of medical treatment, the *mens rea* for murder could readily be established.[99]

G. *Irrelevance of Motive and the Terminal Condition of the Patient*

As was observed during the earlier discussion regarding the criminal liability of doctors for acts which cause the death of the patient, provided the necessary *mens rea* for the crime of murder is established, the motive of the doctor is irrelevant. Thus, if the doctor's omission to provide a patient with medical treatment involves the *actus reus* and *mens rea* for murder, it will be irrelevant to the question of liability that the doctor acted out of compassionate and *bona fide* motives. Further, the fact that the patient in respect of whom treatment was withheld or withdrawn was in a terminal condition, and would in any event have soon died, does not alter the criminal liability of the doctor. Any acceleration of death will suffice, provided only that it is not so minimal or trivial as to be disregarded under the *de minimis* principle.

III. LEGAL EFFECT OF A PATIENT'S RIGHT TO REFUSE TREATMENT ON A DOCTOR'S DUTY TO TREAT

A. *Scope of a Doctor's Duty to Treat*

It was emphasized in the foregoing discussion that an omission to act which results in death will only give rise to criminal liability in circumstances where there is a legal duty to act. Crucial therefore to the question of a doctor's criminal liability for passive euthanasia is the scope of the doctor's duty to his or her patient.

It is generally accepted that a doctor's duty to his or her patient is not absolute.[100] The law does not require that *all* possible treatments and procedures be used in every case. The patient's prognosis may be so poor that the

---

[99] Note for the purposes of the Canadian Criminal Code 1985 (s. 229(ii)) the precise requirement would be that the doctor meant to cause the patient's death or meant to cause the patient bodily harm that he or she knew was likely to cause death and was reckless whether death ensued or not.

[100] Williams, *Textbook of Criminal Law*, above n. 5, at 279–82. There is, increasingly now, case law in support of this proposition: e.g. *Airedale NHS Trust* v. *Bland*, above n. 41; *Rodriguez* v. *British Columbia (Attorney General)* [1993] 3 SCR 519; *Auckland Area Health Board* v. *Attorney General*, above n. 77. In some instances, the legislatures have acted to clarify the situation: e.g. the Consent to Medical Treatment and Palliative Care Act 1995 enacted in South Australia (s.17(2)).

continuation of treatment is futile, and the artificial prolongation of the dying process may in fact be seen as being contrary to the patient's best interests. In such circumstances, where the patient is unlikely to benefit from further treatment, a doctor would not be under a legal duty to provide that treatment.[101] Furthermore, in view of the practical limitations on the availability of medical resources, some consideration of the appropriate allocation of scarce resources and of cost-effectiveness inevitably must come into the decision-making. Especially in light of the general ageing of our population, the demand for medical resources could not be met if every possible measure was obligatory in all cases. Whilst there is widespread agreement that there are limits on the duty of doctors to treat terminally ill patients, the difficulty lies in determining the precise *scope* of that duty and at what point the doctor's duty ceases. There is very real concern amongst many health care professionals about their potential legal liability for the withholding or withdrawing of treatment from a patient. This state of uncertainty obviously has undesirable consequences for medical practice as doctors may, for fear of criminal liability, be reluctant to withhold or withdraw treatment where it would otherwise be appropriate to do so. In turn, the continuation of futile medical treatment is unlikely to promote the interests of patients.

In an attempt to clarify the nature and extent of a doctor's duty to his or her patient, a number of different formulations have been advanced.[102] It is, however, not intended to embark here upon a general examination of the precise scope of a doctor's duty to provide treatment. The purpose of this part is to pursue a more limited line of inquiry; to confine analysis to circumstances where a doctor is under a *prima facie* duty to treat, and then to focus attention on the position of a patient with decision-making capacity, who has given a clear direction that he or she wishes to have no further treatment, and to examine the legal implications of such a direction upon the doctor's legal duty to provide treatment.

Situations may arise where a doctor has in his or her care a patient with decision-making capacity, for whom certain life-prolonging or even life-saving measures would be available, but the patient may request that no further treatment be administered.[103] Since a doctor will not be criminally liable for an omission to treat unless he or she is under a legal duty to

---

[101] This would be the case regardless of whether the patient wishes to receive that treatment: whilst a patient has a right to *refuse* treatment he or she cannot insist upon receiving all possible medical treatment against the medical judgement of the doctor; Kennedy, I., *Treat Me Right* (Oxford, 1988) 321. See also Lamer CJ in *Rodriguez* v. *British Columbia (Attorney General)*, above n. 100, at 560.

[102] e.g. a duty based upon professional standards and customary practice or a duty dependent on the contract pursuant to which the doctor provides medical treatment. For discussion, see Beynon, 'Doctors as Murderers', above n. 73, at 23–8.

[103] The patient may refuse *all* further treatment or may selectively refuse treatment; e.g. declining certain life-prolonging treatment but accepting nutrition and hydration and treatment for pain management.

provide treatment, the fundamental question which arises for determination is the legal effect of the patient's refusal of treatment upon the doctor's duty to treat. Resolution of this question involves consideration of the interrelationship between two disparate and potentially conflicting areas: the patient's common law right to refuse treatment and the criminal law position regarding the legal status of consent of the victim in determining culpability for homicide. In turn, these issues reflect wider interests and competing considerations; the individual's interest in patient autonomy and self-determination on the one hand, and the State's interest in the preservation of human life on the other.

B. The Patient's Common Law Right to Refuse Treatment

The common law has long recognized an individual's right to self-determination over his or her own body, free from interference by others.[104] This right of self-determination is said to express the principle, or value choice, of autonomy of the person. Central to this right to bodily integrity is the common law doctrine of consent. Strictly speaking, every unauthorized touching of a person constitutes an assault and battery[105] and it is only the fact of consent which renders it lawful. Consequently, in the medical context, the administration of medical treatment which involves any touching, without the consent of the patient, will *prima facie* be unlawful[106] and may give rise to both civil liability for damages[107] as well as possible criminal proceedings for assault. Since the unlawfulness stems from the fact of

[104] Engelhardt, T., *The Foundations of Bioethics* (New York, 1986) 264 where he states that it is one of the presumptions of English law that individuals should be secure in their bodies against the unauthorized touching of others. See also *Union Pacific Railway* v. *Botsford* 141 US 250, 251 (1891) where the court stated 'no right is more sacred or is more carefully guarded, by the common law, than the right of every individual to the possession and control of his own person, free from all restraint or interference of others, unless by clear and unquestionable authority of law'. For a general discussion of the principles of self-determination, autonomy and inviolability, see the Law Reform Commission of Canada, Study Paper, *Consent to Medical Care* (Ottawa, 1979) ch. 1.

[105] See *Collins* v. *Wilcock* [1984] 3 All ER 374, 378; *In re F (Mental Patient: Sterilisation)* [1989] 2 WLR 1025, 1066–7, 1082–3; and *Re T (adult: refusal of treatment)* [1992] 4 All ER 649 per Lord Donaldson MR. These principles have also been accepted in Australia; e.g. in the judgments of Nicholson CJ of the Family Court in *In re Jane* [1989] FLC 92-007, 77, 243; *In re Marion* [1991] FLC 92-193, 72,299-78,300.

[106] There are some exceptions, for example in cases of emergency, where treatment is necessary to save the patient's life but the patient is unable to give consent to that treatment (*F* v. *West Berkshire Health Authority* [1990] 2 AC 1, see especially Lord Goff at 73–7; *Re T (adult: refusal of treatment)*, above n. 105, at 653 per Lord Donaldson MR; *Airedale NHS Trust* v. *Bland*, above n. 41, at 889–90 per Lord Mustill). Some statutory exceptions have also been made to the requirement of consent to treatment e.g. public health and mental health legislation.

[107] For an example of a case where a patient successfully sued a doctor for damages in respect of unauthorized medical treatment see *Malette* v. *Shulman* [1991] 2 Med.LR 162. There have also been a number of US cases where the courts have recognized that doctors may be sued for imposing life-sustaining treatment against the wishes of the patient; e.g. *Leach* v. *Shapiro* 13 Ohio App. 3d 393 (1984); *Bartling* v. *Superior Court* 147 Cal. App. 3d 1006 (1983).

touching itself, the contact need not be harmful to the patient for it to give rise to liability nor is there any requirement that the touching be done with hostility.[108] It is, therefore, no defence that the treatment or procedure was skilfully performed or that it was medically necessary and actually benefited the patient.[109] In order to establish a valid cause of action all that needs to be shown is that the treatment was administered in the absence of consent. Where, however, a patient with decision-making capacity has given a legally effective consent to the particular intervention,[110] the patient's consent is a complete defence to any action for damages based on the tort of battery and to any criminal proceedings.[111]

The common law doctrine of 'informed consent' has evolved from these fundamental principles and provides a firm basis for legal recognition of the right of a patient with decision-making capacity to refuse treatment.[112] Pursuant to this doctrine, a doctor is required to make full disclosure to a patient of all proposed medical procedures, the material risks of those procedures, and alternative courses of action. On the basis of the information received from the doctor, the patient is then free to choose amongst the available treatment options. This right of a patient with decision-making capacity to give consent to treatment after having been fully informed as to the material risks of the proposed treatment, logically involves a corresponding right to *refuse* treatment. If a doctor administers treatment without the consent, or indeed, contrary to the express wishes of the patient, the patient's rights are violated. This reasoning has gained wide acceptance and it is now established beyond doubt that patients who have decision-making capacity have a common law right to refuse treatment.[113]

---

[108] *Boughey* v. *R* (1986) 65 ALR 609; *In re F (Mental Patient: Sterilisation)*, above n. 105, at 73 per Lord Goff.

[109] e.g. *Cull* v. *Royal Surrey County Hospital and Butler* [1932] 1 BMJ 1195.

[110] For a consent to medical treatment to be legally effective the medical procedure/ treatment must be one to which the person can give a legally valid consent; the person must have the legal capacity to give a valid consent; and the consent must be a real consent—i.e. it must be voluntarily given in respect of a particular procedure or treatment performed by a particular individual and the person must be aware in broad terms of the nature and purpose of the treatment to which he or she is consenting.

[111] There are some applications of force to which legally effective consent cannot be given for the purpose of the offence of battery; see *A-G's. Reference (No. 6 of 1980)*, above n. 38.

[112] See also the Report of the President's Commission for the Study of Ethical Problems in Medicine and Biomedical and Behavioural Research, *Making Health Care Decisions* (Washington, 1982) 16–17 where the doctrine of informed consent was described as a principle of law embodied within the patient's autonomy or right of self-determination requiring full disclosure to the patient.

[113] In addition to the common law right to refuse treatment, a limited right for competent patients to refuse treatment exists under the statute law of a number of jurisdictions: Article 19.1 of the Civil Code of Lower Canada as amended in 1989; Australia—Vic. Medical Treatment Act 1988, ACT Medical Treatment Act 1994; New Zealand—Bill of Rights Act 1990 s. 11. Legislation is also in place in many US states and also in a number of Canadian and Australian jurisdictions creating mechanisms for future decision-making in the event of incompetency by means of advance directive or durable power of attorney.

The classic exposition of these principles is to be found in the frequently cited judgment of Cardozo J in the American case of *Scholoendorf* v. *Society of New York Hospital*:[114] 'Every human being of adult years and sound mind has a right to determine what shall be done with his own body; and a surgeon who performs an operation without his patient's consent commits an assault for which he is liable in damages'.[115] The issues of patient self-determination and treatment decisions generally, have been most frequently litigated in the USA. A substantial body of case law now exists in which the courts in the USA have sought to balance the patient's right to refuse treatment with a number of State interests including the State's interest in the protection of innocent third parties; the prevention of suicide; the preservation of life; and safeguarding the ethical integrity of the medical profession.[116] Only if the individual's right to self-determination outweighs all the relevant State interests will the right to refuse medical treatment be upheld. Although the courts have, in a number of the earlier cases, denied the right of a patient to refuse treatment and have ordered that treatment be administered against the patient's expressed wishes,[117] the clear trend emerging from more recent case law is that the patient's right to refuse treatment, even life-saving treatment, will be upheld.[118] Since *Cruzan* v. *Director, Missouri Department of Health*,[119] the first 'right to die' case to come before the United States Supreme Court, the legal consensus is stronger than ever.[120]

The patient's right of self-determination has also been acknowledged by the House of Lords in *In re F (Mental Patient: Sterilisation)*[121] in the following terms:

At common law a doctor cannot lawfully operate on adult patients of sound mind or give them any other treatment involving the application of physical force however small, without their consent. If a doctor were to operate on such patients or give them other treatment without their consent, he would commit the actionable tort of trespass to the person.[122]

One of the clearest statements yet of the common law right to refuse treatment was made in the case of *Re T (adult: refusal of medical treat-*

---

[114] 211 NY 125 (1914).   [115] Ibid. at 126.

[116] The relevant State interests have been formulated by the various state courts in the USA, beginning with the seminal *In re Quinlan* case, 355 A2d 647 (1976), and then more comprehensively outlined in *Superintendent of Belcherton State School* v. *Saikewicz* 370 NE 2d 417 and *In re Conroy* 486 A2d 1209 (1985). The existence of State interests which must be balanced against the individual's right to refuse treatment has also been acknowledged by the US Supreme Court in *Cruzan* v. *Director, Missouri Department of Health* 111 LEd. 2d 224 (1990).

[117] e.g. *United States* v. *George* 239 FSupp. 752 (1965); *In re President and Directors of Georgetown College, Inc.* 331 F2d 1000 (1964).

[118] e.g. *In re Farrel* 529 A2d 404 (1987).

[119] See above n. 116.

[120] Meisel, A., 'A Retrospective on *Cruzan*' (1992) 20 *Law Med. & Health Care* 340.

[121] See above n. 105.   [122] Ibid. at 1066–7 per Lord Brandon.

ment),[123] one of the few English cases which has actually involved a refusal of treatment situation. The subject of this case, T, who had been brought up by her mother who was a Jehovah's Witness, was injured in a car accident when she was 34 weeks pregnant. She was admitted to hospital where the possibility of her receiving a blood transfusion was discussed. After a private conversation with her mother, T had indicated to the medical staff, both orally and in writing, that she did not wish to have a blood transfusion if one should become necessary. Following an emergency caesarian operation T's condition deteriorated and she required a blood transfusion. An emergency court hearing was initiated by T's father and her boyfriend (who were not Jehovah's Witnesses) and they sought a declaration that it would be lawful to administer a blood transfusion if, in the clinical judgement of the doctor, that was in the patient's best interests. At first instance, Ward J granted the declaration, holding that in the circumstances, it would not be unlawful for doctors to administer a blood transfusion if that was required in the best interests of the patient. An appeal was brought against this order. The Court of Appeal affirmed the decision of Ward J on the grounds that the patient was not in a physical or mental condition which enabled her to reach a decision binding on the medical authorities and that even if, contrary to that view, she would otherwise have been in a position to reach such a decision, the influence of her mother was such as to vitiate the decision which she expressed. The case is particularly significant for the unequivocal support given to the right of a patient who has decision-making capacity, to refuse medical treatment. In the words of Lord Donaldson MR, with whom Butler-Sloss and Staughton LJJ agreed:

An adult patient who ... suffers from no mental incapacity, has an absolute right to choose whether to consent to medical treatment, to refuse it or to choose one rather than another of the treatments being offered. ... This right of choice is not limited to decisions others might regard as sensible. It exists notwithstanding that the reasons for making the choice are rational, irrational, unknown or even non-existent.

The law requires that an adult patient who is mentally and physically capable of exercising a choice must consent if medical treatment of him is to be lawful, although the consent need not be in writing and may sometimes be inferred from the patient's conduct in the context of the surrounding circumstances. Treating him without his consent or despite a refusal of consent will constitute a civil wrong of trespass to the person and may constitute a crime.[124]

These statements of principle have since been affirmed by the House of Lords in the landmark decision of *Airedale NHS Trust* v. *Bland.*[125] The patient in this case, 21-year-old Anthony Bland, had been in a persistent vegetative state for $3\frac{1}{2}$ years after suffering a severe crushed chest injury in the Hillsborough stadium disaster. As a result of prolonged deprivation of

---

[123] See above n. 105.   [124] Ibid. at 652–3.   [125] See above n. 41.

oxygen he suffered irreversible damage to the brain cortex. All the higher functions of his brain had been destroyed and he could no longer see, hear, feel or be aware of anything. However, as his brain stem continued to function, he was able to breathe unaided. He was being kept alive by means of artificial hydration and nutrition administered through a naso-gastric tube. The unanimous opinion of all the doctors who examined him was that there was no hope of recovery or improvement of any kind. The consultant geriatrician at the hospital where Anthony Bland was being cared for reached the conclusion that it would be appropriate to cease further treatment which would involve withdrawing the artificial feeding and withholding antibiotic treatment in the event that infection occurred. The health authority responsible for Anthony Bland's care, with the support of the parents and family of the patient, applied to the court for declarations that it and the responsible physicians could lawfully discontinue all life-sustaining treatment and medical support measures designed to keep Anthony Bland alive. At first instance Sir Stephen Brown granted the application sought. The Official Solicitor appealed to the Court of Appeal which unanimously upheld the original decision. The Official Solicitor then appealed to the House of Lords contending that the withdrawal of life-support was a breach of the doctor's duty to care for his patient and a criminal act. In a unanimous decision, the House of Lords dismissed the appeal.[126] The House of Lords held that a doctor who has in his care an incompetent patient was under no absolute obligation to prolong the patient's life regardless of the circumstances or quality of the patient's life. Medical treatment, including artificial feeding and the administration of antibiotic drugs, could lawfully be withheld from an insensate patient with no hope of recovery when it was known that the result would be that the patient would shortly thereafter die, provided competent and responsible medical opinion was of the view that it would be in the patient's best interests not to prolong his life by continuing that treatment because such continuance was futile and would not confer any benefit on him. Furthermore, the House of Lords held that the discontinuance of life-support by the withdrawal of artificial feeding or other means of life-support did not amount to a criminal act because if the continuance of that intrusive life-support system was not in the patient's best interests the doctor was no longer under a duty to maintain the patient's life. Rather, the doctor would simply be allowing the patient to die of his pre-existing condition and his death would be regarded in law as exclusively caused by the injury or disease to which his condition is attributable. Their Lordships did however

[126] For general analysis and commentary on this case see Kennedy, I. and Grubb, A., 'Withdrawal of Artificial Hydration and Nutrition: Incompetent Adult: *Airedale NHS Trust* v. *Bland*' [1993] 1 *Med. LR* 359 and Lanham, D., 'Withdrawal of Artificial Feeding from Patients in a Persistent Vegetative State' (1994) 6 *Current Issues in Criminal Justice* 135. For a similar action commenced in Scotland, which was reported in the press at the time this manuscript was being finalized, see *Law Hospital N.H.S. Trust* v. Lord Advocate, *The Times* 20 May 1996.

state that for the time being, doctors should, as a matter of practice, seek the guidance of the courts in all cases before withholding life-prolonging treatment from a patient in a persistent vegetative state.

The House of Lords decision in the *Bland* case has clearly established important principles for the purposes of the law in England with regard to the withdrawal of life-support from patients in a persistent vegetative state. However, the relevance of this decision goes far beyond that rather limited factual situation. Though many important questions undoubtedly remain to be addressed,[127] the principles upon which the House of Lords decision was based were stated in fairly broad terms and are capable of more general application.

The House of Lords decision contains a number of important statements recognizing the unconditional right of a competent adult patient to make his or her own treatment decisions. The judgment of Lord Goff contains the most detailed account:

First it is established that the principle of self-determination requires that respect must be given to the wishes of the patient, so that, if an adult patient of sound mind refuses, however unreasonably, to consent to treatment or care by which his life would or might be prolonged, the doctors responsible for his care must give effect to his wishes, even though they do not consider it to be in his best interests to do so . . . To this extent, the principle of the sanctity of human life must yield to the principle of self-determination, and for present purposes more important, the doctor's duty to act in the best interests of his patient must likewise be qualified. On this basis it has been held that a patient of sound mind may, if properly informed, require that life support should be discontinued.[128]

Lord Mustill also stressed the paramountcy of the patient's choice:

If the patient is capable of making a decision on whether to permit treatment and decides not to permit it his choice must be obeyed, even if on any objective view it is contrary to his best interests. A doctor has no right to proceed in the face of objection, even if it is plain to all, including the patient, that adverse consequences and even death will or may ensue.[129]

Although only Lord Goff specifically referred to the Court of Appeal's decision in *Re T (adult: refusal of treatment)* the rest of their Lordships have implicitly at least given their approval to the reasoning in that case.[130]

Similar statements unequivocally in support of the right of a competent adult patient to refuse treatment can be found in judgments at the highest level in other common law jurisdictions including Canada and Australia. In

---

[127] Lanham, 'Withdrawal of Artificial Feeding from Patients in a Persistent Vegetative State', above n. 126, at 142.

[128] See above n. 41, at 866.

[129] Ibid. at 889. See also Lord Keith at 860 and Lord Browne-Wilkinson at 881–2.

[130] Kennedy and Grubb, 'Withdrawal of Artificial Hydration and Nutrition: Incompetent Adult: *Airedale NHS Trust* v. *Bland*', above n. 126, at 360–1.

the case of *Rodriguez* v. *British Columbia (Attorney General)*[131] in which an order was sought by the appellant that the prohibition on assisting suicide contained in the Canadian Criminal Code 1985 was contrary to certain provisions of the Canadian Charter of Rights and Freedoms reference was made by the Supreme Court of Canada to patients' rights at common law.[132] Sopinka J, delivering the judgment for the majority referred with approval to the House of Lords decision in the *Bland* case, and expressed the Canadian situation in the following terms:

Canadian courts have recognised a common law right of patients to refuse to consent to medical treatment, or to demand that treatment, once commenced, be withdrawn or discontinued. This right has been specifically recognised to exist even if the withdrawal from or refusal of treatment may result in death.[133]

Similarly, the High Court of Australia, in the context of a case concerning the sterilisation of a handicapped minor (*Secretary, Department of Health and Community Services (NT)* v. *JWB and SMB*[134]) has endorsed the fundamental right to personal inviolability. In the words of McHugh J:

It is the central thesis of the common law doctrine of trespass to the person that the voluntary choices and decisions of an adult person of sound mind concerning what is or is not done to his or her body must be respected and accepted, irrespective of what others, including doctors, may think is in the best interests of that particular person . . . the common law respects and preserves the autonomy of adult persons of sound mind with respect to their bodies. By doing so the common law accepts that a person has rights of control and self-determination in respect of his or her body which other persons must respect. Those rights can only be altered with the consent of the person concerned. Thus the legal requirement of consent to bodily interference protects the autonomy and dignity of the individual and limits the power of others to interfere with that person's body.[135]

It is clear from the foregoing case law analysis that it is now a well-established common law principle that a patient who has the requisite

---

[131] See above n. 100. Note also the decision of the Quebec Superior Court in *Nancy B* v. *Hôtel-Dieu de Québec* (above n. 79) discussed below and *Ciarlariello* v. *Schacter* [1993] 2 SCR 119.

[132] For more detailed discussion of this case see pp. 86–94 below.

[133] See above n. 100, at 598. See also Lamer CJ at 560.

[134] [1992] 66 ALJR 300.

[135] Ibid. at 337. Note also the Court of Appeal in the New Zealand case of *Smith* v. *Auckland Hospital Board* [1965] NZLR 191. Reference should also be made to the US Supreme Court decision in *Cruzan* v. *Director, Missouri Department of Health* (above n. 116) though in this case, the right to refuse treatment was analysed in terms of an individual's Fourteenth Amendment liberty interest under the Due Process Clause of the US Constitution. In other US cases, the courts have based their recognition of the right to refuse treatment on both constitutional and common law grounds (e.g. *Superintendent of Belcherton State School* v. *Saikewicz* above n. 116; *Satz* v. *Perlmutter* 362 So. 2d 160 (1978); *Bouvia* v. *Superior Court* 225 Cal. Rptr. 297 (1986)) and in others still, reliance has been placed exclusively on the common law (e.g. *In re Storar* 52 NY2d 363 (1981); *In re Eichner* 52 NY 2d 363 (1981); *Barber* v. *Superior Court* 195 Cal. Rptr. 484 (1983); *In re Conroy* 486 A 2d 1209 (1985)).

decision-making capacity may refuse any treatment, including life-saving treatment. As a matter of principle, the only justification for interference with the patient's right to refuse treatment is if the exercise of that right in some way endangers other persons.[136] Where the patient's refusal of treatment does not pose a risk of harm to others,[137] and provided that the patient has decision-making capacity, the patient's decision ought to be respected, regardless of whether in the opinion of the patient's medical advisers the decision may appear foolish or unreasonable.[138] Moreover, it is now clear that the right to refuse treatment extends not only to patients who presently have decision-making capacity but also to those who have previously given a clear direction in respect of their medical treatment. The development of this proposition for the purposes of the law in England and Wales (where, to date, there is no legislation giving statutory effect to advance directives[139]) began in the case of *Re T (adult: refusal of medical treatment)*[140] referred to earlier. In that case the Court of Appeal held that an anticipatory refusal of treatment must be respected in the same way as the contemporaneous refusal by a competent adult, provided that: the patient had the capacity to decide at the time that the decision was made; that the patient had anticipated and intended his decision to apply to the circumstances that ultimately prevail; and that the patient's decision has not been vitiated due to the effect of outside influence.[141] The House of Lords has since endorsed this reasoning in the case of *Airedale NHS Trust* v.

[136] e.g. in circumstances where a patient purports to refuse medical treatment in respect of a serious contagious disease.

[137] The question has arisen whether this principle of protecting third persons should enable doctors to override a pregnant woman's refusal of treatment so as to protect a viable foetus: see *Re T (adult: refusal of medical treatment)* above n. 105, per Lord Donaldson and *In re S. (adult: refusal of treatment)* [1992] 3 WLR 806 where a declaration was granted permitting an emergency caesarian operation notwithstanding the patient's religious objection. This decision has, however, been subject to considerable criticism and is now of doubtful authority in the light of the strong statements in favour of patient self-determination made in the *Bland* case.

[138] *Smith* v. *Auckland Hospital Board*, above n. 135, at 219. See also *Lane* v. *Candura* 376 NE2d 1232 (1978).

[139] The Law Commission of England and Wales in its Report, *Mental Incapacity* (London, 1995) recommended that legislation should be enacted to give legal effect to advance refusals of treatment (65–82) as well as making provision for continuing powers of attorney (103–31). The government has since effectively shelved this report by announcing a further process of consultation. Note also the earlier report, Age Concern Institute of Gerontology and Centre of Medical Law and Ethics, Working Party Report, *Living Will* (London, 1988) which had also recommended change either by the introduction of living wills on a non-statutory basis or, alternatively, a combination of living wills and durable powers of attorney on a statutory basis, but had called for more debate on the subject before a final decision could be made (77–85). However, the recent House of Lords Select Committee on Medical Ethics, whilst supporting in principle the concept of advance directives, concluded that legislation for advance directives generally was unnecessary: *Report of the Select Committee on Medical Ethics* (London, 1994) Vol. 1, 54–5, 58. It should be noted that under Scottish law an individual is able to appoint someone who is called a tutor dative who has the power, in the event that the person becomes incompetent, to consent to or refuse medical treatment on their behalf.

[140] See above n. 105.   [141] Ibid. at 661–3 per Lord Donaldson.

Bland[142] though it was stressed that in such circumstances, special care would be necessary to ensure that the prior refusal of consent is still properly to be regarded as applicable in the circumstances which have subsequently occurred.[143] The principle outlined in these cases, upholding the legal validity of an anticipatory refusal (or what is sometimes referred to as an 'advance directive' or 'living will') in some circumstances has since been applied by an English court in the case of *Re C.*[144] Although this was only a first instance decision, it has already been recognized as an important case.[145] It is the first case in which the right of a competent adult patient to refuse life-sustaining medical treatment has actually been given effect to and the court specifically upheld the patient's anticipated refusal of treatment. *Re C* involved a 68-year-old male suffering form paranoid schizophrenia who had been a long-term patient at a mental institution. Following an injury to his right foot an infection developed and he was diagnosed as having gangrene. C's doctors recommended amputation of his right leg below the knee as necessary in order to save the life of the patient. However, C refused to consent to amputation of his foot under any circumstances, now or at any time in the future. Following the provision of alternative treatment the immediate threat to his life receded but there was still some risk that the gangrene would redevelop. The hospital refused to give C an undertaking that it would not amputate in the future if that became necessary. C subsequently applied to the court for an injunction restraining the hospital from amputating his foot without his express consent in writing. Thorpe J of the High Court of Justice (Family Division) granted the injunction sought. Relying on the authorities of *Re T (adult: refusal of medical treatment)* and the *Bland* case he held that *prima facie* every adult has the right and capacity to refuse medical treatment, even if such refusal may result in the patient's death or permanent injury to his or her health and that such refusal may take the form of a declaration never to consent in the future or in some future circumstances. Despite the patient's chronic mental illness, the court was able to find that the rebuttable presumption that an adult has the capacity to decide whether to consent to medical treatment had not been displaced, and in so doing laid down some helpful guidelines for the determination of patient competence. By granting the injunction sought by C in this case, this decision has helped to dispel any lingering doubts that anticipated refusals in the form of a living will or otherwise are only directory in nature and not binding.[146]

---

[142] See above n. 41, at 860, 866.   [143] Ibid. at 866 per Lord Donaldson.
[144] [1994] 1 FLR 31.
[145] e.g. Grubb, A., 'Treatment Without Consent: Adult: *Re C (Refusal of Medical Treatment)*' [1994] 2 *Med.LR* 92, 93.
[146] Ibid. at 93.

There is also case law authority recognizing the legal validity of advance directives at common law from other jurisdictions.[147] In *Malette* v. *Shulman*[148] (a case referred to with approval by the Court of Appeal in *Re T (adult: refusal of medical treatment)*) the Ontario Court of Appeal upheld the decision which had been made at first instance for an award of damages against the doctor who had administered a blood transfusion to a Jehovah's Witness contrary to the expressly-stated wishes on a card carried by the patient.[149] Similarly, there have been cases in the USA where the binding force of an advance directive (even in the absence of legislation giving effect to such instruments) has been acknowledged.[150] In the light of the case law developments in these jurisdictions, there is every likelihood that a properly-worded advance directive would also be effective for the purposes of Australian and New Zealand law, to prevent a doctor from lawfully administering treatment that would otherwise be appropriate.[151]

Once it is accepted that a competent adult patient has a legal right to refuse treatment, it follows that that right is legally enforceable. As was noted earlier, a patient can bring an action by way of civil damages or even criminal prosecution for assault if treatment is administered without the patient's consent. Alternatively, in anticipation of a breach or continuing contravention, legal proceedings can be instituted for injunctive relief, restraining the medical practitioner from performing any procedure or administering treatment without the consent of the patient.[152] Accordingly, doctors are under a legal duty to respect the directions of a patient who has decision-making capacity. In addition to the patient's remedies in tort and criminal law, a patient may discharge him or herself from the care of the medical practitioner and seek out a medical practitioner who will respect his or her wishes.[153]

---

[147] In the majority of US states, some provinces in Canada, and also in some Australian jurisdictions legislation exists giving statutory effect to living wills in certain circumstances.

[148] See above n. 107.

[149] The court did, however, note in this case that on the facts before it, it was not concerned with a patient who has been diagnosed as terminally or incurably ill who seeks, by way of advance directive or living will, to reject medical treatment so that he or she may die with dignity.

[150] *In re Conroy* 486 A2d 1209, 1229–30 (1985); *Cruzan v. Director, Missouri Department of Health*, above n. 116.

[151] See also Skegg, P., 'Living Wills and New Zealand Law' (1993) 2 *Bioethics Research Centre Newsletter* 2. In Australia, the Northern Territory has living will legislation (Natural Death Act 1988) which was based on the South Australian Natural Death Act 1983 which has since been repealed by the Consent to Medical Treatment and Palliative Care Act 1995 (SA).

[152] e.g. *Re C*, above n. 144.

[153] Baugham *et al.*, 'Euthanasia: Criminal, Tort, Constitutional and Legislative Considerations', above n. 48, at 1208; Foreman, P., 'The Physician's Criminal Liability for the Practice of Euthanasia' (1975) 27 *Baylor LRev.* 54, 60.

C. Legal Effect of Patient's Refusal of Treatment: Introduction

Against this background of a clearly established right of a competent patient to refuse medical treatment, even life-saving medical treatment, it now becomes necessary to consider the legal effect of such a refusal of treatment upon a doctor's duty towards his or her patient under the criminal law. One is immediately confronted with a fundamental and apparently irreconcilable inconsistency between the criminal law principles in relation to the validity of consent on the one hand, and common law principles regarding patient self-determination on the other. As has already been noted, it is well established that the consent of the victim is no defence to the crime of murder. Even where it can be shown that the consent of the victim went beyond mere acquiescence and involved a firm request that the defendant bring about the victim's death, it would nevertheless be irrelevant for the purposes of the criminal law. Thus, at first glance, it might appear that a doctor's compliance with a patient's refusal of treatment, where that hastens the death of the patient, could result in liability for homicide and the consent of the patient would not be a valid defence. This would seem to be a rather perplexing result which could potentially undermine the right of a patient to refuse treatment. There has been little common law authority directly dealing with this issue and whilst there is a mass of academic literature on the subject of a patient's right to refuse treatment, this particular question has been largely neglected. The failure to adequately address this issue has, in turn, resulted in uncertainty for the medical profession, with doubts frequently expressed by many doctors about their potential liability if they withhold or withdraw treatment at the patient's request, and the patient's death results.

Notwithstanding the criminal law rules regarding the irrelevance of consent to a charge of homicide, the wishes and directions of a patient, who has decision-making capacity, are in fact critical and will, in certain circumstances, exculpate a doctor from criminal liability. From the outset it is vital to identify exactly what the criminal law prohibits. A person cannot give a valid consent to the taking of life where that constitutes a criminal offence. Clearly, therefore, a patient cannot give a valid consent to a doctor to take active steps to take his or her life since that would amount to the criminal offence of murder. But, as we have seen, the basis of a doctor's liability for omissions to treat is predicated upon the existence of a legal duty in respect of that patient. On this reasoning, the patient's refusal of treatment would not amount to consent to a criminal offence. Consequently, the criminal law rules which hold consent irrelevant as a defence to criminal conduct, would have no application.

Since a patient has a legally enforceable right to refuse treatment it should logically follow that a doctor who complies with the instructions of a patient who has decision-making capacity, that treatment be withheld or withdrawn, would not be acting in violation of the criminal law.[154] The patient's refusal of treatment means that there is no duty to treat: the law gives the doctor no authority to act against the patient's wishes so the failure to do so cannot amount to a culpable omission for the purposes of the criminal law. It is also possible that the patient terminates the doctor/patient relationship which gives rise to the doctor's duty to treat. If a patient does terminate the relationship in this way, the doctor's legal duty to the patient would come to an end and the doctor would incur no liability for the consequences of any omission to provide further treatment.[155]

An initial objection may be raised that since the doctor's duty to treat is imposed by law, for the benefit not only of the individual, but also for the benefit of the State, the absolution by the patient is ineffective in relieving the doctor of his duty.[156] In response it can be asserted that although the doctor's duty to treat is imposed by law, the individual's right of self-determination must ultimately prevail and override any interest the State may have in the preservation of the individual's life.[157]

As consent is part of the general theory of law, it is both logical and desirable that its effects should be the same in all branches of law.[158] Under private law principles, the courts have recognized the right of an individual to either give or refuse consent to treatment, and there are strong arguments in favour of the common law rights being given parallel effect under the criminal law. The principal advantage to be derived from the development of a unified doctrine is the guarantee of consistency and uniformity in the application of legal principle. Indeed, if it were otherwise, doctors would be faced with a most unsatisfactory dilemma; they would, on the one

[154] Kennedy, I., 'Switching Off Life Support Machines: the Legal Implications' (1977) *Crim.L.Rev.* 443, 450; Kennedy, I., 'The Legal Effect of Requests by the Terminally Ill and Aged Not to Receive Further Treatment from Doctors' (1976) *Crim.L.Rev.* 217, 229–30; Williams, *Textbook of Criminal Law*, above n. 5, at 279. There are, however, practical problems involved in determining whether the patient has the capacity to make such a decision, with the resulting risk of liability if it is subsequently found that the patient lacked the necessary capacity to refuse treatment; Gurney, E., 'Is there a Right to Die?—A Study of the Law of Euthanasia' (1972) 3 *Cumberland-Samford LRev.* 235, 244.

[155] Kennedy, 'The Legal Effect of Requests by the Terminally Ill and Aged Not to Receive Further Treatment from Doctors', above n. 154, at 229; Meyers, D., *Medico Legal Implications of Death and Dying* (Rochester, New York, 1981) 140.

[156] See Kennedy, 'The Legal Effect of Requests by the Terminally Ill and Aged Not to Receive Further Treatment from Doctors', above n. 154, at 229–30 where this question is raised.

[157] Support for the proposition that the principle of self-determination must prevail over the State's interest in the sanctity of life can be found in the House of Lords decision in the *Bland* case (above n. 41): Lord Keith at 861, Lord Goff at 865–6, and Lord Mustill at 891.

[158] Castel, 'Nature and Effects of Consent with Respect to the Right to Life and the Right to Physical and Mental Integrity in the Medical Field: Criminal and Private Law Aspects', above n. 41, at 318.

hand, be required to comply with the patient's legally enforceable common law right to decline treatment, yet, if no regard was given to the fact of patient consent and the patient's right to refuse treatment, the doctor could be criminally liable if the patient died as a result of his failure to provide treatment. The doctor would, in effect, be compelled to act unlawfully, by providing unauthorized medical treatment in order to avoid liability for the more serious offence of murder, although it could be argued that a doctor in these circumstance could plead the defence of necessity as a defence to an action for criminal assault.[159] Acceptance of this analysis would, however, entail inappropriately subordinating the individual's right of self-determination to the principle of preservation of life.[160] If the right to refuse treatment is to have any real meaning, it must be given parallel effect in the criminal law so that the refusal of treatment by a patient who has decision-making capacity, terminates the doctor's obligation to treat, and thereby absolves the doctor of any liability.[161]

D. The Case Law

Until recently, the only jurisdiction under consideration where these issues have been addressed is the USA. Although the refusal of treatment cases which have been decided in the USA have largely occurred independently of the criminal law, they nevertheless have significant implications for criminal law principles. In upholding patient autonomy and self-determination as the determinative factors in the medical context, the courts in the USA have held, either expressly or by implication, that it would not be unlawful for a doctor to act upon a patient's request that treatment be discontinued.

One of the earliest cases to consider the criminal liability of a doctor for the withdrawal of treatment from a patient was *In re Quinlan*,[162] although the case did not actually involve criminal proceedings.[163] In that case, the

---

[159] For case law authority in support of the existence of a defence of necessity in the criminal law see the Canadian case of *Perka* v. *R* (1985) 14 CCC 3d 385, 417–20 and the Australian case *R* v. *Loughnan* [1981] VR 443. Some of the Australian Code jurisdictions also contain a statutory version of the defence of necessity; see NT Criminal Code 1983 s. 33; WA Criminal Code 1913 s. 25. For the position in the USA, see LaFave and Scott, *Criminal Law*, above n. 2, at 441–3.

[160] Lanham, D., 'The Right to Choose to Die with Dignity' (1990) *Crim.LJ* 401, 406–7.

[161] Law Reform Commission of Canada, Working Paper No. 26, *Medical Treatment and the Criminal Law* (Ottawa, 1980) 73.

[162] See above n. 116.

[163] For a criminal case arising outside the medical context, see *People* v. *Robbins* 443 NYS2d 1016 (1981). In this case a patient suffering from epilepsy and diabetes decided to stop taking all her medication on the basis of religious conviction. The court accepted that a husband had a legal duty to summon care or to administer insulin to his wife when she became incapacitated, but that there would be no breach of that duty if the wife, while capable of doing so, had made a rational decision to forgo medical assistance. It was accepted by the New York Court

New Jersey Supreme Court held that, on the assumption that the removal of the respirator from the patient could be classified as homicide, the death would not come within the scope of unlawful killings proscribed by statute. The court concluded that the termination of treatment pursuant to the constitutional right of privacy is *ipso facto* lawful and that the constitutional protection extends to third parties whose action is necessary to effectuate the exercise of that right. Accordingly, doctors participating in the removal of the respirator would be protected from criminal liability. Although the reasoning of this case was obviously founded on constitutional grounds the case can be interpreted as authority for the wider proposition that where a patient has a right to refuse treatment, whether based upon constitutional principles or the common law, doctors may lawfully comply with the patient's directions, without fear of criminal prosecution. Implicit in this conclusion is the proposition that in circumstances where a competent patient has refused treatment, a doctor is no longer under a legal duty to provide that treatment.

The criminal law issues were more clearly spelt out in the case of *Barber* v. *Superior Court*[164] where the treating doctors actually faced criminal prosecution for murder. The Californian Court of Appeal held that the doctors' omission to continue life-support treatment for a terminally ill and comatosed patient, though intentional and in the knowledge that the patient would die, was not an unlawful failure to perform a legal duty. Although this case actually involved an incompetent patient, the court made it clear that in determining whether a doctor is under a duty to provide medical treatment which is of debatable value, the patient, whenever possible, should be the ultimate decision-maker.

On the basis of these cases, and others decided along similar lines,[165] the position in the USA would appear to be that a doctor can withhold or withdraw treatment at the request of a competent patient without incurring criminal liability, even though the patient's death may result. These cases, particularly the *Barber* case specifically dealing with the question of criminal liability, support the proposition that the refusal of treatment by a competent patient effectively terminates the doctor's duty to provide treatment in such a manner that the subsequent omission of treatment is not a culpable omission for the purposes of the criminal law.

The question of the scope of a doctor's duty for the purposes of the criminal law in circumstances where a patient with decision-making capacity has refused life-saving treatment has recently been considered by the English courts in *Airedale NHS Trust* v. *Bland*.[166] The *Bland* case was a civil

of Appeal, that since treatment could not be administered against her wishes, the State could not impose criminal sanctions on her husband for respecting the wishes of his wife.

[164] See above n. 135.
[165] e.g. *In re Farrel*, above n. 118, at 415–16.   [166] See above n. 41.

case but one which also raised issues of criminal liability, with the health authority seeking a declaration that life-sustaining treatment could lawfully be discontinued and arguments about criminal liability directly brought before the House of Lords by the Official Solicitor.

It is quite clear from the decision of their Lordships that where treatment is determined no longer to be in the patient's best interests the doctor is no longer under a duty to maintain the patient's life.[167] Of course, in the *Bland* case, the court was dealing with a patient who was in a persistent vegetative state so the issue of refusal of treatment by a patient and the legal implications of such refusal for the purposes of the criminal law did not directly arise on the facts. Nevertheless, it is clear from their Lordships' reasoning and *obiter* comments that where a competent patient has refused further medical treatment a doctor would no longer be under a duty to provide that treatment. The clearest statement of the position can be found in the judgment of Lord Browne-Wilkinson:

Where the charge is one of murder by omission to do an act and the act omitted could only be done with the consent of the patient, refusal by the patient of consent to the doing of the act does indirectly provide a defence to the charge of murder. The doctor cannot owe to the patient any duty to maintain his life where that life can only be sustained by intrusive medical care to which the patient will not consent.[168]

Thus, for the purposes of the common law, it now appears to be fairly well established that the refusal of medical treatment by a competent patient in effect absolves the doctor of his or her legal duty to act.

E. The Position Under the Criminal Codes

Separate consideration needs to be given to the position in those jurisdictions where the criminal law has been codified. As was noted earlier, each of the relevant Criminal Codes contains a specific provision to the effect that the victim's consent to death does not affect the question of criminal liability.[169] Questions therefore arise also in Code jurisdictions regarding the legal effect of a patient's refusal of treatment upon the doctor's criminal liability.

---

[167] Ibid. Lord Keith at 861, Lord Goff at 873, and Lord Mustill at 894. Indeed, a number of their Lordships went further, stating that in such circumstances, the continuation of treatment would be unlawful and the doctor must cease treatment. (Lord Browne-Wilkinson at 882–3 and Lord Lowry at 876–7.) See also Smith, G.P., 'Futility and the Principle of Medical Futility: Safeguarding Autonomy and the Prohibition Against Cruel and Unusual Punishment' (1995) 12 *J Contemp. Health Law & Pol'y*. 1, 24.) Note, however, potential problems with this view, for example in the context of organ donation: Kennedy and Grubb, *Medical Law: Text and Materials*, above n. 69, at 1228.

[168] See above n. 41, at 882.

[169] Whilst it could be argued that a clear direction from a patient that his or her death be brought about is not equivalent to mere 'consent', it is likely that the term 'consent' under the Codes would, as at common law, be interpreted to include active requests for death.

The common law principles regarding civil liability for non-consensual touching which underlie the individual's right of self-determination, apply with equal force in the Code jurisdictions.[170] In addition to the rights a patient has at common law, there are a number of provisions in the Codes which seek to protect individuals against any invasion of their bodily integrity.[171] Given that the common law right to refuse unwanted bodily contact is consistent with the approach of the Codes, it logically follows that it may be relevant in determining the scope of the doctor's duty to treat for the purposes of the criminal law in Code jurisdictions.

Recent case law has now confirmed that despite the terms of the various Code provisions regarding the irrelevance of consent to death, a doctor can lawfully comply with a patient's request that no further treatment be administered, even though the patient's death will result. The reasoning which lies behind this conclusion parallels that set out above with respect to those jurisdictions where the criminal law is dealt with at common law; the refusal of treatment by a patient effectively terminates the doctor's duty to provide treatment. In the absence of a duty to provide treatment, the doctor's omission to provide that treatment is not a culpable omission for the purposes of criminal liability under the Codes and no liability can arise. On this reasoning, the provisions invalidating consent are irrelevant, since they only apply where criminal liability is established.[172]

In determining the effect of a patient's refusal of treatment upon the scope of the doctor's duties under the Codes, it is necessary to have regard to the two duty provisions which were noted earlier as being of particular relevance to the question of the liability of doctors for withholding or withdrawing of treatment; the duty to provide necessaries, and the duty to do acts undertaken, the omission of which would be dangerous to human life.

Duty to provide necessaries of life

As was stated above, before a duty to provide the necessaries of life can arise, a person must have 'charge of another, who is unable by reason of age, sickness, unsoundness of mind, detention or any other cause to withdraw himself from such charge'.[173] Under normal circumstances, a doctor

---

[170] For the purposes of Canadian law, note Article 19.1 of the Civil Code of Lower Canada inserted in 1989. In the Northern Territory of Australia certain statutory rights also exist under the Natural Death Act 1988.

[171] e.g. provisions in relation to assault which exist in all Code jurisdictions.

[172] With the exception of the Northern Territory in Australia (s. 26(3)), the relevant Code provisions (see above n. 43) are in terms that consent to death has no effect with regard to criminal responsibility: in the definition section of all the Australian Codes, 'criminal responsibility' is defined as meaning liability to punishment as for an offence.

[173] Canada—Criminal Code 1985 s. 215(1)(c); Australia—NT Criminal Code 1983 s. 149, Qld. Criminal Code 1995 s. 87, Tas. Criminal Code 1924 s. 144, WA Criminal Code 1913 s. 262; New Zealand—Crimes Act 1961 s. 151.

clearly has charge of a sick patient, and the doctor would therefore be under a duty to provide the patient with the 'necessaries of life' which, as was noted earlier, includes medical treatment. The crucial question for the purposes of the present inquiry is the effect that a patient's refusal of treatment has upon this concept of charge and, in particular, whether the patient thereby 'withdraws himself from the charge'. On the basis of the wording of the provision, it is certainly open to argument that in the medical context, a patient who has decision-making capacity, is free to withdraw him or herself from the charge by requesting that treatment be withdrawn or withheld, and this would effectively terminate any duty of the doctor to provide further treatment.[174] If the patient subsequently died as a result of the omission to treat, the doctor would not be criminally responsible, since he or she was no longer under a duty to provide treatment. This interpretation of the provision is in accordance with common law principles outlined above, and would therefore have the advantage of a uniform approach as between Code and common law jurisdictions.

Duty to do acts undertaken

It remains to be considered what effect the patient's refusal of treatment has upon the doctor's duty to do acts undertaken. It is clear that the undertaking may, in certain circumstances, be terminated; by mutual consent, revocation by the patient, or lack of need for medical services. It logically follows that the refusal of treatment by a patient brings to an end the doctor's duty to do those acts with the consequence that any omission to perform that duty which results in the death of the patient is not a culpable omission for the purposes of the criminal law.

One of the few cases specifically to consider the criminal liability of a doctor for the withholding or withdrawing of medical treatment in a Code jurisdiction is the Canadian case of *Nancy B* v. *Hôtel-Dieu de Québec*.[175] This case involved a competent 25-year-old patient who was suffering from an incurable neurological disorder that left her incapable of movement. She had refused further treatment including the respiratory support upon which she was dependent. She sought an injunction against her doctor and the hospital to require them to comply with her decision. Although this case arose in the civil jurisdiction, the Quebec Superior Court also examined the criminal law implications of a doctor's compliance with a patient's request

---

[174] There are a number of early English cases which examine, in a non-medical context, whether the deceased was able to withdraw him or herself from the control or charge of the defendant; *R* v. *Smith* (1865) 169 ER 1533; *R* v. *Chattaway* (1922) 17 Cr. App. R. 7. These cases lend some support to the view that a patient could withdraw from a doctor's charge by requesting that treatment be withdrawn or withheld.

[175] See above n. 79.

that artificial respiratory support be removed. The principal section of the Canadian Criminal Code 1985 considered by the court was section 217 dealing with the duty of persons undertaking acts, the omission of which may be dangerous to life. The court recognized that if strictly interpreted, this provision would have the effect that a doctor who has undertaken treatment is not permitted to terminate that treatment if that involves a risk of life to the patient. The court was, however, anxious to avoid this result and held that the section must be read in context with other provisions in the Code[176] which exclude from criminal liability conduct which can be characterized as 'reasonable'. The court concluded that the conduct of a doctor who stops respiratory support treatment of his or her patient at the freely given and informed request of the patient, so that nature may take its course, could not be characterized as unreasonable. Adopting a broad and liberal interpretation of the Code, the court accordingly held that persons involved in terminating the patient's respiratory support treatment in order to allow nature to take its course would not commit any crime under the Code. The court emphasized that, unlike cases of homicide and suicide which are not natural deaths, if the patient's death takes place after the respiratory support is stopped at the patient's request it would be the result of nature taking its course.

In reaching this conclusion, the court did not specifically consider the effect of section 14 of the Canadian Criminal Code 1985 which invalidates a victim's consent to his or her own death. Implicit, however, in the court's reasoning is the view that in circumstances where a patient has freely and informedly refused treatment, the doctor is no longer under a legal duty to provide that treatment. This decision, based upon a Code in similar terms to the Australian Criminal Codes and the New Zealand Crimes Act 1961, provides support for the proposition that a doctor who withholds or withdraws treatment at the direction of the patient will not incur criminal liability.

Lawful excuse

In the foregoing paragraphs it has been argued that the refusal of treatment by a patient in effect extinguishes the doctor's duty to treat, thereby absolving the doctor from any criminal liability arising from his or her omission to provide treatment. In Code jurisdictions, an alternative argument can be based upon the notion of 'lawful excuse'.

Some support for this interpretation can be found in the New Zealand case of *Auckland Area Health Board* v. *Attorney General*[177] referred to earlier. At issue in that case was whether ventilator support could be removed from a patient who had virtually no brain function and was totally

---

[176] Sections 45, 216, and 219(1).   [177] See above n. 77.

paralysed. Thomas J of the New Zealand High Court found that in view of the patient's hopeless condition, ventilator support could lawfully be removed because it could not, in all the circumstances, be regarded as a necessary of life within the meaning of section 151 of the Crimes Act 1961. Significantly, he continued that even if it could be said that the doctors are under a duty to provide ventilator support to Mr L as a necessary of life, they would be legally justified in withdrawing that support: 'A doctor acting responsibly and in accordance with good medical practice recognised and approved as such in the medical profession would not therefore be liable, in my opinion, to any criminal sanction based upon the application of s 151(1). He or she will have acted with lawful excuse'.

Although not specifically addressed by the court in this case, the same reasoning could be applied in circumstances where a patient who has decision-making capacity has refused life-sustaining medical treatment. Under the relevant provision in the New Zealand Crimes Act 1961 the absence of lawful excuse is specifically referred to in the provision setting out the duty to provide the necessaries of life.[178] This is not the case in other Code jurisdictions.[179] Nevertheless, there is still some room for arguing that the defence of lawful excuse is implicit in the statutory scheme in the other Code jurisdictions. Some support for this view can be derived from the provision in all of the Codes, creating a separate offence of failing to provide necessaries.[180] Under the Code provisions, this offence is established if a person charged with the duty of providing necessaries, fails to do so without lawful excuse. Since lawful excuse is a feature of these provisions dealing with the failure to provide necessaries it could therefore be argued that it should apply uniformly in the interpretation of the duty provisions. And, as argued above, on this view, the refusal of treatment by a competent patient would constitute lawful excuse for omitting to perform duties involving the provision of medical treatment. Dicta in accordance with this interpretation can be found in the judgment of Justice McLachlin in *Rodriguez* v. *British Columbia (Attorney General)*.[181] In discussing the extent of criminal liability for omission his Honour stated: 'Those who are under a legal duty to provide the "necessaries of life" are not subject to criminal penalty where a breach of this duty causes death, if a lawful excuse

[178] Crimes Act 1961 s. 151(1).

[179] But see the Tasmanian Criminal Code s. 152 (dealing generally with criminal responsibility for omissions) where the absence of lawful excuse is stated to be a prerequisite for establishing criminal liability.

[180] Canada—Criminal Code 1985 ss. 215(2) and (3); Australia—NT Criminal Code 1983 s. 183; Qld. Criminal Code 1995 s. 147; Tas. Criminal Code 1924 s. 177; WA Criminal Code 1913 s. 302; New Zealand—Crimes Act 1961 s. 151(2).

[181] See above n. 100. McLachlin J gave one of the dissenting judgments on the issue of the constitutionality of s. 214(b) of the Canadian Criminal Code 1985. For discussion of this case, see pp. 86–99 below.

is made out, for instance, the consent of the party who dies, or incapacity to provide'.[182]

On the basis of the foregoing analysis, it is submitted that in the Code jurisdictions, doctors can lawfully comply with the patient's refusal of treatment, even in circumstances where refusal of treatment amounts to consent to death. This is because the refusal of treatment by a competent patient terminates the doctor's duties under the Codes. Alternatively, it could be argued that since the patient had exercised his or her right to refuse treatment, the doctor had lawful excuse in omitting to perform his or her duty to the patient.[183] As was suggested earlier in the context of the common law position, there are strong arguments in favour of a uniform approach with regard to consent so that the common law right to refuse treatment is given recognition also for the purposes of the criminal law.

Thus it can be concluded that although the criminal law, both at common law and under the Codes, prevents the consent of the victim from being a valid defence to criminal charges, this does not affect the right of a patient to refuse treatment and the capacity of a doctor to comply lawfully with the patient's request, even though the patient's death may result.

CONCLUSION

The object of this chapter has been to examine the present state of the criminal law regarding the practice of active and passive euthanasia in common law jurisdictions with the aim of ascertaining the potential liability of doctors for participation in these practices.

It has been demonstrated that the practice of active euthanasia, even where performed at the request of a patient, constitutes murder in all common law jurisdictions (except for the Northern Territory of Australia where legislation permitting active voluntary euthanasia has recently been passed). If a doctor, at the request of his or her patient, performs an act which causes death, the doctor is potentially liable for murder. For the purposes of establishing criminal liability for acts causing death, no account is taken of the special nature of the doctor/patient relationship, the fact that the acts causing death were performed at the request of the patient, or that they were performed by a doctor acting *bona fide*, out of the highest motives. Moreover, the fact that the patient was in a terminal condition and death was in any event imminent would also be irrelevant.

It has also been shown that passive euthanasia may attract criminal liability. As a result of the special duty owed by doctors to their patients, a

---

[182] Ibid. at 623.
[183] Both of the aforementioned arguments are also potentially available in NSW where the Crimes Act 1900 applies.

doctor who deliberately withholds or withdraws treatment from a patient with the intention of facilitating the patient's death or in the knowledge that this would probably result, is potentially liable for murder if the patient's death in fact results from that omission. Whether or not a doctor is liable in these circumstances will depend on the scope of the doctor's duty to his or her patient. Subject to the doctor's right to refuse to undertake or to withdraw from the care of a patient, the scope of this duty lies within the control of a competent patient, by virtue of the patient's right to either consent to[184] or refuse treatment, or to terminate the doctor/patient relationship.

It follows from the foregoing analysis that a doctor may lawfully perform passive euthanasia at the request of a competent patient: that is, he or she may, at the patient's request, deliberately withhold or withdraw treatment with the intention of facilitating the patient's death. This conclusion, in turn, highlights the law's starkly differential treatment of active and passive euthanasia. A doctor who performs active euthanasia will potentially face criminal liability for murder even in circumstances where the acts causing death were performed at the patient's request. Yet, a doctor who withholds or withdraws treatment at the request of a competent patient, intending that the patient's death will result, will not be criminally liable for the patient's death. Thus, even though the object and end result of active and passive euthanasia are the same, the legal consequences are vastly different.

---

[184] Subject to the qualification that a patient cannot insist upon treatment which is not medically indicated: see above n. 101.

2

Suicide and Assisted Suicide

INTRODUCTION

In some cases, a doctor who is involved in bringing about a patient's death may incur criminal liability for assisting suicide as distinct from homicide. The object of this chapter is to look at the law in relation to assisted suicide[1] and examine the circumstances in which a doctor may be subject to criminal liability for this offence. In the course of this analysis attention will be drawn to relevant analogies between the legal response to active and passive euthanasia on the one hand, as outlined in the preceding chapter, and assisted suicide on the other.

At common law, a person who committed suicide was regarded as a self-murderer or *felo de se* (felon against himself).[2] Consequently, anyone who instigated or aided another to commit suicide was guilty of murder as an accomplice. In England, the Suicide Act of 1961 abrogated the crime of committing suicide[3] and created a new offence of 'aiding, abetting, counselling or procuring the suicide of another'.[4] Under Scottish law, no specific offence of assisting suicide exists but such conduct may be treated as culpable homicide.[5] In the USA, suicide is no longer a crime, but in most states, assisting suicide has been made a specific statutory offence.[6] Similarly, in Canada, all Australian jurisdictions, and New Zealand, suicide and attempted suicide are no longer unlawful,[7] but a statutory offence of assisting suicide has been established.[8]

---

[1] For the purposes of this discussion, the word 'assisted' suicide will be used as a shorthand way to describe the various terms, aid, abet, procure etc. which are contained in the legislation prohibiting assisted suicide.

[2] For a discussion of the history of suicide and its prohibition, see Trowell, H., *The Unfinished Debate On Euthanasia* (London, 1973) 1–11.

[3] Section 1.

[4] Section 2(1).

[5] For example, the survivor of a suicide pact may be guilty of homicide, if he or she actually killed the deceased: see Gordon, G., *Criminal Law of Scotland*, 2nd edn. (Edinburgh, 1978) 727, 765.

[6] See the New York State Task Force on Life and the Law, *When Death is Sought: Assisted Suicide and Euthanasia in the Medical Context* (New York, 1994). In those US jurisdictions without statutes prohibiting assisted suicide, persons who aid in suicides may be subject to prosecution for murder or manslaughter: Smith, C., 'What About Legalized Assisted Suicide?' (1993) 8 *Issues in Law & Med.* 505.

[7] Attempted suicide was, until recently, an offence in the Northern Territory of Australia: Criminal Code 1983 s. 169 (repealed by the Criminal Code Amendment Act 1996).

[8] Canada—Criminal Code 1985 s. 241; Australia—ACT Crimes (Amendment) Ordinance (No. 2) 1990 s. 17(1) and (2), NSW Crimes Act 1900 s. 31C(1) and (2), NT Criminal Code 1983

Some patients who are terminally ill or in intolerable pain will actively seek death and may endeavour to enlist the support of their doctor in achieving this result. Whilst there are, obviously, a number of possible scenarios, two particular situations need to be distinguished: 1) where a doctor assists a patient to commit suicide, by, for example, providing a patient with the necessary medication to commit suicide and supervising its administration; and 2) circumstances where a patient refuses treatment, knowing and intending that death should result and the doctor complies with the patient's refusal by withholding or withdrawing that treatment. In the former case, assisting suicide is almost indistinguishable from the killing of patients on request (or active voluntary euthanasia) which clearly constitutes murder. The latter category involving patient's refusal of treatment may not, at first sight, appear to be suicide at all, but it will be argued that in certain circumstances, refusal of treatment is tantamount to suicide and consideration will be given to the legal position of a doctor who knowingly assists a patient with this purpose.

In part I of this chapter it is proposed to examine the legal requirements for liability for assisting suicide and to ascertain the legal liability of a doctor if he or she responds to a patient expressing the wish to die by either actively assisting the patient in taking his or her own life or by complying with the patient's wish that no further treatment be administered. Consideration is then given in part II of this chapter to important case law developments in which a number of constitutional challenges have been brought against legislation prohibiting assisted suicide in Canada and the USA.

I. ASSISTING SUICIDE: THE LEGAL REQUIREMENTS

As was outlined earlier, following the abolition of the offence of suicide in all jurisdictions, a new statutory offence of assisting suicide was created. Although there are some variations in the wording of the relevant provisions in the various jurisdictions, they are all essentially directed at prohibiting any conduct which involves assisting suicide. The Suicide Act 1961 (England) makes it a statutory crime to 'aid, abet, counsel or procure' a person to commit suicide.[9] Under the Canadian Criminal Code 1985 it is an offence to 'counsel or aid or abet' a person to commit suicide.[10] In Australia, the law in the Australian Capital Territory, New South Wales, South Australia and Victoria, makes it an offence to 'incite, counsel, aid or abet

s. 168, Qld. Criminal Code 1995 s. 108, SA Criminal Law Consolidation Act 1935 s. 13(a)(5), Tas. Criminal Code 1924 s. 163, Vic. Crimes Act 1958 s. 6B(2), WA Criminal Code 1913 s. 288; New Zealand—Crimes Act 1961 s. 179.

[9] Suicide Act 1961 (Eng.) s. 2(1).   [10] Section 241.

another to commit suicide or attempt to commit suicide'.[11] The Criminal Codes in the Northern Territory, Queensland, and Western Australia make it an offence to 'procure or counsel another to kill himself or aid another in killing himself'[12] and under the Tasmanian Code, it is an offence to 'instigate or aid another to kill himself'.[13] Pursuant to the New Zealand Crimes Act 1961 it is an offence to 'incite, counsel, or procure any person to commit suicide' or to 'aid and abet any person in the commission of suicide'.[14] In the USA, the legislation in quite a number of states makes it an offence to 'cause' or 'aid' suicide.[15]

In the English case of *Attorney-General* v. *Able*[16] the court was called upon to consider section 2(1) in the Suicide Act 1961 (England). This case involved the distribution of a booklet entitled 'A Guide to Self-Deliverance' by the Voluntary Euthanasia Society to members of the society. The booklet contained information about various methods of suicide and was prepared with the expressed aim of overcoming people's fear of dying and to reduce the incidence of unsuccessful suicides. The booklet also sought to discourage hasty and ill-considered suicide attempts.

In a civil action brought by the Attorney-General against members of the society's executive committee, a declaration was sought that the future supply of the booklet to persons who were known to be, or likely to be, considering or intending to commit suicide, constituted the offence of aiding, abetting, counselling or procuring the suicide of another, contrary to section 2(1) of the Suicide Act 1961 (England). Although no final determination was made as to whether the distribution of the booklet was in contravention of the legislation,[17] Woolf J did offer some guidance with respect to the interpretation of the provision. His Honour was of the view that in the ordinary case, in deciding whether an offence has been committed, it is preferable to consider the phrase 'aids, abets, counsels or procures' as a whole, but recognized that circumstances could arise which would justify interpreting part of the phrase in isolation. With respect to the meaning of the terminology used in the section, his Honour indicated that whilst 'aiding' requires some form of assistance, it does not require consen-

---

[11] ACT Crimes (Amendment) Ordinance (No. 2) 1990 s. 17(1) and (2), NSW Crimes Act 1900 s. 31C(1) and (2), SA Criminal Law Consolidation Act 1935 s. 13(a)(5), Tas. Criminal Code 1924 s. 163, Vic. Crimes Act 1958 s. 6B(2), WA Criminal Code 1913 s. 288.

[12] NT Criminal Code 1983 s. 168, Qld. Criminal Code 1995 s. 108, WA Criminal Code 1913 s. 288. The Northern Territory provision (as amended by the Criminal Code Amendment Act 1996) expressly extends to assisting an attempted suicide.

[13] Section 163. The term 'instigate' is defined in the interpretation part of the Act to mean 'counsel procure or command'.

[14] Section 179.

[15] LaFave, W. and Scott, A., *Criminal Law*, 2nd edn. (Minnesota, 1986) 651–2.

[16] [1984] 1 All ER 277.

[17] Since the declaration sought could result in treating as criminal conduct which was not in contravention of the criminal law, the declaration was refused.

sus between the accessory and principal or a causal connection between the conduct of the accused and the commission of suicide. 'Abetting' and 'counselling' imply consensus but not causation and 'procuring' implies causation but not necessarily consensus. His Honour went on to make it clear that in order for liability to be established under section 2(1) of the Suicide Act 1961 (England) it must be proved that:

(1)   the accused intended to assist a person to commit suicide;
(2)   while the accused had that intention, he or she provided some assistance to the person contemplating suicide;
(3)   the person committing suicide was thereby in fact assisted or encouraged in taking, or attempting to take his or her own life(—otherwise the alleged offender cannot be guilty of more than an attempt).[18]

With respect to the necessary intention, it was held that an intention to assist another to commit suicide need not involve a desire that suicide should be committed or attempted. Moreover, if these facts can be proved, then it does not make any difference that the person would have tried to commit suicide anyway.[19]

Since this case, there have been instances in England where prosecutions have been brought for assistance in suicide. One such case was *R* v. *Chard*[20] in which the defendant was prosecuted for having provided the deceased with paracetamol pills at her request which she subsequently used to commit suicide. The defendant had given evidence that it had been the deceased's wish to have the option, if she so decided, of taking her own life. Judge Pownall QC of the Old Bailey directed the jury to find the defendant not guilty, finding that there was no evidence to support the charge of aiding and abetting suicide. His Honour held that the defendant had only provided her with an option of taking her own life and that is not enough. Whilst this decision may potentially be seen as a liberalization of the law, caution must be exercised in not overstating the relevance of individual cases which come before the courts by way of prosecution, particularly in the context of a prosecution of a person who has assisted another to die—the interpretation of the law in such cases is often influenced by considerations of sympathy and leniency to the defendant. Unless this approach is confirmed in subsequent cases as representing the law, Woolf J's interpretation of section 2(1) of the Suicide Act 1961 (England) in *Attorney-General* v. *Able* (although made in the context of civil proceedings) remains one of the clearest guides to the criminal law position in England and Wales. In view of the similarity between this provision and the prohibitions on assisting suicide in other common law jurisdictions, the reasoning of Woolf J is likely to be of more general relevance, particularly

---

[18] See above n. 16, at 288.   [19] [1984] 1 All ER 277, 288.
[20] *The Times*, 23 Sept. 1993.

in those jurisdictions where there is little authority on the interpretation of the assisting suicide provisions.

A. A Doctor's Liability for Active Involvement in a Patient's Suicide

In view of the statutory prohibition on assisting suicide and the judicial interpretation it has received, it is readily apparent that, with the exception of the Northern Territory where both active voluntary euthanasia and doctor-assisted suicide have been legalized,[21] a doctor who actively assists a patient to commit suicide will incur criminal liability. Common to all of the statutory provisions is the prohibition on 'aiding suicide' which clearly involves some form of assistance in a person's suicide. To establish a person's guilt as an aider and abettor, it is necessary to show that the person was intentionally assisting or encouraging the commission of the act in question or that he or she was at least ready to assist if required.[22] The prohibition on 'aiding and abetting' suicide is of direct relevance in the medical context since a doctor who, at a patient's request, provides the means of committing suicide is, without doubt, aiding the patient's suicide. In many cases, there would be little difficulty in establishing that the doctor thereby intended to assist the patient to commit suicide[23] (even though the doctor may have hoped that the patient would not do so) and that the patient was in fact assisted or encouraged in taking, or attempting to take his or her own life. In circumstances where the doctor has provided the patient with information and advice, for example, regarding the toxicity of drugs and what would amount to a lethal dose, the doctor's conduct may also attract liability on the basis of 'counselling'[24] or even 'procuring' the patient's suicide.[25] Once the basis for liability for assisted suicide is made

---

[21] Rights of the Terminally Ill Act 1995. For detailed discussion of this Act see pp. 345–57 below. Note also in the USA, the Oregon Death with Dignity Act 1994 which legalizes doctor-assisted suicide; this Act was passed by a majority of citizens in the State of Oregon under a citizen-initiated referendum in November 1994 but is currently the subject of constitutional challenge: see further, pp. 369–73 below.

[22] See below for reference to relevant cases.

[23] The possibility remains of future courts accepting an argument along the lines of the approach adopted in *R* v. *Chard* (above n. 20) that a doctor who provides assistance, for example, the provision of the means to commit suicide, does not thereby intend to assist, but is merely providing the patient with the option of whether or not to commit suicide by making it possible for the patient to do so.

[24] Canada—Criminal Code 1985 s. 241(a); Australia—ACT Crimes (Amendment) Ordinance (No. 2) 1990 s. 17(2), NSW Crimes Act 1900 s. 31C(2), SA Criminal Law Consolidation Act 1935 s. 13(a)(5), NT Criminal Code 1983 s. 168(b), Qld. Criminal Code 1995 s. 108(b), WA Criminal Code 1913 s. 288(2); New Zealand—Crimes Act 1961 s. 179(a). The legislation in a number of Australian jurisdictions also contains a prohibition on inciting another person to commit suicide; ACT Crimes (Amendment) Ordinance (No. 2) 1990 s. 17(2)(a); NSW Crimes Act 1900 s. 31C(2)(a); Vic. Crimes Act 1958 s. 6B(2)(a).

[25] Australia—NT Criminal Code 1983 s. 168(b), Qld. Criminal Code 1995 s. 108(a), WA Criminal Code 1913 s. 288(1); New Zealand—Crimes Act 1961 s. 179(a).

out under the statutory prohibition, the special features which arguably set a doctor's conduct apart from other forms of criminal conduct are irrelevant. Thus, as was seen in the preceding chapter in relation to a doctor's liability for murder, the fact that the doctor was acting *bona fide* and that assistance was provided at the request of the patient within the context of a doctor/patient relationship would not exculpate a doctor from criminal liability. Furthermore, it would be irrelevant that the patient was in a terminal condition and that the patient's death was in any event imminent.

When one comes to consider the factual situations which would come within the statutory prohibition of assisting suicide, it becomes evident that there is, in practice, a fine line between assisting suicide and active voluntary euthanasia which constitutes murder. Essentially, it all depends on the degree of the doctor's involvement. Active assistance in suicide amounts to murder if death occurs as a result of an overt act of the 'assistant'.[26] Where, however, there has simply been participation in the events leading up to the commission of the final overt act, such as providing the means for bringing about death for the patient's own use, the doctor's conduct comes within the prohibition on assisting suicide.[27] Notwithstanding the apparent simplicity of this classification, difficulties may yet arise in determining the appropriate charge in any given case and instances of consent killing are occasionally reduced to assisting suicide.[28]

B. Refusal of Treatment as Suicide and the Legal Position of Doctors

In the foregoing part, it was noted that if a doctor provides active assistance to a patient wishing to commit suicide, by, for example, providing the means by which the suicide is to be effected, the doctor may incur criminal liability under the statutory provisions prohibiting assisted suicide. The fundamental question which now arises for determination is whether a doctor's compliance with a patient's refusal of treatment can ever amount to assisting suicide. In order to answer this question, attention must be directed to the following matters: Can the refusal of treatment by a patient ever amount to suicide?[29] If, in some circumstances, the refusal of treatment *can* amount to

[26] For American case law on this issue see *State* v. *Bouse* 264 P2d 800, 812 (1953); *State* v. *Cobb* 625 P2d 1133 (1981); *In re Joseph G* 34 Cal. 3d 429 (1983).

[27] *In re Joseph* (above n. 26). It has, however, been argued that notwithstanding statutory prohibitions on aiding or instigating suicide, the conduct of the defendant may also constitute murder on the basis of common law principles of causation; see Lanham, D., 'Murder by Instigating Suicide' (1980) *Crim.LRev.* 215, 220–1. This suggestion has been rejected by Williams, G., *Textbook of Criminal Law*, above Ch. 1 n. 5, at 578 n. 3.

[28] Williams, *Textbook of Criminal Law*, above Ch. 1 n. 5, at 580. This is also a reflection of the lenient approach of the law in practice in genuine cases of mercy killing or assisted suicide. For further discussion see p. 129 below.

[29] It should be understood that although suicide is no longer an offence, the question of whether particular conduct constitutes suicide in law is still relevant for the purposes of determining liability for the offence of assisting suicide.

be suicide, is a doctor who accedes to a request by a patient to cease treatment criminally liable for assisting suicide?

Elsewhere, consideration has been given to the fundamental right of a competent patient at common law to refuse treatment including life-saving treatment.[30] The question which now arises for determination is whether the exercise of this right can ever amount to suicide.[31] It is therefore necessary to examine more closely the notion of suicide and its legal requirements.

From the outset, it should be acknowledged that there are some practical obstacles in settling upon an adequate definition of suicide. Suicide has traditionally been anathema in Judaeo-Christian culture, evoking both popular condemnation and legal intervention.[32] Although the law no longer treats suicide or attempted suicide as a crime, in contemporary society, suicide is still socially stigmatized and there are a variety of common legal provisions which reflect continued societal concern over the phenomenon of suicide.[33] Consequently, attempts to define suicide will tend to reflect this social disapproval, and conduct which is regarded as socially acceptable is likely to fall outside the scope of the accepted definition of suicide.

According to the traditional legal definition at common law, suicide is the intentional, voluntary taking of one's own life by a person of sound mind and of the age of discretion.[34] It remains now to be considered how refusal of treatment has been characterized and whether it can ever amount to suicide.

C. Suicide by Omission

A preliminary question of some importance is whether there can be suicide by omission. By definition, suicide involves the taking of one's own life, so the question for determination is whether this must be by some positive conduct or whether an omission to act could amount to suicide. Williams,

---

[30] See pp. 35–44 above.

[31] This discussion is confined to the position of patients who have decision-making capacity, since patients lacking that capacity would be unable to form the necessary intention to commit suicide. It should also be pointed out that what is being considered here is the refusal of treatment by a patient as distinguished from the situation where a person has inflicted injury upon themselves in an attempted suicide and then refuses necessary life-saving treatment.

[32] Cantor, N., *Legal Frontiers of Death and Dying* (Bloomington, 1987) 46.

[33] Ibid. at 46 where he refers to the prohibitions with regard to aiding and abetting suicide, the fact that persons are often hospitalized for psychiatric scrutiny after a suicide attempt, and the fact that bystanders are authorized to use reasonable force to thwart a suicide attempt.

[34] *Clift* v. *Schwabe* (1846) 3 CB 437, approved in *Re Davis* [1968] 1 QB 72. See also St. John Stevas, N., *Life, Death and the Law: Law and Christian Morals in England and the United States* (Bloomington, 1961) 242 where he notes that the definition of suicide generally adopted in the USA is the same as in England, and refers to the case of *Southern Life and Health Insurance Co.* v. *Wynn* 29 Ala. App. 207 (1940).

for example, has suggested that inaction cannot be suicide in law.[35] It is certainly true that suicide is typically associated with affirmative conduct such as taking an overdose of tablets or jumping to one's death.[36] Indeed, the 'cide' in the word suicide entails 'killing' which is commonly contrasted with 'allowing to die'.[37] However, as Lanham suggests,[38] there seems to be no reason in principle why suicide cannot be committed by an omission. Provided there is suicidal intent, omissions resulting in death are not relevantly different from acts. For example, if a person deliberately chooses not to move from the path of an avalanche, or refuses to leave a burning building, it is arguable that the person is in effect, committing suicide.[39] Furthermore, recognition of the possibility of suicide by omission would be consistent with the widespread rejection of technical distinctions between acts and omissions.[40]

There is some, albeit modest, judicial support for the view that there can be suicide by omission. The English case of *Leigh* v. *Gladstone*[41] has been cited in support of this proposition. This case involved the forcible feeding of a suffragette prisoner who was on a hunger strike. Although the issue of preventing suicide was not specifically raised, the court held that the prison officials had a duty to preserve the lives of prisoners and were consequently justified in force-feeding the prisoner.[42] This decision, which is now largely discredited, can be rationalized on the basis that the conduct of the prisoner in refusing food was tantamount to suicide (then a felony) and the prison officials were therefore entitled (*quaere* obliged) to use force to prevent the prisoner from committing suicide by starving herself to death.

There is also authority from a number of other jurisdictions which lends support to the view that there may be suicide by omission. In the US case *In re Caulk*,[43] a prisoner sentenced to life imprisonment had decided to starve

---

[35] Williams, *Textbook of Criminal Law*, above Ch. 1 n. 5, at 613. See also Kennedy, I., 'The Legal Effect of Requests by the Terminally Ill and Aged Not to Receive Further Treatment from Doctors' (1976) *Crim.LRev.* 217, 226 where he questions whether the omission/commission dichotomy applies to suicide.

[36] Cantor, *Legal Frontiers of Death and Dying*, above n. 32, at 47. See also Hale, J., *Pleas of the Crown* (London, 1736) (where suicide or *felo de se* is defined to be 'where a man of the age of discretion, and *compos mentis*, voluntarily kills himself, by stabbing, poison or any other way'), and the interpretation of suicide in *Clift* v. *Schwabe*, above n. 34.

[37] Beauchamp, T. and Perlin, S. (eds), *Ethical Issues in Death and Dying* (Englewood Cliffs, New Jersey, 1978) 99. For discussion of the distinction between 'killing' and 'allowing to die' see pp. 163–4, 191–2 below.

[38] Lanham, D., 'The Right to Choose to Die with Dignity', above Ch. 1 n. 160, at 401, 408.

[39] Cantor, *Legal Frontiers of Death and Dying*, above n. 32, at 47. This analysis is consistent with the definition of suicide proposed by the eminent sociologist Emil Durkheim; 'The term suicide is applied to all cases of death resulting directly or indirectly from a positive or negative act of the victim himself which he knows will produce this result'. Durkheim, E., *Suicide* (Spaulding, J. and Simpson G., translation) (London, 1951) 44.

[40] For discussion see pp. 163–4 below.

[41] (1909) 26 TLR 139.   [42] Ibid. at 142.   [43] 480 A2d 93 (1984).

himself to death and the court was called upon to consider whether the prison authorities could lawfully force-feed the prisoner. The Supreme Court of New Hampshire held that the prisoner's decision to starve himself to death amounted to attempted suicide, and since aiding and abetting suicide was a crime, the prison authorities could lawfully force-feed the prisoner.[44] There is also authority in Canada and Australia to the effect that refusal of food by a prisoner may amount to suicide.[45] In the Australian case of *Schneidas* v. *Corrective Services Commission*[46] the New South Wales Supreme Court was called upon to determine the legal position of prison authorities with respect to a prisoner who had gone on a hunger strike. Lee J was of the view that the prisoner, by denying his body necessary food, was in the course of attempting to commit suicide. His Honour accordingly refused to grant an injunction preventing force-feeding, because to do so would, in effect, involve the court in aiding and abetting the commission of a crime.[47] Apart from the prisoner cases, there have been other instances of judicial recognition that there can be suicide by omission.[48]

It is submitted that as a matter of law, suicide can be committed by an omission. This conclusion is not inconsistent with the traditional common law definition of suicide (that is, the voluntary and intentional taking of one's own life) and derives some support from the modern case law. More importantly, however, this view is supportable as a matter of principle and logic.[49] There appears to be no valid basis for categorically holding that suicide can only be committed by affirmative conduct and that inaction cannot amount to suicide at law.

[44] See also *State ex rel. White* v. *Narick* 292 SE2d 54 (1982); *Re Sanchez* 577 FS 7 (1983); *Van Holden* v. *Chapman* 450 NYS 2d 623 (1982). Cf. *Zant* v. *Prevatee* 286 SE 2d 715 (1982). Lanham has, however, criticized these cases on the grounds that the typical hunger striker is not a would-be suicide since they do not actively seek death but rather life on their terms; 'The Right to Choose to Die with Dignity', above Ch. 1 n. 160, at 409.

[45] See *AG of British Columbia* v. *Astaforoff and AG of Canada* [1984] 4 WWR 385 in which it was held that whilst the patient is competent and able to make a free choice, it would be unreasonable for prison authorities to force-feed her in order to prevent her suicide and they were under no duty to do so.

[46] (Unreported) 8 April 1983, SCNSW.

[47] At the time of this decision, suicide was still an offence in the State of New South Wales. Whilst this may explain the reluctance of the court to be involved in the suicide attempt, it does not affect the court's characterization of the prisoner's refusal of food as an attempt to commit suicide. For comment on this decision, see Potas, I., '*Schneidas* v. *Corrective Services Commission and Ors*' (1983) 7 *Crim. LJ* 353.

[48] e.g. the dissenting judgment of Lynch J in *Brophy* v. *New England Sinai Hospital, Inc.* 497 NE2d 626, 642–3 (1986).

[49] Cantor, N., 'A Patient's Decision to Decline Life-Saving Medical Treatment: Bodily Integrity Versus the Preservation of Life' (1973) 26 *Rutgers LRev.* 228, 255 n. 133 where he suggests that efforts to distinguish suicide from refusal of treatment on the basis of misfeasance versus non-feasance or the immorality of affirmative actions as opposed to passive refusal are unconvincing.

D. Refusal of Treatment as Suicide?

On the assumption that in principle, suicide can be committed by omission, it is necessary specifically to consider whether the refusal of treatment by a patient can ever amount to suicide. It must be emphasized that since suicide or attempted suicide are no longer criminal offences, the significance of this question lies in determining the legal liability of persons who assist another to commit suicide.

It appears to be commonly assumed that refusal of treatment by a patient is not tantamount to suicide. This assumption has undoubtedly been encouraged by the widespread recognition and approval of the patient's common law right to refuse medical treatment, since, as noted earlier, our conception of suicide is influenced by contemporary attitudes. It must, however, be questioned whether the notion of suicide and the right of a patient to refuse treatment are necessarily mutually exclusive. It will be argued that, as a matter of legal principle, it is quite possible that a patient who exercises his or her right to refuse life-saving medical treatment is in fact committing suicide.[50]

The approach of the courts

By far, the majority of cases examining a patient's refusal of treatment in relation to the issue of suicide have come from the USA. In a number of the earlier refusal of treatment cases arising in the USA, the courts drew an analogy between a patient's refusal of treatment and suicide, thereby justifying the court's decision to override the patient's refusal of treatment.[51] So, for example, in *John F Kennedy Memorial Hospital* v. *Heston*[52] the court ordered that a blood transfusion be administered to a Jehovah's Witness who had been seriously injured in a car accident. It was held by the court that: 'If the state may interrupt one mode of self-destruction, it may with equal authority interfere with the other . . . the state's interest in sustaining life in such circumstances is hardly distinguishable from its interest in the case of suicide'.[53] Accordingly, the state's interest in the prevention of suicide and the preservation of life was held to outweigh the patient's right to decline medical treatment.

In more recent cases, however, as greater weight has been given to the individual's right of self-determination, the courts have distinguished be-

---

[50] See also Sherlock, R., 'For Everything there is a Season: The Right to Die in the United States' (1982) *BYULRev.* 545, 558–9. For a contrary view see Lanham, 'The Right to Choose to Die with Dignity', above Ch. 1 n. 160, at 407–10.

[51] e.g. *Application of the President and Directors of Georgetown College Inc.* 331 F2d 1000 (1964); *John F. Kennedy Memorial Hospital* v. *Heston* 58 NJ 576 (1971). *Cf. Erickson Dilgard* 252 NS2d 705 (1962).

[52] 58 NJ 576 (1971).   [53] Ibid. at 581–2.

tween suicide and the refusal of treatment by a patient[54] and consequently, the State's interest in the prevention of suicide has not arisen. The basis for differentiating between refusal of treatment and suicide rests on two main grounds. According to the traditional conception of suicide, as interpreted in a number of US cases, there must be a specific intention to bring about death; and a self-initiated action which causes death. In the more recent refusal of treatment cases, the courts have tended to find both these elements of suicide to be absent.[55] Refusal of treatment by patients has been interpreted by the courts as being aimed at avoiding unwanted treatment, pain or the violation of religious principles, rather than causing one's own death, and therefore the specific intent element has been held to be absent. Furthermore, since the courts have considered the underlying disease or injury—and not the withholding or cessation of treatment—to be the cause of death, they have not considered suicidal refusals to be affirmative acts causing death. The approach of the courts in the USA is well illustrated by *In re Conroy*[56] in which the Supreme Court of New Jersey specifically rejected the analogy between refusal of treatment and suicide and held that a refusal of medical treatment may not properly be viewed as an attempt to commit suicide:

Refusing medical intervention merely allows the disease to take its natural course; if death were eventually to occur, it would be the result, primarily, of the underlying disease, and not the result of self-inflicted injury . . . In addition, people who refuse life-sustaining medical treatment may not harbour a specific intent to die, . . . rather they may fervently wish to live, but to do so free of unwanted medical technology, surgery, or drugs and without protracted suffering.[57]

The relevant issues in this area were starkly raised in the case of *Bouvia* v. *Superior Court*.[58] This case involved a competent 28-year-old quadriple-

---

[54] e.g. *In re Conroy* 486 A2d 1209 (1985); *Bouvia* v. *Superior Court* 225 Cal. Rptr. 297, 306 (1986); *In re Farrel* 529 A2d 404, 411 (1987). See also the decision of the US Court of Appeals for the Ninth Circuit in *Compassion in Dying* v. *State of Washington* No. 94-35534 (9th Cir. March 6 1996) (*en banc*) where this approach was noted. There have, however, been a few isolated exceptions; see the dissenting judgments of Nolan, Lynch and O'Connor JJ in *Brophy* v. *New England Sinai Hospital, Inc.*, above n. 48; the decision of the Missouri Supreme Court in *Cruzan* v. *Harmon* 760 SW2d 408 (1988), per Robertson J at 419–22; the concurring judgment of Justice Scalia of the US Supreme Court in *Cruzan* v. *Director, Missouri Department of Health* 111 LEd. 2d 224, 251-156 (1990); and the joint decision of Miner and Pollack JJ in *Quill* v. *Vacco* No. 60 (2nd Cir. April 2 1996).

Note should also be made of the living will legislation existing in many US states which specifically provides that the withholding or withdrawing of treatment in accordance with a patient's directive does not constitute suicide. In some cases, the courts have relied on this legislation in support of the view that the refusal of treatment does not constitute suicide; e.g. *In re Colyer* 99 Wash. 2d 114 (1983).

[55] e.g. *Superintendent of Belcherton State School* v. *Saikewicz* 370 NE2d 417, 426 (1977); *Bartling* v. *Superior Court* 163 Cal. App. 3d 186, 196 (1984); *Brophy* v. *New England Sinai Hospital, Inc.*, above n. 48.

[56] See above n. 54.   [57] Ibid. at 1224.   [58] See above n. 54.

gic who required permanent hospitalization but whose condition was not terminal.[59] In 1983 Elizabeth Bouvia had expressed the wish to commit suicide and had unsuccessfully sought permission from the court to starve herself to death. In 1986 she again applied to the court, seeking an injunction against her doctors, ordering that the naso-gastric tube with which she was being force-fed be removed. The trial court refused to grant the relief sought. Elizabeth Bouvia then appealed to the California Court of Appeal.

The Court of Appeal held that a competent adult has an absolute right to refuse life-saving treatment, including nourishment and hydration, even if the exercise of this right creates a life-threatening condition. The court rejected arguments that the naso-gastric feeding be maintained in furtherance of the State's interests in the prevention of suicide and the preservation of life. Although the appellant had claimed she did not wish to commit suicide, the trial court had found that she was motivated by a desire to end her life. This view was rejected by the Court of Appeal on the grounds that it was not supported by the evidence. The court effectively evaded the suicide issue by holding that her refusal of medical treatment indicated a decision to 'allow nature to take its course' rather than a decision to commit suicide. In the view of the court, the appellant was not actively seeking to end her life but had merely resigned herself to an earlier death without force-feeding. Although the court had concluded that her rejection of naso-gastric feeding was not motivated by a desire to commit suicide, the Court of Appeal was prepared to concede that in any event, it was irrelevant whether or not she desired to commit suicide because 'if the right to refuse treatment exists, it matters not what "motivates" its exercise'.[60] This latter proposition appears to acknowledge, implicitly at least, that a refusal of treatment by a patient *may* amount to suicide but suggests that the right to refuse treatment is virtually absolute and will be upheld regardless of whether the exercise of that right is tantamount to suicide.[61] However, apart from this concession, which was in any event *obiter*, the approach taken by the *Bouvia* court was essentially in keeping with that articulated by other courts in the USA.[62]

Thus, the suicide issue has been circumvented by the US courts. Regardless of the particular circumstances of the cases before the courts, the refusal of treatment by a patient has generally been distinguished from

[59] She had been diagnosed as likely to live for a further 15 or 20 years.

[60] See above n. 54, at 306.

[61] Fisher, L., 'The Suicide Trap: *Bouvia v. Superior Court* and the Right to Refuse Medical Treatment' (1987) 21 *Loy.LALRev.* 219, 237.

[62] Note, however, the concurring judgment of Compton J, at 307–8 where he acknowledged that Elizabeth Bouvia wanted to die and held that the right to die, 'an integral part of our right to control our own destinies', should include the ability to enlist assistance from others, including the medical profession, in making death as painless and quick as possible'. This judgment obviously has far-reaching implications, being a rare instance of unequivocal judicial endorsement of assisting suicide and arguably even active voluntary euthanasia.

suicide. Consequently, the State's interest in the prevention of suicide has been held not to arise and further, the courts have been able to avoid the question of whether a doctor is unlawfully assisting suicide by complying with a patient's request that treatment be discontinued.

Reference to the refusal of treatment/suicide issue has also been made in a number of cases from other common law jurisdictions. In the Canadian case of *Nancy B* v. *Hôtel-Dieu de Québec*[63] (discussed in the previous chapter[64]) Dufour J of the Quebec Superior Court endorsed the approach taken in *In re Conroy* to the effect that where death occurs following a patient's refusal of treatment it would be the result of the underlying disease and not the result of a self-inflicted injury.[65]

In *Airedale NHS Trust* v. *Bland*[66] (also referred to in the previous chapter[67]) Lord Goff was the only member of the House of Lords to raise the issue of suicide or assisted suicide in circumstances where a doctor acts upon the patient's instructions to refrain from further treatment. His Honour stated:

In cases of this kind, there is no question of the patient having committed suicide, nor therefore of the doctor having aided or abetted him in doing so. It is simply that the patient has, as he is entitled to, declined to consent to treatment which might or would have the effect of prolonging his life, and the doctor has, in accordance with his duty, complied with the patient's wishes.[68]

Whilst it could be argued that the unreported New South Wales decision in *Schneidas* v. *Corrective Services Commission*[69] discussed earlier, lends some modest support to the view that refusal of treatment may constitute suicide, Australian courts when directly faced with these issues are likely to be influenced by the same policy considerations which appear to have shaped the judicial response in the USA and other jurisdictions.

Analysis of the courts' approach

The approach of the courts to this issue is, to a large extent,[70] explicable on the basis of the patient's right of self-determination and the paramountcy which has been attached to that principle. According to Cantor, commenting on the position in the USA,[71] both popular perception and judicial

---

[63] 69 CCC (3d) (1992) 450.   [64] See pp. 51–2 above.

[65] See above n. 63, at 458, 460.

[66] [1993] 1 All ER 821.

[67] See pp. 38–40, 48–9 above.

[68] See above n. 66, at 866. See also Sir Thomas Bingham MR of the Court of Appeal, [1993] 1 All ER 821, 840–1.

[69] See above n. 46.

[70] For reference to a number of other policy considerations possibly underlying the courts' approach, see Matthews, M., 'Suicidal Competence and the Patient's Right to Refuse Life-Saving Treatment' (1987) 74 *Calif.LRev.* 737.

[71] *Legal Frontiers of Death and Dying*, above n. 32, at 47–9.

doctrine have come to regard a dying patient's refusal of treatment as a legitimate form of self-determination, thereby taking it outside the realm of suicide.[72] This widespread respect for individual bodily integrity and self-determination can be seen here to interact with another powerful consideration, namely the common societal aversion to suicide and the tendency to tailor our conception of suicide so as to exclude behaviour which is regarded as acceptable.

Whilst there may be sound policy considerations underlying the courts' approach, it will be argued that the characterization of a patient's refusal of treatment as falling *outside* the realm of suicide on the grounds that the patient lacks a specific intent to die and further, that refusal of treatment does not involve a self-initiated condition, lacks substance and results in an undesirable distortion of legal principles.[73]

Absence of a 'specific intent' to die

Under normal criminal law principles, an individual is generally taken to intend consequences which he or she knows will occur or which are reasonably foreseeable. However, for the purposes of the law of suicide, the courts have held that there must be evidence of a specific intent to die.[74] The requirement of a specific intent in the context of suicide has been justified on the basis that it avoids the inappropriate labelling of some conduct as suicide; for example, the conduct of a person who jumps in front of a car to save another, or who undertakes an heroic but mortally dangerous military mission.[75] This approach, in itself, demonstrates an adaptation of legal principles in order to avoid the result that acceptable behaviour may be classified as suicide. But for present purposes, the major interest lies in the way in which the specific intent requirement is actually applied in the refusal of treatment cases. First of all, let us be clear on what is required by this 'specific intent' requirement. Mere knowledge or foresight of death will not be sufficient. A person has the necessary suicidal intent in circumstances where conduct causing death is deliberately undertaken in order to end his or her life and not for some other purpose. There will inevitably be circumstances where treatment may be refused but the specific intent requirement may be lacking—for example, a Jehovah's Witness who refuses a blood transfusion on the grounds of religious principle but will accept other available treatment, or a patient who declines distasteful or burdensome treatment but does not thereby deliberately seek

---

[72] The position is less clear with regard to a patient whose condition is salvageable; Cantor, *Legal Frontiers of Death and Dying*, above n. 32, at 49–50.

[73] For other commentators criticizing this approach see Fletcher, J., 'The Courts and Euthanasia' (1987–88) 15 *Law, Med. & Health Care* 223, 224–6 and Cantor, *Legal Frontiers of Death and Dying*, above n. 32, at 47.

[74] *Re Davis* (above n. 34) and see above with respect to the position in the USA.

[75] Cantor, *Legal Frontiers of Death and Dying*, above n. 32, at 47.

death.[76] However, it cannot be denied that in some instances, a patient's motives in refusing treatment are indistinguishable from suicidal intent. Take, for example, the situation of a terminally ill patient who declines further medical treatment in order to facilitate an earlier death. In such a case, the patient's rejection of treatment clearly entails a specific intent to die and suggestions to the contrary are simply semantic sleights of hand so as to avoid the conclusion that the patient is in fact thereby committing suicide. Even more obvious are cases where the patient's condition is salvageable or non-terminal and the patient refuses life-saving treatment with the clear intention of orchestrating his or her death; for example, a physically disabled patient who has lost the will to live and rejects further treatment, even nutrition and hydration, as for example, in the *Bouvia* case. Here there is little room for doubt that the patient's decision to refuse treatment entails an intention to bring about his or her death.

Although in many instances, patients who refuse treatment are clearly seeking death, the courts in the USA (where these cases involving competent patients have arisen) have repeatedly held that they lack the necessary intent for that conduct to constitute suicide. There has been a tendency to rationalize this conclusion on the basis that a patient who refuses life-saving treatment would really prefer to live, free of his or her afflictions.[77] This is a patent absurdity which, if followed through to its logical conclusion, would mean that a person deliberately taking his or her life would not be committing suicide if he or she wished it were not necessary.[78]

No self-initiated action which causes death

In their attempts to distinguish refusal of treatment from suicide, the US courts (and to some extent, the courts in Canada and England) have held that the death of a patient following the withdrawal of treatment, is from 'natural causes' (that is, the patient's underlying disease or condition), which were not initiated by the patient. A distinction is then drawn between this situation and suicide which is said to require voluntary, self-initiated action causing death. This analysis is also open to criticism. It was demonstrated earlier that the distinction between acts and omissions is not a valid basis for determining whether certain conduct can amount to suicide. Thus, the refusal of necessary treatment is potentially as much a cause of death over which the person has control, as is the proverbial bottle of barbiturates.[79] The reality is that where death results following the patient's refusal of treatment, the death of the patient at that particular time is due to the

---

[76] Cantor, *Legal Frontiers of Death and Dying*, above n. 32, at 47.

[77] e.g. *Satz* v. *Perlmutter* 362 So. 2d 160, 162–3 (1978).

[78] For criticism of this approach, see Fletcher, 'The Courts and Euthanasia', above n. 73, at 226.

[79] Sherlock, 'For Everything there is a Season: The Right to Die in the United States', above n. 50, at 557.

patient's decision to die rather than the underlying condition of the patient. It is only because of the patient's decision to die and the subsequent refusal of treatment, that the natural processes are 'fatally set in motion'.[80]

The inaccuracy of the current legal analysis is most clearly apparent in cases of refusal of treatment by non-terminal patients. Although the patient's death may be medically avoidable, and indeed the patient may have a potentially long life span if appropriate medical treatment were administered, the patient may decide to refuse further medical treatment. The patient's refusal may extend to nutrition and hydration or other life-saving treatment.[81] In such cases, it is difficult to escape the conclusion that the patient has set in motion the cause of death, and if deliberately done for the purpose of bringing about his or her own death, the patient's conduct constitutes suicide. Yet, even in these circumstances, the courts have maintained their position that refusal of treatment does not amount to suicide, relying on the argument that the patient's death is not self-initiated but results from 'natural causes'.[82] This conclusion is clearly contrary to fact[83] and highlights the distortions which have occurred in this area. It is difficult to deny that where a patient dies following the refusal of nutrition or hydration the patient's death is self-induced.[84] Somewhat ironically, the logic of this conclusion has been accepted in the context of self-initiated starvation by prisoners, where arguably, it is least appropriate.[85] In a number of cases involving hunger strikes by prisoners, the courts have held that the prisoners' conduct amounted to attempted suicide and therefore justified force-feeding.[86] Yet, in analogous cases of patients refusing treatment, including nutrition and hydration, the courts have avoided this conclusion. Clearly what the courts are doing is presenting as a factual premise, what is in reality a normative conclusion about how such conduct should be characterized.[87]

Whilst it may be more obvious in cases involving non-terminal patients, that a refusal of treatment may result in a self-induced death, the same

---

[80] Fletcher, 'The Courts and Euthanasia', above n. 73, at 225.

[81] The courts have generally accepted that the administration of nutrition and hydration by artificial means constitutes 'medical treatment'.

[82] e.g. *Bouvia* v. *Superior Court*, above n. 54; *Brophy* v. *New England Sinai Hospital, Inc.*, above n. 48.

[83] Fletcher, 'The Courts and Euthanasia', above n. 73, at 225.

[84] Matthews, 'Suicidal Competence and the Patient's Right to Refuse Life-Saving Treatment', above n. 70, at 740; Cantor, *Legal Frontiers of Death and Dying*, above n. 32, at 51. See also the dissenting judgments of Lynch and O'Connor JJ in *Brophy* v. *New England Sinai Hospital, Inc.* (above n. 48) and the concurring judgment of Scalia J of the US Supreme Court in *Cruzan* v. *Director, Missouri Department of Health*, above n. 54, at 251–6.

[85] Lanham, 'The Right to Choose to Die with Dignity', above Ch. 1 n. 160, at 409.

[86] e.g. *In re Caulk* 480 A2d 93 (1984); *State ex. rel. White* v. *Narick* 292 SE 2d 54 (1982); *Re Sanchez* 577 FS 7 (1983).

[87] Jarret, C., 'Moral Reasoning and Legal Change: Observations on the Termination of Medical Treatment and the Development of the Law' (1988) 19 *Rutgers LJ* 1017.

reasoning applies with respect to terminal patients; *any* refusal of treatment which hastens death and which is deliberately made for this purpose amounts to suicide and should be recognized as such. Indeed, there have been some isolated instances where some members of the judiciary in the USA have done just that. In most instances, this has been done in order to reject the argument that certain forms of life-saving treatment (such as artificial nutrition and hydration) can be withdrawn.[88] Very rarely has there been positive recognition of the artificiality of the prevailing analysis in the context of extending rather then curtailing patient's rights. For this reason, the comments in the two recent decisions of the United States Circuit Courts of Appeal considering constitutional challenges to legislation prohibiting assisted suicide are particularly interesting.[89] The majority of the Ninth Circuit Court of Appeal in *Compassion in Dying* v. *State of Washington (en banc)*[90] rejected the argument that had been made on behalf of the State that physician-assisted suicide was different in kind to existing life-ending conduct by physicians because it causes deaths that would not result from the patient's underlying disease. After referring to the case of *Cruzan* v. *Director, Missouri Department of Health*[91] in which the United States Supreme Court had sanctioned the removal of a gastronomy tube which was the precipitating cause of Nancy Cruzan's death, the majority in *Compassion in Dying* held: 'Similarly, when a doctor provides a conscious patient with medication to ease his discomfort while he starves himself to death—a practice that is not only legal but has been urged as an alternative to assisted suicide . . . the patient does not die of an underlying ailment. To the contrary, the doctor is helping the patient to end his life by providing medication that makes it possible for the patient to achieve suicide by starvation'. However, as discussed below, the court did go on to question the use of the term 'suicide', even for terminally-ill patients who seek to hasten their death by taking medication prescribed by their physician. The majority in *Quill* v. *Vacco*,[92] a decision of the Second Circuit Court of the United States Courts of Appeal, were equally candid regarding the cause of death in these circumstances. Criticism was made of the conclusion of the court below that withdrawing nutrition and hydration would simply allow nature to take its course and should be distinguished from the situation of a patient intentionally using an artificial death-producing device. After noting some judicial and academic support for the view that withholding or withdrawing of treatment may amount to suicide, Miner and Pollack JJ concluded that the ending of life by means of withdrawing life-support by doctors at a patient's direction is nothing more nor less than assisted suicide. This conclusion was then used to justify their finding that mentally

---

[88] e.g *Brophy* v. *New England Sinai Hospital, Inc.*, above n. 48, O'Connor and Lynch JJ; and Scalia J in *Cruzan* v. *Director, Missouri Department of Health*, above n. 54.

[89] These constitutional developments are dealt with in detail in part II of this chapter.

[90] See above n. 54.   [91] See above n. 54.   [92] See above n. 54.

competent, terminally ill adults who seek to hasten death but are not dependent on life-support are not treated equally to those who are on such life-support and may effectively direct that doctors assist them to commit suicide.[93]

There are, undoubtedly, significant policy considerations which can be used to justify the view that refusals of treatment are to be distinguished from suicide. Although suicide is no longer illegal, there is still a stigma attached and the courts are understandably reluctant to classify as suicide conduct which is socially acceptable. Furthermore, if some cases of refusal of treatment *are* held to be suicide, concerns are likely to arise about the legality of that conduct, both from the perspective of the patient and whether he or she is legally entitled to adopt that course without interference, and from the perspective of the doctor, whether compliance with a patient's request that treatment be discontinued amounts to assisting suicide and may therefore attract criminal liability. Nevertheless, the prevailing approach of creating fictions in order to avoid what in some cases are obvious conclusions is most undesirable and, in the long run, is likely to erode the credibility of the law. Whilst the force of some of the underlying policy considerations must be acknowledged, there are more satisfactory means of dealing with these issues. It would be far preferable if the courts were to recognize that some cases of refusal of treatment *do* amount to suicide and then having recognized this as a starting point, to find more valid grounds to overcome the potential legal difficulties regarding the patient's right to pursue that course and the legal position of the doctor in assisting the patient.

The crux of the matter is that although in certain circumstances, refusal of treatment does amount to suicide, these cases are significantly different from other forms of suicide which the State may have a valid interest in preventing. It will therefore be argued that the competent patient's right to refuse treatment must be respected and upheld notwithstanding that it may be tantamount to suicide, and that doctors who assist patients in carrying out their suicidal intention by withholding or withdrawing treatment at the patient's direction, should be free of criminal liability.

E. Legal Implications of Recognizing Refusal of Treatment as Suicide

It has been suggested in the foregoing pages that in many instances, the refusal of treatment by a patient is in fact tantamount to suicide and should be recognized as such. What then are the implications of this conclusion? Some commentators have accepted the analogy between refusal of treatment and suicide, but have argued that this logically demands that the same

---

[93] For more detailed discussion, see pp. 116–18 below.

State interests which justify the prevention of suicide should apply to prevent the patient's refusal of treatment.[94] This is by no means an inevitable conclusion; the question of whether refusal of treatment is legally tantamount to suicide is not determinative of whether the State can validly compel a patient to undergo treatment.[95]

Although refusal of treatment may legally be equivalent to suicide, there are valid reasons for differentiating between the two.[96] There is obviously no single explanation for the phenomenon of suicide, but there does appear to be widespread agreement that many suicide attempts are the products of mental disorder and not infrequently, represent a cry for help rather than a determined effort to die.[97] If persons attempting to commit suicide are restrained and given assistance, the majority do not make a further attempt.[98] It is, therefore, perfectly valid for the State to intervene to prevent the occurrence of suicide as a general rule, since the State has a valid interest in the prevention of irrational self-destruction.[99] The State's concern in relation to suicide is reflected in the continued legal regulation of some aspects of suicide; although suicide is no longer punishable, aiding or assisting suicide remains a crime, and in some jurisdictions the law permits a person to use reasonable force to prevent suicide.[100]

As a general proposition, State intervention to prevent suicide is justifiable; however, special considerations apply in relation to those suicides which take the form of a refusal of medical treatment. For terminal patients, the choice of death may be a rational one, offering a release from a painful and undignified death.[101] Even where a patient's condition is non-terminal, the patient may be suffering acutely from a debilitated and dependent existence and life on such terms may become unacceptable to the patient.

[94] e.g. Hegland, K., 'Unauthorised Rendition of Lifesaving Medical Treatment' (1965) 53 *Calif.LRev.* 860, 869–71.

[95] Cantor, 'A Patient's Decision to Decline Life-Saving Medical Treatment: Bodily Integrity Versus the Preservation of Life', above n. 49, at 255.

[96] Ibid. at 256–7. In addition to the argument based upon rational as opposed to irrational death Cantor suggests that the sheer magnitude of the suicide problem justifies government intervention and differentiates common suicide from the refusal of treatment cases.

[97] Ibid. at 256.

[98] Skegg, P., 'A Justification for Medical Procedures Performed Without Consent' (1974) 90 *Law QRev.* 512, 524 where he cites Stengel, E. and Cook, N. G., *Attempted Suicide* (1958) 19–24, 126–7, 129 and Stengel, E., *Suicide and Attempted Suicide* (1964) 79–84.

[99] *Superintendent of Belcherton State School* v. *Saikewicz*, above n. 55, at 425; *Bartling* v. *Superior Court*, above n. 55, at 209.

[100] e.g. in Australia, ACT Crimes (Amendment) Ordinance (No. 2) 1990 s. 18; Vic. Crimes Act 1958 s. 463B; NSW Crimes Act 1900 s. 574B; SA Criminal Law Consolidation Act 1935 s. 13(a)(2); Qld. Criminal Code 1995 s. 66.

[101] For support for the view that patient suicide may be rational, see Wanzer, S. et al., 'The Physician's Responsibility Toward Hopelessly Ill Patients: A Second Look' (1989) 320 *New Eng.JMed.* 844, 847–8; Brandt, R., 'The Rationality of Suicide' in Battin, M. and Mayo, D., (eds.) *Suicide: The Philosophical Issues* (New York, 1980) 117 and Werth, J. and Cobia, D., 'Criteria for Rational Suicide' (1995) 25 *Suicide and Life-Threatening Behaviour* 231.

Here again, the choice of death may be entirely rational. In the medical context, the refusal of treatment by a patient is usually a considered and rational decision, based on their medical condition and the circumstances of their continued existence.[102] The State's legitimate interest in the prevention of irrational self-destruction clearly does not arise in these circumstances.

Thus, there is an important distinction to be made between the usual type of suicide and refusal of treatment by a patient aimed at facilitating an earlier death. However, for some time now, the courts in the USA have adopted an inappropriate means of giving effect to this distinction and this approach now appears also to be favoured in other common law jurisdictions such as England and Canada. As we have seen, the US courts have usually denied the connection between suicide and refusal of treatment and have thereby been able to avoid consideration of the State's interest in the prevention of suicide in such cases. In this way, the courts have upheld the right of a patient to refuse treatment even though that refusal closely approximates suicide. It was argued earlier that this line of reasoning is deficient, resulting in unnecessary distortions of fact and law. In its place, an alternative model is suggested; we need to recognize that refusal of treatment may amount to suicide, but must tailor our response to this particular form of suicide so as to take into account the special considerations applying in the medical context. Having regard to the circumstances of the patient and the overriding principle of self-determination, it will be readily apparent that any interest the State may have in the prevention of irrational suicide simply does not apply in such cases.[103] Conversely, because of the special features of the refusal of treatment cases, upholding a patient's right to refuse treatment (even though that refusal may be tantamount to suicide), does not necessarily imply a *general* right to commit suicide free of State intervention.[104]

In the preceding analysis, it has been argued that the refusal of treatment by a patient may be tantamount to suicide. On the assumption that this proposition is indeed correct, it becomes necessary to consider the legal

[102] It is, of course, possible that a patient may have suicidal intentions, quite unrelated to the medical condition which requires life-saving medical treatment; see Lanham, 'The Right to Choose to Die with Dignity', above Ch. 1 n. 160, at 410.

[103] This conclusion will almost inevitably flow in circumstances where the patient's condition is terminal or where the patient is suffering from a debilitating and irreversible condition. Where, however, the patient is potentially salvageable to a healthy existence, the position is less clear; arguably, the State interest in the prevention of suicide is stronger in these circumstances but faithful adherence to the principle of self-determination would protect the right of a patient to refuse treatment in such cases.

[104] Engelhardt, T., *The Foundations of Bioethics* (New York, 1986) 315. But see Cantor, 'A Patient's Decision to Decline Life-Saving Medical Treatment: Bodily Integrity Versus the Preservation of Life', above n. 49, at 258 where he argues that if we uphold refusals of treatment which are suicidal, we must permit all cases of 'serious suicide'; i.e., persons whose decision to die is clearly competent, deliberate, and firm should be permitted to die.

implications of this conclusion for the medical profession. In particular, it is necessary to examine whether a doctor's compliance with the patient's request amounts to the criminal offence of assisting suicide and whether a doctor has a legal right, or indeed, an obligation, to prevent the patient from committing suicide in this way.

Does a doctor's compliance with a patient's refusal of treatment amount to assisting suicide?[105]

This is a question of some considerable importance; if a doctor could incur criminal liability for assisting suicide as a result of his or her acquiescence in the patient's refusal of treatment, it would have the effect of seriously undermining the common law right to refuse treatment. This has already proved to be a matter of practical relevance; in a number of the refusal of treatment cases litigated in the USA, the hospital and medical staff refused to comply with the patient's request on the ground that to do so would involve them in liability for assisting suicide.[106]

In order to ascertain whether a doctor's compliance with the patient's refusal of treatment can amount to assisting suicide,[107] it is necessary to examine the legal requirements in respect of assisting suicide and the case law in this area. It will be argued that if the statutory prohibitions regarding assisted suicide are given a fairly wide interpretation, the conduct of a doctor in acquiescing in the patient's refusal of treatment could theoretically attract criminal liability. Whilst this is obviously an undesirable possibility, the laws in relation to the prevention of suicide have a sound social purpose and it would therefore be inappropriate to distort the meaning of these statutory provisions in order to protect doctors from liability. The better solution to this difficulty is found through the patient's common law right to refuse treatment and reliance upon an argument analogous to that raised earlier in the context of homicide.[108] The essence of this argument, applied here to the issue of suicide, is that since a doctor is legally required to respect the directions of a patient who has decision-making capacity, a doctor's compliance with a patient's refusal of treatment cannot constitute

---

[105] Although this analysis is confined to consideration of the potential liability of doctors, it should be noted that the relatives of a patient could in some circumstances also potentially be liable for assisting the suicide of a patient by their compliance with a patient's refusal of treatment.

[106] *Bouvia* v. *Superior Court*, above n. 54; *Brophy* v. *New England Sinai Hospital, Inc.*, above n. 48.

[107] It should be noted that in the course of withholding or withdrawing life-sustaining treatment some forms of treatment such as palliative care are likely to still be administered. To this extent, one could say that there are relevant acts as well as omissions on the part of the doctor which facilitate the patient's death; however, for the purposes of the present analysis, attention will be focused on the essentially passive nature of a doctor's conduct in withholding or withdrawing treatment.

[108] See pp. 45–7 above.

the criminal offence of assisting suicide, even though the patient's refusal of treatment may be tantamount to suicide and the doctor does in fact provide assistance to the patient.

Can the offence of assisting suicide be established on the basis of *passive* conduct?

As was outlined earlier, in most common law jurisdictions, the offence of suicide has been abolished, but a new statutory offence of assisting suicide has been created, pursuant to which, a person is variously prohibited from aiding, abetting, instigating, counselling, or procuring the suicide of another. Since the conduct under consideration is essentially of a passive nature (the withdrawal or withholding of treatment by a doctor at the request of a patient)[109] a preliminary matter for determination is whether it is possible to aid or abet by omission or whether something in the nature of affirmative conduct is required.

In the jurisdictions under consideration, the only case to specifically consider this matter in the context of determining the legal liability of a doctor for assisting the suicide of his or her patient as a result of withholding or withdrawing treatment, has arisen in the USA. In the case of *Bouvia* v. *Superior Court*[110] referred to earlier, the hospital and treating doctors had argued that Elizabeth Bouvia should not be allowed to refuse medical treatment whilst in their care because that would be tantamount to suicide and they could accordingly be liable for aiding and abetting suicide.[111] The court was therefore called upon to consider the possible liability of the hospital and medical staff for assisting Elizabeth Bouvia's suicide.[112] At first instance, it was held that she was committing suicide by her refusal of treatment and the medical staff would be assisting her suicide if they adhered to her request that she not be force-fed. On appeal, however, this ruling was overturned and it was held that by refusing treatment, she was not committing suicide, but simply letting nature take its course. This conclusion would have been enough to dispose of the suggestion that the hospital and medical staff might have been liable for assisting suicide. Nevertheless, the court went on to consider the possible criminal liability of

---

[109] It will be argued in the following chapter that some cases of withdrawal of treatment involve affirmative conduct, such as turning off artificial life-support or the withdrawal of artificial nutrition and hydration. (For discussion, see pp. 152–69 below.) These forms of withdrawal of treatment have nevertheless usually been classified as omissions rather than acts.

[110] See above n. 54.

[111] Furthermore, it was argued that since the patient was in a public facility, the State would be a party to her conduct and the State could not be forced to commit the crime of aiding and abetting suicide.

[112] The law in relation to assisting suicide in the State of California is contained in s. 401 of the Californian Penal Code which states that 'every person who deliberately aids, or advises, or encourages another to commit suicide is guilty of a felony'.

the hospital and medical staff. The California Court of Appeal was of the view that to establish liability for aiding or abetting suicide, there must be some affirmative act such as providing a gun, poison, knife or other instrumentality by which a person could inflict upon themselves an immediate and fatal injury.[113] Such situations were said to be 'far different than the mere presence of a doctor during the exercise of [a] patient's constitutional rights'.[114] Thus, the appellate court was able to conclude that neither the doctors nor the hospital would be criminally liable for assisting suicide if they were to respect the decision of a competent and informed patient to refuse medical treatment.

On the basis of the *Bouvia* case it would appear that in order to establish liability for assisting suicide, there must be some affirmative conduct on the part of the accused, such as supplying the means for taking one's life, and conduct in the nature of an omission to act would not suffice.[115] On this reasoning, a doctor's compliance with the refusal of treatment by a patient, who has decision-making capacity, would not attract criminal liability for assisting suicide. However, it may be wondered to what extent this reasoning has been influenced by policy considerations and in particular, the natural reluctance of the courts to impose criminal liability on doctors.

There seems to be no reason in principle why the offence of assisting suicide cannot be committed by omission, provided it is accompanied by the necessary intent. This conclusion is supported by an analysis of the wording used in the various statutory prohibitions on assisting suicide. As was noted above, the word 'aid', which has been used in the legislation of most jurisdictions, has been defined as meaning 'to help or assist' and it is certainly possible to envisage circumstances in which a person may, in a general sense, aid another in committing suicide, although not actually taking an active role in the person's suicide; for example, acting as lookout to clear the way for the person to commit suicide, or deliberately failing to seek medical assistance for a person who has attempted to commit suicide with the intention of facilitating that suicide.[116] This interpretation of aiding suicide has the advantage of consistency with the general criminal law principles regarding complicity in crime. For the purposes of those jurisdictions which prohibit 'abetting suicide', it is evident from judicial interpretation of the word 'abet' in the context of parties to offences that there is no

---

[113] See also *In re Joseph G.* 34 Cal. 3d 429, 436 (1983).

[114] See above n. 54, at 306.

[115] This view is also supported by some commentators; e.g. Williams, *Textbook of Criminal Law*, above Ch. 1 n. 5, at 613.

[116] In an English case, *R* v. *Johnson* (unreported) the parents of a girl who had committed suicide after a long period of disablement from multiple sclerosis were convicted of aiding and abetting the suicide of their daughter because of their failure to intervene to prevent her suicide; Note, 'Wrong to do Right' (1990) 38 *VES Newsletter* 1. The case appears to support the proposition that the offence of assisting suicide can be committed by passive conduct which in some way facilitates the person's suicide.

requirement of active conduct or assistance; abetment can be established merely on the basis of a person's presence and acquiescence in certain conduct, where, by their presence, the person intended to and did in fact give encouragement.[117] In any event, in a typical refusal of treatment case, the withholding or withdrawing of life-saving medical treatment would be accompanied by continued medical and physical comfort care from doctors and nursing staff which could readily be interpreted as active assistance or encouragement of the patient in their effort to commit suicide. Even in the absence of such active assistance, the existence of the doctor/patient relationship, which imposes on doctors certain duties with regard to their patients, could be relied on to support the conclusion that the passive conduct of a doctor did amount to assistance.

Whilst there is no case law directly in support of the proposition that a doctor may potentially be liable for assisting the suicide of his or her patient as a result of withholding or withdrawing treatment, there are a number of cases which indirectly at least, may be relevant to this issue. One such case is *Re Kinney*, a decision of the Victorian Supreme Court in Australia.[118] This case involved an unsuccessful suicide attempt by Mr Kinney who was suffering from leukemia and awaiting trial on a murder charge. As a result of an attempted suicide by drug overdose, the patient was in urgent need of medical treatment. The patient's wife sought an injunction to stop St Vincent's Hospital from treating her husband and gave evidence that her husband had indicated to her that he wanted to die. Fullagar J refused to grant the injunction sought, stating that: 'The preventing of medical or surgical treatment amounts to carrying into execution the attempted suicide of the person concerned. *To grant the injunction would be to assist the person to complete his suicide'.*[119] This decision could be interpreted as supporting the proposition that suicide assistance can take the form of an omission; the injunction was sought to prevent treatment, and the court held that granting the injunction would be to assist the person in his suicide, the clear implication being that withholding or withdrawing treatment can amount to assisting suicide.

Another first instance decision in Australia along similar lines was made in the case of *Schneidas* v. *Corrective Services Commission*[120] considered earlier, which involved the force-feeding of a prisoner on a hunger strike. In an application brought on behalf of the prisoner to prevent the prison authorities from force-feeding him, Lee J refused to grant the injunction since it would, in effect, aid and abet the prisoner in committing suicide.[121]

---

[117] *R* v. *Clarkson* (1971) 55 Crim.App.R 445, 448; *R* v. *Russel* [1933] VR 59, 66–7.

[118] (Unreported) 23 Dec. 1988, SC Vic. See also discussion of this case by Skene, L., 'The Fullagar Judgment' (1989) 14 *Legal Service Bulletin* 42.

[119] Ibid. at 4 (author's emphasis).

[120] See above n. 46.

[121] As noted earlier, at the time of this decision, suicide was still a crime in New South Wales.

By analogy, it could therefore be argued that a doctor who withholds or withdraws treatment at the request of a patient pursuant to a patient's suicidal refusal of treatment, in effect assists (aids, abets etc.) the patient in committing suicide.

Since neither of these cases specifically dealt with the question of liability for assisting suicide as a result of passive conduct, such as a doctor's compliance with the patient's suicidal refusal of treatment, one must be careful not to overstate the significance of these decisions. Nevertheless, the cases can be interpreted in support of the view that the offence of assisting suicide could be established on the basis of some relevant omission as distinct from affirmative conduct.

Reference was also made earlier to the English case of *Attorney-General* v. *Able*[122] in which Woolf J was called upon to interpret the English provision dealing with suicide assistance. Whilst this case did not specifically consider whether the offence of assisting suicide can be committed by omission, the principles laid down in that case may nevertheless provide some guidance in interpreting the prohibition on assisting suicide and assessing whether a doctor may be acting unlawfully by complying with a patient's refusal of treatment. Let us assume, for the moment, that refusal of treatment by a patient may be equivalent to suicide and that the offence of assisting suicide can be established on the basis of passive conduct; it could then be argued on the basis of the reasoning in *Attorney-General* v. *Able*, that in some circumstances at least, doctors who withhold or withdraw treatment intend to assist the patient to commit suicide, by their inaction, provide assistance, and the patient is thereby in fact assisted in committing suicide. Thus, the various requirements for the commission of the offence of assisting suicide could arguably be satisfied.[123] According to Woolf J in *Attorney-General* v. *Able*, if these elements can be proved, it does not make any difference that the person would have committed suicide anyway.

It would appear from the foregoing analysis that as a matter of interpretation, the conduct of a doctor in complying with the patient's suicidal refusal of treatment could potentially come within the prohibition on assisting suicide. It therefore becomes very relevant to examine the legal effect of a patient's right to refuse treatment on the doctor's potential criminal liability.

---

[122] See above n. 16.

[123] Probably the most difficult element to establish would be that the doctor *intended* to assist the patient's suicide; it could for example be argued that a doctor who withholds or withdraws treatment on a patient's instructions simply seeks to honour the patient's refusal and does not intend to assist the patient's suicide. It should be noted, however, that Woolf J in *Attorney-General* v. *Able* (above n. 16) held that an intention to assist a person to commit suicide need not involve a desire that suicide should be committed or attempted; for discussion see p. 59 above.

Legal effect of a patient's right to refuse treatment upon a doctor's potential liability for assisting suicide

As outlined in the preceding chapter, the common law principles of informed consent and self-determination prohibit any unauthorized medical intervention except in emergency cases where the patient's consent cannot be obtained.[124] Thus, if a patient, who has decision-making capacity, refuses further medical treatment, the doctor is legally obliged to respect the patient's decision and the failure to do so may attract both criminal and civil liability.[125] Since the doctor cannot continue to treat the patient except with the patient's consent, the doctor cannot be held criminally liable for assisting suicide where he or she simply respects the patient's wishes and withholds or withdraws treatment.[126] As a matter of both law and logic, it cannot be unlawful to do that which by law one is legally required to do.[127] The most satisfactory way in which the legal principles regarding liability for assisted suicide and the refusal of treatment can be reconciled is for the courts to take a broad view of the patient's right to refuse treatment so that the withholding or withdrawal of treatment performed in recognition of that right is exempt from criminal liability even though the legal requirements for establishing liability for assisted suicide against the doctor may be present.[128] Whilst this line of reasoning has not been adopted by the courts, some indirect support for this view can be gleaned from a number of cases decided in the USA dealing with the constitutional right of privacy. One such example is the case of *In re Quinlan*[129] in which the court held that the exercise of the patient's constitutional right of privacy is protected from criminal prosecution and that this protection extends to third parties whose action was necessary to effectuate the exercise of that right.[130] Although rights which are taken to be constitutionally guaranteed obviously have a special status, there is some foundation for the adoption of an analogous argument with respect to protection from criminal liability for those who assist a patient in the exercise of his or her common law right to refuse

---

[124] See pp. 35–45 above.　　[125] See pp. 45–7 above.

[126] Meyers, D., *Medico Legal Implications of Death and Dying* (New York, 1981) 134–5; Williams, *Textbook of Criminal Law*, above Ch. 1 n. 5, at 613.

[127] The defence of necessity may be relevant in this context on the basis that as there is a legal *duty* to comply with the patient's wishes there can be no criminal liability for doing so. Of particular relevance is the Canadian case of *Perka* v. *R* (1985) 14 CCC 3d 385, 417–20 which specifically recognizes the existence of the defence of necessity in circumstances where the defendant is faced with conflicting legal duties.

[128] i.e., that the patient by his or her refusal of treatment is committing suicide, that the doctor intends to assist the patient, and does in fact assist the patient in committing suicide.

[129] See above Ch. 1 n. 116.

[130] See also *Bouvia* v. *Superior Court* (above n. 54) in which the court distinguished between circumstances involving affirmative acts, such as providing the means for the person to commit suicide and 'the mere presence of a doctor during the exercise of [a] patient's constitutional rights'.

treatment. This is of particular relevance in other common law jurisdictions such as the United Kingdom and Australia, where there is fairly widespread acceptance of the right of a patient to refuse treatment, but no equivalent constitutional right.

It should be made clear that the preceding arguments to the effect that doctors should not be criminally liable for the offence of assisting suicide in circumstances where they have complied with a patient's request that life-sustaining treatment be withheld or withdrawn, says nothing about the legality of a doctor providing *active* suicide assistance to a patient. This is because the arguments made have been premised on the fundamental proposition that patients have a right to refuse unwanted medical treatment. Under present law[131] a person has no legal right to active assistance to die[132] although such a right has been claimed on constitutional grounds in a number of recent cases in Canada and the USA which are discussed later in this chapter.[133]

In the foregoing pages, attention has been focused on the potential legal liability for assisting suicide of a doctor who, in compliance with the suicidal request of a patient, with decision-making capacity, withholds or withdraws treatment. A distinct, but nevertheless related matter is whether a doctor ever has the right to intervene so as to prevent the patient from committing suicide, or is even under a duty to do so.

Does a doctor have a right or indeed a duty to prevent suicide?

As we have seen, at one time, suicide and attempted suicide were crimes and it was therefore possible to justify intervention in a person's attempted suicide in order to prevent the commission of a crime.[134] Since suicide has ceased to be criminal in the jurisdictions under consideration, this particular argument no longer applies. Although suicide or attempted suicide are no longer prohibited by the criminal law, as noted earlier, in a number of jurisdictions legislation exists which permits the use of reasonable force to prevent a person from committing suicide. Even in jurisdictions where there is no such provision, it could be argued on policy grounds that well-intentioned intervention in an attempted suicide should not give rise to civil or criminal liability.[135]

---

[131] Even in the Northern Territory of Australia where legislation legalizing active voluntary euthanasia and doctor-assisted suicide has been passed, it does not confer a legally enforceable right on a patient to such assistance. For discussion, see p. 346 below. Note also the legislation passed in the US State of Oregon permitting doctor-assisted suicide: see pp. 370–1 below.

[132] Except in the case of withdrawals of treatment which entail affirmative action. For discussion see pp. 152–69 below.

[133] See pp. 86–124 below.

[134] Williams, *Textbook of Criminal Law*, above Ch. 1 n. 5, at 616–17.

[135] See Kloss, D., 'Consent to Medical Treatment' (1965) 5 *Med. Science & Law* 89, 91–2 and the case of *Meyer* v. *Supreme Lodge Knights of Pythias* 70 NE 111 (1904) in which it was held by a majority of the New York Court of Appeal that a doctor who gave medical treatment to

It has, for example, been argued that where a patient refuses treatment in the knowledge that death will result, the doctor is under an obligation to ignore the patient's request and, under the protection of the plea of necessity, prevent the patient from adopting a course of conduct which would lead to self-destruction.[136] Reliance could purportedly be placed on the English case of *Leigh* v. *Gladstone*,[137] noted earlier, in support of this view.[138] Whilst the principle in that case is potentially wide and may well be capable of extension to the medical context, commentators have overwhelmingly rejected such an approach.[139] The consensus appears to be that reliance upon this authority so as to provide justification to a doctor to override a patient's refusal of treatment would be a most inappropriate infringement of the patient's right of self-determination. Moreover, in view of more recent English authority, particularly the case of *Airedale NHS Trust* v. *Bland*,[140] and recent cases concerning the force-feeding of prisoners,[141] this decision can no longer be taken to represent English law. Thus, *Leigh* v. *Gladstone* cannot validly be used to impose upon doctors a *duty* or for that matter even a *right* to prevent a patient from committing suicide by refusing treatment. The defence of necessity should only apply in emergency situations where the patient is in need of life-saving treatment but the patient's consent to that treatment cannot be obtained.[142] It does not justify overriding the refusal of treatment by a patient, who has decision-making capacity, even where that refusal is clearly suicidal.

A related line of argument that may be advanced is that a doctor is not

---

an attempted suicide, contrary to that person's express wishes, would not be liable in trespass. As Zellick points out (Zellick, P., 'The Forcible Feeding of Prisoners: An Examination of the Legality of Enforced Therapy' (1976) *Pub.Law* 153 at 166), since the facts of this case involved irrational, impulsive suicide, it is not authority for the broad proposition that all intervention in suicide is protected from liability. In circumstances where a well-meaning person intervenes to prevent a suicide, even if such conduct is technically unlawful, it would be most unlikely to give rise to a prosecution or if prosecuted, the person would almost certainly be given an absolute discharge; Williams, *Textbook of Criminal Law*, above Ch. 1 n. 5, at 617.

[136] Kennedy, 'The Legal Effect of Requests by the Terminally Ill and Aged Not to Receive Further Treatment from Doctors', above Ch. 1 n. 154, at 226–7 where he cites Smith, J. C. and Hogan, B., *Criminal Law*, 3rd edn. (London, 1973) 158. This point does not, however, appear to have been made in subsequent editions of this work.

[137] See above n. 41.

[138] As noted earlier, in this case, the court upheld the forced feeding of a suffragette prisoner by the prison authorities and suggested that the prison officers may in fact have been under a *duty* to preserve the prisoner's life.

[139] Kennedy, 'The Legal Effect of Requests by the Terminally Ill and Aged Not to Receive Further Treatment from Doctors', above Ch. 1 n. 154, at 227; Skegg, 'A Justification for Medical Procedures Performed Without Consent', above n. 98, at 525–6.

[140] See above Ch. 1 n. 41.

[141] e.g. *Secretary of State for the Home Department* v. *Robb* [1995] 1 All ER 677. Note also the decision of the Supreme Court of New South Wales, *Department of Immigration* v. *Mok and Another* [1994] 2 Med Law R 102.

[142] In support of this proposition see *In re F (Mental Patient: Sterilisation)* [1990] 2 AC 1, 73–6 per Lord Goff.

obliged to respect a suicidal request by a patient that treatment be terminated, indeed that he or she is obliged to disregard it, since otherwise the doctor would be criminally liable for the offence of assisting suicide.[143] It has been argued that the conduct of a doctor in complying with a patient's suicidal refusal of treatment does, strictly speaking, come within the statutory prohibition on assisting suicide. However, as outlined earlier, a patient who has decision-making capacity has the right to refuse treatment and a doctor may in fact incur both civil and criminal liability for disregarding the patient's directions. It follows therefore that a doctor should be protected from any criminal liability which may arise as a result of the doctor respecting the patient's refusal of treatment. Thus, it would not be legally justifiable for a doctor to force treatment upon a patient on the grounds that it is necessary to do so in order to avoid liability for assisting suicide.

Rational suicide by a patient distinguished from irrational suicide—a reconciliation with State suicide policy

Although as a general proposition, doctors are sometimes free and indeed, even obliged to intervene to avert the consequences of suicide attempts,[144] it has been argued that a doctor is under no legal duty to prevent the rational suicide of a patient with decision-making capacity, who has declined life-saving treatment. Furthermore, it is questionable whether a doctor has a legal right to intervene in these circumstances.

The State has a legitimate interest in the prevention of suicide. As was previously observed, suicide is frequently associated with mental disorder and irrational behaviour and in many instances, attempted suicides represent a plea for help rather than a determined effort to die. Accordingly, laws which are directed to the prevention of suicide[145] are perfectly sound and fulfil an important social service in protecting individuals from irrational self-destruction.

It is imperative, however, to distinguish between two fundamentally different types of suicide; the typical form of suicide or attempted suicide which is the product of irrational and disturbed behaviour on the one hand and, on the other, the situation where a person, who has decision-making capacity, reaches a reasoned and firm decision that he or she wishes to die. For the purposes of the present discussion, the prime example of rational suicide is where a terminal or incurable patient reaches a decision to end his or her life and in furtherance of that decision, seeks to commit suicide, either by refusing necessary medical treatment or by some other means.

---

[143] Kennedy, 'The Legal Effect of Requests by the Terminally Ill and Aged Not to Receive Further Treatment from Doctors', above Ch. 1 n. 154, at 226–8.

[144] For discussion, see Skegg, P., *Law, Ethics and Medicine* (Oxford 1984) 110–13.

[145] For example, the general prohibition on assisting suicide and the provisions which exist permitting physical intervention in order to prevent a person from committing suicide: see above.

Since society has a legitimate interest in the prevention of irrational self-destruction, nothing should impede well-meaning by-standers or medical staff from intervening in clear cases of irrational suicide and imposing medical treatment in an attempt to save the life of that person. Further, where a person is found attempting to commit suicide, and nothing is known about his or her state of mind, it would be reasonable to assume that the attempt is evidence of mental disorder[146] and it would be quite justifiable for concerned persons or members of the medical profession to take whatever steps were necessary to prevent the death of that person. As Skegg points out, doctors are constantly intervening in these circumstances and there can be little doubt that a court would hold their action to be justified.[147]

Where, however, there is clear evidence that a patient, who has decision-making capacity, has made a well-informed, firm, and rational decision that they wish to die, and elects to commit suicide, the decision of the patient should be upheld.[148] In these circumstances, it would be completely inappropriate and misplaced for medical staff to impose medical treatment against the wishes of the patient, on the grounds that they are preventing the patient's suicide. This conclusion has been endorsed by a group of prominent doctors in the USA. In an influential paper, it was accepted that if a terminal patient, not suffering from treatable depression, acts on his or her wish for death and commits suicide, it is ethical for a doctor who knows the patient well to refrain from an attempt at resuscitation.[149]

Legal validation for the foregoing view can be found in the fundamental common law right of a patient, who has decision-making capacity, to refuse medical treatment. Provided there is clear evidence of a firm and informed decision by the patient, the doctor has no right to intervene in the patient's suicide.[150] Further, the validity of the patient's decision to commit suicide should not be dependent on whether the patient's condition is terminal. Whilst it may, from an objective point of view, be easier to understand the decision of a terminal patient to put an end to prolonged suffering and opt for an earlier death, the decision of a salvageable patient to commit suicide may also be perfectly rational. It is a fundamental aspect of an individual's

[146] The available empirical evidence supports the presumption of unsoundness of mind. See also Williams, *Textbook of Criminal Law*, above Ch. 1 n. 5, at 616.

[147] Skegg, 'A Justification for Medical Procedures Performed Without Consent', above n. 98, at 525.

[148] Cantor, *Legal Frontiers of Death and Dying*, above n. 32, at 50–1; Skegg, 'A Justification for Medical Procedures Performed Without Consent', above n. 98, at 524.

[149] Wanzer et al., 'The Physician's Responsibility Toward Hopelessly Ill Patients: A Second Look', above n. 101, at 848. Ten of the twelve doctors expressed their belief that it is not immoral for a doctor to assist in the rational suicide of a terminally ill person by, for example, prescribing drugs.

[150] This should be the case even in those jurisdictions which have specific statutory provision allowing the use of force to prevent suicide. Since the object of these provisions is to prevent *irrational* self-destruction it would be indefensible to invoke these powers in circumstances where it is known that the patient has made a clear and rational decision to commit suicide.

right to bodily integrity and self-determination, that he or she should be free to make his or her own assessment of quality of life and determine when continued existence becomes an intolerable burden.[151] Provided the patient has decision-making capacity and the patient's decision is fully informed, it should be respected by the medical staff.

Recognition that a patient's decision to commit suicide by refusal of treatment should be upheld if it is the product of a reasoned and rational decision has potentially wider implications beyond the medical context and could give rise to an argument that all rational suicides should be permitted.[152] However, the view taken here is that a clear distinction can be drawn between patients who in the exercise of their right of self-determination, are refusing further medical treatment with the intention of committing suicide, and other forms of rational suicide.

II. CONSTITUTIONAL CHALLENGES TO ASSISTING SUICIDE LEGISLATION

In significant developments in Canada and the USA, the courts have been called upon to determine the validity of legislation prohibiting assisted suicide, following challenge to this legislation on constitutional grounds. Even prior to these cases, legal scholars have been debating whether the courts should recognize a constitutional right to commit suicide which would protect the right of the individual to have assistance in taking his or her life in certain circumstances.[153]

The most significant Canadian case to date has been the case *Rodriguez* v. *British Columbia (Attorney General)*[154] which came before the Supreme Court of Canada. The appellant, Sue Rodriguez, 42 years of age, was suffering from amyotrophic lateral sclerosis (Lou Gehrig's disease). This condition causes significant physical deterioration to the point that patients are unable to swallow, speak, or move without assistance, and ultimately, sufferers of this disease lose the capacity to breathe without a respirator or to eat without a gastronomy. At the time of the appeal, Mrs Rodriguez had

---

[151] Cantor, *Legal Frontiers of Death and Dying,* above n. 32, at 51.

[152] Cantor, 'A Patient's Decision to Decline Life-Saving Medical Treatment: Bodily Integrity Versus the Preservation of Life', above n. 49, at 258; Cantor, *Legal Frontiers of Death and Dying,* above n. 32, at 51–2; Zellick, 'The Forcible Feeding of Prisoners: An examination of the Legality of Enforced Therapy', above n. 135, at 170–1; Skegg, 'A Justification for Medical Procedures Performed Without Consent', above n. 98, at 524.

[153] e.g. Engelhardt, T. and Malloy, M., 'Suicide and Assisting Suicide: A Critique of Legal Sanctions' (1982) 36 Sw.LJ 1003; Richards, D., 'Constitutional Privacy, the Right to Die and the Meaning of Life' (1981) 22 *Wm. & Mary LRev.* 327; Kamisar, Y., 'Are Laws Against Assisted Suicide Unconstitutional?' (1993) 23 *Hastings Center R* 32; Carnerie, F., 'Euthanasia and Self-Determinism: Is There a Charter Right to Die in Canada?' (1987) 32 *McGill LJ* 299.

[154] [1993] 3 SCR 519.

a life expectancy of between 2 and 14 months. She did not wish to die immediately but wanted to be able to organize for a qualified physician to set up technological means by which she might, when she was no longer able to enjoy life, by her own hand and at the time of her choosing, end her life. She applied to the Supreme Court of British Columbia for an order that section 241(b) of the Canadian Criminal Code 1985, which prohibits the giving of assistance to commit suicide,[155] be declared invalid on the grounds that it violates her rights under sections 7, 12, and 15(1) of the Canadian Charter of Rights and Freedoms, and is therefore, to the extent that it precludes a terminally ill person from committing 'physician-assisted' suicide,[156] of no force and effect by virtue of section 52(1) of the Constitution Act 1982. The Supreme Court of British Columbia dismissed her application. This decision was affirmed by a majority of the British Columbia Court of Appeal although there was a significant dissent from the Chief Justice of that Court, McEachern CJ, who upheld the appellant's claim and spelt out conditions under which a physician could lawfully assist her to commit suicide.[157]

Sue Rodriguez then appealed to the Supreme Court of Canada but her appeal was dismissed, albeit by the narrowest of margins.[158] The nine judges of the Supreme Court hearing the appeal were sharply divided on the issue with a majority, comprised of La Forest, Sopinka, Gonthier, Iacobucci, and Major JJ, holding that section 241(b) of the Canadian Criminal Code 1985 is constitutional, Lamer CJ and L'Heureux-Dubé, Cory, and McLachlin JJ dissenting.

One of the key issues in this case was whether the prohibition in section 241(b) of the Criminal Code on assisted suicide violated Mrs Rodriguez right to liberty and security of the person under section 7 of the Charter. Section 7 provides: 'Everyone has the right to life, liberty and security of the person and the right not to be deprived thereof except in accordance with the principles of fundamental justice'. The majority, in a joint judgment delivered by Sopinka J, held that liberty and security of the person interests contained in section 7 cannot be divorced from the sanctity of life which is one of the three values protected by section 7. Even where death appears imminent, seeking to control the manner and timing of one's death constitutes a conscious choice of death over life. Life as a value was, therefore,

---

[155] More specifically, this provision prohibits a person from aiding or abetting a person to commit suicide.

[156] For the purposes of discussing this case and the US authorities challenging the constitutionality of legislation prohibiting assisted suicide, the phrase 'physician-assisted suicide' will be used (rather than doctor-assisted suicide which is used elsewhere in this work) because this is the terminology that has been used by the Canadian and US courts.

[157] *Rodriguez v. Attorney General of British Columbia, Attorney General of Canada* (1993) 79 CCC (3d) 1, 2–26.

[158] A few months after the Supreme Court decision was handed down Sue Rodriguez was found dead, having reportedly been assisted to die by an unidentified doctor.

seen as being engaged in this case and had to be considered in the light of the other values mentioned in section 7.

It was accepted by the majority that section 7, when referring to security of the person, encompasses notions of personal autonomy (at least with respect to the right to make choices concerning one's body), control over one's physical and psychological integrity, free from State interference, and basic human dignity. The majority of the court found that the prohibition in section 241(b) which prevents the appellant from having assistance to commit suicide when she is no longer able to do so, deprives her of autonomy over her person and causes her physical pain and psychological distress in a manner which impinges on the security of her person.

Having found that the appellant's security interest was engaged it became necessary to determine whether there had been any deprivation of that interest which was not in accordance with the principles of fundamental justice so as to be in breach of section 7 of the Charter. In determining what are 'principles of fundamental justice' within the meaning of section 7, the majority stated that these principles must be seen as vital or fundamental to our societal notion of justice. They must be capable of being identified with some precision and applied to situations in a manner that yields an identifiable result. The majority held that the principles of fundamental justice must also be legal principles. The appellant had argued that respect for human dignity was a principle of fundamental justice. This proposition was rejected by the majority which held that respect for human dignity, whilst one of the underlying principles on which our society is based, is not a principle of fundamental justice within the meaning of section 7.

The majority found that the blanket prohibition on assisted suicide contained in section 241(b) has as its purpose the protection of the vulnerable. This purpose is grounded in the State interest in protecting life and reflects the policy of the State that human life should not be depreciated by allowing life to be taken. This State policy was said to be part of our fundamental conception of the sanctity of life and it was noted that a blanket prohibition on assisted suicide similar to that contained in the Canadian Criminal Code was the norm among Western democracies. The court interpreted this as indicating that these societies, including Canada, recognize and generally apply the principle of sanctity of life subject to limited and narrow conceptions in which notions of personal autonomy and dignity must prevail. It was stressed that these same societies continue to draw a distinction between active and passive forms of intervention in the dying process. Whilst acknowledging the debate as to whether such distinctions are valid, the majority relied on the fact that the distinctions are maintained and can be persuasively defended. The majority found that to the extent that any consensus did exist, it is that human life must be respected and we must be careful not to undermine the institutions that protect it. After reviewing the common law, the legislative history of the offence, the rationale behind the continued criminalization of assisted suicide and the principles which underlie it, the majority of the court concluded that given the concerns about abuse if assisted suicide were decriminalized and the great difficulty in creating appropriate safeguards to prevent these, it cannot be said that the blanket prohibition on assisted suicide is arbitrary or unfair, or that it is not reflective of fundamental values at play in our society. Thus, the majority concluded, section 241(b) does not infringe section 7 of the Charter.[159]

Quite a different interpretation was given to section 7 of the Charter by the dissenting judges who considered this provision. In a joint judgment, L'Heureux-Dubé and McLachlin JJ held that section 241(b) infringes the right to security of the person included in section 7 of the Charter. This right has an element of personal autonomy which protects the dignity and privacy of individuals with respect to decisions concerning their own body. Their Honours were of the view that the legislative scheme introduced by the Parliament which makes suicide lawful but assisted suicide unlawful has the effect of denying some people the choice of ending their lives solely because they are physically incapable of doing so, thus preventing them from exercising the autonomy over their bodies available to other people. They held that this denial of the ability to end their life is arbitrary and therefore amounted to a limit on the right to security of the person which does not comport with the principles of fundamental justice. L'Heureux-Dubé and McLachlin JJ disagreed with the reliance placed by the majority on the fear of abuse if assisted suicide were to be generally permitted. In their Honours' view, the principles of fundamental justice require that each person, considered individually, be treated fairly by the law. The fear that abuse may arise if an individual is permitted that which she is wrongly denied plays no part at the section 7 stage of analysis but is relevant at the next stage of the analysis where the question is whether a limit imposed contrary to the principles of fundamental justice may nevertheless be saved under section 1 of the Charter as a limit demonstrably justified in a free and democratic society.[160]

Ultimately, however, they decided that section 241(b) could not be justified under section 1 of the Charter. They held that fears that unless assisted suicide is prohibited it will be used as a cloak for murder or that the consent of vulnerable persons may be improperly procured, were not sufficient to override the appellant's entitlement under section 7 to end her life in the manner and at the time of her choosing. It was held that the Criminal Code

---

[159] For a critical analysis of the majority's reasoning in respect to ss. 7 and 1 of the Charter see Weinrib, L., 'The Body and the Body Politic: Assisted Suicide Under the Canadian Charter of Rights and Freedoms' (1994) 39 *McGill LJ* 618.

[160] Section 1 of the Charter is in the following terms: 'The Canadian Charter of Rights and Freedoms guarantees the rights and freedoms set out in it subject only to such reasonable limits prescribed by law as can be demonstrably justified in a free and democratic society'.

already contains sufficient safeguards to meet concerns about consent. Most importantly, unconsented to killings would constitute murder. And, their Honours suggested, if the existing protections under the Code were supplemented by a stipulation requiring a court order to permit the assistance of suicide in a particular case only when the judge is satisfied that the consent is freely given, it would thereby ensure that only those who truly desire to bring their lives to an end obtain assistance. Cory J was substantially in agreement with the reasoning of L'Heureux-Dubé and McLachlin JJ in relation to section 7 of the Charter.

The appellant had also argued that section 241(b) was a violation of her rights under section 12 of the Charter which states that 'everyone has the right not to be subjected to any cruel or unusual punishment'. The majority of the court held that even assuming that 'treatment' within the meaning of section 12 may include that imposed by the State in contexts other than penal or quasi-penal, a mere prohibition by the State on certain action cannot constitute 'treatment' under section 12. Their Honours were of the view that, particularly having regard to the word 'subjecting' in section 12, there must be some more active State process in operation, involving an exercise of State control over the individual. The judges in the minority found it unnecessary to decide this issue, having already upheld the appeal on other grounds.

The final argument relied upon by the appellant was that section 241(b) violated her rights under section 15(1) of the Charter. Section 15(1) provides: 'Every individual is equal before and under the law and has the right to equal protection and equal benefit of the law without discrimination and in particular, without discrimination based on race, national or ethnic origin, colour, religion, sex, age or mental or physical disability'. It had been argued on behalf of the appellant that due to her physical disabilities, she could not, without assistance, commit suicide and the prohibition on assisting suicide in the Criminal Code was depriving her of the option of suicide which was an option open to others. The majority found it preferable not to have to decide the difficult and important issues raised by section 15 of the Charter but rather to assume that the prohibition on assisted suicide in section 241(b) did infringe section 15. This was because in their view, any infringement was clearly justified under section 1 of the Charter as being a limit demonstrably justified in a free and democratic society. In essence, the majority found that the prohibition on assisted suicide is rationally connected to the purpose of section 241(b) which is to protect and maintain respect for human life. This protection is based upon a substantial consensus among Western countries that in order to protect life and those who are vulnerable in society effectively, a prohibition without exception on the giving of assistance to commit suicide is the best approach. Thus, they found that section 241(b) was not overly broad and it had satisfied the proportionality test which is relevant in the application of section 1 of the Charter.

Lamer CJ, dissenting, was the only judge to base his decision primarily on section 15 of the Charter, consequently finding it unnecessary to consider sections 7 and 12 which had been relied on by the other judges. His Honour held that section 241(b) of the Criminal Code infringes the right to equality contained in section 15(1) of the Charter. This is because the effect of the Code provision is to prevent persons, physically unable to end their lives unassisted, from lawfully choosing suicide when that option is in principle available to other members of the public without contravention of the law. Lamer CJ was of the view that the inequality created by section 241(b) can be characterized as a burden or disadvantage, since it limits the ability of those who are subject to this inequality to take and act upon fundamental decisions regarding their lives and persons. Moreover, his Honour held that this inequality is imposed on persons unable to end their lives unassisted solely because of a physical disability, a personal characteristic which is among the grounds for discrimination listed in section 15(1) of the Charter.

Lamer CJ went on to find that section 241(b) of the Code could not be justified under section 1 of the Charter. This was, essentially, because the section failed to meet the proportionality test: whilst agreeing with the majority that the prohibition of assisted suicide is rationally connected to the legislative objective of protecting vulnerable persons from inappropriate coercion, the means chosen to implement this objective did not impair the appellant's equality rights as little as reasonably possible. His Honour found that the reach of the section was over-inclusive: those who were not vulnerable or who did not wish for the State's protection are also brought within the operation of the provision solely as a result of their physical disability. Lamer CJ was of the view that an absolute prohibition that is indifferent to the individual or the circumstances in question cannot satisfy the constitutional duty on the government to impair the rights of persons with physical disabilities as little as reasonably possible. In sharp contrast to the majority judgment, he held that the fear of a slippery slope cannot justify the over-inclusive reach of section 241(b) to encompass not only people who may be vulnerable to the pressure of others, but also persons with no evidence of vulnerability, and, in the case of the appellant, persons where there is positive evidence of freely determined consent. The remedy proposed by Lamer CJ was to declare section 241(b) to be of no force or effect pursuant to section 52(1) of the Constitution Act 1982, but with the effect of the declaration being suspended for one year from the date of the judgment to give Parliament adequate time to decide what legislation, if any, should replace section 241(b). Further, it was proposed to grant Sue Rodriguez a constitutional exemption from the operation of section 241(b) during the period of the suspension, subject to a number of conditions modelled largely on those proposed by McEachern CJ in the court below.[161] Cory J was in agreement with the Chief Justice that section 15(1) of the Charter could be applied to grant to the appellant the relief sought. The remaining minority judges, L'Heureux-Dubé and McLachlin JJ, were in general agreement with the remedy proposed by Lamer CJ, having found for the appellant in relation to section 7 of the Charter.

The decision of the Canadian Supreme Court in the *Rodriguez* case is undoubtedly an important one. It is true that the issue before the court was very narrow, namely whether there is a constitutional right to assisted suicide for persons physically unable to commit suicide unassisted, with the majority of the court finding that there was no constitutional right to assisted suicide in these circumstances. By looking at the issue of assisted suicide generally, the majority arguably did not give adequate attention to the special considerations arising in the context of physician-assisted suicide which are relevant to the issue of abuse and concerns about providing adequate safeguards for the practice. The case can nevertheless be seen as a significant milestone in the history of physician-assisted suicide and voluntary euthanasia in Canada and the common law world generally, not least because of the substantial interest that it has generated in these related issues. Indeed, the overwhelming public sympathy shown for the plight of Sue Rodriguez was an influential factor in bringing about government action to review Canadian law in relation to physician-assisted suicide and active voluntary euthanasia.[162]

One striking feature of the case is the closeness of the court's decision, five of the nine judges rejecting her appeal, the remaining four upholding her claim. Apart from providing Sue Rodriguez with the relief she sought, the remedy allowed by the minority would have placed responsibility on the Canadian Parliament to enact legislation permitting physician-assisted suicide, at least for terminally ill patients who are physically unable to commit

---

[161] These conditions, as modified by Lamer CJ, were as follows: 1) the constitutional exemption may only be sought by way of application to a superior court; 2) the applicant must be certified by a treating physician and independent psychiatrist, in the manner and at the time suggested by McEachern CJ, to be competent to make the decision to end his or her own life, and the physicians must certify that the applicant's decision has been made freely and voluntarily, and at least one of the physicians must be present with the applicant at the time the applicant commits suicide; 3) the physician must also certify: (i) that the applicant is or will become physically incapable of committing suicide unassisted, and (ii) that they have informed him or her, and that he or she understands, that he or she has a constitutional right to change his or her mind about terminating his or her life; 4) notice and access must be given to the Regional Coroner at the time and in the manner outlined by McEachern CJ; 5) the applicant must be examined daily by one of the certifying physicians at the time and in the manner outlined by McEachern CJ; 6) the constitutional exemption will expire according to the time limits set by McEachern CJ; and 7) the act causing the death of the applicant must be that of the applicant him- or herself, and not that of anyone else.

[162] See pp. 382–7 below for discussion of Canadian developments including the setting up of the Special Senate Committee on Euthanasia and Assisted Suicide in 1994.

suicide unaided. Given the narrow margin by which the appellant ultimately failed in having section 241(b) declared unconstitutional, there clearly was considerable support amongst the judges for physician-assisted suicide, at least in some circumstances.[163] Indeed, eight of the nine judges accepted that section 241(b) infringes the patient's rights under section 7 of the Charter (the remaining judge relying instead on section 15 of the Charter). The division in the court in the final outcome was a result of the conflicting views as to who has the onus of establishing that the infringement is justified: according to the majority judgment, determination of whether justification can be established is principally to be determined under section 7 itself, where the onus lies on the individual; whereas in the opinion of the minority, the question of justification falls for consideration under section 1 of the Charter where a heavy onus rests upon the State.[164] The majority were clearly concerned about the dangers of abuse, particularly for the vulnerable, if assisted suicide were permitted; the minority, whilst recognizing the risk of abuse, were not convinced that this factor should override the rights of the individual to a dignified death and felt that there were ways of safeguarding against abuse short of a complete prohibition on assisted suicide.[165]

Thus, although the court was split as to whether the infringements of the appellant's rights could be justified, there was much common ground between the judges. There was agreement that the State has an interest in the protection of life, particularly of the vulnerable members of society, and that ultimately, the State's interest has to be weighed up against the claimed right of individuals to a dignified death by being allowed to determine the time and manner of their death. Significantly, however, there were differences of opinion regarding the importance to be attached to these competing considerations and, of particular relevance, was the disagreement as to whether it would be possible to devise sufficient safeguards in legislation permitting physician-assisted suicide to protect against abuse. What is clear is that the balancing exercise engaged in by the court in determining whether the demonstrated infringement of liberty could be justified, which, to a large extent, also reflects the key issues in the 'euthanasia debate'[166] will inevitably be a central feature in any future attempts in Canada to win judicial support for recognition of a constitutional right to

---

[163] Note also the dissenting judgment of McEachern CJ in the British Columbia Court of Appeal: *Rodriguez v. Attorney General of British Columbia, Attorney General of Canada*, above n. 157. Interestingly, however, the focus of the court's analysis appears to have been assisted suicide in general rather than the more specific issue of physician-assisted suicide which the appellant had specifically raised before the court.

[164] Kennedy, I. and Grubb, A., *Medical Law: Text and Materials*, 2nd ed (London, 1994) 1302.

[165] For analysis of the *Rodriguez* case see Somerville, M., '"Death Talk" in Canada: The *Rodriguez* Case' (1994) 39 *McGill LJ* 602.

[166] For discussion see Ch. 4 below.

die.[167] By virtue of the *Rodriguez* case, some of the principal issues for consideration in any such determination have been defined, not only for the purposes of the specific question which had been before the court regarding the rights of physically disabled patients to physician-assisted suicide, but more generally, regarding the right of patients to have medical assistance in dying.

As noted above, constitutional challenges to the legislative prohibition on assisted suicide have also been brought in a number of US states. This development began in the State of Michigan where a number of challenges were brought on constitutional grounds to the laws which had been enacted in that State specifically prohibiting assisted suicide, in an attempt to curtail the activities of Dr Jack Kevorkian.[168] In May 1993, Judge Stephens of the Wayne County Circuit Court ruled that this law had been improperly enacted and issued a permanent injunction against enforcement. Her Honour also found a due process right to commit suicide but declined to issue a preliminary injunction on this ground, concluding that hearings would be required to determine whether the statute prohibiting assisted suicide placed an undue burden on that right.[169] In a second, independent case, Chief Judge Kaufman of the Wayne County Circuit Court found a due process interest in the decision to end one's life and that the statute impermissibly burdened that interest. A ruling was accordingly made that the Michigan statute prohibiting assisted suicide was unconstitutional in so far as it infringed a person's Fourteenth Amendment liberty interest in committing rational suicide. His Honour held that a person has a constitutionally protected right to commit suicide when a person's quality of life is significantly impaired by a medical condition and the medical condition is extremely unlikely to improve, and that person's decision to commit suicide is a reasonable response to the condition causing the quality of life to be significantly impaired, and the decision to end one's life is freely made without undue influence.[170]

These rulings were, however, subsequently reversed on appeal. The Michigan Court of Appeals, by a majority of 2:1, found that the prohibition on assisted suicide under Michigan law did not violate the United States Constitution, and that the State was free to make it a criminal offence to

---

[167] In the light of the arguments in the *Rodriguez* case it is interesting to note that a completely contrary argument has been put forward in the USA in an attempt to challenge legislation passed in the State of Oregon by a citizen-initiated referendum, permitting physician-assisted suicide. That legislation has been argued to be unconstitutional on the grounds, *inter alia,* that it violates the Americans with Disabilities Act 1990 and discriminates against the terminally ill. See further pp. 372–3 below.

[168] See further p. 136 below.

[169] *Hobbins* v. *Attorney General* (Wayne Cty. Cir.Ct. Mich. 1993).

[170] *People* v. *Kevorkian* No. 93-11482 (Wayne Cty. Cir.Ct. Mich. 1993).

assist another in committing suicide.[171] This was one of a number of issues subsequently appealed to the Michigan Supreme Court in the case of *People* v. *Kevorkian, Hobbins* v. *Attorney General*[172] where a majority of 5:2 rejected the argument that the Michigan statute prohibiting assisted suicide was unconstitutional. The majority of the court was of the view that the decisions of the United States Supreme Court in the cases of *Cruzan* v. *Director, Missouri Department of Health*[173] and *Planned Parenthood* v. *Casey*[174] did not support the conclusion that any persons, including the terminally ill, have a liberty interest in suicide that is protected by the Due Process Clause of the Fourteenth Amendment,[175] stating that 'those who assert such a right misapprehend the nature of the holdings in those cases'. The majority held that the absence of criminal penalties for an act of suicide and the existence of a pragmatic capacity to commit suicide does not lead to the conclusion that there is a constitutional right to do so. Reference was made in this context to the substantial number of jurisdictions which have specific statutes that criminalize assisted suicide, as well as provision made under state legislation for involuntary commitment of persons who may harm themselves as a result of mental illness, and states which allow the use of non-deadly force to thwart suicide attempts. The court stated that: 'Such a right is not expressly recognized anywhere in the Constitution or in the decisions of the United States Supreme Court and cannot be reasonably inferred. In fact, . . . those courts that have found a right to refuse or to continue treatment have done so only after concluding that such refusal is wholly different from an act of suicide'.

The majority concluded its analysis of the issue with the following comments:

We are keenly aware of the intense emotions and competing moral philosophies that characterize the present debate about suicide in general, and assisted suicide in particular. The issues do not lend themselves to simple answers. However, while the complexity of the matter does not permit us to avoid the critical constitutional questions, neither does it, under the guise of constitutional interpretation, permit us to expand the judicial powers of this Court, especially where the question is a policy one that is appropriately left to the citizenry for resolution, either through its elected representatives or through a ballot.

Separate dissenting judgments with regard to this aspect of the majority's holding in the case were delivered by Levin and Mallett JJ. According to

---

[171] *Hobbins* v. *Attorney General* 518 NW 2d 487 (Mich. App. 1994). The majority was comprised of Fitzgerald and Taylor JJ, Shelton J dissented.

[172] 527 NW 2d 714 (1994).

[173] See above n. 54.

[174] 112 S. Ct. 2791 (1992).

[175] See the joint judgment of Cavanagh CJ, and Brickley and Griffin JJ, with whom Boyle and Riley JJ agreed on this issue.

Levin J, the real issue facing the Court is not whether suicide or assisting suicide can be proscribed by law but whether the Due Process Clause of the Constitution bars a state from depriving a competent, terminally ill person, facing imminent death and increasing agony, from obtaining medical assistance. Although it was acknowledged that the issue of assisted suicide is different from the issues of abortion and withdrawal of life-sustaining measures dealt with in previous Supreme Court cases, Levin J found that a reasoned application of the principles stated in *Planned Parenthood* v. *Casey*[176] *and Cruzan* v. *Director, Missouri Department of Health*[177] led to the conclusion that state law restrictions on a person's ability to end his life implicates the interest in personal liberty. He went on to hold that a determination as to whether a competent, terminally ill person has a right to medical assistance to commit suicide could only be made after balancing the State's interest against the person's interest. As distinct from 'irrational suicides' where legitimate State interests generally outweigh a person's interest in ending his life, where the person involved is competent, terminally ill, and facing imminent, agonizing death, the interest of the State in preserving life is weak and the interest of the terminally ill person in ending suffering is strong. Levin J was of the view that the principal argument against assisted suicide is the State's interest in assuring that persons who desire to live are not coerced into committing suicide. He continued:

While this clearly is a concern of great importance, adequate procedures can and have been developed to assure that a terminally ill person's choice to end life is not coerced. Restrictions on medical assistance to commit suicide for the terminally ill should be evaluated according to the undue burden standard enunciated in *Casey*. The undue burden standard permits the state to regulate the process of medically assisted suicide to assure that the person truly (a) is terminally ill, (b) is competent, (c) is suffering agonizing pain (d) faces imminent death (e) desires to commit suicide (f) needs or desires help to do so.

Judge Mallett's decision was along similar lines.[178] His Honour was of the view that the 'right to die' cases establish that a person has a right to determine the extent of his or her suffering when faced with an inevitable death. However, Mallett J rejected the argument of the plaintiffs that a fundamental or absolute right to hasten an inevitable death should be recognized, preferring instead the view that a terminally ill person has such a right only if the person has made a competent decision and is suffering from great pain. His Honour did recognize that the State has certain legitimate interests to assert, including the State interest in the preservation of life, but stated that these interests diminish as death nears for a terminally ill person: the interests are no longer sufficient to outweigh an individual's

---

[176] See above n. 174.   [177] See above n. 54.
[178] The two dissenting judges had in fact each signed the other's decision.

right to self-determination. It is only in other circumstances, going beyond the situation of a terminally ill person who has made a competent decision and is suffering from great pain, that the State may assert its interests. He went on to hold that the Michigan statute prohibiting assisted suicide should be deemed invalid because it bans all assisted suicides, including physician-assisted suicide,[179] and this amounted to an undue burden on the right of the terminally ill to end their suffering through physician-prescribed medications. Mallett J concluded his judgment by putting forward policy justifications for the conclusions reached. He expressed the view that there was no adequate distinction between the right of a terminally ill person to refuse unwanted medical treatment and the right to physician-assisted suicide. In his words, 'There is no sense in disallowing the competent choice to have a physician intervene to relieve intolerable suffering at the end of one's life. Furthermore, such a result conflicts with what many of us would desire when faced with severe pain and inevitable death'. His Honour also referred to the benefits of such recognition, noting that, in contrast to the present time, when individuals are forbidden from consulting with a private trusted physician about such matters, the recognition of a right to make such private decisions would allow open and honest discussion with the patient of all options and consequences.

Dr Kevorkian sought to appeal the majority decision court of the Michigan Supreme Court to the United States Supreme Court but the latter declined to review the case.

Following on from the earlier developments in the State of Michigan, a similar action was brought in the State of Washington in the case of *Compassion in Dying* v. *State of Washington*.[180] In this case, a coalition of plaintiffs, including a number of terminally ill patients, a number of physicians who treat terminally ill patients, and the US organization Compassion in Dying,[181] brought an application before the United States District Court, Western District of Washington at Seattle[182] challenging the constitutionality of the State of Washington's prohibition on assisted suicide, RCW 9A.36.060.[183]

[179] Mallett J actually held the statute to be 'facially' invalid, but it is clear from the Ninth Circuit Courts decision in *Compassion in Dying* (above n. 54) citing the earlier authority of *United States* v. *Salerno* 481 US 739 (1987), that this characterization is inappropriate as there would be circumstances in which the statute can constitutionally be applied.

[180] 850 FSupp 1454 (1994).

[181] A non-profit organization which provides information, counselling, and assistance to mentally competent, terminally ill adult patients considering suicide. See further, pp. 279–80 below.

[182] The case had been brought in the Federal District Court in order to facilitate moving upward toward the Ninth Circuit Court of Appeals in San Francisco and eventually to the US Supreme Court where, if successful, the challenge would invalidate all state laws which prevent a terminally ill patient from requesting and receiving medications which can hasten death. See Editor's note, (1994) 11 *Last Rights* 17.

[183] Pursuant to this provision a person is guilty of promoting a suicide attempt when he knowingly causes or aids another person to commit suicide.

In particular, the plaintiffs relied upon the Fourteenth Amendment to the United States Constitution which declares that the State may not 'deprive any person of life, liberty, or property, without due process of law'. They claimed a liberty interest protected by the Fourteenth Amendment which guarantees adults who are mentally competent, terminally ill, and acting under no undue influence the right to voluntarily hasten their death by taking a lethal dose of physician-prescribed drugs. The plaintiffs contended that individuals in those circumstances have a constitutionally protected right to be free from undue government intrusion in their decision to hasten death and avoid prolonged suffering. The prohibition on assisted suicide was also challenged on equal protection grounds, with reliance being placed on the Equal Protection Clause of the Fourteenth Amendment. The plaintiffs argued that the Washington law RCW 9A.36.060 unconstitutionally distinguishes between two groups of mentally competent, terminally ill adults: those who are dependent on life-support systems who may lawfully obtain assistance in terminating such treatment and thereby hastening death, and those whose treatment does not involve the use of life-support systems who are denied the option of hastening death with medical assistance.

On the basis of these arguments it was asserted that the State of Washington's criminal prohibition against physician-assisted suicide was unconstitutional in so far as it bars physicians from aiding informed, mentally competent, terminally ill adults to commit suicide. The plaintiffs sought a declaratory judgment striking down the statute as unconstitutional, and injunctive relief barring the defendant State of Washington and the Washington Attorney General from enforcing the statute.

In what has already proved to be a very significant development, Rothstein J, Chief District Judge, ruled in favour of a number of the plaintiffs[184] and declared the law in question to be unconstitutional, thereby becoming the first federal court judge to strike down a statute prohibiting assisted suicide on constitutional grounds.[185] Her Honour reviewed decisions of the United States Supreme Court which had recognized a liberty interest in some circumstances including *Cruzan v. Director, Missouri Department of Health*[186] where the majority of the court, although not conclusively deciding whether a patient has a constitutionally protected right to die, acknowledged that a constitutionally protected liberty interest in refusing unwanted life-sustaining medical treatment may be inferred from the

---

[184] The terminally ill patients and the physicians in so far as they raised claims on behalf of their terminally ill patients. Because the physicians and Compassion in Dying had not discussed their claims in the briefs before the court the court did not address them and their applications were denied.

[185] For a critical analysis of this decision, see Bix, B., 'Physician Assisted Suicide and the United States Constitution' (1995) 58 *Mod.LR* 404.

[186] See above n. 54.

court's prior decisions. The question before the court then became whether a constitutional distinction could validly be drawn between refusal or withdrawal of medical treatment which results in death, and the situation in this case involving competent terminally ill individuals who wish to hasten death by self-administering drugs prescribed by a physician. Rothstein J stated that the liberty interest protected by the Fourteenth Amendment is the freedom to make choices according to one's individual conscience about those matters which are essential to personal autonomy and basic human dignity. In her Honour's view, there is no more profoundly personal decision, nor one which is closer to the heart of personal liberty, than the choice a terminally ill person makes to end his or her suffering and to hasten an inevitable death. Thus, she concluded, from a constitutional perspective, a distinction could not be drawn between refusing life-saving medical treatment and physician-assisted suicide by an uncoerced, mentally competent, terminally ill adult.

In determining the constitutional validity of RCW 9A.36.060, the approach adopted by the court was initially to examine the alleged State interests in maintaining a total prohibition on all assisted suicides and then to examine whether the challenged statute places a substantial obstacle in the path of individuals seeking to exercise a constitutionally protected right, thus satisfying the undue burden standard established in previous cases. The conclusion reached by the court was that the challenged statute not only places a substantial obstacle in the path of a terminally ill, mentally competent person wishing to commit physician-assisted suicide, but entirely prohibits it. Rothstein J held that there was no question that such a total ban places an undue burden on the exercise of a constitutionally protected liberty interest. After examining the two main State interests at issue, namely, preventing suicide and protecting people against undue influence from others, it was held that neither of these interests would be impeded by allowing physician-assisted suicide for mentally competent, terminally ill adults. Whilst recognizing the importance and legitimacy of these State interests, it was held that these concerns can be answered by devising safeguards and imposing restrictions on physician-assisted suicide.

With regard to the plaintiffs' argument based upon equal protection, Rothstein J found that the Washington law, by creating an exception for those patients on life-support, yet not permitting competent, terminally ill adult patients such as the plaintiffs the equivalent option of exercising their rights to hasten their deaths with medical assistance, creates a situation in which the fundamental rights of one group are burdened while those of a similarly situated group are not. The court consequently found that RCW 9A.36.060 also violates the equal protection guarantee of the Fourteenth Amendment.

Although finding the State of Washington's prohibition on assisted suicide to be unconstitutional on these grounds,[187] the court declined to enter an injunction barring defendants State of Washington and the Washington Attorney-General from enforcing the statute.

The State appealed Rothstein J's ruling to the United States Court of Appeals for the Ninth Circuit.[188] A majority of a three judge panel reversed Rothstein J's decision, finding Washington's prohibition against physician-assisted suicide constitutional.[189] The majority judgment, delivered by Noonan J with whom O'Scannlain J agreed, found that the conclusion of the District Court that the statute deprived the plaintiffs of a liberty protected by the Fourteenth Amendment and denied them equal protection of the laws could not be sustained. The majority was critical of Rothstein J's interpretation of Supreme Court authority, including the *Cruzan* case. It found that, on the basis of an historical analysis of recognized liberty interests, the plaintiff's claim to a substantive liberty interest had to be rejected. The majority expressed particular disagreement with Rothstein J's conclusion that no distinction could be drawn between the refusal of life-sustaining treatment and a patient seeking medical help to bring about death. Moreover, their Honours held that the statute had been declared unconstitutional without adequate consideration having been given to the interests of the State of Washington and an assessment of whether those interests outweighed any alleged liberty of suicide. Wright J delivered a strong dissenting judgment accepting that the right to die with dignity falls squarely within the privacy rights recognized by the Supreme Court. His Honour agreed with the view of Rothstein J that a constitutional distinction cannot be drawn between refusing life-sustaining medical treatment and accepting physician assistance in hastening death. Wright J concluded that terminally ill, mentally competent adults, like the plaintiff patients, have a fundamental privacy right to choose physician-hastened death, and that the Washington legislation, as applied to those persons, violates the privacy and equal protection guarantees of the Constitution.

The plaintiffs were subsequently successful in their petition for a rehearing *en banc*, a majority of the 25 judges of the Ninth Circuit Court voting to grant a rehearing before an 11-judge panel.[190] This was, of itself, significant

---

[187] The scope of relief ordered by Rothstein J was not entirely clear. It has since been assumed that she did not intend to strike down the entire statute (particularly in view of the fact that the plaintiffs only challenged the 'or aids' provision of the legislation) but rather, only declare the statute invalid in so far as it applied to the prescription of medication to terminally ill, competent adults who wish to hasten their deaths: see the majority judgment in *Compassion in Dying* v. *State of Washington* (above n. 54) given by Reinhardt J of the Ninth Circuit Court of Appeals discussed below.

[188] The US federal system of courts is comprised of 11 federal circuit courts of appeal, of which the Ninth Circuit Court is one.

[189] *Compassion in Dying* v. *State of Washington* 49 F 3d 586 (9th Cir. 1995).

[190] 62 F 3d 299 (9th Cir. 1995).

in view of the infrequency with which such petitions are granted.[191] At the time the manuscript for this book was being finalized, the United States Court of Appeals for the Ninth Circuit handed down its decision in *Compassion in Dying* v. *State of Washington*.[192] In this landmark decision, eight judges of the 11-member Ninth Circuit Court upheld the decision of Rothstein J at first instance, finding in favour of recognizing a constitutional right to physician-assisted suicide for terminally ill competent patients who wish to hasten their deaths by obtaining medication prescribed by their physicians. Judgment for the majority was delivered by Reinhardt J, Browning, Hug, Schroeder, Fletcher, Pregerson, Wiggins, and Thompson JJ concurring. Beezer, Fernandez, and Kleinfeld JJ delivered dissenting judgments.

The majority proceeded along a two-stage line of inquiry: whether a person who is terminally ill has a constitutionally-protected liberty interest in determining the time and manner of his or her death, and if so, whether the Washington statute which prohibits physicians from prescribing life-ending medications for use by terminally ill, competent adults who wish to hasten their own death violates the Due Process Clause of the Fourteenth Amendment. The court explained that, unlike the majority opinion of the three-judge panel that first heard this case on appeal, which had defined the claimed liberty interest as a 'constitutional right to aid in killing oneself', it was taking a broader view of the liberty interest at issue, the relevant interest being defined as an interest in 'determining the time and manner of one's death'. This was justified, *inter alia,* on the basis that the liberty interest that the court was examining encompasses a whole range of acts that are generally not considered to constitute suicide. The court then turned its attention to the appropriate legal standard to be applied in deciding whether or not a liberty interest exists under the Due Process Clause. They referred to the distinction which has traditionally been made between 'fundamental rights' which cannot be limited except to further a compelling and narrowly tailored State interest, and other important interests which are subject to a balancing test that is less restrictive. The majority noted that recent decisions of the Supreme Court suggest that the court may be moving away from this classification system in favour of a continuum approach under which, the more important the individual right or interest, the more persuasive the State's justifications for infringement would have to be. However, it was unnecessary for the court to predict the Supreme Court's future course in order to decide the case before it as, even under the traditional mode of analysis, the liberty interest at issue was such that a balancing test was applicable.

---

[191] The appellants had contended that one of the judges who had overturned the decision at first instance, Noonan J, is a committed Roman Catholic and known opponent of pro-choice.

[192] No. 94-35534 (9th Cir. March 6 1996) *(en banc).*

Consideration was also given to the role of history in determining the existence of important rights or liberty interests. The majority cited authority[193] in support of their view that while historical analysis plays a useful role in any attempt to determine whether a claimed right or liberty interest exists, earlier legislative or judicial recognition of the right or interest is not a *sine qua non*. Indeed, in *Planned Parenthood* v. *Casey*[194] the court had made it clear that the fact that the courts have previously failed to acknowledge the existence of a particular liberty interest or even that the courts have previously prohibited its exercise, is no barrier to recognizing its existence. The majority expressed disagreement with the majority opinion of the three judge panel of the Ninth Circuit Court which had held that an historical analysis alone would be a sufficient basis for rejecting a claimed liberty interest. The majority of the court in the *en banc* hearing was of the view that previous court decisions delineating the boundaries of substantive due process provided general support for the recognition of a liberty interest in determining when and how one's life should end. In addition, the majority held that the more recent decisions of the United States Supreme Court, in *Planned Parenthood* v. *Casey* and *Cruzan* v. *Director, Missouri Department of Health*[195] were fully persuasive and left little room for doubt as to the proper result. On the basis of the Supreme Court's decision in *Casey*, the majority in *Compassion in Dying* (*en banc*) stated that: 'Like the decision whether or not to have an abortion, the decision how and when to die is one of "the most intimate and personal choices a person may make in a lifetime", a choice central to personal dignity and autonomy'. Further, the court found that *Cruzan*, by recognizing a liberty interest that includes the refusal of artificial provision of life-sustaining food and water, necessarily recognizes a liberty interest in hastening one's own death.

Having held that a liberty interest exists in 'determining the time and manner of one's death', or, a 'right to die', the court went on to make it clear that this does not mean that there is a concomitant right to exercise that interest in all circumstances or to do so free from State regulation. This led the court to the next stage of its analysis, namely, whether the State's attempt to curtail the exercise of that interest is constitutionally justified. Detailed consideration was given to the State's interests and how these were to be weighed and balanced against the individual liberty interest in the light of various factors. In relation to the State's interest in preserving life, the court held that although protection of life is one of the State's most important functions, the State's interest is dramatically diminished if the person it seeks to protect is terminally ill and has expressed a wish to die. Reference was made in this context to natural death legislation in the State

---

[193] *Planned Parenthood* v. *Casey* see above n. 174, *Rochin* v. *California* 342 US 165 (1952).
[194] See above n. 174.   [195] See above n. 54.

of Washington[196] which reflected the position taken by the legislature of that State that the interest in preserving life should ordinarily give way to the wishes of the patients, at least in the case of competent, terminally ill adults who are dependent on medical treatment. Attention was then given to the State's more particular interest in deterring the taking of one's life. The court majority held that while the State has a legitimate interest in preventing suicides in general, that interest, like the State's interest in preserving life, is substantially diminished in the case of terminally ill, competent adults who wish to die. The court then set out the steps already taken by the State towards acknowledgment that terminally ill persons are entitled, in a whole variety of circumstances, to hasten their deaths, and that physicians may assist in the process. In particular, the court noted the changes in relation to the patient's right to reject medical treatment, to the point that many states now allow terminally ill patients to order their physicians to discontinue artificial provision of life-sustaining food and water, thus permitting the patients to die by self-starvation. Equally important, in the court's view, was the fact that physicians are now generally permitted to administer death-inducing medication, as long as they can point to a concomitant pain-relieving purpose. The court went on to comment: 'In light of these drastic changes regarding acceptable medical practices, opponents of physician-assisted suicide must now explain precisely what it is about the physician's conduct in assisted suicide cases that distinguishes it from the conduct that the State has explicitly authorized'.

The majority of the court unequivocally rejected the arguments advanced on behalf of the State in support of the view that physician-assisted suicide is different in kind, not degree, from the type of physician-life-ending conduct that is now authorized: the first claimed distinction, the line between commission and omission, was thought to be meaningless in view of the fact that patients are now permitted not only to decline all medical treatment, but to instruct their physicians to terminate whatever treatment they are receiving, thereby actively involving physicians in bringing about their death.[197] The court also dispensed with the second distinction advanced by the State, seeking to differentiate physician-assisted suicide from existing forms of medical conduct, on the basis that assisted suicide causes deaths that would not result from the patient's underlying disease. In the opinion of the court, this distinction no longer has any legitimacy.[198] The third distinction asserted by the State, that physician-assisted suicide requires physicians to provide the causal agent for the patient's death, was also found to be unconvincing having regard to the widespread practice of physicians to provide medica-

---

[196] Washington Natural Death Act RCW 70.122.010.
[197] See pp. 162–3 below for more detailed discussion of this aspect of the majority's opinion.
[198] For more detailed discussion see pp. 72–3 above.

tion to terminally ill patients with the knowledge that it will have a double effect—to reduce the patient's pain and hasten his death.[199]

The majority did acknowledge in their decision that in some respects a recognition of the legitimacy of physician-assisted suicide would constitute an additional step beyond what the courts have previously approved. However, the majority did not believe that the State's interest in preventing that additional step is significantly greater than its interest in preventing the other forms of life-ending medical conduct that physicians now regularly engage in. In sum, the majority found that the State's interest in preventing suicide does not make its interest substantially stronger in the case of physician-assisted suicide than in cases involving other forms of death-hastening medical intervention: to the extent that a difference exists, the majority concluded that it is one of degree and not of kind.

Of particular interest were the majority's comments expressing doubts about the classification of deaths resulting from terminally ill patients taking medications prescribed by their physicians, as 'suicide'. These doubts sprang primarily from the fact that deaths resulting from patients' decisions to terminate life-support systems or to refuse life-sustaining food and water are nor classified as suicide.[200] The majority expressed the belief that there is a strong argument that a decision by a terminally ill patient to hasten by medical means a death that is already in process should not be classified as suicide. On this view, which was merely expressed as *obiter* after the majority already had evaluated the strength of the State's interest in preventing suicide, the State's interest in preventing suicide would not even be implicated in this case.

In addition to the State's claimed interest in preventing suicide, the majority of the court examined the State's interest in preventing deaths that occur as a result of errors in medical or legal judgment. Whilst acknowledging certain practical difficulties, for example, predicting with certainty the duration of a terminally ill patient's remaining existence, the majority members of the court were of the view that sufficient safeguards can be developed by the State and the medical profession to ensure that the possibility of error will ordinarily be remote. Note was made in this context of evidence which suggests that the State's efforts to prohibit assisted suicide are at least partially counter-productive: as a result of the State's ban, some terminally ill adults probably commit suicide although they otherwise might not have done so, and others probably commit suicide sooner than they might have done.

The third of the State interests that the court considered was the State's interest in avoiding the involvement of third parties and precluding the use of arbitrary, unfair, or undue influence. The court specifically recognized

---

[199] This aspect of the court's decision is discussed in more detail at p. 179 below.

[200] For discussion of the prevailing approach of the US courts see pp. 65–8 above.

that there were a number of legitimate State concerns regarding the potential involvement of third parties in cases of assisted suicide, particularly that it may lead to an increase in the incidence of suicide and undermine society's commitment to the sanctity of life. However, the majority was of the view that these concerns diminish in importance in the same way that the State's interest in preventing the act itself diminishes: all are at their lowest when the assistance is provided by or under the supervision or direction of a physician and the recipient is a terminally ill patient.

The majority was critical of the view expressed by Noonan and O'Scannlain JJ when the case was first heard on appeal to the effect that the State prohibition on assisted suicide was necessary to protect the poor and minorities from exploitation on the assumption that they would be particularly targeted for this activity. According to the majority, this reasoning involved the same fallacious argument that had been used in opposition to the legalization of abortion which had never been substantiated in practice. In the opinion of the majority, there is (as with abortion) far more reason to raise the opposite concern, namely that the poor and minorities who historically have received the least adequate health care, will not be afforded a fair opportunity to obtain medical assistance that would allow them to end their lives with a measure of dignity.

Of far more significance for the majority was the concern that infirm, elderly persons will come under undue pressure to end their lives from callous, financially burdened, or self-interested relatives or others who have influence over them. The majority accepted that the risk of undue influence is real and already exists in relation to the withholding or withdrawing of treatment. The judges in the majority did not, however, believe that permitting physician-assisted suicide would significantly add to that risk. In the words of the majority:

While we do not minimize the concern, the temptation to exert undue pressure is ordinarily tempered to a substantial degree in the case of the terminally ill by the knowledge that the person will die shortly in any event. Given the possibility of undue influence that already exists, the recognition of the right to physician-assisted suicide would not increase that risk unduly. In fact, the direct involvement of an impartial and professional third party in the decision-making process would be more likely to provide an important safeguard against such abuse.

The majority judgment also dealt with the concern that physicians, through their involvement in physician-assisted suicide, would become hardened to the inevitability of death and the plight of the terminally ill and that they would treat requests to die in a routine and impersonal manner, rather than affording the careful, thorough, individualized attention that each request deserves. Ultimately, the majority placed their trust in the integrity of the medical profession:

We believe that most, if not all, doctors would not assist a terminally ill patient to hasten his death as long as there was any reasonable chance of alleviating the patient's suffering or enabling him to live under tolerable conditions. We also believe that physicians would not assist a patient to end his life if there were any significant doubt about the patient's true wishes. To do so would be contrary to the physicians' fundamental training, their conservative nature, and the ethics of their profession. In any case, since doctors are highly-regulated professionals, it should not be difficult for the state or the profession itself to establish rules and procedures that will ensure that the occasional negligent or careless recommendation by a licensed physician will not result in an uninformed or erroneous decision by the patient or his family.

However, the majority of the court stressed that they did not dismiss the legitimate concerns that exist regarding undue influence. They accepted that whilst steps can be taken to minimize the danger substantially, imposition of safeguards would not wholly eliminate the concerns. Accordingly, the court stated it was treating these concerns seriously in balancing the competing interests.

The next significant State interest that the majority of the court considered was the State's interest in protecting the integrity of the medical profession.[201] The majority accepted that the State has a legitimate interest in assuring the integrity of the medical profession—an interest that includes prohibiting physicians from engaging in conduct that is at odds with their role as healers. However, the judges in the majority did not believe that the integrity of the medical profession would be threatened in any way by the vindication of the liberty interest at issue here. Rather, they found, it is the existence of a prohibition on assistance in suicide that would create conflicts with physicians' professional obligations and make covert criminals out of honourable, dedicated, and compassionate individuals. In their view, the assertion that the legalization of physician-assisted suicide will erode the commitment of physicians to help their patients rests both on an ignorance of what numbers of physicians have been doing for a considerable time and on a misunderstanding of the proper function of a physician. They referred to the fact that physicians have, for a long time, been discreetly helping terminally ill patients to die, and further that physicians may now openly take actions that will result in the death of their patients—they may terminate life-support systems, withdraw life-sustaining gastronomy tubes, otherwise terminate or withhold all other forms of medical treatment, and may even administer lethal doses of drugs with full knowledge of their 'double effect'. The majority stated:

---

[201] Brief consideration was also given to the State's interest in safeguarding the interests of innocent third parties such as minor children and other dependent family members; however, this interest was held to be of almost negligible weight in circumstances where the patient is terminally ill and his death is imminent and inevitable.

Given the similarity between what doctors are now permitted to do and what the plaintiffs assert they should be permitted to do, we see no risk at all to the integrity of the profession. This is a conclusion shared by a growing number of doctors who openly support physician-assisted suicide and proclaim it to be fully compatible with the physicians' calling and with their commitment and obligation to help the sick.

Reference was also made to a growing body of survey evidence examining physicians' attitudes to providing patients with assistance in dying, and legalization of this practice which supports the view that many physicians do not believe that providing such assistance is in any way contrary to their professional obligations.[202] The court concluded its analysis of this issue by stating:

Recognising the right to 'assisted-suicide' would not require doctors to do anything contrary to their individual principles. A physician whose moral or religious beliefs would prevent him from assisting a patient to hasten his death would be free to follow the dictates of his conscience. Those doctors who believe that terminally ill, competent adults should be permitted to choose the time and manner of their deaths would be able to help them to do so. We believe that extending a choice to doctors as well as to patients would help protect the integrity of the medical profession without compromising the rights or principles of individual doctors and without sacrificing the welfare of their patients.

The final State interest addressed by the court was the fear of adverse consequences: the argument that once we recognize a liberty interest in hastening one's death, it will only be a matter of time before courts will sanction putting people to death, not because they are desperately ill and want to die, but because they are deemed to pose an unjustifiable burden on society. The majority expressed the view that the same sort of nihilistic argument can be offered against any constitutionally-protected right or interest. The judges in the majority accepted that recognition of any rights creates the possibilities of abuse, but noted at the same time, that the court has never refused to recognize a substantive due process liberty right or interest merely because there were difficulties in determining when or how to limit its exercise or because others might some day attempt to use it improperly. The majority referred to the dire predictions which had been made in the context of the abortion debate but which had not materialized and suggested that there is no reason to believe that legalizing physician-assisted suicide will lead to the horrific consequence that its opponents suggest. The court also gave attention to claims that recognizing a due process interest in hastening one's death, even if the exercise of that interest is initially limited to the terminally ill, will prove infinitely expansive because it will be impossible to define the term 'terminally ill'. The majority

---

[202] For detailed discussion of surveys of the medical profession regarding doctors' attitudes to doctor-assisted suicide and active voluntary euthanasia, see pp. 292–332 below.

referred to state natural death legislation where this term has been defined. The judges in the majority accepted that defining the term is not free from difficulty, but thought the experience of the states has shown that the class of the terminally ill is neither indefinable nor undefined. In any event, the court concluded that the purported definitional difficulties provide no legitimate reason for refusing to recognize a liberty interest in hastening one's death.

The majority stated that they did not dispute the contention in the dissenting judgments that the prescription of lethal medication by physicians for use by terminally ill patients who wish to die does not constitute a clear point of demarcation between permissible and impermissible medical conduct. Further, the majority agreed that it may be difficult to make a principled distinction between physician-assisted suicide and the provision to terminally ill patients of other forms of life-ending medical assistance, such as the administration of drugs by a physician. It was recognized that in some instances, the patient may be unable to self-administer the drugs and that the administration by a physician may be the only alternative; however the court specifically stated that the question whether that type of conduct by a physician may be constitutionally protected must be directly answered in future cases. The judges in the majority did, however, go on to say that they viewed the critical line in 'right to die' cases as the one between voluntary and involuntary termination of an individual's life. They considered it less important who administers the medication than who determines whether the terminally ill person's life shall end.

The next stage in applying the balancing test required the court also to consider the means by which the State has chosen to further its interests. The majority found that the Washington statute prohibiting assisted suicide, which involves a total ban, has a drastic impact on the terminally ill. By prohibiting physician assistance, it bars what for many people would be the only acceptable and practical way to end their lives. Whilst rejecting a complete ban on all forms of assisted suicide, the majority held that state regulation was a permissible means of promoting State interests in this area.[203] In the view of the majority, state laws or regulations governing physician-assisted suicide are both necessary and desirable to ensure against error and abuse and to protect legitimate State interests. Their Honours stated that by adopting appropriate, reasonable, and properly drawn safeguards, the State of Washington could ensure that people who choose to have their physicians prescribe a lethal dose are truly competent and meet all of the requisite safeguards. Without endorsing the constitutionality of any particular procedural safeguards, the majority noted that

[203] The court placed reliance on the *Cruzan* decision (above n. 54) in support of its decision to treat a prohibition differently from a regulation.

the State might, for example, require witnesses to ensure voluntariness; reasonable, though short waiting periods to prevent rash decisions; second medical opinions to confirm a patient's terminal status and also to confirm that the patient has been receiving proper treatment, including adequate comfort care; psychological examinations to ensure that the patient is not suffering from momentary or treatable depression; and reporting procedures that will aid in the avoidance of abuse. While recognizing that there is always room for error in any human endeavour, the majority were of the view that sufficient protections can and will be developed by the various states, with the assistance of the medical profession and health care industry to ensure that the possibility of error will be remote.

The majority of the court went on to assess the strength of the liberty interest at issue. As noted earlier in their judgment, an individual's liberty interest in hastening death is at its low point when the person is young and healthy, however, when a mentally competent adult is terminally ill and wishes, free of any coercion, to hasten his death because his remaining days are an unmitigated torture, that person's liberty interest is at its height. And, on the basis of the evidence produced by the plaintiffs in support of their claim that the statute presents an insuperable obstacle to terminally ill persons who wish to hasten their death by peaceful means, the majority of the court was in no doubt that the Washington statute prohibiting all forms of assisted suicide, imposes a burden on the liberty interest.

The court finally turned to the process of weighing and balancing the claimed liberty interest against the State's countervailing interests. Ultimately, the majority of the court held that the liberty interest in choosing the time and manner of death must prevail. The majority stated that the liberty interest at issue is an important one, and in the case of a terminally ill patient, is at its peak, whereas the State's interest in protecting life and preventing suicide is at its weakest. The majority judges did go on to recognize that in the case of life and death decisions, the State has a particularly strong interest in avoiding undue influence and other forms of abuse, but felt that that concern is largely ameliorated because of the mandatory involvement in the decision-making process of physicians, who have a strong bias in favour of preserving life, and because the process itself can be carefully regulated and rigorous safeguards adopted. They were of the view that under these circumstances, the possibility of abuse, even when considered along with the other State interests, does not outweigh the liberty interest at issue. Their Honours noted that Washington State has chosen to pursue its interests by means of what for terminally ill patients is effectively a total prohibition, even though its most important interest could be adequately served by a far less burdensome measure. Moreover, they were of the opinion that the consequences of rejecting the 'as applied' challenge[204] would be disastrous for the terminally ill, while the adverse consequences for the state would be of a far lesser order, and this was a further factor weighing in favour of upholding the liberty interest. Accordingly, the majority held that the 'or aids' provision of the Washington statute is unconstitutional as applied to terminally ill, competent adults who wish to hasten their deaths with medication prescribed by their physicians, as there can be no doubt that Washington's ban on assisted suicide places a substantial obstacle in the path of individuals in those circumstances.[205] In reaching this conclusion, they did not believe that the decision of Hogan J of the Oregon District Court in the case of *Lee* v. *State of Oregon*[206] in relation to the constitutionality of the *Oregon Death with Dignity Act*[207] stood in the way of their decision. The majority found that the reasoning in that case was in direct conflict with their own reasoning and with the legal conclusions that they had reached. They found that in effect, Hogan J had treated a burden as a benefit and vice versa, and in doing so had clearly erred.

Having upheld the plaintiffs' claimed liberty interest, it was unnecessary for the court to decide whether the 'or aids' provision of the Washington statute as it applies to the terminally ill also violates the Equal Protection Clause of the Constitution. The majority did, however, comment that the equal protection argument relied on by Rothstein J was 'not insubstantial'.

In their conclusion, the majority felt compelled to emphasize one final point:

Some argue strongly that decisions regarding matters affecting life or death should not be made by the courts. Essentially we agree with that proposition. In this case, by permitting the individual to exercise the right to choose we are following the constitutional mandate to take such decisions out of the hands of the government, both states and federal, and to put them where they rightly belong, in the hands of the people. We are allowing individuals to make the decisions that so profoundly affect their very existence—and precluding the state from intruding excessively into that critical realm. The Constitution and the courts stand as a bulwark between individual freedom and arbitrary and intrusive governmental power. Under our constitutional system, neither the state nor the majority of the people in a state can

---

[204] An 'as applied' challenge involves a contention that the application of the statute in a particular context would be unconstitutional (in this case, the Washington State prohibition on assisted suicide as it applies to mentally competent, terminally ill adults who wish to seek the help of their physicians in hastening their death). This is to be contrasted with a 'facial' challenge which requires proof that there are no circumstances under which the statute would be valid. See above n. 179.

[205] They also noted that those whose services are essential to help the terminally ill patient obtain and take that medication (e.g. the pharmacist who fills the prescription) are covered by the court's ruling.

[206] *Lee* v. *State of Oregon* 891 F Supp. 1239 (D Or. 1995).

[207] For discussion of this Act, which was passed pursuant to the citizen-initiated referendum process, and the constitutional challenge which was subsequently mounted, see pp. 369–73 below.

impose its will upon the individual in a matter so highly 'central to personal dignity and autonomy'. *Casey*, 112 S. Ct. at 2807. Those who believe strongly that death must come without physician assistance are free to follow that creed, be they doctors or patient. They are not free, however, to force their views, their religious convictions, or their philosophies on all the other members of a democratic society, and to compel those whose values differ with theirs to die painful, protracted, and agonizing deaths.

The main dissenting judgment was given by Beezer J, Fernandez and Kleinfeld JJ essentially joining in Beezer J's dissenting opinion. Contrary to the approach taken by the majority, Beezer J adhered to the traditional distinction between rights which are fundamental and non-fundamental liberty interests. His Honour held that mentally competent, terminally ill adults do not have a fundamental right to physician-assisted suicide. This conclusion was justified on the basis that physician-assisted suicide is neither currently on the list of rights deemed by the Supreme Court to be fundamental nor is it central to personal autonomy or deeply rooted in history as required in order for a liberty interest to be regarded as fundamental.

Beezer J was, however, prepared to find that mentally competent terminally ill adults do have a non-fundamental liberty interest in physician-assisted suicide. This finding was based on the authority of *Planned Parenthood* v. *Casey*,[208] in particular the statement encapsulating the principle of autonomy that 'at the heart of liberty is the right to define one's own concept of existence, of meaning, of the universe, and of the mystery of human life'. Although accepting that decisions about the timing and manner of one's death can plausibly come within a non-fundamental liberty right, Beezer J decided against the plaintiffs on the grounds that the Washington statute prohibiting assisted suicide rationally advances legitimate governmental purposes and therefore does not violate the plaintiff's constitutional substantive due process rights. Beezer J was of the view that the State's interests are all very strong and apply with undiminished vigour to justify the prohibition under the Washington statute of physician-assisted suicide for mentally competent, terminally ill adults.

With regard to the State's interest in the preservation of life, his Honour held that the State's interest is weakened only where continued medical treatment would do nothing more than postpone death. As applied to terminally ill patients seeking physician assisted suicide, the State's interest in preserving life remains at full strength. Beezer J was also of the view that the interests of innocent third parties were implicated, particularly the elderly and infirm, the poor and minorities, and the handicapped, who are at risk of being unwanted and subjected to pressure to choose physician-

---

[208] See above n. 174.

assisted suicide rather than continued treatment. After referring to the inadequacies of pain management, as well as the lack of access to psychiatric services in the USA, Beezer J commented: 'We the courts are asked, in a nation of inadequate and unequal access to medical care for the alleviation of pain and suffering, to create a constitutional right to assisted suicide. Surely this is a case of misplaced priorities'. He went on to reject the proposition that adequate procedural safeguards can be implemented to protect the interests of innocent third parties and cited the Dutch experience in support of this conclusion.[209] His Honour was of the opinion that the only way to achieve adequate protection for these groups is to maintain a bright-line rule against physician-assisted suicide. In addition, he thought that the recognition of a right to physician-assisted suicide could severely disrupt the economic interests of the relatives, partners, and associates of those who commit physician-assisted suicide through the disruption to the established legal order of wills, trusts, life insurance, immunities, and pensions. Significant weight was also given by Beezer J to the State's interest in the prevention of suicide. His Honour was of the view that the State's interest in preventing suicide is distinct from its general interest in preserving life and does not diminish with the onset and advancement of terminal illness. According to Beezer J, the State recognizes suicide as a manifestation of medical and psychological anguish; people with suicidal tendencies are suffering. The State's interest is in addressing and, where possible, relieving that suffering. In relation to the final State interest, in maintaining the ethical integrity of the medical profession, Beezer J held that a right to physician-assisted suicide would violate the State's interest. In support of this view his Honour referred to the provisions under Washington legislation subjecting physicians to professional sanctions for prescribing drugs to their patients in order to assist those patients to commit suicide as well as the AMA Code of Ethics which prohibits physician-assisted suicide.

Following on from his Honour's earlier conclusion that the interest at stake is a non-fundamental liberty interest, he proceeded to assert on the authority of *Reno* v. *Flores*[210] that the statute is therefore subjected only to the 'unexacting' inquiry of whether the statute rationally advances some legitimate governmental purpose. On this basis, he found that the Washington statute does rationally advance four legitimate State interests and therefore is valid under the rational relationship test.

---

[209] It is argued in a later chapter that contrary to the suggestion made in this judgment and the claims of some commentators, the experience in the Netherlands does not provide evidence of abuse resulting from the practice of active voluntary euthanasia or doctor-assisted suicide: see pp. 435–41 below.

[210] 113 S. Ct. 1439 at 1447–9. Note, however, the criticism of this interpretation in the majority judgment where it was stated in the strongest terms that there can be no legitimate argument that rational basis review is applicable in relation to non-fundamental liberty interests and that nothing in the *Flores* case suggests that it is.

Beezer J also held that the Washington statute does not violate the plaintiff's constitutional equal protection rights. He was of the view that the plaintiffs are not similarly situated to patients who wish to refuse or withdraw life-sustaining medical treatment as had been held by Rothstein J, and are therefore not subject to an equal protection analysis. However, he went on to say that even if the two groups—patients refusing unwanted medical treatment and mentally competent, terminally ill adults seeking to commit physician-assisted suicide—were similarly situated, the distinction between them rests solidly on a rational basis, namely the advancement of legitimate legislative goals, and consequently does not violate the plaintiffs' constitutional equal protection rights.

Judge Beezer concluded his judgment with the following comments:

To declare a constitutional right to physician-assisted suicide would be to impose upon the nation a repeal of local laws. Such a declaration would also usurp states' rights to regulate and further the practice of medicine, in so far as a right to physician-assisted suicide flies in the face of well-established state laws governing the medical profession. Finally, the rationales under which we are asked to create this right fail adequately to distinguish physician-assisted suicide as a unique category. If physician-assisted suicide for mentally competent, terminally ill adults is made a constitutional right, voluntary euthanasia for weaker patients, unable to self-terminate, will soon follow. After voluntary euthanasia, it is but a short step to a 'substituted judgment' or 'best interests' analysis for terminally ill patients who have not yet expressed their constitutionally sanctioned desire to be dispatched from this world. This is the sure and inevitable path, as the Dutch experience has amply demonstrated. It is not a path that I would start down.

Fernandez J agreed with Beezer J's dissent, subject to the caveat that he was not convinced that there is any constitutional right whatever to commit suicide. He stated: 'In my view, no one has an even nonfundamental constitutional right to become what our legal ancestors pithily denominated a felo de se'. Kleinfeld J, although joining with Beezer J's dissenting opinion, also expressed his own qualifications. Firstly, he doubted whether there is a constitutional right to commit suicide but found that it was unnecessary to decide whether suicide is a constitutionally protected right because even if it is, the State of Washington has a rational basis for preventing assisted suicide. Secondly, he was of the opinion that Beezer J's response to the statement in the majority judgment regarding the relationship between the provision of pain-killing medication knowing that it will at some dosage cause death, and providing medication for the sole of purpose of causing death, did not go far enough. Beezer J had characterized this as a 'gray area' but in Kleinfeld J's view, the proposition in the majority judgment that there is little, if any, difference for constitutional or ethical purposes between these practices, should be rejected as being 'exactly wrong'.

Kleinfeld J concluded his judgment with comments indicating his belief that the issue of physician-assisted suicide was for the legislature to determine rather than the courts:

It is very difficult to judge what ought to be allowed in the care of terminally ill patients. The Constitution does not speak to the issue. People of varying views, including people with terrible illnesses and their relatives, physicians, and clergy, can, through democratic institutions obtain enlightened compromises of the complex and conflicting considerations. They can do so as least as well as judges can, and nothing in the Constitution prevents them from making the law.

The decision in *Compassion in Dying* v. *State of Washington* is unquestionably of enormous significance. It marks the first time that a constitutional 'right to die' has been unequivocally recognized at this judicial level. The majority judgment of the Ninth Circuit Court provides a detailed and thoughtful analysis of competing considerations on the issue of physician-assisted suicide. The judgment has addressed some notoriously troublesome issues with honesty and candour and has, in the process, highlighted the artificiality of many of the distinctions and assumptions which have traditionally been made. The case is, as a result, likely to encourage re-evaluation of how we regard certain medical practices and where physician-assisted suicide (and potentially active voluntary euthanasia) fit in to the scheme of things from an ethical and legal point of view. The majority position represents a strong statement in support of self-determination, with the majority taking a broad perspective, focusing on the right of an individual to control the timing and manner of his death. By virtue of the sheer number of judges involved, particularly with a majority holding of 8:3 in support of recognizing a constitutional right to physician-assisted suicide for terminally ill competent patients, this decision is the most important to date in the American legal debate over physician-assisted suicide. Moreover, although three of the judges dissented, only one member of the eleven-judge panel, Fernandez J, completely rejected the proposition that a person may have a constitutional right to commit suicide; Beezer J accepted that such a right exists, but found against the plaintiffs on other grounds, and Kleinfeld J simply found it unnecessary to decide. The decision of the majority in this case not only to recognize such a right, but to hold that state legislation prohibiting assisted suicide is in violation of it, has potentially far-reaching implications; indeed, as the majority acknowledged, future courts will need to consider whether recognition of a constitutional right to physician-assisted suicide entails broader recognition of assistance in dying, at least in some circumstances.

Interestingly, the majority judgment given by Reinhardt J rejected the language of 'euthanasia', preferring to use the term 'physician aid in dying' to describe the situation where the physician is directly involved in the administration of drugs to end the patient's life. Reinhardt J defined euthanasia as 'the act or practice of painlessly putting to death persons suffering from incurable and distressing disease, as an act of mercy, *but not at the person's request*',[211] thereby suggesting that it is always performed other than at the person's request. This interpretation is at odds with the well established understanding of the term 'euthanasia' which does not of itself indicate whether death is brought about at the person's request:[212] this is usually specified by including the words 'voluntary' or 'non-voluntary' or 'involuntary', as the case may be.[213] One can only speculate whether this approach simply reflects Reinhardt J's own preference in usage of terms, or whether more should be read into this rejection in the majority judgment of the euthanasia terminology. One could, for example, take the view that the phrase 'physician aid in dying' is a more precise, less emotionally-laden term than 'euthanasia' and therefore is more appropriate in the clinical context where a dispassionate consideration of the relevant issues is required. But regardless of the terminology used, the majority's decision, although principally focused on the constitutional status of physician-assisted suicide, has also made an important contribution to the wider euthanasia debate, particularly in the light of the court's detailed and thoughtful analysis of many of the major arguments which are prominent in that debate.[214]

Soon after the decision in *Compassion in Dying* was handed down, it was reported that an appeal has been lodged to the United States Supreme Court by the Attorney-General for the State of Washington against the Ninth Circuit Court decision. In the meantime, Washington State has requested a 'stay of mandate' which would prevent the majority decision, which potentially applies in the nine states within the jurisdiction of the Ninth Circuit Court,[215] from taking effect until the Supreme Court has ruled on the matter.

In a separate development, also of enormous significance, a constitutional challenge has been upheld against the prohibition on assisted suicide under New York Penal Law.[216] In the wake of the success of *Compassion in Dying* v. *State of Washington* at first instance, a similar action was filed in the United States District Court for the Southern District of New York. This case, *Quill et al* v. *Koppell*[217] was brought jointly by a number of terminally ill, mentally competent patients and physicians involved in the

---

[211] Author's emphasis.

[212] Note, however, the meaning given to euthanasia in the Netherlands: see p. 392 below.

[213] See pp. 7–8 above for discussion of terminology.

[214] For discussion of the euthanasia debate see Ch. 4 below.

[215] Washington, Alaska, Oregon, Montana, Idaho, California, Nevada, Arizona, and Hawaii.

[216] NY Penal Law, ss. 125.15(3) and 120.30 which make it a felony intentionally to aid another person to commit suicide or to promote a suicide attempt by intentionally aiding another person to attempt to commit suicide.

[217] 870 F Supp. 78 (1994).

treatment of terminally ill patients. At first instance Griesa J denied the plaintiffs' motion for a preliminary injunction against the enforcement of the relevant provisions of the New York Penal Law[218] and granted the defendant's cross-motion to dismiss. His Honour found that the physician-assisted suicide at issue in this case did not involve a fundamental liberty interest protected by the Due Process Clause of the Fourteenth Amendment. Further, it was held that the plaintiffs had not shown a violation of the Equal Protection Clause of the Fourteenth Amendment as there was a reasonable and rational basis for the distinction drawn by the New York law between the refusal of treatment at the hands of physicians and physician-assisted suicide.

The plaintiffs appealed from this decision to the United States Court of Appeals for the Second Circuit which has jurisdiction over the States of New York, Connecticut, and Vermont. In April 1996, only a matter of weeks after the historic decision of the Ninth Circuit Court in *Compassion in Dying* v. *State of Washington* (*en banc*), the Second Circuit Court handed down its decision in the case of *Quill* v. *Vacco*[219] in which it reversed in part the decision of Griesa J of the District Court. The court's decision was unanimous, although Calabresi J concurred with the result on different grounds set out in a separate opinion. The leading judgment was written by Miner J with whom Pollack J agreed. In this majority opinion, the court held that physicians who are willing to do so may prescribe drugs to be self-administered by mentally competent patients who seek to end their lives during the final stages of a terminal illness. This holding was based on the court's interpretation of the Equal Protection Clause of the Fourteenth Amendment which directs that all persons similarly circumstanced shall be treated alike. Reference was made to various standards of scrutiny to determine the constitutionality of legislation, noting that the appropriate standard depends on the nature of the legislation being reviewed. Miner and Pollack JJ were of the view that the statutes in question fall within the category of social welfare legislation and therefore are subject to 'rational basis scrutiny' upon judicial review. Their Honours upheld the plaintiffs' contention that the New York law does not treat equally all competent persons who are in the final stages of fatal illness and wish to hasten their deaths. After analysing case-law and legislative developments in relation to the refusal of treatment, the majority observed that those in the final stages of terminal illness who are on life-support systems are allowed to hasten their deaths by directing the removal of such systems; but those who are similarly situated, except for the previous attachment of life-sustaining equipment, are not allowed to hasten death by self-administering pre-

[218] Sections 125.15 and 120.30.
[219] No. 60 (2nd Cir. April 2 1996). The change in case name from *Quill* v. *Koppel* to *Quill* v. *Vacco* came about due to a change of Attorney-General for the State of New York.

scribed drugs. They rejected the distinction which had been relied upon in the court below, between 'allowing nature to take its course', even in the most severe situations, and intentionally using an artificial death producing device. Their Honours commented:

Indeed, there is nothing 'natural' about causing death by means other than the original illness or its complications. The withdrawal of nutrition brings on death by starvation, the withdrawal of hydration brings on death by dehydration, and the withdrawal of ventilation brings about respiratory failure. By ordering the discontinuance of these artificial life-sustaining processes or refusing to accept them in the first place, a patient hastens his death by means that are not natural in any sense. It certainly cannot be said that the death that immediately ensues is the natural results of the progression of the disease or condition from which the patient suffers.

Moreover, the writing of a prescription to hasten death, after consultation with a patient, involves a far less active role for the physician than is required in bringing about death through asphyxiation, starvation and/or dehydration. Withdrawal of life-support requires physicians or those acting at their direction physically to remove equipment and, often to administer palliative drugs which may themselves contribute to death. The ending of life by these means is nothing more nor less than assisted suicide. It simply cannot be said that those mentally competent, terminally-ill persons who seek to hasten death but whose treatment does not include life support are treated equally.

Having found unequal treatment to exist, the court went on to examine whether the inequality was rationally related to some legitimate State interest. The court noted the State's contention that its principal interest is in preserving the life of all its citizens at all times and under all conditions but went on to question what interest the State could possibly have in requiring the prolongation of a life that is all but ended. The court also referred to the decision of the majority of the three-member panel of the Ninth Circuit Court in the case of *Compassion in Dying* v. *State of Washington*,[220] in particular, the identification by the panel majority of certain State interests which were promoted by the maintenance of the Washington prohibition on assisted suicide: the interest in denying physicians 'the role of killers of their patients'; the interest in avoiding psychological pressure upon the elderly and infirm to consent to death; the interest of preventing the exploitation of the poor and minorities; the interest in protecting handicapped persons against societal indifference; and the interest in preventing the sort of abuse which is claimed to have occurred in the Netherlands. However, the majority judges in *Quill* v. *Vacco* were of the view that the New York statutes prohibiting assisted suicide, which are similar to the Washington statute, do not serve any of these State interests in view of the statutory and common law schemes allowing suicide through the withdrawal of life-sustaining treatment. They stated that physicians do not fulfil the role of

---

[220] See above n. 189.

'killer' by prescribing drugs to hasten death any more than they do by disconnecting life-support systems. Likewise, 'psychological pressure' of the elderly and infirm was just as applicable to the withdrawal of life-sustaining equipment as to drugs to hasten death. As there had been no clear indication that there had been a problem in relation to the former, there was no basis for assuming that there would be in relation to the prescription of drugs. In any event, they commented that the State of New York may establish rules and procedures to assure that all choices are free of such pressures. In relation to the protection of the poor and the minorities, they felt it was sufficient to say that these classes of persons are entitled to equal treatment to that which is afforded to all those who may hasten death by means of life-support withdrawal. Finally, as to the interest in avoiding the sort of abuse which their Honours appear to have accepted was occurring in the Netherlands, they stated it was difficult to see how permitting assisted suicide for terminally-ill, mentally competent patients, who would self-administer the lethal drugs, would lead to the practice by physicians of non-voluntary euthanasia. Miner and Pollack JJ also considered the concerns expressed by the Ninth Circuit Court at first instance regarding the lack of clear definition of the term 'terminally ill'. However, they did not think that these concerns were well founded as most physicians would agree on the definition of 'terminally ill', at least for the purposes of the relief sought, and there would be even greater certainty as to when patients were in the final stages of terminal illness. Their Honours commented:

Physicians are accustomed to advising patients and their families in this regard and frequently do so when decisions are made regarding the furnishing or withdrawal of life-support systems. Again, New York may define that stage of illness with greater particularity, require the opinion of more than one physician or impose any other obligation upon patient and physicians who collaborate in hastening death.

Thus, their Honours concluded that the inequality existing between patients who are dependent on life-support systems and those that are not, does not further any legitimate State purpose. Accordingly, the majority held that to the extent that the statutes in question prohibit persons in the final stages of terminal illness from having assistance in ending their lives by the use of self-administered, prescribed drugs, the statutes lack any rational basis and are in violation of the Equal Protection Clause of the Fourteenth Amendment.

Whilst upholding the plaintiffs' arguments regarding Equal Protection, the majority judges rejected the alternative ground for the plaintiffs' complaint based on a violation of a Fourteenth Amendment liberty interest. Following a review of relevant Supreme Court cases concerning the scope of fundamental liberties which qualify for heightened judicial protection, the majority concluded that the right to assisted suicide finds no cognizable basis in the Constitution's language or design, even in the very limited cases of those competent persons who, in the final stages of terminal illness, seek the right to hasten death. Note was made by the majority judges of the reluctance on the part of the Supreme Court to expand the concept of substantive due process, and they went on to say that their position in the judicial hierarchy constrained them to be even more reluctant than the Supreme Court to undertake an expansive approach in this unchartered area. Somewhat surprisingly, there was no discussion of the detailed analysis by the Ninth Circuit Court in the *en banc* hearing where a substantial majority of the judges had upheld a constitutionally protected liberty interest in physician-assisted suicide for terminally ill, competent patients on the basis of the Due Process Clause of the Fourteenth Amendment.

In a separate, concurring opinion, Calabresi J explained that while he agreed with the court that New York's prohibitions on assisted suicide could not stand in view of their potential violation of the Equal Protection and Due Process Clauses of the Fourteenth Amendment, he was of the view that having regard to the history of the statutes and of New York's approach toward assisted suicide, it was not necessary to make a final judgment as to the validity of these statutes. On the basis of an historical survey of the legislative prohibition of assisted suicide he came to the conclusion that the bases of these statutes have been deeply eroded over the last 150 years and few of their foundations remain in place today. More specifically, he noted that the original reason for the statutes—criminalizing conduct that aided or abetted other crimes—is long since gone. Moreover, Calebresi J found that the distinction that has evolved over the years between conduct currently permitted (suicide and aiding someone who wishes to die to do so by removing hydration, feeding, and life-support systems) and conduct still prohibited (giving a competent terminally ill patient lethal drugs which he or she can self-administer) is tenuous at best. Also of relevance was the fact that the legislature, for many years, has not taken any recognizable affirmative step to reaffirm the prohibition of physician-assisted suicide for terminally ill competent patients. Further, it was noted that the enforcement of the laws themselves had fallen into virtual desuetude which raised further doubts about the current support for these laws. Calabresi J went on to explain that although these considerations would not be of much significance in the case of ordinary laws, they become all important in the case of legislation which may be in violation of fundamental substantive constitutional rights or contrary to the requirements of equal protection. In this situation, where the validity of the law is highly suspect, but cannot, in the light of existing Supreme Court authority, be conclusively found to be unconstitutional, Calabresi J held that the courts ought not to decide the ultimate validity of that law without current and clearly expressed statements, by the people or by their elected officials, of the State interests involved. He further contended that in the absence of such statements, the courts have frequently struck down such laws, while leaving open the possibility of reconsideration if appropriate statements were subsequently made. In the matter before him, Calabresi J was satisfied that the court had not been given any clear statements of possible interests that the State actually believes would be served by maintaining the distinction between medical action and medical inaction and this was, in his view, decisive:

> In their absence, how can we say that the distinction, which is anything but obvious, and which results in severe harm to the ability of some, but not all, individuals to determine crucial life and death choices for themselves, is mandated by the state's fundamental needs? And if the state does not affirmatively tell us what it wishes to put on the other side of the scale, how can we make the balance required by *Cruzan* come out in any way but in favour of the individual's freedom to choose between life and death? Whether under Equal Protection or Due Process, then, the absence of a recent, affirmative, lucid and unmistakable statement of why the state wishes to interfere with what has been held by the Supreme Court to be a significant individual right, dooms these statutes.

Thus, by invoking the principle of constitutional remand,[221] Calabresi J was able to join with the other two judges in holding that the statutes were invalid. He did, however, leave open the question of what his view on the merits would be if the State of New York were to reenact existing laws, while articulating the reasons for the distinctions it makes in the laws, and expressing the grounds for the prohibitions themselves.

Even prior to the release of the decision in *Quill* v. *Vacco*, the respective parties had made it clear that if unsuccessful, they would be bringing an appeal to the United States Supreme Court.

In the light of the *Quill* v. *Vacco* case, there have now been two federal appeals courts dealing with 'right to die' questions. As we have seen from the foregoing review, there is now a substantial body of opinion amongst federal court judges in the USA that the general prohibition on assisted suicide is unconstitutional, at least in so far as it prevents physicians from aiding informed, mentally competent, terminally ill adults to commit suicide. Significantly, however, there have been some fundamental disagreements as to the appropriate basis for this conclusion: the Ninth Circuit Court's majority decision resting solely on the basis of constitutionally protected liberty interest under the Due Process Clause of the Fourteenth Amendment, the court finding it unnecessary to come to a conclusion regarding the applicability of the Equal Protection Clause; the Second

---

[221] Calabresi J explained a constitutional remand as doing no more than telling the legislatures and executives of the various states that if they wish to regulate conduct that may come within the protection of the constitution, they must do so clearly and openly: unless they do this, they cannot expect courts to tell them whether what they may or may not actually wish to enact is constitutionally permitted.

Circuit Court decision rejecting this interpretation of the Due Process Clause, but upholding a constitutional challenge based on the Equal Protection Clause. In view of this conflict, attention will be sharply focused on the United States Supreme Court to see whether it agrees to review one or both of these decisions, and if so, what approach is ultimately taken by the Supreme Court in relation to the question of a constitutionally protected right to physician-assisted suicide for terminally ill, competent patients. Given the important and controversial nature of the matter, and the conflict of opinion between the two circuit courts, there is now a strong possibility that the Supreme Court will accept either one or possibly even both these cases for review and ultimately rule on the matter to clarify the constitutional status of legislation prohibiting assisted suicide.[222] If this were to be the case, it may be some time before these constitutional questions are finally resolved.

Predicting the outcome of any such determination is difficult, particularly in view of the divergent interpretations of the Ninth and Second Circuit Courts and the various dissenting opinions that have been given, also in the courts below. With regard to the argument for recognition of a constitutionally protected liberty interest based upon the Due Process Clause, the Supreme Court would, in the first instance, be required squarely to address the question which in *Cruzan* it had been willing to assume, regarding the existence of a constitutionally protected liberty interest in refusing medical treatment. On the assumption that the court does uphold such an interest, the critical question will be whether the scope of this liberty interest can, in the light of previous authority, be extended to encompass the right of a terminally ill, competent patient to physician-assisted suicide. Some commentators have suggested that this is unlikely:[223] it has been argued that the Supreme Court's decision in *Cruzan v. Director, Missouri Department of Health*[224] has demonstrated that the Supreme Court is reluctant to 'constitutionalize' an area marked by divisive social and legal debate and that its inclination, in such cases, is to defer to the states' judgments.

It has also been suggested that in order for the Supreme Court to uphold an interest in physician-assisted suicide (or, as the Ninth Circuit Court of Appeals preferred to express it, an interest in 'determining the time and

---

[222] There have already been reports that prosecution charges in respect of a case of assisted suicide (occurring outside of the medical context) have been suspended awaiting clarification by the Supreme Court regarding the validity of assisting suicide laws. Note, however, that there may be other, less obvious, considerations which may go against the Supreme Court accepting review—it has been suggested that the court may be avoiding review of cases in respect of issues over which the court is sharply divided which includes questions of due process and privacy: *NY Times*, 17 March 1996. It should be noted in this context that the Supreme Court has already once rejected the opportunity to consider whether there is a constitutional right to assisted suicide when it turned down an appeal from Dr Jack Kevorkian: see p. 97 above.

[223] e.g. Kamisar, 'Are Laws Against Assisted Suicide Unconstitutional?', above n. 153.

[224] See above n. 54.

manner of one's death') as an extrapolation from existing 'right to die' cases, the court would have to reconsider a long line of precedent which has held that the refusal of life-sustaining treatment by a patient does not constitute suicide.[225] However, as the majority decision of the Ninth Circuit Court demonstrates, these cases do not present an insurmountable obstacle to the recognition of a constitutional right to physician-assisted suicide for terminally ill, competent patients. In the *Compassion in Dying* (*en banc*) case, the majority judges saw nothing incongruous in recognizing such a right, notwithstanding the cases which have sought to distinguish refusal of treatment from suicide. This was largely due to the broad characterization of the relevant liberty interest as an interest in controlling the time and manner of one's death. And although the majority did give consideration to the State's interest in preventing suicide in evaluating the plaintiff's claim, it did express doubts as to whether deaths resulting from terminally ill patients taking medication prescribed by their physicians should be classified as suicide at all.[226] But there are, in any event, indications in these recent judgments that the courts may be willing to reassess some of the characterizations that have traditionally been accepted, for example, classifying the withdrawal of life-support as an omission, and specifically, in relation to whether ending life by these means, where this is done at the patient's direction, constitutes assisted suicide.[227]

There is also the possibility of a constitutional claim based on the Equal Protection Clause being upheld, although this ground has been less canvassed in previous 'right to die' cases. Certainly in the courts below, there was less obvious disagreement about such a finding, the Second Circuit Court upholding this ground, and the Ninth Circuit Court referring to the argument as 'not insubstantial', but finding it unnecessary to decide the issue.

Even if a constitutionally protected interest in physician-assisted suicide were recognized on Due Process and/or Equal Protection grounds, which would already be a momentous decision for the United States Supreme Court to take, it is likely that the real issue will turn on whether there has been a violation of constitutional rights having regard to relevant State interests. In the *Cruzan* case, Rehnquist CJ, delivering judgment for the majority, made it clear that determining that a person has a liberty interest under the Due Process Clause does not end the inquiry: 'whether the respondent's constitutional rights have been violated must be determined by balancing his liberty interests against the relevant state interests'. Cer-

---

[225] e.g. the majority of the Michigan Supreme Court in *People* v. *Kevorkian, Hobbins* v. *Attorney General*, see above n. 172. For discussion of US authorities where the issue of characterization of refusal of treatment as suicide is considered, see pp. 65–8 above.

[226] See p. 104 above.

[227] With regard to this latter point, see, in particular, the majority opinion in *Quill* v. *Vacco* (see above n. 219) and the majority judgment delivered by Reinhardt J in *Compassion in Dying* v. *Washington* (see above n. 54).

tainly, the *Cruzan* case, which has been the only case on death and dying and the right of privacy ever decided by the United States Supreme Court, provides some indication of the weight the court is likely to attach to particular State interests, especially the State's interest in the protection and preservation of human life. In that case, the court strongly affirmed the State's interest in preserving life, even in respect of a person who was in a persistent vegetative state. The majority stated 'there can be no gainsaying' the State's interest in the protection and preservation of human life—an interest which is demonstrated by states treating homicide as a serious crime and imposing criminal penalties on one who assists another to commit suicide. In relation to the issue before the court in *Cruzan* concerning the role of the State in setting procedural requirements for the withdrawal of treatment from incompetent patients (in particular, the requirement that evidence of the incompetent's wishes at to the withdrawal of treatment be proved by clear and convincing evidence) the majority expressed the view that 'a State may properly decline to make judgments about the "quality" of life that a particular individual may enjoy, and simply assert an unqualified interest in the preservation of human life to be weighed against the constitutionally protected interests of the individual'.

In the light of these comments, there can be little doubt that the State's interest in the protection and preservation of human life is likely to be given significant weight in future cases.[228] It remains to be seen, however, what significance the court would attach to the fact that the plaintiffs in these cases are terminally ill, mentally competent adults who seek medical assistance to commit suicide. The clear choice for the Supreme Court is reflected in the division of opinion in the *Compassion in Dying* case (*en banc*): the majority of the eleven-member panel Ninth Circuit Court took the view that in these circumstances, the State's interests in the preservation of life (as well as the State's interest in the prevention of suicide) are at their lowest whereas the individual's interest in determining the timing and manner of his or her death is at its peak. In contrast, the leading dissenting judgment of Beezer J held that as applied to terminally ill adults seeking physician-assisted suicide, the State's interest in the preservation of life remains at full strength and that the State's interest is weakened only where continued medical treatment would do nothing more than postpone death. The court's assessment of this issue is likely to be crucial to the outcome of its decision, assuming that a constitutionally protected liberty right or interest is first found to be established. Also significant will be the court's approach to the remaining State interests at issue over which the Ninth Circuit Court was divided, in particular, the State's interest in preventing suicide, in avoiding the involvement of third parties, precluding the use of

[228] Note, however, the dissenting judgments of Brennan J (in which Marshall and Blackmun JJ joined) and Stevens J who were in agreement that the State's interest in the preservation of life was outweighed by Nancy Cruzan's interest to be free of unwanted medical treatment.

arbitrary, unfair or undue influence, and in protecting the integrity of the medical profession.

If the decisions in *Compassion in Dying* v. *State of Washington* and *Quill* v. *Vacco* in respect of the due process ground or the equal protection ground are ultimately upheld by the Supreme Court—and one would certainly expect some opposition within the court to such a finding[229]—it would mean that physicians providing assistance to mentally competent, terminally ill patients to commit suicide would fall outside the scope of the general prohibition on assisted suicide under state legislation in the USA. The potential scope of such a finding would be significant, extending far beyond the relatively limited claim at issue in the *Rodriguez* case involving the right to assistance of a competent terminally ill patient who is physically unable to commit suicide unaided. The responsibility would then fall on the states, through their legislatures, to pass legislation regulating the practice of physician-assisted suicide to ensure that appropriate safeguards are in place. The broader ramifications of any such decision may be significant with the potential for future claims based on Equal Protection Grounds seeking to extend the right to have physician assistance in dying also to those who are competent and terminally ill, but are physically unable to commit suicide, thereby directly raising the issue of a constitutionally protected right to active voluntary euthanasia at least in some circumstances.

It has, undoubtedly, been a time of quite extraordinary case law developments in the USA, and with the Supreme Court now likely to rule on these issues in the future, the potential exists for further ground-breaking developments. The impact of the Supreme Court upholding a constitutionally protected interest in physician-assisted suicide, would extend beyond the USA even though there is no comparable constitutional framework in other jurisdictions. Apart from providing a potentially significant impetus for reform in other jurisdictions, there is also the possibility that the issues raised and arguments made in the US constitutional context are carried over to the field of human rights in an attempt to challenge a state's prohibition on doctor-assisted suicide or conceivably, even active voluntary euthanasia.[230]

CONCLUSION

The object of this chapter has been to examine the law in relation to assisted suicide and to consider the potential criminal liability of a doctor who assists

---

[229] See, for example, the judgment of Scalia J in *Cruzan* v. *Director, Missouri Department of Health* (above n. 54) where, although concurring with the decision of the majority, he spoke strongly against giving constitutional recognition to a right to suicide.

[230] For discussion of the human rights dimension see pp. 196–201 below.

a patient to die. Consideration has also been given to recent cases in Canada and the USA which have ruled on the constitutional validity of statutory prohibitions on assisted suicide. Whilst two federal courts in the USA have upheld these challenges (albeit on different grounds), the legal position will remain uncertain until such time as the United States Supreme Court rules on the matter. Leaving aside for the moment the possibility that a constitutionally protected liberty interest in physician-assisted suicide for competent, terminally ill patients is recognized by the United States Supreme Court, which would clearly impact on the capacity of US states to maintain a blanket prohibition on assisted suicide, the present situation is that in all of the jurisdictions under consideration, assisting suicide is a crime. With the exception of the Northern Territory, where both doctor-assisted suicide and active voluntary euthanasia have been legalized,[231] if a doctor actively assists a patient in committing suicide, for example, by supplying the necessary means to bring about the patient's death, the doctor may be criminally liable for assisting suicide. However, by non-action, a doctor may lawfully facilitate the suicide of a patient who wishes to hasten his or her death by refusing treatment. It has been noted that the courts have generally rejected the proposition that refusal of treatment can amount to suicide, and the difficulties with this approach have been discussed. It has been argued in this chapter that although refusal of treatment may in certain circumstances constitute suicide, because patients have a common law right to refuse treatment, a doctor is legally required to comply with a patient's refusal and would therefore not be criminally liable for respecting the patient's decision. Further, it has been suggested that the legitimate State aim of suicide prevention does not justify intervention in the rational suicide of a patient who has decision-making capacity. A doctor is under no duty to intervene so as to avert this form of suicide and arguably has no right to prevent the patient's exercise of self-determination.

On the basis of the analysis in this and the preceding chapter, it can be concluded that patients have a right to refuse medical treatment, including life-saving medical treatment, and a doctor who assists a patient to die by either withholding or withdrawing treatment would not incur criminal liability for either homicide or assisted suicide. There is, therefore, some scope for the lawful practice of passive euthanasia. If, however, a doctor takes active steps in assisting a patient to die, by either providing some assistance to a patient in committing suicide, or in the form of active voluntary euthanasia, he or she may incur criminal liability for assisting suicide or murder, depending on the degree of their involvement in the patient's death.

---

[231] Note also developments in the State of Oregon in the USA: see pp. 369–73 below.

So far, attention has focused on the law regarding active and passive euthanasia performed at the request of the patient, in terms of theoretical liability. In the chapter which follows, attention will turn to an examination of the position in practice in terms of what doctors actually do and how the law is in fact applied.

3

The Position in Practice: Doctors' Practices and the Law Applied

INTRODUCTION

It is evident from the preceding chapters, that there is, in law, a significant distinction between passive and active euthanasia. The position is that passive euthanasia can in certain circumstances be lawfully performed. Conduct constituting passive euthanasia (that is, the deliberate withholding or withdrawing of life-prolonging medical treatment with the object of hastening the patient's death) is in fact, widely practised by the medical profession and accepted as legitimate medical practice.[1] In sharp contrast, with the exception of the Northern Territory of Australia,[2] the law treats active voluntary euthanasia as murder, regardless of the special circumstances, and it is officially condemned by the medical profession. Similarly, a doctor's active involvement in a patient's suicide is unlawful and the practice is rejected by medical organizations.[3] The Hippocratic Oath is often cited as evidence of the medical profession's long tradition of opposi-

[1] e.g. World Medical Association (WMA) *Declaration of Venice on Terminal Illness* (1983) and the WMA *Declaration on Euthanasia* (1987). For discussion of the position in: UK—British Medical Association (BMA) Working Party Report, *Euthanasia: Report of a Working Party to Review the British Medical Associations Guidance on Euthanasia* (London, 1988) 46; US—Statement of the Council of Judicial and Ethical Affairs of the AMA, *Withholding or Withdrawing Life-Prolonging Medical Treatment* March (1986), President's Commission for the Study of Ethical Problems in Medicine and Biomedical and Behavioural Research, *Deciding to Forgo Life-Sustaining Treatment: A Report on the Ethical, Medical and Legal Issues in Treatment Decisions* (Washington, 1983); Canada—Canadian Medical Association (CMA) *Statement on Terminal Illness* (1982) and *Joint Statement on Terminal Illness* (1984); Australia, Australian Medical Association (AMA) *Draft Position Statement: Care of Severely Ill and Terminally Ill Patients* (1996). In relation to New Zealand, see the Report of the Medical Council of New Zealand, *Persistent Vegetative State and the Withdrawal of Food and Fluids* (1993). For an international perspective see Stanley, J., 'The Appleton International Conference: Developing Guidelines for Decision to Forgo Life-Prolonging Medical Treatment' (1992) 18 *Journal of Medical Ethics* 3.
   For the purposes of this work attention is focused on the liability of doctors. It is, however, acknowledged that medical decisions to withhold treatment with the intention of hastening death will usually be made by a doctor, but in practice, are often carried out by the attending nurse.
[2] The position in the Northern Territory is discussed in detail at pp. 344–59 below.
[3] e.g. AMA *Code of Medical Ethics and Current Opinions of the Council of Ethical and Judicial Affairs*, s. 2.211.

tion to active voluntary euthanasia and doctor-assisted suicide.[4] Although doctors are no longer required to swear the Hippocratic Oath, it has in part been incorporated in the ethical codes of the various medical associations in the common law jurisdictions under consideration.[5] Apart from the Hippocratic Oath and the codes of ethical practice which are based upon it, the question of active voluntary euthanasia has been specifically addressed by a number of medical associations. In 1987, the World Medical Association (WMA) issued a *Declaration on Euthanasia* which states:

Euthanasia, that is the act of deliberately ending the life of a patient, even at the patient's own request or at the request of close relatives, is unethical. This does not prevent the physician from respecting the desire of a patient to allow the natural process of death to follow its course in the terminal phase of sickness.[6]

This declaration applies to all member associations of the WMA. The medical associations in the United Kingdom, the USA, and Canada have formulated their own policies on the subject of active voluntary euthanasia, also rejecting the practice.[7]

This chapter will be focusing on the position in practice with respect to active voluntary euthanasia and, to a lesser extent, doctor-assisted suicide. Essentially, the object of this chapter is to highlight the discrepancies between the strict legal position and the position in practice in terms of what doctors actually do and how the law is applied, in order to demonstrate the inadequacies of the present law and the need for re-evaluation of the law's approach. A clear understanding of the position in practice and the extent to which it is at variance with strict legal principles is fundamental to any informed debate on this subject. The analysis in this chapter is, therefore,

---

[4] The relevant part of which provides: 'I will give no deadly medicine to anyone if asked, nor suggest any such counsel'. For critical analysis of the status of the Hippocratic Oath, see p. 244 below.

[5] The modern version of the Hippocratic Oath is now contained in the Declaration of Geneva adopted by the WMA at its meeting in Geneva in 1948 and amended at its meeting in Sydney in 1968. At 3.1.9 it states: 'I will maintain the utmost respect for human life, from the time of conception; even under threat, I will not use my medical knowledge contrary to the laws of humanity'.

[6] Adopted by the 39th World Medical Assembly, Madrid, Spain, October 1987.

[7] BMA, Report, *The Problem of Euthanasia: A Report by a Special Panel Appointed by the Board of Science and Education of the British Medical Association* (1971) (extracted in Trowell, H., *The Unfinished Debate on Euthanasia* (London, 1973) Appendix A, 151–158); BMA Working Party Report, *Euthanasia*, above n. 1, at 67; House of Delegates of the AMA, 1969–78 *Digest of Official Action*, AMA Dec. (1973); Council on Ethical and Judicial Affairs of the AMA, Report, *Euthanasia* (Chicago, 1988) (note also the AMA Council on Ethical and Judicial Affairs, Report 59, *Physician-Assisted Suicide* (1993)); CMA, 'CMA Policy Summary: Physician Assisted Death' (1995) 152 CMAJ 248A. Note also in Australia, the AMA *Draft Position Statement: Care of Severely Ill and Terminally Ill Patients* (1996) where medical interventions intended to end the life of a person are rejected. Whilst the official position of the medical profession is to reject unequivocally active euthanasia, there appears to be increasing dissension within medical associations with regard to this issue. For discussion, see pp. 292–352 below.

intended to lay a foundation for subsequent chapters containing ethical evaluation of active voluntary euthanasia[8] and consideration of reform in this area.[9]

As we have seen, on the basis of existing criminal law principles, any conduct which involves active steps to bring about the death of a patient amounts to murder, regardless of what may appear to be extenuating circumstances; for example, that the patient was in a terminal or incurable condition and had requested that those steps be taken, and that the doctor had acted *bona fide* and out of compassionate motives. Similarly, liability will potentially arise for assisting suicide if a doctor provides a patient with the means to take his or her own life, and the law takes no account of the circumstances of the patient, or the doctor's motive in providing that assistance.

However, if one has regard to the position in practice with respect to active voluntary euthanasia and assisted suicide, it is evident that the law is out of touch with reality. Indications are that patients do request active euthanasia and suicide assistance from their doctors and some doctors are responding to such requests. However, instances of prosecutions against doctors for euthanasia or assisting the suicide of their patients are exceedingly rare. Judging from the few cases which have arisen, and from the experience with cases of mercy killing or assisted suicide occurring outside of the medical context,[10] such cases will generally be dealt with very leniently by the criminal justice system. It will also be shown that other aspects of medical practice, such as turning off life-support or the administration of palliative drugs in the knowledge that they are likely to cause death, which would on strict legal principles attract criminal liability for murder, are characterized in such a way as to avoid the possibility of such liability. It will be argued that the prevailing discrepancies between legal theory and practice, and the deliberate distortion of legal principles, cause serious problems and if allowed to continue, threaten to undermine the law and bring it into disrepute.

This chapter is divided into four parts: part I which sets out the current

---

[8] See Ch. 4.   [9] See Chs. 5 and 6.

[10] For reference to mercy killing cases in the United Kingdom see Reed, N., 'Mercy Killing: Exits: Evidence to the Royal Commission on Criminal Procedure' (1982) 7 *Polytechnic L Rev*, 17 and Leng, R., 'Mercy Killing and the CLRC' (1982) 132 NLJ 76; in the USA, Sander J., 'Euthanasia: None Dare Call it Murder' (1969) 60 *J.Crim.L., Criminology & Police Science* 351, 355–7; Glantz, L. 'Withholding and Withdrawing Treatment: The Role of the Criminal Law' (1987/88) 15 *Law, Med. & Health Care* 231, 232–5; Humphry, D. and Wickett, A., *The Right to Die: Understanding Euthanasia* (Sydney, 1986) especially at 17–20, 91–2, 137–50. See also the Special Senate Committee on Euthanasia and Assisted Suicide, *Of Life and Death: Report of the Special Senate Committee on Euthanasia and Assisted Suicide* (Ottawa, 1995) A-73–A76 and A-77–A79 for reference to a number of Canadian mercy killing cases. For discussion of the position in Australia, see Otlowski, M., 'Mercy Killing Cases in the Australian Criminal Justice System' (1993) 17 *Crim.LJ* 10.

situation with respect to the practice of active voluntary euthanasia and doctor-assisted suicide; part II which examines the law in practice with respect to prosecutions of cases of active voluntary euthanasia and doctor-assisted suicide; part III which outlines the discrepancies between theory and practice; and part IV which analyses the problems with the current legal characterization of the withdrawal of life-support and the administration of palliative drugs which hasten death.

I. PATIENTS' REQUESTS AND DOCTORS' PRACTICES

A. Active Euthanasia and Doctor-Assisted Suicide: Patients' Requests

The object of this section is to examine the extent to which patients actually request active euthanasia or doctor-assisted suicide. Whilst there is obviously no reliable means of accurately measuring the full extent of patient demand, on the basis of available evidence there can be little doubt that *some* patients do specifically request their doctor to assist them to die.[11]

An initial difficulty is that, to a large extent, we are reliant on the doctors dealing with such patients to provide information regarding the frequency of patients' requests for active euthanasia or assisted suicide. For a number of reasons, this is information which doctors may be reluctant to provide. A patient's request to die might be interpreted as a statement of the failure of the medical profession, particularly in light of the profession's traditional role of preservation of life. Furthermore, if some doctors respond to patient requests for active euthanasia or doctor-assisted suicide, it is unlikely to be a subject to which they want to draw attention in view of the present criminality of these practices.

Thus, doctors may have reasons for not disclosing the full extent of patient requests for active euthanasia and assisted suicide, and it is in fact not uncommon for some doctors (or their professional associations) to claim that such requests are rarely made.[12] Furthermore, even if it is accepted that a patient has made such a request, there may be some dispute regarding the proper interpretation of that request; whether it constitutes a genuine wish to die, or whether it is simply indicative of the patient's loneliness, fear, despair, and pain, suggesting the need for support and/or more appropriate pain relief rather than the termination of life.[13] Indeed, in

---

[11] For a discussion of the causes behind a patient's request for euthanasia, see Admiraal, P., 'Justifiable Euthanasia' (1988) 3 *Issues Law & Med.* 361 and p. 239 below.

[12] e.g. Pollard, B., *Euthanasia: Should We Kill the Dying?* (Crows Nest, New South Wales, 1989) 63–6.

[13] e.g. Weddington, W., 'Euthanasia; Clinical Issues Behind the Request' (1981) 246 JAMA 1949.

some instances, the very expression of the patient's request for death has resulted in the patient's decision-making capacity being questioned.[14] Whilst some medical opponents of active voluntary euthanasia have, on the basis of their own experience, disputed the existence of such requests, doctors who are known to have objections to these practices are unlikely to be asked for assistance by their patients.[15]

Although there clearly are difficulties in obtaining accurate and comprehensive information, the available evidence indicates that patients' requests for active euthanasia and doctor-assisted suicide are not uncommon. One of the most reliable sources of information available are the surveys which have been conducted of doctors' experiences in this area. In 1992–93, a survey was conducted in England by means of an anonymous postal questionnaire sampling over 400 doctors, both general practitioners and hospital consultants, in an attempt to explore National Health Service (NHS) doctors' attitudes and practices with regard to active voluntary euthanasia.[16] In one of the questions, doctors were asked whether a patient had ever asked them to hasten his or her death. Of the 273 doctors that answered this question, 163 had been asked by a patient to hasten his or her death, and of these, 124 or 45 per cent, had been asked to hasten death by active means. These findings are comparable with the findings of a more recent national survey conducted in the United Kingdom of over 2,000 general practitioners and hospital doctors which was reported in the medical journal *Doctor*.[17] According to the findings of this survey, approximately one third of doctors had been faced with requests for active assistance, with general practitioners receiving such requests more frequently than hospital doctors.[18]

Similar surveys have also been conducted in other common law jurisdic-

---

[14] The much publicized case of John McEwan in Victoria acutely highlighted the problems which can arise in this area. John McEwan, former Australian water-skiing champion, became a quadriplegic as the result of an accident. After expressing a wish to die and refusing further treatment, he was certified insane. For coverage of this case, see the Parliament of Victoria Social Development Committee, Report, *Inquiry into Options for Dying with Dignity* (Melbourne, 1987) Appendix I.

[15] Kuhse, H. and Young, R., 'A Rejoinder to Some Common Objections to Voluntary Euthanasia', paper delivered to the ANZAAS Symposium; Modern Medical Technology and the Right to Die, No. 222, (1985) 1–2. Some evidence to support this view can be found in a recent survey of South Australian doctors; 50% of the respondent doctors who have treated incurably ill patients and who also believe that assisted dying is sometimes right have been asked by a patient for such help, but only 30% of respondent doctors who have treated incurably ill patients and who do not believe that assisted dying is sometimes right have been asked by a patient for such help; Medical Practitioners Concerned with Assisted Dying, Media Release, 'South Australian Doctors Help Incurable Patients to Die', 28 July 1992.

[16] Ward, B. and Tate, P., 'Attitudes Among NHS Doctors to Requests for Euthanasia' (1994) 308 BMJ 1332. 312 of the 424 questionnaires were returned completed, representing a response rate of 73.6%.

[17] Andrews, J., 'Euthanasia Dilemma Splits the Profession' *Doctor*, 9 Feb. 1995, 43.

[18] 35% of the GPs surveyed had received a request to take active steps whereas only 30% of hospital doctors had been asked by a patient to take active measures to end their lives.

tions. In a small opinion survey conducted in 1991 amongst physicians in the USA (using a sample of 88 physicians)[19] physicians were asked 'How often has anyone asked you to prescribe or administer a lethal dose of medication?'. 56 per cent indicated that this had happened to them at least once. In another more extensive survey recently undertaken in the USA involving a sample of over 700 doctors, 35.2 per cent had been asked to perform active euthanasia one or two times.[20] There is also evidence from other surveys which have focused exclusively on doctor-assisted suicide, that a small, but significant, proportion of doctors have received requests for assisted suicide. In a large study of Oregon doctors conducted in 1995 (responses received from 2,761 of a total 3,944 eligible physicians—a 70 per cent response rate) it was found that 21 per cent of the respondent doctors had been asked for a prescription for a lethal dose of medication within the preceding year.[21] In another recent survey, of physicians in Washington State, based on responses received from 828 physicians of a total 1,453 potential respondents (a 57 per cent response rate), 12 per cent of the responding physicians had received one or more explicit requests for physician-assisted suicide in the past year.[22] In Canada, a large scale survey was undertaken of physicians in Alberta to ascertain their opinions about the morality and legalization of active euthanasia.[23] 258 (19 per cent) of the 1,391 physicians who responded to a postal questionnaire (of a total of 2,002 of the licensed physicians in Alberta who were sampled, a response rate of 69 per cent) confirmed that they had been asked at least once to assist in active euthanasia.[24] Similar surveys conducted in a number of Australian

[19] Ciesielski-Carlucci, C., 'Physician Attitudes and Experiences with Assisted Suicide: Results of a Small Opinion Survey' (1993) 2 *Cambridge Q of Healthcare Ethics* 39. The physicians surveyed were registrants at the First Annual Conference of Healthcare Ethics Committees convened by the International Bioethics Institute in San Francisco in April 1991. Of the 88 physicians sampled, 4 were from a country other than the USA.

[20] Shapiro, R. et al., 'Willingness to Perform Euthanasia: A Survey of Physicians Attitudes' (1994) 154 *Arch.Intern.Med.* 575, 581. Note also the outcomes of other US surveys: Fried, T. *et al.*, 'Limits of Patient Autonomy: Physician Attitudes and Practices Regarding Life-Sustaining Treatments and Euthanasia' (1993) 153 *Arch. Intern.Med.* 722 and Back, A. *et al.*, 'Physician-Assisted Suicide and Euthanasia in Washington State: Patient Requests and Physician Responses' (1996) 275 JAMA 919, 920.

[21] Lee, M. et al., 'Legalizing Assisted Suicide—Views of Physicians in Oregon' (1996) 334 *New Eng. JMed.* 310. This study, which examined the attitudes and practices of Oregon doctors in relation to assisted suicide, was conducted after the passage of the Oregon Death with Dignity Act whilst the legislation was under constitutional challenge: for discussion, see pp. 369–73 below.

[22] Back et al., 'Physician-Assisted Suicide and Euthanasia in Washington State', above n. 20, at 920.

[23] Kinsella, T. and Verhoef, M., 'Alberta Euthanasia Survey: 1. Physician's Opinions About the Morality and Legalization of Active Euthanasia' (1993) 148 CMAJ 1921.

[24] The same researchers have since conducted a nationwide Canadian study sampling 3500 Canadian physicians: of those physicians sampled who have treated patients with terminal illness (81%), 22% had been asked to assist in active voluntary euthanasia and 14% had been asked to assist in physician-assisted suicide.

states have also shown that a significant proportion of Australian doctors have been asked to actively hasten the death of a patient. In Victoria, in a postal survey conducted in 1986 of a sample of 2,000 doctors from the Victorian Medical Register,[25] 48 per cent of the respondents answered affirmatively to a question whether they had, in the course of their medical practice, ever been requested by a patient to hasten his or her death.[26] The same questionnaire was later used in a survey of doctors in New South Wales and the Australian Capital Territory and 47 per cent of the respondent doctors sampled (1,200 responses from a postal survey of 2,000 doctors) in that survey answered affirmatively to this question.[27] Similar findings have been made in analogous surveys undertaken in South Australia.[28] A recent survey of doctors in New Zealand (120 general practitioners sampled nationwide) has also found that a significant proportion of doctors have been asked to perform euthanasia: according to this study, 30 per cent of New Zealand general practitioners have been asked once or twice to assist with euthanasia, 10 per cent have received a euthanasia request on between two and five occasions, and 7 per cent more than five times.[29]

In addition to information obtained from surveys of doctors, the occurrence of patient requests for active euthanasia and suicide assistance has been documented in a number of other ways. Studies have been undertaken of the incidence of requests amongst certain categories of patients. For example, at Daw House, an in-patient hospice and palliative care unit in Adelaide, South Australia, a study found that 6 per cent of patients had made a request for assistance to die.[30] Occasionally, patient requests for active euthanasia or assisted suicide attract widespread media attention.[31] Not infrequently, the medical journals contain case-analyses regarding patient requests for active euthanasia or assisted suicide and how these should be dealt with from a practical and ethical point of view.[32]

Despite the somewhat fragmentary nature of the available evidence, it is

---

[25] Of the 2,000 doctors questioned, 869 doctors (46%) returned completed questionnaires.

[26] Kuhse, H. and Singer, P., 'Doctors' Practices and Attitudes Regarding Voluntary Euthanasia' (1988) 148 MJA 623.

[27] Baume, P. and O'Malley, E., 'Euthanasia: Attitudes and Practices of Medical Practitioners' (1994) 161 MJA 137, 140.

[28] Stevens, C. and Hassan, R., 'Management of Death, Dying and Euthanasia: Attitudes and Practices of Medical Practitioners in South Australia' (1994) 20 *JMed.Ethics* 41 (33%); Medical Practitioners Concerned with Assisted Dying, 'South Australian Doctors Help Incurable Patients to Die', above n. 15, (42%).

[29] Thompson, M., 'Doctors Divided Over Helping Patients Die' (1995) *NZ Doctor*, 28 April, 3.

[30] Hunt, R. et al., 'The Incidence of Requests for Quicker Terminal Course' (1995) 9 *Palliative Med.* 167.

[31] e.g. the very public request of Sue Rodriguez. See p. 86 above.

[32] e.g. Lo, B. et al., 'Ethical Decisions in the Care of a Patient Terminally Ill with Metastatic Cancer' (1980) 92 *Annals Intern.Med.* 107; Higgs, R., 'Cutting the Thread and Pulling the Wool—A Request for Euthanasia in General Practice' (1983) 9 *JMed.Ethics* 45.

indisputable that some patients do specifically seek active euthanasia or suicide assistance from their doctors. However, the true extent of patient demand has not yet been established. Because of the present illegality of active voluntary euthanasia and assisted suicide, patients may be reluctant to make such a request.[33] Note should also be made of the quite frequent occurrence of mercy killing cases outside of the medical context where a family member or friend responds to a patient's request for assistance to die. The fact that requests are made to persons close to the patient and that they feel compelled to act is, to some extent at least, a product of the unavailability of active voluntary euthanasia through lawful and professional means. If active voluntary euthanasia were a lawful option, such requests would be more likely to be referred to the patient's doctor.

B. *Active Euthanasia and Doctor-Assisted Suicide: Doctors' Practices*

In the ongoing debate on the subject of euthanasia, it is frequently asserted or assumed that some doctors are involved in the practice of active voluntary euthanasia and assisted suicide. In this part, an attempt will be made to make some assessment of doctors' involvement in these practices.

Because active voluntary euthanasia and assisted suicide[34] are presently unlawful, significant practical difficulties are encountered in ascertaining the exact extent of these practices. Doctors are naturally reluctant to openly admit any involvement in the practice of active voluntary euthanasia or assisted suicide for fear of criminal prosecution and/or disciplinary action taken against them by their professional organizations.[35] Furthermore, such activities are unlikely to come to the attention of others, since they will usually be performed in a clandestine fashion. Even if other doctors become aware of the involvement of a doctor in these practices, there is some evidence to suggest that most doctors would not report a colleague to legal authorities in these circumstances.[36] Not only is the doctor likely to act

[33] Williams, G., 'Euthanasia' (1973) 41 *Medico-LegalJ* 14–15.

[34] For the purposes of this discussion assisted suicide will be used to refer to active forms of assistance, for example, where the doctor provides the patient with the necessary drugs to take his or her own life. For discussion of the possibility of a doctor's passive conduct (e.g. withholding treatment) constituting assistance in suicide see pp. 76–80 above.

[35] Some support for this view can be gleaned from survey results which indicate that the present illegality of the practice of active voluntary euthanasia has been a significant factor for those doctors who have not responded to patient requests (e.g. Kuhse and Singer, 'Doctors' Practices and Attitudes Regarding Voluntary Euthanasia' above n. 26, at 624). It is possible to extrapolate from this that fear of legal or other damaging professional consequences is likely to be a significant factor in deterring doctors from being open in the practice of active voluntary euthanasia.

[36] Verhoef, M. and Kinsella, T., 'Alberta Euthanasia Survey: 2. Physicians' Opinions About the Acceptance of Active Euthanasia as a Medical Act and the Reporting of Such Practices' (1993) 148 CMAJ 1929, 1931, 1932.

secretly, without onlookers, he or she may also readily conceal the true cause of death by indicating on the death certificate that the deceased died from natural causes.[37] Apart from the fear of criminal prosecution and/or professional disciplinary action, there may be other reasons why doctors may be reluctant to divulge their involvement in these practices. For example, doctors may wish to protect patient confidentiality and indeed may have been specifically requested by the patient not to disclose to anyone the real cause of death. Doctors may also be unwilling to discuss such matters amongst their colleagues for fear of disapproval from their medical peers.[38] There are, consequently, inherent limitations in obtaining reliable and comprehensive information regarding the practice of active voluntary euthanasia and assisted suicide by the medical profession, and the available information is, at times, fragmentary and anecdotal in nature.

Whilst these practical limitations must obviously be acknowledged, there is incontrovertible evidence that a significant proportion of the medical profession is involved in the practice of active voluntary euthanasia and assisted suicide.

Evidence regarding the practices of doctors with respect to active voluntary euthanasia and assisted suicide can be derived from a number of sources, including prosecutions of doctors, surveys of the medical profession, and doctors openly admitting their involvement in these practices.

Prosecutions of doctors for active euthanasia and doctor-assisted suicide

In the USA and the United Kingdom there have been a number of cases involving the prosecution of doctors for their involvement in acts of euthanasia or assisting the suicide of their patients.[39] Although such prosecutions are very rare and cannot be taken to reflect the true extent of the practice of active euthanasia or assisted suicide,[40] they certainly do bear out the contention that such practices do occur from time to time.

Survey evidence of doctors' practices

Provided that they are professionally conducted, and assure the respondents' anonymity, surveys of doctors would appear to offer the most reliable

---

[37] Since autopsies are a relatively rare procedure following the death of a terminal patient, the real cause of death (e.g. the administration of a lethal dose) is unlikely to be discovered.

[38] This is borne out by survey evidence which suggests that only rarely will doctors consult a colleague to discuss such cases: see Back, *et al.*, 'Physician-Assisted Suicide and Euthanasia in Washington State: Patient Requests and Physician Responses', above n. 20, at 923, 924.

[39] See discussion below.

[40] A number of reasons can be advanced for this dearth of prosecutions; as suggested earlier, doctors may, for a variety of reasons, be reluctant to be open in their practice of active voluntary euthanasia or assisted suicide and even in circumstances where active voluntary euthanasia or doctor-assisted suicide are known to be performed, there may be a reluctance on the part of prosecuting authorities to take action against a doctor. See discussion below.

information regarding the practice of active voluntary euthanasia and assisted suicide by the medical profession. A review of the survey evidence from the various jurisdictions reveals that active euthanasia is being performed by a significant number of doctors.[41] In the survey of NHS doctors in England referred to above, doctors were asked whether they had ever complied with a patient's request for active euthanasia. Of the 124 doctors who had been asked for such help, 119 answered this question. 38 of those respondents (32 per cent) indicated that they had taken active steps to end the life of a patient.[42] Very similar results have been recorded in a number of the Australian surveys. In the survey of Victorian doctors noted earlier, 107 (29 per cent) of those doctors who responded to the question whether they had ever taken active steps to bring about the death of a patient who had asked them to do so responded affirmatively.[43] The New South Wales study, using the same survey instrument recorded a positive response rate of 28 per cent to this question.[44] In one of the South Australian surveys referred to earlier, 29 per cent of responding doctors who had ever been asked by an incurably or terminally ill patient actively to assist him or her to die acknowledged having done this for at least one patient.[45] Similarly, there are results available from the USA which also show that active euthanasia is being performed by doctors. In 1987 the Hemlock Society (a national group advocating active voluntary euthanasia[46]) conducted a survey among Californian doctors using the same questionnaire as used in the Monash survey. The questionnaire was sent to 5,000 doctors of whom some 588 responded. 79 of the doctors surveyed (nearly 23 per cent) indicated that they had deliberately taken the lives of terminal patients who had asked to die, and some had done so on more than one occasion.[47] Other less exten-

[41] It should be noted that not all of the surveys which have been undertaken seek to establish the extent of doctors' involvement in these practices; e.g. the survey commissioned by the journal *Doctor* in the UK and many of the US surveys have been limited to determining doctors' *attitudes* rather than doctors' *practices*, possibly due to concern regarding the legal implications of revealing activity which the law presently regards as criminal.

[42] Ward and Tate, 'Attitudes Among NHS Doctors to Requests for Euthanasia', above n. 16, 1332–3.

[43] Kuhse and Singer, 'Doctors' Practices and Attitudes Regarding Voluntary Euthanasia', above n. 26, at 624.

[44] Baume and O'Malley, 'Euthanasia: Attitudes and Practices of Medical Practitioners', above n. 27, at 142.

[45] Medical Practitioners Concerned with Assisted Dying, 'South Australian Doctors Help Incurable Patients to Die', above n. 15. In the other South Australia study, 19% of all respondents answered yes to the question 'Have you ever taken active steps which have brought about the death of a patient?': Stevens and Hassan, 'Management of Death, Dying and Euthanasia: Attitudes and Practices of Medical Practitioners in South Australia', above n. 28, at 43.

[46] See further pp. 276–9 below.

[47] Note, 'Most California Doctors Favour New Euthanasia Law' (1988) 31 *Hemlock Q.* 1–2.

sive surveys conducted in the USA have also confirmed that active euthanasia does take place.[48]

There have been a number of surveys which have attempted to examine the extent of doctors' involvement in assisted suicide. The results of these surveys suggest that a small, but nevertheless significant, proportion of doctors have assisted patients to commit suicide through the provision or prescription of lethal doses of medication.[49] Interestingly, some of the survey evidence from the USA would suggest that doctors in that country are more willing to participate in assisted suicide than active euthanasia.[50] The little evidence that is available from other jurisdictions comparing doctors' involvement in active voluntary euthanasia and doctor-assisted suicide suggests that this is not necessarily the case elsewhere.[51]

Admissions by doctors

Notwithstanding the present illegality of active voluntary euthanasia and doctor-assisted suicide, doctors have, on occasion, openly admitted that they have participated in these practices. Indeed, in recent years there appears to be an increasing number of doctors who have acknowledged that they have actively ended the life of a patient or assisted with a patient's suicide. For example, in the USA, Dr. Timothy Quill described in an article submitted to the *New England Journal of Medicine* how he had prescribed sleeping pills to a patient suffering from leukemia in order that she could

[48] e.g. Ciesielski-Carlucci, 'Physician Attitudes and Experiences with Assisted Suicide: Results of a Small Opinion Survey', above n. 19, at 43; Fried, et al., 'Limits of Patient Autonomy: Physician Attitudes and Practices Regarding Life-Sustaining Treatments and Euthanasia', above n. 20, at 725; Doukas, D., et al., 'Attitudes and Behaviours on Physicians-Assisted Death: A Study of Michigan Oncologists' (1995) 13 *JClin.Oncology* 1055, 1057; Shapiro, R., et al., 'Willingness to Perform Euthanasia: A Survey of Physicians Attitudes', above n. 20, at 581, Back *et al.,* 'Physician-Assisted Suicide and Euthanasia in Washington State', above n. 20, at 923.

[49] e.g. Back et al., 'Physician-Assisted Suicide and Euthanasia in Washington State', above n. 20, at 922 reporting that 24% of the 156 patients who requested physician-assisted suicide received prescriptions and 21 of these died as a result; Lee, 'Legalizing Assisted Suicide— Views of Physicians in Oregon', above n. 21, at 310 where it is reported that of the 21% of doctors who had been asked for a prescription for a lethal dose of medication within the preceding year, 7% indicated that they had complied with this request.

[50] e.g. Ciesielski-Carlucci, 'Physician Attitudes and Experiences with Assisted Suicide: Results of a Small Opinion Survey', above n. 19, at 43 ; Fried, et al., 'Limits of Patient Autonomy: Physician Attitudes and Practices Regarding Life-Sustaining Treatments and Euthanasia', above n. 20, at 725; Doukas, et al., 'Attitudes and Behaviours on Physician-Assisted Death: A Study of Michigan Oncologists', above n. 48, at 1057.

[51] For example, in the survey of doctors in the Australian State of New South Wales, 7% of respondents indicated that they had provided the means for a patient to commit suicide when requested to do so, compared with 28% who had provided active assistance at a patient's request: Baume and O'Malley, 'Euthanasia: Attitudes and Practices of Medical Practitioners', above n. 27, at 140.

kill herself.[52] Another doctor who has openly admitted his involvement in the practice of doctor-assisted suicide is Dr Jack Kevorkian, a retired Michigan pathologist who has assisted the suicide of dozens of patients since 1990.[53] There have also been instances of admissions by doctors that they have performed euthanasia or assisted a patient to commit suicide in the United Kingdom[54] and the other jurisdictions under consideration.[55]

Other admissions to the practice of active voluntary euthanasia have been less public, or have been made anonymously. For example, there have been reports of medical meetings at which doctors have admitted to having administered active euthanasia.[56] Anonymous admissions have generally taken the form of publications and include a much publicized incident in the USA, in which a resident doctor admitted that he had injected a fatal dose of morphine into a 20-year-old patient dying of ovarian cancer.[57]

C. Other Forms of Active Assistance in the Termination of Life

Apart from the deliberate administration of a lethal dose, there are other forms of medical practice which may, in effect, involve active assistance in the termination of life, namely the withdrawal of life-support (for example, turning off a ventilator),[58] and the administration of drugs for the relief of pain and other symptoms which hasten death.

Withdrawal of life-support

Life-support assistance can take a variety of forms; for instance, a ventilator which supports the respiratory function of the patient, or artificial feeding,

---

[52] Quill, T., 'Death and Dignity: A Case of Individualised Decision Making' (1991) 324 *New Eng.JMed.* 691.

[53] For discussion, see below.

[54] Such accounts include that of Dr George Mair who in 1974 published a book in which he openly admitted that he had performed active euthanasia during his time in medical practice: Mair, G., *Confessions of a Surgeon* (London, 1974) 86.

[55] e.g. in Canada, the admission by a Vancouver psychologist, David Lewis, that he had assisted in the suicide of a number of persons with AIDS: Special Senate Committee on Euthanasia and Assisted Suicide, *Of Life and Death*, above n. 10, A-28. For the purposes of Australia, note also the admissions of seven doctors who, in an open letter to the Premier of Victoria, Mr Kennett, have declared that they have helped terminally ill patients to die: *The Age*, 25 March 1995.

[56] e.g. Linacre Centre, Working Party Report, *Euthanasia and Clinical Practice: Trends, Principles and Alternatives* (London, 1982) 11; Fletcher, J., *Morals and Medicine* (Princeton, New Jersey, 1979) 205–6.

[57] Note, 'It's Over, Debbie' (1988) 259 JAMA 272. This admission provoked a storm of protest, particularly because of the manner in which the killing had occurred; the resident had been woken up in the middle of the night, had had no previous contact with the patient, and had only hastily informed himself of her condition without consulting her doctor before administering the lethal dose.

[58] The writing of 'not for resuscitation' orders could also be included in this category since it involves a bodily movement even though it is part of a broader plan of non-intervention.

(for example, intravenous or naso-gastric) which provides a patient with nutrition and hydration. The withdrawal of such life-support measures may arise in a variety of circumstances. It may, for example, be done at the request of a patient who has decision-making capacity and is dependent on life-support.[59] Alternatively, artificial ventilation may be terminated in respect of a brain-damaged or comatosed patient in order to determine whether the patient is able to breathe spontaneously,[60] or because the treating doctors have decided that continuation of life-support is medically futile. It is a fairly common occurrence in medical practice for doctors to withdraw life-support from a patient (which is, in many cases, accompanied by the administration of palliative drugs to ease the patient's distress), and this is widely accepted, even in the most conservative medical circles, to be proper medical practice in appropriate circumstances.[61]

Administration of drugs for the relief of pain and other symptoms which hasten death

Another aspect of medical practice which involves active assistance in the termination of life is the administration of palliative drugs which hasten death. Many patients, particularly those suffering from a terminal condition such as cancer, may experience considerable pain and other distressing symptoms. There are a range of palliative drugs available which may be administered to relieve pain and other symptoms, but which may have the effect of shortening the patient's life. There is some debate about whether the appropriate use of palliative drugs (usually opioids and sedatives in combination) does in fact have the effect of hastening death.[62] Whilst in many cases, the use of palliative drugs will not hasten death and may in fact prolong the life of the patient, there will inevitably be cases where the drugs required to alleviate a patient's pain and distress are likely to have the effect of shortening a patient's life. This may, for example, be due to the effects of increased dosages made necessary due to the progression of the patient's disease, or simply the effect of the patient being kept under heavy sedation. Thus, doctors may face the dilemma of leaving the patient's pain unrelieved, or administering the necessary palliative drugs even though this

---

[59] As, for example in the Canadian case of *Nancy B* v. *Hôtel-Dieu de Québec* 69 CCC (3d) (1992) 450: see pp. 51–2 above.

[60] Skegg, P., *Law Ethics and Medicine*, Revised edn. (Oxford, 1988) 164; Kennedy, I., 'Switching Off Life Support Machines: The Legal Implications' (1977) *Crim.L.Rev.* 443, 445–8.

[61] For evidence of the occurrence and acceptability of this practice, see the President's Commission Report, *Deciding to Forgo Life-Sustaining Treatment*, above Ch. 1 n. 44, at 2–9 (summary of the Commission's conclusions); Hastings Center Report, *Guidelines on the Termination of Life-Sustaining Treatment and Care for the Dying* (Bloomington, 1987) 35–42, 59–62; BMA Working Party Report, *Euthanasia*, above n. 1, at 21.

[62] e.g. National Council for Hospice and Specialist Palliative Care Services, *Key Ethical Issues in Palliative Care* Occasional Paper 3 (London, 1993) 8.

is likely to hasten the death of the patient.[63] Whilst indications are that as a result of increased availability of drugs for pain and symptom control and knowledge of their use, this problem is not as great as it once was, difficulties nevertheless remain. In some instances, the only way to relieve suffering is with doses of pain-killers and sedatives that render the patient permanently unconscious. There can be no doubt that this kind of treatment, in the nature of palliative sedation, will hasten the death of the patient.

It is widely accepted amongst the medical profession that the administration of life-shortening palliative care is, in some circumstances, ethical and constitutes legitimate medical practice.[64]

II. THE LAW IN PRACTICE

All instances of doctors being charged and prosecuted for having performed active euthanasia upon a patient or assisted the suicide of a patient are of obvious relevance in analysing the approach of the law in practice to these activities. However, very few such prosecutions arise and it will be argued that this is in itself significant.[65]

Prosecutions of Doctors for Active Euthanasia or Assisted Suicide[66]

In the USA, the United Kingdom, and Canada, there have been a number of prosecutions of doctors for murder or attempted murder, brought on the grounds of the doctors' involvement in active euthanasia as well as prosecutions against doctors for assisting the suicide of their patients. The first of such cases to arise in the USA was the much publicized prosecution of Dr Hermann Sander in New Hampshire in 1950 for the murder of a patient.[67] Dr Sander had injected air into a vein of his cancer-ridden patient, with the

---

[63] See also Williams, G., *The Sanctity of Life and the Criminal Law* (London, 1956) 287.

[64] According to the Hippocratic Oath, one of the aims of medicine is the prevention of suffering and this is also reflected in the official position of the medical profession; e.g. WMA Policy Statement *Care of Patients with Severe Chronic Pain in Terminal Illness* (1990); BMA Working Party Report, *Euthanasia*, above n. 1, at 40; Council on Ethical and Judicial Affairs of the AMA, Council Report, *Decisions Near the End of Life* (1992) 267 JAMA 2229, 2231.

[65] This is to be contrasted with the many mercy killing cases occurring outside the medical context which come before the courts.

[66] It should be noted that there have also been cases involving the prosecution of nurses for having assisted in the deaths of their patients and these cases have frequently been dealt with leniently in the criminal justice system. For reference to a US case, in which a nurse was acquitted after administering a fatal dose of morphine to a patient, see Humphry, D. (ed.), *Compassionate Crimes, Broken Taboos* (Los Angeles, 1986) 16.

[67] *People* v. *Sander* (unreported) *NY Times*, 10 March 1950. For analysis of this case, see Sachs, T., 'Criminal Law: Humanitarian Motive as a Defense to Homicide' (1950) 48 *Mich.L.Rev.* 1199.

intention of bringing about her death. This was clearly established from the patient's hospital records, in which Dr Sander had made the following entry: 'Patient was given 10cc of air intravenously repeated four times. Expired within 10 minutes after this was started'. At his trial, Dr Sander did not seek to deny that this had occurred. Nor did he attempt to allege that his action was in any way justified.[68] His defence was simply argued on the basis that there was no evidence that he had in fact caused the patient's death.[69] The jury acquitted the doctor of the murder charges, apparently accepting his defence that his acts were not the necessary proximate cause of the patient's death.

Another US case involving the prosecution of a doctor for having administered active euthanasia to a patient is *People* v. *Montemarano*.[70] In that case, Dr Vincent Montemarano was charged with the murder of his 59-year-old patient who was suffering from terminal cancer of the throat. There was evidence before the court that the doctor had administered to the patient a fatal dose of potassium chloride and that the patient had died shortly after. As in the earlier *Sander* case, the issue of euthanasia was not specifically raised by the defence.[71] It was argued on behalf of the doctor that the patient had died before the potassium chloride was administered or alternatively, that the patient had died from other causes. The case was tried before a jury and the doctor was acquitted of all charges.[72]

It should be noted that in neither case was the jury directly confronted with deciding a case of acknowledged medical euthanasia, carried out deliberately by the doctor with the object of terminating the patient's suffering; indeed, it is clear from the earlier analysis of the criminal law in relation to murder[73] that there is no recognized defence at common law applicable in these circumstances. In both cases, the doctors' defence proceeded on the basis that the doctor had not caused the patient's death and the jury in each case apparently accepted these arguments despite considerable evidence to the contrary.[74]

---

[68] Meyers, D., *Medico Legal Implications of Death and Dying* (Rochester, New York, 1981) 121. There appears to be some disagreement amongst commentators as to whether the patient had requested such assistance. Compare for example, Behnke, J. and Bok, S., *Dilemmas of Euthanasia* (Garden City, New York, 1975) 53; and Kamisar, Y., 'Some Non-Religious Views Against Proposed Mercy-Killing Legislation' (1958) 42 *Minn.LRev.* 969, 1019.

[69] Evidence was given at the trial that the patient might already have been dead when Dr Sander gave her the injection and that in any event, 40 cc of air would be insufficient to cause death; see Baugham, W., et al., 'Euthanasia: Criminal, Tort, Constitutional and Legislative Considerations' (1973) 48 *Notre Dame Law.* 1202, 1214.

[70] (Unreported) (1974) Nassau County Court (NY).

[71] Goldsmith, L., 'Physician Acquitted of Charges of Murdering Patient' (1974) 2 *JLMed.* 47, 48.

[72] *NY Times*, 13 Jan. 1974.

[73] See pp. 14–22 above.

[74] Behnke and Bok, *Dilemmas of Euthanasia*, above n. 68, at 53–4; Veatch, R., *Death Dying and the Biological Revolution* (New Haven, 1976) 80.

There have also been a number of other cases which have come before the courts in the USA involving prosecutions against doctors for murder in circumstances suggesting active euthanasia where the doctor was a relative of the deceased. In a 1986 case, Dr Joseph Hassman was charged with the murder of his mother-in-law who had been suffering from Alzheimer's disease. He pleaded guilty to killing her by injecting the pain-killer Demerol into her feeding tube. He was sentenced to 2 years probation, fined $10,000 and ordered to perform 400 hours of community service by a New Jersey Superior Court judge.[75] In imposing the sentence, the judge commented that no purpose would be served by committing the defendant to gaol and suggested that having regard to all the circumstances, gaoling the offender would constitute a serious injustice. In 1988 Dr Peter Rosier was charged with the murder of his wife who had been suffering from terminal cancer. Dr Rosier had admitted to the media, some months after the death of his wife, that he had given his wife drugs at her request so that she could end her life. He pleased not guilty to the charge of murder and notwithstanding factual evidence which clearly indicated Dr Rosier's criminal liability for taking steps to assist his wife to die, he was acquitted by the jury.[76]

Reference should also be made here to Dr Jack Kevorkian mentioned in the preceding chapter,[77] who has, over a period of years, assisted dozens of people to commit suicide. Under the law as it initially stood in the State of Michigan when Dr Kevorkian first assisted patients to commit suicide, assisting suicide was not a specific offence so charges were instead brought for murder. Most of these charges were later dismissed because the prosecution could not show that Dr Kevorkian had activated the suicide device so as to constitute homicide. Legislation was then introduced in the State of Michigan prohibiting assisted suicide. Dr Kevorkian was again charged following his further participation in the deaths of a number of patients. However, he was later acquitted by a Michigan jury of charges that he had violated the Michigan law on assisted suicide, the jury apparently accepting his argument that his main intent had been to relieve suffering and not to cause death.[78] Significantly, a state-wide poll conducted in Michigan found that the great majority of Michigan residents (71 per cent) oppose Dr Kevorkian facing further trials: only 22 per cent thought he should stand trial and of those, not all believed that he should be convicted.[79] Dr Kevorkian has since faced further prosecution under the now-expired Michigan law against assisting suicide but has once again been acquitted of all charges. At the time of writing, he was facing further prosecution in respect of the deaths of a number of patients under Michigan common law.

[77] See p. 94 above.

[75] *People* v. *Hassman* (unreported) *NY Times*, 20 Dec. 1986.
[76] *People* v. *Rosier* (unreported) *Washington Post*, 2 Dec. 1988.
[78] *Washington Post*, 15 May 1994.   [79] *The Globe*, 4 June 1995.

Another noteworthy case is that of Dr Timothy Quill (referred to above), who had publicly admitted assisting a cancer patient to commit suicide. He had been attending the patient for quite a number of years and when the patient requested assistance to die, he provided her with a prescription for barbiturates and information on how to use them in order to commit suicide. As a result of this action, Dr Quill was brought before a grand jury. However, the grand jury refused to indict him on charges of assisting suicide.[80]

In recent years, there have also been a number of prosecutions of doctors in the United Kingdom for the attempted murder of their patients.[81] In 1986, criminal proceedings were brought against Dr Carr for having injected a massive dose of phenobarbitone into a patient who had terminal cancer. The patient had died 2 days later and since natural causes could not be ruled out as the cause of death, the charge was one of attempted murder.[82] The prosecution claimed that the dosage could not possibly be justified on any genuine medical basis and that it had been deliberately administered in order to hasten the death of the patient. As part of the prosecution case it was alleged that the doctor had said that 'he wished the patient should be allowed to die with dignity'. Dr Carr, who had pleaded not guilty to the charge of attempted murder, alleged that the dose had been given in error.[83] This contradicted an earlier statement he had made to the police in which he claimed that he had only administered a fraction of the dose.[84] Despite the weight of evidence against him and a summing-up by the judge hostile to the defence, the jury acquitted the doctor of the charge.[85] This result was hailed by the press as the product of the jury's determination not to brand a doctor a criminal who they believed had acted honourably and mercifully.

A more recent case which has attracted much publicity in the United Kingdom[86] is the prosecution and conviction of Dr Cox for the attempted

---

[80] *NY Times*, 27 July 1991. Although there have been other instances of doctors admitting their participation in the suicide of patients they have generally not resulted in prosecution. This can, in part, be explained by the tendency of the doctors not to disclose the identity of the deceased patient, thereby making it difficult for the prosecuting authorities to prove liability. There does, however, appear to be a distinct disinclination on the part of police and prosecuting authorities to investigate or take action in respect of such cases. See further discussion below.

[81] The prosecutions against doctors in the UK include *R* v. *Arthur* (unreported) *The Times*, 6 Nov. 1981 concerning the prosecution of Dr Leonard Arthur for attempted murder with regard to the death of a Down's syndrome baby, but it is submitted that this case falls outside the ambit of the present analysis, since it did not clearly involve active euthanasia.

[82] *R* v. *Carr* (unreported) *Yorkshire Post*, 12 Nov. 1986.

[83] *Yorkshire Evening Post*, 19 Nov. 1986.

[84] *Yorkshire Evening Post*, 18 Nov. 1986. Dr Carr had initially claimed that he had only injected 150 mgs of phenobarbitone but later accepted that he had given the patient 1,000 mgs.

[85] *The Sunday Times*, 30 Nov. 1986.

[86] e.g. *The Times*, 22 Sept. 1992.

murder of one of his patients.[87] Cox, a rheumatologist, was charged with
attempted murder following the death of a 70-year-old terminally ill patient
who had asked him to put her out of her misery.[88] The deceased, who had
been a patient of Dr Cox for 13 years, had rheumatoid arthritis, complicated
by gastric ulcers, gangrene, and body sores. She was crippled from her
condition and in great pain. There was evidence before the court that she
had repeatedly asked Dr Cox and others to kill her. When other pain-killing
measures failed to bring relief, Cox administered a large dose of potassium
chloride, twice the amount which would normally prove fatal and the patient died within minutes. Cox admitted that he had administered the drug
but maintained that his primary intention was not to kill his patient but
merely to relieve her suffering. Ognall J gave a direction to the jury explaining that if the injection was given by Dr Cox for the primary purpose of
ending the patient's life (as distinct from being primarily aimed at the
alleviation of the patient's pain and suffering) he must be found guilty.
After 8 hours of deliberation, the jury, several overcome with emotion and
weeping, reached a majority verdict of 11–1 against Cox on what the judge
had described as 'the most clear and compelling evidence'.[89] Cox was given
a 12-month prison sentence, but in recognition of the fact that the public
interest would not be served by immediately jailing the consultant, the
sentence was suspended. Ognall J of the Winchester Crown Court described the situation as one in which the consultant had allowed his distress
over the suffering endured by his patient to overcome his professional duty.
His Honour said 'such conduct can never be legally excused. However,
sometimes it can be explained'.[90] In sentencing Cox, Ognall J told him that
his conduct in administering a lethal injection to his patient had not only
been criminal, but also a betrayal of his unequivocal duty as a physician.
Counsel for the defendant had urged the judge to give his client an absolute
discharge in view of the exceptional circumstances of the case but the judge
said that deliberate conduct by a doctor aimed at bringing about the death
of a patient required, as a matter of principle, to be marked by a term of
imprisonment.

The conviction against Cox is of consequence, being one of the rare
instances where a doctor has been found criminally liable for having taken
active steps to hasten the death of a suffering patient. Moreover, it is
significant that a sentence of imprisonment was imposed, albeit one which
was ultimately suspended. The comments made by Ognall J and the course
that he took against Cox indicates that some members of the judiciary

---

[87] *R v. Cox* (1992) 12 BMLR 38 (Winchester CC).

[88] He was evidently charged with attempted murder rather than murder because the deceased's body had been cremated before the police investigation could establish the cause of
death; Note, 'Attempted Murder Conviction of Euthanasia Doctor in England' (1992) 62
VESNSW Newsletter 2.

[89] See above, n. 86.   [90] Ibid.

would be inclined to bring the criminal law to bear against doctors for action taken deliberately to hasten the death of a patient. Although the sentence imposed may, in some respects, appear lenient, the judge had the discretion to impose a lighter penalty, including the possibility of a conditional discharge, which arguably would have been more appropriate in all the circumstances.[91]

In addition to these cases which clearly come within the ambit of active euthanasia, there have also been a number of prosecutions for murder in the United Kingdom in circumstances where the doctor alleged that the death-inducing drugs administered to the patient were for the relief of pain and that therefore, his action did not constitute murder.[92] In both of these cases the doctor was acquitted of the charge.[93]

There have also been a number of cases in Canada involving the prosecution or investigation of doctors for bringing about the deaths of their patients. One of the few Canadian cases involving the prosecution of a doctor for having helped a patient to die was the prosecution of Dr Ernest Pedley in 1973 for the attempted murder of his cancer-stricken wife. Dr Pedley entered a plea of guilty to attempted murder. He was subsequently convicted and a sentence of 6 months imprisonment was handed down.[94] More recently, a doctor from Ontario, Dr Alberto De La Rocha, has been prosecuted for administering a lethal injection to a seriously ill cancer patient who had requested that the ventilator which sustained her breathing be removed. Dr De La Rocha was initially charged with second-degree murder following the death of a patient after the administration of potassium chloride. He subsequently pleaded guilty to a charge of administering a noxious substance and was given a 3-year suspended sentence. The judge hearing the case, Loukidelis J, took the view that this was not a situation where the doctor had acted with euthanasia in mind when he had administered the potassium chloride—rather, it was a situation where potassium chloride was administered to a patient who had stopped breathing and death was only moments away. In all the circumstances, having regard to the purposes of general deterrence and the need to act in the best interests of society, he felt

---

[91] See also Brahams, D., 'Euthanasia: Doctor Convicted of Attempted Murder' (1992) 340 *Lancet* 783 where she suggests that in comparison with the sentences imposed against doctors in a number of recent convictions for criminal recklessness (6 months, suspended), the sentence against Cox was unduly harsh.

[92] *R* v. *Adams* (unreported). See Palmer, H., 'Dr Adams' Trial for Murder' (1957) *Crim.LRev.* 365; *R* v. *Lodwig* (unreported) *The Times*, 16 March 1990. These cases are dealt with in detail below, in the context of the discussion with respect to palliative drugs which hasten death.

[93] In *R* v. *Adams* the defendant was found not guilty after a very favourable direction from the judge, and in *R* v. *Lodwig* (above n. 92) the prosecution did not offer any evidence against the defendant at his trial. See further pp. 172–7 below.

[94] Parker, G., 'You Are a Child of the Universe: You Have a Right to be Here' (1977) 7 *Manitoba LRev.* 151, 165.

that it was unnecessary to order a period of incarceration.[95] In subsequent developments, the Ontario College of Physicians and Surgeons Disciplinary Committee imposed a light penalty, giving Dr Alberto De La Rocha the opportunity to avoid a 90-day suspension by writing a guideline on how to withdraw life-support from terminally ill patients.

In a number of other Canadian cases doctors have been investigated, and in some instances reprimanded for their conduct in assisting patients to die, but no prosecution has proceeded. In June 1992, there were reports of a Canadian case in which a Quebec doctor helped a patient suffering from AIDS to die. The doctor was reprimanded by the Disciplinary Committee of the Quebec Corporation of Physicians, but was not recommended for prosecution.[96] A similar investigation was undertaken of a North Vancouver physician, Dr Peter Graff, in respect of the death of two of his patients who had allegedly died from excessive doses of morphine.[97] The coroner and the College of Physicians and Surgeons of British Columbia conducted separate investigations and both concluded that the doses given greatly exceeded what was necessary to relieve the patients' pain and discomfort. However the College decided not to discipline Dr Graff formally and the Royal Canadian Mounted Police, which also investigated the deaths, decided against laying charges. There have also been reports of similar instance of non-prosecution of a doctor in Manitoba, with prosecutors having apparently decided not to lay criminal charges against a doctor who gave his terminally ill patient multiple doses of morphine.[98] Also of note are the Crown Counsel Prosecution Guidelines which have been developed in the province of British Columbia[99] which specifically address the issues of active euthanasia and doctor-assisted suicide.[100] These guidelines specify additional matters to be taken into account in such cases and make it clear that a prosecution will only be approved where there is a substantial likelihood of conviction and the public interest requires a prosecution. The guidelines

[95] Special Senate Committee on Euthanasia and Assisted Suicide, *Of Life and Death,* above n. 10, A-80–A-83.

[96] Ibid., A-29.

[97] Note, 'BC Physicians Wary of Discussing Experiences Concerning Dying Patients' (1993) 148 CMAJ 1366; Special Senate Committee on Euthanasia and Assisted Suicide, *Of Life and Death*, above n. 10, A-29.

[98] Note, 'Manitoba Doctor Not Charged in the ALS Death' (1994) Vol. 11 No. 2 *Dying with Dignity Newsletter* 8. It is difficult to determine from the brief report that is available on this case whether this was in fact a case of euthanasia or the administration of drugs for the relief of pain and other symptoms. For discussion of this latter issue see pp. 170–84 below.

[99] It should be noted that whilst there is a federal Criminal Code applying in Canada, the administration of justice (including the decision whether charges should be laid) falls within the responsibility of the provinces.

[100] For coverage, see Special Senate Committee on Euthanasia and Assisted Suicide, *Of Life and Death*, above. n. 10, Appendix 1 (A-59–A-63). It should be noted that whilst these guidelines are clearly intended to apply to doctors who assist their patients to die, they potentially apply in all cases where a police report to Crown Counsel reveals that a person motivated by compassion for the deceased participated in causing a death.

also stipulate that in such cases, charging decisions are to be made at the most senior level (Regional Crown Counsel in consultation with the Director of Policy and Legal Services).

Whilst there have been no recorded cases in Australia involving the prosecution of a doctor for having performed active voluntary euthanasia or assisted the suicide of a patient, this dearth of prosecutions cannot be taken as evidence that such cases have not in fact occurred. It is far more likely to be evidence of the invisible nature of such acts[101] and/or the unwillingness of prosecuting authorities to institute proceedings against members of the medical profession. The extent of this reluctance to prosecute has recently been illustrated in the State of Victoria: although seven Victorian doctors have openly admitted that they have assisted terminally ill patients to die,[102] no charges have been laid against them.[103] As a result, the conclusion has already been drawn in some quarters that a situation of *de facto* non-prosecution has been reached in that state.[104]

Perhaps the most significant point to emerge from the foregoing analysis is the sparsity of cases involving the prosecution of doctors for either administering active euthanasia or assisting the suicide of their patients. This contrasts markedly with the available information regarding doctors' practices which strongly suggests that a not insignificant proportion of doctors have performed active voluntary euthanasia or assisted the suicide of their patients. A number of informed suggestions can be put forward by way of possible explanation for this dearth of cases involving prosecutions of doctors. First of all, as noted earlier, in view of the present criminality of active euthanasia and assisted suicide, doctors' involvement in these practices is understandably covert and, therefore, unlikely to come to the attention of others. Furthermore, although such cases are widely known to occur, there appears to be a distinct reluctance by the police and prosecuting authorities to become involved in this area. However, once a matter comes to the attention of the police and prosecuting authorities through the reporting of others or even by the doctor's own admission, the authorities may have little choice but to proceed with a prosecution, provided there is sufficient evidence upon which a reasonable jury, properly instructed, could convict. From an evidentiary point of view, one of the main practical difficulties in securing a murder conviction against a doctor for having killed a patient by administering a lethal dose or by other means is proving that the death of the deceased was caused by the act of the doctor. Particular difficulties are likely to arise in circumstances where the patient was in a terminal condition and had already been receiving large doses of drugs over

---

[101] Crane, D., 'Dying and Its Dilemma as a Field of Research' in Brim, O., *et al.* (eds.), *The Dying Patient* (New York, 1970) 303, 306.
[102] See above, n. 55.
[103] *Australian*, 28 March 1995.   [104] e.g. *Weekend Australian* 1–2 April 1995.

an extended period of time. In these circumstances it may be very difficult for the prosecution to establish that the doctor had caused the patient's death.[105] Lack of evidence may, therefore, be a ground for not instituting, or not proceeding with a prosecution against a doctor. Where a prosecution does proceed, judging from the few cases which have come before the courts, the prospect of securing a murder conviction against a doctor for administering active voluntary euthanasia in a *bona fide* medical context seems fairly remote. Almost invariably, doctors have escaped criminal liability even though, in many instances, the evidence has clearly indicated criminal activity. As the few reported cases have shown, juries are often reluctant to convict doctors who have acted *bona fide* and out of compassionate motives, and are therefore likely to seize upon any defect in the evidence as a reason for acquitting the defendant. Indeed, juries have tended to acquit in circumstances where the evidence and the judge's direction leave them with no legal reason for doing so.[106] It is in fact quite remarkable that the *Cox* case in the United Kingdom was the first time a doctor has been convicted for having taken steps to end the life of a suffering patient.[107]

III. DISCREPANCIES BETWEEN THE CRIMINAL LAW PRINCIPLES AND THE LAW IN PRACTICE

It is evident from the foregoing analysis that a glaring gap exists between the law in theory and the law in practice. Although questions of motive are strictly speaking irrelevant for the purposes of establishing criminal liability, in practice, they will often be decisive in determining the outcome of cases of active euthanasia and doctor-assisted suicide. Without disputing that such cases ought to be dealt with leniently, it is submitted that there are certain fundamental problems with the present legal position which tolerates serious inconsistencies between legal principles and the law in practice. First, there is the concern that because the administration of the law depends to such a large extent on intangible considerations of sympathy, there is no guaranteed consistency of application, thus raising serious questions regarding justice and equality before the law. The second problem is that

---

[105] e.g. *People* v. *Sander* see above n. 67; *People* v. *Montemarano* see above n. 70. Moreover, in practice, difficulties may be encountered in finding a doctor who is willing to give evidence against another doctor, particularly in criminal proceedings.

[106] Perhaps the most remarkable case is that of Dr Sander in which the jury acquitted the defendant even though he had entered on the medical record of the deceased notes to the effect that he had deliberately injected air into the vein of the patient and that the patient had died a short time later; *People* v. *Sander*, above n. 67.

[107] That is, leaving aside cases where the doctor had a familial connection with the deceased and had pleaded guilty to the charge; e.g. *People* v. *Hassman*, above n. 75.

the enormous discrepancies between the law in theory and the law in practice threaten to undermine public confidence in the law and bring it into disrepute. Further, there is the problem that the present *ad hoc* approach fails to establish any legal precedent by which medical decisions in the context of terminal patients can be made and evaluated. A related concern is that there is a very real risk that the illegality and secrecy associated with the practice of active voluntary euthanasia tends to undermine the rights of patients. Separate attention will now be given to each of these above concerns.

A. No Guaranteed Consistency in the Application of the Law

As we have seen, in the majority of cases where doctors have been charged with either active voluntary euthanasia or doctor-assisted suicide, they have been treated with exceptional leniency. The tendency has been for doctors to plead not guilty and for the jury to acquit the doctor of the charges. However, the fact that the administration of the law has been lenient in some cases is no guarantee that a doctor would not be prosecuted and convicted of murder or assisted suicide. Whilst in the majority of cases, doctors have escaped serious criminal liability, there have also been cases in which the criminal law has been much more rigorously enforced. The uncertainty of the present position has been acutely highlighted by the recent conviction of Dr Cox in the United Kingdom for the attempted murder of one of his patients resulting in the imposition of a custodial sentence. The difficulty is that there are no objective criteria or standards to determine the outcome of such cases. It is a basic principle of justice that like cases should be treated alike. However, as a result of the lack of uniform and objective standards applying in such cases, there is significant potential for unequal application of the law and consequently, a very real likelihood of inconsistency of results, and unfairness being done to some offenders.

B. The Law is Brought into Disrepute

Another problem which stems from the present position is that the wide discrepancy between law and practice threatens to bring the law into disrepute. There are two distinct aspects to this argument. First, notwithstanding the criminal law prohibitions with regard to active voluntary euthanasia and assisted suicide, there can be no doubt that some doctors are involved in these practices. In contrast to family mercy killing cases, where it is unlikely that a killing could pass undetected, the practice of medically administered active euthanasia or doctor-assisted suicide is much less likely to come under legal scrutiny and end up before the courts.[108] To have a situation where it is commonly known that the law is being breached by the medical profession yet breaches are usually ignored or pass unpunished, threatens to bring the law into disrepute.

Turning to the second aspect of the problem, there are also serious discrepancies between law and practice in the actual punishment of offenders. Because the present criminal law principles which treat motive as irrelevant, are widely perceived as being inappropriate, devious means are frequently used to circumvent the full rigour of the criminal law. The motive of the offender is in fact being incorporated into decision-making, but only surreptitiously through the use of certain fictions or tactics. This can result in serious distortion of legal principles and widespread connivance to defeat the application of the criminal law. In most of the cases which have come before the courts, doctors have tended to plead not guilty and rely on arguments based on lack of causation or lack of the necessary intention to kill and these arguments have usually been accepted by the jury, often contrary to the weight of the evidence.

The criticism is that the use of such fictions represents a blatant abuse of the law, and when occurring on a regular basis, suggests that the current criminal prohibitions do not reflect common views of reprehensibility. This, in turn, indicates the need to close the gap and bring the overt culture as expressed by the law in accord with the covert culture, as expressed in what people do.[109] Some commentators have in fact stressed the advantages of this gap between law and practice arguing that it preserves the legal prohibition against killing, maintains the deterrent affect of the law, but at the same time provides mechanisms in the criminal justice system to allow for flexibility in the treatment of offenders.[110] However, this view disregards the serious problems which the present hypocrisy produces.

C. Lack of Legal Precedent and Medical Guidance

As a result of the serious discrepancies which exist between the legal principles and the law in practice, there is no established legal precedent with reference to which medical decisions in respect of terminal patients can be made and evaluated.[111] In theory, the medical profession and the

---

[108] See also above regarding the likelihood of the practice being performed in secret and the cause of death being readily concealed.

[109] Gurney, E., 'Is there a Right to Die? A Study of the Law of Euthanasia' (1972) 3 *Cumberland-Samford LRev.* 235, 251.

[110] e.g. Kamisar, 'Some Non-Religious Views Against Proposed Mercy-Killing Legislation', above n. 68; Childress, J., 'Civil Disobedience, Conscientious Objection, and Evasive Noncompliance: A Framework for the Analysis of Illegal Actions in Health Care' (1985) 10 *JMed. & Phil.* 63, 76.

[111] Wilson, J., *Death by Decision* (Philadelphia, 1975) 165.

legal system both reject active voluntary euthanasia and doctor-assisted suicide as acceptable medical practices, yet we know that not infrequently, these practices occur. Furthermore, because active voluntary euthanasia and assisting patient suicide are criminal, doctors will inevitably feel inhibited in discussing these practices with their colleagues in an open and honest way,[112] and consequently will not be able to benefit from criticism or support from their professional peers with regard to their involvement in these practices. This, in turn, jeopardizes the quality of medical decision-making in this area.

D. Patients' Rights are Undermined

One matter of particular concern is that the present situation threatens to undermine the rights and interests of patients. There are a number of possible facets to this argument. One argument is that the situation is discriminatory in that the present criminality of active voluntary euthanasia and assisted suicide inevitably deters some doctors from engaging in these practices.[113] As a result, there is inconsistency of treatment; some patients will have the benefit of practices which are denied to others. It could also be argued that the criminal law prohibitions may in some cases prevent doctors from acceding to a patient's request although they may believe it would be appropriate to do so. A more fundamental concern is that there is a very real risk of abuse if the law condones what is an unregulated practice. Because of the present criminality of the practice of active euthanasia, doctors may engage in the practice without necessarily consulting the patient, motivated by benevolent paternalism and in the belief that they are acting in the patient's best interests. Indeed, if we examine the few cases of medically administered euthanasia which have come before the courts, it is by no means clear that the doctors' actions in these cases were performed at the request of the patient.[114] There is also some evidence from surveys of the medical profession that active euthanasia is not always administered at the patient's request.[115] For doctors to take these decisions upon themselves clearly undermines patient self-determination and the patient's right not to be killed without his or her consent. There is, therefore, the possibility that

[112] See the findings of the study by Back, et al., 'Physician-Assisted Suicide and Euthanasia in Washington State: Patient Requests and Physician Responses', above n. 20, at 923, 924.

[113] See, for example, the survey of Victorian doctors undertaken by Kuhse and Singer, 'Doctors' Practices and Attitudes Regarding Voluntary Euthanasia', above n. 26, at 624 where they note that for a significant proportion of the respondents who had not acted upon a patient's request for active euthanasia, the illegality of the practice had been a factor (65%).

[114] e.g. *People* v. *Sander* see above n. 67.

[115] See Stevens and Hassan, 'Management of Death, Dying and Euthanasia: Attitudes and Practices of Medical Practitioners in South Australia', above n. 28, at 43 where it was found that in approximately half of the cases where doctors had taken active steps to bring about the death of a patient, they had not received a request from the patient.

the present state of the law may in effect be sanctioning such killings without providing adequate protection to unwilling victims.[116] If active euthanasia is in fact being practised, it is imperative that these decisions are based upon the patient's choice rather than the idiosyncratic views of individual doctors.

IV. PROBLEMS WITH THE CHARACTERIZATION OF CERTAIN ASPECTS OF MEDICAL PRACTICE

Other discrepancies between strict legal theory and the law in practice arise in respect of the characterization of certain aspects of medical practice. For the purposes of the present analysis, attention will focus on the practices of withdrawing life-support measures and the administration of drugs for the relief of pain and other symptoms in the knowledge that they are likely to cause death. It will be shown that on strict legal principles, these practices would potentially attract criminal liability for murder, but they are in fact characterized in such a way as to avoid the possibility of criminal liability.

In the preceding chapter, consideration has already been given to the question whether a doctor's compliance with a patient's refusal of treatment could, in principle, amount to assisting suicide, and to the accepted characterization of this form of medical practice.[117] For the purposes of the present analysis, suffice it to say that that is another area where every attempt has been made to interpret the law in such a way as to avoid doctors incurring criminal liability.

A. Withdrawal of Life-Support

As noted earlier, doctors may, in a variety of circumstances, be involved in the removal of life-support from a patient, either at the direction of a patient who has decision-making capacity or in respect of a patient lacking such capacity in circumstances where this medical treatment is no longer medically indicated. For the purposes of this discussion it will be assumed that, as a matter of causation, the relevant conduct in withdrawing life-support did, in fact, cause death to occur at the time that it did, and further, that the doctor either intended to cause the patient's death or was aware that the patient would die at an earlier time than he or she would have if artificial life-support was continued.[118]

---

[116] Kutner, L., 'Due Process of Euthanasia: The Living Will, A Proposal' (1969) 44 *Ind LRev.* 542.

[117] See pp. 65–80 above.

[118] For consideration of the necessary ingredients to establish liability for murder see pp. 13–14 above.

Although it is fairly commonplace for doctors to discontinue life-support, and this is generally accepted to be proper medical practice in appropriate circumstances, it is far from certain that this practice is lawful. Significantly, there is considerable uncertainty on the part of the medical profession and the public generally as to the legality of this practice. In order to determine the legality of conduct involving the withdrawal of life-support it is necessary to ascertain whether this conduct is in law an act terminating life or an omission to provide further life-sustaining therapy. This characterization is vital, since, as outlined in an earlier chapter,[119] the criminal law attributes a different status to 'acts' as distinct from 'omissions' which can have significant legal implications in respect of the legal consequences of such conduct.

The approach of the criminal law to 'acts' which cause death is very clear; they are unconditionally prohibited,[120] regardless of the relationship between the defendant and his or her victim, or whether the victim had requested that he or she be killed. If, however, the withdrawal of life-support equipment is characterized as an 'omission', the analysis proceeds more flexibly[121] and depends on whether the doctor was in all the circumstances under a duty to provide medical treatment. In the absence of a legal duty to provide treatment a doctor would not be criminally liable for his or her omission.

Although the characterization of withdrawal of life-support as either an 'act' or an 'omission' is of central importance in determining the legality of that conduct, there has been relatively little consideration of how this conduct should be characterized. Indeed, because the practice is widely known to occur, without any question of criminal liability arising, it appears to be frequently assumed that this conduct must be an 'omission' in law and therefore lawful.

On the basis of the earlier analysis of acts and omissions in Chapter 1,[122] it would appear that the withdrawal of life-support constitutes an 'act' in the legal sense, since turning off the switch of a ventilator,[123] or physically removing the tubes supplying the patient with artificial nutrition and hydration, clearly involves a 'willed bodily movement' or a 'voluntary muscular contraction'.[124] This conclusion does, of course, have significant legal rami-

---

[119] See pp. 23–5 above.

[120] Fletcher, G., 'Prolonging Life' (1967) 42 *Wash.L Rev.* 999, 1012.

[121] Ibid. at 1006.

[122] See pp. 14–15, 23 above.

[123] In practice, the withdrawal of artificial ventilation may be accompanied by the administration of drugs intended to make the patient comfortable (Schneiderman, L. and Spragg, R., 'Ethical Decisions in Discontinuing Mechanical Ventilation' (1988) 318 *New Eng.J Med.* 984, 987) and this clearly involves additional acts quite apart from turning off life-support.

[124] Since ventilators and other similar forms of artificial life-support run on electricity, once a patient is placed on such a machine, a bodily movement is required to turn the machine off, unless the machine is specially designed otherwise. However, with artificial feeding, it is possible to envisage circumstances where such feeding could be terminated without any bodily

fications. Leaving aside for the moment policy considerations, it would mean that the withdrawal of life-support resulting in the patient's death could potentially expose doctors to criminal liability for murder.[125]

The debate

The question of whether turning off of a life-support system should be classified as an 'act' or an 'omission' has been hotly debated by a number of legal commentators.[126] Whilst there is some disagreement on the matter, the consensus appears to be that withdrawal of life-support from terminal patients should be considered an omission rather than a positive act. This is, perhaps, a predictable result, if one considers the serious consequences which the contrary view would entail. It has already been observed that removal of life-support is a common and widely accepted medical practice. There is, therefore, a natural reluctance to come to the conclusion that doctors performing this practice may be committing murder. Consequently, there has been strong motivation to interpret the actions as something other than acts of killing and every attempt has been made to justify the view that this behaviour constitutes an 'omission', not an 'act'.

Fletcher's classification: 'causing death' versus 'permitting death to occur'

George Fletcher[127] is one of the principal contributors to this debate. He rejects a strict legalistic approach to this issue, which would equate the conduct of a doctor in turning off life-support equipment with that of a hired gunman killing in cold blood and urges that a more sensitive interpretation of the law be adopted. Fletcher proposes that the turning off of a life-support system, such as a mechanical respirator, should be classified as an omission, not an act, and he seeks to justify this proposition on semantic grounds. Whilst acknowledging that turning a respirator off requires physical movement, he argues that this should not be the controlling factor.

movement; for example not refilling the bottle supplying artificial nutrition and hydration. More typically, however, the withdrawal of artificial feeding would involve the removal of artificial feeding tubes from the patient. So, whilst it is conceivable that the withdrawal of artificial feeding could be done by omission, for the purposes of the present discussion, it is assumed that it is generally done in a way which does involve a bodily movement.

[125] In circumstances where the patient has decision-making capacity and has requested that life-support be removed, the patient's conduct could possibly be characterized as suicidal (for further discussion, see pp. 65–73 above). This in turn raises the possibility of the doctor's liability for assisting the suicide of the patient. It will be argued, however, that where the doctor turns off life-support this is an *act* directly connected with the patient's death and the appropriate charge would technically therefore be for murder (assuming the necessary *mens rea* can be established) rather than assisting suicide. An argument will be developed later in this chapter to overcome the conclusion that a doctor would necessarily be liable in these circumstances.

[126] Fletcher, 'Prolonging Life', above Ch. 1 n. 13, 1005–14; Williams, 'Euthanasia', above n. 33, at 20–1; *Textbook of Criminal Law*, Ch. 1 n. 5, at 279–83; Kennedy, 'Switching Off Life Support Machines: The Legal Implications', Above Ch. 1 n. 154.

[127] Fletcher, 'Prolonging Life', above Ch. 1 n. 13.

Instead, he proposes a test for the classification of acts and omissions based on the common usage of the terms 'causing harm' and 'permitting harm to occur'.[128] Fletcher contends that we are equipped with 'linguistic sensitivity' for the distinction between these terms which reflects a common sense perception of reality, and that we should employ this sensitivity in classifying the conduct of a doctor in turning off life-support. If a patient is beyond recovery and on the verge of death, turning off a respirator would normally be regarded as 'permitting a patient to die' rather than 'causing death'.[129] In these circumstances, the decision to withdraw life-support is equivalent to not employing it in the first place. On this basis, he is able to conclude that turning off a respirator should be classified as an omission, notwithstanding that it involves some bodily movement.[130] And whilst he concedes that some omissions may cause harm, he argues that in the context of withdrawal of life-sustaining therapy, the law must focus on the doctor/patient relationship to define legal consequences, allowing customary standards to be the controlling factor.

Clearly, however, Fletcher's proposed method of classification, based on the common usage of the terms 'causing harm' and 'permitting harm to occur', depends, to a large extent, on the condition of the patient. He acknowledges as much by his reference to 'a patient beyond recovery and on the verge of death' and his comments to the effect that one would baulk at saying that turning off a respirator in these circumstances is causing death. It logically follows that in some circumstances, turning off a respirator, or other form of life-support, *does* amount to 'causing death' rather than 'permitting death to occur' and would accordingly be classified as an 'act', not an 'omission'. For example, if someone turned off a respirator which had maintained a fully conscious and reasonably healthy poliomyelitis patient for several years and which could have continued to do so for years to come, one could quite naturally describe such conduct as 'causing death'.[131] It may, therefore, be wondered whether such a variable test could operate satisfactorily in practice, particularly where the final determination appears to involve a qualitative judgment as to the condition and prognosis of the patient. In the interests of certainty and consistency in the application

---

[128] Ibid. at 1007.   [129] Ibid.

[130] Ibid. at 1012–104. For criticism of Fletcher's reasoning see Skegg, P., 'The Termination of Life-Support Measures and the Law of Murder', above Ch. 1 n. 9, at 430–2 where he argues that it does not accommodate those circumstances where the conduct in question could naturally be described in terms of *either* permitting or causing death. Skegg asserts that whilst it is perfectly natural to speak of the withdrawal of artificial respiration from a patient who is beyond recovery and on the verge of death as 'permitting death', many people would probably consider it no less natural to speak of such conduct as 'causing death to occur at the time when it did'.

[131] Skegg, 'The Termination of Life-Support Measures and the Law of Murder', above Ch. 1 n. 9, at 430. Moreover, according to Skegg, there are some situations which are capable of being classified as *either* causing death or permitting death to occur.

of legal principles, it could be argued that the conduct of turning off life-support must be uniformly classified as *either* an act or an omission, and should not be determined by reference to external considerations.

Williams' reference to 'the substance of the matter'

Glanville Williams[132] is also of the view that turning off a respirator is an omission but he justifies this conclusion on different grounds. The essence of Williams' argument is that the moral and legal rule which distinguishes between acts and omissions must be interpreted in accordance with 'the substance of the matter'.[133] He accepts that giving up trying to keep a patient alive may involve positive action, in the sense of willed movement, for example, disconnecting a respirator that is keeping the patient alive. He argues, however, that this need not be regarded as an 'act' for the purposes of the moral and legal rule, because *in substance* it merely puts into effect a decision to take no further steps. To justify his view that stopping a respirator is not, in substance, an act of killing, Williams examines the manner in which such machines operate. He argues that if a respirator only worked as long as the doctor turned a handle and the doctor stopped turning, he would be regarded as merely omitting to save the patient's life. Alternatively, if the respirator worked electrically but was made to shut itself off every 24 hours, a deliberate failure to restart would be an omission. From this premise, he argues that it can make no moral difference that respirators are made to run continuously and therefore need to be stopped. Thus, he concludes, turning the respirator off is not a positive act of killing the patient but rather a decision to let nature take its course.

On the basis of the test put forward by Williams, the classification of conduct as an act or an omission would be made by the court on a case by case basis, according to 'the substance of the matter'. There are in fact, distinct similarities between this approach and the test proposed by Fletcher which requires consideration of whether the conduct in question can be said to have 'caused death' or merely 'permitted death to occur'. Both would ultimately require a determination by the court, based on the particular facts of the case, and the court's inquiry would inevitably turn on the question of whether it was, in the circumstances, appropriate to withdraw treatment.[134]

Williams' approach is open to the same objection as Fletcher's arguments, namely that identical conduct (that is, physically turning off or withdrawing life-support), could be classified either as an act or an omis-

---

[132] *Textbook of Criminal Law*, above Ch. 1 n. 5, at 282–3; 'Euthanasia', above n. 33, at 20–1.
[133] 'Euthanasia', above n. 33, at 20–1.
[134] This determination will depend on the condition and prognosis of the patient and, as Williams acknowledges (*Textbook of Criminal Law*, above Ch. 1 n. 5, at 283), this approach leaves it very much up to the individual doctor to determine whether life has any value for the patient.

sion, depending on the surrounding circumstances. On Williams' analysis, if
life-support is turned off at the request of the patient or pursuant to a *bona
fide* medical decision to cease further treatment, a court would be likely to
find that any physical acts involved should be disregarded, because in
substance, the medical staff were merely putting into effect a decision to
take no further steps. Where, however, a machine is turned off for other
than *bona fide* medical reasons, for example, in order to avoid a night shift
attendance on the patient, the conduct could be regarded as, in substance,
an act of killing.

In view of the general criminal law principles which continue to uphold
the acts/omissions dichotomy, there is, understandably strong motivation
for preferring to classify 'turning off' as an omission rather than an act so as
to avoid the spectre of doctors incurring criminal liability. Notwithstanding
the commendable motives of legal commentators and jurists in their attempts to justify this position, there remains a fundamental difficulty with
this approach. Skegg[135] has raised the objection that this classification only
works satisfactorily in circumstances where there is an appropriate duty
relationship between the patient and the person who switches off the machine and that in the absence of such a relationship, serious difficulties arise.
Taking this reasoning to its logical conclusion, it would allow strangers to
interfere and kill the patient by turning off life-support equipment; if the
removal of life-support is held to be an omission, the stranger would commit no crime since he or she was under no legally recognized duty to act. A
possible answer to this objection, raised by both Williams and Skegg, is that
the withdrawal of life-support should only be classified as an omission in
circumstances where there is a legally recognized duty relationship between
the parties. So, if an intruder who owes no duty to the patient switches off
a life-support system, his conduct will be treated as an act of murder.[136] But,
as Skegg acknowledges, this explanation is open to the objection that it is
undesirable that the same physical movements should be classified either as
an act or an omission, depending on who it was that switched off the
machine.[137] As was suggested earlier, in the interests of certainty and uni-

---

[135] Skegg, 'The Termination of Life-Support Measures and the Law of Murder', above Ch.
1 n. 9, at 432.

[136] Williams, *Textbook of Criminal Law*, above Ch. 1 n. 5, at 282 where he takes this
reasoning further, arguing that the intruder has no responsibility for or authority in respect of
the patient—he or she does not take part in the decision whether to continue medical treatment or not, so what he or she does is a positive act of intervention. An alternative analysis is
that where an unauthorized person interferes with the treatment of a patient they pull onto
themselves a duty of care such that they could be liable for an omission to act. It is interesting
to note in this context, that a murder charge has recently been laid against a male nurse in the
Australian State of Victoria for allegedly turning off a dying woman's life-support machine:
Australian, 9 May 1996.

[137] Skegg, 'The Termination of Life-Support Measures and the Law of Murder', above Ch.
1 n. 9, at 432.

formity in the application of the law, it is important that the classification of acts and omissions be determined without reference to what are arguably peripheral considerations.

Kennedy's analysis

Not all commentators support these attempts to justify the practice of turning off life-support systems by classifying turning off as an omission. Kennedy, for example, rejects this approach as 'elaborate and unsatisfactory'.[138] In his view, to describe the turning off of life-support as an omission does some considerable violence to ordinary English usage and represents an attempt to solve the problem by logic-chopping. Kennedy argues that in circumstances where a patient is dependent on life-support, and the doctor knows that the patient will die if the life-support measures are removed, in determining the liability of the doctor in withdrawing life-support, a distinction must be drawn between: (i) the situation where the patient requests that further support be terminated; and (ii) where life-support is turned off without the consent of the patient. In the former case, a doctor's compliance with the patient's request would not attract criminal liability; not because it is an omission to treat rather than an act of killing, but on a number of other interrelated grounds. First, he argues, there is the libertarian premise that a person's position should not be irremediably worsened by another's conduct. Turning off life-support permits other factors to intercede and thrusts the decision back on the patient. Secondly, he argues in favour of what he refers to as the 'red light' rule; that it is better to have a clear, albeit crude, general rule condemning all acts of killing and inviting leniency in cases of justifiable transgression. Thirdly, from an evidentiary point of view, he argues that there is a significant distinction between the termination of life-support and other forms of active killing such as stabbing which are potentially more open to abuse. Finally, he suggests that since a patient requesting termination of life-support is a relatively rare phenomenon, the criminal law can respond to it as a tolerable and justifiable exception to basic criminal law rules. In the second situation, however, where life-support is intentionally terminated without the knowledge and the consent of the dependent patient, the conduct clearly amounts to murder regardless of the actor's motive.

In effect, Kennedy avoids characterizing the relevant conduct of withdrawing life-support as either an 'act' or an 'omission'. He is, however, at pains to point out that the conduct we are considering involves *discontinuation* of treatment, and that there is an important distinction between a request by a patient that treatment be discontinued which is complied with

[138] 'Switching Off Life-Support Machines: The Legal Implications', above Ch. 1 n. 154, at 444.

on the one hand, and a request by a patient that someone stabs him or her to death which is complied with on the other. Whilst the former does not, on his analysis, attract liability, the latter does.[139]

The truth of the matter is that the acts/omissions dichotomy presents a real dilemma in cases where the discontinuation of treatment involves a willed bodily movement. Clearly, steps taken to turn off artificial ventilation or remove artificial feeding tubes are performed pursuant to a decision to omit further treatment in respect of a patient (either at the patient's direction, or where a decision is made in respect of a patient who lacks decision-making capacity) and it is beyond doubt, that in some circumstances, this course of action will be appropriate. This does not, however, alter the fact that technically speaking, these various forms of withdrawal of medical care involve 'acts' in the sense of 'willed bodily movements' or 'muscular contractions'. The position is, perhaps, clearest in relation to the issue of removal of life-support equipment; as one commentator has argued, once life-support equipment has begun to operate on a patient, it is fallacious to argue that a cessation of such treatment is a mere omission and not an act in the legal sense.[140] The doctor must physically turn the switch to the off position and this entails positive action.[141]

The approach of the courts: characterization in practice

It is, in all the circumstances, not surprising that the courts, when faced with difficult questions of characterizing medical conduct, have generally glossed over the issue or have simply assumed that withdrawal of treatment constitutes an omission, notwithstanding that it may involve some positive action.

Since the issue of withdrawal of life-support has been most frequently litigated in the USA, most of the relevant cases come from that jurisdiction. In a number of US cases the courts have upheld the right of a patient to refuse treatment, even in circumstances where that involves having ventilators or artificial feeding tubes disconnected.[142] However, these cases have generally been non-criminal in nature, so the question of classification of

---

[139] Although not expressly stated by Kennedy, a convincing way of distinguishing between discontinuance of treatment and other forms of active intervention such as stabbing or the administration of a lethal injection performed at the request of the patient, is by relying on the patient's right to refuse treatment and the fact that a doctor may lawfully act on the patient's request—indeed is obliged to do so, if he or she is to avoid liability for battery. This argument is developed further below.

[140] Cannon, W., 'The Right to Die' (1970) 7 *Hous.LRev.* 654, 659.

[141] For other commentators who are of the view that turning off life-support is an act, not an omission, see, for example, Sharpe, G., *The Law and Medicine in Canada*, 2nd edn. (Toronto, 1987) 303; Lanham, D., 'The Right to Choose to Die with Dignity' (1990) 14 *Crim.LawJ* 401, 428.

[142] e.g. *Satz* v. *Perlmutter* 362 So.2d 160 (1978); *Bartling* v. *Superior Court* 163 Cal.App. 3d 186 (1984); *Brophy* v. *New England Sinai Hospital, Inc.* 497 NE 2d 626 (1986).

withdrawal of life-support which is relevant to the question of criminal liability has only been indirectly addressed, if at all.[143]

A notable exception was the case of *Barber* v. *Superior Court*[144] involving a criminal prosecution of two doctors for murder and conspiracy to commit murder for their conduct in removing life-support equipment and intravenous tubes supplying nutrition and hydration to a dying patient. Quite clearly, therefore, determination of whether the doctors' conduct in removing the life-support equipment and feeding tubes was an 'act' or an 'omission' was central to the doctors' criminal liability. Although the conduct in question involved positive action in the sense of 'willed bodily movements', the court nevertheless held that the cessation of these life-support measures was not an affirmative act but rather a withdrawal or omission of further treatment. The approach taken by the court seems to be akin to that suggested by Williams that account must be taken of 'the substance of the matter'. The court was of the view that:

Even though these support devices are, to a degree, 'self propelled', each pulsation of the respirator or each drop of fluid introduced in the patient's body by intravenous feeding devices is comparable to a manually administered injection or item of medication. Hence 'disconnecting' of the mechanical devices is comparable to withholding the manually administered injection or medication.[145]

Thus, the court held that for the purpose of assessing a doctor's liability, withdrawal of life-support equipment or intravenous tubes should be regarded as equivalent to initially withholding the procedures. Since the conduct could be characterized as an omission, the legality of the conduct turned on the question of the scope of the doctors' duty and the doctors were held not to be liable.

In more recent years, the question of characterization of withdrawal of life-support and the legality of this practice has also arisen in other jurisdictions, including the United Kingdom in the case of *Airedale NHS Trust* v. *Bland*[146] which was discussed at length in an earlier chapter.[147] One of the arguments advanced by the Official Solicitor in that case was that the discontinuance of the existing regime of artificial feeding constituted positive acts of commission intended to lead to the death of Anthony Bland and were therefore criminal. The House of Lords, however, rejected this characterization, holding that the discontinuation of life-support should be categorized as an omission rather than an act.

---

[143] One explanation for the failure of the courts in the USA to address this issue is the emphasis which has been given in many cases to the patient's constitutional right to refuse treatment which has led to an assumption by the courts that doctors would not incur criminal or civil liability for taking steps in facilitating the exercise of that right: e.g. *In re Quinlan* 355 A2d 647 (1976).

[144] *Barber* v. *Superior Court* 195 Cal.Rptr. 484 (1983).

[145] Ibid.   [146] [1993] 1 All ER 821.   [147] See pp. 38–40, 48–9 above.

Lord Goff explained the situation in the following terms:

It is true that it may be difficult to describe what the doctor actually does as an omission, for example where he takes some positive steps to bring the life support to an end. But discontinuation of life support is, for present purposes, no different from not initiating life support in the first place. In each case, the doctor is simply allowing his patient to die in the sense that he is desisting from taking a step which might, in certain circumstances, prevent his patient from dying as a result of the pre-existing condition; and as a matter of general principle an omission such as this will not be unlawful unless it constitutes a breach of the duty to the patient.[148]

His Lordship then went on to differentiate this situation involving conduct by a doctor from that of an interloper who maliciously switches off a life-support machine. In his view, these circumstances need to be distinguished because, although the interloper may perform exactly the same act as the doctor who continues life-support, his doing so constitutes interference with the life-prolonging treatment then being administered by the doctor. Accordingly, his Lordship reasoned, whereas the doctor, in discontinuing life-support is simply allowing his patient to die of a pre-existing condition, the interloper is actively intervening to stop the doctor from prolonging the patient's life, and such conduct cannot possibly be categorized as an omission.

Other members of the House of Lords were in agreement that the conduct proposed in respect of Anthony Bland should be classified as an omission. For example, Lord Browne-Wilkinson, whilst acknowledging that the removal of the naso-gastric tube is undoubtedly a positive act, similar to switching off a ventilator in the case of a patient whose life is being sustained by artificial ventilation stated: 'in neither case should the act be classified as positive, since to do so would be to introduce intolerably fine distinctions'.[149]

One of the difficulties with the approach of the House of Lords on this issue is that the characterization of the conduct apparently depends on who is involved: if a doctor discontinues life-support, albeit doing certain positive acts, that should be characterized as an omission; if life-support is discontinued by some intermeddling third party, that would constitute an act. As was suggested earlier in the course of evaluating the leading commentators' contribution to this debate, it is unsatisfactory that the same physical movements should be classified differently, depending on who it is that discontinues the life-support. That there are inherent difficulties in the current legal analysis was in fact acknowledged by Lord Mustill. After reaffirming the crucial distinction between acts and omissions—the distinction between taking active steps to terminate a patient's life and the situation as in the *Bland* case, where a course of conduct involving the

---

[148] See above n. 146, at 867–8.   [149] Ibid. at 881. See also Lord Mustill at 894–5.

withdrawal of treatment has the aim of terminating the patient's life, his Lordship stated:

The acute unease which I feel about adopting this way through the legal and ethical maze is I believe due in an important part to the sensation that however much the terminologies may differ the ethical status of the two courses of action is for all relevant purposes indistinguishable. By dismissing this appeal I fear that your Lordships' House may only emphasise the distortions of a legal structure which is already both morally and intellectually misshapen. Still, the law is there and we must take it as it stands.[150]

In addition to these authorities, there have also been a number of cases in which the courts have accepted that doctors have acted properly in withdrawing artificial life-support from brain-damaged patients.[151] Thus, in prosecutions of persons whose conduct had led the victim to be dependent on life-support, the courts have held that the conduct of the doctor in disconnecting life-support did not break the chain of causation between the initial injuries and the death. Although decided in quite a different context, these cases tend to support the view that the withdrawal of life-support is characterized by the courts as an omission to provide further treatment, rather than an act which causes death.

Thus, in cases involving the withdrawal of treatment, for example, disconnecting life-support equipment or the removal of artificial feeding tubes, the courts have generally proceeded on the basis that these are essentially cases of omission notwithstanding that they may entail some positive action. This conclusion is, however, difficult to justify on strict legal principles. The removal of life-support clearly does involve an 'act' in the strict legal sense, and, provided the other necessary requirements are fulfilled, it would *prima facie* constitute murder if the patient's death results.

One of the rare instances where a court has not attempted to characterize the withdrawal of life-support as an omission is the New Zealand case of *Auckland Area Health Board* v. *Attorney-General*[152] (also noted earlier[153]) involving the removal of a ventilatory life-support system from a patient. In this case the attention of the court focused on whether or not this conduct could be justified (either on the basis that there was no duty to continue the life-support or because the doctor had lawful excuse for withdrawing it) rather than on whether or not it constituted an act or an omission. Indeed, in the course of analysis, reference was made to the 'act of discontinuing life-support' yet this description of the conduct was not seen as being decisive of the issue. This case is noteworthy as being an exception to the approach usually taken by the courts to the characterization of the removal

---

[150] See above n. 146, at 885. Note also the comments of Lord Goff at 867. For more general discussion about the moral and ethical equivalence of acts and omissions see pp. 191–4 below.
[151] e.g. *Finlayson* v. *H.M. Advocate* [1978] SLT (Notes) 60; *R* v. *Malcherek* [1981] 1 WLR 690.
[152] [1993] 1 NZLR 235.   [153] See pp. 27, 52–3 above.

of life-support. Significantly, in the landmark decision of the United States Court of Appeals for the Ninth Circuit in the case of *Compassion in Dying v. State of Washington*[154] the majority of the Court, in justifying its decision to declare the state prohibition on assisted suicide unconstitutional as applied to terminally ill competent patients, drew attention to the meaningless distinction between commission and omission. It was described as 'a distinction without a difference now that patients are permitted not only to decline all medical treatment, but to instruct their doctors to terminate whatever treatment, artificial or otherwise, they are receiving. In disconnecting a respirator, or authorising its disconnection, a doctor is unquestionably committing an act; he is taking an active role in bringing about the patient's death'. The significance of this aspect of the court's ruling is that it represents one of the clearest judicial statements highlighting the artificiality of the prevailing approach of the courts in the characterization of the withdrawal of life-support.[155] As we have seen, the court's attention in this case was focused on the constitutionality of the Washington prohibition on assisted suicide, rather than the legal position of doctors involved in the withdrawal of life-support. It is clear, however, that in adopting this analysis, the majority were not suggesting that doctors involved in such conduct should attract criminal liability. Rather, it was assumed that such conduct is lawful, notwithstanding that it involves positive action, and this was an influential factor in the court's reasoning in upholding a liberty interest in physician-assisted suicide for competent, terminally ill adults.

Policy considerations

There are undoubtedly significant policy considerations behind the approach of the courts and the views of many commentators in finding that the withdrawal of life-support is in law an omission, not an act. As noted earlier, the withdrawal of life-support is now fairly well established medical practice, and there is naturally a reluctance to interpret that practice in such a way as to raise the spectre of doctors incurring criminal liability. Indeed, it would seem that every possible effort has been made to interpret the conduct of the doctors in such a way as to sanction their practices and avoid the possibility that this conduct may be criminal.

'Killing' and 'letting die'

Quite apart from its relevance to the issue of criminal liability, the acts/ omissions distinction has been influential in shaping attitudes in relation to the taking of human life. Commentators have seized on this distinction in

---

[154] No. 94-35534 (9th Cir. March 6 1996) (*en banc*). For detailed discussion of this case see pp. 101–15 above.
[155] See also the majority opinion in *Quill* v. *Vacco* No. 60 (2nd Cir. April 2 1996). For discussion of this case see pp. 116–21 above.

order to distinguish between the humane termination of medical care on the one hand and unlawful killing on the other and this reasoning is also reflected in the official statements of some medical organizations with regard to the withholding of treatment and the practice of active euthanasia.[156] Distinctions have been drawn between 'causing death' and 'allowing death to occur' or between 'killing' and 'letting die'. However, euphemisms such as 'letting die' or 'allowing death to occur' are inherently misleading and tend to obscure the real issues. The difficulty is that terms such as 'killing' or 'allowing to die' are often used not only in a descriptive sense, but are also intended to convey normative connotations. For example, 'allowing to die' is often used to communicate approval of the fact that death will occur as distinct from 'killing' which has connotations of illegitimate taking of life.[157] Further, these terms tend to imply a number of invalid assumptions. For instance, these distinctions give rise to the assumption that acts of killing cause death, whereas, omissions to provide treatment, or 'letting die' do not. However, this assumption is clearly unfounded since an omission to provide treatment can in some circumstances be properly regarded as a cause of death. These terms are also objectionable on the grounds that they appear to suggest that only acts of killing are proscribed as unlawful and that omissions to act are legally permissible. This suggestion is also quite unwarranted since the doctor's duty to his or her patient may also give rise to liability for omissions to act.

Although these distinctions between 'killing and letting die' or 'causing death and allowing death' to occur are, to a large extent, based on invalid and unfounded assumptions, they have nevertheless gained considerable currency. In practice, the usage of these terms would tend to encourage the characterization of the withdrawal of life-support as an omission; (that is, a 'letting die' or 'allowing death to occur' as distinct from 'causing death' or 'killing') in order to convey the broad acceptability of this practice.

Distinction between withholding and withdrawing medical treatment

There are also other implications flowing from a strict adherence to the acts/omissions distinction. If the withdrawal of life-support is held to be an act, this would result in a distinction being drawn between initially withholding treatment, which on any analysis, is clearly an omission, and withdrawing treatment once instituted, which would be classified as an act and which

---

[156] e.g. Statement of the Council of Judicial and Ethical Affairs of the AMA, *Withholding or Withdrawing Life-Prolonging Medical Treatment*, March 1986, which states that 'for humane reasons, with informed consent, a physician may do what is medically necessary to alleviate severe pain, or cease or omit treatment to permit a terminally ill patient to die when death is imminent. However, the physician should not intentionally cause death'.

[157] President's Commission Report, *Deciding to Forgo Life-Sustaining Treatment*, above Ch. 1 n. 44. at 64.

would, therefore, attract different legal consequences. However, this is thought to be a most unsatisfactory distinction to draw in practice.[158] As a preliminary objection, although the nature of the distinction may at first sight seem clear enough, cases that obscure it abound.[159] But, apart from the difficulties in the application of such a distinction, its adoption is likely to have serious implications. As pointed out by the President's Commission in its Report, *Deciding To Forgo Life-Sustaining Treatment,*[160] if the view is taken that treatment, once started cannot be stopped, or that stopping requires much greater justification than not starting, this may result in treatment being continued for longer than is optimal for the patient, even to the point where it is causing positive harm with little or no compensating benefit.

According to the President's Commission, an even more troubling wrong occurs when treatment that might save life or improve health is not started because the health care personnel are afraid that they will find it legally difficult to stop the treatment if it proves to be of little benefit and greatly burdens the patient.[161] Thus, the commission was concerned that the erection of a higher requirement for cessation might unjustifiably discourage vigorous initial attempts to treat seriously ill patients that sometimes succeed.[162] The commission was of the view that the distinction between withholding and withdrawing treatment is not of itself of moral significance; if there is justification for not commencing a treatment, the same grounds should also be sufficient for ceasing it. The commission concluded, neither law nor public policy should mark a difference in moral seriousness between stopping and not starting treatment.

There are clearly valid reasons why there should be no distinction between withholding medical procedures and terminating such procedures once instituted. In a number of cases the courts have recognized these

---

[158] Ibid. at 73–7. See also the Hastings Center Report, *Guidelines on the Termination of Life-Sustaining Treatment and Care for the Dying,* above n. 61, at 130–1.

[159] See President's Commission Report, *Deciding to Forgo Life-Sustaining Treatment,* above Ch. 1 n. 44, at 74 for some examples which tend to obscure the distinction; disconnecting a respirator would count as stopping—but if the patient is on a respirator and the power fails, does failure to use a manual bellows system count as stopping or not starting? And what of medical therapies which require repeated applications of an intervention? Does failure to continue to reapply the intervention count as stopping or as not starting?

[160] Above Ch. 1 n. 44, at 75.

[161] Ibid. See also House of Lords, *Report of the Select Committee on Medical Ethics* (London, 1994) Vol 1, 51.

[162] Indeed, as argued by the President's Commission (President's Commission Report, *Deciding to Forgo Life-Sustaining Treatment,* above Ch. 1 n. 44, at 76), if there is any basis to draw a moral distinction between withholding and withdrawing treatment, it should work the opposite way; greater justification ought to be required to withhold than to withdraw treatment. This is because the effects of treatment will often be highly uncertain before the treatment has been tried. However, once the treatment has been implemented and it is clear that it is not helpful to the patient, there is then actual evidence, rather than mere surmise, to support discontinuing the treatment.

problems and have specifically stated that no such distinction will be made.[163] As we have seen, one way of achieving this result (but not necessarily the *only* way), is to hold that withdrawal of life-support amounts to an omission, in the same way that withholding treatment is in law an omission.[164]

A critique of the present legal analysis

Although there are clearly significant policy considerations involved, it is submitted that there are some fundamental problems inherent in the present legal analysis. To hold that the withdrawal of life-support constitutes an omission is simply a policy decision which ignores the reality that this conduct involves 'willed bodily movements' or 'voluntary muscular contractions'. Problems arise because the prevailing interpretation involves legal fictions and the distortion of accepted legal principles. This is particularly serious having regard to the importance of the acts/omissions distinction in determining criminal liability. There are undoubtedly difficulties with the acts/omissions distinction. Not only is the distinction between acts and omissions often very difficult to draw in practice, in many cases it fails to provide an adequate foundation for the moral and legal evaluation of events leading to death.[165] One cannot ignore the fact that strict adherence to the acts/omissions dichotomy leads to some very fine distinctions, which arguably are morally and ethically unsustainable.[166] For example, is it valid to hold that the ending of a programme of dialysis is a mere 'omission', whilst switching off a ventilator is an 'act', even though they are both directed at the same end, namely discontinuing life-support? The overwhelming consensus amongst commentators appears to be that in substance, there is no difference between these forms of medical practice and that it is most inappropriate for liability for homicide to depend on artificial distinctions of this kind.[167] As we have seen, the response of most commentators has been to argue that although we are here dealing with conduct which can technically be described as acts, it should, nevertheless, be classified as an omission. The difficulties that have been encountered in this area have led other commentators to completely reject the current conceptual framework of acts and omissions.[168] However, if we accept the need to

---

[163] e.g. in the USA, the cases of *Barber* v. *Superior Court*, above n. 144, at 490; *In re Conroy*, above Ch. 1 n. 116, at 1234. See also *Airedale NHS Trust* v. *Bland*, above n. 146, at 875 per Lord Lowry.

[164] e.g. the approach taken in *Barber* v. *Superior Court*, above n. 144.

[165] President's Commission Report, *Deciding to Forgo Life-Sustaining Treatment*, above Ch. 1 n. 44, at 64.

[166] Williams, 'Euthanasia and Abortion', (1966) 38 *UColo.LRev.* 178, 183.

[167] Smith, J. C. and Hogan, B., *Criminal Law*, 6th edn. (London, 1983) 51.

[168] e.g. Devettere, R., 'The Imprecise Language of Euthanasia and Causing Death' (1990) 1 *JClin.Ethics* 268, 273.

operate within the existing legal and ethical framework, the conclusion seems inescapable that the withdrawal of life-support must be classified as an act, not an omission.

If the withdrawal of life-support is characterized as an act, the obvious conclusion would appear to be that the commission of that act will constitute murder if it is accompanied by the necessary *mens rea*. Furthermore, having regard to the rules negating consent to acts which cause death, it would appear to be irrelevant that the patient had directed that life-support be withdrawn. Despite the seeming inevitability of these conclusions, it is submitted that there is an alternative method of analysis which retains the traditional acts/omissions distinction, but nevertheless, acknowledges that, in some instances, doctors may lawfully perform acts which cause death.

A possible solution

If we are to adhere to the acts/omissions dichotomy, the most acceptable means of overcoming present difficulties is to recognize that, in appropriate circumstances, withdrawal of treatment will be justifiable and will not result in criminal liability, even though it involves an act in the sense of a 'willed bodily movement' or 'voluntary muscular contraction' which may have been accompanied by the necessary *mens rea* for murder.

The situation is clearest in cases involving a competent patient who directs that life-support be discontinued: if the patient's fundamental right of self-determination is taken to its logical conclusion, it should enable the patient to refuse further treatment even though the implementation of that refusal may require the medical staff to take positive action (for example, the act of turning off life-support equipment or the removal of artificial feeding tubes) which is directly connected to the patient's death. This was certainly the view of the President's Commission, which stated in unequivocal terms:

For competent patients, the principle of self-determination is understood to include a right to refuse life-sustaining treatment, and to place a duty on providers and others to respect that right. Providers, in turn are protected from liability when they act to aid a patient in carrying out that right. Active steps to terminate life-sustaining interventions may be permitted, indeed required, by the patient's authority to forgo therapy even when such steps lead to death.[169]

This statement has subsequently been endorsed by the courts in the USA.[170] Not only does a patient have the right to refuse treatment, the corollary of this right is that non-consensual treatment amounts to a battery. On the assumption that life-support such as artificial ventilation or

---

[169] President's Commission Report, *Deciding to Forgo Life-Sustaining Treatment*, above Ch. 1 n. 44, at 72.
[170] *In re Conroy*, above Ch. 1 n. 116, at 1234.

artificial feeding is seen as medical treatment,[171] the patient's withdrawal of consent would render the continuation of that treatment a non-consensual touching and therefore a battery.[172] Thus, a doctor would have legal justification for removing life-support at the direction of the patient, notwithstanding that such removal may entail conduct of a positive nature. The doctor would simply be removing the source of a battery, which in law he or she is required to do, and thereby would be respecting the patient's right to refuse treatment.[173] In these circumstances, the doctor should be protected from any criminal liability in respect of that conduct. Whilst this reasoning has rarely been spelt out it is entirely consistent with recent case law from a number of jurisdictions[174] and contemporary developments regarding the patient's right of self-determination.[175]

Even in circumstances where the patient is not competent, there may be grounds to conclude that the removal of life-support, although involving positive conduct, would not be unlawful. It may be that a formerly competent patient had made an advance directive regarding his or her treatment wishes which covers the situation of removal of life-support.[176] Provided the evidentiary requirements for the recognition of such a directive were satisfied,[177] doctors could lawfully implement the patient's wishes (indeed, would be legally obliged to do so) in the same way that they are required to act on the directions of a presently competent patient. In the absence of an advance directive or alternatively, legislation allowing the patient to appoint an agent to make health care decisions on the patient's behalf, an argument could still be made out that the conduct of a doctor in discontinuing life-support which is medically futile and no longer benefits the patient is lawful, notwithstanding that it involves an act as distinct from an omission. One possible basis for this conclusion is the proposition put forward by a number of judges in the *Bland*[178] case to the effect that a doctor would be under a duty to discontinue treatment which is no longer of benefit to the

---

[171] This has been accepted by the courts in a number of jurisdictions; e.g. *Barber* v. *Superior Court*, above n. 144; *Airedale NHS Trust* v. *Bland*, above n. 146.

[172] Some support for this view can be derived from the English case of *Fagan* v. *Metropolitan Police Commissioner* [1969] 1 QB 439.

[173] Skegg, *Law, Ethics and Medicine*, above n. 60, at 180. See p. 47 above for consideration of the possible reliance by doctors on the defence of necessity in order to avoid criminal liability.

[174] e.g. *In re Farrel* 529 A2d 404 (1987); *Nancy B* v. *Hotel-Dieu de Quebec*, above n. 59.

[175] Respect for the patient's right to refuse treatment may also be reflected in arguments based on lack of the necessary *mens rea* to convict for murder. It could, for example, be argued that a doctor who has acted upon the request of a competent patient that artificial life-support measures be removed should not be criminally liable even though he or she knew that death would probably result since the doctor's intention was to uphold the patient's right to refuse treatment rather than bring about the death of the patient. Acceptance of this argument would, however, involve legal recognition of the principle of 'double effect' which has to date not been accepted into the criminal law; for further discussion see below.

[176] See pp. 42–4 above for discussion of the legal status of advance directives.

[177] Note above, p. 43.   [178] See above n. 146.

patient.[179] This can be seen as part of an overriding duty on the part of doctors to act in the best interests of their patients.[180] If this proposition is correct, it could be relied upon to argue that it must be legal for a doctor to do that which he or she is legally obliged to do, even though that may involve positive conduct leading to the death of the patient.

If we take the step of recognizing that the withdrawal of life-support is indeed an act rather than an omission, we then have to determine what effect this conclusion has on criminal law principles generally regarding acts which cause death. In particular, consideration has to be given to whether this necessarily leads to the conclusion that patients can authorize other acts which cause death, such as the administration of a lethal injection. Indeed, concern about this very possibility underlies the reluctance of many commentators to accept that the withdrawal of life-support is an act, fearing that this would result in an erosion of the general legal prohibition of active killing.

Proponents of active voluntary euthanasia may wish to argue that it logically follows from the acceptance of the withdrawal of life-support as an act that a patient who has decision-making capacity can authorize *any* acts which cause death. Realistically, however, any change to the legality of the practice of active voluntary euthanasia is unlikely to be achieved in this way. Whilst a number of commentators have either accepted that the withdrawal of life-support is in fact an act, or have rejected outright the acts/ omission doctrine as determinative of liability, they have at the same time argued for the retention of the general legal prohibition on active killing. This, they claim, can be achieved by drawing a distinction between an act of discontinuance of medical treatment and other acts of commission, such as giving a lethal injection.[181] It is suggested here that one recognizes the withdrawal of artificial life-support as an act which doctors may lawfully perform at the request of the patient, but, at the same time, acknowledging that this does not, of itself, lead to the conclusion that a doctor may, under present law, perform other acts causing death at the request of the patient. This would have the advantage of intellectual honesty and consistent legal reasoning, avoiding the distortions and legal fictions which the present position entails. Alternatively, it may be desirable to legislate in this area to remove any doubt about the legality of doctors turning off life-support in appropriate circumstances.

[179] Ibid. at 882–3 per Lord Browne-Wilkinson and Lord Lowry, at 876–7. See further p. 49 n. 167 above.

[180] Note also Lord Goff at 868 who invoked this as the basis of the exception for doctors' immunity from liability with regard to the administration of drugs for relief of pain and other symptoms but which may hasten death. See discussion below.

[181] e.g. Cantor, N., *Legal Frontiers of Death and Dying* (Bloomington, 1987) 34; Kennedy, 'Switching Off Life Support Machines: The Legal Implications', above Ch. 1 n. 154, at 449.

B. Administration of Drugs for the Relief of Pain and Other Symptoms

In the context of the care of terminal patients, cases may arise in which palliative drugs required to alleviate pain and other distressing symptoms are likely to have the effect of shortening the patient's life. As was acknowledged earlier, the proper use of palliative drugs will not necessarily hasten death: indeed, they may extend the life of the patient by increasing mobility and functioning, reducing dependency, and increasing the zest for life. The purpose of this analysis is to examine the situation where palliative drugs necessary to provide relief from pain or other distressing symptoms are administered in the knowledge that they are likely to hasten the patient's death and the patient does in fact die as a result.

Palliative drugs may be administered in a wide range of circumstances: they may be administered at the request of or with the consent of a patient who has decision-making capacity, or the doctor may determine on behalf of the patient that such a course is appropriate, for example, in circumstances where the patient lacks the capacity to decide.[182] Although, as noted earlier, it appears to be widely accepted amongst the medical profession that the administration of potentially life-shortening palliative care is in some circumstances ethical and constitutes legitimate medical practice, it is open to question whether this practice is in fact lawful.

Under existing criminal law principles for murder outlined in Chapter 1,[183] liability will be established for acts which cause death if they are performed with an intention to cause death or in the knowledge that death will probably result. Provided the necessary *mens rea* and *actus reus* can be established, the doctor's motive or the fact that the patient consented to the act causing death would be irrelevant to the issue of liability. Nor would it make any difference that the patient was in any event dying since hastening of death is sufficient to establish criminal liability.[184] Thus, upon a strict interpretation of the criminal law, doctors are potentially liable for murder if they administer palliative drugs in the knowledge that death will probably result even though their intention is to alleviate the patient's condition.[185] This conclusion obviously has far-reaching implications, having regard to the realities of medical practice and the wish of doctors to act in their

---

[182] For the purposes of this analysis, attention will be focused on the situation involving terminal patients. It should be noted, however, that the issue of palliative drugs which shorten life may also arise in respect of non-terminally ill patients who are experiencing pain and suffering. For discussion, see Caswell, D., 'Rejecting Criminal Liability for Life-Shortening Palliative Care' (1990) 6 *J Contemp. Health Law & Pol'y* 127, 132–3, and Somerville, M., 'Pain and Suffering at the Interfaces of Law and Medicine' (1986) 36 *U. Toronto LJ* 286, 299–301.

[183] See pp. 15–16, 31–2 above.

[184] See pp. 18–19 above.

[185] Alternatively, the doctor may face manslaughter charges, e.g. in circumstances where the *mens rea* for murder cannot be established.

patient's best interests and where possible relieve a patient's pain and other distressing symptoms.

It is widely assumed that doctors are not acting unlawfully if they administer palliative drugs which are likely to hasten the death of a patient, provided that the doctor's intention was to alleviate pain and other symptoms and not bring about the patient's death.[186] Certainly, no attempt is made to restrict this practice, or to prosecute doctors who thereby hasten the death of their patients.[187]

As with the issue of turning off life-support, this assumption regarding the legality of the practice of administering palliative drugs which hasten death is largely based on policy considerations. Whilst the deliberate administration of a lethal dose clearly constitutes murder, many people see a distinction between palliative care and active voluntary euthanasia. Indeed, there is much resistance to any attempt to characterize the practice of administering palliative drugs as euthanasia.[188] Because of the widespread acceptability of the practice, and the natural desire to avoid the possibility of doctors incurring criminal liability, the criminal law is assumed not to be applicable. Furthermore, it is indisputable that many patients require drugs for the relief of pain and other symptoms, often in high dosages. If strict criminal law principles were to be applied, doctors would be encouraged to practice defensive medicine and this would result in tighter, less sensitive administration of palliative drugs. Thus, there are powerful policy considerations which have influenced the legal characterization of this medical practice.

The law as interpreted by the courts

Whilst there have been few cases which have raised the issue of the legality of administering palliative drugs which hasten death, the case law which does exist strongly suggests that doctors will not incur criminal liability if, in appropriate circumstances, they administer drugs for pain relief which hasten death even though the doctor knew that death was likely to result.

---

[186] For the purposes of this discussion, attention is focused on the potential liability of doctors for the administration of palliative drugs which may hasten death. It is, however, acknowledged that in practice it may be the case that the doctor prescribes the drugs but the nurse is left to actually administer them; see Johnstone, M., *Bioethics—A Nursing Perspective* (Sydney, 1989) 249.

[187] One of the rare exceptions was the case of *R* v. *Lodwig* (above n. 92) considered below.

[188] e.g. Louisell, D., 'Euthanasia and Biathanasia: On Dying and Killing' (1973) 22 *Catholic ULRev.* 723, 731; Church Assembly Board for Social Responsibility, *On Dying Well: An Anglican Contribution to the Debate on Euthanasia* (London, 1975) 61. See also Caswell, 'Rejecting Criminal Liability for Life-Shortening Palliative Care', above n. 182, at 129, 131 n. 13 where he argues that palliative care is different from active euthanasia, but acknowledges that the distinction often becomes blurred. Note, however, the practice of some commentators to refer to the administration of drugs for the relief of pain and other symptoms as 'indirect euthanasia'; e.g. MacKinnon, P., 'Euthanasia and Homicide' (1983–4) 26 *Crim.LQ* 483.

The *Adams* case

The leading case in this area is the 1957 English case of *R* v. *Adams*[189] which involved the prosecution of a doctor, John Bodkin Adams, for having allegedly murdered a patient. The prosecution's case was that Adams had deliberately killed an elderly patient by the administration of large doses of morphine and heroin in order that he would benefit under her will. The defence case was that the drugs had been administered to relieve the patient's pain and it thereby raised the question of whether doctors were entitled to adopt a course of treatment which would have the effect of shortening the patient's life. Adams was in fact acquitted, but the case has become of lasting significance because of Devlin J's direction to the jury. Whilst a direction to the jury would not usually have much precedent force, this case is something of an exception, largely because of the eminence of the judge, the significance of the legal issue under consideration, and because it was one of the first common law authorities directly dealing with this issue.[190]

Devlin J began by pointing out that shortening life constitutes murder and that the law does not recognize a special defence of preventing severe pain. His Honour then went on to say:

But that does not mean that a doctor who is aiding the sick and the dying has to calculate in minutes or even hours, and perhaps not in days or weeks, the effect on the patient's life of the medicines that he administers or else be in peril of a charge of murder. If the first purpose of medicine, the restoration of health, can no longer be achieved, there is still much for a doctor to do, and he is entitled to do all that is proper and necessary to relieve pain and suffering, even if the measures he takes may incidentally shorten life.[191]

Devlin J stressed that this was not because there is any special defence for doctors, but simply the result of interpreting cause of death in a 'common sense' way. His Honour said that if a patient's death is hastened by the administration of medical treatment, no people of common sense would say that the doctor caused her death:

They would say that the cause of death was the illness or the injury or whatever it was which brought her into hospital, and the proper medical treatment that is administered and has an incidental effect of determining the exact moment of death, or may have, is not the cause of death in any sensible use of that term.[192]

---

[189] (Unreported) (1957). See Palmer, 'Dr Adams' Trial for Murder', above n. 92. The judge in this case, Devlin J, as he then was, subsequently wrote a book about this trial; Devlin, P., *Easing the Passing* (London, 1985).

[190] The issue of administration of palliative drugs has been raised in a number of later cases, see for example, *R* v. *Lodwig* (above n. 92) and *R* v. *Cox*, (above n. 87) discussed below.

[191] For a transcript of the instructions to the jury see Williams, *The Sanctity of Life and the Criminal Law*, above n, 63, at 289.

[192] Ibid.

Whilst the interpretation of this direction to the jury is not without difficulty,[193] the clearest interpretation is that it rests on the legal doctrine of causation.[194] There are, however, limits on the scope of the principle expounded by Devlin J. It is only envisaged to apply in circumstances where the patient is beyond recovery and where the treatment administered is in accordance with proper medical practice.[195] Within these limits, the decision has been widely cited as authority for the proposition that doctors may administer necessary pain-relieving drugs which incidentally shorten life without fear of prosecution.[196]

Although the practical effect of the decision has received considerable support, Devlin's legal basis for arriving at that decision has attracted criticism. Williams, in particular, has criticized the causation analysis on the grounds that it conceals rather than reveals the valuation that is being made.[197] He points out that if a terminally ill patient dies from respiratory failure or pneumonia as a result of the administration of morphine, medically speaking, the death would not be caused by the underlying disease but by the morphine and he expresses some difficulty with the view that for legal purposes, the causation is precisely the opposite.

An alternative analysis: the common law doctrine of necessity

Williams argues that the common law doctrine of necessity provides a better explanation for exempting the doctor from criminal liability.[198] In his view, the doctrine of necessity refers to a choice between competing values in circumstances where the ordinary rule has to be departed from in order to avert some greater evil. He points out that in the context of use of pain-relieving drugs, there are situations where the doctor is faced with the choice of administering what is likely to be a fatal dose if the patient's pain

---

[193] e.g. Smith, J. C. and Hogan, B., *Criminal Law*, 5th edn. (London, 1983) 313; Kennedy, I. and Grubb, A., *Medical Law: Text and Materials* (London, 1994) 1205–7.

[194] Williams, *The Sanctity of Life and the Criminal Law*, above n. 63, at 289. That this was in fact what Devlin J meant was clarified some years later when, in the course of a lecture, he stated that 'proper medical treatment consequent upon illness or injury plays no part in legal causation; and to relieve the pains of death is undoubtedly proper medical treatment'. See Devlin, P., *Samples of Law Making* (London, 1962) 95.

[195] This is clear from Devlin J's reference to what is 'proper and necessary' to relieve pain and suffering and to 'proper medical treatment'. On the basis of this decision, commentators have suggested that the principle would not apply where a larger amount of a drug is administered than is necessary to reduce the pain and suffering to reasonable levels or where safer alternatives exist to the drug actually chosen; e.g. Skegg, *Law, Ethics and Medicine*, above n. 60, at 139.

[196] After the decision in the *Adams* case, the *Daily Telegraph* published a statement by the Director of Public Prosecutions to the effect that he did not wish to challenge Devlin's direction to the jury and that he could only agree with it; see Harvard, L., 'The Influence of the Law on Clinical Decisions Affecting Life and Death' (1983) 23 *Med. Science & Law* 157, 161.

[197] Williams, *The Sanctity of Life and the Criminal Law*, above n. 63, at 289–90.

[198] Ibid. at 286, 290.

is to be relieved, or leaving the patient without adequate relief. Williams argues that the doctor's actions in administering the fatal dose must be excused on the basis of the defence of necessity, since there is no way of relieving the pain without ending life.

The approach suggested by Williams has considerable merit. It avoids the manipulation of the doctrine of causation in order to escape the conclusion that since the doctor had foreseen that death would result from the administration of pain-relieving drugs, he or she should be legally responsible for his or her conduct. It is far preferable to deal with the issue directly and, if necessary, create a new defence, rather than to distort existing legal principles to accommodate a desired outcome. Furthermore, since the defence of necessity is only envisaged as an exceptional departure from the normal rule, it preserves intact accepted criminal law principles regarding the *mens rea* and *actus reus* for murder.

Although conceptually sound and receiving support from some eminent jurists,[199] the doctrine of necessity has not, to date, been invoked by the courts to justify the administration of palliative drugs which incidentally hasten death, and there is case law, particularly in England, which suggests that the defence of necessity is not available as a defence to murder.[200]

R v. Adams *and the doctrine of 'double effect'*

It has been suggested by some commentators that the effect of the *Adams* case has been to incorporate into English law the doctrine of 'double effect'.[201] This doctrine, stemming from Catholic moral theology,[202] is essentially based on a distinction between results which are *intended* and those which are merely *foreseen* as a non-intended consequence of one's action. Under this principle, it may sometimes be morally legitimate to act while foreseeing, but not intending, an undesirable result of one's action, but it is never morally legitimate to act with the intention of producing that result.[203]

---

[199] Williams, above n. 63, at 284, 286–8, 290; Moore, G., 'The Common Law Doctrine of Necessity' in Church of England, National Assembly Board for Social Responsibility, *Decisions About Life and Death: A Problem of Modern Medicine* (London, 1965) 49, 50. Other commentators are less confident that reliance on the defence of necessity is the solution; e.g. Caswell, 'Rejecting Criminal Liability for Life-Shortening Palliative Care', above n. 182, at 136–7 where he expresses the concern that whilst the availability of the defence of necessity may help deal with isolated cases it does not provide clear guidance to doctors.

[200] *R v. Dudley* (1884) 14 QBD 273; *R v. Howe* (1987) 85 Crim.App.R 32, 39–41.

[201] See Kennedy and Grubb, *Medical Law*, above Ch. 1 n. 69, at 1205–6 for discussion of this possibility.

[202] For a contemporary statement of the position of the Catholic Church with regard to this doctrine see Pope Pius XII, 'Religious and Moral Aspects of Pain Prevention in Medical Practice' (1957) 88 *Ir.Ecclesiastical Rec.* 193, 193–209.

[203] For discussion of the principle of double effect see Kelly, G., *Medico-Moral Problems* (St. Louis, Missouri, 1958) 12–16. Kelly states that in order for the principle of double effect to apply, certain conditions must be fulfilled; 1) the action, considered by itself and independently of its effects, must not be morally evil; 2) the evil effect must not be the means of producing the good effect; 3) the evil effect is sincerely not intended, but merely tolerated; 4) there must be a proportionate reason for performing the action, in spite of its evil consequences.

Thus, a doctor can legitimately administer palliative drugs which hasten death if his or her primary aim is to relieve the patient's suffering, though foreseeing that this may indirectly hasten the death of the patient. However, a doctor may never deliberately give a patient an overdose with the intention of killing the patient.

One possible interpretation of Devlin J's direction to the jury in the *Adams* case is that in circumstances involving administration of palliative drugs, a doctor will not be criminally liable unless he or she actually intended to bring about the death.[204] However, the difficulty with this interpretation is that it is inconsistent with strict criminal law principles. As Williams observes:

There is no legal difference between desiring or intending a consequence as following from your conduct, and persisting in your conduct with the knowledge that the consequence will inevitably follow from it, though not desiring that consequence. When a result is foreseen as certain it is the same as if it were desired or intended.[205]

Although the doctrine of double effect is sometimes invoked to justify the administration of palliative drugs which incidentally hasten death,[206] the reality of the matter is that the distinction between *intending* and merely *knowing* that death will probably result from one's acts is a distinction that has never made a difference to the criminal law.[207] According to well established principles, provided the defendant subjectively knew that the administration of drugs would be life-threatening, criminal liability for homicide can theoretically be established even though the doctor's primary intention was to relieve the patient's suffering.

Despite the dubious basis for this justification for the use of palliative drugs which are likely to hasten the death of the patient, this analysis based on the concept of double effect was recently endorsed by the House of Lords Select Committee on Medical Ethics[208] and it continues to find support in the case law.

The law in England in the light of the Adams case

Whilst the analytical basis of the *Adams* case may be open to interpretation, it does appear to have become authority, at least in England, for the following proposition; a doctor may lawfully administer to a patient *in extremis* palliative drugs in such quantities to relieve the patient's suffering, even though the doctor knows that the patient is likely to die as a result, subject, however, to the proviso that those drugs are administered for the

---

[204] Kennedy and Grubb, *Medical Law*, above Ch. 1 n. 69, at 1205–6.

[205] *Sanctity of Life and the Criminal Law*, above n. 63, at 286. See also Kennedy and Grubb, *Medical Law*, above Ch. 1 n. 69, at 1206.

[206] e.g. BMA Working Party Report, *Euthanasia*, above n. 1, at 40.

[207] See pp. 15–16, 31–2 above for discussion of the *mens rea* for the crime of murder.

[208] House of Lords, *Report of the Select Committee on Medical Ethics* (London, 1994) HL Paper 21, Vol. 1, 49–50.

purpose of relieving pain and other symptoms and not to kill the patient. Leaving aside for the moment policy considerations which clearly favour doctors being able to administer appropriate pharmacological relief for pain and other distressing symptoms, it is readily apparent that the *Adams* case represents quite a remarkable exception to existing criminal law principles. It is well established that motive or desire is not normally relevant to preclude the imposition of criminal liability for conduct which causes death, in circumstances where those consequences were intended or at least foreseen. Given the significance of this departure from criminal law principles, it is, perhaps, surprising that there has not been a clearer statement of the basis of the exception. Indeed, some commentators have questioned the authority of the *Adams* case and have suggested that there may still be some uncertainty about the law as it concerns the use of pain-killing drugs which incidentally shorten life.[209] Nevertheless, review of relevant cases decided in England since the *Adams* case indicates that this exception to criminal liability has now become fairly well accepted. In *Airedale NHS Trust* v. *Bland*,[210] considered earlier, Lord Goff (with whom the other members of the House of Lords generally agreed), referred with approval to the 'established rule' that a doctor may, when caring for a patient who is, for example, dying of cancer, lawfully administer pain-killing drugs despite the fact that he knows that an incidental effect of that application will be to abbreviate the patient's life.[211] There have also been a number of cases dealing with disabled newborns, which tend to support the view that doctors may lawfully administer drugs for the relief of pain and other symptoms which have the effect of hastening the patient's death.[212] One of the more recent examples is *In re J (Wardship: Medical Treatment)*[213] arising in the court's wardship jurisdiction. The baby in this case was profoundly handicapped but not terminally ill and the question at issue was whether the court could sanction the withholding of future resuscitation by mechanical ventilation. Lord

---

[209] e.g. Lord Edmund Davies, 'On Dying and Dying Well: Legal Aspects' (1977) 70 *Proc. Royal Soc.Med.* 71, 74; Trowell, *The Unfinished Debate on Euthanasia*, above Ch. 2 n. 2, at 35–6.

[210] See above n. 146.

[211] Ibid. at 868. This part of Lord Goff's judgment has been cited by one commentator in support of an alternative analysis of the pain-killing drug exception established in the *Adams* case: having rejected arguments based on double effect or causation as fundamentally flawed, Grubb suggests that the most coherent argument is that a doctor is not in breach of his duty to his patient when he administers pain-relieving drugs which incidentally shorten the patient's life—an argument which he acknowledges, requires acceptance of the proposition that consideration of a doctor's duty is relevant not only when death follows from the omission to treat a patient but also when it results from acts. Note, 'Attempted Murder of Terminally Ill Patient' [1993] 1 *Med.LR* 232, 234.

[212] e.g. *R* v. *Arthur* (unreported) (1981) (discussed by Gunn, M., and Smith, J. C., 'Arthur's Case and the Right to Life of a Down's Syndrome Child' (1985) *Crim.LRev.* 705); *In re C (A Minor) (Wardship: Medical Treatment)* [1989] 3 WLR 240.

[213] [1991] 2 WLR 140.

Donaldson MR, who delivered the principal judgment for the court, expressed the following view:

What doctors and the court have to decide is whether, in the best interests of the child patient, a particular decision as to medical treatment should be taken which *as a side effect* will render death more or less likely. This is not a matter of semantics. It is fundamental. At the other end of the age spectrum, the use of drugs to reduce pain will often be fully justified, notwithstanding that this will hasten the moment of death. What can never be justified is the use of drugs or surgical procedures with the primary purpose of doing so.[214]

Although these comments were made in a civil case concerning the medical treatment of a minor, they are potentially of wider relevance and appear to endorse the use of palliative drugs which are likely incidentally to hasten death on the basis of the doctrine of double effect.

Notwithstanding these cases, the present immunity of doctors from prosecution for the practice of administration of palliative drugs which are likely to hasten death rests on the somewhat tenuous authority of the *Adams* case and the compliance of prosecuting authorities with this state of affairs. A number of recent prosecutions of doctors in England has shown that the legal position of doctors in administering drugs for the relief of pain and other symptoms is far from certain.[215] In 1990, Dr Thomas Lodwig had been charged with the murder of a 48-year-old male patient who was in the terminal stages of cancer. The patient had been receiving heroin in increasing dosages for the purposes of pain relief. However, in the days preceding his death, this regimen was no longer effective and the patient was suffering severe and uncontrollable pain. In an attempt to relieve the patient's distress, Dr Lodwig gave the patient a mixture of potassium chloride and lignocaine. The patient died a few minutes later. Potassium chloride is known to be lethal, but there was some evidence to suggest that when used in combination with pain-killers, it could accelerate their pain-killing effect.[216] Dr Lodwig was committed for trial but when the matter came before the court the prosecution offered no evidence against him and the judge directed that a verdict of not guilty be entered.[217] Although the prosecution of Dr Lodwig was eventually dropped, the case has certainly highlighted the legal vulnerability of doctors in these circumstances.

The issue of palliative drugs was also raised in the prosecution against Dr Cox referred to earlier.[218] Dr Cox had administered a large and undiluted

[214] Ibid. at 149 (emphasis in the original).   [215] See above n. 92.

[216] Two eminent doctors from St. Bartholomew's Hospital, where Dr Lodwig had completed his training, had been involved in research regarding the use of potassium chloride with pain-killers to accelerate their analgesic effect and reported encouraging results from their clinical trials; *The Times*, 16 March 1990.

[217] The principle reason that the prosecution was dropped was because of uncertainty regarding the cause of death; *The Times*, 16 March 1990.

[218] See pp. 143–5 above.

dose of potassium chloride to his patient from which the patient died within minutes. Cox had argued that his primary intention in administering the drug was not to kill the patient but to relieve her suffering. Justice Ognall, in his direction to the jury, explained the situation in the following terms, using language invoking the concept of double effect:

There can be no doubt that the use of drugs to reduce pain and suffering will often be justified notwithstanding that it will, in fact, hasten the moment of death . . . what can never be lawful is the use of drugs with the primary purpose of hastening the moment of death . . . The distinction that the law requires you to draw is this. Is it proved that in giving that injection in that form and in those amounts Dr Cox's primary purpose was to bring the life of Lillian Boyes to an end? If it was then he is guilty. If on the other hand it was or may have been his primary purpose in acting as he did to alleviate her pain and suffering then he is not guilty and that is so even though he recognised that in fulfilling that primary purpose he might or even would hasten the moment of her death.[219]

The jury's verdict of guilty in this case was clearly premised on the assumption that Dr Cox had intended to kill the patient, albeit for merciful motives.

The position in other jurisdictions

Whilst there is scant authority in the other jurisdictions under consideration directly in support of an exception to criminal liability in circumstances where death is hastened by the administration of palliative drugs, it appears to be widely assumed that doctors administering drugs to relieve their patient's pain and distress will not incur criminal liability. In the USA for example, although few cases have specified the drug exception to homicide, the practice of administering drugs to relieve pain and other symptoms, even if it hastens death, is generally accepted as legal, despite the fact that it might technically be regarded as homicide.[220] Cantor writes: 'There is a tacit understanding that prosecution would never be undertaken, even if causal connection between the analgesic and death could be established. [M]edical practice has won de facto legal acceptance because of widespread acknowledgment of its humane grounding'.[221]

One of the rare instances where the courts in the USA have acknowledged the practice and drawn attention to the anomalous nature of the legal exception is the decision of the Ninth Circuit Court of the United States Court of Appeals in the case of *Compassion in Dying* v. *State of Washington*. Reinhardt J, giving judgment for the majority in that case, rejected the

---

[219] See above n. 87.
[220] President's Commission Report, *Deciding to Forgo Life-Sustaining Treatment*, above Ch. 1 n. 44, at 78–82.
[221] Cantor, *Legal Frontiers of Death and Dying*, above Ch. 2 n. 32, at 35.

argument that had been advanced on behalf of the State that physician-assisted suicide is different in kind from the type of physician life-ending conduct that is now authorized because, amongst other things, it requires physicians to provide the causal agent of patient's deaths. His Honour stated:

Contrary to the State's assertion, given current medical practices and current medical ethics, it is not possible to distinguish prohibited from permissible medical conduct on the basis of whether the medication provided by the doctor will cause the patient's death. As part of the tradition of administering comfort care, doctors have been supplying the causal agent of patient's deaths for decades. Physicians routinely and openly provide medication to terminally ill patients with the knowledge that it will have a double effect—reduce the patient's pain and hasten his death.

Reinhardt J went on to refer to various Reports of the Council of Ethical and Judicial Affairs of the AMA which acknowledge that the patient's death is a possible side effect of palliative treatment, and that increasing the appropriate medication for a patient may depress respiration and cause death. His Honour went on to say:

The euphemistic use of 'possible' and 'may' may salve the conscience of the AMA, but it does not change the realities of the practice of medicine or the legal consequences that would normally flow from the commission of an act one has reason to believe will likely result in the death of another. In the case of 'double effect' . . . we find the act acceptable . . . because the act is medically and ethically appropriate even though the result—the patient's death—is both foreseeable and intended . . . There can be no doubt, therefore that the actual cause of patient's death is the drug administered by the physician or by a person acting under his supervision or direction.

In other common law jurisdictions such as Canada,[222] Australia, and New Zealand it has also been assumed that doctors will not incur criminal liability for providing necessary palliative care, even though this is likely to hasten the death of the patient, notwithstanding that there is little direct authority in support of such an exception.

In Canada, at least, there has been some acknowledgment by the Supreme Court that the practice of administering palliative drugs which are likely to hasten death occurs without doctors incurring criminal liability. In *Rodriguez* v. *British Columbia (Attorney General)* (discussed in detail in the preceding chapter[223]) reference was made by a number of the judges to the issue of palliative care given to relieve pain and suffering, even though the effect of that treatment may be to shorten the patient's life.[224] By distin-

---

[222] For discussion of the Canadian law and practice see Special Senate Committee on Euthanasia and Assisted Suicide, *Of Life and Death*, above n. 10, at Ch. 4.

[223] See pp. 86–94 above.

[224] [1993] 3 SCR 519, 560 (Lamer CJ, dissenting) and 606 (Sopinka J).

guishing this situation from euthanasia or assisted suicide the court has given tacit approval to the practice.[225]

It is, however, very difficult to identify a coherent legal basis for the exception, particularly for the purpose of those jurisdictions whose Codes contain an unequivocal statement to the effect that a person who is responsible for hastening the death of another is deemed to have killed that person.[226] Whilst it is likely that the courts in these countries would ultimately be inclined to take the view that the *Adams* case represents the common law position, the current uncertainty of the present situation has been highlighted by law reform bodies in a number of jurisdictions recommending the introduction of legislation to clarify the legal status of this practice.[227] In response to these concerns, legislation has now been introduced in a number of Australian jurisdictions to make it clear that doctors and health care professionals involved in the provision of palliative care are not at risk of criminal liability.[228]

In Australia, one possibility which may be explored in the future, as a possible alternative to the reasoning in the *Adams* case, is the exception referred to in *R* v. *Crabbe*. Although only *obiter*, it was suggested in a joint judgment of the High Court of Australia that not every fatal act done with the knowledge that death or grievous bodily harm will probably result is murder. The court went on to say that the act may be lawful, that is, justified or excused by law, and gave the example of a surgeon who performs a hazardous but necessary operation, in circumstances where he or she could foresee that the patient's death was probable. After raising this possibility and noting that it was not necessary for the court to discuss it in the present case, the court did, with apparent approval, refer to academic writers who have pointed out that in deciding whether an act is justifiable, its social purpose or social utility is important. In the light of the comments in this case it is possible, at least for the purposes of the Australian common law jurisdictions, that the courts would accommodate the practice of doctors administering palliative drugs which are likely incidentally to hasten the

---

[225] Note also the New Zealand case of *Auckland Area Health Board* v. *Attorney-General* [1993] 1 NZLR 235, 252 in which reference was made, with approval, to Devlin J's instruction to the jury in the *Adams* case.

[226] Canada—Criminal Code 1985 s. 226; Australia—Tas. Criminal Code 1924 s. 154(d), WA Criminal Code 1913 s. 273; New Zealand—Crimes Act 1961 s. 164.

[227] e.g. Law Reform Commission of Canada, Report No. 20, *Euthanasia, Aiding Suicide and the Cessation of Treatment* (Ottawa, 1983) 22–3 and restated in the later report, Report No. 30, *Recodifying Criminal Law* (Ottawa, 1987) 185–6; and in Australia, e.g. the Western Australia Law Reform Commission, Report *Medical Treatment for the Dying* (Perth, 1991) 25–7; South Australian Select Committee, Second Interim Report, South Australian Select Committee on the Law and Practice on Death and Dying (Adelaide, 1992), 4–6.

[228] ACT Medical Treatment Act 1994 s. 23, Qld. Criminal Code 1995 s. 82, SA Consent to Medical Treatment and Palliative Care Act 1995 s. 17.

patient's death within this concept of socially justifiable risk. This would presumably be done within the conceptual framework of the doctrine of necessity which, as noted earlier, has been put forward by some commentators as an alternative to the approach in the *Adams* case. But there is, admittedly, a significant difference between the taking of a risk for the purpose of saving life (for example, performing a hazardous operation) and a situation where a doctor causes the patient's death in an attempt to relieve pain. It must be remembered, however, that we are considering here patients who are in a terminal condition and for whom palliative treatment is the only realistic option. In these circumstances, the social utility of reducing the pain and suffering of dying patients through the provision of palliative treatments would need to be weighed against the possibility that the patient's death is likely to be hastened as a result of that treatment. In the present medico-legal environment, it is quite possible that the courts would accept that the need to minimize pain and suffering is paramount and that a defence to homicide is thus made out. It is submitted that such an interpretation would offer a preferable means for creating an exception to criminal liability to the prevailing approach as laid down in the *Adams* case.

A critique of the present law

It should be stressed from the outset that there can be no real dispute about the social desirability of the practice of administering palliative drugs and the recognized need for doctors to be able to provide patients with adequate relief of pain and other distressing symptoms. Thus, the following critique of the present legal position is not in any way aimed at changing current medical practice. Rather, the object is to demonstrate that the prevailing assumptions regarding the legality of this practice are irreconcilable with established criminal law principles and that the law is clearly being manipulated in order to sanction what is widely regarded as legitimate medical practice. Clearly, doctors must be able to administer lawfully the necessary palliative drugs to relieve their patients' pain and other symptoms but it is argued that a more satisfactory basis for the legal exception needs to be developed.

Resort to legal fictions

As we have seen, the legality of administering drugs for the relief of pain and other symptoms, but which are likely to have the effect of hastening death has only directly arisen for consideration in England in the *Adams* case and later cases which have considered the issue. Whichever analysis of the *Adams* case is adopted, that is, based on either the causation arguments or the principle of double effect, the case is completely contrary to established legal authority. As Devlin J himself acknowledged,[229] under ordinary criminal law principles the hastening of an inevitable death is murder. Whilst there may well be practical difficulties in establishing causation in cases where a patient has died following the administration of palliative drugs, it is simply legal sophistry to say that this is never the relevant cause of death in law. Similarly, with regard to the double effect doctrine, the distinction between intending to kill and merely foreseeing that death will probably result from one's acts has never been relevant for the purpose of establishing criminal liability. The reality is that on accepted principles of intention and causation for the crime of murder, a doctor who administers palliative drugs which he or she knows will probably hasten the patient's death, has the necessary *mens rea* and if death results, has in law caused that death. The fact that the doctor's motive was to relieve the patient's pain or other distressing symptoms, or that the patient had consented to the treatment, would not protect a doctor from criminal liability.

Thus, there is clearly a wide gulf between strict criminal principles on the one hand, and on the other, the law as presently interpreted in the *Adams* case, or, as is the case in other jurisdictions, that which is simply assumed to apply: although strictly speaking, the practice constitutes murder, the law has acknowledged, and acquiesced in, the practice.[230] In those jurisdictions where the courts have actually considered the matter, it is interesting to observe how the courts have almost surreptitiously manipulated the law to accommodate this practice, without clearly and unequivocally stating an exception to established criminal law principles. Indeed, one detects a distinct reluctance to deal openly with the matter and provide an appropriate defence in respect of this practice.[231] This is, perhaps, understandable, in that the courts do not want to be seen creating special defences for doctors or to be sanctioning what may be regarded by some as medical euthanasia. Nevertheless, these considerations do not justify the use of illogical legal fictions. It is simply not valid to reinterpret or gloss over established principles in order to produce a desired result. The real danger is that manipulation or distortion of established legal principles tends to undermine the credibility of the law and threatens to bring it into disrepute.

Unworkable distinctions

The other major criticism of the prevailing legal position is that it involves very fine, and arguably unworkable, distinctions. On the authority of the *Adams* case, there is a distinction between the administration of drugs for

---

[229] Palmer, 'Dr Adams' Trial for Murder', above n. 92, at 375 where he cites Devlin J's summing-up to the jury: 'It did not matter whether Mrs Morrell's death was inevitable and that her days were numbered. If her life were cut short by weeks or months it was just as much murder as if it were cut short by years'.

[230] Cantor, *Legal Frontiers of Death and Dying*, above Ch. 2 n. 32, at 35.

[231] Skegg, *Law, Ethics and Medicine*, above n. 60, at 78.

relief of pain and other symptoms which are known to be likely to hasten the death of the patient, and the administration of a lethal dose intended to kill the patient; the former is lawful, whereas the latter constitutes the crime of murder. Indeed, the terminology used is in itself significant; the incidental 'shortening of life' or 'hastening of death' is often used in contradistinction to 'killing' the patient, thereby concealing the reality that the administration of palliative drugs may equally kill a patient.

Although the distinction between killing and merely hastening death in the process of relieving the patient's pain has gained considerable currency, the dividing line can be impossibly fine as has been illustrated in a number of the recent prosecutions coming before the courts.[232] Ultimately it seems to depend on what was in the mind of the doctor when he or she administered the drugs in question—was it to relieve the patient's pain and other symptoms or to kill the patient? Whilst this may, in many instances, be a fairly straightforward proposition, circumstances can be envisaged which tend to blur the distinction. For example, what if it is necessary to kill the patient in order to relieve his or her pain and distress? It might be suggested that in these circumstances the doctor's primary intention is to relieve the patient's pain and other symptoms and the hastening of death is simply an incidental consequence. Realistically, however, it is more likely that the doctor's intention in these circumstances is to kill both the pain and the patient.[233] Moreover, with the increasing use of palliative sedation in extreme cases of suffering, whereby the patient is rendered permanently unconscious, the distinction between active euthanasia and palliative care virtually disappears. Indeed, as some specialists in the palliative care field have acknowledged, palliative sedation is in effect, a form of slow active euthanasia.[234]

There is also the real concern that the principle of double effect encourages dishonesty of intent on the part of health care professionals and, by ignoring or diminishing the causal connection between the treatment and the hastened death, dangerously undermines the acceptance of professional responsibility for the outcomes of palliative treatment.[235] It has been forcefully argued that good clinical practice demands that the important conse-

---

[232] e.g. *R* v. *Lodwig* see above n. 92. In practice, much depends on the drugs administered and whether they have any pain-relieving qualities, in which case the doctors intentions may be ambiguous. If they do not (e.g. *R* v. *Cox* where a large dose of potassium chloride was administered) it is difficult to avoid the conclusion that the doctor's intention was to kill the patient.

[233] See Hunt, R., 'Palliative Care: The Rhetoric–Reality Gap' in Kuhse, H. (ed.), *Willing to Listen, Wanting to Die* (Melbourne, 1994) 115, 125 for an example of a doctor supporting this view in the context of a person's dying process. For further comment on the complexities of clinical intentions, see Quill, T., 'The Ambiguity of Clinical Intentions' (1993) 329 *New Eng.JMed.* 1039.

[234] e.g. Hunt, 'Palliative Care: the Rhetoric–Reality Gap', above n. 233, at 125.

[235] Ibid. at 125–6.

quences of treatment options be considered and discussed with patients and that it is both poor practice and morally evasive simply to turn a 'blind eye' to the fact that a palliative treatment may shorten life.

Furthermore, if administering drugs to relieve pain and other symptoms is permissible despite the possibility that death may be hastened, but administering drugs with the intention of euthanasia is not, it is possible that some doctors will perform active euthanasia under the guise of palliative care, and there is evidence to suggest that this does in fact occur.[236] Thus, as Williams observes, since many of the available analgesics have the effect of hastening death, a situation of benevolent hypocrisy prevails.[237]

Uncertainty in practice

Another major criticism of the present legal position is that it is still precariously uncertain, particularly in those jurisdictions where the issue has not directly come before the courts. Whilst it is more than likely that the *Adams* approach would be accepted, this cannot be guaranteed. In a climate of uncertainty regarding the legality of administering palliative drugs which are likely to hasten death, there is the risk that doctors may be unwilling to provide adequate relief for pain and symptoms, thereby forcing patients to endure unnecessary pain and suffering.[238]

It is clearly undesirable that doctors should face the possibility of criminal liability as a result of acting humanely to relieve a patient's pain and other distressing symptoms. Some commentators have stressed that, in any event, it is unlikely that these practices are discovered, or if discovered, that they can be proved and successfully prosecuted.[239] This may well be so but it must be wondered whether the present situation is satisfactory. Palliative care is of such importance that doctors ought to be able to administer confidently to the needs of their patients without raising the spectre of criminal liability. It would be far preferable if there were a clearer statement of the legal exception which protects doctors from liability in circumstances where drugs are administered for the purpose of relieving pain and distress, but which are likely to have the effect of hastening the death of the patient.

[236] e.g. Maguire, D., *Death by Choice* (New York, 1984) 37.

[237] Williams, G., 'Euthanasia' (1970) 63 *Proceedings for the Royal Society of Medicine* 663, 665.

[238] See also Caswell, 'Rejecting Criminal Liability for Life-Shortening Palliative Care', above n. 182, at 138; Western Australia Law Reform Commission, Report *Medical Treatment for the Dying*, above n. 227, at 25–6.

[239] e.g. Church Assembly Board for Social Responsibility, *On Dying Well*, above n. 188, at 58. In circumstances where the patient is suffering from a terminal condition and is in a debilitated state it will often be difficult to establish that the patient died from the drugs rather than the underlying illness. Difficulties are compounded in circumstances where the patient has become habituated to the use of a drug, with the result that increased dosages may have the same effect as a standard dose would have on a normal patient.

CONCLUSION

The object of this chapter has been to highlight the serious discrepancies which exist between the strict legal position and the position in practice with regard to active voluntary euthanasia and where relevant, doctor-assisted suicide, in order to demonstrate the inadequacies of the present law and the need for re-evaluation of the law's approach to these issues. It has been shown that despite the criminal law prohibition of active voluntary euthanasia as murder, there is significant evidence to indicate that this practice does occur: it is not uncommon for patients to request active euthanasia and there is evidence from all jurisdictions that a significant proportion of doctors do comply with such requests. However, the likelihood of a doctor being prosecuted and convicted of the murder of a patient is fairly remote. The same holds true for doctor-assisted suicide; although there is incontrovertible evidence that this practice occurs there are virtually no prosecutions. In those few cases where prosecutions have resulted, doctors have almost invariably been acquitted, although the conviction of Dr Cox in the United Kingdom for attempted murder has demonstrated the legal vulnerability of doctors who engage in these practices.

It has also been shown that other aspects of medical practice, such as turning off life-support and the administration of palliative drugs knowing that they are likely to cause death, although on strict legal principles attract criminal liability for murder, have been deliberately characterized in such a way as to avoid such liability.

It is, therefore, evident that significant inconsistencies exist between the law in theory and the law in practice. In effect, the criminal justice system has acquiesced in certain medical practices involving the termination of life by manipulating and distorting legal principles to avoid the full rigours of the criminal law. It has been argued that the present position is most unsatisfactory and threatens to undermine the credibility of the law. There is a need for greater honesty and clarity in this area to overcome the existing discrepancies and anomalies. It must be acknowledged that active voluntary euthanasia is already being performed, albeit surreptitiously, and that there are other medical practices, which, although widely accepted, are strictly speaking contrary to established criminal law principles. The law appears to condone some medical 'acts' which hasten the death of a patient such as the removal of artificial life-support and the administration of drugs for relief of pain and other symptoms, yet, theoretically at least, maintains a strict legal prohibition on the practice of active voluntary euthanasia. Given the obvious similarities between these various medical acts in terms of outcome and intention, and arguably, also morality, one may well question whether the line between lawful and unlawful conduct has been appropriately drawn. Does it really make sense for the law to permit a patient to direct the discontinuance of artificial life-support and thereby bring about an earlier death, yet deny the patient direct assistance in the form of a lethal dose? Arguably not, and there are strong arguments to suggest that established criminal law principles with regard to homicide are simply inappropriate in the contemporary context of medically administered active voluntary euthanasia. The fact that doctors are unlikely to be exposed to liability, or if exposed, will almost certainly be dealt with leniently, is not an adequate response. It is quite unacceptable that doctors who feel compelled to respond to a patient's request for active euthanasia presently run the risk of serious criminal liability. If society has reached the stage where such medical conduct is regarded as acceptable and not deserving of punishment, this should be more directly reflected in our laws rather than doctors and those involved in the administration of the criminal justice system having to rely on subterfuge and questionable techniques of liability avoidance.

Consideration also needs to be given to the rights and interests of patients. So long as active voluntary euthanasia remains an illegal and covert practice, its administration will inevitably be inconsistent, and it will not equally be available to all who seek it. There is also the very real concern that whilst the practice of active voluntary euthanasia exists but remains unregulated, patients' rights and interests are not adequately protected.

Since the law already permits certain acts which cause death in connection with implementing the withdrawal of life-support and in administering palliative drugs, it is, in fact, only a small step to say that, in some limited circumstances, active voluntary euthanasia should also be allowed. In light of the available evidence that death-inducing acts are already taking place, it would be preferable to formalize current practices, in order to regulate and protect against abuse and to overcome discrepancies between legal theory and practice. The present connivance and hypocrisy of the law is no credit to the legal profession and certainly leaves doctors in an untenable position. There is a strong case for the law to confront directly the question of active voluntary euthanasia, for instilling greater clarity and certainty in this area, and to provide appropriate protection for doctors, who act *bona fide* in their patients' best interests. However, the question of reform is not just a legal issue, and there are obviously a whole host of considerations to be taken into account in determining whether the law should be changed so as to allow doctors to perform active euthanasia at the request of a patient. It is to this issue that attention will turn in the following chapter dealing with the euthanasia debate.

4

The Euthanasia Debate

INTRODUCTION

The object of this chapter is to review and analyse critically the 'euthanasia debate'. The debate regarding the practice and legalization of active voluntary euthanasia has existed for many years[1] and there is already a wealth of literature on this subject from a variety of disciplines, including law, medicine, theology, and philosophy. Consequently, this chapter seeks to review the existing literature to consider the principal arguments that have been advanced both for and against the legalization of active voluntary euthanasia. Although many of the issues are legal in nature, this chapter necessarily involves consideration also of non-legal arguments. An attempt will be made to analyse critically the competing arguments and arrive at some conclusion as to whether active voluntary euthanasia should be legalized. It must be emphasized that the principal concern here is what the law ought to be rather than the question of the morality of active euthanasia apart from the law. For the purposes of this analysis, the issue of active voluntary euthanasia will be considered in general terms only, without reference to any particular proposal for legalization, leaving for later consideration how legalization could be most appropriately effected.[2]

It must be recognized from the outset that the debate about active voluntary euthanasia is in many respects indeterminable and intractable. Euthanasia is a controversial subject which inevitably provokes intense emotional debate and gives rise to strong convictions which do not readily lend themselves to consensus. Where such conflicts of values exist, with seemingly little middle ground, it is unlikely that a resolution can be reached which will meet with universal approval. Indeed, in a society with a plurality of widely differing moral views and convictions, one cannot expect unanimity on this issue.

Despite the difficulties in this area, there is a pressing need for the issue of active voluntary euthanasia to be addressed. Attitudes to death have been changing. What has traditionally been a taboo subject is now increas-

---

[1] For commentators dealing with the historical aspects of the euthanasia debate see Gruman, G., 'An Historical Introduction to Ideas About Voluntary Euthanasia' (1973) 4 *Omega* 87; van der Sluis, I., 'The Movement for Euthanasia, 1875–1975' (1979) 66 *Janus* 131. See also p. 1, n. 1 above.

[2] See Ch. 8 dealing with options for reform.

ingly being openly discussed, and a more personal conception of death is emerging. The medicalization of terminal care and increasing attention to patient rights generally, have also encouraged greater interest in the euthanasia debate. Public opinion appears to be increasingly in favour of permitting active euthanasia in carefully regulated circumstances, and the campaign for reform of the law is gathering momentum.[3] As we have seen, legislation permitting active voluntary euthanasia has recently been passed in the Northern Territory of Australia, and bills are pending in other jurisdictions.[4] Now, more than ever, there is a need to examine dispassionately the euthanasia debate and determine whether active voluntary euthanasia should be legalized.

Although the focus of this chapter is the euthanasia debate, much of the discussion also applies to doctor-assisted suicide. Whilst there are obviously some differences between the two practices, in particular, the extent of the doctor's involvement in bringing about the death of the patient,[5] the position taken in this work is that the differences are not of great significance.[6]

This chapter is divided into three parts: part I dealing with the case for legalizing active voluntary euthanasia, part II dealing with the case against legalization, and part III examining the legal philosophers' debate; the role of the criminal law.

I. THE CASE FOR LEGALIZATION OF ACTIVE VOLUNTARY EUTHANASIA

There have, over the years, been many proponents of active euthanasia, who have campaigned for its legalization including eminent figures such as Williams[7] and Fletcher.[8] Whilst all euthanasia proponents are in favour of the legalization of active euthanasia, a difference of opinion exists as to whether it should be strictly limited to voluntary euthanasia, or whether, in some circumstances non-voluntary (as distinct from involuntary) euthanasia should also be permitted.[9] Consistent with the object of this work, the

---

[3] See Ch. 5.   [4] See Ch. 6.

[5] In the case of active voluntary euthanasia, the doctor is directly involved in the act of killing: in the case of doctor-assisted suicide, the doctor only provides indirect assistance to the patient who takes his or her own life.

[6] See below.

[7] e.g. Williams, *The Sanctity of Life and the Criminal Law*, above Ch. 3 n. 63; 'Euthanasia' (1973) 41 *Medico-Legal J* 14.

[8] e.g. Fletcher, J., *Morals and Medicine* (Princeton, New Jersey, 1979) 172–210; 'Ethics and Euthanasia' (1973) 73 *Am.J Nursing* 670. Other notable commentators who have contributed to the debate in favour of active euthanasia include Kohl, M. (ed.), *Beneficent Euthanasia* (Buffalo, New York, 1975) and Morris, A., 'Voluntary Euthanasia' (1970) 45 *Wash.LRev.* 239.

[9] e.g. Kohl, *Beneficent Euthanasia*, above n. 8; Williams, *The Sanctity of Life and the Criminal Law*, above Ch. 3 n. 63, at 310–12. See pp. 7–8 above for definition of these terms.

pro-euthanasia arguments considered in this chapter will only be dealing with active voluntary euthanasia.

A. *Self-Determination: An Argument from Liberty*

The main argument in support of the legalization of active voluntary euthanasia is based on the principle of autonomy or the right to self-determination.[10] According to this principle, each person has value and is worthy of respect, is the bearer of basic rights and freedoms, and is the final determinant of his or her destiny.[11] Proponents argue that an individual who has decision-making capacity, has the right to control his or her own body and should be able to determine how and when he or she will die as long as this does not interfere with the rights of others. It is this human self-determination, the capacity of individuals to choose and pursue their particular life-plan, which is said to give persons their special moral status[12] and is an essential component of the dignity that attaches to rational personhood.[13]

Proponents argue that maintenance of the present legal prohibition on active voluntary euthanasia is an unjustifiable infringement of the liberty of those persons who would choose to be killed.[14] It has been argued that to deny active voluntary euthanasia is a form of tyranny; an attempt to control the life of a person who has his or her own autonomous view about how that life should go, and that this constitutes an ultimate denial of respect for persons.[15] According to proponents of euthanasia, in order to uphold the patient's interest in self-determination, doctors should be free to act upon the request of an informed and mentally capable patient for active voluntary euthanasia without fear of criminal liability.

If the principle of self-determination is accepted as the appropriate foundation for the legalization of active voluntary euthanasia there would be no need objectively to examine quality of life considerations—indeed, it would be quite inappropriate to do so. Any attempt to impose a qualitative assess-

---

[10] Smith, G. P., 'All's Well That Ends Well: Toward a Policy of Assisted Rational Suicide or Merely Enlightened Self-Determination?' (1989) 22 *UCalif. Davis* 275; Arras, J., 'The Right to Die on the Slippery Slope' (1982) 8 *Social Theory & Practice* 285, 293–4. Opponents of legalization have, however, taken the view that the right to self-determination does not extend to allowing an individual to choose to be killed; e.g. Callahan, D., 'Can We Return Death to Disease?' (1989) 19 *Hastings Center* R 4, 5.

[11] Gula, R., 'Moral Principles Shaping Public Policy on Euthanasia' (1990) 14 *Second Opinion* 73, 78.

[12] Rawls, J., 'Rational and Full Autonomy' (1980) 77 *JPhil.* 524.

[13] Dyck, A., 'An Alternative to the Ethics of Euthanasia' in Weir, R. (ed.), *Ethical Issues in Death and Dying* (New York, 1977) 281, 285.

[14] Euthanasia Society, *A Plan for Voluntary Euthanasia*, Revised edn. (London, 1962) 5–9.

[15] Harris, J., 'Euthanasia and the Value of Life' in Keown, J. (ed.), *Euthanasia Examined: Ethical, Clinical and Legal Perspectives* (Cambridge, 1995) 6, 19.

ment of the patient's life as a basis for active euthanasia would be a violation of the requirement of justice[16] and would be completely contrary to the
principle of patient autonomy. Different patients will inevitably have different goals and values which can best be respected by giving effect to the
patient's interest in self-determination and allowing the patient to make
decisions based on his or her own quality of life assessment. Thus, subject to
any requirements of enabling legislation,[17] the sole consideration should be
the patient's choice, based on the patient's *subjective* assessment of his or
her circumstances whether motivated by a fear of pain, suffering, dependency, or other causes.

Further, it must be understood that strict adherence to the notion of self-
determination necessarily dispels any reliance upon utilitarian principles as
a basis for active euthanasia. The arguments of some proponents for the
legalization of active euthanasia rest on a form of utilitarian humanism
which demands the decriminalization of certain acts of euthanasia and
suicide.[18] On pure utilitarian principles, active euthanasia would be justified
in circumstances where the patient, and persons involved in the care of the
patient, are suffering a balance of pain over pleasure and where the killing
of the patient would, on utilitarian calculations, produce the greatest good
for the greatest number. However, this reveals a fundamental weakness in
utilitarian arguments as a basis for strictly voluntary euthanasia, in that
they apply with equal force to cases of involuntary euthanasia—a practice
which must be unequivocally deplored. According to utilitarian principles,
provided there is a balance of pain over pleasure, active euthanasia
would be justified if it could maximize benefits overall, regardless of
whether the patient can or would give consent.[19] Thus, the interests of
the individual patient are subordinated to the interests of the majority.
Because of this possible manipulation of utilitarian arguments towards non-
voluntary and involuntary euthanasia, utilitarianism ought to be rejected
as a moral theory justifying active voluntary euthanasia.[20] In contrast,
however, the autonomy-based principle of self-determination, essentially
anti-utilitarian in nature, is not susceptible to the same arguments for

---

[16] Grisez, G. and Boyle, J. M., *Life and Death with Liberty and Justice: A Contribution to the Euthanasia Debate* (Notre Dame, Indiana, 1979) 214–50.

[17] For discussion, see Ch. 8.

[18] e.g. Williams, *The Sanctity of Life and the Criminal Law*, above Ch. 3 n. 63, at 277–312 and the analysis of Williams' argument by Richards, D., 'Constitutional Privacy, the Right to Die and the Meaning of Life', above Ch. 2 n. 153, at 335–6.

[19] Richards, 'Constitutional Privacy, the Right to Die and the Meaning of Life', above Ch. 2 n. 153, at 335–401.

[20] Ibid. at 401. Some philosophers have attempted to overcome these objections by arguing for the acceptance of rule-utilitarianism rather than act-utilitarianism (for discussion see Hospers, J., *An Introduction to Philosophical Analysis* (London, 1967) 604–12) or by substitut-
ing calculations based on happiness with consideration of interests; see Rachels, J., *The End of Life: The Morality of Euthanasia* (Oxford, 1986) 156–8.

extension to non-voluntary or involuntary forms of killing, and therefore constitutes the only acceptable basis for the legalization of active voluntary euthanasia.

B. The Patient's Right to Refuse Treatment: Is there a Morally Valid Distinction between Passive and Active Euthanasia?

In support of arguments based on the patient's interest in self-determination, proponents frequently draw attention to the inconsistency of the present law which permits a patient to induce an earlier death by refusing treatment, yet categorically prohibits a patient from seeking active assistance in dying.[21]

As outlined in Chapter 1, the patient's interest in self-determination finds expression in the important legal right to bodily integrity.[22] It is now well accepted that a fully informed patient who has decision-making capacity, has the right to refuse any life-sustaining medical treatment, notwithstanding that death may result. This right is grounded in the importance of respecting a patient's autonomy and self-determination in health care decisions, including decisions concerning the manner and timing of death. Proponents argue that if the law recognizes the patient's autonomy and self-determination as justification for passive euthanasia, it is logically inconsistent to refuse to recognize the same interests as a justification for active euthanasia.[23] This argument, based on the inconsistency of the present law, derives significant support from the claim by many philosophers and ethicists that there is no morally relevant difference between passive euthanasia—deliberately letting a patient die—and active euthanasia—the killing of a patient; both involve the intentional termination of life.[24] Moreover, it is argued that to deny active assistance to a patient who seeks it, is not only an infringement of that person's interest in self-determination, but may also be contrary to the patient's 'best interests', since the alternative of letting die may be neither swift nor painless.[25] Furthermore,

---

[21] Kuhse, H., 'Euthanasia—Again' (1985) 142 MJA 610; Winkler, E., 'Reflections on the State of Current Debate Over Physician-Assisted Suicide and Euthanasia' (1995) 9 *Bioethics* 313.

[22] See pp. 34–45 above.

[23] e.g. Kuhse, H., 'The Case for Active Voluntary Euthanasia' (1986) 14 *Law, Med. & Health Care* 145.

[24] There is a growing body of literature on the moral significance of the killing/letting die distinction, much of which was spawned by the argument presented by James Rachels, in his article 'Active and Passive Euthanasia' (1975) 292 *New Eng.JMed.* 78 which challenged the conventional doctrine that there is an important moral difference between killing and letting die. For other commentators in support of the moral equivalence view see Fletcher, 'Ethics and Euthanasia', above n. 8, at 675; Kuhse, H., *The Sanctity of Life Doctrine in Medicine: A Critique* (Oxford, 1987) 123–35.

[25] Kuhse, H., 'Active and Passive Euthanasia—Ten Years into the Debate' (1986) 1 *Euthanasia Rev.* 108, 117; Battin, M., 'The Least Worst Death' (1983) 13 *Hastings Center R* 13, 13–14.

since not all terminal or incurable patients are dependent on life-sustaining treatment, they do not all have the option of inducing death by refusing treatment, except perhaps by slowly starving and dehydrating themselves to death. It could, therefore, be argued that the present law is discriminatory in its operation since it does not offer to all patients the same opportunity of inducing an earlier death.[26]

Whilst many commentators support the view that there is no morally relevant difference between active and passive euthanasia, others have argued for the retention of the distinction. Some commentators have sought to defend the validity of the distinction on moral grounds arguing that a morally relevant difference exists which justifies maintenance of the prohibition against active euthanasia or 'killing'.[27] Others have claimed that irrespective of philosophical arguments, a distinction is discernible in practice in view of the willingness of doctors to allow patients to die, contrasted with their intuitive opposition to active voluntary euthanasia.[28] This claim can, however, be quickly countered on the basis that it purports to treat a value judgement as evidence and, furthermore, suggests that there is unanimity within the medical profession on the issue of active euthanasia which is clearly not the case.[29] What this alleged distinction does reveal is that there is an element of self-deception operative here which may assist doctors in justifying their conduct in permitting patients to die.

There are others still, including the influential President's Commission for the Study of Ethical Problems in Medicine and Biomedical and Behavioural Research, in its Report *Deciding to Forgo Life-Sustaining Treatment*, who are prepared to acknowledge that the distinction between acts and omissions leading to death is not of itself morally relevant, yet nevertheless argue for maintenance of the current prohibition of active voluntary euthanasia on practical grounds.[30] For example, concern is frequently expressed about the irrevocability of active euthanasia, allowing no opportunity for a change of mind or to correct mistakes, but the most serious concerns stem

---

[26] Note in this context the equal protection arguments that were raised in *Compassion in Dying* v. *State of Washington* No. 94-35534 (9th Cir. March 6 1996) (*en banc*) and which were upheld in *Quill* v. *Vacco* No. 60 (2nd Cir. April 2 1996) in relation to physician-assisted suicide. For discussion see pp. 101–21 above.

[27] e.g. Keyserlingk, E., *Sanctity of Life or Quality of Life in the Context of Ethics, Medicine and Law* (Ottawa, 1979) 123–6; Beauchamp, T., 'A Reply to Rachels on Active and Passive Euthanasia' in Beauchamp, T. and Perlin, S. (eds.), *Ethical Issues in Death and Dying* (Englewood Cliffs, New Jersey, 1978) 246–58.

[28] Gillett, G., 'Euthanasia, Letting Die and the Pause' (1988) 14 *JMed. Ethics* 61. See also Maguire, D., *Death by Choice* (Garden City, New York, 1984) 98 where he argues that omissions and commissions are different realities and since morality is based on reality a *real* difference could be expected to make a *moral* difference.

[29] Parker, M., 'Moral Intuition, Good Deaths and Ordinary Medical Practitioners' (1990) 16 *JMed. Ethics* 28, 29. For discussion of the views of the medical profession see pp. 292–332 below.

[30] President's Commission for the Study of Ethical Problems in Medicine and Biomedical and Behavioural Research, *Deciding to Forgo Life-Sustaining Treatment: A Report on the Ethical, Medical and Legal Issues in Treatment Decisions* (Washington, 1983) 65–73; Capron, A., 'The Right to Die: Progress and Peril' (1987) 2 *Euthanasia Rev.* 42, 53–9.

from a fear of abuse and other negative social consequences if active voluntary euthanasia were to be legalized. A rebuttal of these practical arguments will be presented later in this chapter.

There is no doubt at all that the existing prohibition on active voluntary euthanasia places significant limits on the self-determination of some patients. This has been recognized by many of those resisting legalization yet has not been seen as sufficient justification for any change to the present law. A prime example of this approach is to be found in the Report of the President's Commission. The commission acknowledged that policies prohibiting direct killing may conflict with the important value of patient self-determination but nonetheless went on to find this limitation on individual self-determination to be an acceptable cost of securing the general protection of human life.[31]

This reasoning is open to criticism. Particularly if one accepts the force of the argument that there is no intrinsic moral difference between active and passive euthanasia, there appears to be no valid justification for refusing to uphold the patient's self-determination in cases of active voluntary euthanasia. The practical arguments against the legalization of active voluntary euthanasia (for example, the possibility of error and abuse) can be adequately addressed through the introduction of appropriate regulation and safeguards and do not justify undermining the patient's right of self-determination. The only acceptable limitation on the patient's right to make decisions for him or herself is the requirement that the patient has decision-making capacity and is in a position to make an informed choice.

Analogy with suicide

Another argument frequently advanced in support of legalization of active voluntary euthanasia proceeds by way of analogy to the law of suicide. The argument begins with the proposition that since it is not unlawful for a person to commit or attempt to commit suicide,[32] the law, implicitly at least, recognizes the right of an individual to take his or her life. From this premise it is argued that if an individual does have the right to take his or her life, he or she should be able to seek the assistance of others in achieving this end.[33]

A right to commit suicide?

Some commentators have argued for a moral right to commit suicide, at least in some circumstances.[34] The real issue, however, for the purposes of

---

[31] President's Commission Report, *Deciding to Forgo Life-Sustaining Treatment*, above n. 30, at 73.

[32] For a discussion of the law dealing with suicide and attempted suicide, see pp. 56–7 above.

[33] Rachels, J., 'Barney Clark's Key' (1983) 13 *Hastings Center R* 17, 19; Fletcher, J., 'The Courts and Euthanasia' (1987–88) 15 *Law, Med.&Health Care* 223, 228.

[34] e.g. Battin, M., 'Suicide: A Fundamental Human Right?' in Battin, M. and Mayo, D. (eds.), *Suicide: The Philosophical Issues* (New York, 1980) 267–85; and Charlesworth, M., *Life, Death, Genes and Ethics* (Crows Nest, New South Wales, 1989) 70–1.

the present discussion, is whether an individual has a *legal right* to do so. The answer to this question must be in the negative, particularly in view of the continuing prohibition on assisting suicide and the laws which uphold intervention in the suicide of another.[35] The most accurate assessment of the current position is that the decriminalization of suicide and attempted suicide has not created any positive or legally enforceable *right* to commit suicide—it has merely given persons the *liberty*, subject to certain constraints, of choosing to end their own lives without thereby incurring criminal liability.[36] It could, nevertheless, still be argued that if persons are generally at liberty to commit suicide, they should also be free to seek the assistance of others in achieving their aim and, if necessary, to authorize another to take active steps to bring about their death. Further to this argument, if a third person complies with a request for assistance that person ought not be penalized since they are simply facilitating what the individual is at liberty to do. It must be emphasized that this argument does not necessarily entail general endorsement of suicide and suicide assistance. In many instances, suicidal persons are psychologically disturbed and should be prevented from implementing their plan. There are, however, cases where the choice of death is rational and where it would be entirely inappropriate to intervene, for example, in circumstances where a terminal or incurable patient seeks death as a relief from his or her suffering.

Significance of third party involvement

On the assumption that there is some validity in the analogy between suicide and active voluntary euthanasia, a crucial question which needs to be addressed is what significance, if any, should be attached to the fact that active voluntary euthanasia involves the direct assistance of a third party? Some commentators have argued that an important distinction exists between suicide on the one hand, which is an autonomous and self-regarding act, and assisted suicide or active voluntary euthanasia on the other, which requires the involvement and assistance of a third party.[37] This third party involvement, they argue, constitutes a crucial difference because the conduct changes from being a purely private act to a form of public action with ramifications extending beyond the parties involved. Moreover, it has been suggested that if the argument for active voluntary euthanasia is based on dignity of human freedom and self-determination, then it is inconsistent to ask someone else to assist.[38] However, this objection ignores the practical

[35] See p. 74, n. 100 above.
[36] Note, however, recent developments in the USA, where a constitutionally protected liberty interest in physician-assisted suicide has been recognized for competent, terminally ill patients: see pp. 94–124 above.
[37] Callahan, 'Can We Return Death to Disease?', above n. 10, at 4.
[38] Linacre Centre, Report of a Working Party, *Euthanasia and Clinical Practice: Trends, Principles and Alternatives* (London, 1982) 28–9.

realities of patients *in extremis* who are often physically unable to secure the means to a quick and easy death and may even be unable to self-administer the fatal dose if it were made available to them. It also disregards persons who are unable to commit suicide due to physical disability. On humanitarian grounds, it could be argued that it would be more compassionate and humane to assist those who wish to die but who are unable to kill themselves unaided by either directly administering active voluntary euthanasia or providing medical assistance in suicide to ensure that death is assured and achieved in a dignified manner.

Whilst it is conceded that the involvement of third parties in cases of doctor-assisted suicide and active voluntary euthanasia does differentiate these cases from autonomous suicide, it is disputed that this significantly alters the character of the acts to such a degree that they should necessarily be prohibited. The more relevant consideration is whether the patient has requested assistance. If the choice of death represents an exercise in patient autonomy and self-determination, this choice ought to be respected and it should be permissible to assist the patient in achieving his or her aim. The debate regarding third party involvement does, however, draw attention to the need also to respect the autonomy of others in dealing with a patient who seeks death.

Autonomy of others

According to accepted principles of autonomy and liberty, individuals should be free to pursue their own life choices, provided that this does not violate the rights of any third parties. In promoting the self-determination and autonomy of the patient, care must be taken not to interfere with the autonomy of others. In particular, doctors should not be required to abdicate their autonomy in favour of that of the patient. The position of third parties, and their right to remain free of involvement in the practice of active euthanasia, can be ensured by making it clear under any legislation permitting active voluntary euthanasia that doctors are under no *duty* to perform active euthanasia at the request of a patient, but may, in appropriate circumstances, be free to do so if they choose.[39]

A right to die?

Any attempt to analyse whether there is a 'right to die', or whether such a right should exist encounters enormous difficulties. To begin with, the

---

[39] But see the view of Grisez and Boyle, *Life and Death with Liberty and Justice,* above n. 16, at 163 where it is argued that the legalization of active voluntary euthanasia would infringe on the liberty of citizens to stand aloof from the practice regardless of whether they are personally involved in its administration.

popular notion of a right to die is virtually meaningless in view of the fact that, ultimately, death is inevitable for everyone. Moreover, the right to die is ambiguous in that it can mean anything from a right not to be kept alive against one's will to a more positive right to seek assistance to die. For the purposes of the present discussion, it will be assumed that the expression 'right to die' is intended to convey a right to active assistance in bringing about one's death. Understood in this way, it can be stated that there is at present no legally recognized right to die because as we have seen, with the exception of the Northern Territory of Australia,[40] active voluntary euthanasia is prohibited under the criminal law of all common law jurisdictions under consideration.

Active voluntary euthanasia as a human right?

On the basis of current human rights instruments, there appears to be little scope for arguing that there is a positive human right to die. No express provision is made in any of the human rights instruments for such a right. It could, however, be argued that a right to die, or at least a liberty to be assisted in securing an earlier death, can be established on the basis of other provisions contained in human rights instruments such as the right to life or the right to privacy or security of the person. All of the common law countries under consideration are parties to human rights instruments which contain such rights: the United Kingdom, the USA, Canada, Australia, and New Zealand are parties to the International Covenant on Civil and Political Rights and the United Kingdom has also signed and ratified the European Convention on Human Rights. Pursuant to these instruments, state parties or individuals[41] can bring a matter before the relevant human rights tribunal: the United Nations Human Rights Committee appointed under the ICCPR in respect of matters arising under that Covenant or the European Commission of Human Rights in respect of matters arising under the European Convention on Human Rights. The European Commission of Human Rights can investigate and report and can refer cases to the European Court of Human Rights.[42]

To date, there have been no cases where any of these human rights bodies have been called upon directly to consider the implications of human rights instruments on the issue of active voluntary euthanasia. There has, however, been some consideration of assisted suicide under Article 8 of the

---

[40] It should be noted that the Rights of the Terminally Ill Act 1995 (NT) does not create a positive right to such assistance, but simply makes it lawful for a doctor to comply with a patient's request in certain circumstances. For discussion see p. 346 below.

[41] Individuals only have standing in those states where the state has agreed to be bound by the Optional Protocol to the ICCPR. For the purposes of the countries under consideration, it should be noted that this step has not been taken by the USA.

[42] This is subject to the requirement in Article 46 of the European Convention on Human Rights that the state party has recognized its jurisdiction. The UK has fulfilled this requirement.

European Convention on Human Rights. In the case of *R* v. *UK*[43] the European Commission considered the admissibility of a complaint of the applicant, a member of the Voluntary Euthanasia Society (then known as EXIT), who had been convicted and sentenced to 18 months' imprisonment for aiding and abetting suicide and for conspiring to aid and abet suicide. *Inter alia*, the applicant complained that his conviction and sentence under section 2 of the Suicide Act 1961 constituted a violation of his right to respect for private life contrary to Article 8 of the Convention. It was argued that the offering of assistance to those who wanted to commit suicide falls within the domain of private life. The Commission held that the aiding and abetting of suicide cannot be described as falling into the sphere of private life protected under Article 8 of the Convention; on the contrary, the acts of aiding, abetting, counselling, or procuring suicide are excluded from the concept of privacy by virtue of their trespass on the public interest in protecting life as reflected in the criminal law provisions of the Suicide Act 1961. The Commission did, however, acknowledge in passing that assistance in suicide (and, by implication, any legislation prohibiting such conduct) might be thought to touch directly on the private lives of those who sought to commit suicide but this issue was clearly distinct from the circumstances of the application before the Commission.

Whilst there have been no cases directly raising the issues of an individual's right to active voluntary euthanasia or assistance in suicide, it is quite possible that in the future, a case could be brought before one of these bodies seeking to challenge the existing criminal law prohibition on assistance in dying on the grounds that such laws are inconsistent with human rights instruments, relying on one or more of a number of possible arguments.

All human rights instruments make provision for the 'right to life'.[44] On one view, a claim for active voluntary euthanasia could be seen as inconsistent with this right to life even though it involves intervention which the patient has consented to.[45] However, as is argued later in this chapter, in order to be at all meaningful, the right to life must be capable of waiver, and opting for an earlier death does not derogate from a person's right to life. For present purposes, an argument could be made that this provision prohibits any law which prevents a person from exercising a choice to end his or her life, with the assistance of that person's doctor.[46] Some support for

---

[43] (1983) 33 DR 270.

[44] e.g. International Covenant on Civil and Political Rights Article 6 (para. 1): 'Every human being has the inherent right to life. This right shall be protected by law. No one shall be arbitrarily deprived of his life'. See also Article 2 of the European Convention on Human Rights.

[45] Feldman, D., *Human Rights and Civil Liberties in England and Wales* (Oxford, 1993).

[46] Kennedy, I. and Grubb, A., *Medical Law: Text and Materials*, 2nd edn. (London, 1994) 1289.

this view can be found in the case of *Rodriguez* v. *British Columbia (Attorney General)*[47] which was considered in an earlier chapter.[48] In that case, the Supreme Court of Canada was required to consider whether the prohibition on assisted suicide under section 241(b) of the Canadian Criminal Code was contrary to the provisions of the Canadian Charter of Rights and Freedoms including section 7 which states that 'Everyone has the right to life, liberty and security of the person and the right not to be deprived thereof except in accordance with the principles of fundamental justice'. Whilst most of the judges (both those in the majority and the minority) relied on the individual's right to security[49] rather than the right to life in reaching their decision, Cory J (in dissent) was of the view that dying is an integral part of living and is therefore entitled to the constitutional protection provided by section 7.[50] Cory J concluded that the right to die with dignity should be as well protected as any other aspect of the right to life and accordingly held that this protection extended to incapacitated persons seeking assistance to die. This case is certainly an interesting example of how an expansive interpretation might be given to the 'right to life' as contained in human rights instruments.[51] However, having regard to human rights jurisprudence, it is doubtful whether the right to life can validly be interpreted as guaranteeing a positive right to die. The tendency has been not readily to imply the negative of a positive right; thus the right to life arguably does not entail a right to be assisted to die.

It is possible that an argument in support of an individual's right to seek assistance to die might be based on the right of privacy contained in a number of human rights instruments. It has, for example, been suggested that Article 8 of the European Convention on Human Rights which states *inter alia* that everyone has the right to respect for his private life, may be invoked as a basis for protecting an individual's right to seek assistance to die. Indeed, the decision of the European Commission in *R* v. *UK* noted earlier, clearly acknowledges that the prohibition on aiding and abetting suicide may be an interference with the right of a person seeking to commit suicide to respect for private life. Article 8 has been given a wide interpretation so as to protect a range of individual interests. It is therefore quite possible that it could be interpreted as protecting a patient's choice of how to die.[52] The right to privacy provision in the International Covenant on

[47] *Rodriguez* v. *British Columbia (Attorney General)* [1993] 3 SCR 519.
[48] See pp. 86–94 above.
[49] See discussion below.
[50] See above n. 47, at 630.
[51] Note also the decision of Hamilton CJ in the Irish Supreme Court decision, *In the Matter of a Ward of Court* [1995] 2 ILRM 401, where he held that the right to life which is recognized by the Irish Constitution necessarily implies the right to have nature take its course and to die a natural death. However, he went on to state that it does not include the right to have life terminated or death accelerated.
[52] Kennedy and Grubb, *Medical Law*, above Ch. 1 n. 69, at 1303.

Civil and Political Rights, although cast in somewhat different terms,[53] is open to the same sort of interpretation. However, the protections afforded under these provisions are not absolute. For example, the right to privacy under the European Convention on Human Rights is qualified by Article 8(2) which countenances interference with this right if it is in accordance with the law and is necessary in a democratic society for the protection of health or morals or for the protection of the rights and freedoms of others. Similarly, the right to privacy provision under the International Covenant on Civil and Political Rights only protects against 'arbitrary or unlawful interference'. These qualifications, particularly the explicit proviso in Article 8(2) of the European Convention on Human Rights, introduce consideration of the type of policy arguments which were raised by some of the judges in the *Rodriguez* case in the course of determining whether the infringement of Sue Rodriguez's rights which they found to be established under section 7 of Charter could be justified under the Charter.[54] Of particular relevance would be whether the prohibition on assisted death was a necessary and proportional response to achieve the purpose underlying it, that is, the protection of human life and the prevention of abuse.[55] This clearly leaves some room for interpretation as is illustrated by the division of the court in the *Rodriguez* case: the conclusion of the majority of the Canadian Supreme Court was that given the concerns about abuse if assisted suicide were decriminalized, the legislative prohibition on assisted suicide, although amounting to a deprivation of the plaintiff's interests, was consistent with the principles of fundamental justice. However, the minority judges, whilst accepting that there are dangers of abuse, were of the view that the State had not satisfied the onus of demonstrating that abuse cannot be prevented by permitting physician-assisted suicide in carefully regulated circumstances and by the fact that the existing criminal law prohibition in respect of unconsented to killing would apply to such conduct.

Another possible argument in support of human rights recognition of assisted dying might be based on the provision guaranteeing 'liberty and security of the person' (particularly the reference to 'security of the person') contained in a number of human rights instruments.[56] The Canadian

---

[53] See Article 17(1): 'No one shall be subjected to arbitrary or unlawful interference with his privacy, family home or correspondence, nor to unlawful attacks on his honour or reputation'.

[54] The majority considered this by reference to s. 7 itself which contains a proviso 'except in accordance with the principles of fundamental justice'; a number of the judges in the minority instead based their interpretation on s. 1 of the Charter which provides that a law which violates the principles of fundamental justice under s. 7 may be saved under s. 1 if the State proves that it is reasonable and demonstrably justified in a free society. See further pp. 87–9 above.

[55] Kennedy and Grubb, *Medical Law,* above Ch. 1 n. 69, at 1303.

[56] See the International Covenant on Civil and Political Rights Article 9(1): 'Everyone has the right to liberty and security of the person'. See also Article 5 of the European Convention on Human Rights.

Charter of Rights and Freedoms (section 7) contains a similar provision which, as noted earlier, was given detailed consideration by the Canadian Supreme Court in the *Rodriguez* case. The issue before the court in the *Rodriguez* case was quite narrow in its terms, turning on the rights of physically handicapped persons who would be unable to commit suicide. Nevertheless, the acceptance by the judges of the court that the right to security of the person in section 7 of the Charter encompasses notions of personal autonomy protecting choices concerning one's body, is of wider significance and may in the future influence the development of human rights jurisprudence in this area.[57] To date, however, the interpretation of the protection of liberty and security of the person under international human rights instruments has been given a more limited interpretation centred on freedom from arbitrary arrest and detention which must be protected by the State.

Finally, a somewhat tenuous argument may be made based on a provision contained in a number of human rights instruments to the effect that 'No one shall be subject to cruel, inhuman or degrading treatment or punishment'.[58] The two main issues which arise for consideration are whether the State's conduct in prohibiting assistance in dying constitutes 'treatment', and if so, whether the State is subjecting a citizen to it by merely prohibiting help. Consideration of the interpretation given to a similar provision in the Canadian Charter of Rights and Freedoms by the Canadian Supreme Court in the *Rodriguez* case is instructive. There it was held by the majority[59] that even assuming that 'treatment' within the meaning of section 12 may include that imposed by the State in contexts other than penal or quasi-penal, a mere prohibition by a State on certain action cannot constitute treatment under section 12. Further, it needs to be shown that the State has subjected the individual to the treatment complained of. The majority held that in order to do this, there must be some more active State process in operation involving an exercise of State control over the individual, whether it be positive action, inaction, or prohibition. According to Sopinka J giving judgment for the majority, 'To hold that the criminal prohibition in section 241(b) without the appellant being in any way subject to the state administrative or justice system, falls within the bounds of section 12 would stretch the ordinary meaning of being "subjected to . . . treatment" by the state'.[60]

It is apparent from the foregoing discussion that a number of possible arguments can be made in support of the view that the interests at stake with regard to active voluntary euthanasia and doctor-assisted suicide should be

[57] Note also the decision of Wilson J in *R* v. *Morgentaler* [1988] 1 SCR 30 in which he gave a broad interpretation of s. 7 holding that the right to 'liberty' protected an individual's autonomy over personal decisions intimately affecting that person's private life.
[58] e.g. International Covenant on Civil and Political Rights Article 7.
[59] The dissenting judges found it unnecessary to consider s. 12 of the Charter.
[60] See above, n. 100, 47 at 612.

recognized as fundamental human rights. However, in the absence of any clear authority in support, it is perhaps doubtful that such recognition will be given on the basis of current human rights instruments. Thus, the possibility of striking down laws which prohibit active voluntary euthanasia or doctor-assisted suicide on the basis that they are in contravention of human rights instruments appears, at this stage, to be rather remote. This is not to say that human rights considerations are completely irrelevant: even in the absence of a specific human right which can be claimed, human rights norms may be influential in the wider debate with respect to legalization.

Should there be a right to die?

If one accepts the principle of self-determination as the basis for active voluntary euthanasia, it remains to be determined what legal status should be given to the patient's interest in choosing an earlier death. In particular, it must be decided whether patients *should* have a right to die. In this context, an important distinction must be drawn between the right to die as expressed in terms of a basic human right (although not necessarily legally enforceable) and a legal right. The recognition of the right to die as a human right would create duties on the part of the State (for example, in relation to the amendment of its laws which prohibit doctors from giving assistance in dying); it would not confer on individuals any legally enforceable right to active voluntary euthanasia or impose any obligation on doctors to participate in its administration.

The situation is more problematic where the right to die is expressed in terms of a legally enforceable right. Apart from problems of definition, there are potential difficulties in adopting a strict rights-based model as the basis for legalization of active voluntary euthanasia. Although the notion of 'rights' is expansive and, in its wider sense, can be used to encompass a variety of legal concepts,[61] strictly speaking, rights (as distinct from liberties or privileges) are correlative with duties. Thus, the creation of any *right* to active euthanasia tends to imply a corresponding *duty* on the part of someone to become actively involved in bringing about death, although it is acknowledged that a right could conceivably be framed in a way which avoids the imposition of a duty on any particular person. For example, a 'right' to assistance could be created, but at the same time allowing conscientious objection for those doctors who are opposed to providing such assistance. Certainly in the US constitutional context, the courts have already indicated that the recognition of a constitutional right to physician-assisted suicide does not entail any duty on the part of any doctor.[62]

---

[61] Hohfeld, W., *Fundamental Legal Conceptions* (Cook, W. ed.), (New Haven, 1919) 6–7, 36–8.

[62] See the decision of the majority of the US Court of Appeals for the Ninth Circuit in the case of *Compassion in Dying* v. *State of Washington* see above Ch. 2 n. 54.

Another possibility is for the right to active voluntary euthanasia to be framed simply in terms of a right of one person to authorize another to kill him or her intentionally and directly[63] but without creating a right to demand such assistance.

There is broad agreement amongst euthanasia advocates that it would be inappropriate to impose a duty on any person to take the life of another. Although such a duty would uphold the autonomy of the patient who requests assistance, it is recognized that it would be an unjustifiable interference with the autonomy of others. It is primarily to avoid the implication of any such duty and the resulting infringement of the autonomy of third parties that a strictly rights-based model has been widely rejected as an appropriate basis for the legalization of active voluntary euthanasia.[64]

Self-determination and the liberty to choose an earlier death

The dilemma which confronts us is to find some way to give effect to the autonomy and self-determination of the patient, but, at the same time, to protect the autonomy of others. This dilemma can best be resolved by holding that the patient's right of self-determination does not necessarily translate into an enforceable legal *right* to demand assistance to die. The patient's interest in self-determination can be appropriately protected by recognizing a *liberty*[65] to choose an earlier death and have the assistance of a doctor to bring it about. If the patient's interest is expressed in terms of a liberty rather than a legal right it would not be legally enforceable and would not create any duties upon others to accede to a patient's request for death.[66] Thus, a doctor willing to assist would be *permitted* to perform active euthanasia at the request of a patient without being under any duty to do so. The creation of a liberty would nevertheless be significant in that persons desiring active voluntary euthanasia would not be restrained from exercising that choice, and provided they have a doctor willing to comply with their request, they may lawfully secure a quick and painless death. Indeed, the mere knowledge that active voluntary euthanasia is available in the event that suffering becomes unbearable would in many instances be sufficient to

---

[63] e.g. the discussion by Kamisar, Y., 'Physician-Assisted Suicide, The Last Bridge to Active Voluntary Euthanasia' in Keown (ed.), *Euthanasia Examined,* above n. 15, at 225.

[64] e.g. Williams, P., 'Rights and the Alleged Rights of Innocents to be Killed' (1976–77) 87 *Ethics*; Trowell, H., *The Unfinished Debate on Euthanasia* (London, 1973) 116–21; Velleman, J., 'Against the Right to Die' (1992) 17 *JMed.&Phil.* 665.

[65] For a definition of a 'liberty', see, for example, Grisez and Boyle, *Life and Death with Liberty and Justice,* above n. 16, at 453 (defined as the absence of imposed constraints to pursuing one's own purposes in one's own way); Feinberg, J., *The Moral Limits of the Criminal Law* Vol. I *Harm to Others* (New York, 1984) 7 (the absence of legal coercion).

[66] See Trowell, *The Unfinished Debate on Euthanasia,* above Ch. 2 n. 2, at 120–1; Hohfeld, *Fundamental Legal Conceptions,* above n. 61, 7, at 38–50.

put patients in control and remove the fear of having to endure intolerable pain or other distress.[67]

It is clear from the foregoing analysis that the principle of self-determination is central to the case for legalization of active voluntary euthanasia. Consideration will now turn to a number of other arguments which support the case for legalization.

C. Prevention of Cruelty: An Argument from Mercy

Another argument, which is a cornerstone of the case for the legalization of active voluntary euthanasia, is the need to alleviate pain and suffering and to prevent cruelty.[68] Proponents argue that to maintain the legal prohibition on active voluntary euthanasia amounts to cruel and degrading treatment and that cruelty is an evil which must be avoided so far as possible. They argue that in circumstances where there is no reasonable prospect of meaningful recovery, considerations of commonsense and compassion demand that patients should be allowed a merciful release from prolonged and useless suffering. Further, as noted earlier, reliance on the passive form of euthanasia will not necessarily guarantee a swift and painfree death. If active voluntary euthanasia were legalized, doctors would be able to comply with a patient's request to die and the merciful and kindly treatment of patients would be promoted.

A potential conflict exists between the duty to prevent cruelty and relieve suffering, and the doctor's duty to save life. This conflict can best be resolved by holding that where a patient has voluntarily requested active euthanasia, the greater duty is to accede to the patient's request and avoid unnecessary suffering.[69] Although legalizing active voluntary euthanasia would not totally eliminate all pain and suffering associated with terminal illness, it would significantly reduce the burden on patients by placing the power to end a miserable existence under the patient's own control.[70] This empowerment of the individual may in turn improve the quality of the remaining time, and may in fact assist the patient to live longer, confident in the knowledge that assistance is available if needed.

The argument from prevention of suffering and cruelty has been more positively stated by Kohl who has advocated the principle of 'beneficent

---

[67] This proposition is supported by the findings of the Remmelink study in the Netherlands; see pp. 428, 441 below.

[68] e.g. Williams, G., 'Euthanasia Legislation: A Rejoinder to the Non-Religious Objections' in Downing, A. and Smoker, B. (eds.), *Voluntary Euthanasia: Experts Debate the Right to Die* (London, 1986) 156, 156–7.

[69] More detailed consideration of the role of the medical profession is presented below, pp. 242–7.

[70] Morris, 'Voluntary Euthanasia', above n. 8, at 254.

euthanasia'.[71] Kohl argues that active euthanasia is 'kind' treatment, and since society and its members have a *prima facie* obligation to treat members kindly, it follows that beneficent euthanasia is a *prima facie* obligation. It should be noted that Kohl supports not only active voluntary euthanasia but also non-voluntary euthanasia in some circumstances. Nevertheless, the value of Kohl's contribution to the debate has been to highlight that active euthanasia is a means of minimizing suffering and maximizing kind and loving treatment of patients. However, for the reasons outlined above, the notion of a *prima facie* obligation to provide euthanasia must be rejected, at least in so far as it implies that a *duty* is cast upon any particular individual to perform an act of euthanasia.

Opponents of euthanasia have sought to undermine arguments based upon the prevention of cruelty and need for merciful treatment by suggesting that the concepts of 'mercy' and 'prevention of cruelty' are flexible, capable of differing interpretations, and that this may, with time, result in an ever-increasing category of candidates for active euthanasia.[72] Further, it is claimed that the concern of proponents is often not with the pain and suffering of the patient but of the family, relatives, and friends who must witness the patient's last days.[73] However, these arguments have no validity in the present context of a proposal for active *voluntary* euthanasia which is firmly based on the fundamental principle of self-determination. The crucial issue is not whether the doctors believe it would be merciful to terminate life, or the need to relieve the understandable anguish of loved ones, but whether the patient seeks active euthanasia as a release from his or her suffering.

D. *Promotion of Human Dignity*

Closely related to the foregoing arguments based on self-determination and the prevention of cruelty is the argument that legalization of active voluntary euthanasia is necessary in order to promote human dignity. Proponents argue that the notion of human dignity demands that individuals have control over significant life decisions, including the choice to die, and that this control is acknowledged and respected by others.[74] This argument is well encapsulated by Fletcher where he states that 'to prolong life uselessly, while the personal qualities of freedom, knowledge, self-possession and

[71] See Kohl, M., *The Morality of Killing: Sanctity of Life, Abortion and Euthanasia* (London, 1974) 106; 'Voluntary Beneficent Euthanasia' in Kohl, *Beneficent Euthanasia*, above n. 8.

[72] e.g. Dyck, A., 'The Good Samaritan Ideal and Beneficent Euthanasia: Conflicting Views of Mercy' (1975) 42 *Linacre Q* 176, 180–1.

[73] e.g. Parker, G., 'You are a Child of the Universe: You Have a Right to be Here' (1977) 7 *Man.LJ* 151, 155.

[74] e.g. Moore, M., 'The Case for Voluntary Euthanasia' (1974) 42 *UMKCLRev.* 327, 332.

control, and responsibility are sacrificed, is to attack the moral status of a person'.[75]

Advances in medical technology have greatly increased the capacity of the medical profession to prolong life. In many cases, however, death can be merely forestalled and patients may face the prospect of a prolonged and agonizing death. For many patients, the principal fear is not of pain or even death itself, but of loss of control of bodily and mental functions and the resulting helplessness and dependence on others—in short the depersonalization of the dying. Patients may understandably wish to spare themselves and their loved ones the indignity of a prolonged death and creeping mental and physical deterioration. Indeed, it is this concern for the circumstances of one's dying that has largely fuelled the campaign for 'death with dignity' and has led to the introduction in some jurisdictions of 'natural death' legislation giving legal effect to living wills and legislation providing for the appointment of enduring powers of attorney to make health care decisions.[76]

The present law permits passive euthanasia, but this will not guarantee a patient a humane and dignified death. On the contrary, a 'natural death' achieved by the refusal of treatment may be particularly unpleasant and undignified.[77] According to proponents, preservation of human dignity can only be assured with the acceptance of active voluntary euthanasia, and the recognition of the liberty of the individual to determine the manner and timing of his or her death.

Opponents of euthanasia have challenged this reasoning on two fronts. First, they claim that *all* individuals have intrinsic worth and dignity and it would therefore be immoral to sanction the death of any individual. Indeed, they argue, it is because of their respect for human worth and dignity that they steadfastly disapprove of active voluntary euthanasia.[78] Secondly, they assert that the argument based on the notion of human dignity logically entails that all who live in an unalterably undignified form of existence ought to be killed.[79] Both of these arguments are misconceived. The first argument is flawed because it proceeds on a different notion of 'dignity' than that which is being claimed here, namely the power to control important aspects of one's life including matters of life and death. Acceptance and preservation of human dignity in this sense in no way purports to deny the intrinsic worth and dignity of all human beings regardless of their health or

---

[75] *Morals and Medicine*, above Ch. 3 n. 56, at 191.   [76] See further, p. 36, n. 113 above.

[77] e.g. Battin, 'The Least Worst Death', above n. 25, at 13–14.

[78] e.g. British Medical Association (BMA) Working Party Report, *Euthanasia: Report of a Working Party to Review the British Medical Associations Guidance on Euthanasia* (London, 1988) 40; Gormally, L., 'A Non-Utilitarian Case Against Voluntary Euthanasia' in Downing and Smoker (eds.), *Voluntary Euthanasia*, above n. 68, at 72, 82–8.

[79] See Kluge, E., *The Practice of Death* (New Haven, 1975) 154–7 for an analysis of this argument.

condition.[80] The second argument, reminiscent of the objections raised against the prevention of cruelty argument, also fails because it ignores the important correlation between preserving human dignity and upholding the patient's interest in self-determination. If self-determination is accepted as the touchstone, there can be no suggestion that persons will be disposed of, on the basis of some objective assessment of whether their life lacks dignity. It is through the recognition of the principle of self-determination that respect is shown for individuals and human dignity is promoted.

E. What is Morally Right Should be Made Legally Permissible

Another argument advanced by some proponents, is that since active voluntary euthanasia is acknowledged by many to be *morally* right, it should be made *legally* permissible.[81] In furtherance of this argument, attention is drawn to the conflicting demands placed on individual doctors faced with a request for active euthanasia; on the one hand, the desire to act mercifully and relieve the patient's suffering and on the other, the concern to be law-abiding and avoid violation of the criminal law. Proponents argue that this places doctors in an intolerable situation and that society has a duty to make legally permissible conduct that is merciful and widely recognized as morally right.[82]

It is certainly true that despite the forceful objections of some commentators, there has been widespread support from a variety of sources for the view that in certain circumstances, active voluntary euthanasia is morally justified.[83] Subject to possible negative consequences which may flow from the legalization of active voluntary euthanasia, which will be dealt with below, a strong argument can be made that the law should reflect prevailing morality. This argument will be developed later in this chapter in the part dealing with the role of the criminal law. It should be noted, however, that the arguments presented in this work in support of legalization of active voluntary euthanasia do not necessarily depend on the acceptance of the morality of the practice—indeed, it is acknowledged that there is no moral consensus on this issue.

One possible counter-argument which will be dealt with more fully in the context of the case against legalization is that an important distinction exists

---

[80] Kohl, 'Voluntary Beneficent Euthanasia', above n. 71, at 132–4 where he examines the different interpretations of 'dignity'. See also below, the discussion of Dworkin's thesis regarding the sacredness of human life and the need to respect the dignity of individuals.

[81] e.g. Russell, R., *Freedom to Die: The Legal Aspects of Euthanasia*, Revised edn. (New York, 1977) 235–6; Williams, G., 'Euthanasia and Abortion' (1966) 38 *UColo.LRev.* 178, 182.

[82] Russell, *Freedom to Die,* above n. 81, at 235.

[83] Support has come from theologians; e.g. Joseph Fletcher (Episcopal Minister); Daniel Maguire (Catholic philosopher); lawyers (e.g. Glanville Williams); doctors (e.g. Rodney Syme and Malcolm Parker); and ethicists and philosophers (e.g. Marvin Kohl and Robert Young).

between the morality of the individual case and the appropriateness of developing a public policy permitting active voluntary euthanasia. In fact, many opponents of legalization are prepared to concede the morality of active voluntary euthanasia in exceptional circumstances, but vigorously reject the introduction of legislation to cover such cases which would institutionalize the practice. The validity of this position in turn depends on an assessment of the practical objections to the legalization of active voluntary euthanasia which will be undertaken later in this chapter.

F. Formalize Current Practices

A further argument in support of the legalization of active voluntary euthanasia is that we need to formalize existing practices. There are two separate aspects of this argument: first, the argument that since the practice of active euthanasia already occurs, we need to institutionalize and regulate that practice with the adoption of proper safeguards in order to protect against the risk of abuse; and secondly, that the practice should be legalized to overcome existing discrepancies between legal theory and practice. Both of these arguments will now be considered in turn.

The need to regulate and protect against abuse

Reference was made in the preceding chapter to available evidence which indicates that some doctors, at least, are already involved in the practice of active voluntary euthanasia even though this contravenes the criminal law.[84] As many of the opponents of legalization have pointed out, the mere fact that the law is being broken is not of itself a valid ground for legal change.[85] There are, however, certain difficulties inherent in the present situation which call for a re-evaluation of the prohibition of active voluntary euthanasia. Because the practice is presently illegal, it is performed covertly leaving little opportunity for consultation[86] or regulation. It was also noted that even where fellow doctors become aware of a doctor's involvement in active voluntary euthanasia, they are likely to maintain the secrecy and not report their colleague to the legal authorities.[87] Decisions are more likely to be made on the basis of the participating doctor's own conscience and his or her willingness to take risks rather than the compelling nature of the pa-

[84] See pp. 134–8 above.

[85] e.g. Grisez and Boyle, *Life and Death with Liberty and Justice*, above n. 16, at 146.

[86] This conclusion is supported by survey findings which have shown that doctors only rarely consult colleagues about patient requests for assistance in dying: see Back, A., et al., 'Physician-Assisted Suicide and Euthanasia in Washington State: Patient Requests and Physician Responses' (1996) 275 JAMA 919, 923, 924.

[87] Verhoef, M. and Kinsella, T., 'Alberta Euthanasia Survey: 2. Physicians' Opinions About the Acceptance of Active Euthanasia as a Medical Act and the Reporting of Such Practices' (1993) 148 CMAJ 1929, 1931, 1932.

tient's request.[88] Particularly in light of the paternalistic nature of the medical profession, this may result in a situation where active euthanasia is performed by a doctor on the basis of what he or she perceives to be the patient's best interests, but without the express consent of the patient. There is, in fact already evidence which suggests that in the hidden practice of euthanasia as it exists, active euthanasia is not always performed at the request of the patient.[89] This is clearly contrary to the fundamental principle of self-determination and the requirement of voluntariness in the practice of active euthanasia. Further, since some doctors may be more willing than others to contravene the criminal law, the option of active euthanasia is not presently available to all patients, thereby causing potential injustice to some.[90]

The essence of the proponents' argument is that if the practice already occurs, it is preferable for it to be legalized and brought out into the open in order that appropriate safeguards can be implemented to protect against abuse.[91] There is good reason to believe that the risk of abuse and idiosyncratic decision-making would be reduced if a form of active voluntary euthanasia was legally available and the need for secrecy was overcome.[92] If a lawful means is established for doctors assisting patients to die which, subject to certain conditions, provides an immunity from criminal liability, it stands to reason that doctors would prefer to seek the protection of the law by complying with its terms rather than take the risk of incurring serious criminal liability. Legalization of active voluntary euthanasia would promote open discussion of the issues and would thereby contribute to the quality of decision-making. Legalization would also ensure that active voluntary euthanasia would be an option available to all patients subject only to the right of a doctor to decline to become involved in the practice. Patient self-determination would thereby be promoted.

The need to overcome discrepancies between legal theory and practice

The second part of the proponents' argument concerns the need to overcome existing discrepancies between legal theory and practice. Proponents

---

[88] Quill, T., et al., 'Care of the Hopelessly Ill: Proposed Criteria for Physician Assisted Suicide' (1992) 327 *NewEng.JMed.* 1380, 1383.

[89] e.g. the findings of Stevens, C. and Hassan, R., 'Management of Death, Dying and Euthanasia: Attitudes and Practices of Medical Practitioners in South Australia' (1994) 20 *JMed.Ethics* 41.

[90] e.g. Humphry, D., 'Euthanasia for the Elite' (1986) 1 *Euthanasia Rev.* 203; Institute of Medical Ethics, Working Party on the Ethics of Prolonging Life and Assisting Death, Discussion Paper, 'Assisted Death' (1990) 336 *Lancet* 610, 611.

[91] Levisohn, A., 'Voluntary Mercy Deaths' (1961) 8 *JForensic Med.* 57, 69; Institute of Medical Ethics, Discussion Paper 'Assisted Death', above n. 90, at 611.

[92] Quill et al., 'Care of the Hopelessly Ill: Proposed Criteria for Physician Assisted Suicide', above n. 88, at 1383. For a contrary view see Somerville, M., 'The Song of Death: The Lyrics of Euthanasia' (1993) 9 *JContemp.Health Law&Pol'y* 1, 41.

point out that even though there is evidence to suggest that some doctors are engaged in the practice of active voluntary euthanasia which constitutes murder, if one has regard to the realities of the law in practice, it is unlikely that a doctor would be prosecuted, or if prosecuted, that he or she would be convicted. From this premise, they argue that the law in operation in effect condones the practice of active voluntary euthanasia. Proponents go on to assert that the present disparity between legal theory and the law as it operates in practice is unsatisfactory, engendering cynicism and disrespect for the law.[93] Further, it is argued, that whilst it is most unlikely that a doctor would be prosecuted and convicted, there is, nevertheless, no guarantee of this;[94] indeed, the very informality of the present situation invites arbitrary and capricious results. Moreover, it is argued to be unsatisfactory that doctors who are acting *bona fide* and at the request of the patient should be exposed to the risk of prosecution. Thus, proponents are of the view that active voluntary euthanasia ought to be legalized in order to close the gap between legal theory and practice, and to ensure that doctors who perform active voluntary euthanasia are not vulnerable to criminal prosecution.[95]

The problems which stem from the present disparity between law and practice are serious and constitute good cause to re-evaluate the present criminal law prohibition on active voluntary euthanasia. A strong case can be made out that legalization of the practice is necessary in order to overcome these difficulties and to provide legal guidance for the making of medical and ethical decisions regarding the termination of life.

Arguments have also been advanced against legislating to overcome the present discrepancies between law and practice.[96] It has, for example, been argued that notwithstanding the occasional contravention of the law, the existing prohibition plays an important part at the macro or societal level in preventing many more cases of active euthanasia, a significant proportion of which would be non-voluntary and which would not in any event be legalized.[97] Significantly, though, those who seek to make these arguments are not suggesting that in all cases where the prohibition on active voluntary euthanasia is ignored the law should be invoked to prosecute: they acknowledge that although conduct may be illegal, in some circumstances at the level of the individual case prosecution is inappropriate.[98] The validity of

[93] See further pp. 149–50 above.

[94] This has been demonstrated by the prosecution and conviction of Dr Cox in the UK for the attempted murder of his patient. For discussion see pp. 143–5 above.

[95] e.g. Levisohn, 'Voluntary Mercy Deaths', above n. 91.

[96] e.g. Somerville, 'The Song of Death: The Lyrics of Euthanasia', above n. 92, at 42–3.

[97] e.g. Grisez and Boyle, *Life and Death with Liberty and Justice*, above n. 16, at 148; Kamisar, 'Some Non-Religious Views Against Proposed Mercy-Killing Legislation' (1958) 41 Minn.LRev. 969, 1042; Somerville, 'The Song of Death: The Lyrics of Euthanasia', above n. 92, at 43; New York State Task Force on Life and the Law, *When Death is Sought: Assisted Suicide and Euthanasia in the Medical Context* (New York, 1994) 140–1.

[98] e.g. Somerville, 'The Song of Death: The Lyrics of Euthanasia', above n. 92, at 43.

these arguments against legalization depends, to a large extent, on the so-called 'wedge argument' which will be considered later in this chapter. For present purposes, it can be stated that there is no evidence that the legalization of active voluntary euthanasia would lead to an increase in active non-voluntary or involuntary euthanasia; these forms of euthanasia are currently prohibited by the criminal law and would remain so.

G. Public Demand and Support for Active Voluntary Euthanasia

The case for legalization is further bolstered by evidence of growing public demand and support for active voluntary euthanasia. Opinion polls have been periodically conducted in the United Kingdom, the USA, Canada, and Australia to gauge public attitudes to whether active voluntary euthanasia ought to be legalized, and the results of these polls indicate increasing public support for its legalization.[99]

Opponents have been quick to challenge the relevance of such polls. At one level, they are critical of the manner in which the polls are conducted, particularly the way in which questions are framed.[100] It has also been argued that care needs to be taken with how such polls are to be interpreted. Attention has been drawn to inconsistencies within the same surveys and to the fact, in the light of the US citizen-initiated referendum experience,[101] that poll results have not always been an accurate predictor of legislative outcomes.[102] More fundamentally, however, some opponents have challenged the relevance of opinion polls in shaping law and public policy, arguing that it is not necessarily appropriate to base the law on the opinion of the majority.[103] There is, they argue, no guarantee that the opinions polled are based on an informed understanding of the issues, and even if opinions are informed and valid, opponents question whether the moral worth of an argument is to be judged by the number of those who subscribe to it.

Apart from the opinion polls, further evidence of public support and demand for legalization of active voluntary euthanasia is to be found in the emergence and growth in all jurisdictions of voluntary euthanasia societies actively campaigning for reform of the law in this area.[104] Moreover, the issue of active voluntary euthanasia has increasingly been brought before

---

[99] Waller, S., 'Trends in Public Acceptance of Euthanasia Worldwide' (1986) 1 *Euthanasia Rev.* 33. For further discussion see pp. 257–68 below.

[100] e.g. BMA Working Party Report, *Euthanasia*, above Ch. 3 n. 1, at 41–2; Keyserlingk, E., 'Public Opinion on Legalizing Active Euthanasia' (1987) 3 *Humane Med.* 139.

[101] See further pp. 364–8 below.

[102] Somerville, 'The Song of Death: The Lyrics of Euthanasia', above n. 92, at 21 referring to Initiative 119 in Washington State.

[103] e.g. BMA Working Party Report, *Euthanasia*, above Ch. 3 n. 1, at 42.

[104] See pp. 268–89 below.

the public by the media, and the community response has generally been favourable.[105]

Whilst it is, admittedly, very difficult accurately to assess the state of public opinion, available evidence regarding opinion polls and the growth of the voluntary euthanasia movement would appear to indicate that there is significant and increasing public demand and support for legalization. Since the role of the law is, at least in part, to meet the real needs of the community, evidence of public demand and support for legalization of active voluntary euthanasia can only operate to strengthen the case for reform. More detailed consideration will be given to the relevance of public opinion and the role of the law later in this chapter.

Another consideration which should be noted concerns the implications of a legalized form of active voluntary euthanasia for mercy killings generally. Mercy killings or assisted suicides in the family context arise quite frequently, often in circumstances where a loved one has persistently begged for assistance to die. If active voluntary euthanasia were an option legally available in such circumstances, it would be likely to reduce the occurrence of such family mercy killings which are inevitably performed inexpertly, often by crude and undignified means, and result in serious criminal liability for the mercy killer, although in many cases, mitigated by the leniency of the criminal justice system. Clearly it is preferable to ensure that where possible, a professional medical assessment is made and that the patient's death is brought about in accordance with specified safeguards for the performance of active voluntary euthanasia.

H. The Case For Legalization: An Evaluation

In the foregoing part, an attempt has been made to present and analyse the various arguments that have been raised in support of the legalization of active voluntary euthanasia. It has been demonstrated that a number of powerful and convincing arguments can be raised in support of such legalization, the most important of which is undoubtedly the libertarian principle of patient self-determination. It is submitted that on the strength of these arguments, taken together, a *prima facie* case exists for changing our laws to permit doctors to take active steps to end the lives of their patients at the patient's request.

An important aspect of the proponents' argument is that their claim for active voluntary euthanasia concerns a *liberty*; a claim to be free to seek assistance in determining the manner and timing of one's death. Proponents argue that in a free society, it is the *restraint* of liberty that must be justified, not the existence of liberty, and that the criminal law should not be invoked

---

[105] See pp. 289–90 below.

to repress conduct unless this is demonstrably necessary on social grounds.[106] Thus, it is argued, the onus lies upon those objecting to the legalization of active voluntary euthanasia to demonstrate why there should be restrictions on the liberty of the individual to seek and receive assistance in bringing about his or her death. According to this view, opponents will have to convince proponents what compelling public interest demands that patients are denied a choice of a painfree and dignified death. If the opponents fail to discharge this onus, then we are left with compelling arguments for legalization which ought to be acted upon.

Consideration must now turn to the case against legalization of active voluntary euthanasia, to determine whether any of the objections raised by opponents are of sufficient force to justify the restraint of individual liberty and self-determination.

II. THE CASE AGAINST LEGALIZATION OF ACTIVE VOLUNTARY EUTHANASIA

The arguments advanced by opponents of the legalization of active voluntary euthanasia can be divided into two categories; doctrinal or deontological arguments on the one hand, and pragmatic or consequentialist objections on the other.[107] Arguments falling into the first category are absolutist and theoretical in nature, whereas pragmatic or consequentialist arguments focus on the practical consequences of legalization. According to the doctrinal approach, active voluntary euthanasia is intrinsically wrong, regardless of the circumstances. Many of the religious and moral arguments fall within this category. This category also includes a number of moral and philosophical arguments against legalization. Opponents of euthanasia adhering to this approach, the most notable of whom are Sullivan and Kelly, argue that in view of the inherent wrongfulness of active voluntary euthanasia, it should remain subject to unqualified prohibition.[108]

However, a significant proportion of opponents are willing to concede that there are powerful arguments for the toleration of active voluntary euthanasia in individual cases, but contend that the institutionalization of the practice is so fraught with risks and difficulties that it cannot be countenanced. Thus, the objection to active voluntary euthanasia is not necessarily based on the alleged wrongfulness of the individual act, but on the undesir-

---

[106] Williams, 'Euthanasia Legislation: A Rejoinder to the Non-Religious Objections', above n. 68, at 157; Morris, 'Voluntary Euthanasia', above n. 8, at 254–5.

[107] See also Fletcher, 'The Courts and Euthanasia', above Ch. 2 n. 73, at 228.

[108] Sullivan, J., *The Morality of Mercy Killing* (Westminster, Maryland, 1950); Kelly, G., *Medico-Moral Problems*, above Ch. 3 n. 203, at 115–16.

able consequences which it is feared may result if the practice is legalized.[109] These arguments are best characterized as pragmatic or consequentialist objections. It is proposed to deal with these different categories of objection in turn.

A. Doctrinal Arguments Against Active Voluntary Euthanasia

Religious arguments against active voluntary euthanasia

The following discussion will be focused on the Judaeo-Christian tradition which is the principal source of religious opposition to the practice of active voluntary euthanasia.[110] Notwithstanding some individual dissenters,[111] the Judaeo-Christian tradition has consistently condemned the practice of active voluntary euthanasia, and of all denominations, the Catholic Church has been most prominent in its opposition.[112]

Sanctity of human life

Central to this opposition to active voluntary euthanasia is the fundamental belief in the sanctity of human life. Although no longer an exclusively religious concept, the principle of sanctity of life clearly does have religious origins. Essentially, this principle holds that human life is sacred, has intrinsic value, and must therefore be respected and preserved.[113] According to Christian tradition, life is a gift from God, and supreme dominion over life belongs to God alone. Human responsibility for life is one of 'stewardship'; man does not have absolute control over his own life, but merely holds it in trust for God. Only God, the Creator of life, has the right to decide at what moment a life shall cease, and any direct killing of the innocent without the authority of God is wrong and against the natural law.[114] The fact that the

---

[109] e.g. Kamisar, 'Some Non-Religious Views Against Proposed Mercy-Killing Legislation', above Ch. 3 n. 68, at 975.

[110] For a discussion of other religious viewpoints regarding the practice of euthanasia, see Larue, G., *Euthanasia and Religion: A Survey of the Attitudes of World Religions to the Right to Die* (Los Angeles, 1985).

[111] e.g. Joseph Fletcher, an Episcopal minister, and Daniel Maguire, a Catholic philosopher, who have been prominent advocates for the legalization of active voluntary euthanasia.

[112] The opposition of the Roman Catholic Church to euthanasia dates back to the time of St. Augustine. At various times in the history of the Catholic Church, official church pronouncements have condemned euthanasia (see Kelly, *Medico-Moral Problems*, above Ch. 3 n. 203, at 115–18) including the recent Encyclical of Pope John Paul II, *Evangelium Vitae* (The Gospel of Life) released in 1995. Note also the Sacred Congregation for the Doctrine of the Faith, *Declaration on Euthanasia* (1980).

[113] The principle of sanctity of life is, however, not an absolute principle and is, therefore, distinguishable from 'vitalism' which holds that human life is an absolute value in itself and that every effort must be made to preserve life. See Keyserlingk, *Sanctity of Life or Quality of Life*, above n. 27, at 30–5.

[114] Gula, R., 'Euthanasia: A Catholic Perspective' (1987) 68 *Health Progress* 28, 29.

individual killed had given his or her consent does not alter the wrongfulness of the act. Similarly, suicide has always attracted religious sanction. Thus, man has the use of life, but may not destroy it at will, and to choose to do so involves a rejection of God's sovereignty.

The objection has been raised that if this 'divine monopoly theory' is carried through to its logical conclusion, it would mean that it is immoral to prolong life, since this is just as much an interference with God's sovereignty as is prematurely ending life.[115] However, according to Christian tradition, the prolongation of life by human intervention is justified on the grounds that it demonstrates respect for the value of human life, thereby confirming, rather than denying, God's dominion.

As was noted earlier, the sanctity of life doctrine should not be seen as a concept based solely in religion. As Ronald Dworkin has argued,[116] there is a secular as well as a religious interpretation of the idea that human life is sacred. A review of the euthanasia literature illustrates that there are certainly some commentators who would seek to invoke these secular reasons—moral, rational, and medical—for respecting sanctity of life and rejecting euthanasia.[117] Dworkin, on the other hand, argues that this very sacredness is a crucial argument *for* rather than against euthanasia.[118] The essence of Dworkin's thesis is that in order to respect individual patients' dignity and the intrinsic value of their lives, we must allow individuals freedom of conscience to make mortal decisions for themselves. Further, he argues whatever view we take on the subject of euthanasia, we want the right to decide for ourselves and we should therefore be ready to insist that any genuine constitution of principle will guarantee that right for everyone.[119]

Prohibition against intentional killing

Closely related to the principle of God's sovereignty is the prohibition against killing contained in the Ten Commandments. The Sixth Commandment states 'thou shalt not kill' which would seemingly prohibit all intentional killing, even for merciful motives. It has, however, been argued that the interpretation 'thou shalt not kill' is an inaccurate translation from the original Hebrew and that a more precise translation would be 'thou shalt do no murder', namely unlawful killing.[120] On this view, active euthanasia

---

[115] Fletcher, *Morals and Medicine*, above Ch. 3 n. 56, at 192–3; Magurie, *Death by Choice*, above Ch. 3 n. 236, at 118–19.

[116] *Life's Dominion: An Argument About Abortion and Euthanasia* (London, 1993) 195.

[117] e.g. Fenigsen, R., 'A Case Against Dutch Euthanasia' (1989) 19 *Hastings Center R* (Spec. Supp.) 22, 24.

[118] *Life's Dominion*, above n. 116, at 196.

[119] Ibid. at 239.

[120] Fletcher, *Morals and Medicine*, above Ch. 3 n. 56, at 196; Williams, *The Sanctity of Life and the Criminal Law*, above Ch. 3 n. 63, at 279.

performed at the request of a patient would not be in contravention of the Sixth Commandment.

Furthermore, examination of the biblical prohibition against direct killing in its proper context reveals that it was never understood as an absolute prohibition on the taking of human life.[121] Judaeo-Christian tradition has always recognized that in certain circumstances intentional killing may be permissible, for example, in the context of just war, capital punishment, and legitimate self-defence.[122] Thus, the biblical prohibition on killing is not an absolute principle but rather reflects the need to protect human life from arbitrary killing without community sanction. However, in the context of life and death decisions, the Commandment prohibiting killing has been understood as preventing the termination of human life, even for merciful reasons.

The value of human suffering

Another ground of religious objection to the practice of active voluntary euthanasia stems from the Christian belief in the value of human suffering. According to Christian teaching, physical suffering is not an absolute evil, devoid of purpose. Rather, it is seen as having a special place in God's divine plan for the universe, allowing an opportunity for the sufferer's spiritual growth and a means of redemption.[123] Furthermore, those who are in contact with a suffering patient are given an opportunity to practice Christian charity.[124] Thus, the practice of active voluntary euthanasia is rejected as a denial of the spiritual significance of suffering.

However, this objection to the practice of active voluntary euthanasia based on a belief in the value of human suffering has been subject to vigorous attack from a number of commentators.[125] Williams points out that for anyone acquainted with the reality of suffering in illness, this argument must seem both absurd and intolerant.[126] Further, as Fletcher observes, if suffering were indeed part of God's divine plan which must, therefore, be accepted, we should not be able to give our moral approval to anaesthetics or to provide any medical relief of human suffering.[127] This inconsistency regarding the place of suffering is itself reflected in Christian teaching; although the value of redemptive suffering is extolled, it is widely accepted that suffering can, in appropriate circumstances, be relieved,

---

[121] Gula, 'Euthanasia: A Catholic Perspective', above n. 114, at 30.

[122] Sullivan, *The Morality of Mercy Killing*, above n. 108, at 33–9; Fletcher, *Morals and Medicine*, above Ch. 3 n. 56, at 196.

[123] Kluge, *The Ethics of Deliberate Death* (New York, 1981), 32–3.

[124] Sullivan, *The Morality of Mercy Killing*, above n. 108, at 47.

[125] e.g. Fletcher, *Morals and Medicine*, above Ch. 3 n. 56, at 196; Williams, 'Euthanasia and Abortion', above Ch. 3 n. 166, 180; Maguire, *Death by Choice*, above Ch. 3 n. 236, 194.

[126] Williams, 'Euthanasia and Abortion', above Ch. 3 n. 166, at 180.

[127] Fletcher, *Morals and Medicine*, above Ch. 3 n. 56, at 196–8.

and the choice of whether or not to do so is a personal decision of conscience.[128]

Status of religious objections to euthanasia

It is evident from the foregoing review that religious opposition to the practice of active voluntary euthanasia is based on a number of interrelated arguments including adherence to the principle of the sanctity of life, the biblical prohibition against direct killing, and the value of human suffering. However, by their very nature, religious arguments based upon absolute adherence to faith are not really open to ethical reasoning or debate and may not accord with public opinion.[129] Consequently no attempt will be made to debate the merits of these religious arguments. Rather, it will be argued that religious objections are of limited practical relevance in determining whether the practice of active voluntary euthanasia should be legalized.

Religious arguments will naturally be convincing to those who accept the religious viewpoint but they clearly do not have universal relevance. Religion is a matter of personal commitment, and objections to active voluntary euthanasia based purely on religious views should not dominate the law nor impinge on the freedom of others. Whilst the convictions of believers must obviously be respected, it must be recognized that in a pluralistic and largely secular society, the freedom of conviction of non-believers must also be upheld. It was stressed in the earlier part of this chapter that the main argument in the case for legalization of active voluntary euthanasia is the principle of autonomy or self-determination. Taking this principle into account, a powerful argument can be advanced to the effect that prohibitions on active voluntary euthanasia based purely on religious beliefs should not be applied by law to those who do not share that belief where this is not required for the welfare of society generally.[130] Only if the legal prohibition on active voluntary euthanasia is removed will everyone be able to live according to their own convictions; those who oppose active voluntary euthanasia could reject it for themselves, and those who are in favour of the practice are not forced to live against their convictions. It is entirely inappropriate for adherents to religious views to insist that their beliefs should be binding on all others.

---

[128] For a statement of the position of the Catholic Church, see the address of Pope Pius XII, 'Religious and Moral Aspects of Pain Prevention in Medical Practice' (1957) 88 *Ir. Ecclesiastical Rec.* 193. Note also the Anglican position: Church of England, National Assembly Board for Social Responsibility, *On Dying Well: An Anglican Contribution to the Debate on Euthanasia* (London, 1975) 21, 39–50.

[129] Fletcher, 'The Courts and Euthanasia', above Ch. 2 n. 73, at 228–9.

[130] Williams, *The Sanctity of Life and the Criminal Law*, above Ch. 3 n. 63, at 278; Morris, 'Voluntary Euthanasia', above n. 8, at 248–51.

Active voluntary euthanasia inconsistent with the inalienable right to life

Another doctrinal argument against active voluntary euthanasia is that it is inconsistent with the inalienable right to life. According to this argument, derived from human rights philosophy,[131] individuals have certain inherent and inalienable rights including the right to life.[132] Consequently, active euthanasia performed at the request of a patient is *never* morally justifiable since it is a violation of this inalienable right. For strict adherents to a right to life philosophy, this argument would appear to be beyond controversy. The present criminal law which prevents a person from giving a legally effective consent to his or her own death can certainly be understood as supporting the view that individuals have an inalienable right to life.[133] However, some philosophers, including Feinberg, have persuasively argued that active voluntary euthanasia can be reconciled with the inalienable right to life.[134] Feinberg points out that if the opponents' argument regarding the impermissibility of active voluntary euthanasia is correct, it would effectively mean that the so called 'right to life' is in fact a mandatory right which entails a duty to live.[135] This conclusion reveals the fallacy of the initial premise. It stands to reason that if something is a right at all then it must be capable of being given up. The right to life can be reconciled with acceptance of active voluntary euthanasia by recognizing that although the right to life is inalienable, it can be *waived* in the exercise of one's discretion whether to continue to live. Thus, a rational request for active euthanasia is simply an exercise of one's right to life, in the sense of being able to exercise one's own choice, rather than an attempt to alienate the inalienable.[136]

Acceptance of active voluntary euthanasia would create a duty to kill

Another fundamental objection to active voluntary euthanasia is that the creation of a right to seek active euthanasia would impose on others a correlative duty to kill.[137] As was acknowledged earlier in this chap-

[131] e.g. in the works of Locke, J., *Second Treatise*, in *Two Treatises of Government*, (Laslett, P. (ed.)), Revised edn. (New York, 1965); Rosseau, J., *The Social Contract and Discourses* (London, 1913); Kant, I., *The Metaphysics of Morals* (I. Kant, introduction, translation and notes by Gregor, M.) (Cambridge, 1991).

[132] Support for the existence of a right to life can also be derived from international human rights instruments; see pp. 197–8 above.

[133] See pp. 19–21 above.

[134] Feinberg, J., 'Voluntary Euthanasia and the Inalienable Right to Life' in Feinberg, J., *Rights, Justice, and the Bounds of Liberty* (Princeton, New Jersey, 1980) 220–75. See also Kohl, M., 'Euthanasia and the Right to Life' in Spicker, S. and Engelhardt, H. (eds.), *Philosophical Medical Ethics* (Holland, 1975) 73.

[135] Kluge, *Ethics of Deliberate Death*, above n. 123, at 103.

[136] Feinberg, 'Voluntary Euthanasia and the Inalienable Right to Life', above n. 134, at 220–75.

[137] A number of opponents of legalization have raised this objection; e.g. Campbell, T., 'Euthanasia and the Law' (1979) 17 *Alta.L.Rev.* 188, 189; Potts, S., 'Looking for the Exit Door: Killing and Caring in Modern Medicine' (1988) 25 *Hous. L Rev.* 509.

ter,[138] it is certainly true that the concept of rights, in its strict sense, has generally been understood to entail correlative duties or obligations. However, this is seriously flawed as an absolute argument against the legalization of active voluntary euthanasia, since it proceeds on the assumption that a scheme of legalized euthanasia would necessarily create legal rights and duties. As was earlier observed, a strict rights-based model is not a suitable basis for implementing active voluntary euthanasia. Whilst it would be possible to frame a right to active voluntary euthanasia in a way which avoids the imposition of any duty, the language of 'rights' does inevitably carry this connotation, so, to avoid any misunderstanding, it would be preferable if it were dispensed with.[139] If active voluntary euthanasia were to be legalized, it would be far preferable to avoid this rights/duties analysis altogether by vesting in patients a *liberty* to seek active euthanasia and *permitting* doctors to perform active euthanasia at the request of a patient without creating any *duty* to do so.

B. Practical Arguments Against Active Voluntary Euthanasia

As noted earlier, the objections of many opponents of euthanasia are based, not on the inherent wrongfulness of individual acts of active voluntary euthanasia (which they concede may be moral and in the interests of the individual in exceptional cases), but arise out of concern for the long term consequences if the practice of active voluntary euthanasia is institutionalized.[140] On the basis of this argument, no matter what view one takes of individual instances of active voluntary euthanasia, as a matter of social policy we ought to enforce a rigorous rule against it.[141] This is because at the macro or societal level, the unacceptability of active voluntary euthanasia is such that the best case arguments for it at the individual level are outweighed.[142] One of the leading opponents of active voluntary euthanasia on pragmatic grounds is undoubtedly Kamisar, through his much celebrated work, 'Some Non-Religious Views Against Proposed "Mercy-Killing" Legislation' in which a range of practical objections to the legalization of active voluntary euthanasia are raised.[143] Unlike doctrinal objections, which can more readily be dismissed on the grounds that they are 'uncritical universal negatives, not open to ethical reasoning or conscientious judgment',[144] ob-

---

[138] See p. 201 above.   [139] See p. 202 above.

[140] e.g. Kamisar, 'Some Non-Religious Views Against Proposed Mercy-Killing Legislation', above Ch. 3 n. 68, at 975; Somerville, 'The Song of Death: The Lyrics of Euthanasia', above n. 92.

[141] Rachels, *The End of Life*, above n. 20, at 172.

[142] Somerville, 'The Song of Death: The Lyrics of Euthanasia', above n. 92, at 27.

[143] Above Ch. 3 n. 68.

[144] Fletcher, 'The Courts and Euthanasia', above Ch. 2 n. 73, at 229.

jections based on pragmatic considerations are, by their very nature, of greater practical relevance, requiring close and careful examination. Significantly, many of these practical arguments have recently been addressed in a number of important decisions in the USA in the context of examining the constitutional status of the legislative prohibition on assisted suicide in so far as it applies to competent, terminally ill patients.[145]

The wedge argument

The most popular objection to the legalization of active voluntary euthanasia is the 'slippery slope' or 'thin edge of the wedge' argument. The wedge argument against active voluntary euthanasia has two forms.[146] One form of the argument is that the legalization of active voluntary euthanasia *logically entails* non-voluntary and involuntary euthanasia. It will be demonstrated that this form of the argument ignores the vital distinction between voluntary euthanasia on the one hand, and non-voluntary and involuntary euthanasia on the other.[147] The second form of the wedge argument is that whilst the legalization of active voluntary euthanasia does not logically entail involuntary euthanasia, this will inevitably be the result if the first domino is allowed to fall. Thus, according to this version of the wedge argument, the legalization of active voluntary euthanasia would lead to widespread involuntary euthanasia and the termination of lives no longer considered socially useful. The classic statement of the wedge argument is to be found in the scholarly writing of Kamisar, but it is also a basis of Christian opposition to euthanasia.[148] The argument has gained new impetus in the modern medical context where there is growing concern over limited medical resources and escalating health care costs.[149] The fear is that the perceived economic benefits which may be derived from the legalization of active voluntary euthanasia could result in an expanding category of patients for whom active euthanasia is permitted.

Almost without exception, proponents of the wedge argument refer to the atrocities which took place in Nazi Germany in support of their contention that taking the first, albeit small, step on the slippery slope, will result in wrongs of ever-increasing magnitude.[150] However, closer examination of German history reveals that the concept of euthanasia from which the Nazi

---

[145] *Compassion in Dying* v. *State of Washington (en banc)* (above Ch. 2 n. 54); *Quill* v. *Vacco* (above Ch. 2 n. 54): for discussion see pp. 101–21 above. Note also *Rodriguez* v. *British Columbia (Attorney General)*, above n. 47. For discussion see pp. 86–94 above.

[146] van der Burg, W., 'The Slippery Slope Argument' (1991) 102 *Ethics* 42, 43.

[147] See pp. 7–8 above for consideration of this distinction.

[148] e.g. Sullivan, *The Morality of Mercy Killing*, above n. 108, at 54–7.

[149] e.g. Twycross, R., 'Assisted Death: A Reply' (1990) 336 *Lancet* 796, 797.

[150] Kamisar, 'Some Non-Religious Views Against Proposed Mercy-Killing Legislation', above Ch. 3 n. 68, at 1030–41.

atrocities allegedly developed, was completely removed from the contemporary notion of active voluntary euthanasia as a merciful release from suffering performed at the patient's request.

The programme of euthanasia in Germany had its origins in a highly influential book written by Binding and Hoche in 1920, *Die Freigabe der Vernichtung Lebensunwerten Lebens. Ihr Mass and ihre Form*.[151] The German word 'lebensunwerten' translates to mean 'life not entitled to be lived'. In this work, Karl Binding, a leading jurist, and Alfred Hoche, a well known psychiatrist, advocated the killing of 'worthless people' in order to relieve society of the burden of their care. The book was immensely popular, and its underlying concept of some people simply not being worthy to live, was to subsequently shape German medical and ethical thinking. The essence of this concept was that some lives are completely devoid of value and should therefore be terminated. Initially, in the 1930s, programmes were introduced for the elimination of incurables, the mentally-ill, and defective. However, with the growth of Nazi fanaticism, the concept of 'a life not worth living' later came to be used as a justification for genocide.[152] The argument of euthanasia opponents is that the atrocities of Nazi Germany had started from small beginnings, namely with the acceptance of the attitude that there is such a thing as 'a life not worth living' and therefore, active voluntary euthanasia must not be legalized, lest the same consequences result.

The Nazi experience is undeniably a lasting blemish on humanity, and no attempt will be made to diminish the horror or significance of this period in German history. However, the Nazi analogy is simply inapplicable to the contemporary notion of active voluntary euthanasia. The Nazi programme of euthanasia was essentially based on eugenics. It was neither voluntary nor based on compassion but, rather, was motivated by the desire to preserve the purity of the 'Volk' and rid the country of useless mouths to feed. Reflection on these past experiences certainly serves as a salutary warning of the dangers inherent in a policy of euthanasia based on the concept of 'a life not worth living' which, because of its indeterminacy, invites extension and abuse. However, the contemporary notion of active voluntary euthanasia which is being advanced in this work, is based upon quite a different premise, namely the patient's freedom of choice and right of self-determination. The suggestion made by some commentators[153] that the

---

[151] Binding, K. and Hoche, A., *Die Freigabe der Vernichtung Lebensunwerten Lebens. Ihr Mass and ihre Form* (Leipzig, 1920).

[152] For detailed analysis of the history of euthanasia in Germany, see: van der Sluis, 'The Movement for Euthanasia, 1875–1975', above n. 1, at 137–48, 154–60; Alexander, L., 'Medical Science Under Dictatorship' (1949) 241 *New Eng.J.Med.* 39.

[153] e.g. Sherlock, R., 'Public Policy and the Life Not Worth Living: The Case Against Euthanasia' (1980) 47 *Linacre Q* 121; Rice, C., *The Vanishing Right to Life* (Garden City, New York, 1969) 61.

concept of active voluntary euthanasia necessarily involves acceptance of a policy that certain lives are not worth living is flatly rejected as being both misleading and inaccurate. As was stressed above, respect for a patient's right of self-determination does not involve an objective assessment about the value or worth of that life.

It is frequently alleged that proponents of active voluntary euthanasia have a broader secret agenda, with objectives extending well beyond euthanasia performed at the person's request. Indeed, it has been suggested that the strategy of the euthanasia movement has been deliberately to use the wedge principle to their own advantage; to secure initially the legalization of active voluntary euthanasia; and once this becomes accepted as standard practice, they will introduce more ambitious and far-reaching reforms.[154] Whilst the general thrust of the euthanasia movement in recent years has been confined to legalization of active voluntary euthanasia, there are undoubtedly some extremists amongst the euthanasia advocates, particularly those drawing their support from utilitarian arguments, who would be in favour of a broader basis for active euthanasia.[155] However, a very real and significant distinction exists between voluntary euthanasia on the one hand, and involuntary or even non-voluntary euthanasia on the other, and this distinction must be firmly borne in mind in evaluating the wedge argument. Provided that the individual's choice is treated as determinative, there is a sufficiently clear line to prevent the imposition of active euthanasia on non-consenting patients. What must be emphasized is that the objective of active voluntary euthanasia is the promotion of individual autonomy and self-determination rather than any sinister aim of human disposal. Recognition of patient autonomy and self-determination is thus a clear limiting principle against abuse. So long as this crucial distinction between voluntary and non-voluntary/involuntary euthanasia is understood, the first form of the wedge argument, namely that legalization of active voluntary euthanasia logically entails involuntary euthanasia, can be rejected.

The wedge argument in its second form, based upon the inevitable slide towards involuntary euthanasia, is a stronger argument and seemingly more difficult to refute. Notwithstanding the popularity of this argument, there has been wide recognition that it is an argument which must be treated with caution since it could be used as a basis for the opposition of virtually any social policy.[156] Furthermore, since we are dealing with the fundamental

---

[154] e.g. Kamisar, 'Some Non-Religious Views Against Proposed Mercy-Killing Legislation', above Ch. 3 n. 68, at 1015.

[155] e.g. Kohl, *The Morality of Killing*, above Ch. 4 n. 71; Williams, *The Sanctity of Life and the Criminal Law*, above Ch. 3 n. 63, at 310–12.

[156] e.g. Williams, *The Sanctity of Life and the Criminal Law*, above Ch. 3 n. 63, at 280–1; President's Commission Report, *Deciding to Forgo Life-Sustaining Treatment*, above Ch. 1 n. 44, at 29–30. See also the comments in the majority decision of the US Court of Appeals for the Ninth Circuit in the case of *Compassion in Dying* v. *State of Washington*, see above Ch. 2 n. 54.

notion of self-determination, it becomes necessary to weigh up whether the risks posed by the legalization of active voluntary euthanasia are both sufficiently grave and sufficiently certain to outweigh the patient's right of self-determination. There would be little dispute regarding the gravity of the risk of involuntary and even non-voluntary euthanasia. However, in order for the wedge argument to be persuasive, it must be evident that the feared consequences which are alleged to flow from the legalization of active voluntary euthanasia are reasonably likely to occur. The mere *possibility* that a law permitting active voluntary euthanasia may be broadened in the future is not a sufficient justification for refusing to allow its enactment. Since a strong moral case can be presented for the legalization of active voluntary euthanasia, it is incumbent on the opponents of reform to provide convincing evidence that these feared consequences are indeed likely. It is at this point that the wedge objection fails to stand up to scrutiny. Having earlier dispensed with the Nazi analogy, there is simply no compelling evidence to suggest that the acceptance of active voluntary euthanasia on a strictly limited basis would be the 'thin edge of the wedge'. Indeed, there is significant evidence to the contrary; since 1970, active voluntary euthanasia has been practised in the Netherlands, yet, contrary to the claims of some opponents, there is no convincing evidence to suggest that this has represented a step onto the slippery slope, leading to involuntary euthanasia.[157] Moreover, it could be argued, by analogy, that the liberalization of the law with regard to infanticide and suicide during the course of this century has not resulted in a diminution in respect for human life. Opponents of legalization would probably contend that the experience with abortion since it was made legal in some circumstances, is evidence of a slippery slope if the crucial step is taken to liberalize the law. Their argument would be that what began as simply permission for doctors to perform abortions under certain restricted terms has now become an expectation that abortion is available on demand.[158] It is impossible to refute the proposition that abortion is today far more freely available than it was prior to the introduction of legislation permitting it in certain circumstances. However, the relevance of the abortion analogy to the issue of active voluntary euthanasia is limited indeed. It may suggest that eligibility criteria for persons seeking active voluntary euthanasia (for example, with regard to their condition, age etc[159]) may be tested over time, which may in turn suggest the need for rigorous enforcement of any such conditions. But, that is as far as it goes. It most certainly cannot be taken as evidence of a likely

---

[157] For discussion of the extent of the practice of euthanasia in the Netherlands see pp. 427–41 below.

[158] House of Lords, *Report of the Select Committee on Medical Ethics* (London, 1994) Vol. 1, 26.

[159] For discussion of proposed criteria, see pp. 470–81 below.

slide from voluntary to non-voluntary or involuntary euthanasia if the practice were to be legalized. Such a claim could only be made if there was evidence that the liberalization of abortion law so as to allow the practice in certain circumstances at a woman's request had led to abortions being performed on women without their consent. This is simply not the case, so the 'abortion analogy' does not hold up to scrutiny as a serious objection to the legalization of active voluntary euthanasia. Some commentators have in fact argued that if anything, the abortion experience has shown that many of the original fears were unfounded: many believed that permitting abortion in early pregnancy would logically necessitate the legalization of late abortions—even on the delivery table at the end of pregnancy—and infanticide, whereas the liberalization of abortion law has not had this effect.[160] Nor is there any evidence to suggest that the legalization of abortion has undermined our commitment to life generally.[161]

A further requirement for the acceptability of a slippery slope argument which is sometimes put forward is that there must be an alternative that is less susceptible to this danger.[162] In this respect, the slippery slope arguments which are commonly made fail to satisfy the necessary burden of proof. As we have seen, active euthanasia is already practised, albeit in a hidden and secretive fashion, and there is absolutely no evidence to demonstrate that this state of affairs provides any protection against slippery slopes. To the contrary, as was argued earlier, there is good reason to believe that a practice which is open, carefully regulated, and subject to public scrutiny, will provide greater protection from abuse. In the final analysis, the wedge objection is an argument easily raised, but totally unsupportable and should therefore be rejected as a valid basis for opposition to the legalization of active voluntary euthanasia.[163]

It has, however, been acknowledged by critics of the standard slippery slope arguments that such arguments may have greater force in the legal context.[164] With regard to the 'logical' version of the slippery slope argument the reasoning is that the passing of laws permitting certain conduct introduces a new element in the body of legal norms from which courts must make their own theory of law. Thus, it could be argued that the legalization of active voluntary euthanasia would, through incremental steps, eventually

---

[160] Weinrib, L., 'The Body and the Body Politic: Assisted Suicide under the *Canadian Charter of Rights and Freedoms*' (1994) 39 *McGill LJ* 618, 637–8.

[161] See also the decision of the majority of the US Court of Appeals for the Ninth Circuit in the case of *Compassion in Dying* v. *State of Washington(en banc)* see above Ch. 2 n. 54.

[162] van der Burg, 'The Slippery Slope Argument', above n. 146, at 61.

[163] Commentators have sought to find support for their rejection of slippery slope arguments by drawing on other examples of deliberate killing which have defied the slippery slope analysis: e.g. Rachels, *The End of Life*, above n. 20, at 174–5; Browne, A., 'Assisted Suicide and Active Voluntary Euthanasia' (1989) 2 *Can.JLJuris.* 47; Williams, 'Euthanasia and Abortion', above Ch. 3 n. 166, at 181.

[164] van der Burg, 'The Slippery Slope Argument', above n. 146, at 61–3.

result in the legal permissibility of active euthanasia for patients who are not competent.[165] Pressure for such an extension might well be expected in the USA where the courts have traditionally sought to equate the rights of competent and incompetent patients and where constitutional arguments may be advanced in support. Attempts at a similar extension may possibly even be made in other countries such as the United Kingdom, where, in the context of withdrawal of treatment decisions, the courts have made it clear that a line cannot properly be drawn between competent and incompetent people in a way that denies appropriate withdrawal of treatment from the latter.[166] In the context of life-sustaining treatment, the courts in the USA have held it to be unreasonable to continue life-sustaining treatment that the patient would not have wanted just because the patient now lacks the capacity to express his or her wishes.[167] Accordingly, through the doctrine of substituted judgment, the right of a competent patient to refuse treatment has been extended to incompetent patients, exercisable by a surrogate decision-maker who is to decide what the patient would have decided in the circumstances if he or she were competent.

The possibility of pressure being exerted for a similar extension in favour of incompetent patients if a law permitting active voluntary euthanasia was introduced, is perhaps the most plausible slippery slope concern. There are, however, counter arguments which go some way towards dispelling these concerns or at least putting them in their proper context. To begin with, the point needs to be made that even if such predictions were realized, the sort of practice which is being contemplated here of active euthanasia being performed on incompetent patients, at the request of a surrogate decision-maker based upon what the patient would have wanted, is quite distinct from the claims by those alleging a slippery slope of wide scale involuntary euthanasia to rid society of the weak and vulnerable. And if one was to draw on the experience in the USA with regard to the application of the substituted judgment doctrine in the context of life-sustaining treatment decisions, there is every indication that the courts would apply strict tests or procedures to safeguard the rights of incompetent patients.[168] Having said that, it must be stressed that the essence of this work is that anything other than strictly voluntary euthanasia performed at the request of a presently competent patient is unacceptable and we therefore need to be satisfied that this extension from voluntary to non-voluntary euthanasia is not likely to occur. Consistent with the earlier rebuttal of more general slippery slope arguments it is disputed that this development is so logically linked with the

[165] Callahan, D., 'Aid-In-Dying: The Social Dimension' (1991) 118 *Commonweal* 476, 478–9.

[166] e.g. *Airedale NHS Trust* v. *Bland* [1993] 1 All ER 821.

[167] Brock, D., 'Euthanasia' (1992) 65 *Yale Journal of Biology and Medicine* 121, 128.

[168] Neeley, G., 'The Constitutional Right to Suicide, the Quality of Life and the "Slippery Slope": An Explicit Reply to Lingering Concerns' (1994) 28 *Akron LRev.* 53, 63–5.

legalization of active voluntary euthanasia that it would necessarily occur: to suggest as much amounts to a denial of capacity of reasoned and balanced judgment on the part of the State's law-making bodies. In responding to concerns about the future practice of euthanasia if active assistance at a patient's request were legalized, we must not discount the rationality of human beings and their ability to make sensible and wise choices.

Elsewhere in this work, support has been given to the view that there is no moral difference between active and passive euthanasia: that this conduct is essentially similar in terms of intention and outcome.[169] There may, however, still be reasons why, for some purposes at least, a distinction needs to be drawn between these two forms of euthanasia on the basis of the fundamental issues of patient competence and voluntariness. Where patients lack the necessary decision-making capacity to make their own health care decisions, provision must be made for decisions to be made on their behalf, be it through some form of advance directive, or through the appointment of a decision-making agent, or through some other mechanism for substituted consent. In many cases the decision-maker will be called on to decide whether the medical treatment which has been provided to the patient should now be withdrawn. This sort of practice, particularly where it is informed by knowledge of what the patient would have wanted in the circumstances, appears entirely justifiable and appropriate. Analysing the situation from a rights perspective, since competent patients have a virtually absolute right to refuse treatment, it appears logical to recognize the same right for incompetent patients, exercisable by a surrogate decision-maker, enabling the withholding or withdrawing of medical treatment in appropriate circumstances. But the situation with regard to active voluntary euthanasia is different. As has been stressed earlier, this work does not seek to assert 'rights', even for competent patients. Rather, it has been argued the law should recognize a liberty in those who are competent and fully informed to seek active voluntary euthanasia in certain circumstances. So this, in itself, represents an important distinction between termination of lifesaving treatment and active voluntary euthanasia. Despite this difference the temptation may exist to try to have the same 'liberty' recognized also for incompetent patients. There are, however, powerful arguments going against such an extension which make it unlikely that our law-makers would countenance such a move. To begin with, as legalization of active voluntary euthanasia could only realistically be achieved by legislation, there is plenty of opportunity for enacting rules and distinctions to break any supposed connection between the position of competent and incompetent patients, thus impeding the tendency to slide.[170] Moreover, it must be

---

[169] See pp. 54–5, 191–2 above.

[170] Weinrib, 'The Body and the Body Politic: Assisted Suicide under the *Canadian Charter of Rights and Freedoms*', above Ch. 2 n. 159, at 638.

understood that any extension of the law could only be by subsequent legislative enactment or through case law developments based on constitutional or similar arguments regarding the applicability of such a law. Before any such attempt to extend the law could succeed, the lawmakers, be it the legislatures or the courts, would have to weigh up the interests involved in extending rights to incompetent patients against the greater potential for misuse and abuse if active euthanasia is permitted for patients who are not competent. On any objective assessment of the euthanasia issue, it has to be accepted that there are some risks involved if active voluntary euthanasia were to be legalized. Clearly, therefore, an important part of any scheme for legalization is to ensure that there are stringent safeguards to minimize the level of risk and protect against abuse. The most fundamental requirement is the voluntariness of the request: indeed, as we have seen, respect for the patient's self-determination is one of the principal justifications for permitting active voluntary euthanasia. The crucial point for present purposes is that this element of voluntariness can only be satisfactorily provided for if active euthanasia is strictly limited to patients who presently have decision-making capacity. As is argued in a later chapter,[171] even a clearly articulated request for active voluntary euthanasia in an advance directive cannot provide the same degree of certainty that this continues to accord with the patient's wishes as the stated wishes of a patient who presently has decision-making capacity. So, in order to maximize the autonomy of patients who seek euthanasia but at the same time ensuring that we do not overstep the mark and take on unnecessary risks which may result in harm to those who have not requested and do not wish euthanasia, the line must firmly be drawn at presently capable patients. Only in this way can we ensure fully voluntary consent which can be tested before active voluntary euthanasia is performed. These considerations would have to weigh very heavily in any assessment of whether the practice of active euthanasia should be extended to patients who are not competent and would be compelling reasons for not taking this step. Thus, it is argued, whilst it is possible, even likely, that attempts would be made to extend the ambit of any euthanasia legislation to allow the practice also for incompetent patients, such attempts would probably be unsuccessful, especially in the light of the widespread support for the view that active euthanasia should be limited to patients who have decision-making capacity, who request it as a result of their present situation and prognosis for recovery.

Some commentators have sought to refute the wedge objection on different grounds; they point out that passive euthanasia is now common practice and since there is no intrinsic moral difference between active and passive euthanasia, they argue that if indeed there is a 'slippery slope' then we are

---

[171] See pp. 481–4 below.

already on it.[172] Thus, it is argued, there is no logical basis for objection to active voluntary euthanasia since it is essentially equivalent to the existing practice of passive euthanasia. Moreover, attention is drawn to other practices involving the termination of life such as the turning off of life-support and the administration of palliative drugs which are likely to cause death, which are in some respects similar to active voluntary euthanasia. It is further argued that rather than seeking to prohibit active voluntary euthanasia, it would be better to bring all life and death decisions out into the open where there can be the widest possible debate and public scrutiny.

The validity of this argument depends on acceptance of the view that there is no morally relevant difference between passive and active euthanasia—which as noted above, is a view by no means universally endorsed. This line of argument does, however, highlight the artificiality in maintaining unduly rigid distinctions between active and passive voluntary euthanasia, when they are often so similar, at least in terms of intention and outcome.

For all of the foregoing reasons, slippery slope arguments do not provide a sufficient justification to retain the existing prohibition on active voluntary euthanasia; while the possibility of bad consequences should encourage us to proceed cautiously, it should not prevent us from proceeding at all.[173]

Effect on social fabric of society

Closely connected with the wedge argument is the objection that the legalization of active voluntary euthanasia would have the effect of substantially damaging the moral and social fabric of society. It is argued that any lessening of the traditional common law prohibition on killing would dehumanize society and result in a reduced respect for human life. There is particular concern that persons involved in the practice of active euthanasia, whether directly or indirectly, would become brutalized and less caring and vigilant about the value of human life. For some opponents, the main objection stems from concern that by legalizing active voluntary euthanasia, the practice will become routinized and institutionalized and consequently will come to be seen as establishing the norm.[174]

In a sense these arguments are simply a restatement of the wedge argument; it is feared that if the barriers to killing are lowered, the practice of active euthanasia may be extended beyond that which is originally envisaged. However, apart from concerns about 'slippery slopes', this argument also appears to suggest that a society which allows active voluntary euthanasia is inevitably morally and socially inferior to a society which prohibits its practice. To begin with, one may wonder how the moral and social

---

[172] Kuhse, H., 'The Alleged Peril of Active Voluntary Euthanasia: A Reply to Alexander Morgan Capron' (1987) 2 *Euthanasia Rev.* 60, 67–70.

[173] Rachels, *The End of Life*, above n. 20, at 175.

[174] Somerville, 'The Song of Death: The Lyrics of Euthanasia', above n. 92, at 43.

quality of society can reliably be gauged, and there is a temptation to summarily reject this objection on the grounds that it is impossibly vague and indeterminable. But if we are to take this objection seriously, it is clear that it can be countered on a number of grounds. To begin with, one might seek to challenge the premise on which these arguments are based, namely that acts of euthanasia performed at a patient's request are qualitatively different from other medical interventions and non-interventions at the end of life.[175] As was argued in an earlier chapter,[176] there is in fact much in common between active voluntary euthanasia, and the existing practices of passive euthanasia performed at the patient's request, as well as the termination of life-support and the administration of life-shortening palliative care, which are accepted as lawful practices under existing law. Moreover, it has long been accepted that certain forms of killing are justifiable, for example, killing in war, or in self-defence, yet there has been no convincing evidence to suggest that this has damaged the essential fabric of society. It therefore seems invalid to assert categorically that to allow active euthanasia performed at the request of the patient in order to relieve the patient's pain and suffering will necessarily diminish respect for the sanctity of life and result in the moral and social decline of society. In fact, if we look to the Netherlands, where active voluntary euthanasia is now quite openly practiced by doctors, there has been no evidence of such decline.[177] Indeed, it could be argued that facilitating a gentle and easy death at the patient's request is a moral advance rather than a moral decline; active euthanasia, at the patient's request, is a merciful and benevolent act which promotes desirable virtues in society, and since it furthers the principle of individual self-determination, it enhances, rather than diminishes, respect for human life.[178] The arguments of Dworkin referred to above can be used in direct support of this view. On these grounds it could be argued that the present prohibition of active voluntary euthanasia, far from protecting the integrity of society, contributes to its brutalization. For the foregoing reasons, these objections to the practice of active voluntary euthanasia based upon the feared consequences for the social fabric of society fail to provide convincing grounds against the legalization of active voluntary euthanasia.

Problems in ascertaining patient consent, feared abuses and risk of error

Consideration will now turn to a number of objections to legalization of active voluntary euthanasia which focus on the problems of ascertaining a

[175] For an example of the original premise, see Somerville, 'The Song of Death: The Lyrics of Euthanasia', above n. 92, at 56.
[176] See pp. 152–86 above.
[177] See pp. 435–41 below.
[178] Angell, M., 'Euthanasia' (1988) 319 *New Eng.JMed.* 1348, 1350.

truly voluntary consent from the patient as well as concerns about feared abuse and risk of error if active voluntary euthanasia were legalized. It will be demonstrated that these are essentially paternalistic arguments which, if accepted, would have the effect of unjustifiably limiting patient autonomy.

Voluntariness and patient consent

A major objection which has been raised to the legalization of active voluntary euthanasia relates to the issue of patient competence and decision-making capacity, and the difficulties involved in determining whether the patient's request for death represents a free and rational choice.[179] There are a number of facets to this argument. One aspect of the argument is that patients in the final painful stages of a terminal illness may be so affected by pain, mental anguish, or the stupefying effects of pain-relieving drugs that they are incapable of giving a free and rational consent. There is some evidence to suggest that patients with advanced terminal cancer often experience repeated episodes of cognitive failure caused by medication or organic changes associated with the dying process.[180] The mental and physical condition of a seriously ill patient may fluctuate and the patient may be subject to confusional states[181] impairing the patient's decision-making capacity. Even where an apparently clear request for active euthanasia has been made, the patient may subsequently vacillate in his or her decision. It is argued by opponents that as a result of possible confusion, impairment, and vacillation, it often becomes very difficult to gauge accurately the reliability of a patient's request. Furthermore, it is not uncommon for terminal patients to suffer from depression,[182] and opponents maintain that a request for death may simply be an impulsive and transient response to the patient's difficult circumstances and may, therefore, be inherently unreliable.[183] Attention has also been drawn to the fact that there is a high incidence of undiagnosed treatable depression amongst patients, particularly the elderly.[184] In addition, opponents claim that there may be problems in interpreting a patient's request: what may appear to be a voluntary

---

[179] e.g. Kamisar, 'Some Non-Religious Views Against Proposed Mercy-Killing Legislation', above Ch. 3 n. 68, at 985–90; Rice, *The Vanishing Right to Life*, above n. 153, at 55–7.

[180] e.g. Bruera, E. et al., 'Cognitive Failure in Patients with Terminal Cancer: A Prospective Study' (1992) 7 *J Pain &Symptom Management* 192.

[181] e.g. Stedeford, A., 'Confusional States' in Twycross, R. and Ventafridda, V. (eds.), *The Continuing Care of Terminal Cancer Patients* (New Haven, 1980) 179–92.

[182] See Kubler-Ross, E., *On Death and Dying* (New York, 1969) 75–98 where she identified five emotional stages that a dying patient could experience, including depression.

[183] Some evidence can be cited in support of these claims from studies which have concentrated on the correlation between the desire for death and depression: see Brown, H. et al., 'Is it Normal for Terminally Ill Patients to Desire Death?' (1986) 143 *Am.J Psychiatry* 208; Chochinov, H. et al., 'Desire for Death in the Terminally Ill' (1995) 12 *Am.J Psychiatry* 1185.

[184] Conwell , Y. and Caine, E., 'Rational Suicide and the Right to Die: Reality and Myth' (1991) 325 *New Engl.J Med.* 1100, 1101.

request to die may in fact be a call for help or support and may not reflect the patient's autonomous choice.[185]

These objections must be taken seriously, since the voluntariness of the patient's consent is undoubtedly of vital importance to the question of legalization of active voluntary euthanasia. However, the problems concerning the reliability of a terminal patient's request for death should not be overstated.[186] With regard to the first basis of the objection, the decision-making capacity of patients cannot be categorically denied simply because they are in a terminal state. This would represent an unjustifiable infringement of patient autonomy. Whilst some patients may be so affected that they are no longer able to exercise an autonomous choice, there will be others who will be capable of doing so even in the terminal stages of their illness. Further, it should be pointed out that these problems are not unique to the issue of active voluntary euthanasia. The issues of patient decision-making capacity and voluntariness of consent arise in virtually all areas of medical practice, including cases of refusal of treatment. Although there may be difficulties in determining whether a patient has decision-making capacity in a particular case, it would be unrealistic to suggest that a patient can never give a valid consent to the withdrawal of treatment. Similarly with active voluntary euthanasia; although difficulties will inevitably be encountered in ascertaining the voluntariness of a patient's consent, these difficulties are not insurmountable and certainly do not justify a blanket prohibition on the practice. Indeed, it would be inconsistent to accept that a patient can voluntarily choose passive euthanasia by refusing treatment, but not active euthanasia, since both involve the choice of an earlier death.[187]

Concerns regarding the interpretation of a patient's request for active euthanasia can also be countered. Whilst some situations are truly ambiguous, serious requests for active euthanasia can be separated from those that reflect symbolic gestures for assistance or attention.[188]

It is submitted that the various concerns of the opponents regarding voluntariness of patient consent can be adequately addressed through appropriate regulation of the practice of active voluntary euthanasia.[189] For

---

[185] Zwart, H., 'Psychology, Self-Determination and the Veil' in Aycke, O. and Smook, M. (eds.), *Right to Self-Determination*, Proceedings of the 8th World Right to Die Societies (Amsterdam, 1990) 33; Lynn, J., 'The Health Care Professional's Role When Active Euthanasia Is Sought' (1988) 4 *J Palliative Care* 100.

[186] Some support for the stability of patient preferences can be derived from a study conducted by Everhart and Pearlman dealing with patients' attitudes to life-sustaining treatment; Everhart, M. and Pearlman, R., 'Stability of Patient Preferences Regarding Life-Sustaining Treatments' (1990) 97 *Chest* 159. In this study it was found that despite significant changes in health status and mood, treatment preferences were stable over time.

[187] Kuhse, 'The Case for Active Voluntary Euthanasia', above n. 23 at 147.

[188] Churchill, L., 'Examining the Ethics of Active Euthanasia' (1990) 5 *Med. Ethics for the Physician* 16, 17.

[189] For further discussion, see pp. 478–84, 485 below.

example, legislation permitting active voluntary euthanasia could specify as preconditions that: a professional assessment is made of the patient's decision-making capacity; the patient is appraized of sufficient facts to give an 'informed consent'; that the patient's request must be repeated on several occasions over an extended period of time before it is acted upon; and that the patient be allowed to revoke the request at any time, regardless of the patient's physical or mental condition. Such measures would largely reduce the possibility of doctors acting upon requests which are not completely voluntary.

Feared abuses and other problems

(i) Possibility of abuse by unscrupulous parties. Closely connected with the issue of voluntariness of the patient's consent is the objection that the legalization of active voluntary euthanasia would result in abuses of the practice.[190] Abuse may take a number of forms.[191] It may be in the nature of interpersonal abuse involving unscrupulous family members who manipulate a patient's request for euthanasia or possibly, in collusion with doctors, take advantage of the law permitting active voluntary euthanasia to conceal a conspiracy to murder a patient.[192] Apart from possible participation in such criminal activity, there are other possible forms of 'professional abuse' which doctors might conceivably be involved in, including manipulation of relevant information about diagnosis and prognosis, withholding of adequate pain relief, or using euthanasia as a means of covering up their medical mistakes. Given the weight of professional authority and the power to influence patient choices, whether for malevolent or benevolent (albeit paternalistic) motives, the potential clearly exists for doctors to abuse their professional position. Concerns have also been raised about institutional abuse whereby policies operate so as to narrow the range of actual choices open to the patient.

It cannot be disputed that abuses may occur if active voluntary euthanasia were legalized; the reality is that all laws are potentially open to abuse. All the same, this objection does not appear to be compelling. First, as has been argued elsewhere in this work,[193] the present practice of active euthanasia in an illegal and unregulated form is likely to involve some degree of abuse and there is every reason to believe that legalization, with appropriate regulatory procedures, would reduce the possibility of covert and im-

---

[190] President's Commission Report, *Deciding to Forgo Life-Sustaining Treatment*, above Ch. 1 n. 44, at 79–80.

[191] For consideration of types of possible abuse, see Battin, M., 'Voluntary Euthanasia and the Risks of Abuse: Can We Learn Anything from the Netherlands?' (1992) 20 *Law, Med.&Health Care* 133.

[192] e.g. Kass, L., 'Neither for Love Nor Money: Why Doctors Must Not Kill' (1989) 94 *Public Interest* 25, 35–6.

[193] See pp. 150–2 above.

proper conduct. And, as a number of commentators have pointed out,[194] the possibility of abuse already exists with respect to passive euthanasia, which in some cases, may in fact offer a greater opportunity for improper conduct since the patient's death may be easier to conceal than from a killing by more direct means.

In any event, the possibility, or even the strong likelihood, of some abuse occurring if active voluntary euthanasia is legalized is not of itself sufficient to prohibit the practice completely, if, as has been suggested, there are powerful arguments for legalization. Whilst abuses will inevitably result, the risk of abuse can be minimized by the imposition of stringent safeguards regulating the practice.[195]

(ii)   Pressure on the patient. Some opponents argue that abuse may take a more subtle form of pressure being exerted on the patient to request active euthanasia.[196] Their argument is that chronically and terminally ill patients are often vulnerable and perceive themselves to be a burden on others. Attention has also been drawn to the situation of the elderly in the community and the discrimination they already suffer.[197] If active voluntary euthanasia were to become readily available, eligible patients may feel under a *duty* to request it, particularly if relatives or hospital staff exert pressure on patients to do so and thereby relieve them of the financial and social burden of their care. Thus, it is argued that legalizing active voluntary euthanasia would be to risk putting to death many patients who do not genuinely wish to die but who are pressured into requesting active euthanasia. Special concerns have also been raised, that if legalized, euthanasia will be an option that doctors will actively promote and which their patients may feel obliged to accept due to their dependence in the relationship.[198] Even in circumstances where the patient has initiated the request, concerns have been expressed that the involvement of the doctors may constitute pressure on the patient to proceed as some patients would be too embarrassed or intimidated to express uncertainty about their decision after initially making a request.[199]

[194] e.g. Kuhse, 'The Alleged Peril of Active Voluntary Euthanasia: A Reply to Alexander Morgan Capron', above n. 172, at 65; Richter, 'The Hastings Centre and Euthanasia' (1988) 3 *Euthanasia Rev.* 56, 65–6.

[195] Safeguards could, for example, include the requirement that the patient's request be witnessed by two independent persons, that official records be kept, and that the attending doctor's diagnosis is confirmed by another doctor. See further pp. 470–92 below.

[196] e.g. Kamisar, 'Some Non-Religious Views Against Proposed Mercy-Killing Legislation', above Ch. 3 n. 68, at 990–1; van der Sluis, I., 'How Voluntary is Voluntary Euthanasia?' (1988) 4 *JPalliative Care* 107, at 107–8.

[197] Osgood, N., 'Assisted Suicide and Older People—A Deadly Combination: Ethical Problems in Permitting Assisted Suicide' (1995) 10 *Issues Law&Med.* 361.

[198] See New York State Task Force on Life and the Law, *When Death is Sought*, above n. 97, at 121–2.

[199] Ibid. at 84.

These are, essentially, arguments relating to the voluntariness of the patient's consent and reflects the paternalistic stance of many of the opponents of legalization. Problems of coercion and consent have had to be dealt with in other areas of medical practice, including refusal of treatment decisions, and there is no reason to assume that the problem is going to be significantly different in relation to active voluntary euthanasia. As part and parcel of the legalization of active voluntary euthanasia, it would not be impossible to devise procedures which would minimize the risk of the patient's consent being undermined by subtle coercion or influence from family or other sources. For example, as part of the procedure for the assessment of a patient's request for active euthanasia, possible sources of coercion would have to be investigated to ensure that the patient's request is truly voluntary. It is far more appropriate and consistent with principles of self-determination to try and guard against coercion and improper influence, rather than to deny to all the possibility of electing an earlier death. It must also be stressed that whilst evidence of improper pressure or coercion would clearly undermine a finding of voluntariness, the mere fact that a person is in part motivated by altruistic reasons, such as not wanting to be a burden on their relatives, should not, of itself, lead to the conclusion that the patient's request is unreliable.[200] To do so would be to undermine the patient's right of self-determination including the liberty to have regard to the needs and interests of others in making decisions in respect of their own health care.

Concerns about pressure from doctors also appear unwarranted. To suggest that doctors would become active proponents of active voluntary euthanasia and would themselves be putting pressure on patients to seek this option disregards well established principles guiding medical practice[201] which would require that active voluntary euthanasia would only be contemplated as a measure of last resort. Indeed, if we look to the position in the Netherlands where active voluntary euthanasia is practised relatively openly with some degree of legal tolerance, indications are that Dutch doctors regard this practice very seriously as one that should only be considered where all other possible options have been exhausted.[202] There is certainly no evidence to suggest that it is a practice which doctors in the Netherlands actively promote or encourage for their patients. Moreover, as

---

[200] Gunderson, M. and Mayo, D., 'Altruisim and Physician Assisted Death' (1993) 18 *JMed.&Phil.* 281. Note also the comments of the majority in *Compassion in Dying* v. *State of Washington* (see above Ch. 2 n. 54) where, in the context of considering State regulation of physician-assisted suicide, the majority commented that: 'While state regulation can help to ensure that patients do not make rash, uninformed, or ill considered decisions, we are reluctant to say that, in a society in which the costs of protracted health care can be so exorbitant, it is improper for competent, terminally ill adults to take the economic welfare of their families and loved ones into account'.

[201] e.g. attempting to cure patients where possible and doing no harm.

[202] See p. 429 below.

we have seen, doctors already play an important role in other critical health-care decisions, for example, regarding refusal of treatment decisions and the administration of palliative care, and there is no valid basis to suggest that this role is misused or exercised in such a way that brings pressure to bear on patients. In any event, safeguards could be included under legislation permitting active voluntary euthanasia which would help to overcome any risk of pressure from the patient's own doctor, such as the involvement of an independent doctor to verify patient consent and to establish the genuineness of the patient's request.[203]

(iii)   Possibility of error. A number of the arguments that have been advanced against legalization of active voluntary euthanasia have been based on the possibility of error in diagnosis or prognosis or the possibility of a cure being discovered which may save the life of the patient. These objections can, however, readily be countered on the grounds that they are unjustifiably paternalistic and are completely contrary to the fundamental principle of patient self-determination.

(a)   Possibility of mistaken diagnosis or prognosis. A common objection to the legalization of active voluntary euthanasia is that doctors are fallible and may be mistaken in their diagnosis of illness or in their assessment of prognosis for recovery.[204] Opponents point out that if a doctor mistakenly diagnoses a patient as terminal, and on the basis of that diagnosis, the patient requests and receives active euthanasia, a life will have been unnecessarily and irreversibly extinguished: unlike in the case of passive euthanasia, where a patient may survive a prognostic mistake, if active euthanasia is administered, the mistake becomes self-fulfilling.[205] Accordingly, it is argued, in order to avoid the risks of mistaken diagnosis or prognosis, active voluntary euthanasia must be completely prohibited.

While the chance of mistaken diagnosis or prognosis in cases of advanced terminal illness is highly improbable, it cannot be ruled out entirely; the possibility of error exists in all human actions. These risks can, however, be minimized by requiring that the patient is seen by more than one doctor before active voluntary euthanasia is authorized. But most importantly, the patient must be informed of the possibility of error, in order that he or she can make an informed and rational choice.[206] It is a fundamental part of autonomous decision-making that the patient be allowed to weigh up the

[203] See further, pp. 484–6 below regarding possible legislative safeguards.

[204] e.g. Kamisar, 'Some Non-Religious Views Against Proposed Mercy-Killing Legislation', above Ch. 3 n. 68, at 993–8; Rice, *The Vanishing Right to Life*, above n. 153, at 57–9.

[205] Capron, 'The Right to Die: Progress and Peril', above n. 30, at 55. But see the response of Kuhse, 'The Alleged Peril of Active Voluntary Euthanasia: A Reply to Alexander Morgan Capron', above n. 172, at 62 where she points out that there are also many cases where a patient's decision to refuse life-sustaining treatment will make a mistaken prognosis equally self-fulfilling.

[206] Arras, 'The Right to Die on the Slippery Slope', above n. 10, at 301–2.

available information and elect to act upon it even if there is a small chance that the information may be incorrect. Whilst the possibility of mistaken diagnosis or prognosis requires extreme caution before a patient's condition is declared 'hopeless', it does not constitute an adequate objection to the legalization of active voluntary euthanasia.

(b)   Possibility of a cure. A related clinical objection is that a cure or some measure of relief may be discovered within the natural life expectancy of the patient.[207] Supporters of this argument contend that the administration of active voluntary euthanasia would foreclose the possibility of the patient being able to benefit from any new discovery and that it should, therefore, be prohibited.

It is certainly true that medical science is constantly advancing and the possibility always exists that a cure may be found for a condition previously considered hopeless. However, from a practical point of view, this possibility will only be of relevance to patients who have undergone euthanasia shortly before the discovery became readily available for use and who would have been able to expect a complete recovery from their condition. The reality is that usually, a considerable time elapses between the announcement of a new medical discovery and its implementation and availability for use. Even if the cure were immediately available, it would be unlikely to be able to reverse the condition of those patients with advanced terminal illness who are most likely to be seeking active voluntary euthanasia.[208] Ultimately, it comes down to a question of patient choice. As part of the counselling that a patient would receive before a request for active euthanasia is acted upon, the patient should be informed of the possibility (albeit remote) of a cure being discovered for his or her particular condition. This would be especially important in circumstances where a doctor is aware of a new medical break-through which is soon to become available. In this way, the patient can be fully informed before a decision is made with respect to active voluntary euthanasia. It is then for the patient, in the exercise of his or her self-determination, to evaluate the possible advantages of waiting for a possible cure as against seeking an early release from his or her suffering. It would be most unreasonable to deny all patients the freedom to elect active voluntary euthanasia on the ground that for some this interference with their free choice may mean the possibility of a cure.

The foregoing analysis of objections based on problems in ascertaining patient consent, feared abuses, and risk of error gives rise to fundamental questions regarding patient autonomy. Opponents of legalization of active voluntary euthanasia are undoubtedly sincere in their wish to protect patients from the risk of error or abuse and to avoid a request being acted

---

[207] Kamisar, 'Some Non-Religious Views Against Proposed Mercy-Killing Legislation', above Ch. 3 n. 68, at 998–1005.

[208] Morris, 'Voluntary Euthanasia', above n. 8, at 261–2.

upon which does not reflect the patient's genuine wishes. The question which must, however, be addressed is whether such objections are justifiable. More particularly, this involves the need to balance, on the one hand, the liberty interests of those patients who voluntarily seek active euthanasia and, on the other, the need to protect those who may be vulnerable to abuse or coercion from others or who may be mistakenly killed if active voluntary euthanasia were legalized.[209] If the present prohibition on active voluntary euthanasia is retained, the choice of some patients will be denied and they will be forced to suffer against their will. If, however, active voluntary euthanasia is legalized, there will be some risk of unwilling casualties as a result of error and abuse. The approach of opponents of legalization has been to sacrifice the autonomy of patients genuinely seeking active euthanasia for the benefit of those who may be harmed if active voluntary euthanasia is legalized. Some opponents have attempted to justify their conclusion with claims that in numerical terms, the number of vulnerable persons who would be at risk if active voluntary euthanasia were legalized would be greater than those who would be forced to suffer against their will if the present prohibition is retained.[210] Apart from the fact that such numerical claims are purely speculative and may in fact be completely unfounded, it could be argued that the question raised is, in any event, far more complex, involving a balancing of values.[211] Ultimately, the principle of patient autonomy must prevail, notwithstanding that this may entail some risk of error and abuse, particularly since these risks can be adequately guarded against by the introduction of appropriate safeguards. It is also quite possible that legalization would not in fact produce more mistakes and abuse than non-legalization.[212]

Practical difficulties in formulating criteria for active voluntary euthanasia

Another objection, which is really an extension of some of the preceding arguments, is that even if the concept of active voluntary euthanasia were accepted in principle, it would be extremely difficult, if not impossible, to formulate a legislative provision sufficiently precise to allow active voluntary euthanasia in appropriate cases, yet providing adequate safeguards

[209] See also Fletcher, J. C., 'Is Euthanasia Ever Justifiable?' in Wiernik, P. (ed.), *Controversies in Oncology* (New York, 1982) 297, 314, 318; Lynn, 'The Health Care Professional's Role When Active Euthanasia Is Sought', above n. 185, at 102; Feinberg, J., 'Overlooking the Merits of the Individual Case: An Unpromising Approach to the Right to Die' (1991) 4 *Ratio Juris.* 131.
[210] e.g. Fletcher, 'Is Euthanasia Ever Justifiable?', above n. 209, at 314.
[211] See also Feinberg, 'Overlooking the Merits of the Individual Case: An Unpromising Approach to the Right to Die', above n. 209, at 140–51.
[212] For development of this argument, see Newman, N., 'Euthanasia: Orchestrating "The Last Syllable of . . . Time"' (1991) 53 *UPitt.LRev.* 153, 177–8.

against abuse.[213] Put more bluntly, it is sometimes contended that specific plans for active voluntary euthanasia are simply unworkable; if adequate provision were to be made to ensure that the patient has given a voluntary and informed consent, that the patient's condition has been confirmed by consultation with other doctors, and that potential mistakes and abuses have been guarded against, the procedure would become so cumbersome and time-consuming that it would be unable to fulfil its objective of providing the means for a swift and painless death. Indeed, Kamisar, one of the most forceful critics of legalization of active voluntary euthanasia, has suggested that euthanasiasts are seeking a goal which is inherently inconsistent: a procedure for death which provides ample safeguards against abuse and mistake and which is, at the same time, 'quick' and 'easy' in operation.[214]

The fact that it would be difficult to devise guidelines does not mean that this cannot or should not be undertaken. Whilst it is inevitable that an appropriate regulatory procedure for the legalization of active voluntary euthanasia will, to some extent, cause delays in providing the desired result, this is not a valid reason to reject legalization; indeed, one must question whether it would in fact be appropriate to have a euthanasia procedure which is 'quick and easy' in operation. The gravity and irreversible nature of the decision demand a process of careful review and deliberation. Moreover, opponents have tended to exaggerate the extent of the regulatory machinery necessary to implement effectively active voluntary euthanasia and the degree to which this will impede doctors being able to provide the assistance requested. As the recent developments in the Northern Territory has shown, there is no reason why a procedure cannot be developed which provides necessary protection to ensure the voluntariness of patient consent and to protect against abuse, but at the same time is accessible and workable.[215]

Euthanasia is an unnecessary and inappropriate response

An alternative form of argument proceeds on the basis that active voluntary euthanasia is an unnecessary and inappropriate response to the patient's circumstances. There are a number of distinct components to this line of reasoning; that in light of developments in modern palliative care, there is no significant qualitative nor quantitative need for active voluntary euthanasia; that the final days of a patient's life may bring unexpected joy and fulfilment which the patient should not be denied; and that in any event,

---

[213] Kamisar, 'Some Non-Religious Views Against Proposed Mercy-Killing Legislation', above Ch. 3 n. 68, at 978–85.
[214] Ibid. at 982.
[215] For discussion of the Northern Territory legislation see pp. 345–57 below.

legislative change is unnecessary since the present laws deal adequately with the situation. Each of these assertions will be examined in turn.

Capacity for pain relief

Opponents of euthanasia are frequently heard to say that legalization of active voluntary euthanasia is unnecessary in light of modern developments in palliative care.[216] It is alleged that modern analgesics and narcotics can control pain and represent a safer and more positive response to the problems of the terminally or incurably ill than active voluntary euthanasia.

Whilst it is true that there have been significant advancements in recent years in the area of palliative care, and that in most instances, dying patients can be made comfortable and their pain can be relieved, specialists in the area concede that it is not possible to eliminate pain in all cases.[217] Furthermore, the practical realities of medical care often fall far short of the results achievable through optimal treatment.[218] This, in turn, raises another argument made by some opponents: if active voluntary euthanasia were legalized, some people would choose to die in order to escape improper treatment of pain and other symptoms, and that inequities in the health care system would mean that the poor would be particularly disadvantaged.[219] In response to such concerns, it should be stressed that every effort should be made to maximize individuals' opportunity for receiving optimal palliative care with the aim of making the lives of terminally ill patients as comfortable as possible and reduce to a minimum the number of people who would seek an earlier release from their suffering. However, as suggested earlier, the reality often falls short of the ideal. The choices that individuals will make are clearly influenced by the circumstances in which they find themselves as is already the case with respect to other medical decision-making. As part of the exercise of self-determination, individuals should be able to choose active voluntary euthanasia as a means of escaping a situation which is for them intolerable, including circumstances where the palliative care

---

[216] Kamisar, 'Some Non-Religious Views Against Proposed Mercy-Killing Legislation', above Ch. 3 n. 68, at 1008–11.

[217] e.g. Hockley, J. *et al.*, 'Survey of Distressing Symptoms in Dying Patients and their Families in Hospital and the Response to a Symptom Control Team' (1988) 296 BMJ 1715, 1715–17. See also the Statement of the Australian Association for Hospice and Palliative Care Inc, *Position Statement on Voluntary Active Euthanasia* (1995). For further discussion, see pp. 324–5 below.

[218] Mills, M. *et al.*, 'Care of Dying Patients in Hospital' (1994) 309 BMJ 583. According to a study, reported in this article, of the care of dying patients in general hospitals in Scotland (although admittedly conducted some years before the article was published), basic interventions to maintain patients' comfort were often not provided. Contact between nurses and dying patients was minimal; distancing and isolation of patients by most medical and nursing staff were evident and this isolation increased as death approached. The conclusions reached in this study was that the care of many of the dying patients observed in these hospitals was poor.

[219] Bernhoft, R., 'The Human Costs of Euthanasia: A Risk/Benefit Analysis of Physician Assisted Suicide' (1993) 15 *Clinical Therapeutics* 1185, at 1186.

available is inadequate. In any event, it is important that this concern is put into perspective: the reasons behind patient requests for active voluntary euthanasia are multifarious and as explained in the argument which follows, the provision of even optimal palliative care by no means guarantees that such requests will not be made.

Even if it *were* possible to relieve all physical pain, that would not obviate the need for active voluntary euthanasia. For many patients, there are aspects of dying that drugs and other forms of palliative care cannot alleviate, including the suffering and distress of their condition, the mental and emotional anguish, and the fear of dependency and degradation.[220] Significantly, the available evidence suggests that the factors prompting a request for active euthanasia are, in many cases, not intractable physical pain but unbearable or senseless suffering.[221] Particular factors that have been highlighted are concerns about loss of control, being a burden, being dependent, and loss of dignity.[222] As a matter of personal dignity, autonomy, and self-determination, patients in such circumstances should have the liberty to choose death. Thus, whilst palliative care clearly constitutes a vital part of the overall care for terminal patients and may, if made widely available, help to reduce the need for active voluntary euthanasia, it can by no means obviate the need for it entirely. Further it should be emphasized that for many patients, simply knowing that active voluntary euthanasia would be available if circumstances required it would be significant: providing patients with this reassurance may offer them the opportunity to live their final days in peace without necessarily exercising that option.

Quantitative need for euthanasia not large

Another argument raised by the opponents of euthanasia is that legalization is unnecessary since there is no great demand for active euthanasia in practice.[223] Although there are enormous difficulties involved in accurately quantifying the extent of demand for active voluntary euthanasia, evidence was presented in the preceding chapter that some patients do request active euthanasia, notwithstanding the present illegality of the practice,[224] and if it

---

[220] For medical recognition of unrelieved pain and other distressing symptoms in the dying, see Hockley et al., 'Survey of Distressing Symptoms in Dying Patients and their Families in Hospital and the Response to a Symptom Control Team', above n. 217, at 1715–17.

[221] Sneiderman, B., 'Euthanasia in the Netherlands: A Model for Canada?' (1992) 8 *Humane Med.* 104, 108. See also the findings of the Remmelink survey in the Netherlands which found that for a majority of patients, loss of dignity was the principal reason behind the request and in only a small minority of case was pain the sole reason: see p. 429 below.

[222] See Back et al., 'Physician-Assisted Suicide and Euthanasia in Washington State', above Ch. 3 n. 20, at 924, reporting on concerns of patients requesting physician-assisted death from the perspective of their physicians.

[223] Kamisar, 'Some Non-Religious Views Against Proposed Mercy-Killing Legislation', above Ch. 3 n. 68, at 1011.

[224] See pp. 130–4 above.

were to be legalized, more patients would undoubtedly articulate such requests. In the light of the available information, it is reasonable to assume that if active voluntary euthanasia were legalized it would be an option sought by only a small minority of patients.[225] Even so, that arguably already constitutes sufficient justification for legalizing the practice.[226] The arguments advanced in support of active voluntary euthanasia are based on fundamental principles and do not rely for their validity on claims regarding the extent of demand for the practice.

Adequacy of present position

A rather interesting argument advanced by some opponents is that legislation covering active voluntary euthanasia is unnecessary since present law and practice adequately deal with the situation and any legislative change would open the floodgates to unnecessary deaths.[227]

Essentially this is an argument for retaining the status quo, but on closer examination this argument discloses the blatant hypocrisy of many of the opponents. It seems that they are willing to acknowledge that doctors may, in appropriate cases, administer active euthanasia without attracting legal sanction, yet are unwilling to condone any change in the law which legalizes this practice. This puts doctors in an impossible situation; the conflicting message that they are given is that although active voluntary euthanasia is unlawful, the law may turn a blind eye to its administration in practice.[228] Whilst it is unlikely that a doctor would be prosecuted for murder it is undesirable that doctors should be exposed to the risk of criminal liability. The recent conviction of Dr Cox in the United Kingdom for the attempted murder of his patient has brought into sharp focus the legal vulnerability of doctors who respond to a patient's request for active euthanasia.[229] Moreover, the present practice of active euthanasia is necessarily informal and covert, and is, therefore, more likely to be discriminatory and subject to abuse. If, as a society, we have reached a situation where we accept the

---

[225] Some guide as to the demand for active voluntary euthanasia if it were legalized can be gleaned from the Netherlands where the practice, although not actually legalized, has received some official support. The Remmelink survey (discussed pp. 423–35 below) found that there are approximately 9,000 explicit requests for active euthanasia or assisted suicide each year in the Netherlands which has a population of approximately 14 million and an annual total of approximately 130,000 deaths. Significantly, in only a small proportion of these cases was active voluntary euthanasia in fact performed.

[226] See also Williams, 'Euthanasia Legislation: A Rejoinder to Non-Religious Objections', above n. 68, at 156, 164.

[227] Kamisar, 'Some Non-Religious Views Against Proposed Mercy-Killing Legislation', above Ch. 3 n. 68, at 1041–2.

[228] Nowell-Smith, P., 'Death By Request as a Right' (1987) 2 *Euthanasia Rev.* 80, 86; Williams, 'Euthanasia Legislation: A Rejoinder to Non-Religious Objections', above n. 68, at 156, 157–8.

[229] For further discussion of this case, see pp. 143–5 above.

practice of active voluntary euthanasia in appropriate cases but wish doctors to avoid prosecution, it would be much more satisfactory to formalize
the situation by legalizing active voluntary euthanasia in carefully regulated
circumstances. As suggested in the preceding chapter, there are powerful
arguments in favour of closing the gap between the law on the books and
the law in practice.[230]

The patient can always commit suicide

Another basis on which some opponents of euthanasia argue that legislative
change is unnecessary is that patients who are serious about wanting death
always have the option of committing suicide.[231] For some opponents the
concept of suicide is preferable to active voluntary euthanasia since it
removes doubt as to the voluntariness of the act and avoids the problems
associated with third party involvement in the patient's death. Indeed, it has
been questioned why anyone physically capable of suicide should feel entitled to demand of others that they become involved in their killing, with the
further claim being made that those who have the capacity but lack the will
to accomplish their own end should be considered poor candidates for
euthanasia due to their vacillation about self-destruction.[232]

There are a number of counter arguments which can be made. Committing suicide is by no means an easy thing to do. Information about the
means of committing suicide may be difficult to obtain and suicide attempts
without medical information and/or help are often messy, undignified, and
ultimately unsuccessful. In many instances, those patients who would be
likely to seek active voluntary euthanasia (patients who have reached an
advanced stage of terminal illness) are no longer in a position to take their
own lives. They are often immobilized by their condition and simply do not
have the means available to commit suicide without the co-operation of
others. Moreover, some persons may find the concept of suicide repugnant,
yet would willingly avail themselves of the option of active voluntary euthanasia administered by a doctor. Further, it could be argued that if suicide is
to be the only option available to patients, it would tend to encourage
persons who are aware of their hopeless condition to act while they are still
physically able to do so, thereby possibly depriving them of extra time
which they may have enjoyed, had medically administered active voluntary
euthanasia been available. Another consideration is that the present blanket prohibition on assisted suicide makes it problematic for individuals to

---

[230] See pp. 148–52 above.

[231] e.g. Kamisar, 'Some Non-Religious Views Against Proposed Mercy-Killing Legislation',
above Ch. 3 n. 68, at 1011; Grisez, 'Suicide and Euthanasia' in Horan, D. and Mall, D. (eds.),
Death, Dying and Euthanasia (Frederick, Maryland, 1980) 742, 803.

[232] Mullen, P., 'Euthanasia: An Impoverished Construction of Life and Death' (1995) 3
JLaw &Med. 121, 125.

undertake their deaths in the company of their loved ones, because of the fear of exposing them to criminal liability.[233] All in all, there is much to be said for a formalized approach, permitting medically assisted dying so that patients can be secure in the knowledge that help will be available if it becomes necessary.

Final days

A further argument is that one can never know what the final days of life for a dying patient will hold and that by allowing active voluntary euthanasia, we may foreclose the possibility of some profound good such as reconciliation, reaffirmation, or realization.[234]

Undoubtedly for some patients, their final days in the face of impending death may yield unexpected and invaluable experiences. However, this is not a valid argument for denying the individual the liberty to choose an earlier death. It would be unjustifiably paternalistic to insist that patients must endure a prolonged dying in the hope that this will be a rewarding experience. The wishes of a patient who has decision-making capacity ought to be respected, even though this may result in lost spiritual or emotional opportunities for him or her.

Effect on the doctor/patient relationship

A further objection which is frequently raised by opponents to euthanasia is that any change to the law permitting doctors to administer active voluntary euthanasia would have serious implications for the relationship between doctor and patient.[235] This argument is often supported with claims that doctors are opposed to active voluntary euthanasia and do not wish to become involved in its practice.[236]

Opponents argue that the traditional role of doctors in the community, based on the Hippocratic Oath,[237] has been that of healer, trusted with the responsibility of saving and prolonging life and that to cast doctors in the role of administering active euthanasia would undermine and compromise the objectives of the medical profession and destroy the trust and confidence that is essential to the success of the doctor/patient relationship.[238]

---

[233] Dickens, B., 'When Terminally Ill Patients Request Death: Assisted Suicide Before Canadian Courts' (1994) 10 *JPalliative Care* 52, 55.

[234] Gillett, 'Euthanasia, Letting Die and the Pause', above n. 28, at 67.

[235] Trowell, *The Unfinished Debate on Euthanasia*, above Ch. 2 n. 2, at 128–31; St. John Stevas, N., *Life, Death and the Law: Law and Christian Morals in England and the United States* (Bloomington, 1961) 275.

[236] e.g. St. John Stevas, *Life, Death and the Law*, above n. 235, at 275.

[237] *Inter alia*, the Oath provides; 'I will give no deadly medicine to anyone if asked, nor suggest any such counsel'. For a modern translation of the Hippocratic Oath see Edelstein, L., *The Hippocratic Oath* (Baltimore, 1943).

[238] e.g. BMA Working Party Report, *Euthanasia*, above Ch. 3 n. 1, at 18–20; Keyserlingk, *Sanctity of Life or Quality of Life*, above n. 27, at 128.

Doctors would be viewed by their patients as killers instead of healers, and patients—in any event a vulnerable group—would feel threatened because of their doctor's possible participation in active euthanasia. Thus, opponents argue, the prohibition on active euthanasia must remain in order to preserve the doctor/patient relationship and to ensure that patients can at all times feel that their doctor will act as the guardian of life.[239] Apart from the need to protect the doctor/patient relationship, concerns have also been raised regarding the possible psychological consequences to doctors if they participate in the practice of active voluntary euthanasia.[240] For example, fears have been expressed that to allow a doctor to kill a patient, even at the patient's request, is to desensitize the doctor to the value of human life.

First of all it should be noted that the objection based on the potential damage to the doctor/patient relationship is not an absolute argument against the legalization of active voluntary euthanasia; euthanasia need not necessarily be performed by the medical profession and it would be possible to frame legislation in such a way so that doctors are not involved.[241] However, doctors are clearly the most appropriate group of persons to administer active voluntary euthanasia in view of their contact with and knowledge of the patient, and their medical expertise which is necessary to facilitate a painless and dignified death. Moreover, doctors practice under well-recognized codes of ethics and have the professional integrity and organization to administer and monitor the implementation of active voluntary euthanasia. And whilst it is true that professional medical associations are, with some isolated exceptions, overwhelmingly opposed to active voluntary euthanasia, surveys of members of the medical profession indicate that the great majority of doctors believe that if legalized, the practice should be medicalized (that is, it should be performed only by doctors and performed at medical sites) and a significant proportion would personally be willing to participate in the practice.[242] Furthermore, as outlined in the preceding chapter, there is overwhelming evidence to suggest that some doctors already perform active euthanasia.[243]

Assuming then, that if active voluntary euthanasia were to be legalized, doctors would be the ones to administer it, consideration needs to be given to the substance of the opponents' argument that permitting doctors to perform active voluntary euthanasia would be contrary to the traditional

---

[239] Trowell, *The Unfinished Debate on Euthanasia*, above Ch. 2 n. 2, at 130–1.

[240] e.g. Misbin, R., 'Physicians' Aid-in-Dying' (1991) 325 *New Eng.JMed.* 1307, at 1309.

[241] Provision could, for example, be made for active euthanasia to be performed by friends or relatives of the patient, or by trained lay persons. One suggestion, which would avoid the involvement of ordinary medical practitioners, has been advanced by Crisp, R., 'A Good Death: Who Best to Bring It?' (1987) 1 *Bioethics* 74, 77–9 where he suggests that if active voluntary euthanasia were to be legalized it should become part of an area of medical specialization in the care of the terminally ill.

[242] See pp. 292–332 below.　　　[243] See pp. 134–8 above.

role of the medical profession and would adversely effect the doctor/patient relationship.

Properly understood, the goals of medicine are to prolong and preserve life and cure disease, but at the same time, to relieve pain and suffering.[244] These goals are potentially conflicting: the prolongation of life may prolong suffering, and conversely, in order to relieve pain and suffering, it may be necessary to shorten life.[245] Importantly, it must be recognized that in some cases, life cannot be saved nor disease cured. In these circumstances, the doctor's role in alleviating suffering is of paramount importance and the administration of active euthanasia at the patient's request can be seen as a legitimate part of the doctor's role as health care professional; the principle of patient autonomy should be sufficient to override the imperative to save life while still honouring the doctor/patient relationship in continuing to relieve suffering. And whilst opponents frequently argue that the Hippocratic Oath prohibits doctors from acceding to patient's requests for active voluntary euthanasia, this objection has little force in contemporary society, where a literal interpretation of the Oath is of limited practical relevance.[246]

Further, it can be argued that legalization of active voluntary euthanasia would not necessarily have adverse effects on the doctor/patient relationship. If one has regard to the position in the Netherlands, where active voluntary euthanasia is now openly practised, there does not appear to have been any erosion of the trust between patients and their doctors.[247] In fact, for many people, the knowledge that their doctor could assist in administering active euthanasia at their request would have a positive effect, fostering greater confidence, and relieving anxiety about an agonizing and undignified death.[248] Thus, contrary to the claims of opponents, the legalization of

[244] Cassel, E., 'The Nature of Suffering and the Goals of Medicine' (1982) 306 *New Eng.J Med.* 639.

[245] Parker, 'Moral Intuition, Good Deaths and Ordinary Medical Practitioners', above n. 29, at 32.

[246] Quite a number of commentators have cast doubt on the status of the Hippocratic Oath; some have suggested that even in its day, the Oath did not represent the views of the majority of doctors: (e.g. Devettere, R., 'Reconceptualising the Euthanasia Debate' (1989) 17 *Law, Med.& Health Care* 145, 147); others have suggested that notwithstanding the terms of the Oath, the Hippocratic tradition was not opposed to active voluntary euthanasia (e.g. Carrick, P., *Medical Ethics in Antiquity* (Dordecht, 1985) 154–9) and some commentators have highlighted the selective use that is at times made of 'the Hippocratic tradition', noting that there are many aspects of the Oath which have become hopelessly outdated—one example is abortion—although prohibited under the Oath, abortion is a fairly common medical practice (Momeyer, R., 'Does Physician Assisted Suicide Violate the Integrity of Medicine?' (1995) 20 *J Med.&Phil.* 13, 18). See also the discussion in the majority decision of the US Court of Appeals for the Ninth Circuit in *Compassion in Dying* v. *State of Washington (en banc)* (see above Ch. 2 n. 54), discussed at pp. 103–7 above.

[247] See the Institute of Medical Ethics, Discussion Paper 'Assisted Death', above n. 90, at 611 and pp. 440–1 below dealing with the position in the Netherlands.

[248] Cohen, H., 'Euthanasia as a Way of Life' (1991) 43 *Hemlock Q* 7, 7–8.

doctor-administered active voluntary euthanasia could have the effect of strengthening the doctor/patient relationship. Support for this view can be derived from public opinion polls which show overwhelming support for doctors being able to administer active voluntary euthanasia.[249] To suggest that doctors performing active voluntary euthanasia would be viewed as 'killers' ignores the fact that the legalization of active euthanasia would be subject to stringent safeguards, requiring patient consent, and providing that any termination of life not in accordance with those requirements would remain unlawful and punishable as homicide.[250] There is good reason to believe that the public's trust and confidence in the medical profession will not decrease if its members are sure that active euthanasia will not be administered without their explicit request.[251] Moreover, doctors are bound by strict codes of ethics and can, on the whole, be trusted to act responsibly if empowered to perform active voluntary euthanasia, particularly if there is an appropriate regulatory framework.

Another important consideration, closely interrelated with the status of the doctor/patient relationship, concerns whether doctors' participation in assisting patients to die can be reconciled with the professional integrity of doctors. One of the claims of opponents is that the professional integrity of the medical profession will be imperilled if doctors are permitted to assist patients to die. However, convincing arguments have been put forward that the practice of voluntary doctor-assisted death as a last resort does not violate the doctor's professional integrity.[252] Four basic duties or norms of medicine have been identified: the duty to practice competently, to avoid harming patients unduly, to refrain from medical fraud, and to preserve patients' trust. Whilst *prima facie* there is a duty to refrain from assisted suicide and active voluntary euthanasia, under these norms, voluntary doctor-assisted death in exceptional circumstances in response to unrelievable suffering is permissible and consistent with professional integrity. Further support for rejecting the validity of this concern can be drawn from an examination of the reality of medical practice: as discussed elsewhere in this work,[253] doctors are already involved in the practices of assisted suicide and active voluntary euthanasia as well as other forms of active conduct that hastens the death of their patients such as terminating life-support systems or administering palliative drugs for the relief of pain and symptoms with

---

[249] See pp. 257–68 below.

[250] See also Davies, J., 'Raping and Making Love are Different Concepts: So are Killing and Voluntary Euthanasia' (1988) 14 *JMed.Ethics* 148, 148–9.

[251] See also Leenen, H., 'Dying with Dignity: Developments in the Field of Euthanasia in the Netherlands' (1989) *Med.&Law* 517, 519; Kuhse, 'The Alleged Peril of Active Voluntary Euthanasia: A Reply to Alexander Morgan Capron', above n. 172, at 64.

[252] See Miller, F. and Brody, H., 'Professional Integrity and Physician-Assisted Death' (1995) 25 *Hastings Center R* 8.

[253] See pp. 134–9 above.

full knowledge of their 'double effect'.[254] In these circumstances, it becomes increasingly difficult to contend that legalization of active voluntary euthanasia and doctor-assisted suicide will jeopardize the integrity of the medical profession, particularly in view of the growing evidence that many doctors do not believe that providing such assistance is in any way contrary to their professional obligations.

The final aspect to the opponents' objection to the involvement of doctors in the practice of active voluntary euthanasia based on the possible detrimental psychological effects on doctors can also be rejected. There is no doubt at all that taking steps to bring about the death of a patient at the patient's request is a serious matter about which doctors would have to deliberate very carefully. Indeed, the very difficulty of such decisions can be seen as an important safeguard for the practice of active voluntary euthanasia. Under a scheme of legalized active voluntary euthanasia, doctors' participation would be entirely voluntary, thereby minimizing any risk of trauma or damage. It must also be borne in mind that active euthanasia would be an option sought by only a small minority of patients so the occasions on which a doctor would participate in its performance would be few and far between. In any event, the concept of active voluntary euthanasia cannot be judged in isolation. It has been argued earlier in this work that doctors are already involved in conduct which hastens death in the form of omissions to provide treatment, the termination of life support, and the administration of palliative drugs for the relief of pain and other symptoms.[255] In these circumstances, it is difficult to allege that the voluntary participation of a doctor in active euthanasia at the request of a patient would be likely to have a detrimental psychological effect on doctors. Moreover, it could be argued that there are also problems in retaining the status quo; doctors may become desensitized to human suffering if they feel they are denied by law the means to alleviate that suffering.[256]

In the light of the foregoing evaluation, it would appear that many of the arguments which have been raised against the involvement of doctors in the administration of active voluntary euthanasia indicate that the objections made are based on professional interests rather than concern for the well-being of patients.[257] The claims which have been made regarding the implications of legalization of active voluntary euthanasia upon the interests of the medical profession are largely without foundation. Doctors opposed to active voluntary euthanasia would have nothing to fear as participation by doctors in the practice would be entirely voluntary: doctors would be under

---

[254] See also *Compassion in Dying* v. *State of Washington* (see above Ch. 2 n. 54) discussed at pp. 101–15 above.

[255] See pp. 127, 138–40 above. For analysis of these practices, see pp. 152–86 above.

[256] Misbin, 'Physicians' Aid-in-Dying', above n. 240, at 1309.

[257] Preston, T., 'Professional Norms and Physician Attitudes Toward Euthanasia' (1994) 22 *JL&Med.* 36.

no duty to perform active voluntary euthanasia, rather, those wishing to assist patients who request active voluntary euthanasia would be permitted to do so in certain circumstances without the fear of attracting criminal liability. Given the demand and widespread support for active voluntary euthanasia there is good reason to believe that the professional standing of doctors would not be diminished.

Legalization would discourage medical research and developments in palliative care

A further argument which has been advanced against the legalization of active voluntary euthanasia is that it would discourage the search for new cures and progress in palliative care.[258] Opponents argue that the prohibition on active euthanasia has been an important impetus in the development of humane terminal care and research for cures for terminal conditions. If we now permit active voluntary euthanasia, we will be jeopardizing future developments in these areas to the detriment of the majority of patients. A related argument is that the availability of active voluntary euthanasia is likely to contribute to the medicalization of the dying, diverting attention and resources from difficult social and personal aspects of the needs of dying and suffering persons.[259]

In evaluating these arguments it is important to note that mixed views are held in respect of active voluntary euthanasia amongst those involved in the provision of palliative care. Whilst many are opposed to the legalization of active voluntary euthanasia,[260] some palliative care specialists have supported legalization[261] and there has been recognition on the part of some professional palliative care associations of the need for proper debate about the role of active voluntary euthanasia in the palliative care context.[262]

Few would wish to disagree with the proposition that research efforts should be encouraged and that every attempt should be made to devise more humane forms of terminal care; indeed this may help to reduce the number of patients who would request active euthanasia as a solution to their situation. However, it cannot be assumed, as the euthanasia opponents appear to have done, that legalization of active voluntary euthanasia

---

[258] e.g. Potts, 'Looking for the Exit Door: Killing and Caring in Modern Medicine', above n. 137, at 504–5; Twycross, R., 'Debate: Euthanasia—A Physician's Viewpoint' (1982) 8 *J Med. Ethics* 86, at 91.

[259] Burgess, M., 'The Medicalization of Dying' (1993) 18 *J Med.&Phil.* 269.

[260] e.g. Dame Cicely Saunders, of St. Christopher's Hospice, London, (see Du Boulay, S., *Cicely Saunders: The Founder of the Modern Hospice Movement* (London, 1984)); Twycross, R., 'Where There is Hope There is Life: A View from the Hospice' in Keown, *Euthanasia Examined*, above n. 15, at 141.

[261] e.g. Hunt, R., 'Palliative Care—The Rhetoric-Reality Gap' in Kuhse, H. (ed), *Willing to Listen: Wanting to Die* (Melbourne, 1994).

[262] e.g. the Australian Association for Hospice and Palliative Care Inc., *Position Statement on Voluntary Active Euthanasia*, above n. 217. For further discussion, see pp. 324–5 below.

would necessarily have the effect of discouraging medical research and progress in palliative care.[263] Since active voluntary euthanasia would more than likely be an option only sought by a small minority, justification would remain for continuing research and improvements in terminal care for the great majority of patients. It is, in any event, misguided to regard active voluntary euthanasia as in any way competing with medical research and developments. Rather, what proponents wish to achieve is to expand the options available to patients, by offering active voluntary euthanasia as a last resort for patients who have explored other options but found them to be unsatisfactory.

C. Evaluation of the Case For and Against Active Voluntary Euthanasia

In the preceding part, attention has focused on the objections that have most frequently been raised against the legalization of active voluntary euthanasia. In assessing these arguments, it must be emphasized that we are dealing with the issue of legalization of active *voluntary* euthanasia. So, whilst many of the arguments may be perfectly valid objections to non-voluntary or involuntary euthanasia, the crucial distinction between voluntary euthanasia on the one hand, and involuntary or non-voluntary euthanasia on the other, must be firmly borne in mind.

The basis for opposition to legalization of active voluntary euthanasia has come from a variety of sources, and includes religious, moral, and philosophical objections, but the most serious challenge to the pro-legalization case undoubtedly stems from objections based on practical arguments. There is, in fact, a significant area of common ground in the euthanasia debate in that many commentators would agree that legalization of active voluntary euthanasia would give rise to the risk of abuse, mistake, and other undesirable consequences. However, a fundamental difference of opinion exists as to the appropriate response in these circumstances. Opponents vigorously argue that legalization, even under strict conditions, would create unacceptable risks and that the benefits which would be gained would be far outweighed by the dangers to society.[264] Thus, they argue, the risks and dangers are too great to warrant a change to the existing law. Proponents, on the other hand, emphasize the importance of patient autonomy. They contend that the risks and dangers associated with legalization do not justify an absolute prohibition of active voluntary euthanasia and that they

---

[263] See also the decision of the majority of the US Court of Appeals for the Ninth Circuit in *Compassion in Dying* v. *State of Washington* (see above Ch. 2 n. 54) for a similar view, although the court was there considering the issue in the context of the legalization of doctor-assisted suicide.

[264] e.g. Kamisar, 'Some Non-Religious Views Against Proposed Mercy-Killing Legislation', above Ch. 3 n. 68, at 976.

can be adequately dealt with by appropriate regulation and the imposition of rigorous safeguards. Further, they argue that the criminal law should not intervene in the exercise of individual liberty unless there are compelling social interests requiring it to do so.[265]

III. THE LEGAL PHILOSOPHERS' DEBATE: THE ROLE OF THE CRIMINAL LAW

The euthanasia debate gives rise to fundamental questions about the rights and interests of individuals weighed against the values and interests of society as a whole. The aim of this part is to examine the role of the criminal law and ascertain the circumstances in which State intervention in individual autonomy is justified. Specific consideration will then be given to the proper scope of the criminal law with regard to active voluntary euthanasia.

A. *The Libertarian Premise: The Prevention of Harm*

Of the competing views regarding the appropriate basis for criminal law intervention,[266] the most convincing argument is the libertarian premise that individuals should be free to do as they please, provided that their conduct does not cause harm to others; in short, the 'harm principle'.[267] The classic exposition of this view is by John Stuart Mill, in his now famous *On Liberty*,[268] where he wrote that:

The only purpose for which power can rightfully be exercised over any member of a civilised community against his will is to prevent harm to others. His own good, either physical or moral, is not a sufficient warrant. He cannot rightfully be compelled to do or to forbear because it will be better for him to do so, because it will make him happier, because in the opinion of others, to do so would be wise or even right.[269]

According to this view, the principal role of the criminal law is to protect society and its members against harm and to punish behaviour which threatens or harms public interests. This involves not only protection from physical injury, but also the protection of fundamental social values and

---

[265] e.g. Morris, 'Voluntary Euthanasia', above n. 8, at 254.

[266] For discussion of some of the possible justifications for State intervention in the affairs of the individual, see, for example, Feinberg, J., *The Moral Limits of the Criminal Law*, a four volume series comprised of Vol. I *Harm to Others* (New York, 1984); Vol. II *Offense to Others* (New York, 1985); Vol III *Harm to Self* (New York, 1986); and Vol. IV *Harmless Wrongdoing* (New York, 1988).

[267] For detailed analysis of the meaning of 'harm', see Feinberg, *Harm to Others*, above n. 266, at 31–64.

[268] 2nd edn. (London, 1859).   [269] Ibid. at 72.

interests.[270] Individual freedom is qualified only by the restraint necessary for the protection of the bodily integrity and freedom of others. Prevention of self-caused harm is not a valid ground for intervention with a person's autonomous choices. As was seen in an earlier chapter, the common law has traditionally accorded the highest value to the preservation and protection of human life.[271] The common law tradition, as reflected in the criminal law sanctions, regards human life as sacred and inalienable and prohibits anyone from licensing their own self-destruction. The prohibition of homicide constitutes a fundamental component of the criminal law's protection of human life. This prohibition is obviously necessary for the protection of society and its members, since killing is normally a harm, violating the right to life of the person killed. Thus, a clear rule against active killing is entirely justified.

The question arises as to whether a merciful killing at the patient's request should be treated as any other homicide. Although killing will usually constitute a harm, this is not always the case. Killing of a person is only wrongful and constitutes a harm where it deprives a person of their right to life.[272] Where, however, a person has a rational interest in dying and has expressed a clear wish to do so, the killing of that person violates no rights and therefore, does not constitute a 'harm' in the accepted sense.[273] In the absence of harm to any individual, there is arguably no need for the criminal law prohibition of murder to apply. Furthermore, even if it were accepted, for argument's sake, that the State has a legitimate interest in the lives of its citizens such that it may prevent a healthy person from taking his or her life, in circumstances where a person is terminally or incurably ill and expresses a wish to die, the State can claim no compelling social interests justifying interference with the individual's liberty to choose a quick and painless death.[274] Indeed, in the case of active voluntary euthanasia, it is difficult to see how acceding to the request of a terminal or incurable patient for a release from suffering can, in any practical sense, endanger society. If we are to respect the individual's right to liberty, we must allow him or her to seek an earlier death with the assistance of others.[275]

[270] Law Reform Commission of Canada, *Our Criminal Law* (Ottawa, 1976) 16.

[271] See pp. 18–21 above.

[272] Brody, B., 'A Non-Consequentialist Argument for Active Euthanasia' in Brody, B. and Engelhardt, T., *Bioethics: Readings and Cases* (Englewood Cliffs, New Jersey, 1987) 161–5; Richards, 'Constitutional Privacy, the Right to Die and the Meaning of Life', above Ch. 2 n. 153, at 358–9.

[273] Feinberg, *Harm to Others*, above n. 266, at 116.

[274] Williams, 'Euthanasia Legislation: A Rejoinder to the Non-Religious Objections', above n. 68, at 157. See now also the reasoning of the court in *Compassion in Dying* v. *State of Washington*, above Ch. 2 n. 54.

[275] Note also Rachels, *The End of Life*, above n. 20, at 181–2 where he argues that Mill's principle applies not only to acts which are entirely self-regarding (e.g. suicide) but also to individuals who voluntarily agree to act together; this is still a private affair and no one else's interests need be involved.

Opponents will, once again, seek to rely on the 'wedge argument' as a basis of justifying the maintenance of the existing prohibition on active voluntary euthanasia, arguing that the present law provides a valuable barrier against unlawful killing which we must be careful to preserve. Consideration has already been given to the counter-arguments to the wedge objection and no attempt will be made here to retrace that ground. What may be observed, however, for the purposes of the present analysis, is the inconsistency of the present law which permits human life to be taken deliberately in some circumstances without criminal consequences, yet categorically prohibits the taking of life at the request of a fully informed patient who has decision-making capacity. So, for example, in cases of war, capital punishment and self-defence, the criminal law has made some concession to the sanctity of life principle and accepts that there may be good reason for the intentional termination of life. Some important public interest seems to have been recognized sufficient to justify these cases of killing, despite the general presumption of the law against the taking of life. Yet, according to current criminal law principles, the consent of the patient is not regarded as sufficient justification to absolve another person from criminal liability for assisting the patient to die.

B. The Present Limits of Consent

In the earlier analysis of the criminal law in Chapter 1, attention was drawn to the very significant limits that are placed on consent for the purposes of the criminal law.[276] It was shown that on the basis of established principles, one cannot licence the infliction of death on oneself by another.[277] Indeed, the consent of the victim is, strictly speaking, irrelevant to the issue of liability for homicide. The question arises, however, why should an individual not be able to validly dispose of his or her right to bodily integrity by requesting to be killed, provided that no harm is thereby caused to others? In other contexts the consent of the individual is all important, for example with regard to medical treatment, even life-sustaining medical treatment, with the consequence that the administration of treatment without the consent of a patient who has decision-making capacity would generally be unlawful. It could, accordingly, be argued that an individual should have the same right to consent or not to consent to active voluntary euthanasia and consent ought not be vitiated on questionable public policy grounds.

It must be understood that what is being claimed here is not a general right that all individuals be free lawfully to consent to their own death. Indeed, it is acknowledged that the State has a direct interest in maintaining the lives of healthy and productive citizens and maintaining social order,

---

[276] See above pp. 19–21.
[277] Williams, G., 'Consent and Public Policy' (1962) *Crim.LRev.* 74 (Part 1), 154 (Part 2).

and that the introduction of a general right to consent to one's death could undermine these legitimate State interests. Rather, what is being claimed is a more limited entitlement for terminal and incurable patients that they may give a legally effective consent to a doctor to bring about their death. In these circumstances, the State does not have a sufficient interest in the timing and manner of the patient's death to justify negating the patient's consent.

C. Relationship Between Law and Morality

It was suggested earlier in this chapter that the principle role of the criminal law is to protect society and its members against harm and to punish behaviour which threatens or harms public interests.[278] Another issue which must be addressed is the relationship between law and morality, and what bearing this has upon the question of legalization of active voluntary euthanasia. Is active voluntary euthanasia immoral, and further, is the answer to this question determinative of whether it should be subject to criminal sanction?

There has been a long-standing debate about the proper role of the criminal law, and more particularly, whether the criminal law should be used to attempt to enforce morality, even though immorality will cause no tangible harm to others.[279] The leading exponent of the view that the criminal law does have a role in enforcing morality has been Lord Devlin in his much acclaimed work, *The Enforcement of Morals.*[280] Devlin's thesis is that the law exists for the protection of society, not merely for the benefit of the individual, and in order to discharge its function, the law must protect the community of ideas, political and moral, without which no society can exist. In support of his thesis, Devlin seeks to demonstrate that the criminal law is in fact based upon moral principles and to illustrate this proposition, he refers to the attitude which the criminal law adopts towards consent. He argues that the reason an individual cannot consent to an offence against himself is because it is an offence against society, in that it threatens one of the great moral principles upon which society is based—the sanctity of human life. Thus, he concludes, there is only one explanation of what has hitherto been accepted as the basis of the criminal law; that there are certain standards of behaviour or moral principles which society requires to be observed, the breach of which is an offence not merely against the person who is injured, but against society as a whole.

[278] See pp. 249–50 above.
[279] For the principal contributions to this debate, see the *Report of the Committee on Homosexual Offences and Prostitution* (London, 1957) Cmnd. 247 (referred to as the *Wolfenden Report*); Mill, J., *On Liberty*, above n. 268; Devlin, P., *The Enforcement of Morals* (London, 1965); Hart, H., *Law, Liberty and Morality* (London, 1962).
[280] Above n. 279.

However, many commentators disagree with the proposition put forward by Devlin that the enforcement of a common morality is within the proper scope of the criminal law.[281] The primary objection to Devlin's moral theory is that the legal enforcement of morals will seriously impinge upon individual freedom and self-determination. The view is widely held that there are some areas of private morality and individual conscience which simply ought not to be subject to legal sanction. With particular reference to Devlin's reasoning regarding the irrelevance of consent, it has been argued that the rules excluding the victim's consent as a defence to criminal charges do not in any event necessarily support his contention that the function of the law is to enforce moral principles, and instead may perfectly well be explained as a piece of paternalism, designed to protect individuals against themselves.[282]

Even if one disagrees with Devlin's principal thesis, one has to recognize that morality is not completely irrelevant to the criminal law. It seems obvious that some relationship between law and morality exists, in that much of what is criminal conduct will also incur the moral condemnation of the community. And conversely, the law draws its strength from the common morality. There can, however, be no simplistic correlation;[283] the fact that something is immoral does not necessarily mean that it should consequently be unlawful, and conversely, whether or not something is lawful is not in itself determinative of the morality of that conduct.

In the light of the foregoing analysis, we are now in a position to consider the issue of active voluntary euthanasia and the proper role of the criminal law in this area. Is active voluntary euthanasia immoral? The position taken in this work is that it is not, and that would certainly be the view of most proponents of active voluntary euthanasia.[284] However, in our pluralistic society, there is no community consensus regarding the morality of active voluntary euthanasia. But, the significant point is that once one accepts that there is no one-for-one correspondence between law and morality, it becomes unnecessary to pronounce decisively on the morality of active voluntary euthanasia. Thus, even if active voluntary euthanasia *is* immoral, that does not in itself constitute sufficient justification for maintaining the existing legal prohibition of the practice.[285] By the same token, it is accepted that evidence of the morality of active voluntary euthanasia will not of itself be

---

[281] e.g. the *Wolfenden Report*, above n. 279; Hart, *Law, Liberty and Morality*, above n. 279.

[282] Hart, *Law, Liberty and Morality*, above n. 279, at 30–4.

[283] Note also Lord Hailsham, 'The Law, Politics and Morality' (1988) *Denning LJ* 59, 60–1.

[284] As Kohl notes (*Beneficent Euthanasia*, above n. 8; xvi), it is possible to take the view that active voluntary euthanasia is morally wrong but should nevertheless be legalized. He points out, however, that this is not widely argued for in the literature.

[285] Kohl, *Beneficent Euthanasia*, above n. 8; Flew, A., 'The Principle of Euthanasia' in Downing and Smoker, *Voluntary Euthanasia: Experts Debate the Right to Die*, above n. 68, at 40, 40–1.

a decisive argument for its legalization. Indeed, as we have seen, there are many opponents who argue that although active voluntary euthanasia may be moral in individual cases, it ought nonetheless to be prohibited. However, the practical arguments against legalization have already been countered, and in the absence of convincing evidence of likely harm to others resulting from a patient's choice to opt for an earlier death, the question of active euthanasia is essentially a matter of private choice which should be left to the individual patient in the exercise of his or her self-determination. As one commentator has suggested, the proper place for debating the ethics or morality of assistance in dying is in the individual conscience of the person concerned.[286] This applies not only to persons seeking assistance but also to the doctors to whom the request is made who must decide for themselves their attitude to providing such assistance.

Furthermore, in assessing the appropriate relationship between law and morality, it should not be overlooked that it is possible that the enforcement of morality may itself lead to harm, far in excess of any possible harm that the prohibited practices themselves may entail. In the context of the law's continuing prohibition of active voluntary euthanasia this is a very real possibility. The prohibition is aimed at protecting the sanctity of life, but denying a patient the choice of an earlier death may violate the patient's dignity and self-determination and cause unnecessary suffering. Thus, in any analysis of the role of the law and the relationship between law and morality, one cannot ignore the costs involved in invoking the criminal law.

D. Relationship Between Law and Public Opinion

Related to the foregoing discussion about law and morality is the issue of public opinion and the extent to which the law should reflect the wishes of the community. This is a relevant issue in the euthanasia debate, in view of growing public support for the legalization of active voluntary euthanasia.

The appropriate relationship between the law and public opinion has long been a matter for dispute. There is, for example, debate as to whether the law ought to follow behind public opinion, so that it can count on the support of the community as a whole, or whether its role is to lead or fortify public opinion.[287] From the outset it should be acknowledged that the mere fact that there is public support for something cannot be taken as evidence that it ought to be legalized. The relevance of public opinion must be more carefully justified than crude reliance on support in numbers.

While the criminal law obviously fulfils a number of roles, it has been argued in this work that its primary role is to protect society and its mem-

---

[286] Boyd, K., 'Euthanasia Back to the Future' in Keown, *Euthanasia Examined*, above n. 15, at 72, 78.
[287] *Wolfenden Report*, above n. 279, at para. 16.

bers from harm. This protective function is complemented by the criminal law's educative role, seeking to encourage law-abiding behaviour, and punishing those who threaten or harm public interests. Because of the criminal law's role in primarily protecting, and also educating the community, public support for the legalization of active voluntary euthanasia can never, of itself, be sufficient justification for reform of the law. Public opinion may quite possibly be misguided or misinformed, or may have failed to take into account the full implications of legalization. Before the case for reform is made out, it must be shown that the consequences of legalization of active voluntary euthanasia have been addressed, and that no harm is likely to result to society or its members if the practice is legalized. Within these confines, public opinion should have a role in shaping the law, indicating, as it does, prevailing morality and the needs of the community. After all, ultimately, the law must serve the community and it must, therefore, be responsive to real social needs. It is widely recognized that if a law is markedly out of tune with public opinion, it will quickly fall into disrepute. Thus, while evidence of community support for legalization of active voluntary euthanasia is not of itself decisive, it is undoubtedly a relevant factor in determining the appropriateness of legalization, and in the chapter which follows, evidence will be provided of growing public support for the legalization of active voluntary euthanasia.[288]

In the preceding analysis an attempt has been made to demonstrate that active voluntary euthanasia differs significantly from other proscribed forms of killing and that in light of these differences, the present criminalization of active voluntary euthanasia is beyond the proper scope of the criminal law. On libertarian principles, it has been argued that the State may only impose criminal sanctions in respect of conduct which is likely to cause serious harm to others. As there is no evidence that legalization of active voluntary euthanasia would be likely to cause such harm, retention of the existing prohibition cannot be justified.

The present law which prohibits active voluntary euthanasia is a violation of the individual's liberty and self-determination. The choice whether to live or die is essentially a private choice, and individuals should be permitted to live their lives according to their own life choices, free of coercion or paternalistic interference. The liberty of the individual is paramount and must be preserved to the extent that it does not constitute a danger to society. The optimum way of maximizing individual freedom with regard to active voluntary euthanasia, but at same time, ensuring protection of society and its members, is through the creation of a carefully defined exception to the general prohibition against killing. Recognition of such an exception is not inconsistent with the fundamental belief that human life has value and

---

[288] See pp. 257–68 below.

must be protected wherever possible. Indeed the criminal law's prohibition of murder will continue to protect the right to life of all persons from unrequested killing. Further, removal of the present prohibition would tend to promote justice and equity, in that the opportunity to seek active assistance in dying would become openly available to all and the practice of active voluntary euthanasia would be subject to rigorous safeguards to protect against abuse. There will always be those who are implacably opposed to a change in the law but because we are dealing here with *voluntary* euthanasia the right of opponents to reject euthanasia for themselves is not impinged on by creating the opportunity for others who seek it to exercise that choice.

CONCLUSION

As noted at the outset of this chapter, differences of opinion will always exist as to whether or not active voluntary euthanasia ought to be legalized. In the final analysis, the objections raised by the opponents are not sufficiently compelling to undermine the strong *prima facie* case which has been established for legalization of active voluntary euthanasia. The practical concerns which have been raised about the effects of legalization do not warrant a blanket prohibition and can be met by the implementation of appropriate regulations and safeguards. Further, having regard to the proper scope of the criminal law, it has been shown that there are no pressing social interests which demand retention of the criminal law prohibition. In our pluriform society, the most appropriate course to maximize individual freedom and self-determination is to remove the present legal prohibition so that all individuals will be free to live according to their own beliefs.

Thus, it is submitted, active voluntary euthanasia is acceptable in principle, and re-evaluation of the criminal law prohibition is required. However, the practical objections which have been raised must be given serious consideration in any process of reform. The challenge which lies ahead is to formulate a legislative proposal which reduces the potential risks to an acceptable level, without interfering too severely with individual autonomy and self-determination.

5

The Changing Climate for Reform

INTRODUCTION

The object of this chapter is to examine the changing climate for reform with regard to active voluntary euthanasia. This involves consideration of a number of related issues: (i) public opinion which appears to be increasingly in support of the legalization of active voluntary euthanasia performed by doctors for terminally ill or incurable patients; (ii) the development of voluntary euthanasia organizations campaigning for the legalization of active voluntary euthanasia; and (iii) developments within the medical profession indicating growing support for the concept of active voluntary euthanasia. Although these areas of change are very much interrelated, for the purposes of exposition, it will be necessary to deal with them separately. This chapter is accordingly divided into three parts: part I dealing with opinion polls, part II dealing with the voluntary euthanasia movement, and part III tracing changes within the medical profession.

I. PUBLIC OPINION

Although there have, over time, been some fluctuations in public opinion on the issue of active voluntary euthanasia, opinion polls undertaken in the various common law jurisdictions under consideration indicate growing public support in favour of its legalization.

A. United Kingdom

In the United Kingdom, opinion polls on the subject of active voluntary euthanasia date back to the 1930s. During that decade, the issue of legalization of active voluntary euthanasia had been brought to public attention through the activities of the newly established Voluntary Euthanasia Society in London and the concerted attempts at legislative reform made in 1936.[1] According to a Gallup Poll conducted in 1938, 62 per cent of those polled believed that 'those suffering from an incurable disease should be allowed the option, under proper medical safeguards, of voluntary death',

---

[1] See p. 269 below.

compared to 22 per cent who disagreed. By 1950, however, when Gallup conducted the same poll, the support for active voluntary euthanasia had dropped to 55 per cent, with 24 per cent of those polled disagreeing with the proposition that incurable patients should have the option of a voluntary death. Although attempts to explain this decline in support for active voluntary euthanasia are merely speculative, it is quite possibly attributable to the negative connotations of the concept of euthanasia following the inhuman practices in Nazi Germany.

Since 1950, public acceptance of active voluntary euthanasia has gradually been increasing in the United Kingdom, although survey results reveal some fluctuations in public attitudes. In a 1976 National Opinion Poll, responses were sought to the following question: 'Some people say that the law should allow adults to receive medical help to an immediate peaceful death if they suffer from an incurable physical illness that is intolerable to them, provided they have previously requested such help in writing. Please tell me whether you agree or disagree with this'. Of those polled, 69 per cent indicated their agreement with this statement, 17 per cent disagreed and 14 per cent were undecided. Another survey was conducted 3 years later, also by National Opinion Polls, but asking a quite different question. Respondents were asked: 'Do you agree that, if a patient is suffering from a distressing and incurable illness, a doctor should be allowed to supply that patient with the means to end his own life, if the patient wishes to?' 62 per cent of those surveyed agreed, 22 per cent disagreed and 16 per cent were undecided. Because of the difference in survey question used in the 1976 and the 1979 polls, little weight can be attached to any discrepancies between these results. Of greater statistical relevance are the 1985, the 1989 and the 1993 surveys conducted by National Opinion Polls, where the same question was used to that in the 1976 National Opinion Poll.[2] The results of these polls, when analysed in connection with the 1976 poll, provide some indication of changes in public attitudes on the subject of active voluntary euthanasia in the United Kingdom over this period (see Table A). In the period 1976–1993, the proportion of the population in agreement with the statement had risen from 69 per cent to 79 per cent, a 10 per cent increase for that period, with only 10 per cent against in the most recent 1993 poll. There was also some reduction in the category of 'undecided' from 14 per cent in 1976 down to 11 per cent in 1993, although this has been subject to fluctuation, falling to 8 per cent in 1985.

The results of the 1976, 1985, 1989, and 1993 National Opinion Polls do not show any statistically significant difference in terms of sex or economic class, but there is a definite age divergence, with younger respondents tending to be more in favour of active voluntary euthanasia than the older

---

[2] Note, however, in the 1993 poll, the word 'immediate' preceding 'peaceful death' was omitted.

TABLE A: United Kingdom—National Opinion
Poll results

	For	*Against*	*Undecided*
1976	69%	17%	14%
1985	72%	21%	8%
1989	75%	16%	9%
1993	79%	10%	11%

age groups. Religious affiliation is also clearly a significant factor. Although members of all the main religious denominations, (including Roman Catholics), show a majority in favour of active voluntary euthanasia, Roman Catholics are less likely to support active voluntary euthanasia than are members of the Church of England or atheists.[3]

On the basis of the National Opinion Polls conducted regularly since 1976, which provide the most reliable indication of public opinion in the United Kingdom on this issue, there is clearly evidence of growing public support for active voluntary euthanasia.

B. USA

Numerous polls have been conducted in the USA by a number of research organizations over the past 40 or so years to assess public attitudes on the subject of active voluntary euthanasia.[4] The principal research organizations to conduct opinion polls on this subject in the USA have been Gallup (Gallup National Opinion Research Center), Roper, and Harris, each using their own survey question.[5] Results of the various polls indicate a substantial growth in acceptance of active voluntary euthanasia by the American public since the late 1940s (see Table B).

[3] According to the most recent poll results, the highest figure of support for active voluntary euthanasia for a religious denomination was the Church of Scotland (85%), with the Church of England at 80% and 73% of Roman Catholics in favour. Atheists recorded 93% agreement.

[4] For discussion of opinion poll results in the USA with regard to active voluntary euthanasia, see Russell, R., *Freedom to Die: The Legal Aspects of Euthanasia*, Revised edn. (New York, 1977) Chs. 4–7 (and supplement to first edition, 387–9); Ostheimer, J., 'The Polls: Changing Attitudes Towards Euthanasia' (1980) 44 *Public Opinion Q* 123.

[5] Gallup Poll question: 'When a person has a disease that cannot be cured, do you think that doctors should be allowed by law to end the patient's life by some painless means if the patient and his family request it?'

Roper Poll question: 'When a person has a painful and distressing terminal disease, do you think doctors should or should not be allowed by law to end the patient's life if there is no hope of recovery and the patient requests it?'

Harris Poll question: 'Do you think that the patient who is terminally ill, with no cure in sight, ought to have the right to tell his doctor to put him out of his misery, or do you think this is wrong?'

TABLE B: USA—Gallup, Harris, and Roper
Poll results

Gallup Poll/National Opinion Research Centre		
For	*Against*	*Undecided*
1947 37%	54%	9%
1950 36%	54%	10%
1973 53%	40%	7%
1982 61%	34%	5%
1983 63%	32%	3%
1990 65%	31%	4%
1996 75%	22%	3%

Harris Poll		
For	*Against*	*Undecided*
1973 37%	53%	10%
1977 49%	38%	13%
1981 56%	41%	3%
1985 61%	36%	3%

Roper Poll		
For	*Against*	*Undecided*
1986 62%	27%	10%
1988 58%	27%	14%
1990 64%	24%	13%

Harris Polls, which have been undertaken at regular intervals in the period 1973–85, reveal a marked increase in support for active voluntary euthanasia in that period from 37 per cent in favour in 1973 (53 per cent against and 10 per cent undecided) to 61 per cent in favour in 1985 (36 per cent against and 3 per cent undecided). Roper Polls, which have been conducted in the USA in the period 1986–90, also indicate an overall increase in the level of public support for active voluntary euthanasia from 62 per cent in 1986 to 64 per cent in 1990.[6] However, most significant of all are the Gallup Polls gauging attitudes with respect to medically-administered active voluntary euthanasia which cover the period 1947–96.

[6] In a separate development, a nationwide public opinion survey was undertaken in 1991 sponsored by the Harvard School of Public Health and the *Boston Globe* which revealed that almost two-thirds (64%) of Americans favour active voluntary euthanasia performed at the request of a terminally ill patient. For a discussion of these findings, see Blendon, R. et al., 'Should Physicians Aid Their Patients in Dying?: The Public Perspective' (1992) 267 JAMA 2658.

According to the Gallup Poll results, public approval in the USA had grown from 37 per cent in 1947 (54 per cent disagreeing and 9 per cent undecided) to 75 per cent in 1996 (with 22 per cent disagreeing and only 3 per cent undecided).

There are obvious difficulties in analysing the results of polls which have been derived from a number of separate surveys, using different survey questions. It is, nevertheless, possible to make some general observations regarding trends in survey results obtained.[7] According to the research by the Gallup National Opinion Research Center, acceptance of active voluntary euthanasia has grown among all major population subgroups, but change has been greatest among Catholics and the younger age groups. There appear to be no significant differences in responses based upon sex, political affiliation, or geographical area of the respondents. The results of some polls indicate that age of the respondents is a factor, with a higher approval rating amongst younger age groups. Religious affiliation is of some significance, in that Catholics are less likely to support active voluntary euthanasia than Protestants, or non-religious persons. Respondents with higher education, professional status, and income tend to be more accepting of the concept of active voluntary euthanasia. The race of the respondents appears to also be a relevant factor, with substantially fewer black Americans supporting active voluntary euthanasia.[8]

Whilst there are some discrepancies in the results as between the various research organizations, possibly attributable to the different questions those organizations have used, overall, the polls in the USA reveal a steady growth in community acceptance of active voluntary euthanasia over recent decades. According to the most recent Gallup Poll, three-quarters of the population now support medical assistance in dying in certain circumstances.

C. Canada

Canadian polls over the past two decades also indicate a significant increase in support for active voluntary euthanasia. Since 1968, Gallup Canada have regularly conducted polls using the same poll question in which respondents were asked: 'When a person has an incurable disease that causes great suffering, do you, or do you not think that competent doctors should be allowed by law, to end the patient's life through mercy killing, if the patient

---

[7] For general commentary and analysis, see Jorgenson, D. and Neubecker, R., 'Euthanasia: A National Survey of Attitudes Towards Voluntary Termination of Life' (1980–81) 11 *Omega* 281; Marzen, T., 'Euthanasia: The Handwriting on the Wall' (1988) 3 *Euthanasia Rev.* 44, 46; Ostheimer, 'The Polls: Changing Attitudes Towards Euthanasia', above n. 4.

[8] See, for example, the results of the 1986 Roper Poll, discussed by Marzen, 'Euthanasia: The Handwriting on the Wall', above n. 7, at 46 which indicated that only 46% of black Americans supported active voluntary euthanasia, with 39% against and 15% undecided.

TABLE C: Canada—Gallup Poll results

	For	Against	Undecided
1968	45%	43%	12%
1974	55%	35%	10%
1979	68%	23%	9%
1984	66%	24%	10%
1989	77%	17%	6%
1990	78%	14%	8%
1991	75%	17%	9%
1992	77%	17%	6%
1995	75%	17%	8%

has made a formal request in writing?' Although there have been some fluctuations, these polls of Canadian public opinion reveal growing public support for active voluntary euthanasia (see Table C). In the most recent poll, conducted in 1995, 75 per cent of Canadians surveyed supported the view that a doctor should be allowed by law to end the life of an incurable suffering patient at the patient's request, with only 17 per cent opposed and 8 per cent undecided.

Analysis of the Canadian Gallup Poll results over recent years suggests that a number of factors appear to be relevant in determining people's attitudes to active voluntary euthanasia. Age of the respondents is a relevant factor, with the proportion of respondents in favour of active assistance to die being significantly lower among those over 50 years than among younger people. Other factors which appear to be of some relevance include the sex of the respondents, with males marginally more in favour of allowing a doctor to end the life of a patient than are females, as well as education and income, with the better educated and higher earning respondents more likely to be in favour of allowing a doctor to end the life of a patient at the patient's request. There also appear to be some regional variations, with the highest proportion giving an affirmative answer in Quebec and the lowest in the prairie states.

The Gallup Polls regularly undertaken since 1968, using the same survey question, represent a fairly accurate guide as to changing community attitudes in Canada to the issue of active voluntary euthanasia.[9] These polls reveal a marked shift in public opinion since the 1968 poll, from a 45 per cent rate of approval to 75 per cent: this represents a 30 per cent increase in public acceptance during the 27-year period 1968–95.

---

[9] The information from Gallup Polls has been confirmed by the results from other polls taken in Canada: e.g. the 1993 Angus Reid Poll which found that 76% of Canadians support the 'right to die' for patients who wished to end their lives.

TABLE D: Australia—Morgan Gallup Poll results

	For	*Against*	*Undecided*
1962	47%	39%	14%
1978	67%	22%	11%
1983	67%	21%	12%
1986	66%	21%	13%
1987	75%	18%	7%
1989	71%	20%	9%
1990	77%	17%	6%
1991	74%	20%	7%
1992	76%	18%	6%
1993	78%	15%	7%
1994	78%	13%	9%
1995	78%	14%	8%

D. Australia

Since the early 1960s, opinion polls have been conducted regularly in Australia by the Morgan Research Centre to gauge the attitude of Australians to active voluntary euthanasia.[10] Whilst there has been some vacillation in public attitudes over time, the results of the Morgan Gallup Polls over the past two decades reveals an increase in public support in Australia for allowing a doctor to give a patient a lethal dose at the patient's request[11] (see Table D).

The most recent Morgan Gallup Poll, taken in 1995, indicates that 78 per cent of those surveyed were in favour of active voluntary euthanasia, with only 14 per cent against and 8 per cent undecided. This represents a significant increase from the 1962 Gallup Poll results according to which 47 per cent of those surveyed were in favour of active voluntary euthanasia, 39 per cent against and 14 per cent undecided: a 31 per cent increase in public acceptance of active voluntary euthanasia over a 33-year period. Not only has there been a distinct increase in levels of support, with a corresponding decline in those opposed to active voluntary euthanasia, but the proportion of respondents who are undecided has decreased (from 14 per cent in 1962

[10] In the polls conducted since 1983, those surveyed were asked: 'If a hopelessly ill patient, in great pain with absolutely no chance of recovering, asks for a lethal dose, so as not to wake again, should a doctor be allowed to give a lethal dose, or not?' The original question was in slightly different terms: 'If a person who is terminally ill, or injured with no chance of recovery, asks for a lethal dose so as not to wake again, or asks for some other help to die, should that person be helped to die or not?'

[11] Similar results have been obtained in New Zealand. According to a 1994 Morgan Poll published by TIME Magazine, 68% of those polled supported active voluntary euthanasia, 20% against and 12% undecided. This represented a slight drop in support compared with the results for the 1992 poll.

to 8 per cent in 1995), suggesting that more people have made up their minds on the issue.

The results do not reveal any consistent trends with regard to federal voting intention or with regard to the sex of those polled, though in the more recent polls, there appears to be evidence of greater support for active voluntary euthanasia amongst men than women. Analysis of the results on the basis of the age of the respondents indicates that the numbers in favour of active voluntary euthanasia were greater in the younger age groups, and older people were least likely to favour a doctor being allowed to administer a lethal dose. The religious affiliation of respondents is also a relevant factor in determining their attitudes to active voluntary euthanasia, although perhaps not as significant as one might expect. There is evidence which suggests that regular church-goers are much less likely to support active voluntary euthanasia than non-regular churchgoers, agnostics, or atheists. Of those who are religiously affiliated, Roman Catholics are less likely to support active voluntary euthanasia than are Anglicans or members of the Presbyterian or Uniting Church. Nevertheless, despite the Catholic Church's opposition to euthanasia, recent polls indicate that a significant majority of Catholic respondents are in favour of a doctor being allowed to give a patient a lethal dose.

E. Evaluation of Opinion Poll Results

It is evident from the foregoing review of opinion polls conducted in the United Kingdom, the USA, Canada, and Australia that there has been growing public support for active voluntary euthanasia in all jurisdictions under consideration. In the United Kingdom, National Opinion Polls conducted since 1976 show a steady increase in public support, with a shift from 69 per cent in favour in 1976 to 79 per cent in favour in 1993, a 10 per cent increase for the 17-year period 1976–93. In the USA reliable poll results dating back to 1947 indicate a marked shift from 37 per cent in favour in 1947 to 75 per cent in favour in 1996; an increase of 38 per cent. In Canada, polls conducted by Canadian Gallup indicate a shift in public opinion since 1968 from a 45 per cent rate of approval to 75 per cent in favour in 1995, representing a 30 per cent increase in public acceptance during the 27-year period 1968–95. Finally, in Australia, Gallup Polls indicate there has been a 31 per cent increase in public support for active voluntary euthanasia since 1962, from 47 per cent in favour in 1962 to 78 per cent in favour in 1995.

Caution must be exercised in comparing poll results from different countries, where the polls have been conducted by different organizations, using different survey questions. Notwithstanding these limitations, it is possible to make some general observations, regarding trends in public opinion. There is, in fact, a remarkable degree of consistency in the public opinion results on the issue of active voluntary euthanasia obtained in the United Kingdom, the USA, Canada, and Australia. According to the most recent results, 79 per cent were in favour in the United Kingdom, 75 per cent in favour in the USA, 75 per cent in favour in Canada and 78 per cent in favour in Australia. The unavoidable conclusion is that these polls reflect a growing demand for law reform to allow active voluntary euthanasia, with an overwhelming majority of respondents in favour of legalization. Indeed, to have public support in excess of 75 per cent, as the poll results from a number of these jurisdictions suggest, reflects quite an extraordinary degree of agreement on the issue. Looking at the overall position over the last couple of years where there have only been minor fluctuations, it is likely that the level of public support has now stabilized at close to 80 per cent.

Apart from the overall trend towards greater acceptance of active voluntary euthanasia evident in all jurisdictions, there are a number of more specific similarities which should be noted. There is some evidence to suggest that the age of the respondent is a relevant factor in determining attitudes to active voluntary euthanasia. Younger persons are more likely to support active voluntary euthanasia, and support decreases as the age of the respondent increases.[12] Another factor which seems to be relevant in influencing attitudes to voluntary euthanasia is the religious affiliation, if any, of the respondent. Whilst there has been a noticeable increase in support for active voluntary euthanasia from Catholics evidenced in the poll results, there still appears to be some correlation between religious affiliation (particularly Catholic) and anti-euthanasia attitudes; generally speaking, persons who are religious are less likely to support active voluntary euthanasia than persons who are not; and more particularly, Catholics are less likely to support active voluntary euthanasia than members of other religious denominations or persons who are not religiously affiliated. The sex of the respondent is yet another factor which appears to be of some, albeit marginal, significance in influencing attitudes to active voluntary euthanasia, with males slightly more inclined than females to be in favour of allowing a doctor to assist a patient to die.

In taking an overview of all jurisdictions, it is also interesting to observe the decrease over time in the percentage of persons who were unable to answer the survey question although here, too, there have been some fluctuations over time; in the United Kingdom it has declined since 1976 from 14 per cent to 11 per cent in 1993; in the USA the various

[12] See Waller, S., 'Trends in Public Acceptance of Euthanasia Worldwide' (1986) 1 *Euthanasia Rev.* 33, 44–6 also for possible reasons behind these variations.

polls also indicate an overall decline (for example, on the basis of the Gallup Poll results there has been a decline from 9 per cent in 1947 to 3 per cent in 1996);[13] in Canada it has declined since 1968 from 12 per cent to 8 per cent in 1995, and in Australia, it has fallen since 1962 from 14 per cent to 8 per cent in 1995. This reduction in the number of people who are undecided on the issue of active voluntary euthanasia can probably be attributed to increased public debate on the subject over the past decade or so, with the result that more people have considered the matter and formed an opinion as to whether active voluntary euthanasia should be made lawful.

The literature is sparse on reasons behind this shift in public opinion with regard to the legalization of active voluntary euthanasia. Whilst any explanation can at best be speculative, a number of inferences can be drawn. In recent decades, the issue of active voluntary euthanasia has been increasingly brought to the attention of the public. The media has played a significant role in promoting the debate about active voluntary euthanasia as have the voluntary euthanasia societies which have been established in all jurisdictions.[14] As a result of growing community debate on the subject, the public is better informed about the issue and has increasingly swung its support behind the legalization of active voluntary euthanasia. Other factors contributing to the increasing preparedness of the public to sanction active voluntary euthanasia are the changing attitudes to death and the diminishing significance of religious and cultural strictures against the taking of life. Accompanying this changed outlook to death and dying, there has been increased attention to patients' rights and the principles of patient autonomy and self-determination. There is evidence of growing concern amongst members of the public that they may fall victim to developments in medical technology. This has resulted in a desire for individuals to re-establish control over the manner of their dying. The public is also likely to be sensitive to changing attitudes within the medical profession on the subject of active voluntary euthanasia, with media reports of doctors indicating their support for the practice and on occasion being involved in its administration.

In sum, the clear message to law reformers is that the public is overwhelmingly in favour of active voluntary euthanasia and would support the introduction of legislation to legalize this practice in certain circumstances. As was noted in an earlier chapter, inevitably, there are those who question reliance on public opinion polls, either on the grounds that the poll questions are so vague and ambiguous that they produce unreliable results, or

---

[13] This is not supported by evidence from the Roper Polls which in fact indicate an increasing proportion of undecided respondents, but these results are not necessarily representative since they were taken over a short period (1986–90).

[14] These developments are discussed further at pp. 268–90 below.

on the ground that public opinion is an inherently unsafe and inappropriate basis for developing law and social policy.[15]

It must be conceded that some of the survey questions used could have been more clearly and appropriately expressed and that this in turn may have some bearing on the responses that those questions would elicit.[16] Indeed, due to the research initiated by the US organization, the Euthanasia Research and Guidance Organization (ERGO!), evidence now exists to demonstrate that the language used does make a difference in determining the acceptability of a proposal permitting euthanasia.[17] In part, the problem stems from the need for consistency in the survey question if one is attempting to follow trends in public opinion over an extended period of time. Thus, once a survey question has been in use for a time, it gains a certain currency, and is unlikely to be significantly changed, even though a contemporary compilation of the issues would perhaps be differently expressed. Having conceded some difficulties with some of the survey questions currently in use, these difficulties must not be overstated. They certainly cannot be legitimately invoked to undermine or discredit the overall impact of the opinion polls which provide overwhelming evidence of growing public support for active voluntary euthanasia. In this regard, it is very interesting to note the results of a poll commissioned by the anti-euthanasia organization, The World Federation of Doctors Who Respect Human Life (British Section) and the Human Rights Society in 1987 to make their own assessment of public attitudes to euthanasia. Significantly, notwithstanding questions which arguably were slanted away from choice, a majority of the sample (comprised of over 1,800 adults throughout Great Britain) were in favour of active euthanasia in some circumstances.[18]

More fundamental is the objection that, notwithstanding widespread public support for active voluntary euthanasia, it is, in any event, not appropriate to base the law on the opinion of the majority.[19] In response it

[15] Grisez, G. and Boyle, J. M., *Life and Death with Liberty and Justice* (Notre Dame, Indiana, 1979) 14; Somerville, M., 'The Song of Death: The Lyrics of Euthanasia' (1993) 9 *J Contemp. Health Law & Pol'y* 1, 21. For further discussion, see pp. 210–11 above.

[16] Dissatisfaction has, for example, been expressed with the nature of some of the questions used in the US polls: see Ostheimer, 'The Polls: Changing Attitudes Towards Euthanasia', above n. 4, at 124, where he asserts that the wording used in the Gallup Poll question, particularly, the reference to ending the patient's life 'by some painless means' is ambiguous. He also suggests that the reference in the Harris Poll question, to 'put out of one's misery' is unsatisfactory because of its tendency to precondition a negative response.

[17] ERGO!, 'What's in a Word?: The Results of a Roper Poll of Americans on How They View the Importance of Language in The Debate Over The Right to Choose to Die' (1993).

[18] 23% thought that euthanasia should be made legal in all cases when the patient requests it; 49% believed that euthanasia should be made legal only when a patient who requests it is suffering from a severe illness and is in a lot of pain; 19% believed that the law should not be changed so as to allow euthanasia; 9% were undecided. MORI 1987.

[19] British Medical Association, Working Party Report, *Euthanasia: Report of a Working Party to Review the British Medical Associations Guidance on Euthanasia* (London, 1988) 42. For analysis of this argument, see pp. 254–6 above.

can be argued that although strength of numbers is not, of itself, a valid basis for a change in the law, where, as is the case with regard to active voluntary euthanasia, there are weighty substantive arguments in favour of reform,[20] evidence of public demand for such change can only operate to strengthen that case. Moreover, it must be stressed that what is sought by proponents for active voluntary euthanasia is permissive legislation only: the law can, as it does in respect of other controversial issues, show what is permissible, ultimately leaving it to individuals to decide for themselves whether this is an option they wish to pursue.

It must be emphasized that these changes in community attitudes have come about over a number of decades, so the process of change has been gradual. There is, however, some evidence to suggest that the pace of change has accelerated in the past decade,[21] reflecting the increased level of public interest in the subject and the growing momentum of the voluntary euthanasia movement during this period. On the basis of the more recent results, levels of community support appear to have stabilized with more than three-quarters of the community in these various jurisdictions in favour of legalization.

II. THE VOLUNTARY EUTHANASIA MOVEMENT

The upsurge in public support for active voluntary euthanasia in recent decades has also been manifest in growing community action. The voluntary euthanasia societies which have been established in all of the common law jurisdictions under consideration have been working towards legalization and they have greatly contributed to the growing momentum of the voluntary euthanasia movement. In response to these developments, there has also been organized opposition to the legalization of active voluntary euthanasia from various 'right to life' groups as well as other anti-euthanasia organisations specifically established to counter the growing campaign for legalization.

A. Organizational Support for the Legalization of Active Voluntary Euthanasia

United Kingdom

There are two voluntary euthanasia societies in the United Kingdom; the Voluntary Euthanasia Society representing England and Wales, based in

---

[20] See the discussion at pp. 188–212 above.

[21] See, for example, the Morgan Gallup Poll results for Australia in the period 1986–95 during which there was a 12% increase in public support. Note also a similar development in Canada for the period 1984–95 during which there was an 9% increase.

London, and the Voluntary Euthanasia Society of Scotland based in Edinburgh.[22] The history of the London-based society is of special interest because of its early origins and its active involvement since the mid-1930s in efforts to secure legislative reform. Also of interest is the controversy surrounding the society in the early 1980s in connection with the publication of a suicide manual and the imprisonment of two members for having assisted the suicide of a number of persons.

Voluntary Euthanasia Society (England and Wales)

The origins of the Voluntary Euthanasia Society, established in 1935, and the early attempts at legislative reform in 1936 are well documented.[23] Most commentators agree that the contemporary movement for active voluntary euthanasia in the United Kingdom began with a Presidential address by Dr C. Millard in 1931 to the Society of Medical Officers of Health, entitled 'A Plea for the Legalization of Voluntary Euthanasia'. Millard's address was subsequently published,[24] together with a proposed draft bill for the legalization of active voluntary euthanasia,[25] and it received widespread publicity. In the years which followed, Millard communicated with members of the medical and other professions who were interested in his proposal, and in 1935, the Voluntary Euthanasia Legalization Society was officially formed under the Presidency of Lord Moynihan, with the specific purpose of promoting the draft bill which Millard had proposed.[26] Under the guidance of Millard, in his capacity as Honorary Secretary, and Lord Moynihan as President—both well respected doctors—the society enjoyed the support of many of Britain's most distinguished doctors, public figures, and clergymen. Although the Voluntary Euthanasia (Legalization) Bill introduced by Lord Ponsonby in the House of Lords in November 1936 was ultimately unsuccessful, it stimulated considerable public interest and discussion of the issue, and brought many new members and supporters to the society. In the ensuing years, the society, with Millard as its chief spokesman, continued to campaign for legalization of active voluntary euthanasia, though it was in

[22] For a number of years there was a third organization in the United Kingdom, called New Exit. It was established in 1983 as a splinter group of the Voluntary Euthanasia Society (Britain) but ceased to exist in 1988.

[23] For literature tracing the history of the society, see, for example, Trowell, H., *The Unfinished Debate on Euthanasia* (London, 1973) 14–15; Williams, G., *The Sanctity of Life and the Criminal Law* (London, 1956) 293–302.

[24] Millard's address was published in *Public Health* Nov. (1931) and was released as a pamphlet shortly afterwards.

[25] The Voluntary Euthanasia (Legalisation) Bill. For discussion of this bill see p. 334 below.

[26] The stated aim of the society was 'to create a public opinion favourable to the view that an adult person suffering from a fatal illness, for which no cure is known, should be entitled by law to the mercy of a painless death if and when that is his expressed wish: and to promote this legislation'.

fact some decades before voluntary legislation was again introduced into Parliament.[27]

With the outbreak of the Second World War and the negative connotations given to the word 'euthanasia' as a result of the Nazi atrocities, there was a definite reduction in activities and publication pertaining to euthanasia in the early 1940s and a perceived shift in public sentiment away from active voluntary euthanasia. The Voluntary Euthanasia Society nevertheless remained active during this time, continuing in its efforts to secure reform. The society, which had begun as the Voluntary Euthanasia Legalization Society, had at one time discarded the words 'voluntary' and 'legalization' from its name, but in 1969 reinstated the word 'voluntary', so that it became The Voluntary Euthanasia Society.

In 1979, following its annual meeting, the society changed its name to 'EXIT'. In the same year, a proposal had been mooted for the publication by the society of a practical guide to rational suicide—a 'do-it-yourself' manual as a stopgap expedient pending the legalization of active voluntary euthanasia. Although the majority of members supported this proposal, the executive of the newly named EXIT society was divided over the matter. After the election of a new executive and appropriate amendments to the society's constitution so as to bring such a publication within its purview, the society eventually proceeded with the publication of a booklet on methods of suicide in 1981, entitled *A Guide to Self-Deliverance*. Sales of the booklet were restricted to members of at least 3 months' standing who were over 25 years of age, and each copy was numbered so that its purchaser could be traced if necessary. However, the legality of the publication and distribution of this booklet were subsequently challenged by the Director of Public Prosecutions. Initially, criminal prosecution was threatened on the grounds of contravention of section 2 of the Suicide Act 1961 (England). The proceedings which did in fact result took the form of an application brought by the Attorney-General to the High Court for a declaration of illegality under section 2 of the Suicide Act 1961 (England). In a hearing which came before the court in April 1983, Woolf J refused to grant the Attorney-General's application, holding that the publication of such material was not of itself unlawful.[28] However, he held that whether or not the distribution of these booklets was legal would depend on whether there was, at the time, an intention to assist those who are contemplating suicide and further, that the person contemplating suicide was in fact assisted or

---

[27] In 1950, the activities of the society had resulted in a debate in the House of Lords on a motion in favour of the principle underlying voluntary euthanasia; however, the motion was withdrawn without a vote due to strong opposition. It was not until 1962 that a new bill was drafted and publicly proposed, which was introduced into Parliament some years later where it was defeated after being put to the vote (Voluntary Euthanasia Bill 1969).

[28] *Attorney-General* v. *Able* [1983] 3 WLR 845. For more detailed analysis of this case, see pp. 58–9 above.

encouraged, by reading the booklet, to attempt to take his or her own life. Woolf J was of the view that the legality of publication and distribution could not be determined in advance based on hypothetical circumstances— in each case, the jury would have to decide whether the necessary facts were proved. In the light of this decision, the society decided against further publication and distribution of the booklet. However, the publicity surrounding the booklet, even prior to its actual release, and then in connection with the resulting litigation, proved to be a boon to the society, resulting in a substantial increase in its membership.[29]

At about the same time, the society attracted adverse publicity, when the then Secretary of the society, Nicholas Reed, and a long-time volunteer worker for the society, Mark Lyons, were tried for their involvement in assisting suicide and conspiracy to assist suicide. Reed was found guilty on four counts and was sentenced to $2\frac{1}{2}$ years imprisonment. On appeal, this was later reduced to 18 months. Lyons was also found guilty on a number of counts, but since he had been in custody awaiting trial for nearly a year, he was released on a 2-year suspended sentence. Although the society was quick to dissociate itself from the Reed-Lyons affair, affirming its intention to operate within the limits of the law, its public image was seriously damaged as a result of this case. The society's objectives had never endorsed the concept of active euthanasia or assisted suicide for depressed or disturbed people, so it was particularly damaging when evidence at the trial revealed that some of the individuals who had been helped or offered help to commit suicide were mentally ill, depressive, or alcoholics. Indeed, according to the former chairman of the executive committee, the society subsequently found it an uphill struggle for some years thereafter to regain its reputation as a respectable pressure group rather than as a 'suicide club', as *The Times* newspaper had dubbed it.[30]

In 1981, the society dropped the name EXIT and reverted back to its former name, 'The Voluntary Euthanasia Society' which it has since retained. The society's principal object is to promote legislation which would allow an adult person, suffering from a severe illness to which no relief is known, to receive an immediate painless death, if that is the patient's expressed wish.[31] Over the years, the society has been active in its efforts to secure reform of the law in this area, having been responsible for commissioning opinion polls, lobbying politicians, campaigning for reform, and preparing draft legislation for the legalization of active voluntary euthanasia.[32] The society publishes a newsletter three times a year and its repre-

[29] When the news broke that the booklet would be published, membership soared with 6,527 new members in 1980.
[30] *The Times*, 31 Oct. 1981.
[31] Booklet published by the Voluntary Euthanasia Society, *The Last Right* (London, 1988) 1.
[32] See pp. 334–6 below.

sentatives frequently accept invitations to speak to various groups and conduct media interviews to discuss the society's aims and activities. The society is also involved in the promotion and distribution of 'advance directives'. It has campaigned for the statutory recognition of such directives, and has been involved in the preparation of draft legislation.[33]

Membership of the society is steadily increasing and is open to all who sympathize with the society's objects. In the wake of the activities of the British Medical Association Working Party on Euthanasia in 1988 (discussed below[34]), the society established a medical group made up of doctor members of the society. This group has extended its membership to include nurses, and other health care workers.

Voluntary Euthanasia Society of Scotland

The Voluntary Euthanasia Society of Scotland (originally named 'Scottish EXIT' but then renamed the Voluntary Euthanasia Society of Scotland in 1993), was established in 1980 as a breakaway organization from the English organization EXIT as it was then known. Prior to that time, a Scottish regional branch of EXIT had been operating in Scotland—'Scottish Region EXIT'. However, disagreement had arisen between the executive of EXIT and the Scottish branch over plans by the Scottish branch to publish a booklet on self-deliverance. When the Acting Chairman of EXIT forbade publication of the proposed booklet, the Scottish members decided to declare independence from EXIT and to continue as a separate entity. Thus, the newly created Scottish EXIT, taking advantage of more lenient conditions that prevail under Scottish law in relation to assisted suicide,[35] became the first organization to publish a booklet on self-deliverance. The publication entitled *How to Die with Dignity*[36] was first released in September 1980, and since then has been available for strictly private distribution amongst members of the society. Following an international collaboration funded by the Voluntary Euthanasia Society of Scotland and the Hemlock Society in the USA, an International Drug Consensus Working Party was established to investigate the suitability of drugs and methods for self-deliverance. This has led to the production of a supplement to the original book called *Departing Drugs*,[37] published in 1993 which is claimed to be the first thoroughly researched and scientific compendium of drugs and methods for self-deliverance.

The principal aim of the Voluntary Euthanasia Society of Scotland is to secure reform of the law so as to permit active voluntary euthanasia, and to this end, the society is involved in a wide range of activities, including public

[33] Medical Treatment (Advance Directives) Bill.   [34] See pp. 297–302 below.
[35] For further consideration of the legal position in Scotland, see p. 56, n. 5 above.
[36] Mair, G., *How to Die with Dignity* (Glasgow, 1980).
[37] In Scotland the book has been released as the *Supplement to How to Die with Dignity*.

meetings, media interviews, press publicity and lobbying of politicians. The Voluntary Euthanasia Society of Scotland is also involved in a major initiative with the Institute of Law and Ethics in Medicine at Glasgow University to examine the feasibility of a law on doctor-assisted suicide for the United Kingdom and to put forward draft legislation.

USA

In the wake of developments in the United Kingdom, the Euthanasia Society of America was founded in 1938.[38] The founder and first President of the society was the Reverend Charles Francis Potter, a humanist and prolific writer of books on religion. As had been the case in the United Kingdom, the Euthanasia Society of America was involved in early but unsuccessful attempts to introduce legislation to legalize active euthanasia. A euthanasia bill was prepared by the society formulated broadly along the same lines as the 1936 English Bill and was submitted, with some differences in content, to the New York State and Nebraska assemblies in the late 1930s.[39] However, neither bill was enacted. Initially, the aims of the Euthanasia Society of America had extended to the legalization of non-voluntary euthanasia in certain circumstances. In the light of the results of a survey of doctors conducted by the society in 1941, which indicated substantial approval for voluntary as distinct from non-voluntary euthanasia, it was decided to confine the activities of the society strictly to voluntary euthanasia.

During the 1940s and early 1950s, concerted efforts were made by the society to introduce legislation in New York to permit active voluntary euthanasia, but these efforts were repeatedly thwarted for lack of a sponsor for the legislation. Parallel attempts in other US states also proved fruitless. In view of the previous failed attempts at legislative reform, the society decided that further attempts would be futile until a more favourable climate of opinion had been created. However, the society's efforts at legislative reform had at least succeeded in drawing attention to the society and its objectives and attracting some prominent supporters for its cause, including many doctors and clergy.

In the course of the 1960s, under the new Presidency of Donald McKinney, a Unitarian minister, there was some reassessment of the organization's goals with increasing emphasis on the right of the individual to consent to or refuse treatment. Although there were some who still believed in pressing for legislation for the legalization of active voluntary

---

[38] For historical coverage of the position in the USA see Russel, *Freedom to Die*, above Ch. 4 n. 81, at Chs. 4–7.

[39] The Nebraska Bill differed from both the New York Bill and the legislation which had been proposed in the United Kingdom on the grounds that it authorized a limited form of non-voluntary euthanasia of minors and incompetent adults. It was also broader in scope in that it provided that active euthanasia could be performed even where the illness was not terminal.

euthanasia, the majority of the then board of directors saw education of the public and the health care professions as the primary need, and the activities of the society were directed towards education rather than legislation. Pursuant to this shift in focus, the society established the Euthanasia Educational Fund in 1967 (subsequently named the Euthanasia Educational Council in 1972), a tax-exempt branch of the society, the function of which was to disseminate information and promote discussion on the issues involved in death and dying. In the mid 1970s, when the prospects of introducing legislation had improved, the politically active counterpart of the council, the Euthanasia Society of America, was reactivated as the 'Society for the Right to Die' to promote state 'right to die' legislation.[40] In 1978, the Euthanasia Educational Council changed its name to 'Concern for Dying'. For some years, the Society for the Right to Die and Concern for Dying were affiliated, operating as separate arms of the American 'right to die' movement and sharing the same office premises. Because of the Euthanasia Educational Council's tax exempt non-profit status, euthanasia supporters were encouraged to send donations which were in turn partly used to finance the activities of the Society for the Right to Die.[41] However, the tensions underlying the differing orientations of the two groups eventually led to a complete split in 1979.

Concern for Dying, with its essentially educational outlook, continued with its programme of public and professional education and dissemination of its living will. In addition to the publication of a quarterly newsletter which commenced in 1975, and reports on legal, medical, and ethical developments in the care of the dying, Concern for Dying produced a significant amount of literature on the subject of death and dying[42] as well as a number of educational films and videotapes. A major programme activity of Concern for Dying was the Interdisciplinary Collaboration on Death and Dying. First established in 1978, the Interdisciplinary Collaboration on Death and Dying (known as the Collaboration) was developed as a professional educational programme on terminal care decision-making for students and practitioners in law, medicine, nursing, social work, theology, health care administration, and related professions, with the aim of improving participants' understanding and skill in dealing with the needs of the terminally ill and their families. Another initiative introduced by Concern for Dying was the establishment of a living will registry in 1983, whereby individuals can, for a small fee, have a copy of their living will kept on a computerized file in a central location. During the 1980s, Concern for Dying began to diversify its activities into the judicial and legislative areas. A legal advisory

---

[40] Society for the Right to Die, *The First Fifty Years 1938–88* (New York, 1988).

[41] Humphry, D. and Wickett, A., *The Right to Die: Understanding Euthanasia* (Sydney, 1986) 119.

[42] e.g. *The Living Will and Other Advance Directives* (1986).

service was established to handle the numerous inquiries from attorneys for information about the legal status of non-statutory advance directives and other legal questions pertaining to the terminally ill. Concern's staff attorney and committee members have been involved in a number of court cases, giving legal advice as well as filing *amicus* briefs in a number of landmark cases. The organization has also been involved in drafting model 'right to refuse treatment' legislation.

Following its official separation from Concern for Dying in 1979, the more politically active group, the Society for the Right to Die, continued with its campaign for 'right to die' legislation and has been instrumental in securing reform in this area.[43] However, the split between the two organizations resulted in an expansion of the society's programme into educational and judicial arenas, while continuing with its legislative activities. In addition to the publication and distribution of its newsletters, the society produced numerous publications dealing with living wills and relevant legislation and generally on the subject of 'death with dignity'.[44] In 1984, a legal department was established and the society has been involved in many 'right to die' court cases, with staff attorneys acting as advocates or more usually, submitting *amicus* briefs in support of the patient's right to refuse life-sustaining treatment. The society has also been active in the medical field. In 1985, the society established a medical relations department, with the aim of promoting closer contact between the society and health care facilities. The society has regularly sponsored conferences for doctors to foster the exchange of views on 'right to die' issues among medical practitioners. In 1982 the society convened a conference of ten of the nation's most prominent doctors with the aim of establishing comprehensive guidelines on the doctors' responsibility towards hopelessly ill patients and their families. This initiative led to the publication of an authoritative article in the *New England Journal of Medicine*[45] which was subsequently incorporated in the society's own publication, *The Physician and the Hopelessly Ill Patient: Legal, Medical and Ethical Guidelines*,[46] and has been widely distributed amongst the health care community. Encouraged by the success of the 1982 conference, the doctors were convened by the society for a second time in 1987 in order to continue their analysis of the appropriate role of

---

[43] In 1978 the society was involved in drafting model living will legislation in conjunction with the Yale Legislative Services at the Yale Law School. The draft legislation has subsequently been used as a legislative model in a number of jurisdictions; Society for the Right to Die, *The First Fifty Years 1938–88*, above n. 40, at 4–5.

[44] The society's publications include *Handbook of Living Will Laws 1981–84* (New York, 1984); *The Handbook of 1985 Living Will Laws* (New York, 1985); *Handbook of Living Will Laws*, 1987 edn. (New York, 1987); and *The Physician and the Hopelessly Ill Patient* (New York, 1985).

[45] Wanzer, S. et al., 'The Physician's Responsibility to the Hopelessly Ill Patient' (1984) 310 *New Eng.J.Med.* 955.

[46] Society for the Right to Die (New York, 1985).

doctors with regard to dying patients. Nine of the original ten participants were present (one of the doctors had since died), and there were three additions. This second conference resulted in a follow-up publication in the *New England Journal of Medicine*,[47] once again attracting considerable publicity and interest from both within and outside the medical profession.

Unlike the founders of the original Euthanasia Society of America, neither Concern for Dying nor the Society for the Right to Die have openly advocated active voluntary euthanasia. Instead, their activities have been focused on recognition of the patient's right to refuse treatment, acceptance of living wills, and matters generally falling within the category of 'passive' euthanasia. Although there was a marked difference in strategy between the two organizations in the late 1970s, by the end of the 1980s, both organizations had recognized the respective merits of educational and legislative initiatives in achieving their aims, and this was reflected in the diversification of their activities. This had, however, resulted in a duplication of programmes and ineffective use of limited resources. In 1990, Concern for Dying and the Society for the Right to Die began negotiations for the merger of the two organizations and in September 1991 they officially merged to create a new organization under the name 'Choice in Dying'. By combining their resources and membership, the two former bodies have been able to create a more efficient and influential organization to pursue their common objectives.

The Hemlock Society USA

In 1980 Derek Humphry, a journalist and author who had emigrated from England some 2 years earlier, and his second wife, Anne Wickett, established the Hemlock Society, a non-profit educational and research organization. In a media interview,[48] Humphry explained that his motivation for the formation of the society was the experience of helping his first wife, Jean, who was suffering from cancer, to commit suicide and later publishing a book on the subject entitled *Jean's Way*.[49] According to Humphry, the experience of writing the book, and the reactions he received to it, got him caught up in the whole issue and led him to establish the Hemlock Society as a way to pursue the issue intelligently through research, writing, and publishing books. The Hemlock Society derives its name from the root plant Hemlock, a poisonous umbelliferous plant. It was decided to use this name for the newly created organization because of its connotations with rational suicide which the society supports. Unlike Choice in Dying and the two organizations from which it developed which have limited their activi-

---

[47] Wanzer, S. et al., 'The Physician's Responsibility Toward Hopelessly Ill Patients: A Second Look' (1989) 320 *New Eng.J Med.* 844.

[48] *Medicine in the News*, 2 April 1986.

[49] Humphry, D. and Wickett, A., *Jean's Way* (New York, 1978).

ties to the pursuit of passive euthanasia, the Hemlock Society supports the option of active voluntary euthanasia for the terminally ill and has for some time been one of its leading proponents in North America. In 1981, the Hemlock Society was granted status as a non-profit, educational corporation, which means that all donations, gifts, and legacies made to the society are tax deductible. This was a development of considerable practical significance, since the society is financially dependent on donations, as well as membership fees and the sale of its books.

Membership of the Hemlock Society has steadily grown since its establishment in 1980 and currently stands in excess of 40,000 members. As the influence and popularity of the Hemlock Society has increased, many chapters of the society have been set up throughout the USA. The society was originally based in Los Angeles, California, but has since been relocated and is now based in Denver, Colorado. The Hemlock Society is a founder member of the World Federation of the Right to Die Societies. The stated principles of the society are to seek to promote a climate of public opinion which is tolerant of the right of people who are terminally ill to end their lives in a planned manner. The Hemlock Society believes that the final decision to terminate life is ultimately one's own. It believes this action, and most of all its timing, to be an extremely personal decision, wherever possible taken in concert with family and friends. The society speaks only to those people who have mutual sympathy with its goals. However, views contrary to its own which are held by other religions and philosophies are respected. The society does not encourage suicide for emotional, traumatic, or financial reasons in the absence of terminal illness, and supports the work of those involved in suicide prevention programmes.

Amongst the principal objectives of the society is the promotion of dialogue to raise public consciousness of active voluntary euthanasia through the news media, public meetings, and with the medical and legal professions and others, and to support the principle of legislation to permit a dying person lawfully to request a doctor to help him or her to die. In pursuit of its stated principles and objectives, the society engages in a wide range of activities. Its representatives, particularly Derek Humphry, who for many years was the Executive Director of the society, developed a high media profile, frequently giving interviews as well as engaging in many television and radio debates with ethicists, doctors, and lawyers throughout the country as well as abroad. A quarterly newsletter[50] is issued to members, providing up-to-date information on issues of death and dying. The Hemlock Society is particularly notable for its numerous publications on suicide, assisted suicide, active voluntary euthanasia, and related issues.[51] It boasts

---

[50] Originally the *Hemlock Quarterly*—renamed *Time Lines* in 1994.
[51] Titles include Humphry and Wickett, A., *Jean's Way*; above n. 49; Humphry, D., *Let Me Die Before I Wake* (Eugene, Oregon, 1981); Portwood, D., *Commonsense Suicide* (Los

many of its own titles, including the first US guide to self-deliverance, *Let Me Die Before I Wake*, by Derek Humphry which was released in 1981. This book takes the form of case histories that illustrate the concept of active voluntary euthanasia: in the context of true stories of suicides by terminally ill people, lethal drug dosages are disclosed. The publication of this book caused considerable controversy, including condemnation from other voluntary euthanasia organizations in the USA, primarily on the grounds that such material is likely to be the subject of abuse. *Let Me Die Before I Wake* was initially only available to Hemlock members, but was subsequently released for general sale. It has proved to be the society's best selling title, with over 60,000 copies sold in the first 5 years of its release, as well as reportedly being a heavily borrowed item in public libraries. Humphry has since written another book on the subject, *Final Exit: The Practicalities of Self-Deliverance and Assisted Suicide for the Dying* which has also proved to be enormously successful.[52] *Final Exit* is a detailed manual on how to commit suicide, explicitly setting out information about drug dosages, as well as giving guidance to doctors and nurses about helping people to die. As with the earlier publication *Let Me Die Before I Wake*, *Final Exit* has been the subject of controversy, primarily because of fears that it would be abused by people suffering depression or severe anxiety.

Reflecting on the achievements of the society, Humphry has explained that the first 5 years of its work were devoted to raising public consciousness of the issue through its books, newsletters, conferences, and media briefings.[53] By 1985, the view was taken by the representatives of the society that public support for active voluntary euthanasia was at a level sufficient to promote legislative activities and since then, the society has been pressing for legislation which would permit 'physician aid in dying'.[54] In planning a strategy for legislative activity, it was decided to retain the Hemlock Society as the intellectual underpinning of the movement, specializing as it does, in research and publication, and to start a new organization which would have the appropriate legal status to engage substantially in active politics. The Hemlock Society provided financial support for the creation of a sister organization for the purpose of changing state law to permit 'physician aid in dying' for the terminally ill. The new organization, Americans

Angeles, 1983); Larue, G., *Euthanasia and Religion: A Survey of the Attitudes of World Religions to the Right to Die* (Los Angeles, 1985); Humphry and Wickett, *The Right to Die*; above Ch. 3 n. 10; Humphry, D. (ed.), *Compassionate Crimes, Broken Taboos* (Los Angeles, 1986); Johnson, G., *The Right to Die, Voluntary Euthanasia* (Los Angeles, 1987); Risley, R., *Death with Dignity: A New Law Permitting Physician Aid-In-Dying* (Eugene, Oregon, 1989); Humphry, D., *Final Exit: The Practicalities of Self-Deliverance and Assisted Suicide for the Dying* (Eugene, Oregon, 1991).

[52] (1991) reported by *Publishers Weekly* to be a best selling non-fiction book; for some time it held top position in the advice category of the *New York Times* best-seller list.

[53] Humphry, D., 'Physicians and Euthanasia' (1988) 3 *Euthanasia Rev.* 79, at 81–2.

[54] See further, pp. 364–74 below.

Against Human Suffering, was established in 1986 and became the political arm of the Hemlock Society, with a different tax status, thereby allowing it to engage in law reform activities. In collaboration with the new organization Americans Against Human Suffering, the Hemlock Society has campaigned for the introduction of 'physician aid in dying' legislation in a number of US states including the Oregon initiative which resulted in the passage of legislation in the State of Oregon, permitting physician-assisted suicide.[55] Americans Against Human Suffering has since been renamed 'Americans for Death with Dignity'. Its mission statement is to create a legal right in the USA so that every mentally competent adult has the choice of a physician-assisted humane and dignified death when he or she becomes terminally ill. To this end, the group continues to campaign for the legalization of active voluntary euthanasia. The Hemlock Society now has a new political arm 'Pro-USA' and a new mobilization fund. The society is now referred to as the 'Hemlock Society USA'.

Compassion in Dying

In 1993 a new group was established in Seattle, Washington State, called Compassion in Dying. This development came about following a split within the Hemlock Society, after the society had made it clear that counselling and assistance with rational suicide was not part of the society's programme. The new organization, Compassion in Dying, aims to support terminally ill persons in choosing to die without pain, without suffering, and with personal assistance if necessary to accomplish an end to life through rational suicide in morally compelling cases. In addition to assisting in suicide, Compassion in Dying seeks to offer advice on pain management and hospital care and to arrange for spiritual support when requested.

Compassion in Dying claims that the present law on assisting suicide in the State of Washington (as in most other states[56]) which prohibits aiding or causing a person to commit suicide is aimed at the protection of the emotionally disturbed or mentally ill and does not apply to Compassion in Dying's goals of aiding rational suicides. Compassion in Dying has made it clear that it does not provide direct assistance in dying by administering lethal injections or providing a means of ending life, but will, in appropriate cases which meet its criteria, help patients obtain prescriptions for barbiturates and other medications from their own doctor, or, if requested, provide confidential information about suitable medications for suicide. Compassion in Dying has a multidisciplinary Advisory Committee which is comprised of a number of doctors, a lawyer, a nurse, a psychologist, a minister, and a grief counsellor. When the organization is approached by an individual for suicide assistance, the doctors will examine and confirm the

---

[55] For discussion of these legislative developments, see pp. 364–74 below.
[56] See p. 56 above.

terminal prognosis, review the medical records, and then consult with the patient's own doctor. If the patient's doctor is unwilling to prescribe medications for suicide, the patient will be assisted to find another doctor.

Compassion in Dying has also recently been involved in sponsoring lawsuits in the States of Washington and New York, testing state laws prohibiting assistance with suicide.[57] It claims that the laws in these states and other jurisdictions in the USA are unconstitutional in so far as they are applied to mentally competent, end-stage terminally ill adult patients seeking medications from their doctors to self-administer for the purpose of hastening death. Decisions in each of these actions have recently been handed down, both upholding a constitutionally protected interest in physician-assisted suicide in certain circumstances.[58] Appeals are now likely to be brought before the United States Supreme Court in respect of these decisions, and in the event that the United States Supreme Court agrees to accept review, Compassion in Dying will be continuing its support for these constitutional challenges.

ERGO!

Another recent development in the USA has been the establishment of a new organization ERGO!—the Euthanasia Research and Guidance Organization. ERGO!'s mission statement is to:

Make the movement for the right to choose to die better informed about the complexities of [the] subject. It does not compete with other groups, seeking rather to provide information to assist them better to carry out their functions. ERGO! is not a membership organisation but derives its supporters from individuals and organisations that subscribe to its services as a not-for-profit information clearing house.

One of its pioneers and current President is Derek Humphry (formerly Executive Director of the Hemlock Society). The goals and strategies of ERGO! include to identify public policy issues and conduct ongoing research; to disseminate research findings to policy makers, medical professionals, 'right to die' societies, legal and health professionals, legislators, and the public, nationally and internationally; to provide education in all aspects of 'aid in dying', and to develop guidelines for implementing the most humane means for physician 'aid in dying'.

Canada

There are two principal voluntary euthanasia societies in Canada: Dying with Dignity and The Right to Die Society of Canada.[59]

---

[57] See pp. 97–121 above.

[58] See *Compassion in Dying* v. *State of Washington* No. 94-35534 (9th Cir. March 6 1996) (*en banc*) and *Quill* v. *Vacco* No. 60 (2nd Cir. April 2 1996) discussed at pp. 101–121 above.

[59] There have been other organizations in existence including Goodbye, A Right to Die Society which was established in 1991 to promote active voluntary euthanasia, and Fondation

Dying with Dignity

The largest of the organizations, Dying with Dignity established in 1980, is a national organization based in Toronto, Ontario. In its promotional literature, Dying with Dignity describes itself as 'a Canadian society concerned with the quality of dying'. The stated aims of the society are to inform and educate Canadians about the right to a good death, to promote a better understanding among the general public and health care professionals regarding the issues of death and dying, to distribute and encourage recognition of the living will in Canada, and to encourage medical and legal recognition of active voluntary euthanasia. Dying with Dignity is a non-profit registered charitable organization, and donations to it are consequently tax deductible.

Dying with Dignity engages in a wide range of activities in pursuit of its objectives. The society issues a quarterly newsletter, provides speakers for meetings, and offers its library resources to the public. Its staff, principally consisting of an Executive Director, supplemented by volunteer assistance, handle numerous telephone inquiries and letters and also seek to provide a counselling service about options for the terminally ill. Maryilynne Seguin, founding member and currently Executive Director of the organization, has explained that Dying with Dignity counsellors do not suggest to patients that they consider euthanasia or assisted suicide.[60] Nor do they obtain medication for that person or administer medications to an individual. Rather, it is the role of a counsellor advocate to support a person in their decision. They are also prepared to negotiate on a client's behalf for their right to die with dignity. In furtherance of its stated aims, the society is also involved in the promotion and distribution of its own living will and durable power of attorney, and has endorsed legislative developments to give legal recognition to these mechanisms for future decision-making.

In its efforts to educate Canadians about the right to a good death and to promote a better understanding among the general public and health care professionals regarding the issues of death and dying, the society has played an active role in the media. Representatives of the society are regularly invited to appear on radio and television interviews and talkback shows and frequently hold interviews with the print media. Other educationally orientated activities organized by the society include a regular public forum on health care issues as well as sponsorship of conferences.

Dying with Dignity has been actively fostering a co-operative working

Responsable Jusqu'a la fin, (Foundation Responsible Until the End) established in 1986 to promote the right to die in accordance with existing laws in the Province of Quebec and to secure recognition of the living will.

[60] Seguin, M., 'Freedom to Choose' in Oki, T. (ed.), *The Living Will in the World* Proceedings of the 9th International Conference of the World Federation of the Right to Die Societies, Kyoto, Japan (Tokyo, 1992), 147, 152.

relationship with the medical profession in Canada. It has established dialogue with a number of medical organizations and has conducted a number of surveys of doctors to gauge respondents' awareness of and attitudes to the living will, which have generally promoted a positive response from the doctors surveyed.[61] The extent of this co-operative relationship is reflected in the fact that the medical organizations have been co-sponsors of the public forums organized by Dying with Dignity which often feature speakers from the medical profession. The society has also been involved in various other initiatives intended to promote an appreciation within the medical community of its role and aims. In 1989, Dying with Dignity convened a special meeting of doctors and lawyers, with the aim of informally exchanging ideas on topics of mutual concern, including patients' rights within the health care system, medical and legal recognition of the living will and durable power of attorney for health care, and the need, if any, for protective legislation for doctors honouring the wish of a patient to die with dignity.

Over its relatively short history, Dying with Dignity has enjoyed growing acceptance and support for its aims. However, there had been complaints from some members on the grounds that the society was not sufficiently vocal or active in promoting the issue of active voluntary euthanasia. No doubt encouraged by evidence of growing community and professional support, there has, in recent years, been some reassessment of the society's policy position. This has resulted in a shift of emphasis in the aims and activities of the organization, with a strengthening of the organization's commitment to active voluntary euthanasia. A voluntary euthanasia declaration has been prepared and distributed and the objective of securing legalization is now more openly advocated. The society has also established a registry for the durable power of attorney for health care and the voluntary euthanasia declaration.

Membership in Dying with Dignity has been increasing steadily over recent years, much of which the society attributes to its media activities, as well as to a growing awareness in the community of the issues that it espouses. The organization also reports an increase in institutional membership which, it believes, reflects growing social acceptability of the organization in Canada.[62] Dying with Dignity has established branches in a number of centres across Canada for the purpose of providing a closer contact for members in these communities. The national body provides resources to assist these groups in their operation.

The Right to Die Society of Canada

In 1991 the Right to Die Society of Canada, was formed, based in Victoria, British Columbia. The Right to Die Society of Canada has been established

---

[61] Note, 'Ontario Physicians Respond' (1987) Vol. 4 No. 4 *Dying with Dignity Newsletter* 1.
[62] Report of the Executive Director (1990) Vol. 7 No. 3 *Dying with Dignity Newsletter* 3.

to provide a mechanism by which Canadians supporting the introduction of legislation permitting 'physician aid in dying' for the terminally ill can achieve law reform. Unlike other 'right to die' societies in Canada which are registered charities and are consequently prevented by Revenue Canada guidelines from being politically active in lobbying for legislative change, the Right to Die Society of Canada has a different tax status and is accordingly free to pursue its law reform goals. The society has sought to pursue its objectives in a number of ways including the dissemination of information, political lobbying, and through the courts. In 1992 the society initiated court action on behalf on Sue Rodriguez to challenge the constitutionality of the provision of the Canadian Criminal Code which prohibits assisted suicide.[63]

The Right to Die Society of Canada produces a substantial journal entitled *Last Rights* which has recently featured a series of special editions to advance the existing momentum for reform. The society has also developed a database on the Internet through its Last Rights Information Centres, the World Wide Web Service 'DeathNET', to provide information about current events in this area in Canada and internationally. The society has been actively involved in lobbying members of Parliament with regard to 'right to die' issues and claims some credit for the decision of Liberal Senator Joan Nieman to call for a parliamentary inquiry, resulting in the establishment of the Senate Special Committee on Euthanasia and Assisted Suicide in 1994 chaired by Senator Nieman.[64] In the wake of the recently released Report by the Senate Special Committee which rejected both active voluntary euthanasia and doctor-assisted suicide, the society has launched a new initiative for members to become more deeply involved in the assisting of suicide of individuals who ask for such assistance. This is intended to demonstrate the society's commitment to the cause and to force a change in the law.

Australia

Since the mid-1970s, a number of voluntary euthanasia societies have been established in Australia. Such societies now exist in all Australian states and territories. The first to be established in February 1974[65] were the Australian Voluntary Euthanasia Society, based in New South Wales (later renamed the Voluntary Euthanasia Society of New South Wales), and the Voluntary Euthanasia Society of Victoria. In the 1980s, a number of further societies were formed in Australia: the West Australian Voluntary Euthanasia Society in March 1980, the South Australian Voluntary Euthanasia Society in 1983, the Voluntary Euthanasia Society of Queensland in 1987,

---

[63] See further, pp. 86–94 above.   [64] See further, pp. 382–7 below.
[65] Similar developments occurred in New Zealand with the establishment in 1978 of voluntary euthanasia societies in Auckland and Wellington.

and the Voluntary Euthanasia Society of Tasmania in 1992. The most recently formed society is the Northern Territory Voluntary Euthanasia Society which was established in 1995. A number of the societies have created branches to service better their members. Most of the voluntary euthanasia societies are incorporated.

The justification for the creation of separate societies in Australia is primarily because of this country's federal structure and of the fact that the reforms being sought are in the criminal law field and are therefore a matter within the responsibility of the state and territory legislatures. As a result, the campaign for reform has been focused at the state and territory level. However, with the rapid expansion of the voluntary euthanasia movement in the 1980s, there was growing recognition of the need for closer co-operation between the state organizations, and in 1987 the Australian societies joined in a Federation of Australian Voluntary Euthanasia Societies in an attempt to co-ordinate their activities.[66] In 1988, one of the New Zealand societies, the Voluntary Euthanasia Society (Auckland) was admitted to the Federation, which then became the Federation of Australasian Voluntary Euthanasia Societies. However, this organization did not operate as effectively as was hoped, and has since been disbanded.

Thus, although all of the Australian societies pursue similar objectives and policies, each is a separate and autonomous body and they have generally pursued their activities independently. Most of the societies are, however, affiliated with the World Federation of Right to Die Societies, formed in 1980.[67] The main objective of all the Australian societies is, essentially, to promote public understanding and acceptance of active voluntary euthanasia and to secure reform of the law. The statement of aims contained in the literature for the Victorian, New South Wales, and Queensland societies is fairly representative, namely to 'promote legislation giving effect to the widely held public opinion that any person suffering, through illness or disability, severe pain or distress for which no remedy is available, should be entitled by law to a painless and dignified death in accordance with that person's expressed direction'.

For some time, the view was taken by the executive bodies of most of the societies that the legalization of active voluntary euthanasia is a long-term goal, and their efforts were accordingly concentrated on more readily achievable objectives. These objectives have included encouraging people to make a 'living will' or advance directive, increasing patients' awareness

---

[66] The terms of reference for FAVES were as follows: 'To present the views of member societies at a national level, to co-ordinate and facilitate the activities of voluntary euthanasia societies throughout Australia, to promote and assist the formation of further voluntary euthanasia societies, to arrange national and regional conferences, to publish a national newsletter and other literature relevant to voluntary euthanasia and to represent the Australian voluntary euthanasia movement internationally'.

[67] For discussion of the role of the World Federation, see pp. 286–88 below.

of their rights, ensuring that pain control education is an integral part of medical training, and lobbying governments to set up more hospices. In some states, the voluntary euthanasia societies have played an active role with regard to the passage of legislation dealing with the refusal of treatment and passive euthanasia.[68]

In more recent years, however, the societies have been very active in their attempts to secure reform with regard to active voluntary euthanasia, engaging in a wide range of activities. To a large extent, these are directed at increasing public awareness and acceptance of active voluntary euthanasia. In pursuit of these aims, the societies issue regular newsletters, handle many telephone calls and inquiries, and generally seek to disseminate information to the community about active voluntary euthanasia. All of the societies have published educational material outlining their aims and the relevant issues in the debate regarding legalization of active voluntary euthanasia.[69] Many of the societies have secured notable patrons to assist in promoting their societies' objectives. Representatives of the societies frequently present lectures at the request of various groups and organizations, appear on television, and give radio interviews. Public meetings are regularly arranged by the societies, often with well-known guest speakers, as well as seminars, workshops, and educative displays.

The societies are also involved in more direct attempts at securing reform for active voluntary euthanasia, including political campaigning and the preparation of submissions to governmental and law reform commission inquiries. In recent years, a number of the societies have undertaken specific steps towards the introduction of legislation for the legalization of active voluntary euthanasia. In 1988 the South Australian Voluntary Euthanasia Society established a Task Force to examine and report on the possibilities for legislative reform and to formulate plans for introducing active voluntary euthanasia legislation in South Australia. The Task Force drafted a paper entitled, a 'Discussion Paper on Decriminalizing Voluntary Euthanasia in South Australia' (1989), and has since produced a draft bill for the legalization of active voluntary euthanasia. In the State of Victoria, legislation has been developed by the Voluntary Euthanasia Society for the legalization of doctor-assisted suicide which it sees as an intermediate goal. The Victorian society also played a particularly active role in supporting the

---

[68] This was the case in Victoria with regard to the major inquiry by the Parliament of Victoria Social Development Committee into Options for Dying with Dignity and the resulting Medical Treatment Act 1988 (Vic.), and more recently in South Australia, in relation to the work of the South Australian Parliamentary Select Committee on the Law and Practice Relating to Death and Dying and the resulting Consent to Medical Treatment and Palliative Care Act 1995 (SA).

[69] e.g. booklets such as that produced by the South Australian Voluntary Euthanasia Society *The Right to Choose: The Case for Voluntary Euthanasia*, 3rd edn. (Adelaide, 1995), as well as brochures and information sheets.

reform initiative in the Northern Territory by providing information to those involved in the introduction of this legislation, and by a number of its members presenting submissions to the Northern Territory Select Committee on Euthanasia.[70]

Efforts have also been made by some societies to promote dialogue within the medical profession on the subject of active voluntary euthanasia. Invitations have been extended to the medical profession to the societies' public meetings and seminars, and the societies have also been responsible for the publication and distribution of material directed at the medical profession, such as the booklet *Voluntary Euthanasia and the Medical Profession: An Invitation to Dialogue* produced by the South Australian Voluntary Euthanasia Society in 1990. A number of the societies have now set up groups of doctors and nurses to work on health care aspects of voluntary euthanasia.

In a recent development, a Voluntary Euthanasia Coalition has been formed in the State of New South Wales: the Coalition of Organisations for Voluntary Euthanasia (COVE) comprising the New South Wales Voluntary Euthanasia Society, the AIDS Council of New South Wales, the New South Wales Council for Civil Liberties, the New South Wales Young Lawyers and the Doctors' Reform Society.[71]

Membership of the Australian voluntary euthanasia societies is open to all adults who are in agreement with the societies' aims. Over the years, the societies have attracted members from a wide range of social, economic, political, philosophical, and religious backgrounds. Membership has increased substantially since the societies were first established, with particular growth having been experienced since the 1980s coinciding with increased media exposure and public debate on the subject.

International developments: The World Federation of Right to Die Societies

The first international meeting on voluntary euthanasia was held in Tokyo in 1976, followed by a meeting in San Francisco in 1978. As a result of these early meetings, the World Federation of Right to Die Societies was founded in Oxford in 1980, with 27 groups from 18 countries joining as founding members. Whilst there have been some fluctuations, membership in the federation has remained fairly constant and presently stands at over 35 with

[70] See pp. 344–59 below for discussion of the developments in the Northern Territory. It should be noted that there was no voluntary euthanasia society in existence in the Northern Territory at the time, although one has since been established, following the introduction of these reforms. See above.

[71] See COVE's policy document, *Twelve Principles for Euthanasia Law Reform* which was distributed at the launch of COVE in November 1995.

representation from most voluntary euthanasia organizations throughout the world.[72] The World Federation of Right to Die Societies, deliberately named in such a way that it would cover all voluntary euthanasia and 'right to die' societies—whether proponents of passive and/or active euthanasia—aims to establish voluntary euthanasia organizations in every country and to secure, throughout the world, the legalization of the right of self-determination in dying.[73] As a federation, its major role is the co-ordination on an international basis of the member societies. Its major organizational activity is the biennial meeting held in connection with the biennial international euthanasia conference. These conferences, hosted by members of the federation, have been held in Melbourne (1982), Nice (1984), Bombay (1986), San Francisco (1988), Maastricht (1990), Kyoto (1992), and Bath (1994). The meeting of representatives of the member societies at the international conferences is regarded as invaluable, offering the opportunity for reporting of news from each member society and acting as a medium for dialogue and exchanging ideas among member organizations. The federation publishes a *World Right to Die Newsletter* twice a year. Under the World Federation's Constitution, its affairs are to be managed by its Board of Directors which consists of a President, Vice President, Secretary, Newsletter Editor, and Treasurer plus a number of Directors at large.

As a world federation, the various member societies are able to present a unified policy position on particular issues, in circumstances where a co-ordinated international approach is required. There have in recent years been a number of such initiatives. In 1988 the federation made a submission to the Human Rights Commission of the United Nations. In the spirit of compromise, it was agreed that the submission be confined to passive euthanasia, so that the views of all member societies could be represented.[74] The object of this submission was for the incorporation of the right of dying with dignity as an Appendix to the Charter of Human Rights of 1948, in the hope that the United Nations would subsequently encourage its member countries to introduce suitably reformed laws which affirm patients' right to die with dignity. Since that time there have been a number of further international initiatives. Dr Helga Kuhse, in her capacity as President of the World Federation of Right to Die Societies, has written to the World Medical Association requesting that this group re-examine its position with respect to active voluntary euthanasia. Letters have also been sent to the World Health Organisation and the Council of Europe in an attempt to

---

[72] See Note, 'Profiles of World Federation of Right to Die Societies Members' (1989) 15 *World Right-to-Die Newsletter* 2–5.
[73] By-Law of World Federation of Right to Die Societies, Article II.
[74] Note, 'World Federation Submission to United Nations' (1988) Vol. 5 No. 2 *Dying with Dignity Newsletter* 1.

obtain advisory status for the world federation as a non-governmental organization.

Another noteworthy development has been the formation in 1993 of a European Division of the World Federation, the European Federation of Right to Die Societies. The prime objective of this union is to strengthen the movement in Europe for choice in dying. In May 1993, the seven countries in attendance at the second meeting of the European Division of the World federation (Belgium, England, France, Scotland, Switzerland, Netherlands, and Germany) agreed on the following statement:

The European Division of the World Federation of Right to Die Societies supports the right of everyone to self-determination in dying. When competent, this includes the right to withhold consent to life-prolonging treatment. The same rights should apply to people who are no longer competent, but have previously made their views clearly known. Everyone should have the right to appoint someone to speak on their behalf in these circumstances. Positive help to die for an incurably ill and/or intolerably suffering person, who persistently requests that help, should be part of good medical practice. This should apply to persons who have previously made their wishes known as above. Strict guidelines and controls will be necessary and these will vary from country to country.

The European Division of the World Federation will explore ways of presenting a common policy and will seek representation on European organizations such as the Council of Europe. The European Division has already played an active role in providing evidence to the House of Lords Select Committee on Medical Ethics in the United Kingdom as well as to legislative bodies in Luxembourg and Belgium which are looking at the issue of voluntary euthanasia.[75]

Voluntary euthanasia societies: a global perspective

It is evident from the foregoing review that in the past few decades, there have been significant developments in the voluntary euthanasia movement with the emergence and expansion of voluntary euthanasia societies in the United Kingdom, the USA, Canada, and Australia. The developments in these jurisdictions have been parallelled by similar developments in other parts of the world. Virtually all of the societies report steadily increasing membership and growing community support and acceptance of their cause. There is a widely-held view amongst members and supporters of these societies that this is a movement 'whose time has come'.[76] This in turn has been reflected in increased reform activity. Initiatives are under-way in a number of jurisdictions aimed at securing the introduction of legislation

[75] See pp. 336–9 below for further discussion of the House of Lords Select Committee.
[76] e.g. Note, 'Now is the Time' (1990) Vol. 7 No. 1 *Dying with Dignity Newsletter* 7; Note, 'Voluntary Euthanasia is "an Idea Whose Time Has Come" Says Derek Humphry' (1992) 78 *VESV Report* 3.

permitting active voluntary euthanasia. In historic developments, some success has already been achieved with the acceptance of a citizen-initiated referendum proposal for the legalization of physician-assisted suicide in the State of Oregon in the USA in 1994 and, even more significantly, the passage of legislation in the Northern Territory in 1995 for the legalization of both active voluntary euthanasia and doctor-assisted suicide.[77]

B. Increased Media Coverage, and Public Figures in Support

Another factor contributing to the public awareness and acceptance of active voluntary euthanasia is the substantial increase in media coverage of the issue in the form of radio and television programmes and press reports. Not only has there been a significant increase in the extent of the media coverage, but there appears also to be growing sympathy in the media's treatment of the subject.[78] The public interest in the subject of active voluntary euthanasia has been stimulated by a variety of items regularly presented through the media, including coverage of reform initiatives, reports of increasingly favourable opinion poll results, of doctors assisting their patients to die, and television dramatizations dealing with euthanasia. Widespread publicity and concern about the AIDS epidemic has also contributed to the momentum of the voluntary euthanasia movement, with media reports of AIDS sufferers seeking active euthanasia accompanied by claims that these requests are generally dealt with sympathetically by the medical profession.[79]

Over the years, the voluntary euthanasia cause has also been promoted by prominent public figures who have indicated their support for legalization. For example, in the United Kingdom, the acclaimed writer Arthur Koestler did much to contribute to public awareness and acceptance of active voluntary euthanasia through his support of the British Voluntary Euthanasia Society,[80] and through his much publicized suicide pact with his

---

[77] See pp. 344–59 below.

[78] This is exemplified by an editorial in *The Times*, 'Rights and Wrongs of Dying', 28 Oct. 1991 which suggested that the issue of active voluntary euthanasia should not be left unresolved indefinitely and that it should be the subject of a full-scale public inquiry. More recently, in response to the conviction of Dr Cox in the United Kingdom (discussed at pp. 143–5 above), there were a number of newspaper items which dealt with the case very sympathetically; e.g. *Sunday Telegraph*, 20 Sept. 1992; *The Times*, 21 Sept. 1992; *Guardian*, 22 Sept. 1992; *Daily Express*, 23 Sept. 1992. Note also the editorial in *The Economist*, 17 Sept. 1994 giving support to active voluntary euthanasia and the article entitled 'Wise Decisions on the Right to Die' published in the *NY Times*, 4 April 1996 in response to the Ninth and Second Court decisions declaring the State prohibition on assisted suicide in Washington and New York to be unconstitutional in so far as it applies to competent, terminally ill patients. For discussion of these cases, see pp. 100–21 above.

[79] e.g. *Australian*, 7 April 1987.

[80] Koestler was for a time Vice-Chairman of the Society and had written the preface to the society's booklet, *A Guide to Self-Deliverance*.

wife after he became incurably ill with Parkinson's disease and leukemia.[81] Similarly, in other jurisdictions, the voluntary euthanasia movement has been fuelled by statements of support from well-known figures.[82]

There have also been occasions over the years when members of the judiciary have shown their sympathy and even support for a change to the law to allow doctors to assist patients to die in appropriate circumstances.[83] More recently, cases involving challenges to the validity of legislation prohibiting assisted suicide have arisen in Canada and the USA. In the *Rodriguez*[84] case, the Supreme Court of Canada upheld the validity of this legislation but there were a number of significant dissents to this decision which demonstrated considerable sympathy for persons in the situation of the appellant, seeking medical assistance to die.[85] As a result of the cases in the USA in which a constitutional challenge to the State prohibition on assisted suicide has been upheld,[86] and clear support has been given to the right of competent, terminally ill patients to determine the time and manner of their deaths, the courts themselves have become instrumental in bringing about reform.

C. Organized Opposition to the Legalization of Active Voluntary Euthanasia

While the voluntary euthanasia movement has clearly been advancing, so has the opposition to euthanasia from certain groups, and this can be seen as a direct consequence of the changing climate for reform.[87] Since the commencement of the modern voluntary euthanasia movement, any public support for euthanasia, and attempts to introduce legislative reform, have invariably attracted protest from certain quarters. Anti-euthanasia sentiment was particularly strong in the 1950s, attributable, at least in part, to the revulsion to the Nazi crimes.

As previously noted,[88] the churches, especially the Roman Catholic Church, have traditionally been opposed to the notion of active voluntary euthanasia, and have been quite vocal in their condemnation of any propos-

---

[81] *Time*, 21 March 1983.

[82] For example, in Australia, the (now retired) Governor General, Bill Hayden AC has recently spoken out in support of legalization of active voluntary euthanasia: *Australian*, 22 June 1995.

[83] See, for example, the concurring opinion of Compton J in *Bouvia* v. *Superior Court* 225 Cal. Rptr. 297 (1986) and the judgment of Lord Browne-Wilkinson in *Airedale NHS* v. *Bland* [1993] 1 All ER 821.

[84] [1993] 3 SCR 519.

[85] See the dissents of Lamer CJ, L'Heureux-Dubé, Cory, and McLachlin JJ. Note also the dissent of McEachern CJ of the British Columbia Court of Appeal (1993) 79 CCC (3d) 1.

[86] For detailed discussion of these cases see pp. 100–21 above.

[87] For historical coverage of the opposition to euthanasia, see Russell, *Freedom to Die*, above Ch. 4 n. 81, at 59–214.

[88] See pp. 213–16 above.

als for its legalization. Despite the churches' opposition, there have always been individual dissenters from within who have been willing to indicate publicly their support for legalization.[89] Even the churches themselves have, in more recent times, indicated a willingness to re-examine traditional views pertaining to life and death. Some churches have, for example, introduced their own initiatives to examine the problems associated with death and dying, including the issue of euthanasia.[90] Since the mid-1960s, there has been increasing discussion of the issue of euthanasia in church-sponsored periodicals, including articles openly supporting active voluntary euthanasia. Today, the churches have generally come to accept what is, in effect, passive euthanasia (although the terminology of 'euthanasia' is rejected), in recognition of the problems associated with medical advancements and the futile prolongation of life. Support has also been given to the practice of administering to a dying person drugs for the alleviation of pain, even though they may hasten death.[91] More significantly, there has even been backing for active voluntary euthanasia, at least in some circumstances, from a number of notable Catholic and Protestant theologians.[92] In recent years, there have been quite a number of ordained clergy from a broad spectrum of denominations who have indicated their support.[93] The general proposition remains, however, that the churches have been amongst the most significant opponents of the practice.

In addition to the traditional opposition from the churches, 'right to life' groups have also been vocal opponents of euthanasia. Alongside their campaign efforts to prohibit abortion, 'right to life' organizations have vigorously opposed any proposals for the legalization of active voluntary euthanasia, and even 'natural death' and 'living will' legislation which permits only passive euthanasia in some limited circumstances has attracted opposition. Whilst upholding the general right of patients to control their

[89] e.g. Sullivan, *The Morality of Mercy Killing* (Westminster, Maryland, 1950) 19–21.

[90] For example the Church of England, National Assembly Board for Social Responsibility established an inquiry and in 1965 published a report entitled, *Decisions about Life and Death: A Problem of Modern Medicine* (London, 1965). See also the Church of England, National Assembly Board for Social Responsibility, *On Dying Well: An Anglican Contribution to the Debate on Euthanasia* (London, 1975).

[91] See further, p. 216 above.

[92] e.g. Daniel Maguire (Professor of Theology); Richard McCormick (Catholic moral theologian); Paul Ramsey (Protestant Minister, Professor of Religion). For reference to the views of these commentators see Ch. 4. Note also the views of Reverend Dr Kenneth Boyd: Boyd, K., 'Euthanasia Back to the Future' in Keown, J., *Euthanasia Examined: Ethical, Clinical and Legal Perspectives* (Cambridge, 1995) 72.

[93] In the United Kingdom: e.g. Rev. D. Jenkins, Bishop of Durham, 'Why Not Choose Death in the End' (1991) 7 *Care of the Critically Ill* 6. In the USA: e.g. Rev. J. Brooke (United Church of Christ) is Executive Director of the Californian-based organization, Americans for Death with Dignity. There was also considerable support from some clergy for 'Initiative 119', the 1991 proposal to introduce 'physician aid in dying' legislation in Washington State with a mixed denominational group being formed 'Interfaith Clergy for YES on Initiative 119'. For further discussion of Initiative 119 see pp. 366–8 below.

own treatment, 'right to life' organizations are opposed to any deliberate termination of life, whether by passive or active means. As the voluntary euthanasia movement has gained in intensity, a number of new organizations have been established for the purpose of counteracting this development and fighting against the legalization of active voluntary euthanasia. For example, in 1987, the International Anti-Euthanasia Task Force was formed in the USA, which includes, amongst its stated purposes, to promote and defend the right of all persons to be treated with respect, dignity, and compassion and to resist attitudes, programs, and policies which threaten the lives and rights of those who are medically vulnerable.[94] In the United Kingdom a new organization was created in 1991 under the name of ALERT which aims to campaign against the legalization of active voluntary euthanasia. ALERT issues a regular newsletter[95] and is affiliated with the International Anti-Euthanasia Task Force.

These anti-euthanasia developments can be seen as a direct response to the modern voluntary euthanasia movement and to the growing success of the campaign for the legalization of active voluntary euthanasia.

III. SIGNS OF CHANGE FROM WITHIN THE MEDICAL PROFESSION

As noted earlier, although conduct amounting to 'passive euthanasia' is now widely accepted as an appropriate form of medical practice, the medical profession has traditionally been opposed to the concept of active voluntary euthanasia and has steadfastly resisted efforts to secure its legalization.[96] However, despite this traditional opposition to active voluntary euthanasia, some prominent and respected doctors have openly supported the voluntary euthanasia cause and have in fact played a significant role in the voluntary euthanasia movement.[97] Developments within the medical profession in more recent years indicate that professional medical organizations need to re-examine their official stance on the issue of active voluntary euthanasia. Not only are there continuing reports of some more outspoken members of the profession indicating their involvement in the practice and support for legalization, there is also growing evidence to suggest that attitudes to the issue of active voluntary euthanasia have undergone considerable change within the profession generally. Reliable sur-

[94] See pamphlet, International Anti-Euthanasia Task Force, Human Life Center, University of Steubenville.

[95] The newsletter is entitled ALERT *Euthanasia Update.*

[96] See pp. 127–8 above.

[97] For detailed historical coverage of the position in the USA and the United Kingdom, see Russell, *Freedom to Die,* above Ch. 4 n. 81, at Chs. 4–7.

veys of the medical profession undertaken in all jurisdictions under consideration have shown that a substantial proportion of doctors are in favour of the legalization of active voluntary euthanasia and would be willing to engage in the practice if it were made legal. Moreover, a significant proportion are already involved in the practice, notwithstanding its present illegality.[98] In the light of this evidence, it is becoming increasingly apparent that the professional medical associations no longer represent the views of their members on this issue and that a major reassessment of the associations' traditional opposition to active voluntary euthanasia is now long overdue.

Some progress towards reform has already been made at the official levels of the medical profession. There has been widespread acceptance of medical conduct which amounts to passive euthanasia as being consistent with legitimate medical practice. The practical endorsement of passive euthanasia by the medical profession does, to a large extent, reflect growing recognition of the limits of modern medical technology and of the importance of patient autonomy and self-determination in deciding upon treatment choices. As argued in an earlier chapter,[99] these principles apply with equal force to active voluntary euthanasia, so the foundation has been laid for broader recognition of the need to respect patients' health care decisions. Significantly, there is also now growing awareness of, and support for living wills amongst the medical profession.[100]

There are further indications that the medical profession may, in the longer term, be amenable to reform on the issue of active voluntary euthanasia. In recent years, there appears to be greater willingness on the part of the profession to re-evaluate its stance with regard to active voluntary euthanasia, and to debate openly the issues involved. This is clearly evidenced by the increased attention to the issue of active euthanasia in the medical literature, as well as the growing number of medical conferences, symposia, seminars, and meetings where the issue has been discussed. Further, as outlined below, in a number of jurisdictions, medical associations have actually initiated inquiries to reassess their traditional opposition to the legalization of active voluntary euthanasia. The significance of these developments must be considered against the traditionally accepted view that active euthanasia is contrary to the doctor's role as healer, and the resulting sensitivity of the medical profession in broaching this subject.

There has also been a number of other factors operating within the medical profession which have, in a more general way, contributed to the process of reform towards recognition of active voluntary euthanasia. One such factor is the increasing attention being given to the subject of medical

---

[98] See pp. 134–8 above. [99] See pp. 188–93 above.
[100] For example, the British Medical Association (BMA) has issued a statement strongly supporting the principle of an advance directive: 'BMA Statement on Advance Directives' (1992) and (1994) (revised).

ethics generally. Over the past 10 years or so, quite a number of research centres and institutions have been established in the common law jurisdictions under consideration, devoted to teaching and research in this field,[101] and institutional ethics committees have also come into prominence. Growing recognition of the importance of medical ethics has resulted in a reassessment of medical curricula in most jurisdictions to include some teaching of medical ethics.[102] The significance of these developments with regard to active voluntary euthanasia has been its effect in stimulating debate on the issue within the medical profession.

Another development within the medical profession, which has indirectly assisted the voluntary euthanasia cause, has been growing attention to the needs of the dying, embracing not only medical matters but also the emotional and psychological needs of terminal patients. Though previously a much neglected area, since the 1960s, there has been a significant upsurge in research and interest on this subject. The practical limits of modern medical technology are increasingly being recognized, and there has been a recasting of priorities from attempting to preserve life at all cost to easing the passing of dying patients. This development has been manifest in a number of ways, including an outpouring of literature on the subject of death and dying, and increasing attention to the subject in the medical curriculum. There have also been significant advancements in relation to hospice and palliative care. The modern hospice movement which emerged in the 1960s and 1970s largely through the work of Dame Cicely Saunders, of St Christopher's Hospice, London,[103] has, as its paramount aim, the improvement of the quality of life for the terminally ill. The provision of appropriate palliative and hospice care for terminally ill patients is now increasingly being seen as part of mainstream medicine. Although active voluntary euthanasia has generally been rejected as an unnecessary and unacceptable option by many organizations and individuals involved in the delivery of hospice and palliative care,[104] these developments are nevertheless of relevance to the voluntary euthanasia cause in that they reflect a changed attitude within the medical profession to the needs of the dying and may

[101] In the United Kingdom, e.g. the Institute of Medical Ethics; in the USA, e.g. the Kennedy Institute of Ethics at Georgetown University, Washington and the Hastings Center, New York; in Canada, e.g. the Center for Bioethics, Clinical Research Institute of Montreal; and in Australia, the establishment of the Monash Centre for Human Bioethics.

[102] For literature reflecting the changing approach of the medical profession to the teaching of medical ethics, see Chambers, D., 'Ethics or Medical Ethics' (1984) 24 *Med. Science & Law* 17, and the *Report of a Working Party on the Teaching of Medical Ethics* (The Pond Report) (London, 1987).

[103] See Du Boulay, S., *Cicely Saunders: The Founder of the Modern Hospice Movement* (London, 1984).

[104] e.g. Dame Cicely Saunders, of St. Christopher's Hospice, London, above n. 103; Twycross, R., 'Where There is Hope There is Life: A View from the Hospice' in Keown, *Euthanasia Examined*, above Ch. 4 n. 15, at 141.

thereby encourage greater acceptance of active voluntary euthanasia within the health care professions. In more recent years, there has even been some support for the concept of active voluntary euthanasia from professionals within the palliative care field.[105]

It should be noted, however, that although there has been a shift towards greater understanding and acceptance of active voluntary euthanasia within the medical profession generally, there have also been elements within the profession which remain steadfastly opposed to the concept and have vigorously countered any proposals for the legalization. At the international level, an organization of doctors has been established (World Federation of Doctors who Respect Human Life) to prevent the legalization of active voluntary euthanasia. The World Medical Association continues to oppose active voluntary euthanasia and the official stance of the overwhelming majority of medical associations remains one of opposition.

Separate consideration will now be given to the position in the key jurisdictions under consideration.

A. United Kingdom

As was noted above, the origins of the modern voluntary euthanasia movement in the United Kingdom stem from the work of Dr Millard in the 1930s, and since that time, many British doctors have publicly expressed their support for the legalization of active voluntary euthanasia.[106] However, the official position of the medical profession has been consistently to condemn any such proposal. There have, nevertheless, been a number of significant developments, prominent amongst them the inquiries initiated by the British Medical Association (BMA) first in 1969, and more recently, in 1988, to examine the problem of euthanasia. Although the legalization of active voluntary euthanasia was ultimately rejected by both of these inquiries, the fact that these inquiries were even undertaken is a matter of some significance, demonstrating an apparent willingness on the part of the BMA to undertake a review of its traditional opposition to active voluntary euthanasia. The BMA is one of the few professional medical associations to undertake a review of this kind in the common law jurisdictions under consideration. That this occurred in the United Kingdom can best be understood in light of the repeated efforts by voluntary euthanasia proponents in that jurisdiction, dating back to the mid 1930s, to introduce legislation permitting active voluntary euthanasia.

---

[105] See pp. 247–8 above.
[106] Since the inception of the VES in 1935, doctors have been actively involved in the running of the society, with a number of well known doctors holding senior positions in the society; e.g. Lord Moynihan, eminent surgeon, was the first President of the society and more recently, Dr Jonathon Miller has held office as Vice-President.

Another significant development in the United Kingdom has been the growing evidence from surveys that substantial support exists for the legalization of active voluntary euthanasia amongst members of the medical profession. These survey results contradict the findings of the BMA reports that the profession remains opposed to the legalization of active voluntary euthanasia. Moreover, the BMA purports to represent the majority of doctors in the United Kingdom.[107] However, on the basis of these survey results, there is strong evidence to suggest that the rejection of active voluntary euthanasia in the official reports of the BMA, most recently in 1988, is contrary to the views of the medical profession in the United Kingdom as a whole.

The BMA policy, first declared in 1950, has been unequivocally to condemn active voluntary euthanasia.[108] In 1969, the representative body of the BMA passed a resolution confirming this position and instructing the BMA council to give this view full publicity.[109] Pursuant to this resolution, the Board of Science and Education of the BMA appointed a panel of ten doctors, chaired by Dr Hugh Trowell, to consider the problem. However, the panel was effectively bound by the earlier resolution of the representative body in 1969 condemning active voluntary euthanasia, so its role was not really to examine the problem afresh, but simply to supply suitable arguments in support of the decision which had already been made. It was, in all the circumstances, not surprising that the report of the special panel, released in 1971, roundly condemned active voluntary euthanasia.[110] The report contained most of the standard arguments which had previously been raised in the euthanasia debate. It was, for example, claimed that most people, even those suffering from cancer, die in peace and dignity, thereby implying that active voluntary euthanasia was unnecessary and that doctors saw no need for legislation. In response to suggestions that some doctors were already performing active voluntary euthanasia, the panel expressed the view that if this does occur, it is confined to the very few and cannot be condoned. In rejecting legislation permitting active voluntary euthanasia, much emphasis was placed on the perceived dangers of such legislation and the impossibility of providing adequate safeguards. The report concluded that:

Euthanasia legislation would be a licence for the killing of human beings . . . Euthanasia cannot be accepted by the medical profession; in rejecting it doctors will be

---

[107] Approximately 80% of doctors in the United Kingdom belong to the BMA.

[108] See Trowell, *The Unfinished Debate on Euthanasia*, above Ch. 2 n. 2, at 19–20. For a statement of the current BMA position see BMA, *Medical Ethics Today: Its Practice and Philosophy* (London, 1993) 175–9.

[109] Trowell, *The Unfinished Debate on Euthanasia*, above Ch. 2 n. 2, at 19–20.

[110] BMA, *The Problem of Euthanasia: A Report by a Special Panel Appointed by the Board of Science and Education of the British Medical Association* (London, 1971) (extracted in Trowell, *The Unfinished Debate on Euthanasia*, above Ch. 2 n. 2, Appendix A, 151–8).

supported by the majority of laymen, who share the belief that the deliberate killing of a helpless person can never be condoned . . . Killing patients is no part of the work of doctors and nurses.[111]

The report met with sharp criticism from the Voluntary Euthanasia Society.[112] The society accused the panel of having reached its conclusions even before it had commenced to sit, and claimed that in doing so, the panel had failed to address adequately fundamental issues, including the patient's right of self-determination. The society also alleged that the panel had ignored relevant information from National Opinion Poll surveys of general practitioners conducted in 1964 and 1965. These surveys revealed that nearly half of the practitioners polled had been confronted with a request for active euthanasia (48.6 per cent), many believed that if active voluntary euthanasia were made legal in certain circumstances, appropriate safeguards could be devised (44.3 per cent answered yes, 43.5 per cent answered no to this question) and further, more than one-third of the respondents (35.8 per cent) said that they would be prepared to administer active voluntary euthanasia if it became legally permissible.

For many years, the 1971 report of the special panel was taken to represent the position of the BMA, and it was not until 1986 that steps were taken for a review of the association's guidelines on euthanasia. At the 1986 annual representative meeting of the BMA, a resolution was passed urging the BMA 'to reconsider its policy on euthanasia'. The BMA's council subsequently approved a recommendation from the association's central ethical committee providing for the establishment of a working party on euthanasia and setting out its terms of reference.[113] The working party, chaired by Sir Henry Yellowlees, met during 1987–88. In May 1988, its report was considered at a meeting of the BMA's council at which the council agreed that the report should be published to restate the association's advice on euthanasia.

As with the earlier BMA report, the 1988 report of the working party[114] restates many of the well established arguments against active voluntary euthanasia which were considered in the preceding chapter.[115] The report

---

[111] Trowell, *The Unfinished Debate on Euthanasia,* above Ch. 2 n. 2, at 157–8.

[112] Voluntary Euthanasia Society, 'Doctors and Euthanasia: A Rejoinder to the British Medical Association's Report "The Problem of Euthanasia"' (1971) (extracted in Trowell, *The Unfinished Debate on Euthanasia,* above Ch. 2 n. 2, Appendix B, 161–71).

[113] The terms of reference for the Working Party were: to examine: a) problems relating to euthanasia, terminal illness, and suicide; b) UK law relating to suicide and homicide; c) guidance and instructions given by different religions, e.g. Protestant, Catholic, Jewish, Hindu, Buddhist; d) the present theoretical position in the UK as stated in the BMA *Handbook of Medical Ethics*; and e) current practice and trends in euthanasia in other countries, for example the Netherlands. (See the Foreword to the Report).

[114] BMA, Working Party Report, *Euthanasia,* above Ch. 3 n. 1.

[115] For example, that euthanasia is unnecessary (at 12); that its legalization would be socially dangerous and would undermine the doctor/patient relationship (at 17–20, 59).

upholds the distinction between active and passive euthanasia and recommends that an active intervention to terminate another person's life should remain illegal. Whilst acknowledging the importance of patient autonomy and the right of patients to decline treatment, the working party was of the view that patients do not have the right to demand treatment which doctors cannot in good conscience provide. The working party stated that requests for active voluntary euthanasia are requests for doctors to act in ways that are at variance with all their training and inclinations, and that the medical profession has a right to limit patient autonomy where the patient demands some treatment or action that runs counter to settled and informed medical opinion. It was found that an active intervention by a doctor to terminate a patient's life falls within this category, and patients should not be able to require their doctors to collaborate in their death. In the words of the working party: 'We do not, at present, see that any general policy condoning medical interventions to terminate life can be reconciled with the commitments of good medical practice. As a profession, we must stand by the commitments that lead us to preserve life and meet suffering creatively'.[116]

Evidence of public opinion polls indicating widespread agreement with the idea of active voluntary euthanasia was summarily dismissed, *inter alia*, on the grounds that the working party did not accept that 'tailoring what is morally right to the opinion of the majority is necessarily correct'.

The working party sought to bolster its views by invoking the distinction between intention and consequences, which it described as an important reference point in the moral assessment of any action. Thus, the distinction between active and passive euthanasia was justified on the basis that a decision to withdraw treatment which has become a burden and is no longer of continuing benefit to a patient, has a different intent to one which involves ending the life of a person. On the same grounds, the working party was prepared to accept drug treatment which may involve a risk to the person's life if the sole intention is to relieve illness, pain, distress, or suffering. However, the working party warned that any doctor, compelled by conscience to intervene to end a person's life, would have to be prepared to face the closest scrutiny of this action that the law might wish to make.

The report concludes with a restatement of the central position of the working party:

The law should not be changed and the deliberate taking of a human life should remain a crime. This rejection of a change in the law to permit doctors to intervene to end a person's life is not just a subordination of individual well being to social policy. It is instead, an affirmation of the supreme value of the individual, no matter how worthless and hopeless that individual may feel.[117]

[116] BMA, Working Party Report, *Euthanasia*, above Ch. 3 n. 1, at 19–20.
[117] Ibid. at 69.

The report of the working party is undoubtedly of significance, ostensibly involving a full review of the BMA's guidance on euthanasia. This is to be contrasted with the report prepared by the special panel in 1971, since the panel was effectively bound by an earlier resolution of the representative body condemning euthanasia. The working party report therefore represents the first major review of the association's guidelines ever to be undertaken.

The report has, however, attracted considerable criticism from a variety of sources.[118] It has been criticized on the grounds that it is a superficial document which fails to present fairly the arguments of the opponents, even to the point of misrepresenting the opponents' position. Furthermore, the report has been criticized for its conservatism and lack of originality. In particular, it has been attacked on the grounds that it perpetuates traditional, but arguably irrelevant, distinctions between active and passive euthanasia, and between intention and consequences. Critics claim that, as a result, the report is flawed by inconsistencies and fails adequately to deal with the complex problems in this area.

A particularly disturbing criticism which has been levelled at the report is that it gives the impression of bias towards a predetermined outcome, leaving the reader in some doubt as to whether there was a genuine attempt to review critically the BMA's guidance on euthanasia. Because the traditional opposition of the medical profession to active voluntary euthanasia is so deeply entrenched, it was all the more necessary for the inquiry to be conducted objectively and impartially. One of the specific complaints made by the Voluntary Euthanasia Society which illustrates its concern in this regard was that when it became necessary for one of the members of the working party (Dr Jonathon Miller, known for his pro-euthanasia views) to withdraw from the project, the chairman of the working party refused to accept a doctor sympathetic to, or at least open-minded about active voluntary euthanasia as a substitute.[119]

Aside from these criticisms, probably the most serious shortcoming of the report is its cursory treatment of opinion poll results gathered in the United Kingdom. Over the years, a number of opinion polls have been commissioned by the Voluntary Euthanasia Society to ascertain the views of general practitioners and the public generally on the issue of active voluntary euthanasia. Of particular relevance to this report was a telephone survey of some 300 British general practitioners, commissioned by the Voluntary Euthanasia Society and carried out by National Opinion Poll Market Re-

---

[118] e.g. Nowell-Smith, P., 'Euthanasia and the Doctors—A Rejection of the BMA's Report' (1989) 15 *JMed. Ethics* 124; Higgs, R., 'Not the Last Word on Euthanasia' (1988) 296 BMJ 1348; Beloff, J., 'Why the BMA is Wrong' (1989) Jan. *VES Newsletter* 1.

[119] Minutes of the Annual General Meeting (1988) 35 *VES Newsletter* 2.

search Ltd in 1987.[120] As part of that survey, general practitioners were asked: 'Some people say that the law should allow adults to receive medical help to an immediate peaceful death if they suffer from an incurable physical illness that is intolerable to them, provided they have previously requested such help in writing. Do you agree or disagree with this?' 30 per cent of respondent general practitioners said that they agreed with this statement, 59 per cent said that they disagreed with it and 9 per cent had mixed views. A further question was then put to the general practitioners to gauge whether they would consider performing active voluntary euthanasia if the law were changed. The question was in the following terms: 'At the moment euthanasia is illegal. Suppose the law is changed to permit voluntary euthanasia and there was a patient on your list, whose case you knew well, who suffered from an incurable physical illness that was intolerable to them. If that patient made a signed request that you end his/her life, would you consider doing so or not?' 35 per cent of the general practitioners polled said that they would definitely consider euthanasia in these circumstances and 10 per cent said that they might possibly do so. The remainder said that they would not consider euthanasia in these circumstances. These results indicate considerable support within the medical profession in the United Kingdom for active voluntary euthanasia and consequently cast serious doubt on some of the assumptions made in the working party report.

To a large extent, the arguments raised in the report against active voluntary euthanasia were based on the need to uphold the traditions of the medical profession, with various references to active euthanasia running counter to doctors' intuition, counter to settled and informed medical opinion, and the basic ethical commitments of medicine.[121] Such comments clearly imply that there is widespread agreement within the profession on the issue of active voluntary euthanasia; indeed, the whole tenor of the report is to assert categorically that active voluntary euthanasia is condemned by the medical profession as a whole. Significantly, however, no attempt was made by the working party to provide evidence in support of these assertions, for example, by conducting a survey of its members to assess their views on the subject.

In presenting its case for reform, the Voluntary Euthanasia Society had submitted results of opinion polls to the working party as evidence of support for active voluntary euthanasia amongst both the general public and general practitioners in the United Kingdom. The treatment of this evidence in the report is unsatisfactory, to say the least. Not only is the crucial evidence from the survey of general practitioners completely omit-

[120] National Opinion Poll Market Research, *Attitudes Towards Euthanasia Among Britain's GPs,* NOP Market Research Ltd. (London, 1987).
[121] BMA Working Party Report, *Euthanasia,* above Ch. 3 n. 1, at 19–20.

ted, but the position of the Voluntary Euthanasia Society is seriously misrepresented. The report states: 'The Voluntary Euthanasia Society (VES) has attempted to strengthen the case for active termination of life by conducting public opinion polls which purport to show widespread agreement with the idea of voluntary active euthanasia'.[122]

The language used here, in particular, the word 'purport' carries overtones that the results were somehow manipulated or fabricated, and incorrectly suggests that the Voluntary Euthanasia Society had itself conducted the polls in question, when, in fact, the working party had been given documentation which clearly indicated that the polls had been conducted by National Opinion Poll Market Research Ltd. Further, the report sought to attack the form of questions used in the polls without fairly presenting the full picture. The report is also to be criticized for its bald claim that opinion poll evidence is in any event suspect. As has already been noted, the working party rejected the idea that one should tailor what is morally right to the opinion of the majority. This approach may well be sound, but the report fails to acknowledge that this argument can work both ways: if doctors' views are not in accord with the general population, they cannot plead their own majority opinion to have any more weight than their arguments warrant. Instead, the report reflects double standards, with frequent reliance being made on arguments based on majority medical opinion.

Even more telling was the complete failure of the report to address the opinion poll evidence which indicates a substantial proportion of doctors in the United Kingdom support active voluntary euthanasia and would consider practising it if it were made legal. Evidence had been made available to the working party regarding attitudes of British general practitioners on the subject of active voluntary euthanasia which would have been particularly relevant in light of the fact that the working party had made no attempt to gather its own evidence with regard to these matters. However, this material, which would cast serious doubt on the view expressed in the report that the medical profession universally condemns legalized active euthanasia, is not referred to in the report.

Although the report has attracted considerable criticism, the process of inquiry undertaken by the BMA has nevertheless been significant, indicating some preparedness on the part of the British medical profession to reevaluate its stance with regard to active voluntary euthanasia. Whilst ultimately reiterating the medical profession's traditional opposition to active euthanasia, the report has undoubtedly made some contribution to the reform process by fostering debate on the issue within the medical profession and the community generally. However, in the light of the survey

---

[122] Ibid. at 41.

evidence regarding medical opinion on the subject, serious doubt must be cast on the underlying assumption in the report that active voluntary euthanasia is condemned by the medical profession as a body. This evidence, and its notable omission in the report, must clearly affect the credibility and validity of the report as a whole. It should be noted that since the 1988 report, the BMA has reaffirmed its opposition to the legalization of active voluntary euthanasia.[123]

Another noteworthy development in the United Kingdom which supports earlier findings about doctors' attitudes to active voluntary euthanasia is the survey undertaken in 1993 among a sample of some 400 National Health Service doctors (involving comparable numbers of general practitioners and hospital consultants) by means of a postal questionnaire.[124] A number of the survey questions were directed to establishing the attitudes of respondents to active euthanasia. In one of these questions the doctors were asked whether they thought that the law on euthanasia in Britain should be similar to that in the Netherlands. 47 per cent of the respondent doctors agreed, 33 per cent disagreed and 19 per cent were undecided. In another question, doctors were asked whether they would consider practising active euthanasia if it was legal. Almost half of the respondents (46 per cent) indicated that they would consider practising active euthanasia in these circumstances (33 per cent disagreed and 21 per cent were undecided)—significantly more than the 35 per cent in the survey of general practitioners in 1987. There was greater support for legalization of active voluntary euthanasia and willingness to practise it amongst general practitioners than amongst the consultants. Significant associations were found to exist between a doctor holding a religious belief, the belief that the law should not be changed, and being unwilling to practise active euthanasia if it became legal.

These findings have largely been confirmed by a major national survey of general practitioners and hospital doctors in the United Kingdom undertaken by the popular medical journal *Doctor*.[125] Of a total of 2,150 respondent doctors, over a third (35 per cent) had received requests from patients to take active steps, and more than a quarter (27 per cent) said that they had wished to comply at some time with a request for active euthanasia. The survey also found that general practitioners were more likely to want to comply with such requests than hospital doctors—51 per cent of the general practitioners who had been asked for active euthanasia by a patient wanted to comply with the request, compared with 47 per cent of hospital doctors.

[123] 1993 BMA Annual General Meeting, reported in *The Times*, 30 June 1993.
[124] Ward, B. and Tate. P., 'Attitudes Among NHS Doctors to Requests for Euthanasia' (1994) 308 BMJ 1332. Reference was made earlier to the results of this survey with regard to patients' requests for euthanasia and doctors' practices: see pp. 131, 135–7 above.
[125] Andrews, J., 'Euthanasia Dilemma Splits the Profession' (1995) *Doctor* 9 Feb., 43.

Those general practitioners who had received multiple requests were more likely to say that they wanted to comply and they were also more likely to want to change the law on euthanasia. 44 per cent of the respondent doctors supported a change to the law to make active voluntary euthanasia legal. Support for change to the law was greatest amongst those doctors who had more recently qualified, and doctors who had received more requests for active voluntary euthanasia. 43 per cent of the respondent doctors said that they would consider practising active voluntary euthanasia if it were legalized. There were some consistent geographical differences in the experience and attitudes of the respondent doctors. For example, the general practitioners in Northern Ireland were far less likely to receive requests for active euthanasia than elsewhere, and less than one-third said they had wished to comply with a request, compared with 63 per cent of the respondent doctors from the South West of England. The survey report states that reasons for these differences are unclear but that religious beliefs, for example, in Northern Ireland, may play a part. Differences in outcome were also noted across age categories, with younger doctors (described for the purposes of this study as under 35 years of age) being more likely to support active voluntary euthanasia and consider practising it if it were legalized than older doctors (over 55 years of age): more than half of the general practitioners who would consider practising it were under the age of 35, while 6 out of 10 of those who would not were over 55.

Another interesting finding of this study was that the great majority of the respondent doctors (83 per cent) believed that their training did not equip them to deal with euthanasia and they felt ill-prepared to cope with euthanasia requests from patients. Significantly, the issue of *Doctor* which reported this survey contained an editorial, which drew attention to the extent of support amongst doctors for change to the law and questioned what the key medical organizations were doing to canvass their members' views or to offer support, advice, and training.[126]

Taken together, the results of the survey of the National Health Service doctors and that undertaken by the journal *Doctor*, reveal considerable consistency in results, with almost half of the respondent doctors in support of reform of the law (47 per cent NHS, 44 per cent *Doctor*), and very similar numbers indicating that they would consider practising active voluntary euthanasia if it were legal (46 per cent NHS, 43 per cent *Doctor*).

The reaction to the prosecution of Dr Cox in 1992 is further evidence of the changing attitude of the British medical profession to the issue of active voluntary euthanasia. As noted in an earlier chapter, Dr Cox was convicted of the attempted murder of one of his patients who had died following the

---

[126] 'It's Time to Speak Out on Euthanasia' (1995) *Doctor* 9 Feb., 27.

administration of a lethal dose of potassium chloride.[127] His conviction, and the imposition of a 12-month suspended prison sentence, came as a shock to many doctors who had tended to assume that a jury would not convict in these circumstances. The *Cox* case has, as a result, been cause for serious reflection within the medical profession regarding the state of the present law. In an editorial in the leading *British Medical Journal*, the editor, Richard Smith, wrote that it was time for the British to think deeply about euthanasia.[128] Commenting on the reaction to the verdict and sentence, he noted that the law is in effect the codification of the will of the people, and when there is such tension between a legal verdict and the people's thinking then it is time to reconsider the law. He suggested that a Royal Commission be established to examine this issue, and went on to foreshadow the need for legislation to bring the law in step with modern thinking and to clarify what is acceptable.

Following his conviction, Dr Cox's case came before the General Medical Council's professional conduct committee which is the doctors' regulatory body. Cox pleaded guilty to the charge but told the committee that although he had expedited the death of his patient, it was in any case imminent. The committee, which has wide powers, including the power to strike a doctor off the medical register, reprimanded and admonished Dr Cox, but gave permission for him to continue working as a hospital consultant. This is unquestionably a very lenient outcome and suggests that the committee sympathized with, if not condoned, the doctor's actions.

Also worthy of note is the recent editorial which was published in the July 1995 issue of the *Lancet* which expressly renounces its earlier position as stated in 1960 when it had pleaded for decisions about hastening death to be left to doctors, not codified in law.[129]

Another important development in the United Kingdom with regard to the subject of active voluntary euthanasia has been the work of the Institute of Medical Ethics Working Party on the Ethics of Prolonging Life and Assisting Death. In response to frequent calls for review, the Institute of Medical Ethics set up a multi-disciplinary working party to investigate and report on the ethics of prolonging life and assisting death. The individuals invited to serve on the working party were drawn from a number of disciplines, and were chosen with the intention of representing a broad spectrum of ethical viewpoints on the subject. In September 1990, the working party released a discussion paper, published in the *Lancet*,[130] in which it examined in what circumstances, if any, a doctor is ethically justified in assisting

---

[127] See pp. 143–5 above.

[128] Smith, R., 'Euthanasia: Time For a Royal Commission' (1992) 305 BMJ 728.

[129] 'The Final Autonomy' (1995) 346 *Lancet* 259.

[130] Institute of Medical Ethics, Working Party on the Ethics of Prolonging Life and Assisting Death, 'Assisted Death' (1990) 336 *Lancet* 610.

death.[131] After considering some of the commonly raised objections to assisting death, and the moral debate as to whether there is any difference between killing and letting die, the working party suggested that in circumstances where a patient is suffering from a terminal illness, where distressing symptoms cannot be relieved, and the patient asks to have his or her life ended, the balance of the moral argument shifts towards asking why death should not be assisted; the greater the unrelieved pain and distress, the more ethical is a doctor's decision to assist death if the patient desires it. The majority of the working party concluded that:

A doctor, acting in good conscience, is ethically justified in assisting death if the need to relieve intense and unceasing pain or distress caused by an incurable illness greatly outweighs the benefit to the patient of further prolonging his life ... Assistance of death, however is not justified until the doctor and the clinical team are sure that the patient's pain and distress cannot be relieved by any other means—pharmacological, surgical, psychological, or social.[132]

The discussion paper of the working party, and in particular, its endorsement of assisted death in certain circumstances, is clearly a development of enormous significance. It represents an unequivocal rejection of the position of the BMA working party in its 1988 report and is likely to be the focus for ongoing debate in this area in the United Kingdom.

B. USA

As has been the case in the United Kingdom, many notable and respected doctors in the USA have given their support to the legalization of active voluntary euthanasia and have contributed significantly to the voluntary euthanasia movement.[133] However, the American Medical Association (AMA)—the largest medical association in the USA—and other professional medical associations, whilst endorsing passive euthanasia in some circumstances,[134] have consistently rejected active voluntary euthanasia.[135]

Despite this official rejection, there are clear indications of growing support within the medical profession generally for legalization of active voluntary euthanasia, or 'physician aid in dying,' as it is often referred to in the USA. Some of the most reliable indicators of changing attitudes on this issue are the various opinion poll surveys which have been conducted over the years. These surveys provide strong evidence that a growing number of doctors are in favour of legalization and would be prepared to practise

---

[131] For the purposes of the discussion paper, 'assisting death' is used to refer to an act by a doctor with the deliberate intention of hastening the death of a patient with a terminal illness.
[132] Institute of Medical Ethics, Discussion Paper 'Assisted Death', above n. 130, at 613.
[133] For detailed historical coverage of the position in the USA see Russell, *Freedom to Die*, above Ch. 4 n. 81, at Chs. 4–7.
[134] See p. 127 n. 1 above.   [135] See p. 128 above.

active voluntary euthanasia if it were made legal. In addition to these surveys, there have been a number of other developments in the USA in recent years, paralleling developments in other jurisdictions, which reflect growing interest and support within the medical profession for active voluntary euthanasia. These developments strongly suggest that the traditional opposition of the AMA and similar organizations may no longer reflect the views of the majority of their members. Whilst no official inquiry has yet been undertaken by the professional medical associations in the USA to review the profession's traditional opposition to active voluntary euthanasia, there may be some evidence of a possible softening of the official position of the AMA.

Over the years, quite a number of surveys of doctors' attitudes to active voluntary euthanasia have been conducted in the USA, including a number of small scale surveys in the 1960s and 1970s which found only fairly modest support (in the range of 15–30 per cent).[136] In the late 1980s, a number of surveys were undertaken of the medical profession in California in the light of a reform initiative being proposed in that state for the legalization of active voluntary euthanasia[137]—a survey commissioned by the Hemlock Society in 1987 to gauge attitudes and practices of Californian doctors with regard to active voluntary euthanasia[138] and a survey undertaken by the San Francisco Medical Society reported in 1988.

One of the matters that the Hemlock survey (involving some 588 respondents) sought to assess was the extent to which the illegality of active voluntary euthanasia was a relevant factor in the decision-making for those doctors who had rejected a patient's request for active euthanasia. Illegality clearly played a role for a majority of these doctors (79.5 per cent). Of the doctors who had rejected a patient's request to hasten death, 16.5 per cent did so solely because the action was illegal, 23 per cent gave this as the primary reason for rejecting the request, while 40 per cent said that this was part of the reason. 20 per cent said that the illegality of the action was not at all the reason for rejecting the request.[139]

The Hemlock survey also sought to ascertain doctors' attitudes to taking active steps to bring about a patient's death at the patient's request. When asked if it was sometimes right to agree to hasten a patient's death, 62.5 per

---

[136] Williams, R., 'Our Role in the Generation, Modification and Termination of Life' (1969) 124 *Arch. Internal Med.* 215 (survey of members of the Association of American Physicians and the Association of Professors of Medicine); Brown, N. et al., 'The Preservation of Life' (1970) 211 JAMA 76 (survey of doctors at two Seattle hospitals).

[137] For discussion of these developments, see pp. 364–6 below.

[138] The survey instrument used for the Hemlock survey was identical to that developed earlier by Kuhse and Singer for the survey of attitudes and practices of doctors in the Australian State of Victoria discussed below.

[139] Note, 'Most California Doctors Favour New Euthanasia Law' (1988) 31 *Hemlock Q* 1–2.

cent of the respondent doctors said it was sometimes right to do so, while 37.5 per cent disagreed.

Respondents were also asked whether it would be a good thing if a situation similar to that prevailing in the Netherlands existed in California, allowing doctors to end the lives of patients in certain circumstances without the risk of criminal prosecution. 67 per cent of the respondents agreed that it would be a good thing, and more than half (58 per cent) of the doctors felt that their professional medical association should take a similar stand to that taken by the Royal Dutch Medical Association.[140] The doctors were also asked whether the law should be changed to permit active voluntary euthanasia. More than two-thirds (68.7 per cent) believed that the law should be changed. Just over one half (51 per cent of the respondents) said that they would practise active voluntary euthanasia if it were legal.

Also in 1988, but some months after the release of the results of the Hemlock survey in California, the findings were published of a survey of doctors undertaken by the San Francisco Medical Society. The aim of this survey was to gauge the attitudes to active voluntary euthanasia of members of the Society in the light of reform initiatives being proposed in the State of California for the legalization of active voluntary physician-assisted euthanasia.[141] The survey covered some 1,743 San Francisco doctors, 676 of whom responded (a total response rate of 38.8 per cent). The overwhelming majority of the doctors surveyed supported the view that patients should have the option of requesting active voluntary euthanasia when faced with incurable terminal illness: 70 per cent in favour, with only 23 per cent against.[142] Another of the questions was directed at ascertaining members' views as to the doctors' role with regard to active voluntary euthanasia. More than half (54 per cent) were of the view that if legal, active voluntary euthanasia should be carried out by physicians, while 26 per cent disagreed (11 per cent unsure and 9 per cent giving no answer to this question). On the question of preparedness to perform active voluntary euthanasia if it were made legal, 45 per cent of the respondents indicated that they would, 35 per cent said no (18 per cent were unsure and 2 per cent gave no answer).

The survey conducted by the San Francisco Medical Society is significant. It was the first survey of its kind undertaken by a professional medical association in any of the jurisdictions under consideration.[143] Not only was an anonymous opinion survey of members undertaken, but the results of the survey were made public. Prior to the survey, the San Francisco Medical

[140] For discussion of the position in the Netherlands, see Ch. 7.

[141] Heilig, S., 'The SFMS Euthanasia Survey: Results and Analyses' (1988) *San Francisco Med.* 24–6 May, 34.

[142] Ibid. at 24. 7% of respondents were unsure and 1% did not answer this question.

[143] The Canadian Medical Association has since surveyed the opinion of its members: see discussion on pp. 314–18 below.

Society did not have an official position on the subject of active voluntary euthanasia and on the basis of the survey results, the society decided not to take any such position, deferring to the individual and personal convictions of each member physician. This course of events can only be seen as evidence of a growing willingness within the medical profession to obtain an informed view on the subject and possibly re-evaluate its traditional opposition to the legalization of active voluntary euthanasia.

Since these two surveys were undertaken in California, there have been quite a number of other surveys of doctors' attitudes and practices in other parts of the USA which provide insights into the changing attitudes of the medical profession with regard to active voluntary euthanasia. In 1988, a large poll of doctors' attitudes and practices was conducted by the Center for Health Ethics and Policy Graduate School of Public Affairs, University of Colorado at Denver.[144] This survey involved a questionnaire sent to all of the 7,095 doctors in Colorado of which a total of 2,218 responded. Although dealing primarily with passive euthanasia, the survey revealed that 60 per cent of the respondent doctors had attended patients for whom they believed active voluntary euthanasia would be justifiable if it were legal, and of those who had encountered such patients, 58.9 per cent indicated that they would have personally been willing to administer a lethal drug if such measures were allowed by law.

Following the defeat in Washington State of Initiative 119 which would have legalized physician-assisted suicide and active voluntary euthanasia,[145] a postal survey was undertaken of physicians in the State of Washington in 1992.[146] Responses were received from 938 of the 1,355 physicians who had been sent a questionnaire (a response rate of 69 per cent). The questionnaire sought physicians' opinions with respect to both active voluntary euthanasia and physician-assisted suicide. 54 per cent of the respondents thought that euthanasia[147] should be legal in some situations (38 per cent disagreed, 8 per cent neutral). 53 per cent of the respondents were of the view that physician-assisted suicide[148] should be legal in some situations (37 per cent disagreed, 10 per cent neutral). As to their willingness to participate in these practices, 33 per cent of respondents stated that they would be

---

[144] *Withholding and Withdrawing Life-Sustaining Treatment: A Survey of Opinions and Experiences of Colorado Physicians* (Colorado, 1988).

[145] See further pp. 366–8 below.

[146] Cohen, J. et al., 'Attitudes Toward Assisted Suicide and Euthanasia Among Physicians in Washington State' (1994) 331 *New Eng.JMed.* 89. For the purposes of discussing this and other US surveys below, the term 'physician' rather than 'doctor' is used in accordance with the terminology used in the USA.

[147] The wording used in the survey was the 'deliberate administration of an overdose of medication to an ill patient at his or her request with the primary intent to end his or her life'.

[148] This was described in the survey instrument as 'the prescription of medication (e.g. narcotics or barbiturates) or the counselling of an ill patient so he or she may use an overdose to end his or her life'.

willing to perform euthanasia (58 per cent disagreed, 9 per cent neutral) compared with 40 per cent who stated that they would be willing to assist a patient in committing suicide (49 per cent disagreed, 10 per cent neutral).

In other studies in the USA of physicians' attitudes to physician-assisted suicide it has been shown that there is substantial support for legalization of this practice.[149] In a large study of Oregon physicians[150] conducted after the passage of the Oregon Death with Dignity Act but whilst it was under constitutional challenge, it was found that 60 per cent of the respondents thought that physician-assisted suicide should be legal in some cases.[151] Nearly half of the respondents (46 per cent) indicated that they might be willing to prescribe a lethal dose of medication if it were legal to do so. The authors of this study conclude that Oregon physicians have a more favourable attitude to physician-assisted suicide and are more willing to participate than other groups of physicians previously surveyed in the USA.

A number of the recent studies have sought to examine variables in physicians' attitudes towards the practice of euthanasia. In a 1991 survey of physicians' attitudes conducted in Wisconsin it was found that religious affiliation was the demographic characteristic most significantly associated with respondent physicians' willingness to perform euthanasia, with Christian fundamentalists and Catholics being far less willing to perform euthanasia in any circumstances, compared with Protestant and Jewish respondents and those of no specified religion. There was also some correlation between speciality type and willingness to perform legalized euthanasia, with practitioners in family or general practice generally being more willing to perform it.[152]

The significance of religious affiliation to attitudes to physician-assisted death has been further highlighted in a study of the attitudes and behaviour of Michigan oncologists.[153] This study involved a questionnaire which had been mailed out to all oncologists in the State of Michigan in 1993 (sample size of 250). Responses were received from 154 physicians (overall response rate 61.6 per cent). This study found that respondent oncologists who listed no religious affiliation had significantly more favourable attitudes to physician-assisted suicide and active euthanasia than Catholics and Protes-

---

[149] Apart from the Oregon study, mentioned below, note also a recent study of Michigan doctors: when asked to choose between legalization of physician-assisted suicide and a complete ban, 56% supported legalization (37% preferred a ban and 8% were uncertain.): Bachman, J. et al., 'Attitudes of Michigan Physicians and the Public Toward Legalizing Physician-Assisted Suicide and Voluntary Euthanasia' (1996) 334 *New Eng.J Med.* 303, 306.

[150] Questionnaires were sent to 3,944 physicians; 2,761 responded: a response rate of 70%.

[151] Lee, M. et al., 'Legalizing Assisted Suicide—Views of Physician in Oregon' (1996) 334 *New Eng.J Med.* 310, 311.

[152] On this point see also Duberstein, P. *et al.*, 'Attitudes Toward Self-Determined Death: A Survey of Primary Care Physicians' (1995) 43 *J Am.Geriatric Society* 395, 399.

[153] Doukas, D. et al., 'Attitudes and Behaviours on Physician-Assisted Death: A Study of Michigan Oncologists' (1995) 13 *J Clin.Oncology* 1055.

tants. With regard to one of the questions put: 'would you provide the means or instruction by which a patient could take his or her own life', 45 per cent of the group with no religious affiliation responded affirmatively compared with 25 per cent of the Jewish oncologists, 10 per cent of the Catholics, and 9 per cent of the Protestants. In another question, the oncologists were asked whether they would ever administer medication with the intent to cause death. 18 per cent of the group with no religious affiliation responded affirmatively, compared with 12 per cent of the Jewish oncologists, 10 per cent of the Protestants, and 5 per cent of the Catholics. The researchers conclude that in the light of these results, religious conviction may play a powerful role in future debate on the place of physician-assisted dying in health care.

Similarly, in studies principally focused on physicians' attitudes to the legalization of physician-assisted suicide, religion has been shown to be the most important personal characteristic influencing attitudes to legalization: those who considered religion very important in their lives were much less likely both to support legalization and to consider personal involvement in physician-assisted suicide than were people for whom religion was less important.[154] Another factor which has been identified as of some relevance is age, there being a slight tendency for older respondents to be less likely to support legalization.[155]

When compared with the available survey results from the 1960s and 1970s which had indicated support for active voluntary euthanasia in the range of 15–30 per cent, the more recent results appear to reflect growing support amongst the medical profession for active voluntary euthanasia (and physician-assisted suicide), with results now ranging from 54 per cent (State of Washington) to 70 per cent (San Francisco survey) in support of reform. This development is consistent with the increase in support for active voluntary euthanasia reflected in public opinion polls in the USA as a whole.

Whilst the survey evidence provides perhaps the clearest indication of changing attitudes to active voluntary euthanasia and physician-assisted suicide amongst physicians in the USA, there have been a number of other noteworthy developments which reflect growing acceptance of these practices within the medical profession. A striking development which clearly signals change in this area is the increased level of informed debate on the subject. It is a subject which is now openly being discussed amongst the

---

[154] Bachman, et al., 'Attitudes of Michigan Physicians and the Public Toward Legalizing Physician-Assisted Suicide and Voluntary Euthanasia', above n. 149, 308. See also Lee, et al., 'Legalizing Assisted Suicide—Views of Physician in Oregon', above Ch. 3 n. 21, 312, 314.

[155] Bachman, et al., Attitudes of Michigan Physicians and the Public Toward Legalizing Physician-Assisted Suicide and Voluntary Euthanasia', above n. 149, at 308, but see the contrary finding by Lee, et al., 'Legalizing Assisted Suicide—Views of Physician in Oregon', above Ch. 3 n. 21, at 312, 314.

medical profession and frequently features in the pages of the medical journals and other medical literature in the USA. More and more physicians, many of whom are well-known and respected, have publicly declared their willingness to re-examine the appropriateness of the current prohibitions on active voluntary euthanasia and physician-assisted suicide.[156]

Illustrative of this trend has been the emerging consensus amongst a group of eminent physicians regarding care of the dying. This came about through the initiative of the Society for the Right to Die (now called Choice in Dying) which had sponsored a number of conferences for a select group of physicians in the USA from diverse professional and institutional backgrounds, with the object of establishing guidelines in the care of dying patients.[157] The deliberations and conclusions of this panel of eminent physicians have subsequently been published in a series of special articles in the *New England Journal of Medicine*[158] and have attracted widespread publicity. At the second of these conferences, a group of twelve physicians considered the physicians' response to the dying patient who is rational and desires suicide or euthanasia. In the publication which followed, tacit approval was given to physician-assisted suicide, with ten of the twelve physicians supporting the view that it is not immoral for a physician to assist in the rational suicide of a terminally ill patient. And whilst active voluntary euthanasia was not openly advocated, the matter was dealt with in a sympathetic and even-handed manner, with the group refraining from outright condemnation of the practice. Although euthanasia opponents have sought to undermine the relevance of these conferences, and the resulting publications,[159] these developments are of obvious significance. Not only have they attracted widespread publicity, but they have undoubtedly been influential in promoting understanding and acceptance within the medical profession of physician-assisted suicide and even active voluntary euthanasia.

Another noteworthy development was the publication of an article in the *American Medical Association Journal*, in which a doctor admitted to having taken active steps to hasten the death of a patient dying of cancer. The article, entitled 'It's Over Debbie',[160] which appeared in the 8 January 1988 issue of the journal, briefly recounted the experience of a resident doctor who was called up in the middle of the night to attend to Debbie, a 20-year-old female patient, dying of ovarian cancer. Her only words to the doctor

---

[156] e.g. Angell, M., 'Euthanasia' (1988) 319 *New Eng.JMed.* 1348; Cassel, C. and Meier, D., 'Morals and Moralism in the Debate Over Euthanasia and Assisted Suicide' (1990) 323 *New Eng.JMed.* 750.

[157] See p. 276 above.

[158] Wanzer, et al., 'The Physician's Responsibility to the Hopelessly Ill Patient', above n. 45; Wanzer, et al., The Physician's Responsibility Toward Hopelessly Ill Patients: A Second Look', above Ch. 2 n. 101.

[159] For example, alleging bias in the selection of doctors in the group, and the fact that they were sponsored by the Right to Die Society which is a pro-euthanasia organization.

[160] (1988) 259 JAMA 272.

were 'let's get this over with', to which the doctor responded by administering 20 mg of morphine intravenously. The doctor recollected in this piece how Debbie's breathing slowed, became irregular, and then ceased within a few minutes. The article, and its anonymous presentation in the journal, without editorial comment, stimulated substantial reaction from the medical profession, as well as the public, the media, and legal authorities. The weight of opinion was against the resident's actions, with criticism even extending to the editors of the journal for publishing the article.[161] In a subsequent editorial, George Lundberg, defending his decision to publish the manuscript, stated that the article proceeded through the normal peer review process, and after some editorial debate, the decision was taken to publish it in order to provoke responsible debate within the medical profession and the public about active voluntary euthanasia in the USA.[162] According to Lundberg, by publishing 'It's Over Debbie', the journal demonstrated its belief that the ethics of euthanasia must be debated anew.[163] Although the publication of this article and the actions of the resident described therein have attracted much criticism, both from within and outside the medical profession, even from proponents of euthanasia,[164] it nevertheless marks a significant development within the medical profession in the USA. The fact that the item was published in the prestigious journal of the AMA, and the subsequent defence of that decision by the editor, clearly demonstrate a more open-minded attitude to active voluntary euthanasia and represents acknowledgment of the need to openly discuss the issue. Whatever else this publication may have achieved, it certainly succeeded in its aim of prompting debate within the medical profession and the public about active voluntary euthanasia in the USA.

Interest in the subject of active voluntary euthanasia has also been stimulated as a result of a number of widely publicized cases of physician-assisted suicide. One of the most forthright proponents of physician-assisted suicide in the USA is Dr Jack Kevorkian who has assisted in the suicide of dozens of patients.[165] From the outset, Dr Kevorkian has been very public in his advocacy of physician-assisted suicide, and has succeeded in attracting much publicity to the voluntary euthanasia cause. The reaction to Dr Kevorkian's conduct from the medical profession in the USA has been somewhat mixed: amongst some vocal opposition,[166] he also received con-

---

[161] See the letters to the editor arising from this publication; (1988) 259 JAMA 272, 2094–8.

[162] Note, '"It's Over, Debbie" and the Euthanasia Debate' (1988) 259 JAMA 2142.

[163] Lundberg, G., 'Debate Over the Ethics of Euthanasia' (1988) 259 JAMA 2143.

[164] It has, for example, been argued that the actions of the doctor in this case were completely inappropriate because he knew virtually nothing of the patient's condition or circumstances and had acted impulsively on the basis of an ambiguous request.

[165] For discussion, see p. 142 above.

[166] e.g. Weir, R., 'The Morality of Physician-Assisted Suicide' (1992) 20 *Law, Med. & Health Care* 116, at 119–20.

siderable support.[167] These cases, and the controversy surrounding Dr Kevorkian, have certainly prompted debate within the medical profession regarding physician-assisted suicide and active voluntary euthanasia. Significantly, in 1995 a new organization was formed in the State of Michigan by a group of doctors called Physicians from Mercy which has publicly endorsed the concept of medically-assisted dying. According to the groups' declaration of principles, the intention is to establish guidelines and protocols for merciful, dignified, medically-assisted termination of life under appropriate circumstances.

Another case of physician-assisted suicide which, in comparison with the activities of Dr Kevorkian, has attracted overwhelmingly favourable publicity is that involving Dr Timothy Quill. As noted in an earlier chapter, this case came to light as a result of an admission by Dr Quill, published in the *New England Journal of Medicine*.[168] Dr Quill escaped liability on charges of assisting suicide as a result of the grand jury's refusal to indict. He later explained that his purpose behind publishing the account was to provoke greater public discussion of the treatment of terminally ill patients.[169] His confession was welcomed by many doctors and ethicists as helping to remove taboos preventing doctors from discussing how they have helped their patients to die, and paving the way for a reassessment of the doctors' role.[170] In the light of his experiences, Dr Quill has since written a book entitled *Death with Dignity: Making Choices and Taking Charge*[171] as well as numerous other publications,[172] and has taken an active role in trying to encourage informed debate on these issues.

Significantly, there has been some indication of a possible willingness to review the AMA's official opposition to active voluntary euthanasia and physician-assisted suicide in the future. In a report released in 1991, the AMA's Council on Ethical and Judicial Affairs noted the increasing support for the proposition that physicians should be allowed deliberately to end a patient's life upon the patient's request.[173] Whilst reiterating its position that physicians must not perform active voluntary euthanasia or par-

---

[167] A survey of doctors was conducted in the wake of the Kevorkian case by *American Press* in July 1990 in which an opinion poll was sent to 100 doctors: 30 per cent of the doctors polled said that the actions of Dr Kevorkian in assisting in the suicide of a patient should be legal. Note should also be taken of the editorial that appeared in the *NY Times* in December 1993 in support of physician-assisted suicide.
[168] Quill, T., 'Death and Dignity: A Case of Individualised Decision Making' (1991) 324 *New Eng.JMed.* 691. See further, p. 137 above.
[169] *NY Times*, 27 July 1991.
[170] For an illustration of the favourable reaction to the actions of Dr Quill, see Jecker, N., 'Giving Death a Hand: When the Dying and the Doctor Stand in a Special Relationship' (1991) 39 *JAm.Geriatrics Society* 831.
[171] (New York, 1993).
[172] e.g. Quill, T., 'Risk Taking by Physician in Legally Gray Areas' (1994) 57 *Alb.Law Rev.* 693.
[173] AMA, Council on Ethical and Judicial Affairs, *Decisions Near the End of Life* (1991) 245.

ticipate in assisted suicide, the council recommended that a more careful examination of the issue is necessary. In particular, it observed that there is currently little data in the USA regarding the number of requests for active euthanasia or assisted suicide, the concerns behind the requests, the types and degree of intolerable and unrelievable suffering, or the number of requests that have been granted by health care providers. The council suggested that before active voluntary euthanasia can be considered a legitimate medical treatment in the USA, the needs behind the demand for physician provided euthanasia must be examined more thoroughly and addressed more effectively. The report concluded with a recommendation that the societal risks of involving physicians in medical interventions to cause patients' deaths is too great to condone active voluntary euthanasia or physician-assisted suicide at this time. This report is significant in so far that it demonstrates the preparedness of the AMA to investigate the issue further and possibly re-evaluate its stance with regard to active voluntary euthanasia and physician-assisted suicide at some later stage.

However, in a subsequent report, released in 1993, the Council on Ethical and Judicial Affairs revisited the issue of physician-assisted suicide and confirmed its traditional opposition.[174] After examining the ethical issues involved, the council rejected physician-assisted suicide as fundamentally inconsistent with the physician's professional role and instead made recommendations aimed at improving the quality of palliative care for terminally ill patients.

C. Canada

There have also been important developments in Canada which indicate some shift in the attitudes of the medical profession on the issue of active voluntary euthanasia. Unlike the medical associations in the other jurisdictions under consideration, for some time, the Canadian Medical Association (CMA) had not taken an official position on the subject. The CMA's Code of Ethics does not mention euthanasia or physician-assisted suicide, although the Code has traditionally been interpreted as opposing these practices. In the face of developments in the Canadian courts, including the *Rodriguez* case[175] and criticism of the CMA for not having an explicit policy, the CMA Board of Directors decided on 1 March 1993 that the Committee on Ethics would develop a policy statement on euthanasia for consideration by the General Council at the 1994 Council Meeting. To this end, it was announced that the CMA was to conduct a survey of doctors to determine members' views on euthanasia. It was also announced that a series of papers

---

[174] AMA, Council on Ethical and Judicial Affairs, Report 59, *Physician Assisted Suicide* (1993).

[175] See above Ch. 1 n. 100. For discussion see pp. 86–94 above.

on euthanasia and physician-assisted suicide would be published in the *Canadian Medical Association Journal*. These articles were intended to provide information to individual doctors about the relevant issues and to encourage debate on the subject, with the aim of assisting doctors and the CMA as a whole, to reach a position on the subject of active voluntary euthanasia. The ultimate goal was to facilitate a contribution by the CMA that would reflect the well-informed views of Canadian doctors.

Following this educational initiative through the publication of a series of articles, first in the *Canadian Medical Association Journal*,[176] then in booklet form,[177] the Committee on Ethics was instructed by the Board of Directors to develop a policy on 'physician aid in dying' and also by the General Council to study the issue further and report back. In the meantime, the survey to ascertain members' views on the subject of active voluntary euthanasia was undertaken. The survey, co-sponsored by the Centre for Bioethics at the University of Toronto and the CMA, was conducted by means of an anonymous questionnaire mailed to a group of 2,990 physicians comprised of both CMA members and non-members. Preliminary results of the survey, based on the responses of 923 of the physicians sampled, were released during the August 1993 annual meeting of the CMA.[178] These results indicated overwhelming support amongst physicians for the CMA to take a stand on euthanasia and assisted suicide (89.4 per cent). The results revealed that most physicians (60.5 per cent) believe that the association should support some type of change in law concerning physician-assisted suicide and active voluntary euthanasia, whilst less than a third (28.9 per cent) wanted the association to oppose any change to current laws which outlaw participation by physicians in either assisted suicide or active voluntary euthanasia. In relation to specific options for reform, 35 per cent of the respondent physicians were in favour of modification of the Criminal Code to permit euthanasia in certain cases; 27.2 per cent supported modification of the Criminal Code to permit physician-assisted suicide in certain cases; 32 per cent supported decriminalization of euthanasia, assuming legislation to prevent abuse; and 28 per cent supported decriminalization of physician-assisted suicide, assuming legislation to prevent abuse: comprising a total of 60.5 per cent of respondents who supported one or more of the four options that would involve legislative change.

The Chairman of the Committee on Ethics, Douglas Sawyer, made it clear that the survey results would be taken into account by the committee in preparing a position paper, so as to ensure that the paper would recognize the views of the profession. The position proposed by the Committee

---

[176] The five part series was published in Volume 148 (1993).

[177] CMA, *Canadian Physicians and Euthanasia* (1993).

[178] Sullivan, P., 'Take a Stand on Euthanasia, Assisted Suicide, MDs tell CMA in Survey Released During Annual Meeting' (1993) 149 CMAJ 858.

on Ethics was to recognize that the legalization of active voluntary euthanasia is a decision society must make.[179] The position was encapsulated in the following statement: 'The CMA is convinced that the question of legalizing physician assisted death is a matter of conscience for physicians, and therefore it does not intend to advocate a particular position on this matter ... Doctors should be free to participate in the societal and political debate according to their own beliefs'.[180]

Thus, the proposal of the Committee of Ethics was essentially one of neutrality on the issue of whether active voluntary euthanasia should be legalized, leaving it instead as a matter of individual conscience for doctors. The policy statement proposed by the Committee on Ethics set out a number of conditions and safeguards, should legislators decide to change Canada's existing laws and legalize active voluntary euthanasia. The conditions included provision of adequate palliative care services to all Canadians and strengthening of suicide prevention programmes. The statement also said that no doctor should be compelled to participate in active voluntary euthanasia or physician-assisted suicide and that any legislative change should be for a strictly limited period and then systematically evaluated.

There was, however, criticism of this proposed policy statement from some quarters in the CMA, and at the 1994 Annual Meeting of the association, an alternative resolution, rejecting active voluntary euthanasia, was put to a vote by members of General Council and was supported by a fairly narrow majority (94 to 73, 18 abstentions). The CMA has since released a Policy Statement on Physician Assisted Death published in the *Canadian Medical Association Journal*.[181] The association's policy is that members should specifically exclude participation in active voluntary euthanasia and physician-assisted suicide. It goes on to state that the CMA recognizes that it is the prerogative of society to decide whether the laws dealing with active voluntary euthanasia and physician-assisted suicide should be changed and that the CMA wishes to contribute the perspective of the medical profession to the examination of the legal, social, and ethical issues. The statement urges that before any change in the legal status of active voluntary euthanasia or physician-assisted suicide is considered, areas of concern identified by the association should be addressed, including adequate palliative care services to be made available to all Canadians; maintenance and strengthening of suicide-prevention programmes; a study to be undertaken of medical decision-making during dying; opportunity for the public to comment on

---

[179] Rafuse, J., 'CMA Rejects Neutral Stand, Comes Out Firmly Against MD Participation in Euthanasia' (1994) 151 CMAJ 853.

[180] A very similar approach was taken by the Committee on Ethics of the Alberta Medical Association: Committee on Ethics, 'Alberta Medical Association: Statement Reflecting the Range of Ethical Opinions on Abortion and Euthanasia' (1991) *Alberta Doctors Digest* Aug/Oct 11.

[181] 'CMA Policy Summary: Physician Assisted Death' (1995) 152 CMAJ 248A.

any proposed legislative change; and the need to consider whether any proposed legislation can restrict active voluntary euthanasia and physician-assisted suicide to the circumstances intended. This Statement, approved by the Board of Directors in October 1994, was the basis of the CMA's submission to the Special Senate Committee on Euthanasia and Assisted Suicide.[182]

In the light of the results of the survey regarding Canadian doctors' attitudes to euthanasia, it is questionable whether the position adopted by the CMA actually reflects the view of the majority of members of the association or Canadian doctors generally. Somewhat ironically, this outcome completely goes against the stated goals of the CMA's Committee on Ethics which had hoped to develop a position that reflected the views of Canadian doctors. The survey results had indicated that the doctors polled wanted the CMA to take a stand on the issue, and in view of the degree of support for change to the law (a total of 60 per cent supporting a change to the law either in the form of active voluntary euthanasia or physician-assisted suicide[183]), this would presumably have meant adopting a position in support of legislative change of some kind.

Apart from the survey organized for the purpose of the CMA, there is other survey evidence from Canada which indicates a considerable degree of support for the legalization of active voluntary euthanasia. In 1991 a postal survey was undertaken of doctors in Alberta.[184] A total of 2,002 physicians were sent a questionnaire and responses were returned by 1,391 (69 per cent response rate). The survey revealed a division of opinion among Alberta physicians regarding the morality of euthanasia—44 per cent of the respondents believed that it is sometimes right to practise euthanasia, 46 per cent did not. Just over half (51 per cent) of the respondent physicians stated that the law should be changed to permit patients to request active euthanasia. A little over a quarter of the physicians (28 per cent) stated that they would practise active euthanasia if it were legalized. A large majority (at least 70 per cent) of respondents were of the view that if it were to be made legal, active euthanasia should be medicalized by restricting it to be performed by physicians and to be taught at medical sites. Religious affiliation and activity were found to be the strongest determinant of attitudes to euthanasia. Amongst the respondents, Catholic physicians were the least likely to believe that active voluntary euthanasia was morally acceptable (31 per cent) or to indicate their willingness to practise it if it were legalized (19 per cent), whereas physicians with no specified religion

---

[182] See further, pp. 382–6 below.

[183] See above.

[184] Kinsella, T. and Verhoef, M., 'Alberta Euthanasia Survey: 1. Physicians' Opinions About the Morality and Legalization of Active Euthanasia' (1993) 148 CMAJ 1921 and 'Alberta Euthanasia Survey: 2. Physicians' Opinions About the Acceptance of Active Euthanasia as a Medical Act and the Reporting of Such Practice' (1993) 148 CMAJ 1929.

or non-orthodox Jews were the most likely to support active voluntary euthanasia in principle (63 per cent and 60 per cent respectively) and indicate their willingness to practise it if it were made legal (46 per cent and 36 per cent respectively). Moreover, there was a direct correlation between the degree of religious activity and the level of support for euthanasia— physicians whose religious activity was regular were substantially less willing to practise active euthanasia if legalized, compared with those who were not religiously active (14 per cent compared with 40 per cent).[185]

The results from the Alberta survey are not directly comparable with the CMA survey as different questions had been used in the survey instrument. In particular, on the issue of law reform, the CMA survey had sought doctors' opinions on a number of options—legalization or decriminalization of active voluntary euthanasia as well as physician-assisted suicide, with a majority of over 60 per cent in favour of some form of legislative change, whereas the Alberta survey focused exclusively on whether active euthanasia should be legalized. Nevertheless, the surveys do provide evidence that a considerable number of doctors believe that active euthanasia should be legalized (51 per cent Alberta survey, 35 per cent CMA survey, with a further 32 per cent supporting decriminalization of active voluntary euthanasia), that it should become a medicalized practice (70 per cent Alberta survey), and that a significant minority of them would be willing to perform active voluntary euthanasia if it were legal (28 per cent Alberta survey).

D. Australia

The Australian Medical Association (AMA) is the largest medical association in Australia of which approximately half of Australian doctors are members. The official position of the AMA with regard to active voluntary euthanasia has always been one of opposition.[186] However, recent events in Australia indicate that in adopting this position, the association may not be reflecting the views of its members, nor of Australian doctors generally.

For some years now there have been occasional expressions of support for active voluntary euthanasia from members of the medical profession in Australia,[187] and even forthright admissions of involvement in the prac-

---

[185] The general trend of these results from the survey of Alberta doctors has since been confirmed in a nationwide Canadian study by the same researchers, of a sample of 3,500 physicians, the results of which had just been reported in the media as this work was finalized. This study did, however, find significant regional differences in attitudes regarding the morality of active voluntary euthanasia and in relation to personal practice. It also confirmed the correlation between level of religious activity and acceptance of the morality and legalization of active voluntary euthanasia and physician-assisted suicide.

[186] See p. 128, n. 7 above.

[187] e.g. Dr John Woolnough (see *Australian*, 22 June 1973); Parker, M., 'Moral Intuition, Good Deaths and Ordinary Medical Practitioners' (1990) 16 *J Med. Ethics* 28; Syme, R., 'A Patient's Right to a Good Death' (1991) 154 MJA 203.

tice.[188] However, in terms of actual evidence of the attitudes of Australian doctors to the issue of active voluntary euthanasia, the more significant developments have been the surveys of doctors' attitudes and practices which have been undertaken in a number of Australian jurisdictions over recent years. The first survey to be conducted was the 1987 survey of attitudes and practices of doctors in Victoria, conducted by Professor Peter Singer and Dr Helga Kuhse from the Monash Centre for Human Bioethics.[189] The findings were based on responses received from 869 respondents from a total of 2,000 Victorian doctors to whom questionnaires were sent (46 per cent response rate).[190] Doctors who had refused to act on a patient's request for active euthanasia were asked to what extent the illegality of the conduct had been a factor in their decision. The responses indicated that the illegality was a factor in the rejection of the request for a majority of these doctors (65 per cent); 5 per cent indicated that they rejected the request solely on this ground; and a further 15 per cent said that they rejected the request primarily for this reason, leaving 45 per cent of doctors for whom illegality was 'in part' a reason for the rejection of the request. For 35 per cent of the doctors, it was not a reason at all.

Another of the survey questions was directed at ascertaining doctors' attitudes to taking active steps to bring about a patient's death. Of those surveyed, 62 per cent believed that it was sometimes right for a doctor to take active steps to bring about the death of a patient who had requested this, whilst 34 per cent thought that it was not.[191] Support for a doctor to take active steps came from doctors in all age groups but was greatest among the younger doctors. There was also majority support amongst most religious groups except Roman Catholics. Doctors who were members of the AMA tended to have similar views to doctors as a whole.

The survey also sought to ascertain doctors' views of the Netherlands situation. More than half of the doctors indicated that they did think that it would be a good thing if the Netherlands situation existed in Australia—59 per cent, compared with 37 per cent who answered no to this question. A slightly smaller majority (52 per cent) were of the view that their professional organization (which for the majority of the doctors surveyed was the AMA) should take a similar stand to that of the Royal Dutch Medical Association, whilst 43 per cent of doctors did not think so.

As to doctors' attitudes to legalization of active voluntary euthanasia, 60

---

[188] See p. 137 above.

[189] Kuhse, H. and Singer, P., 'Doctors' Practices and Attitudes Regarding Voluntary Euthanasia' (1988) 148 MJA 623. The authors of this survey have also completed a related survey to gauge the attitudes and practices of nurses in Victoria: Kuhse, H. and Singer, P., 'Euthanasia: A Survey of Nurses' Attitudes and Practices' (1992) 21 *Australian Nurses J* 21.

[190] For further information about this survey, see pp. 132–3 and 136 above.

[191] See also the findings of a survey of New Zealand doctors (a poll of 120 general practitioners nationwide) which found that 49% of general practitioners overall said doctors should be prepared to help with euthanasia and 43% rejected the idea: Thompson, M., 'Doctors Divided Over Helping Patients Die' (1995) *NZ Doctor* April 3, 28.

per cent of the respondents indicated support for a change to the law to permit active voluntary euthanasia in some circumstances (37 per cent were against such change). When asked whether they would practise active voluntary euthanasia if it were legal, 40 per cent of the doctors said that they would, 41 per cent said that they would not and the remainder did not answer this question.

A similar survey has also been conducted in South Australia in 1992 to ascertain the views of South Australian doctors on assisted dying.[192] The findings of this survey, based on a sample of 1,000 South Australian doctors, has tended to confirm the results of the more extensive Monash survey. 61 per cent of the respondent doctors were of the view that it is sometimes right for a doctor to take active steps to bring about the death of a terminally ill or incurable patient who has requested the doctor to do this. Over half of the respondent doctors (56 per cent) indicated that they would like to see a law introduced, based on the judicial guidelines allowing actively assisted dying in the Netherlands.[193] Approximately half of the respondent doctors (48 per cent) indicated that they would be prepared actively to assist an incurably ill patient to die if they were asked by the patient and the law permitted it.

In 1993 a survey modelled on the earlier Victorian study by Kuhse and Singer was conducted in the State of New South Wales and the Australian Capital Territory.[194] A questionnaire was sent to 2,000 doctors randomly selected from the Medical Register of New South Wales (which includes medical practitioners in the Australian Capital Territory.) Responses were received from 1,268 doctors (a response rate of 65.2 per cent). Of the practitioners who had refused requests for active voluntary euthanasia or doctor-assisted suicide, the respondents were fairly evenly divided as to whether illegality had been a factor in their decision. It had played a role in the decision for 51 per cent of the respondents—29 per cent indicated that their decision was based in part on legal issues, 19 per cent said illegality was the primary reason, and 3 per cent based their decision wholly on the illegality of the act. 48 per cent of the respondents claimed that illegality was not at all an issue in the decision.

A clear majority of the respondents (59 per cent) believed that it is sometimes right for a doctor to take active steps to bring about the death of a patient who had requested this. With respect to a related question on

[192] Medical Practitioners Concerned with Assisted Dying, Media Release, 'South Australian Doctors Help Incurable Patients to Die' 28 July 1992.

[193] Note also the study by Stevens, C. and Hassan, R., 'Management of Death and Dying and Euthanasia: Attitudes and Practices of Medical Practitioners in South Australia' (1994) 20 *JMed.Ethics* 41, which found, on the question of attitudes to change to the law, 45% were in favour of legalization of active voluntary euthanasia and 39% were opposed.

[194] Baume, P. and O'Malley, E., 'Euthanasia: Attitudes and Practices of Medical Practitioners' (1994) 161 MJA 137.

doctor-assisted suicide, which had not appeared in the earlier Victorian survey, 56 per cent of respondents indicated that is was sometimes right for a doctor to provide the means to suicide. 59 per cent of the respondents were of the view that the Netherlands situation with regard to active voluntary euthanasia should be introduced in Australia, and 52 per cent believed that their professional organization should take a stand and approve active voluntary euthanasia. There was greater support amongst respondents for a change to the law to permit active voluntary euthanasia (58 per cent of respondents) as opposed to doctor-assisted suicide (46 per cent). Exactly half of the respondents indicated that if active voluntary euthanasia was legal and an incurably ill patient requested them to hasten his or death, they would comply with the request.

The nature of respondents' religious affiliation was found to be a significant determinant in shaping attitudes and practices to active voluntary euthanasia.[195] 70 per cent of the respondents identified themselves with a religious faith, with the remaining 30 per cent of the respondents indicating that they had no such affiliation. The responses of the 'non-theists' (agnostics and atheists) were compared with the answers of those who professed any religion ('theists'). The 'non-theists' were the most sympathetic to the idea of active voluntary euthanasia and physician-assisted suicide. They were 1.6 times as likely to practise active voluntary euthanasia as were all 'theists'. 'Non-theists' were more than twice as likely to know of other doctors who practised active voluntary euthanasia and were more than three times more likely to think active voluntary euthanasia to be sometimes right, compared with 'theist' practitioners. Further, 'non-theists' were significantly more likely to favour the Dutch arrangements, and to indicate support for professional responsibility regarding euthanasia policies and the need for legal changes compared to all 'theist' doctors. Of those respondents who did identify with a religion, Catholics were significantly different from other doctors in the strength and extent of their opposition to active voluntary euthanasia. Protestant practitioners fell midway between the Catholic practitioners and the 'non-theists', whereas Jewish practitioners were almost as supportive of active voluntary euthanasia and physician-assisted suicide as 'non-theists'.

A correlation was also noted between the age of the respondents and attitudes to euthanasia. Respondents under 40 years of age were more likely to believe it is sometimes right to practise active voluntary euthanasia and to believe that the law should be changed to allow its practice than older respondents (over 60 years of age). Some differences were also noted in the responses of general practitioners (who comprised close to half of the

---

[195] This was the subject of a separate publication based on the same survey results: Baume, P. et al., 'Professed Religious Affiliation and the Practice of Euthanasia' (1995) 21 *JMed.Ethics* 49.

respondents: 44.6 per cent) compared with other groups of practitioners, with general practitioners being significantly more likely to have reported treating terminally ill patients and practising active voluntary euthanasia. At the same time, the present illegality of the practice was significantly more likely to prevent general practitioners compared with other groups of practitioners from acceding to a request for active voluntary euthanasia.

Interestingly, the overall responses of this survey were almost identical to the earlier Victorian survey, suggesting that there had been virtually no change in the intervening 5-year period and that there was no significant difference between these Australian jurisdictions. Moreover, in view of the similarity of results also from the South Australian survey referred to above, it is reasonable to suggest that the responses from the doctors in these Australian jurisdictions would be broadly representative of Australian doctors generally. The overwhelming conclusion to be drawn from these surveys is that the majority of Australian doctors support active voluntary euthanasia with approximately 60 per cent in support of a change in the law, and almost half of the respondent doctors indicating that they would be willing to practise active voluntary euthanasia if it were legal. The attitude of doctors to change in the law is consistent with the views of the Australian public generally, although the level of support is slightly less amongst the medical profession.[196]

A significant outcome of these surveys is the fact that a majority of the doctors who responded to the questionnaire, (most of whom were members of the AMA), thought that their professional association should take a stand on the issue similar to that which has been taken by the Royal Dutch Medical Association. This result must raise serious questions about the current policies of the AMA and other major medical organizations in Australia on the subject of active voluntary euthanasia and their capacity to represent the views of their members.

Although the issue of active voluntary euthanasia has, from time to time, been raised at council meetings, neither the AMA nor other professional medical associations in Australia have to date conducted any surveys or polls of their members, or doctors generally, concerning attitudes to active voluntary euthanasia. Moreover, following the release of the survey results and the calls for review that those results provoked, the official representatives of the AMA have affirmed the association's opposition to active voluntary euthanasia and denied that the results demonstrated a widespread desire among members to change the association's ethical position on the matter. To date, the only branch of the AMA which has undertaken a review of its position with regard to active voluntary euthanasia has been the South Australian Branch. The Branch Council of the AMA in South

---

[196] Approximately 60% compared with approximately 75% amongst the general public. For discussion of trends in public opinion on active voluntary euthanasia see pp. 257–68 above.

Australia established a working party on euthanasia which in 1990 prepared a Report for Council. The report itself was not made publicly available, but the position of the South Australian Branch of the Association as reflected in its submission to the South Australian Select Committee on the Law and Practice Relating to Death and Dying,[197] remains one of opposition.

The AMA has recently released a Position Statement on the *Care of Severely Ill and Terminally Ill Patients* in which the association affirms its opposition to active interventions which are intended to end the life of a patient.[198] Significantly, however, this statement does acknowledge that there is a wide divergence of views on the legitimacy or otherwise of euthanasia and doctor-assisted suicide in Australian society generally and within the Australian medical profession and that there are some instances where satisfactory relief of suffering cannot be achieved.

In sharp contrast to the position taken by most Australian medical organizations, the Doctors' Reform Society has publicly endorsed active voluntary euthanasia. Established in 1973, the Doctors' Reform Society is an organization which aims to promote reform and improvement in Australian health services and changes in Australian society conducive to the health of the Australian people. It seeks to pursue these aims by promoting informed debate among doctors, by publication of the journal *New Doctor*, and by participation in the democratic processes of our society.[199] At its national conference in Brisbane in 1988, the society formally adopted a policy statement in which it supported the legalization of active voluntary euthanasia.[200] The society has advocated the creation of a patients' bill of rights, which would include the right to be able to request a medically-assisted death when suffering a fatal and distressing illness.[201] The statement goes on to provide that patients' rights should be protected by legislation, particularly with regard to the 'right to die'. On the specifics of implementation of such a proposal, it is stated that legislation allowing both passive and active euthanasia should be based on the Netherlands criteria:

(i)   only doctors may carry out euthanasia;

(ii)   individual doctors are free to refuse to carry out euthanasia;

(iii)   there must be an explicit request by the patient which leaves no room for doubt concerning the patient's desire to die;

(iv)   the patient's decision must be well-informed, free and enduring;

(v)   there is no acceptable alternative (for the patient) to improve his/her condition;

---

[197] For discussion see pp. 340–2 below.

[198] AMA *Position Statement: Care of Severely Ill and Terminally Ill Patients* (1996).

[199] See the statement of aims and philosophy in the society's journal, *New Doctor*.

[200] Note, 'Doctors' Reform Society Policy Statement' (1988) 49 *New Doctor* paras. 3.1.12 and 3.3.

[201] Ibid. at para. 3.1.12. See also para. 3.1.11 recommending recognition of the right not to have life needlessly prolonged when suffering a fatal and distressing illness.

(vi) the doctor must exercise due care in making the decision and consult another independent medical practitioner.[202]

Another noteworthy development has been the establishment in South Australia of a doctors' organization entitled Medical Practitioners Concerned with Assisted Dying. This organization, working in consultation with the South Australian Voluntary Euthanasia Society, has put forward a proposed law for medical 'aid in dying' along similar lines to the position prevailing in the Netherlands.[203]

Apart from the survey results discussed above, there are a number of other more general indicators of the attitudes of doctors in Australia with regard to active voluntary euthanasia. There has been more extensive and open discussion of the subject in recent years, both in the context of formal and informal meetings of professional medical associations and at medical conferences. In 1994 the Australian Medical Association organized a national forum on euthanasia (*National Forum on the Ethical and Legal Issues in Relation to the Dying Person*), which included guest speakers presenting a range of different viewpoints. There has also been increasing coverage of the issue in Australian medical journals, including the prestigious *Medical Journal of Australia*. Numerous articles have been published on the subject which adopt a neutral and even-handed stance, and in the past few years, more and more doctors have been writing in defence of active voluntary euthanasia. In a recent editorial of the *Medical Journal of Australia*, there is an appeal for frank and dispassionate debate. The editor, Martin Van Der Weyden, writes: 'The time has surely come for society to openly address the taboo of dying. Active euthanasia should be widely discussed in an open forum free of the polemics of opponents and advocates, and without the political, religious and legal prohibitions that have stifled the debate'.[204]

Another significant development reflecting the changing climate for reform was the publication in 1993 of an issues paper by the Royal Australasian College of Physicians canvassing the arguments for and against active voluntary euthanasia.[205] In explaining the college's decision to produce an issues paper on the subject, it was stated that it was done with the aim of helping College Fellows contribute to the debate in the public arena and in their interactions with patients, colleagues, and the college, and to assist them in the difficult end of life decisions which they confront on a daily basis.

In another important development, the Australian Association for Hospice and Palliative Care Inc. issued a Position Statement on Voluntary

[202] Above n. 200, at para. 3.3.

[203] Medical Practitioners Concerned with Assisted Dying, 'South Australian Doctors Help Incurable Patients to Die', above n. 192.

[204] 'Medicine and the Community—the Euthanasia Debate' (1995) 162 MJA 566.

[205] *Ethics: Voluntary Euthanasia, Issues Involved in the Case For and Against* (Sydney, 1995).

Active Euthanasia in 1995. The Association's position is that legalization of active voluntary euthanasia is not a substitute for the proper provision of palliative care services to all Australians and that currently accepted palliative care does not include the deliberate ending of life, even if this is requested by the patient. The statement does, however, acknowledge that while pain and symptoms can be addressed, complete relief is not always possible in all cases, even with optimal palliative care. The statement goes on to recognize that there is a wide divergence of views about voluntary euthanasia in Australian society and also within the caring professions, including the palliative care community, and that some people rationally and consistently request active voluntary euthanasia. It goes on to welcome open and frank discussion within the community and particularly the health professions, about all aspects of death and dying, including active voluntary euthanasia.

The recent passage of legislation in the Northern Territory permitting active voluntary euthanasia and doctor-assisted suicide[206] as well as the forthright admissions of a group of Victorian doctors publicized through their open letter to the Premier of that state which was then followed by an appeal by 70 Victorian doctors for a review of the laws prohibiting voluntary euthanasia[207] have also contributed to the heightened level of awareness and debate on the issue in Australia within the medical profession and amongst the public generally.

E. International Developments: The Appleton International Conference

Another significant development which has given recognition and qualified support to active voluntary euthanasia has been the Appleton International Conference. This development began in 1987 with an international working conference for practising clinicians regarding decisions to withhold or withdraw treatment.[208] Participants were drawn internationally from nearly a dozen countries and their deliberations led to the preparation of model guidelines with regard to forgoing treatment.[209] A further conference was held in 1991 to continue the development of internationally recognized guidelines with regard to forgoing life-prolonging medical treatment. At this conference, consideration was, *inter alia*, given to requests for intervention intended to terminate life (active voluntary euthanasia). Although

---

[206] For discussion, see pp. 345–57 below.

[207] *Herald/Sun* 3 November 1995. As to the open letter containing admissions of involvement in assisting patients to die, see further p. 138, n. 55 above.

[208] Stanley, J., 'The Appleton International Conference: Developing Guidelines for Decisions to Forgo Life-Prolonging Medical Treatment' (1992) 18 *J Med. Ethics* 3.

[209] These guidelines were published as 'The Appleton Consensus: Suggested International Guidelines for Decisions to Forgo Medical Treatment' in the *Journal of the Danish Medical Association* (1989).

there was by no means unanimity on the issue, the following guidelines
were suggested concerning requests for active euthanasia:

Patients having decision-making capacity who are severely and irremediably suffering from an incurable disease sometimes ask for assistance in dying. Such requests
for active termination of life by a medical act which directly and intentionally causes
death may be morally justifiable and should be given serious consideration. Doctors
have an obligation to try to provide treatment and care that will result in a peaceful,
dignified, and humane death with minimal suffering. There is a particular obligation
upon the doctor confronted with a request for euthanasia or other assistance in
dying to undertake a scrupulously careful enquiry into the circumstances of the
request to see if alternative courses of action might be helpful in removing or
alleviating the cause or causes that led to the request. Attention should focus upon:
(a) physical distress, which might be removed by better palliative treatment,
(b) the possibility of significant mental depression which might be susceptible to
    treatment, and
(c) the perception of being an undue burden upon family members and other
    carers, which might be helped by counselling and more adequate support
    facilities.

It is recognised that participation in doctor-assisted dying for those patients who
persist in their wish to die in spite of all measures to reduce their suffering will reflect
different cultural and societal norms in individual countries. Whether statutory
legalization of the international termination of life by doctors is desirable is the
subject of continuing international debate.[210]

These carefully worded guidelines which have gained international exposure are clearly intended to convey a degree of acceptance for active voluntary euthanasia. In so doing, they reflect the enormous changes that have
occurred with regard to this subject, and in their own right, mark a significant milestone.

F. Changes Within the Medical Profession: An Evaluation

From the foregoing review of developments within the medical profession
in the United Kingdom, the United States, Canada, and Australia with
regard to the issue of active voluntary euthanasia, it is readily apparent that
despite the official opposition of professional medical organizations, there
is growing evidence of a changed outlook on the subject on the part of many
doctors. Whilst there are some variations in the format and outcomes of the
surveys which have been undertaken in the various jurisdictions, there is
unquestionably a strong degree of support from within the profession for a
change to the law to permit active voluntary euthanasia. In some jurisdictions, this now represents the majority view (for example in the USA with

---

[210] Stanley, 'The Appleton International Conference: Developing Guidelines for Decisions
to Forgo Life-Prolonging Medical Treatment', above n. 208, 6–7. Note the dissent to this
guideline by five of the 24 participants.

support ranging between 54 per cent–70 per cent of respondents, and Australia where there is a support rate of approximately 60 per cent). In other jurisdictions, it falls short of a majority (for example, the United Kingdom, where on the basis of the different surveys, support has ranged from 44 per cent–47 per cent), but nevertheless comprises a substantial proportion of the medical profession. Also very significant is the relatively high proportion of doctors who have indicated that they would be willing to be involved in the practice of active voluntary euthanasia if it were legalized (for example, in the United Kingdom ranging from 43 per cent–46 per cent, and in Australia, between 40 per cent–50 per cent). It is interesting to compare these results with the findings as to the proportion of doctors who have acted upon a patient's request for active euthanasia. Available survey results from a number of jurisdictions indicate that between one quarter and one third of those doctors who have been asked by a patient to perform euthanasia have acceded to the patient's request.[211] This discrepancy suggests that for a significant proportion of doctors, the present illegality of the practice is a significant factor in their non-participation. This is confirmed by the survey findings which indicate that for a majority of those doctors who had rejected a request for active euthanasia, the illegality of the practice had played some role in the decision (for example, in the USA, according to the Hemlock survey, 79.5 per cent, and in Australia, between 51 per cent–65 per cent), in some cases being the sole reason for the rejection of the request.

In a number of the surveys from different jurisdictions religion was found to be the most significant factor to influence attitudes to euthanasia. According to survey evidence from the USA, Canada, and Australia, doctors who are Roman Catholic are substantially less likely to support active voluntary euthanasia or be willing to practise it if legalized, compared with doctors from other religious denominations such as Protestants. Those with no specified religious affiliation were the most likely to support active voluntary euthanasia. A number of the surveys also took account of the age of respondents and area of practice (general practitioner or other) and found these factors to be significant variables. For example, in relation to age, it was found that the respondents in the younger age categories (defined variously as below 35 years of age or below 40 years of age) were more likely to support legalization of active voluntary euthanasia than doctors in the older age brackets (defined in the different surveys as 55 or 60 years or more): for example, in Australia, the survey of doctors in New South Wales and the Australian Capital Territory. This is entirely consistent with the results of polls amongst the general population. Younger respondents were also more likely to be willing to practise active voluntary euthanasia if it

[211] See pp. 135–7 above.

were legalized (for example, in the United Kingdom, *Doctor* survey). The survey findings also provide some evidence to suggest that general practitioners may take a more liberal attitude to active voluntary euthanasia compared with other groups of practitioners. For example, in surveys in the United Kingdom, the USA, and Australia, it was found that general practitioners, on the whole, indicated greater willingness to practise active voluntary euthanasia if it were legalized. It has been suggested that this greater willingness may relate to the characteristics of doctors who choose to go into general practice, it may relate to their training, or it may relate to professional values that develop from the broader based, longer term relationships that such doctors have with their patients compared with other specialities who may define differently those activities that fall outside the physician's reference.[212]

Another important finding which stems from one of the surveys in the United Kingdom is that the great majority of doctors (83 per cent) feel they are not given adequate guidance on the issue, and generally feel ill-prepared to cope with requests for euthanasia.[213] The survey results also indicate support for the medical associations taking a more positive stance on the issue (for example, in the USA 58 per cent, Australia 52 per cent). Significantly, there is strong support for the view that if active voluntary euthanasia is to be legalized, the practice should be performed by a doctor (for example, according to the Alberta survey in Canada, 70 per cent, in the USA, in the San Francisco study, 54 per cent).

On the basis of a number of surveys of doctors in the USA there is some evidence to suggest that doctors, at least in that country, would prefer to assist a patient to commit suicide rather than perform active voluntary euthanasia. This is reflected in survey findings regarding levels of participation in the two practices.[214] Differences have also been demonstrated re-

---

[212] Shapiro, R. et al., 'Willingness to Perform Euthanasia: A Survey of Physicians Attitudes' (1994) 154 *Arch.Intern.Med.* 575, 584.

[213] See also the findings of a New Zealand survey of general practitioners (a sample of 120 general practitioners nationwide) which found that general practitioners see a need for some professional guidelines on the subject, with two to one in favour of some form of protocol being prepared: Thompson, 'Doctors Divided Over Helping Patients Die' above Ch. 3 n. 29.

[214] e.g. Doukas et al., 'Attitudes and Behaviours on Physician-Assisted Death: A Study of Michigan Oncologists', above Ch. 3 n. 48, at 1057 where, of the oncologists surveyed, 18% had actively participated in assisted suicide as compared with 4% who had performed active voluntary euthanasia. See also Ciesielski-Carlucci, C., 'Physician Attitudes and Experiences with Assisted Suicide: Results of a Small Opinion Survey' (1993) 2 *Cambridge Q Healthcare Ethics* 39 and Fried, T. et al., 'Limits of Patient Autonomy: Physician Attitudes and Practices Regarding Life-Sustaining Treatments and Euthanasia' (1993) 153 *Arch.Intern.Med.* 722. Compare these findings with the results of an Australian survey of doctors in New South Wales and the Australia Capital Territory which found that only 7% of respondents indicated that they had provided the means for a patient to commit suicide when requested to do so, compared with 28% who had provided active assistance at a patient's request: see Baume and O'Malley, 'Euthanasia: Attitudes and Practices of Medical Practitioners', above Ch. 3 n. 27. Note also the recent Canadian study conducted nationwide by Verhoef and Kinsella (see

garding doctors' willingness to engage in these practices if they were to be legalized.[215] Nevertheless, it would appear that the level of support for legalization amongst doctors in the USA is roughly the same as between the two practices.[216]

Whilst the change in attitude of members of the medical profession to medical assistance in dying can be demonstrated relatively easily, through survey and other evidence, it is more difficult to state with any certainty the reasons behind these changes. A number of tentative suggestions can, however, be made which reinforce the important interrelationship between the changing attitude of the medical profession on the issue and changes in public opinion generally. Amongst possible reasons behind this clear shift in medical opinion is the increasingly open attitude in the community to death and dying. Although active voluntary euthanasia remains a crime, much of the taboo formerly surrounding the subject has disappeared and doctors are, therefore, increasingly willing to present their views on the subject. Doctors, as members of the community, can be taken to reflect, at least to some extent, the attitudes of the wider population which are unquestionably moving towards acceptance of active voluntary euthanasia. Moreover, as the evidence of public support for active voluntary euthanasia mounts, more and more doctors would be likely to acknowledge this development and respond to it, regardless of what their own personal views on the subject may be. This is particularly the case in view of the declining influence of medical paternalism and the growing recognition of the importance of patient autonomy and self-determination.

In the light of the overwhelming evidence of growing acceptance within the medical profession for active voluntary euthanasia, there is a strong case to suggest that if the professional medical associations are to remain rel-

n. 185 above) which found that nationally, physicians' opinions were virtually identical concerning acceptance of the morality, legalization, and personal practice of both active voluntary euthanasia and physician-assisted suicide.

For an interesting explanation as to why there may be a preference in the USA for physician-assisted suicide over active voluntary euthanasia see Pabst Battin, M., 'Holland and Home: On the Exportability of Dutch Euthanasia Practices' in Aycke, O. and Smook, M. (eds.), *Right to Self-Determination* (Amsterdam, 1990) 124, 131.

[215] e.g. the study of Cohen et al., 'Attitudes Toward Assisted Suicide and Euthanasia Among Physicians in Washington State', above n. 146 which found that 33% of respondents would be willing to perform euthanasia as compared with 40% who would be willing to assist a patient to commit suicide.

[216] See above, Cohen et al., 'Attitudes Toward Assisted Suicide and Euthanasia Among Physicians in Washington State', above n. 146 which found that 54% of respondents thought euthanasia should be legal in some circumstances, compared with 53% of respondents who thought that physician-assisted suicide should be legal in some circumstances. Compare this, however with the findings of the survey of doctors in New South Wales and the Australian Capital Territory which found greater support for a change in the law to permit active voluntary euthanasia (58%) as opposed to doctor-assisted suicide (46%). See Baume and O'Malley, 'Euthanasia: Attitudes and Practices of Medical Practitioners', Ch. 3 n. 27. For discussion see above.

evant and representative of the views of their members, they must urgently re-examine their traditional opposition to the practice. Moreover, if such a review is to be effective and responsive to the needs of the medical profession as a whole, it is essential that a genuine effort is made to gauge the views of members of the profession. Indeed, as suggested above, it was primarily for this reason that the review undertaken by the BMA in 1988, whilst undoubtedly a development of major significance, ultimately failed to address the real issues in this area. It should go without saying that once members' views are ascertained, the medical associations should ensure that they are taken into account in the formulation of policy on euthanasia. In this regard, some criticism could be made of the CMA which, after gathering information about doctors attitudes to reform which had shown widespread support for change to the present laws, ignored the recommendations of its Committee on Ethics and adopted a position of opposition to active voluntary euthanasia, clearly contrary to the views of many of its members.

In evaluating the current situation within the medical profession, it would be a mistake not to acknowledge the strength of opposition to any change. Indeed, in some of the survey results, views of the respondent doctors have been sharply divided, for and against legalization of active voluntary euthanasia (for example, in one of the surveys in the United Kingdom, 44 per cent in favour of reform, 54 per cent against). Significantly, in a number of the surveys, religious affiliation and activity has been identified as one of the most significant factors to shape attitudes to active voluntary euthanasia. However, these differences are merely reflective of the trend shown in opinion poll results of the general population noted above, namely that there is a correlation between religious affiliation and the levels of support for active voluntary euthanasia. As was argued in an earlier chapter,[217] religion is a matter personal to individuals which must of course be respected, but given our pluralistic society, it should not be permitted to dominate legal or social policy. In view of the polarized attitudes within the profession, with strongly held views on both sides of the debate, the most appropriate option would be (as had been recommended by the CMA's Committee on Ethics) for medical associations to acknowledge this diversity of views and take a neutral stand on the issue, leaving it to individual members to determine their own views on the subject as a matter of individual conscience.[218] There is a precedent for such an approach within the medical profession in respect of abortion—the profession has taken a neutral approach to the issue, leaving it to the discretion of individual doctors

[217] See pp. 216–17 above.
[218] Note in this regard the approach taken by the San Francisco Medical Society discussed above.

whether they become involved in the practice.[219] Indeed, it seems contradictory for the profession to recognize individual conviction and conscience of doctors in one context but not the other.[220] In order to preserve the freedom of choice of all doctors, it is essential that any legislative proposal for reform of active voluntary euthanasia ensures free exercise of doctors' discretion as to whether or not they should participate in the practice. It certainly does not seem justifiable for the medical associations to continue to ignore the growing evidence of support for change within the profession. It must, however, be recognized that the situation poses a dilemma for the medical associations. Notwithstanding irrefutable evidence which suggests that members support active voluntary euthanasia and indeed, that many doctors are already engaged in the practice, the associations would obviously be reluctant to be seen openly to be condoning a position which is in conflict with the criminal law and which appears to run counter to their traditional beliefs. What this highlights is the need for a co-ordinated, interdisciplinary approach to law reform if legislation is to be enacted permitting active voluntary euthanasia.

It has also been shown that apart from survey evidence of doctors' attitudes to active voluntary euthanasia, in all the jurisdictions under consideration, there have been quite a number of other more general developments within the medical profession which have contributed to the process of reform. Widespread acceptance of conduct amounting to passive euthanasia, changing attitudes to death and dying, the development of hospice and palliative care, and increased debate within the medical profession and the community generally on the subject of assisted dying are just some of the developments which have contributed to a growing understanding and acceptance of active voluntary euthanasia. The extent of this change, also from an international perspective, is evident from the deliberations of the Appleton International Conference which has led to the development of guidelines for medical practitioners concerning requests for active euthanasia.

CONCLUSION

The object of this chapter has been to outline the key features in the changing climate for reform of the law with regard to active voluntary euthanasia. Evidence from opinion poll results has shown that a large majority of people in all common law jurisdictions under consideration support the legalization of active voluntary euthanasia. The degree of com-

[219] See the WMA Statement on Therapeutic Abortion (1983).
[220] SAVES, 'The World Medical Association and Voluntary Euthanasia' (1995).

munity support is reflected in the expansion of the voluntary euthanasia movement, with the establishment and growth of voluntary euthanasia societies in all jurisdictions. Intermeshed with these developments, there has been a significant shift of opinion from within the medical profession towards acceptance of active voluntary euthanasia, although the implications of this shift are yet to be fully recognized by the official medical organizations. The analysis in this chapter evidences a clear trend towards greater acceptance of active voluntary euthanasia. In some jurisdictions, in particular, the United Kingdom and the USA, this development dates back a number of decades, whilst in others it is of more recent origin. However, in all jurisdictions, there are indications that the trend has been gathering momentum in recent years, with ever increasing demands for changes to the present law. In the chapter which follows, consideration will be given to the measures which have to date resulted from this changing climate for reform.

6

Moves Towards Reform

INTRODUCTION

The foregoing chapter has concentrated on the changing climate for reform within the medical profession and the community generally on the issue of active voluntary euthanasia, documenting the growing evidence of acceptance of the practice and support for its legalization. Specific attention will now be given to the official response to these changes in the form of law reform commission and parliamentary inquiries and the legislative developments that have occurred with regard to the legalization of active voluntary euthanasia in the common law jurisdictions under consideration. To date, the Northern Territory in Australia is the only jurisdiction in the world to have enacted legislation legalizing the practice. In the State of Oregon in the USA, a citizen-initiated referendum in support of laws allowing physician-assisted suicide has been passed, but this legislation is currently being challenged in the courts on constitutional grounds.

This chapter begins with an evaluation of the position in the United Kingdom in view of the long history of reform initiatives in that jurisdiction. Attention will then be devoted to the Australian position, with particular reference to the recent developments in the Northern Territory. In the remainder of the chapter, consideration will also be given to reform developments which have occurred in the USA, and Canada.

I. UNITED KINGDOM

The United Kingdom has a long history of reform efforts to introduce legislation for the legalization of active voluntary euthanasia due to the early development of the voluntary euthanasia movement in that country.[1] The Voluntary Euthanasia Society in London was the first such society to be established in the common law world and has, since its inception in 1935, actively pursued the introduction of active voluntary euthanasia legislation. Quite a number of bills have been prepared and introduced into Parliament but these reform efforts have been unsuccessful. Apart from these legisla-

---

[1] For historical coverage of the legislative developments in the UK, see Gould, J. and Lord Craigmyle (eds.), *Your Death Warrant? Implications of Euthanasia: A Medical, Legal and Ethical Study* (New Rochelle, New York, 1971).

tive activities, there have also been a number of governmental inquiries which have considered the issue of mercy killing, and more recently, the House of Lords Select Committee on Medical Ethics has specifically considered the issue of active voluntary euthanasia.

A. Legislative Developments

In 1936, a bill, known as the Voluntary Euthanasia (Legalization) Bill which was promoted by the newly established British Voluntary Euthanasia Legalization Society,[2] was introduced into the House of Lords by Lord Ponsonby. Under this Bill, in order to be eligible for active voluntary euthanasia, a patient had to be over 21 years of age, suffering from an incurable and fatal illness, and was required to sign a form in the presence of two witnesses asking to be put to death. Before a patient's request for active euthanasia would be approved, a complicated legal procedure would have to be complied with, including investigation of the case by a 'euthanasia referee' and a hearing before a special court. If the necessary conditions were satisfied, a license would be issued permitting active voluntary euthanasia to be administered by a doctor in the presence of an official witness.[3] The Bill was given a first reading, but was rejected by the House of Lords on the second reading by a vote of 35 to 14. It was subsequently acknowledged by the Voluntary Euthanasia Legalization Society that the cumbersome safeguards included in the Bill had largely been responsible for its defeat, with opponents of the legislation having objected that it would bring too much formality into the sickroom.[4]

Under the guidance of Professor Glanville Williams, a notable supporter of active voluntary euthanasia,[5] new legislation was developed during the 1960s for legalization which provided for a much simplified procedure with a minimum of formality.[6] The revised Bill authorized a doctor to administer active euthanasia to a consenting patient thought, on reasonable grounds, to be suffering from an 'irremediable condition',[7] and who had, not less than 30 days previously, signed a declaration requesting the administration of

---

[2] For discussion see p. 269 above.

[3] Helme, T., 'The Voluntary Euthanasia (Legalisation) Bill (1936) Revisited' (1991) 17 *JMed. Ethics* 25.

[4] See Euthanasia Society, *A Plan for Voluntary Euthanasia*, Revised edn. (London, 1962) 10.

[5] See, for example, Williams, G., *The Sanctity of Life and the Criminal Law* (London, 1956) 302 where he sets out his suggestions for reform; and 'Voluntary Euthanasia—The Next Step', an address delivered by Professor Williams on the occasion of the 1955 Annual General Meeting of the Euthanasia Society.

[6] The Euthanasia Society, *A Plan for Voluntary Euthanasia*, above n. 4.

[7] 'Irremediable condition' was defined in clause 1 of the Bill to mean 'a serious physical illness or impairment reasonably thought in the patient's case to be incurable and expected to cause him severe distress or render him incapable of rational existence'.

active euthanasia. In addition to streamlining the procedure for the administration of active voluntary euthanasia, the Bill contained a number of other significant changes from the earlier legislation. One such change was the substitution of the requirement of an 'irremediable' condition for the requirement of a 'fatal' condition which had been contained in the previous proposal, thereby considerably extending the range of cases to which active voluntary euthanasia would become applicable. Another noteworthy new feature of this Bill was that it allowed for an advance declaration, enabling persons to request in advance the administration of active euthanasia in the event of their suffering from an irremediable condition at some future date. The Bill also sought to provide protection to doctors and nurses who, in good faith, administered active voluntary euthanasia in accordance with the legislation.[8] In 1969 Lord Raglan introduced into the House of Lords a Voluntary Euthanasia Bill modelled along these lines (with minor modifications). However, the Bill was rejected on the second reading by a vote of 61 to 40. Although the bill was defeated, the vote in the House reflected a substantial increase in support since the 1936 Bill. Moreover, many of those who voted against the 1969 Bill indicated that they supported it in principle, but objected to some of the specific details of the legislation.[9]

The society's campaign for the legalization of active voluntary euthanasia has continued to the present time. In the early 1980s, a new draft bill was prepared[10] and representations were made to Members of Parliament with the aim of gauging support for the proposed legislation. Since that time, a number of early day motions have been tabled in support of active voluntary euthanasia which have been endorsed by quite a number of parliamentarians. In 1990 Mr Roland Boyes introduced a Voluntary Euthanasia Bill into the House of Commons under the '10 minute rule' which allows bills to be debated (10 minutes for and against) and, if successful at this stage, to be printed and officially presented.[11] The proposal was, however, defeated by 101 votes to 35. Subsequent efforts by Mr Piara Khabra to present a Voluntary Euthanasia Bill were unsuccessful due to lack of parliamentary time. In 1991, an all-party parliamentary group for voluntary euthanasia was established on the initiative of Lady Nicol.[12] The group was chaired by the medical peer, Lord Winstanley, Liberal Democrat spokesman on health,[13]

---

[8] Clause 5. The 1936 Bill did, implicitly at least, create an immunity for doctors; see clause 1.

[9] For example, the Bill was criticized on the grounds of poor drafting, vague definition of terms, and procedural difficulties.

[10] Voluntary Euthanasia Bill, Provisional Draft 1983.

[11] The 10-minute rule provides an opportunity for a backbencher Member of Parliament to raise an issue. If a bill is successful at this stage, it simply means that the person putting forward the bill has the opportunity for the bill to be printed. There is, however, no chance of it directly becoming legislation through the 10-minute rule procedure.

[12] Note, 'All Party Parliamentary Group' (1991) 43 *VES Newsletter* 9.

[13] Note, 'Euthanasia: New Issue for Conscience' (1991) 303 BMJ 1422.

and claimed the support of many MPs and peers with supporters of the group drawn from both Houses and the main political parties. Under the aegis of this group, a bill to confirm the legal status of advance directives was introduced into the House of Lords as a Private Member's Bill by Lord Allen of Abbeydale. Following the establishment of the House of Lords Select Committee in 1993 this Bill was not debated in the House of Lords but simply referred to the committee. Following the death of Lord Winstanley in July 1993 the group disbanded but in 1995 a new group, the All-Party Parliamentary Advance Directives Group, was formed at the instigation of Mr Piara Khabra, who is currently the chair.

The society is presently campaigning to have a Private Member's Bill introduced into Parliament. This is dependent on persuading one of the society's MP supporters to agree to introduce such legislation, and then for that Member to be drawn in the ballot in the House of Commons, allowing that Member the opportunity of introducing a Private Member's Bill.

B. Official Inquiries

There have, over the past few decades, been a number of official inquiries in the United Kingdom which have considered the issue of mercy killing and recommended against any change to the law to make it the subject of a separate offence.[14] However, as these inquiries have focused on the more general question of mercy killing as distinct from the more specific issue of medically administered active voluntary euthanasia, these findings are only of limited relevance to the discussion in this chapter. Of much greater significance was the establishment in 1993 of the House of Lords Select Committee on Medical Ethics. This committee was set up in the wake of two important cases in England: the case of Tony Bland in which the Law Lords had ruled that doctors could stop artificial feeding[15] and had called on Parliament to consider the issue of medical assistance in dying; and in the previous year, the conviction of Dr Cox[16] which had catapulted the issue of euthanasia into the public arena. The committee's terms of reference were wide ranging, including consideration of a person's right to withhold consent to life-prolonging treatment and the position of persons who are no longer able to give or withhold consent. With respect to the issue of euthanasia, the committee's terms of reference were to 'consider whether and in what circumstances actions that have as their intention or a likely conse-

---

[14] *Royal Commission on Capital Punishment* (London, 1953) Cmnd. 8932, paras. 177–80; Criminal Law Revision Committee, Fourteenth Report, *Offences Against the Person* (London, 1980) Cmnd. 7844, para. 115. Note also the Report of the Select Committee, *Murder and Life Imprisonment* (London, 1988–89) HL Paper which rejected a proposal for the creation of a special defence for cases of mercy killing.

[15] See further pp. 38–9 above.

[16] For discussion of this case see pp. 143–5 above.

quence the shortening of another person's life may be justified on the grounds that they accord with that person's wishes or with that person's best interests . . . and in so doing, to pay regard to the likely effects of changes in law or medical practice on society as a whole'.

In the course of conducting its inquiry, the Committee received evidence from many organizations and interested groups as well as letters from many individuals. In addition, the committee made a visit to the Netherlands towards the end of its inquiry to discuss the experience in that jurisdiction.

In its report,[17] the committee strongly endorsed the right of a competent patient to refuse consent to any medical treatment, for whatever reason. It was, however, of the view that the right to refuse medical treatment is far removed from the right to request assistance in dying. Whilst acknowledging the strength of the arguments which have been advanced in support of voluntary euthanasia, the committee came to the conclusion that ultimately, these arguments are not sufficient reasons to weaken society's prohibition of intentional killing which is the cornerstone of law and social relationships. The committee did accept that there are individual cases in which euthanasia may be seen by some to be appropriate. But, in the opinion of the committee, individual cases cannot reasonably establish the foundation of a policy which would have such serious and widespread repercussions. Further, it was stated that the issue of euthanasia is one in which the interests of the individual cannot be separated from the interests of society as a whole.

One reason that the committee gave for this conclusion was that it did not think it possible to set secure limits on voluntary euthanasia. The committee was of the opinion that it would be next to impossible to ensure that all acts of euthanasia were truly voluntary and that any liberalization of the law was not abused. Moreover, the committee stated that to create an exception to the general prohibition of intentional killing would inevitably open the way to its further erosion whether by design, by inadventure, or by the human tendency to test the limits of any regulation. These dangers, the committee felt, were such that any decriminalization of voluntary euthanasia would give rise to more, and graver problems than those that it sought to address.

The committee also expressed concern that vulnerable people—the elderly, the lonely, sick, or distressed—would feel pressure, whether real or imagined, to request early death. The committee accepted that for the most part, requests resulting from such pressure or from remediable depressive illness would be identified as such by doctors and managed appropriately. Nevertheless, the committee felt that the message which society sends to vulnerable and disadvantaged people should not, however, obliquely, encourage them to seek death, but should ensure them of society's care and

---

[17] *Report of the Select Committee on Medical Ethics* (London, 1994) HL Paper 21, Vol. 1.

support in life. The committee went on to extol the benefits of palliative care as the preferred method of relieving the pain and distress of terminal illness.

The committee concluded that rejection of euthanasia as an option for the individual, in the interests of the wider social good, entails a compelling social responsibility to care adequately for those who are elderly, dying, or disabled. To this end, a number of recommendations were made, including recommendations that high quality palliative care should be made more widely available; research into new and improved methods of pain relief and symptom control should be adequately supported; and that training of health care professionals should prepare them for the weighty ethical responsibilities which they carry, by giving greater priority to health care ethics, and counselling and communications skills.

In addition, the committee, in keeping with the approach adopted in the earlier inquiries into mercy killing, recommended against the creation of a new offence of mercy killing. Further, the committee recommended no change in the law on assisted suicide. It did, however, strongly endorse the recommendations of a previous select committee[18] that the mandatory life sentence for murder should be abolished to allow greater flexibility in sentencing.

A number of observations can be made regarding the House of Lords Select Committee Report. The first thing to note is that it is somewhat surprising, in all the circumstances, that the committee's report, including the committee's recommendations regarding voluntary euthanasia, was unanimous. Given the diversity of views that are generally held with respect to active voluntary euthanasia, one would have expected at least some dissent from the majority position. The very unanimity of the report suggests that the committee is not representative of the wider views of British society, particularly having regard to the outcome of opinion polls in the United Kingdom. Moreover, the committee's conclusion that intentional killing is always wrong and must be unequivocally prohibited is contrary to the view of a substantial proportion of British doctors.[19]

One of the main reasons given by the committee for its rejection of active voluntary euthanasia was the committee's concern regarding abuses and difficulties in controlling the practice if the law were changed to permit it under certain circumstances. However, notably absent from the committee's deliberation was any consideration of the problems or dangers inherent in the present situation of a hidden and unregulated practice. By failing to advert to the difficulties with the law as it stands, the conclusions of the report with respect to increased risks lose much of their force. Also to be noted is the fact that the committee's deliberations regarding euthanasia

---

[18] Report of the Select Committee, *Murder and Life Imprisonment* above n. 14, at 78.
[19] Boyd, K., 'The Price of Euthanasia' (1995) Jan. *VES Newsletter* 1, 2.

make no reference to the Netherlands position. There is some discussion in a separate Appendix to the report of the committee's visit to the Netherlands (Appendix 3), but there is no explanation as to why such little weight appears to have been given to the Dutch experience. Finally, the committee's pronouncements regarding palliative care offer little comfort to those whose pain and distress cannot be adequately relieved or whose experience with dying falls short of the ideal. As has been argued in an earlier chapter,[20] advancements with regard to palliative care are certainly to be encouraged and may help to reduce the need for euthanasia, but will never obviate the need altogether.

Although the Report of the House of Lords Select Committee on Medical Ethics unanimously rejected the legalization of active voluntary euthanasia, the very fact that this committee was established to inquire into the issue is of itself of some significance, demonstrating an awareness on the part of Parliament that it is a matter of societal concern which has to be addressed. In this respect, the committee's deliberations can be seen as part of a longer term reform process. In the short term, however, there is no evidence of any willingness on the part of the British Government to move on the issue. In its official response to the Select Committee's Report, the Government has strongly supported the committee's rejection of the case for legalization of euthanasia.[21]

II. AUSTRALIA

Undoubtedly, the most significant development to have occurred in Australia has been the passage of legislation permitting active voluntary euthanasia and doctor-assisted suicide in the Northern Territory. To begin with, a brief account will be given of developments in Australia leading up to these reforms. As in the United Kingdom, the more general issue of mercy killing has been considered by a number of law reform bodies in various Australian jurisdictions to determine whether it should the subject of a separate offence, taking it outside the category of murder.[22] However, as was recognized in at least one of these inquiries,[23] quite different issues are involved in cases of mercy killing by family or friends, and cases of active

---

[20] See pp. 247–8 above.

[21] *The Government Response to the Report of the Select Committee on Medical Ethics* (London, 1994) Cmnd. 2553.

[22] Law Reform Commissioner of Victoria, Report No. 1, *Law of Murder* (Melbourne, 1974) 20; South Australian Criminal Law and Penal Methods Committee, Fourth Report, *The Substantive Criminal Law* (Adelaide, 1977) 57–8; Law Reform Commissioner of Victoria, Working Paper No 8, *Murder: Mental Element and Punishment* (Melbourne, 1984).

[23] Law Reform Commissioner of Victoria, Working Paper, *Murder: Mental Element and Punishment* above n. 22. at 30.

voluntary euthanasia performed in the medical context, so these deliberations are, at best, only of indirect relevance to this work.

In addition, there have been a number of Australian inquiries dealing generally with dying with dignity, the terms of reference for which have been sufficiently broad to allow consideration of the issue of active voluntary euthanasia. In 1985, the all-party Parliament of Victoria Social Development Committee was given a brief to inquire into a number of issues related to the treatment of dying patients. The committee's terms of reference were potentially far-reaching, including consideration of:

(i)   whether it is desirable and practicable for the government to take legislative or other action establishing a right to die;

(ii)   the fundamental question as to whether, and under what circumstances, if any, a person should have a right to die; and

(iii)   the right of an individual to direct that in certain circumstances he or she be allowed to die, or be assisted in dying and the form which such a direction should take.

Regrettably, however, the issue of active voluntary euthanasia was given scant consideration. A major factor in this regard was that the matter was exclusively examined in the context of determining whether it was appropriate to take action establishing a 'right to die' rather than under one of the other terms of reference which would have provided a more suitable basis from which to proceed the analysis. Because of the inherent vagueness of the concept of a 'right to die', the committee concluded that it was neither desirable or practicable to legislate or take other action to establish such a right. A number of the committee's other terms of reference, directing inquiry into the right of an individual to be 'assisted in dying' were interpreted by the committee as not encompassing euthanasia. Although arguably broad enough to permit consideration of active voluntary euthanasia as a form of assistance in dying, these particular terms of reference were read down by the committee so as to exclude consideration of this subject. This represented a fairly significant limitation on the scope of the committee's inquiry, virtually foreclosing serious consideration of active voluntary euthanasia.

Some years later, in the State of South Australia, a Select Committee on the Law and Practice Relating to Death and Dying was appointed by the South Australian House of Assembly. Included amongst its terms of reference, the committee was to examine to what extent, if any, community attitudes towards death and dying may be changing and to what extent if any the law relating to death or dying needs to be clarified or amended. This term of reference was sufficiently broad to include the issue of active voluntary euthanasia, and it was in fact interpreted by the committee as encompassing this issue. Although the committee had from an early stage in its deliberations acknowledged the view of some people in the community that active voluntary euthanasia should be decriminalized and become an accepted part of medical practice,[24] the committee ultimately came down against the legalization of active voluntary euthanasia. In rejecting the arguments that had been advanced by the South Australian Voluntary Euthanasia Society in support of the case for legalization, the committee expressed the view that the fact that some patients and doctors may resort to illegal means of ending life is not in itself sufficient justification for legalizing the practice. Reference was made to evidence put before the committee regarding the growth of the voluntary euthanasia movement, results of public opinion polls, surveys of the medical profession, and published articles in support of legalization of active voluntary euthanasia. However, the committee stated that these materials did not persuade it that parliament should legislate in this area, since there is a significant difference between the expression of personal support for legalizing active voluntary euthanasia and the acceptance of responsibility for provision in law of this power. The committee also noted that: 'The fact that there is no precedent in the world for legalized voluntary euthanasia, despite popular pressure in many countries, is evidence of reluctance by even the most radical legislators to adopt a course of action which could have far-reaching and unforeseen consequences'.[25]

Whilst acknowledging the need to relieve suffering of patients, the committee was of the view that this was not a goal which should be achieved by means of medically assisted death. The committee expressed the belief that if the other recommendations made in its report regarding appropriate care for the dying were adopted, there would be significant relief of suffering, as well as enhancement of individual dignity, greater comfort for families, and improved development of professional skills.

Although rejecting the legalization of active voluntary euthanasia, the committee's report is significant in that it did at least openly address the issue and acknowledge the growing demand for legalization of the practice. It could be argued that there might have been more complete canvassing of the arguments in support of legalization, in particular the need for upholding patient self-determination. Essentially, the reasons given for rejecting any change in this area reflect conservative views about the implications of legalization and concern about untested consequences. Unfortunately, the current Netherlands' experience where active voluntary euthanasia has for some time been practised by the medical profession with relative openness,

---

[24] South Australian Select Committee of the House of Assembly on the Law and Practice Relating to Death and Dying, *Interim Report of the Select Committee of the House of Assembly on the Law and Practice Relating to Death and Dying* (Adelaide, 1991).

[25] South Australia Select Committee of the House of Assembly on the Law and Practice Relating to Death and Dying, *Second Interim Report of the Select Committee of the House of Assembly on the Law and Practice Relating to Death and Dying* (Adelaide, 1992) 52.

was not studied in depth by the committee, though the committee did note concerns which have been expressed about the cumulative impact on that society of medically assisted death. Since the Netherlands is the only jurisdiction where active voluntary euthanasia is practised by the medical profession with some degree of official acceptance, any serious and comprehensive analysis of the issue of legalization of active voluntary euthanasia would require a detailed examination of the position in that jurisdiction.[26]

Even prior to the historic developments in the Northern Territory in May 1995, there had been growing indications that a serious effort would be made in Australia for the legalization of active voluntary euthanasia. Interest was sparked in the Australian Capital Territory (ACT) by the quite unexpected announcement of the ACT branch of the Australian Labour Party in June 1991 that it had adopted the concept of active voluntary euthanasia as party policy in the following terms: 'If a patient who has been counselled consistently requests assistance to die and two doctors are of the view that there is little or no prospect of substantial improvement of the patient's condition, then it should not be an offence for a doctor to assist the patient to die'.

It was at the time stated to be a long term proposal which the ACT Labor government would implement, following a process of extensive community consultation. The adoption of this policy by the ACT branch of the Australian Labor Party represented quite a milestone in the history of active voluntary euthanasia in Australia, being the first time that a political party has officially endorsed its legalization.

The first significant legislative move toward the legalization of active voluntary euthanasia in Australia came from Independent Mr Michael Moore who, in June 1993, introduced into the ACT Legislative Assembly the Voluntary and Natural Death Bill 1993. This Bill sought to make provision with respect to both withholding and withdrawing of treatment, and active voluntary euthanasia. It also sought to provide a mechanism for future decision-making in the event of the patient's incompetency by means of the appointment of a power of attorney. Pursuant to the Bill, a person of sound mind and who has attained the age of 18 years may make a direction that in the event that he or she suffers from a terminal illness, extraordinary measures shall not be applied to him or her, or a drug for the purpose of inducing his or her death shall be administered or provided to him or her. The Bill further provided that where a person is capable of administering or assisting to administer a drug to induce death to himself or herself, they should do so.

In addition, the Bill made provision for an adult of sound mind to confer

---

[26] For discussion of the Netherlands position, see Ch. 7 below.

on another person (the grantee) the power to consent on their behalf to the withholding or withdrawing of extraordinary measures from the grantor, or the administration or provision of a drug to induce the death of the grantor in the event that the grantor is suffering from a terminal illness and there is an absence of thought or perception in the grantor.

The Voluntary Euthanasia Bill contained a number of preconditions before a direction from a patient (or the patient's agent) for assistance in dying could be complied with. These included that the request (whether in writing or made orally) is witnessed by two persons who are not relatives of the person making the direction or entitled to any portion of the estate of the terminally ill person; that the medical practitioner must inform the person about the nature of his or her illness, alternative forms of treatment that may be available and the consequences of remaining untreated; and that the medical practitioner must not comply with a direction unless he or she has consulted another medical practitioner who has not been involved in the treatment of the patient, and that practitioner has agreed to the granting of the request.

Shortly after its introduction in the ACT Legislative Assembly, the Voluntary and Natural Death Bill 1993 was referred to a Parliamentary Select Committee on Euthanasia which was set up to inquire into and report on the Bill by March 1994. In the meantime, the Labor Party announced that it would not be supporting the legislation as the party was not yet ready to implement its policy and the community required more time to debate the matter. After a period of public consultation, the three member committee, (with Michael Moore as chair) came to the conclusion that the provisions of the Bill enabling an individual to seek assistance in dying should not be proceeded with at this stage.[27] In so deciding, the committee acknowledged the apparently ever-increasing community support for voluntary euthanasia, but also the very strong representation of views from a number of influential sectors in the community opposing the euthanasia provisions of the Bill. However, a recommendation was made that Michael Moore be given leave to bring in a Bill dealing with the withholding and withdrawing of medical treatment and related matters, and this did in fact result in the subsequent passage of the Medical Treatment Act 1994 (ACT).

Although the Voluntary and Natural Death Bill 1993 (ACT) had little prospect of success, particularly in view of the loose drafting for which the legislation had been widely criticized, it was nevertheless significant, representing the first occasion that a bill for the legalization of active voluntary euthanasia has been introduced in an Australian parliament.

As was suggested earlier, undoubtedly the most significant development to have occurred with respect to active voluntary euthanasia in Australia or

[27] Legislative Assembly for the Australian Capital Territory, Select Committee on Euthanasia, *Voluntary and Natural Death Bill 1993* (Canberra, 1994).

the common law world generally has been the enactment of legislation in the Northern Territory of Australia which permits active voluntary euthanasia in carefully defined circumstances. Apart from the Netherlands, where active voluntary euthanasia is practised quite openly, but remains an offence under the Dutch Penal Code (although guidelines for the practice have recently been given some statutory recognition under regulations[28]), the only other jurisdiction to have legislated in this area is the US State of Oregon where legislation permitting doctor-assisted suicide put forward by way of citizen initiated referendum was passed in November 1994. However, the introduction of this legislation, which in any event, does not encompass a more direct form of assistance in the form of active voluntary euthanasia, has been blocked due to a constitutional challenge to its validity.[29]

In February 1995, the then Chief Minister of the Northern Territory, the Honourable Marshall Perron, tabled a Private Member's Bill in the Northern Territory Legislative Assembly for the legalization of active voluntary euthanasia and doctor-assisted suicide. This in itself was significant, being the first time in Australian history that a government leader had introduced such legislation. The Bill, entitled the Rights of the Terminally Ill Bill 1995, was then referred to a parliamentary select committee, the Northern Territory Select Committee on Euthanasia, for consideration. The Select Committee conducted public hearings in the Northern Territory during April 1995. It also received numerous written submissions from residents in the Northern Territory as well as other parts of Australia. In mid-May 1995, the Select Committee reported back to the Assembly. Its report, *The Right of the Individual or the Common Good?*[30] contained many recommendations for amendments to the initial Bill as well as recommendations regarding the improvement of palliative care services in the Northern Territory and the need for public education with regard to the legislation. However, the committee quite deliberately chose not to make recommendations as to whether or not legislation permitting active voluntary euthanasia should be introduced, its chairman explaining that pursuant to its terms of reference, the committee's role was to gather evidence and submissions for the consideration of the members of the Legislative Assembly so that an informed debate could take place in the Parliament. Shortly prior to the Bill being returned to the Assembly, its architect, Chief Minister Marshall Perron announced his resignation, explaining that he wanted all members of the Assembly to be able to vote on the Bill in accordance with their conscience, without the debate being influenced in any way by his position as political leader.

Upon the return of the Bill to the Assembly, after some debate, a vote of

---

[28] See Ch. 7 for discussion of the Netherlands' position.
[29] See further below.   [30] (Darwin, 1995).

13 to 12 was taken that the Bill be read for a second time.[31] In the committee stage of the debate, numerous amendments were made to the legislation, most of which were introduced by Marshall Perron himself and by the leader of the Australian Labor Party Opposition. These amendments, which implemented to a large extent the recommendations of the Select Committee, effected some quite significant changes, particularly in relation to the strengthening of the safeguards in the legislation. The Bill was ultimately passed by the 25-member Northern Territory Assembly on 25 May 1995 by a majority of 15 to 10 after a marathon 14-hour debate which ended in the early hours of the morning. Unlike most of the parliaments in Australia, the parliament in the Northern Territory is comprized of one house only, so this single historic vote guaranteed the passage of the Rights of the Terminally Ill Bill. The Act has since received the Administrator's assent, and is due to commence on 1 July 1996.

The general scheme of the legislation is to make it lawful in certain circumstances for a medical practitioner to assist with the termination of a patient's life at the patient's request, thereby creating an exception to the prohibition on homicide and assisting suicide under the Northern Territory Criminal Code 1988.[32] The Rights of the Terminally Ill Act[33] provides in section 4 that a patient who in the course of a terminal illness is experiencing pain, suffering and/or distress to an extent unacceptable to the patient, may request that his or her medical practitioner give assistance to terminate his or her life. In the original bill, no specific definition of terminal illness was provided in the definition section of the legislation, although it was quite clear from the substantive provisions that the legislation was only intended to apply in circumstances where a patient is suffering from an illness from which the patient is, within reasonable medical judgement, likely to die within 12 months. In accordance with the recommendations of the Select Committee, this set period of 12 months was removed from the original bill. 'Terminal illness' is now expressly defined in the legislation as an illness[34] which, in reasonable medical judgement, will, in the normal course, without the application of extraordinary measures or of treatment unacceptable to the patient, result in the death of the patient. This represented a significant change to the legislation, overcoming the great practical difficulty of predicting likely life expectancy for patients who are terminally ill. The legislation, as amended, provides the option of assistance in dying to those patients

---

[31] Trollope, S., 'Legislating a Right to Die: The Rights of the Terminally Ill Act 1995 (NT)' (1995) 3 *JLaw&Med.* 19.

[32] For discussion of the general criminal law principles under the Criminal Code 1983 (NT) see Chs. 1 and 2.

[33] A copy of this Act and the Regulations enacted under it are contained in the Appendix at the rear of this work; see pp. 503–19.

[34] 'Illness' is defined in s. 3 as including injury or degeneration of mental or physical faculties.

whose condition will result in death regardless of available treatment, as well as those whose condition may not strictly be terminal, but who reject certain life-saving treatment as being unacceptable to them, provided that there is some degree of imminence of death in the absence of that treatment[35] (for example, a patient with motor neuron disease who is ventilator dependent) and that the other conditions of the legislation are satisfied.

The key section which empowers a doctor to comply with a patient's request and to assist lawfully in ending the patient's life is section 5. This section provides that where a terminally ill patient has requested a medical practitioner to provide assistance in terminating his or her life pursuant to a certificate of request (contained in the Schedule to the Act), a medical practitioner may, if satisfied that the conditions contained in the legislation have been met, assist the patient to terminate the patient's life in accordance with the legislation. Even though section 5 is expressed in discretionary terms, thereby giving doctors a choice as to whether or not to provide assistance, it goes on to state expressly that the medical practitioner may, for any reason, *refuse* to give assistance. This additional wording has clearly been included to counter any concern that doctors who are opposed to assisting the suicide of a patient or administering active voluntary euthanasia would be compelled to participate in these practices if they were made legal.[36] Thus, despite the language of the title of the legislation (*Rights* of the Terminally Ill Act[37]) it clearly confers no right on an individual to demand assistance to die: rather it allows a patient to make a request and for a doctor to choose to comply with that request provided certain conditions are met. The Act further seeks to protect the freedom of a doctor to choose either to participate or not to participate under the legislation by making it an offence for a person to give or promise any reward or advantage (other than a reasonable payment for medical services) or by any means cause or threaten to cause any disadvantage to a medical practitioner or other person for refusing to assist, or for the purpose of compelling or persuading the medical practitioner or other person to assist or refuse to assist in the termination of a patient's life under the legislation (section 6).

As noted, the legislation is framed in terms of a medical practitioner assisting a patient to terminate his or her life. The term 'assist' is defined in the interpretation section (section 3) as including the prescribing of a substance, the preparation and the giving of a substance to the patient for self-administration, and the administration of a substance to the patient. The legislation therefore clearly encompasses cases of doctor-assisted suicide in which the medical practitioner assists his or her patient to die by providing

[35] See s. 7(1) discussed below.
[36] See also the immunity provisions in s. 20(2) and (4) of the Act which reinforce the right of a doctor to refuse to participate in assisting a patient to die.
[37] Emphasis added.

the means by which the patient takes his or her own life, as well as cases of active voluntary euthanasia where the medical practitioner is more directly involved, through the administration of a substance which brings about the death of the patient. The Act itself provides no direction as to what substances may be suitable for this purpose but it does stipulate in a later provision (section 7(2)) that in assisting a patient under the Act, a medical practitioner must be guided by appropriate medical standards and such guidelines, if any, as are prescribed, and shall consider the appropriate pharmaceutical information about any substance reasonably available for use in the circumstances. The Rights of the Terminally Ill Regulations which have been enacted under the Act (see section 21) set down some guidelines for the performance of active voluntary euthanasia and doctor-assisted suicide but do not prescribe any particular drugs or combination of drugs to be used.

The original bill had not specified any minimum period of practice for medical practitioners before they were eligible to provide assistance to a patient at his or her request to terminate the patient's life. The Select Committee had been concerned about inexperienced medical practitioners being involved in the practice of active voluntary euthanasia and accordingly recommended that only medical practitioners with at least 5 years' experience should make decisions under the legislation, and this is now a requirement under the legislation.[38] It should be noted that the legislation does contemplate that assistance to terminate a patient's life may be provided by a 'health care provider' on the instruction of a medical practitioner. 'Health care provider' is defined in the Act as, in relation to a patient, including a hospital, nursing home, or other institutions (including those responsible for its management) in which the patient is located for care or attention, and any nurse or other person whose duties include or directly or indirectly relate to the care or medical treatment of the patient. Section 16(1) makes it clear that an action taken in accordance with the Act by a medical practitioner or a health care provider on the instructions of a medical practitioner does not constitute an offence under Part VI of the Criminal Code. Where assistance is provided by a health care provider, the medical practitioner must at least remain present while the assistance is given and until the death of the patient (section 7(1)(p)).

A critical part of the legislation is section 7 which sets out the conditions under which a medical practitioner may provide assistance to a patient to end the patient's life. Section 7(1) provides that a medical practitioner may assist a patient to end his or her life only if the following conditions are met:

---

[38] 'Medical practitioner' is defined in s. 3 as a medical practitioner who has been entitled to practise as a medical practitioner (however described) in a state or a territory of the Commonwealth for a continuous period of not less than 5 years and who is resident in, and entitled under the Medical Act to practise medicine, in the territory.

(a)   the patient has attained the age of 18 years;
(b)   the medical practitioner is satisfied, on reasonable grounds, that—
    (i)   the patient is suffering from an illness that will in the normal
           course and without the application of extraordinary measures,
           result in the death of the patient;
    (ii)   in reasonable medical judgement, there is no medical measure
           acceptable to the patient that can reasonably be undertaken in
           the hope of effecting a cure; and
    (iii) any medical treatment reasonably available to the patient is
           confined to the relief of pain and/or suffering with the object of
           allowing the patient to die a comfortable death.

The original Bill had contained a requirement that the medical practitioner's opinion be confirmed by a second medical practitioner who has
examined the patient. During the course of amendments made to the legislation prior to its passage, this requirement was tightened up to ensure the
independence of the second medical practitioner. In addition, a requirement was added to section 7(1)(c) that the second medical practitioner must
hold a diploma of psychological medicine or its equivalent. By requiring the
second medical practitioner to have some background in psychiatry or
psychology, the focus of this precondition was to verify the patient's mental
state, in particular that the patient is not suffering from a treatable clinical
depression in respect of the illness. However, as was pointed out in the
course of the original legislative debate by parliamentarians opposed to the
legislation, the decision to define the category of second medical practitioner principally by reference to their qualification to determine the patient's mental state was made at the expense of not providing for expert
confirmation of diagnosis and prognosis by a doctor specializing in the field
of the patient's terminal illness.

Since the passage of the legislation, it has come to light that the 'diploma
of psychological medicine' referred to in this section is an obsolete qualification. An amendment Bill has recently been brought before the Northern
Territory Parliament to address this difficulty. The Rights of the Terminally
Ill Amendment Bill 1995 (NT) was introduced in November 1995 and
passed with only minor amendment in February 1996 (Rights of the Terminally Ill Amendment Act 1996). The effect of this amendment is to replace
the provision requiring the second medical practitioner to hold a diploma of
psychological medicine or its equivalent with a twofold requirement: the
patient must be examined by a second medical practitioner and by a qualified psychiatrist, both of whom must be independent from the first medical
practitioner.[39] The significance of this amendment is that the two distinct

[39] See s. 7(1)(c) which specifies that neither the second medical practitioner nor the qualified
psychiatrist can be a relative or employee of or a member of the same medical practice as the
first medical practitioner or each other.

aspects of the role of second medical practitioner as originally provided for, namely confirming the opinion of the first medical practitioner regarding the patient's condition and prognosis and confirming that the patient is not suffering from a treatable clinical depression in respect of the illness, are now to be performed by specialists in each of these areas. As was noted, the principal impetus for this amendment was to rectify the difficulty regarding the 'diploma of psychological medicine' referred to under the original Act. This has been achieved by now setting down a more stringent requirement that the patient be examined by a qualified psychiatrist[40] (section 7(1)(c)(ii)) who must confirm that the patient is not suffering from a treatable clinical depression in respect of the illness (section 7(1)(c)(iv)) before a doctor can proceed to assist a patient to die under the Act. Having removed the requirement that the second medical practitioner have qualifications in psychological medicine or its equivalent (this role of assessing the patient's mental state now falling within the responsibility of a psychiatrist) the opportunity has been taken to amend the legislation to ensure that the second medical practitioner has appropriate expertise in the area of the patient's terminal illness. The new section 7(1)(c)(i) stipulates that the second medical practitioner must hold prescribed professional qualifications, or have prescribed experience in the treatment of the terminal illness from which the patient is suffering.[41] One of the key preconditions for the performance of active voluntary euthanasia or assisting the suicide of a patient under the Act is that the second medical practitioner examine the patient and confirm the findings of the first medical practitioner with regard to the existence and seriousness of the illness; that the patient is likely to die as a result of the illness; and the patient's prognosis.[42]

A further precondition to a medical practitioner assisting a patient to end his or her life is contained in section 7(1)(d) which requires that the

[40] Defined in s. 3 of the legislation as a person (a) entitled under a law of a state or territory of the Commonwealth to practise as a specialist in the medical speciality of psychiatry; (b) a specialist whose qualifications are recognized by the Royal Australia and New Zealand College of Psychiatrists as entitling the person to fellowship of that College; or (c) a person employed by the Commonwealth or a State or Territory of the Commonwealth, or an Agency or authority of the Commonwealth or a State or Territory, as a specialist or consultant in the medical speciality of psychiatry.

[41] The Working Party on the Implementation of the Rights of the Terminally Ill Act had made detailed recommendations on the requisite professional qualification or prescribed experience for the second medical practitioner; Working Party, *Report on the Implementation of the Rights of the Terminally Ill Act* (Darwin, 1996). As enacted, The Rights of the Terminally Ill Regulations provide that for the purposes of section 7(1)(c)(i) of the Act, the medical practitioner shall hold a qualification in a medical speciality related to the terminal illness of the patient recognised by a medical specialised college in Australia and which entitles the medical practitioner to fellowship of the college. Note also the requirement stemming from the definition of 'medical practitioner' in s. 3 (see n. 38 above) including the requirement of residency in the Northern Territory.

[42] This is now set out in s. 7(1)(c)(iii).

illness is causing the patient severe pain or suffering. The wording of this provision came about following amendment to the original Bill which had required that the illness be one which is causing the patient severe 'pain or suffering or distress'. In an effort to tighten up the legislation, 'distress' has been removed as a separate ground justifying a medical practitioner to provide assistance to a patient to end his or her life, although it does still appear in section 4 (together with pain and suffering) to describe those patients who may request assistance under the legislation to terminate their lives.

Further, section 7(1)(e) requires that the medical practitioner has informed the patient of the nature of the illness and its likely course, and the medical treatment, including palliative care, counselling, psychiatric support, and extraordinary measures for keeping the patient alive that might be available to the patient. In relation to this requirement, the legislation specifically provides that where a patient's medical practitioner has no special qualification in the field of palliative care, the information to be provided to the patient regarding the availability of palliative care is to be given by some other medical practitioner who does have the necessary qualifications (s. 7(3)).

Section 7(1) of the Act goes on to require as preconditions for a medical practitioner providing assistance under the legislation that:

(f)	after being informed by the medical practitioner in accordance with section 7(1)(e) of the Act, the patient indicates to the medical practitioner that the patient has decided to end his or her life;

(g)	the medical practitioner is satisfied that the patient has considered the possible implication of the patient's decision to his or her family;

(h)	the medical practitioner is satisfied, on reasonable grounds, that the patient is of sound mind and that the patient's decision to end his or her life has been made freely, voluntarily and after due consideration.

The next of the preconditions for assistance refers to the execution of a certificate of request by the patient, or in circumstances where a patient is physically unable to sign the certificate of request, a person acting on his or her behalf in accordance with section 9 of the Act. That section makes it clear that this must be someone other than the medical practitioner or qualified psychiatrist referred to in s. 7(1)(c) or a person who is likely to receive a financial benefit directly or indirectly as a result of the death of the patient. One of the more significant amendments made to the legislation in the course of its passage was the inclusion of a 'cooling off' period between the time of the initial request for assistance and the giving of assistance to the patient to terminate his or her life. Section 7(1)(i) stipulates that there must be a period of least 7 days between the time that the patient indicates to the medical practitioner that he or she has decided to end his or her life, and the signing of the certificate of request. Pursuant to section 7(1)(n), a further 48 hours must elapse from the time of signing the certificate of request before that request can be acted upon. The combined effect of these provisions is that a person's life cannot be ended until at least 9 days after the initial request for assistance was made.

Section 7(1) of the Act then continues with a number of provisions dealing with the signing and witnessing of a certificate of request. It requires that:

(j)　the medical practitioner has witnessed the patient's signature on the certificate of request or that of the person who signed on behalf of the patient, and has completed and signed the relevant declaration on the certificate;

(k)　the certificate of request has been signed in the presence of the patient and the first medical practitioner by another medical practitioner (who may be the same medical practitioner who has examined the patient pursuant to section 7(1)(c)(i)) after that medical practitioner has discussed the case with the first medical practitioner and the patient and is satisfied, on reasonable grounds, that the certificate is in order, that the patient is of sound mind and the patient's decision to end his or her life has been made freely, voluntarily and after due consideration, and that the above conditions have been complied with.

A further requirement introduced by way of amendment to the original Bill which was made following the recommendations of the Select Committee concerns the use of an interpreter where the medical practitioners do not share the same first language as the patient. This amendment was seen as being of particular importance in the Northern Territory where there is a large Aboriginal population who do not speak English as a first language. Section 7(4) of the Act provides that a medical practitioner must not assist a patient under the Act where the medical practitioner or any other medical practitioner or qualified psychiatrist who is required under the legislation to communicate with the patient does not share the same first language as the patient, unless there is present at the time of that communication and the time that the certificate of request is signed by or on behalf of the patient an accredited interpreter in the first language of the patient.[43] The Act further requires that where the assistance of an interpreter is required, the certificate of request must be signed by the interpreter confirming the patient's understanding of the request for assistance.

---

[43] This provision has been the subject of recent amendment. Under the original Act, s. 7(4) referred to an interpreter who holds a level three accreditation. This requirement has since been removed and substituted with a requirement that the person hold a prescribed qualification for interpreters in the first language of the patient, thus leaving the details of this requirement to be dealt with under the regulations: see the Rigths of the Terminally Ill Regulations.

Another precondition is that the medical practitioner has no reason to believe that he or she, the countersigning medical practitioner or a close relative or associate of either of them, will gain a financial advantage (other than a reasonable payment for medical services) directly or indirectly as a result of the death of the patient (section 7(1)(m)).

Section 7(1) of the legislation further stipulates as a condition for a medical practitioner to provide assistance to a patient that:

(o)   at no time before assisting the patient to end his or her life has the patient given to the medical practitioner an indication that it was no longer the patient's wish to end his or her life.

This particular formulation was the product of an amendment made to the original Bill which had required the medical practitioner to have no reasonable grounds for doubting that it continues to be the patient's wish to end his or her life. This earlier formulation cast the onus on the doctor to be satisfied, at the time of providing assistance in dying, that the patient did in fact want the doctor to proceed. On the recommendation of the Select Committee this provision was amended so as to place the onus on the patient to indicate that they have changed their mind. This means that in circumstances where a patient's mental condition has deteriorated, possibly to the point of incompetence, a doctor may nevertheless proceed to act upon the patient's request, provided that the doctor has no reason to believe that the patient would not want him or her to do so. As the legislation stands, there is no requirement that the patient is competent at that time or that the doctor must confirm that the patient wishes him or her to provide assistance. Provided the other requirements of the legislation are met (including an initial request for assistance which is confirmed in writing by the execution of a certificate of request by the patient whilst competent), a doctor may proceed to provide assistance in dying, regardless of the mental state of the patient at that time, so long as there has been no indication from the patient that this no longer represents his or her wishes. Whilst this approach ensures that patients are not excluded from receiving assistance on the grounds of intervening incompetence, it would have been preferable and more consistent with the other rigorous safeguards in the legislation, to have a requirement that the patient's wishes must be confirmed immediately prior to assistance being given. This is particularly the case in view of the fact that it may have been some time ago that the patient signed the certificate of request: apart from the requirement under the Act that a minimum of 48 hours must have elapsed since the certificate of request was signed, the Act is silent as to the timing of a doctor acting upon a patient's request.

The final precondition under section 7(1) of the legislation is that:

(p)   the medical practitioner himself provides the assistance and/or is and remains present while the assistance is given and until the death of the patient.

Important amendments made to the original Bill were the restrictions placed on medical practitioners providing assistance to a patient to end his or her life in circumstances where palliative care options have not been exhausted. To begin with, as noted earlier, section 7(3) makes it clear that where a patient's medical practitioner has no special qualifications in the field of palliative care, the information to be provided to the patient on the availability of palliative care shall be given by a medical practitioner who has such special qualifications in the field of palliative care as are prescribed.[44] Section 8 of the Act prohibits a medical practitioner from assisting a patient under the Act, if, in his or her opinion, after considering the advice of the second medical practitioner, there are palliative care options reasonably available to the patient to alleviate the patient's pain and suffering to levels acceptable to the patient. This provision in effect precludes a patient from rejecting reasonable palliative care options. Where reasonable palliative care options are available, they must at least be tried. It is only in circumstances where such palliative care has been provided but does not alleviate the patient's pain and suffering to levels acceptable to the patient that a medical practitioner can proceed to provide a patient with assistance to terminate his or her life. The Act further directs that where palliative care options have been provided and have brought about remission of the patient's pain and suffering, but subsequently fail to continue to do so, the medical practitioner may only provide assistance to the patient under the Act if the patient has reaffirmed his or her original request.

In order to safeguard the voluntariness of a request for assistance by a patient, the Act confers on patients the right to rescind a request for assistance at any time and in any manner (section 10). The Act goes on to direct that where a patient rescinds a request, the patient's medical practitioner must, as soon as practicable, destroy the certificate and note that fact on the patient's medical record.

The Act also seeks to protect against improper conduct by making it an offence for a person to procure the signing or witnessing of a certificate of request by deception or improper influence (section 11—carrying a penalty of $20,000 or imprisonment for 4 years.) Moreover, the Act provides that a person found guilty of such an offence under the legislation forfeits any

---

[44] The Rights of the Terminally Ill Regulations state that for the purposes of section 7(3) of the Act, 'special qualification' is taken to include competence by reason of ability, knowledge and skills acquired through experience. The Regulations go on to prescribe the necessary qualifications for a medical practitioner who under section 7(3) provides information to the patient on the availability of palliative care.

financial or other benefit the person would otherwise obtain, directly or indirectly, as a result of the death of the patient, whether or not the death results from assistance given under the Act.

Part 3 of the Act deals with the keeping of relevant medical records and the reporting of cases to the Coroner. The original Bill had referred to the keeping of medical records, without specifying on whom the record-keeping obligation was to fall, nor imposing any penalty in the event of breach. However, amendments were made at the time of passage of the legislation and under section 12 of the legislation, as enacted, the responsibility for keeping relevant records rests with the medical practitioner who assists the patient to terminate his or her life. The Act provides that a medical practitioner who assists a patient to terminate a patient's life under the legislation must keep, as part of the patient's medical record:

(a) a note of any oral request of the patient for such assistance;

(b) the certificate of request;

(c) a record of his or her opinion as to the patient's state of mind at the time of signing the certificate of request, and certification of the medical practitioner's opinion that the patient's decision to end his or her life was made freely, voluntarily and after due consideration;

(d) the reports of the second medical practitioner and qualified psychiatrist referred to in section 7(1)(c); and

(e) a note by that medical practitioner:
    (i)   certifying as to the independence of the second medical practitioner and the qualified psychiatrist and the residential and period of practice qualifications of the patient's medical practitioner;
    (ii) indicating that all requirements under the Act have been met;
    (iii) indicating the steps taken to carry out the request for assistance.

Failure to keep records as required may results in the imposition of a penalty of $10,000 or imprisonment for 2 years.

Pursuant to section 14, a medical practitioner who has assisted a patient to die under the Act, must, as soon as practicable after the death of the patient, report the death to the Coroner by sending the Coroner a copy of the death certificate under the Registration of Births Deaths and Marriages Act 1962 and so much of the medical record of the patient (including those items which must be kept pursuant to section 12) as relates to the terminal illness and death of the patient. This provision, which, on the recommendation of the Select Committee, was expanded from the requirement contained in the original Bill that only a copy of the death certificate be sent to the Coroner, provides an opportunity for the Coroner to scrutinize the relevant documentation with a view to assessing whether the requirements of the legislation have been satisfied.

Under the Act, the Coroner is vested with the responsibility of advising the Attorney-General of the number of patients who died as a result of assistance under the legislation each year. The Attorney-General is, in turn, required to report the number, in such manner or report as he or she thinks appropriate, to the Legislative Assembly. Further the Coroner may at any time report to the Attorney-General on the operation of the Act or any matter affecting the Act's operation. Upon receipt of such a report, the Attorney-General is required to table a copy in the Assembly within 3 sitting days of the Assembly after the Report has been received.

Another important feature of the legislation are the immunities it creates in respect of civil or criminal or professional disciplinary action for persons acting in good faith in compliance with the legislation (section 20). It is this provision which ensures that the usual criminal law prohibitions with regard to homicide and assisting suicide (contained in the Northern Territory Criminal Code 1983 sections 162 and 168 respectively[45]) do not apply in circumstances where there has been full adherence to the legislative requirements. The Act also expressly provides for the effect of a request for assistance under the legislation, or the rescinding of such a request, on the construction of wills, contracts, and insurance or annuity policies (sections 18 and 19).

As a result of the passage of the Rights of the Terminally Ill Act, the Northern Territory has become the first jurisdiction in the world to enact laws permitting active voluntary euthanasia. As was explained in an earlier chapter, because of the constitutional arrangements in Australia, the subject of active voluntary euthanasia involving criminal law and health issues falls within the jurisdiction of individual states and territories.[46] Although the Act's operation is confined to the Northern Territory, as it does not contain a residency requirement, there would be nothing to prevent terminally ill residents in other parts of Australia (or, for that matter, from other countries) travelling to the Northern Territory in order to make use of this legislation.

The Rights of the Terminally Ill Act has been carefully framed, containing many safeguards to ensure that assistance from a doctor in the form of active voluntary euthanasia or doctor-assisted suicide is properly regulated and only available in strictly defined circumstances. Particular attention is given under the legislation to ensure that the patient's decision to request assistance is fully informed, genuinely held, and made entirely voluntarily. Moreover, the legislation respects the autonomy, not only of the patient, but also of doctors by making it clear that they should be free to decide whether to provide assistance to a patient to end his or her life. Signifi-

---

[45] For discussion of the criminal law principles with respect to homicide and assisting suicide see Chs. 1 and 2.

[46] See p. 13, n. 2 above.

cantly, notwithstanding the Act's title which may suggest otherwise, the Rights of the Terminally Ill Act does not confer any rights on a patient to have active voluntary euthanasia performed.[47] An important feature of the legislation is the involvement of an independent medical practitioner who is required to confirm the first medical practitioner's diagnosis and prognosis and that the patient is likely to die as a result of the illness. As a result of the recent amendments to the Act as originally enacted, the requirements for medical consultation have been tightened up, with the inclusion of a requirement that the second medical practitioner have prescribed qualifications or experience in the treatment of the terminal illness from which the patient is suffering and a separate requirement that the patient must be examined by a qualified psychiatrist to confirm the patient's mental state. Also significant are the mechanisms for the full reporting of cases to the Coroner so as to provide a further independent check that the guidelines are adhered to. The legislation seeks to strike a balance between the availability of euthanasia and access to and reasonable use of palliative care options by requiring that the patient be informed of palliative care options by a doctor with qualifications in that area, and that no assistance to terminate the life of the patient be provided where the medical practitioner believes that there are palliative care options reasonably available to the patient to alleviate the patient's pain and suffering to levels acceptable to the patient. Thus, assistance in dying is an option of last resort under the legislation. The Select Committee had made recommendations about the need to allow time before the commencement of the legislation for health care providers to inform themselves of the latest techniques in palliative care and euthanasia and for any additional palliative care measures to be put in place. One of the amendments made to the legislation during the committee stage was the insertion of a commencement clause to allow the Government to delay the commencement of the legislation until it is satisfied that the necessary regulations have been prepared[48] and other preconditions have been met including the establishment of a hospice, the employment of palliative care specialists in the Northern Territory health system, and the implementation of euthanasia education programmes throughout the Northern Territory, particularly amongst the aboriginal communities. At the time of writing, it had just recently been announced

---

[47] For discussion as to the role of rights in this area see pp. 201–2 above.

[48] A four-member Working Party (Working Party on the Implementation of the Rights of the Terminally Ill Act) has been established comprised of representatives from the Northern Territory Attorney-Generals' Department and the Health Department, to make recommendations to the Attorney-General *inter alia* with regard to the introduction of appropriate regulations under the legislation. The Report of the Working Party has recently been tabled in the Northern Territory Parliament (*Report on the Implementation of the Rights of the Terminally Ill Act*, n. 41 above), and at the time of writing, regulations had just been finalized: see the Rights of the Terminally Ill Regulations 1996, a copy of which is contained in the Appendix at the rear of this work, pp. 503–13.

that the legislation would commence on 1 July 1996, although this news was greeted with concern from some quarters that this left inadequate time for effective implementation of the euthanasia education programme. Clearly, those wishing to avail themselves of the legislation are anxious for it to come into effect as soon as possible. There has already been one heart-rending account of how a woman, Marta Alfonso-Bowes, had travelled to the Northern Territory in the hope of lawfully being able to obtain assistance to die when she chose to do so, only to find that the legislation was not yet in operation. She subsequently committed suicide whilst she was still able to do so herself, rather than risk waiting for the legislation to come into operation.[49]

The Northern Territory Rights of the Terminally Ill Act has clearly been influenced by the guidelines which have been developed in the Netherlands for the practice of euthanasia as well as by legislative models put forward in other jurisdictions. However, in the final analysis, in comparison with other legislative proposals, it represents a cautious approach to this difficult issue, requiring exhaustive criteria to be satisfied before a medical practitioner is permitted to give assistance in dying. One of the few questions that one might raise is that the legislation falls short of requiring that the patient's wishes must be confirmed at the time assistance in dying is given—it is sufficient that the patient has given no indication that this no longer accords with his or her wishes. There is also some basis for suggesting that the mechanisms in place under the legislation for retrospectively scrutinizing cases where assistance has been provided, could be more rigorous.[50] Under the legislation the Coroner must collect the documentation that is submitted to him or her in connection with assisted deaths under the Act and report the number of deaths annually to the Attorney-General. The Coroner is given no specific power under the legislation to assess the adequacy of the supporting documentation or otherwise investigate the deaths reported. In order for the Coroner to play an effective role in providing procedural protection against the possibility of abuse it would be preferable if he or she were given the specific power to investigate fully each death.

Predictably, there has been mixed reaction to the legislation. Whilst it has been applauded from some quarters including the pro-euthanasia lobby and HIV-AIDS groups, the legislation has been strongly resisted by main-stream churches, 'right to life' groups, and the Australian Medical Association (AMA). Prior to its passage, an intensive campaign of opposition was mounted against the legislation by these forces, including the establishment of a new group called the 'Coalition Against Euthanasia' formed by the Catholic Church and the Northern Territory branch of the AMA. This

[49] 'The "Marta Alfonso-Bowes Memorial Award"' (1996) 2 *NT VES Newsletter* 5.
[50] See also Ranson, D., 'The Coroner and the Rights of the Terminally Ill Act 1995 (NT)', (1995) 3 *JLaw&Med.* 169.

campaign has continued since the passage of the legislation. The AMA at its National Conference held only days after the historic passage of the legislation voted overwhelmingly to endorse the World Medical Association's condemnation of voluntary euthanasia as unethical. Concern has been raised about fear of the legislation among the aboriginal communities in the Northern Territory, and it has been suggested that there should be a ban on the legislation coming into force. There have also been commentators who have suggested that the availability of euthanasia under the legislation has been so circumscribed as to be virtually unworkable and that the legislation will inevitably have to be amended, thus representing the first stage of a 'slippery slope'. Whilst there has been a considerable outpouring of critical commentary since the enactment of the legislation,[51] most of the criticism appears to stem from an 'in principle' objection to legalization rather than a sustained attack on the terms of the legislation and the safeguards that it provides.

Since the enactment of the Rights of the Terminally Ill Act various attempts have been made by its opponents to prevent the legislation coming into operation. Calls were made for the Governor General of Australia to exercise his discretion to disallow the legislation;[52] however, as was widely expected, the Governor General chose not to invoke this power. Similar representations were made by the Northern Territory branch of the AMA to the then Prime Minister, Paul Keating, seeking his intervention to veto the legislation,[53] however the Prime Minister declined to intervene. There have also been calls from some quarters for the legislation to be debated afresh by the Northern Territory Parliament in view of the changed composition of the Parliament since the legislation was passed. At the time the amendment Act was before the Parliament in February 1996, unsuccessful attempts were made by a member of the Australian Labor Party Opposition, legal affairs spokesman Mr Neil Bell, to have the legislation repealed. Further attempts to repeal the legislation have been foreshadowed for later in the year, but any such move is thought unlikely to win the necessary majority support of the Parliament. The Northern Territory Government

[51] e.g. Mullen, P., 'Euthanasia: An Impoverished Construction of Life and Death' (1995) 3 *JLaw&Med.* 121; Mendelson, D., 'The Northern Territory's Euthanasia Legislation in Historical Perspective' (1995) 3 *JLaw&Med.* 136; Gillett, G., 'Ethical Aspects of the Northern Territory Legislation' (1995) 3 *JLaw&Med.* 145; Ashby, M., 'Hard Cases, Causation and Care of the Dying' (1995) 3 *JLaw&Med.* 152; Buchanan, J., 'Euthanasia: The Medical and Psychological Issues' (1995) 3 *JLaw&Med.* 161.

[52] Because the Northern Territory is a territory of the Commonwealth of Australia, the Governor General has the power to disallow the legislation within 6 months of the Bill being assented to by the Administrator of the Northern Territory.

[53] *Australian*, 11 December 1995. The Federal Parliament has the constitutional power to make laws for any Territory of Australia pursuant to s. 122 of the Commonwealth of Australia Constitution 1901, but this power has never been used to override a law enacted by a Territory.

has taken the view that although not all its members had voted for the legislation in the original conscience vote, now that that historic vote has been taken, the Government's role is to implement the legislation.[54]

The full impact of these ground-breaking developments in the Northern Territory remains to be assessed. The Working Party on the Implementation of the Rights of the Terminally Ill Act has, under its terms of reference, been given the task of developing a mechanism to monitor and evaluate the implementation of the legislation but at the time of writing, these recommendations had not yet been made. Obviously there can be no objective evaluation of the operation of the legislation in practice until the legislation has been in operation for a reasonable period of time. However, there are already indications that the successful passage of the Rights of the Terminally Ill Act has heightened interest in the issue of active voluntary euthanasia elsewhere in Australia, and several bills have been put forward in other Australian jurisdictions, with further bills foreshadowed.

Even prior to the historic passage of the Northern Territory legislation, a Private Member's Bill was introduced in the South Australian Parliament by Mr John Quirke MP, for the legalization of active voluntary euthanasia and doctor-assisted suicide. This Bill, entitled the Voluntary Euthanasia Bill 1995, which was introduced on 9 March 1995, sought to make provision for a medical practitioner to assist the death of patients who are terminally ill and who have requested assistance, subject to certain safeguards. Under the proposed Bill, an adult person of sound mind and who has been diagnosed as suffering from a terminal illness that is likely to cause the person's death within 12 months could make a request for active voluntary euthanasia or assisted suicide. Before formally making such a request which would have to be in writing in the form prescribed in the Schedule to the legislation (unless the person was unable to write in which case the request could be made orally), the person would have to be fully informed of the diagnosis and prognosis of his or her condition; the forms of treatment that may be available for the condition and their respective risks, side effects, and likely outcomes; and the proposed euthanasia procedure, risks associated with the procedure and feasible alternatives to the procedure. A request for euthanasia would have to be made in the presence of a medical practitioner and one other adult witness, both of whom must certify that the person who made the request appeared to be of sound mind, and to understand the nature and implications of the request, and was not apparently acting under duress. The preconditions under the Bill for a medical practitioner to provide assistance to a patient in the form of active voluntary euthanasia or doctor-assisted suicide included: that the patient has made a request for

---

[54] *Weekend Australian*, 13–14 April 1996.

assistance under the legislation and there is no reason to believe that the request has been revoked; that the patient is suffering from a terminal illness that is likely to cause his or her death within 12 months from the date of the request; that the medical practitioner is of the opinion that euthanasia is appropriate in the circumstances of the case; that another medical practitioner who is not involved in the day to day treatment or care of the patient has personally examined the patient and has signed a certificate, confirming that the patient is suffering from a terminal illness that is likely to cause his or her death within 12 months from the date of the request and that euthanasia is appropriate in the circumstances of the case; and that the medical practitioner is satisfied that no person who has signed the request or certificate of confirmation will gain a financial advantage (other than reasonable payment for medical services) directly or indirectly as a result of the death of the patient. The Bill also contained a conscientious objection clause to the effect that a medical practitioner may decline to carry out a request for the administration of euthanasia on grounds of conscience or other grounds, but in those circumstances must inform the patient that another medical practitioner may be prepared to consider the request. Provision was also made for a medical practitioner who provides assistance under the legislation to make a report to the State Coroner within 7 days in accordance with the prescribed form which must be accompanied by a copy of the request for euthanasia and the certificate of confirmation given by the second medical practitioner.

On 27 July 1995, the South Australian House of Assembly voted overwhelmingly against a second reading of the Voluntary Euthanasia Bill 1995, 30 votes to 12. This meant that the legislation did not even proceed to the committee stage where it could be debated and voted on clause by clause, before a final vote would be taken whether the Bill should be passed. This fairly decisive defeat of the bill may be seen as something of a reaction to the developments in the Northern Territory. However, in comparison with the Northern Territory legislation, the South Australian Bill was much less detailed and contained fewer safeguards and this no doubt contributed to the decision by many members of the South Australian House of Assembly to reject the bill. Mr Quirke has since indicated that he may introduce another bill at a later stage. Anne Levy, a member of the South Australian Legislative Council has also indicated her intention to introduce her own euthanasia bill.

Within days of the landmark passage of the Northern Territory legislation, the New South Wales Australia Labor Party approved a plan to introduce a voluntary euthanasia bill into Parliament and allow members a conscience vote on the legislation. Upper House Member of Parliament, Mr Paul O'Grady was subsequently given approval by Caucus to introduce a euthanasia bill as a Private Member's Bill. A bill was being prepared, but in

January 1996 Mr O'Grady resigned from the Upper House because of ill health. An informal parliamentary working group on euthanasia has since been established representing a diversity of political ideology. According to the group's spokesperson, Liberal backbencher Mr Jeremy Kinross, the group plans to introduce a voluntary euthanasia bill along similar lines to the Northern Territory legislation in the New South Wales Upper House.[55]

In the ACT, Independent Michael Moore reintroduced a modified version of his earlier euthanasia Bill (discussed above) in the ACT Legislative Assembly, this time, in the form of an amendment to the Medical Treatment Act 1994. The Medical Treatment (Amendment) Bill, tabled on 20 September 1995, contained more detailed and exacting safeguards than the previous proposal,[56] however it still made provision for the appointment of an agent who would have the legal authority to request active voluntary euthanasia on the patient's behalf.

In view of the ACT Labor Party 1991 policy in support of the legalization of active voluntary euthanasia, a Caucus decision was taken to disallow a conscience vote, which would have meant that ALP members would have been required to vote in favour of the Bill. However, following objection from some members, it was resolved that in principle support for legalization would be retained, but that Labor MPs who did not abide by the policy of support for active voluntary euthanasia would not be disciplined by the party. A number of Labor Members of Parliament did in fact vote against the legislation resulting in its defeat, 10 votes to 7. Given the extraordinarily broad terms of the legislation, this was already quite a remarkable result.

In the light of developments to date and the continued interest that the Northern Territory legislation inevitably generates, especially once it commences operation, the issue of active voluntary euthanasia is likely to remain on the political agenda in Australia with parliaments in a number of Australian jurisdictions being called on to consider the issue in the not too distant future.[57]

Consideration will now be given to some of the more important reform developments in the USA and Canada, including legislative efforts to introduce laws permitting active voluntary euthanasia, and government-initiated law reform commission and parliamentary inquiries touching on the issue.

---

[55] *Weekend Australian*, 6–7 April 1996.

[56] For example, the introduction of a requirement that the patient must be suffering severe pain or distress caused by the illness which cannot be controlled by medical treatment or palliative care to the satisfaction of the patient, the involvement of a second medical practitioner in confirming diagnosis of terminal illness, and a procedure for reporting cases of active voluntary euthanasia or doctor-assisted suicide to the Coroner.

[57] It should be noted that in August 1995, a Private Member's Bill providing for active voluntary euthanasia (the Death with Dignity Bill 1995) had been introduced into the New Zealand Parliament by a National Party backbencher, Mr Michael Laws, but was heavily defeated by the Parliament: *Australian*, 17 Aug. 1995.

III. USA

The USA also has a long history of reform efforts to introduce legislation for the legalization of active voluntary euthanasia. The earliest Bill dates back to 1906, and in the decades which followed, particularly in the period between the late 1930s and the late 1950s, quite a number of voluntary euthanasia bills have been prepared and introduced into various state legislatures without success. In more recent times, renewed efforts have been made for the introduction of legislation. Since the mid-1980s, the organization Americans Against Human Suffering (now renamed, Americans for Death with Dignity) has been campaigning for the introduction of legislation permitting physician[58] 'aid in dying' in a number of states through the voter-initiative mechanism. The various physician 'aid in dying' bills which have been proposed have, in the main, covered both physician-assisted suicide and active voluntary euthanasia. However, in November 1994, this campaign for reform resulted in the passage of more limited legislation in the State of Oregon permitting physician-assisted suicide in certain circumstances. The significance of this development has been overshadowed by the fact that the new law which was to come into effect in December 1994 has been blocked as a result of a challenge to its constitutional validity. In addition to these developments, based upon the voter-initiated referendum process, quite a number of bills for the introduction of physician-assisted suicide and active voluntary euthanasia have been introduced in various US states. Apart from legislative developments, also noteworthy are the government inquiries at the federal and state level which have addressed the issues of active voluntary euthanasia and physician-assisted suicide and whether legalization is appropriate.

As a result of recent case law developments in the USA, these legislative efforts to secure legalization of physician-assisted suicide and active voluntary euthanasia have, to some extent, been overtaken. Two separate courts of the US Federal Court of Appeals (the Ninth Circuit and the Second Circuit Courts of Appeals) have ruled in favour of a constitutionally recognized interest in physician-assisted suicide for competent, terminally ill patients, although relying on different constitutional grounds in coming to this conclusion.[59] Applications for appeal are expected in respect of both of these decision and it remains to be seen whether the United States Supreme Court agrees to review either or both of these decisions. Unless there is an

---

[58] As for earlier discussions of the US position, the term 'physician' will principally be used in accordance with the usage in that country.

[59] *Compassion in Dying* v. *State of Washington* No. 94-35534 (9th Cir. March 6 1996) (*en banc*); *Quill* v. *Vacco* No. 60 (2nd Cir. April 2 1996). For detailed discussion see pp. 101–21 above.

authoritative ruling from the Supreme Court overturning these decisions, doctors in the states within the jurisdiction of these two circuit courts of appeal will be free to assist competent, terminally ill patients to commit suicide. However, the courts in these two historic decisions have acknowledged the need for state legislatures regulating the practice of physician-assisted suicide to ensure adequate safeguards are in place to protect against abuse.

A. Legislative Developments

The first voluntary euthanasia Bill to have been brought before the legislature in the USA, and for that matter, in any English-speaking country in the world, was the Bill for the legalization of active voluntary euthanasia for certain incurable sufferers introduced in the State of Ohio in 1906 as a Private Member's Bill.[60] Under the proposed legislation, an adult of sound mind, who had been fatally hurt or was so ill that recovery was impossible, or who was suffering from extreme physical pain without hope of recovery, could express to his or her doctor the wish to die. Provided that three further doctors agreed that the case was hopeless, they were empowered to make arrangements to put the person out of pain and suffering with as little discomfort as possible. Although proceeding to a first reading, the Bill was defeated by a vote of 79 to 23.

In February 1937, a euthanasia bill largely modelled on the 1936 British Bill was introduced into the Nebraska State legislature by Senator Comstock, and sponsored by Dr Philbrick, a retired doctor. The Nebraska Bill differed from the British Bill in two important respects: first, by allowing an application to be made on behalf of a minor or incompetent adult, who was suffering from an incurable or fatal disease; and secondly, by providing that active euthanasia could be performed even where the illness was not terminal. The Bill was referred to a committee and was postponed indefinitely, having never been submitted to a vote. There was also an unsuccessful attempt to introduce a similar bill into the New York legislature but without the provisions with regard to minors and incompetent adults.

By 1938, the Euthanasia Society of America was established,[61] and for many years was the driving force behind efforts to secure legislative reform with regard to active voluntary euthanasia. In response to growing indications of community support for active voluntary euthanasia by the mid 1940s, the Euthanasia Society of America began a campaign in New York

---

[60] Russell, R. *Freedom to Die: The Legal Aspects of Euthanasia*, Revised edn. (New York, 1977) 60–1 and see generally for historical coverage of legislative developments in the USA.
[61] For discussion see pp. 273–4 above.

to secure the legalization of active voluntary euthanasia. In 1947 a euthanasia bill was presented to the New York legislature. This Bill, also based on the 1936 British Bill, provided that any person of sound mind, over 21 years of age, and suffering from severe physical pain caused by disease for which there is no known remedy, could, by written petition, apply to have active euthanasia administered. As under the 1936 British Bill, a complicated legal procedure was involved, pursuant to which a commission was to be appointed by the court to investigate the patient's request. Subject to a favourable report from the commission, the court would grant the patient's petition permitting the administration of active euthanasia. However, the Bill met with opposition and by the end of 1949 had still not been introduced into the New York legislature. In 1952, a further attempt was made to get the New York state legislature to consider this legislation, but the Bill once again failed to reach the legislature, despite evidence of wide support for the proposal from doctors, the clergy, and the community.

In the decades which followed, further unsuccessful attempts were made to pass active voluntary euthanasia legislation in a number of US jurisdictions. In 1950, a bill was proposed for the State of Connecticut and was introduced, with some modifications, into the Connecticut General Assembly in 1959 at the initiative of the state chapter of the Euthanasia Society. This Bill, which was couched in similar terms to the New York Bill, was also defeated. In the light of these set-backs, the Euthanasia Society of America decided that further legislative efforts would be fruitless and resolved to shift its campaign for reform towards educational activities. The Bills which were subsequently introduced into the legislatures of a number of US states were initiated independently of the activities of the Euthanasia Society and were substantially similar to the 1969 Voluntary Euthanasia Bill proposed in the United Kingdom. In 1969, the Health and Welfare Committee of the Idaho House of Representatives put forward a Voluntary Euthanasia Bill to legalize the painless inducement of death at the request of a patient suffering from an irremediable condition. Notwithstanding quite detailed safeguards built into the legislation, it failed to pass. The next attempt at legislative reform was in Oregon in 1973 when a Voluntary Euthanasia Bill was introduced by a group of Senators into the Oregon legislature. However, this Bill was tabled after a single hearing. In the same year, a bill to legalize active voluntary euthanasia was introduced into the Montana State legislature but this Bill was also defeated.

In recent years attempts have been made in a number of states, to introduce physician 'aid in dying' legislation through the voter-initiated referendum process available in certain states allowing citizens to introduce fully drafted legislation if they obtain a certain number of signatures on a petition (based on a percentage of voter population) within a specified time. The first state to be targeted for reform was California because of its reputation as the bellwether state for many social reforms. The Humane and Dignified Death Act 1988[62] sought, by amendment to the Californian Constitution, to extend the right of privacy to include the right of the terminally ill to physician 'aid in dying'. More particularly, the object of the legislation was to confer on all competent, terminally ill adults the right to request and receive voluntary, humane, and dignified physician 'aid in dying' under carefully defined circumstances.[63] In order to achieve this objective, the Act sought to build on the existing law by enlarging the Californian Natural Death Act 1976 and including a durable power of attorney of health care within the legislation.

In order to come within the scope of the proposed legislation, a competent adult would have to sign a directive in the presence of two disinterested witnesses.[64] Before signing the directive, the patient would be required to inform his or her family and indicate that he or she has considered the family's opinion though the patient would retain the right of final decision, provided he or she remained competent. In the directive, a patient would be required to specify that it was his or her wish that his or her life be not prolonged artificially or that his or her life be ended with the help of a physician on request. The patient would also be required to designate an agent to make health care decisions on his or her behalf in the event that he or she becomes incompetent, and must specifically stipulate whether the agent has the power to request physician 'aid in dying' on his or her behalf. Once duly executed, a directive would remain in effect for a period of 7 years, but could be revoked at any time. A number of conditions would have to be met before a physician would legally be able to comply with a patient's directive. First, there would have to be a validly executed directive presently in force. Secondly, two physicians would have to certify that the patient's condition was 'terminal'.[65] Thirdly, if the patient became incompetent after being certified terminally ill, the patient's agent could request physician 'aid in dying' on behalf of the patient but the decision would have to be reviewed by a three person ethics committee. In this way, the proposed Act sought to make provision for physician 'aid in dying' for patients who are no longer competent to make their own decisions.

[62] Although widely referred to as an 'Act,' this legislation was never enacted.

[63] 'Aid in dying' was defined as any medical procedure that will terminate the life of a qualified patient swiftly, painlessly, and humanely. For analysis of the legislation see Risley, R., *Death with Dignity: A New Law Permitting Physician Aid-in-Dying* (Eugene, Oregon, 1989) 47; Clarke, D., 'Physician Assisted Aid in Dying: A California Proposal' (1988) 2 *Euthanasia Rev.* 207.

[64] For reference to the Humane and Dignified Death Act 1988 see Risley, R. and White, M., 'Humane and Dignified Death Initiative for 1988' (1986) 1 *Euthanasia Rev.* 226–37.

[65] 'Terminal condition' was defined under the legislation as one which, regardless of application of life-sustaining procedures, is incurable and, within reasonable medical judgement, will lead to death within 6 months.

The Humane and Dignified Death Act 1988 also proposed protection for physicians and other health care workers from civil, criminal and administrative liability when complying with the patient's directive in accordance with the legislation. The legislation additionally provided that the failure of a physician to effectuate the directive would not give rise to liability. However, the wilful refusal by a physician to transfer the patient to a physician who would comply with the directive would constitute unprofessional conduct. Further, the Act provided that nothing in the legislation should be construed to condone, authorize, or approve mercy killing or to permit any affirmative or deliberate act to end life except as provided for under the legislation.

Whilst clearly following the format of living will legislation introduced in many jurisdictions in the USA since the mid-1970s, the proposed Humane and Dignified Death Act 1988 represented a significant departure from the existing living will legislation in seeking to permit physician 'aid in dying' (that is encompassing both active voluntary euthanasia and physician-assisted suicide), subject to certain conditions and safeguards. The scope of the proposed legislation was potentially quite broad, permitting physician 'aid in dying' at the request of a competent patient as well as providing a mechanism for the patient to appoint an agent to request 'aid in dying' on his or her behalf in the event that he or she becomes incompetent. The Californian initiative drew considerable opposition from 'right to life' and medical groups, including the Californian Medical Association, primarily on the grounds that legalization of physician 'aid in dying' would be too open to abuse to be justifiable. Efforts to introduce this legislation in California in 1988 were ultimately unsuccessful, due to a failure to collect the required number of signatures within the specified time-frame to qualify the initiative for the ballot. This was later put down to a lack of funding, weak organization, and inexperience.

The next state targeted for the introduction of legislation permitting physician 'aid in dying' was Washington where the 'Death with Dignity Initiative' (also known as Initiative 119) was mounted. In May 1990, campaigners began to gather signatures in support of the petition for the introduction of legislation in Washington State permitting physician 'aid in dying'. Under Washington State law, a minimum of 150,001 signatures must be collected in order to qualify an initiative for the referendum process. However, this number was far exceeded and a total of 223,000 signatures was in fact collected, qualifying the initiative for the November 1991 ballot.

The legislative proposal under Initiative 119 was similar to the Humane and Dignified Death Act 1988 which had been proposed in California.[66] In

---

[66] The full title to this legislation was An Act Relating to the Natural Death Act and Amending RCW 70.122.010, 70.122.020, 70.122.030, 70.122.040, 70.122.050, 70.122.060, 70.122.070, 70.122.080, 70.122.090, 70.122.100, and 70.122.900. There were, in fact, two distinct

order to qualify for physician 'aid in dying', a person would need to be examined by two physicians, one of whom must be the attending physician. Both physicians would have to certify that the patient's condition was 'terminal'.[67] Further, the patient would need to indicate in writing a request for 'aid in dying'[68] at the time such a medical procedure was desired and the request would need to be witnessed by two disinterested persons. Thus, the Washington initiative was clearly confined to competent patients requesting 'aid in dying' on their own behalf. In this respect, it was substantially narrower than the earlier Californian proposal.

The Washington initiative also provided that a directive could be revoked at any time and that no physician who provides 'aid in dying' to a qualified patient in accordance with the provisions of the legislation shall be subject to prosecution or be guilty of any criminal act or unprofessional conduct. As under the Californian proposal, no health care facility or physician would be obligated to administer 'aid in dying'. However, if the physician or facility was unwilling to do so, they would be required to transfer the patient to another health care facility and/or physician who would be willing to carry out the patient's request.

Proponents for Initiative 119 presented a sophisticated campaign and were supported by a variety of professional groups including clergy, lawyers, doctors, nurses, social workers, and hospice workers.[69] However, as with the earlier campaign in California, considerable opposition was encountered, particularly from 'right to life' groups and Roman Catholic Church leaders. In the build-up to the November ballot, these forces financed an aggressive television campaign against the initiative, deploring it for lack of safeguards. The initiative was also opposed by the Washington State Medical Association.[70] Public opinion polls taken prior to the ballot

components to Initiative 119; the 'aid in dying' proposal which is discussed here, and a proposal to extend the Washington Natural Death Act 1979, by clarifying that artificially administered nutrition and hydration is a life-sustaining procedure which may be withdrawn, and extending the definition of 'terminal condition' to include irreversible coma and persistent vegetative state.

[67] As under the earlier Californian proposal, 'terminal condition' was defined as an incurable or irreversible condition which in the opinion of the physicians, exercising reasonable medical judgement, will result in death within 6 months.

[68] 'Aid in dying' was defined under the legislation to mean 'aid in the form of a medical service, provided in person by a physician, that will end the life of a conscious and mentally competent qualified patient in a dignified, painless and humane manner, when requested voluntarily by the patient through a written directive in accordance with this chapter at the time the medical service is to be provided'.

[69] e.g. Washington Citizens for Death with Dignity; the Interfaith Clergy for Yes on Initiative 119; Lawyers for Yes on Initiative 119; Nurses for Yes on Initiative 119; and Physicians for Yes on Initiative 119.

[70] In a random survey of its membership, 51% of the 2,000 respondents voted to oppose the initiative, with 49% in support. In the light of this close poll result, the association did not initially campaign against the initiative. However, following a House of Delegates vote against the measure and with support from the American Medical Association, it embarked, quite late in the piece, on a campaign against the legislation: *Am.Med. News* 18 Nov. (1991).

suggested that the initiative would be successful. However, in a state-wide referendum held on 5 November 1991, the initiative was defeated by a narrow margin. Of some 1.3 million voters (apparently the biggest recorded turnout for a state referendum in Washington), 54 per cent voted against with 46 per cent in favour.[71]

For many, the defeat of the initiative came as a surprise, particularly in the light of opinion poll results gathered over recent years, also in the USA,[72] which indicate majority support for active voluntary euthanasia. A number of factors can be advanced which may help to explain the referendum result.[73] There is no doubt that the opposition's campaign against the initiative took its toll in the electorate. There was also some adverse publicity arising from the suicide of Anne Wickett, the former wife of Derek Humphry, the then Executive Director of the Hemlock Society and one of the key supporters of the legislation. There may have also been some public backlash to the activities of Jack Kevorkian and his 'suicide machines' which were again before the public in the period shortly prior to the November ballot. More fundamentally, some of those in the community who in principle support active voluntary euthanasia may not have been satisfied with the particular form of the proposal: there were, for example, complaints that the legislative proposal was loosely worded and lacked a precise regulatory mechanism for the practice of physician 'aid in dying'.

Despite its defeat, Initiative 119 was an historic development, being the first time ever that voters have had the opportunity to pass electoral judgement on the subject of physician 'aid in dying'. The initiative was also significant for the widespread support it received from a variety of professional groups. It must also be emphasized that although it was ultimately unsuccessful, it was supported by a substantial minority and the final result was really very close.

In 1992, renewed efforts were made for the introduction of physician 'aid in dying' legislation in the State of California. The 'California Coalition for Death with Dignity' was formed between Hemlock chapters in that state, and the organization Americans Against Human Suffering (which at that time had been renamed 'Californians Against Human Suffering'), to campaign for the introduction of physician 'aid in dying' legislation. The legislation, a slightly modified version of the earlier Humane and Dignified Death Act 1988 was renamed the Death with Dignity Act. It differed from the Washington proposal in a number of respects. One additional requirement under the Californian proposal was that the request for 'aid in dying' had to be an 'enduring request'. It also had provision for psychological counselling and record-keeping and required that the family must be informed of the patient's intent. As under the earlier Californian proposal,

---

[71] *NYTimes*, 7 Nov. 1991.   [72] See pp. 259–61 above.
[73] Carson, R., 'Washington's I-119' (1992) 22 *Hastings Center R* 7.

the legislation provided for the appointment of a health care attorney who can make decisions on behalf of the patient in the event that the patient becomes incompetent, including a request for 'aid in dying'. In this respect the legislation was broader than the Washington proposal. This proposal, known as Proposition 161, was sufficiently supported to qualify for the ballot but was defeated in the November 1992 ballot by 54 per cent to 46 per cent—exactly the same margin as for the Washington Initiative 119. This loss was attributed to insufficient financial backing to compete with the well funded opposition campaign, particularly coming so soon after the earlier initiatives which had depleted the organizations' financial resources.[74]

The most significant legislative development in the USA to date has occurred in the State of Oregon. In November 1994, legislation was enacted in the State of Oregon legalizing the practice of physician-assisted suicide in certain circumstances, although, as was noted above, the commencement of this legislation has been stalled due to a constitutional challenge.[75] After having qualified for the ballot under the voter-initiated referendum process, the Death with Dignity Act (better known as 'Measure 16') which was sponsored by Oregon Right to Die, was put to voters in the State of Oregon on 8 November 1994 and was passed by a narrow margin—51 per cent in favour, 49 per cent against. This marked an historic event—it was the first time that voters in the USA had approved a voter-initiated measure in this area and Oregon thereby became the first jurisdiction in the world (this pre-dating the developments in the Northern Territory of Australia) to legalize physician-assisted suicide. The narrow scope of the legislation in comparison with previous initiatives and the quite rigorous safeguards it contains[76] probably help to explain how this initiative succeeded where previous efforts had failed, notwithstanding an expensive advertising campaign run by opponents of the legislation. Also of significance was that the fact that the Oregon Medical Association, as well as a number of other organizations including the Oregon Association of Pharmacists and the Oregon Hospice Association, decided not to oppose the initiative, preferring instead to adopt a neutral position with respect to the legislation.[77] This contrasts with the position in the States of California and Washington where the relevant States' medical associations had opposed broader initiatives.

The Oregon Death with Dignity Act permits physicians to prescribe drugs for a terminally ill adult patient who asks for it in order to end his or her life in a humane and dignified manner. It does not permit a physician to be involved in the administration of a lethal drug and specifically provides

[74] For detailed discussion of this legislative proposal and its shortcomings, see Humphry, D., *Lawful Exit: The Limits of Freedom in Help in Dying* (Oregon, 1993) 98–132.

[75] For discussion, see pp. 371–2 below.

[76] For a contrary view see Capron, A., 'Sledding in Oregon' (1995) 25 *Hastings Centre R* 34.

[77] The measure was, however, opposed by the American Medical Association which criticized its state affiliate, the Oregon Medical Association, for failing to take a stand on the issue.

that mercy killing or active voluntary euthanasia are not allowed. The legislation is limited to adult patients, who are residents of Oregon, who are capable[78] and suffering from a terminal disease[79] which is expected to result in death within 6 months. In order to receive a prescription under the legislation for drugs to end his or her life, a patient must make an initial oral request for assistance, followed by a formal written request. Further, the legislation requires that the patient reiterate his or her request by making a second oral request before a physician may prescribe death-inducing medication. There is a minimum 15-day waiting period imposed under the legislation from the time of the initial request and the writing of the prescription. There is a further requirement that a minimum of 48 hours must elapse between the patient's written request and the writing of a prescription under the Act. In order to be valid, the written request must be in the form prescribed in the Act, signed and dated by the patient, and witnessed by at least two individuals (other than the patient's attending physician) who, in the presence of the patient, attest that to the best of their knowledge and belief, the patient is capable, acting voluntarily, and is not being coerced to sign the request. At least one of the witnesses must be independent of the patient—not related to the patient, or entitled to any portion of the estate of the patient, or an owner, operator or employee of a health care facility where the qualified patient is receiving medical treatment or is a resident. Moreover, the Act specifically provides that the patient's attending physician cannot be a witness.

The legislation makes it clear that no person is under any duty to participate in the provision of medication to a patient to end his or her life. However, if a health care provider[80] is unable or unwilling to carry out a patient's request and the patient transfers his or her care to a new health care provider, the prior health care provider must, if requested, transfer a copy of the patient's relevant medical records to that new health provider.

The legislation casts a number of responsibilities on those physicians who are able and willing to assist patients to die by means of physician-assisted suicide. Upon receiving a request, the attending physician (defined as the physician who has the primary responsibility for the care of the patient and the treatment of the patient's terminal illness) must make the initial determination of whether the patient has a terminal disease, is capable, and has made the request voluntarily. It is also the responsibility of the attending

[78] 'Capable' is defined under the legislation as patients who have the capacity to make and communicate health care decisions.

[79] 'Terminal disease' is defined as an incurable and irreversible disease that has been medically confirmed and will, within reasonable medical judgement, produce death within 6 months.

[80] Defined as a person licensed, certified, or otherwise authorized or permitted by the law of the State of Oregon to administer health care in the ordinary course of business or practice of a profession and includes a health care facility.

physician to inform the patient of his or her medical diagnosis, his or her prognosis, the potential risks associated with taking the medication to be prescribed; the probable result of taking the medication to be prescribed; and the feasible alternatives, including, but not limited to, comfort care, hospice care, and pain control. It is a requirement under the legislation that a consulting physician (defined as a physician who is qualified by speciality or experience to make a professional diagnosis and prognosis regarding the patient's disease) must confirm the diagnosis and also the fact that the patient is capable and acting voluntarily. If, in the opinion of the attending physician or the consulting physician, a patient may be suffering from a psychiatric or psychological disorder, or from depression causing impaired judgement, the patient must be referred to a psychiatrist or psychologist for counselling. No medication to end the patient's life may be prescribed until the person performing the counselling determines that the patient is not suffering from a psychiatric and psychological disorder or depression causing impaired judgement.

The attending physician is required under the Act to request that the patient notify next of kin of his or her request for medication; however, the patient's refusal or inability to do so will not be a ground for denying the patient's request. The attending physician must inform the patient that he or she has the opportunity to rescind the request at any time and in any manner. At the expiration of the 15-day waiting period following the patient's initial oral request, the physician must again offer the patient the opportunity to rescind before writing out a prescription for medication under the Act. Further, the patient's physician must verify, immediately prior to writing the prescription for medication, that the patient is making an informed decision.[81] The legislation requires that the attending physician fully document in the patient's record all stages of the process, including all oral and written requests by a patient for medication to end his or her life; both the attending physician's and consulting physician's diagnosis and prognosis and verification that the patient is capable, acting voluntarily, and has made an informed decision, and a note by the attending physician confirming that all requirements under the Act have been met and setting out the steps taken to carry out the request, including a notation of the medication prescribed. The Act also requires the Oregon Health Division to review annually a sample of medical records maintained pursuant to the Act, to make rules to facilitate the collection of information regarding compliance with the Act, and to generate and make available to the public an annual statistical report of this information.

All persons participating in good faith in compliance with the Act are

---

[81] 'Informed decision' is defined as a decision by a patient to request and obtain a prescription to end his or her life that is based on the appreciation of the relevant facts and after being fully informed by his or her physician regarding diagnosis, prognosis, risks etc.

immune from civil or criminal liability or professional disciplinary action. The legislation makes it clear that this extends to being present when a patient who has satisfied the requirements of the legislation, takes the prescribed medication to end his or her life.

The Act also creates certain offences in respect of any person coercing or exerting undue influence on a patient to request medication, or altering or forging a request for medication. It expressly provides that these penalties are in addition to any criminal penalties applicable under other laws for conduct which is inconsistent with the Act.

The Oregon Death with Dignity Act was due to come into operation on 8 December 1994 but within days of coming into force, legal action was taken to block the legislation. A group of plaintiffs (including physicians and terminally ill patients) represented by a lawyer from the National Right to Life Organization, instituted an action against the State of Oregon. The plaintiffs argued that the law discriminates against terminally ill patients and people with religious objections by depriving terminally ill persons in the State of Oregon of the protection of the criminal prohibition against assisted suicide and the law that provides for commitment of mentally ill persons. It was also argued that the law contravenes the Americans with Disabilities Act, the Religious Freedom Restoration Act, the First Amendment rights of freedom to exercise religion and to associate, and the Equal Protection and Due Process clauses of the Fourteenth Amendment of the United States Constitution. A temporary restraining order was issued on 7 December 1994, the day before the legislation was due to take effect. The plaintiffs then brought a motion for a preliminary injunction postponing the implementation of the legislation until the constitutional issues are resolved. A preliminary injunction was granted on 27 December 1994 by Hogan J of the United States District Court for the District of Oregon, pending a trial to review the constitutional questions. This was justified on the grounds that there was a possibility of irreparable harm to the First Amendment rights of the plaintiffs if the injunction were not granted, and further, that issuance of the injunction was in the public interest.[82] The full hearing of the constitutionality of the Oregon Death with Dignity Act commenced in the Oregon District Court on 18 April 1995. On 3 August 1995, Hogan J ruled that the legislation was unconstitutional and granted a permanent injunction against the defendants.[83] The ruling was based on Hogan J's finding that the legislation was in violation of the Equal Protection clause of the Fourteenth Amendment of the Constitution. Particular concern was expressed about the inadequacy of safeguards to ensure appropriate mental evaluation of the patient before a physician is permitted to prescribe medication for the patient to commit suicide. In view of this

[82] *Lee* v. *Oregon* 869 F Supp. 1491 (D Or. 1994).
[83] *Lee* v. *Oregon* 891 F Supp. 1239 (D Or. 1995).

aspect of the plaintiffs' case being upheld, the court found it unnecessary to decide the motions related to the other claims made. The sponsors of the law, Oregon Right to Die, subsequently lodged an appeal with the Ninth Circuit Court of Appeals. In the meantime, an eleven-member bench of the Ninth Circuit Court of Appeals has handed down its ruling in the case of *Compassion in Dying* v. *State of Washington*[84] in which the court struck down a Washington statute prohibiting assistance in suicide in so far as it applies to competent, terminally ill patients seeking physician-assisted suicide. In the course of the judgment, the majority specifically referred to the challenge to the Oregon physician-assisted suicide law and rejected Hogan J's decision as being directly contrary to their reasoning and the legal conclusions that the court had reached. In the light of the *Compassion in Dying* decision, which in any event also applies in the State of Oregon,[85] the way has now largely been cleared for the Oregon law to come into force, subject only to a reversal by the United States Supreme Court. At the time of writing, efforts were underway by the proponents of the Oregon legislation to have the injunction imposed by Hogan J blocking the commencement of the legislation lifted, directly through application to Hogan J, as well as by means of appeal from this decision to the Ninth Circuit Court of Appeals.

Although its implementation has been delayed, the passage of the Oregon Death with Dignity Act has been hailed as an important watershed for the right to die debate in the USA. The legislation itself represents a very moderate and cautious approach to the issue of physician 'aid in dying'. It has been acknowledged that by limiting the legislation to physician-assisted suicide, many people who would wish to have assistance in dying would be excluded from its operation. The fact that a majority of voters in the State of Oregon supported this measure has no doubt boosted hopes for the successful introduction of similar measures in other US jurisdictions.

In addition to these developments based on the citizen-initiated referendum process, since 1992, bills have been introduced in quite a number of US states for the introduction for some form of 'aid in dying'.[86] In some cases, the legislation has been limited to physician-assisted suicide,[87] in other cases the legislation has sought to permit medically administered active voluntary euthanasia.[88] Whilst none of these bills has yet been successful, this degree

---

[84] See above Ch. 2 n. 54.

[85] Oregon is one of the nine states within the jurisdiction of the Ninth Circuit Court of Appeals.

[86] These include the States of New Hampshire, Iowa, Maine, Washington, Massachusetts, Wisconsin, New Mexico, and Texas.

[87] e.g. in New Hampshire, An Act Relative to Death with Dignity for Certain Persons Suffering Terminal Illness 1992.

[88] e.g. in Iowa, An Act Relating to the Provision of Assistance-in-Dying, and Providing Penalties 1992.

of legislative activity on the subject is quite unprecedented in the USA and has marked a new era in the campaign for the introduction of legislation permitting active voluntary euthanasia and physician-assisted suicide. Moreover, the recent decisions of the Ninth and Second Circuit Courts of Appeals which have removed any legal impediment for physicians in the states affected by these decisions[89] to assist competent, terminally ill patients to commit suicide, have provided a potentially powerful stimulus for the introduction of legislation permitting physician-assisted suicide in certain circumstances. As was noted earlier, the course of future developments in these jurisdictions now depends on whether the Supreme Court will review these decisions and the outcome of any such determination. In the event that the Supreme Court either rejects to review, or accepts to review and upholds the principle of a constitutionally protected interest in physician-assisted suicide in certain circumstances, the onus will very much be on the state legislatures in these jurisdictions to introduce legislation so as to regulate the practice of physician-assisted suicide, ensuring appropriate controls and safeguards are put in place. Indeed, the introduction of such regulatory legislation was strongly recommended by the courts in these landmark cases, particularly by the majority in *Compassion in Dying* v. *State of Washington*.[90]

B. Government Inquiries

There have been a number of Government inquiries in the USA, both at the federal and state level, which have addressed the issue of active voluntary euthanasia. In the course of its work with regard to decisions to forgo life-sustaining treatment, the President's Commission considered the question whether the law should be changed to permit active voluntary euthanasia.[91] However, the Commission was of the view that it would not be appropriate to legalize such conduct. Whilst recognizing the artificiality of some of the distinctions which are made in the health care context, in particular, the distinction between acts and omissions, the Commission came to the conclusion that the legal prohibition on active killing should be sustained. It expressed the view that:

Weakening the legal prohibition to allow a deliberate taking of life in extreme circumstances would risk allowing wholly unjustified taking of life in less extreme circumstances. Such a risk would be warranted only if there were substantial evidence of serious harms to be relieved by a weakened protection of life, which the Commission does not find to be the case.[92]

---

[89] See p. 115, n. 215 above for reference to the states affected by these decisions.

[90] See above Ch. 2 n. 54. For discussion see pp. 108–9 above.

[91] President's Commission for the Study of Ethical Problems in Medicine and Biomedical and Behavioural Research, *Deciding to Forgo Life-Sustaining Treatment: A Report on the Ethical, Medical and Legal Issues in Treatment Decisions* (Washington, 1983).

[92] Ibid. at 72.

In examining the implications of its conclusion, the Commission acknowledged that one serious consequence of maintaining the legal prohibition against killing of terminally ill patients could be the prolongation of suffering. However, in the opinion of the commission, this possibility was insufficiently weighty to justify a change in legal policy:

In the final stages of some diseases, such as cancer, patients may undergo unbearable suffering that only ends with death. Some have claimed that sometimes the only way to improve such patients' lot is to actively and intentionally end their lives. If such steps are forbidden, physicians and family might be forced to deny these patients the relief they seek and to prolong their agony pointlessly.

If this were a common consequence of a policy prohibiting all active termination of human life, it should force a reevaluation of maintaining the prohibition. Rarely however, does such suffering persist when there is adequate use of pain relieving drugs and procedures.[93]

The Commission also recognized that policies prohibiting direct killing may conflict with the important value of patient self-determination:

This conflict will arise when deliberate actions intended to cause death have been freely chosen by an informed and competent patient as the necessary or preferred means of carrying out his or her wishes, but the patient is unable to kill him or herself unaided, or others prevent the patient from doing so. The frequency with which this conflict occurs is not known, although it is probably rare. The Commission finds this limitation on individual self-determination to be an acceptable cost of securing the general protection of human life afforded by the prohibition of direct killing.[94]

And in an earlier part of the Commission's report, where consideration was given to the possible liability of doctors under the criminal law, the commission stated that:

Since neither wrongful shortening of life by physicians nor the failure to give appropriate medical treatment for fear of the criminal law appears to be prevalent, society seems to be well served by retaining its criminal prohibition on killing, as interpreted and applied by reasonable members of the community in the form of prosecutors, judges and jurors.[95]

First, it should be noted that the Commission's report was primarily concerned with forgoing life-sustaining treatment, so the Commission's comments on legalizing active voluntary euthanasia were simply incidental to its principal inquiry. It is therefore not unreasonable to suggest that the issue of active voluntary euthanasia may not have received as full and detailed consideration as it would deserve, and further that the commission is unlikely to have had before it all the relevant evidence and information to make a fully informed decision on this difficult question. The Commission's report is nevertheless significant in that it was one of the first government

---

[93] Ibid. at 73. [94] Ibid. [95] Ibid. at 35–6.

inquiries in the common law jurisdictions under consideration to have given serious consideration to the possibility of legalizing active voluntary euthanasia performed in the medical context.

Central to the Commission's rejection of active voluntary euthanasia is the concern that its legalization would result in abuse and erosion of proper respect for human life. However, there is remarkably little argument or evidence of any kind to substantiate this assertion which, in turn, casts doubt on the Commission's findings.[96] Moreover, in examining the consequences of maintaining the legal prohibition against killing terminally-ill patients at their request, scant consideration was given to the abuses and problems resulting from the hidden and unregulated practice of active euthanasia.

Despite the Commission's rejection of any change to the law, the willingness of the Commission to accept the possible need to re-evaluate the present prohibition is of itself significant, reflecting recognition that the law's prohibition on direct killing is not immutable and may require adaptation to meet changing circumstances. Further, it should be noted that since the Commission released its report in 1983, there have been significant developments with regard to the issue of active voluntary euthanasia[97] which would arguably justify a different conclusion today.

In recent years, task forces have been established in a number of US states to examine the issue of physician 'aid in dying' and make recommendations to state legislatures. In 1985, the Governor of New York, Mario Cuomo, convened the Task Force on the Life and the Law to recommend public policy on issues raised by medical advances. Although assisted suicide and euthanasia were not on the agenda initially presented to the Task Force, it chose to examine and report on these practices in order to contribute to the debate unfolding in New York and nationally, in the USA. In its report,[98] the Task Force comprized of 24 members, of various backgrounds and ethical and religious beliefs, unanimously recommended against any change to New York laws prohibiting assisted suicide and euthanasia.

The Task Force was principally concerned with the social risks of legalization. It advocated that for the purposes of public policy and medical practice, a line must be drawn between forgoing medical interventions and assistance to commit suicide or the performance of euthanasia. Members of the Task Force were unanimously of the view that legalization of assisted suicide and euthanasia would pose profound risks to many patients. They felt that regardless of how carefully any guidelines are framed, the practice

[96] Winkler, E., 'Forgoing Treatment: Killing vs. Letting Die and the Issue of Non-Feeding' in Thornton, J. and Winkler, E., *Ethics and Aging: The Right to Live and the Right to Die* (Vancouver, 1988) 155, 162.

[97] See Ch. 5.

[98] *When Death is Sought: Assisted Suicide and Euthanasia in the Medical Context* (New York, 1994).

of assisted suicide and euthanasia would be affected by the social inequalities and bias underlying the delivery of health care. In their view, the practices would pose the greatest risks to those who are poor, elderly, members of a minority group, or without access to good medical care. Further it was thought that the clinical safeguards that have been proposed to prevent abuse and error would not be realized in many cases. To illustrate their concerns, the Task Force noted that most doctors do not have a long-standing relationship with their patient or information about the complex personal factors relevant to evaluating a request for suicide assistance or euthanasia. Attention was also drawn to the widespread failure of American medicine to treat pain adequately or to diagnose or to treat depression in many cases.

The Task Force also raised concerns about the longer term implications for society if assisted suicide and euthanasia are legalized. It was suggested that legalization would affect our perceptions about one person assisting another to die and that over time, the sense of gravity about these practices would dissipate. The Task Force members were particularly concerned that the criteria and safeguards that have been proposed for assisted suicide and euthanasia would be extended in clinical practice and law, for example, beyond patients who are terminally ill and patients who are able to give consent.

The policy recommendations made by the New York State Task Force reflect a concern to protect society from the dangers of error and abuse which they believe will result from legalization. To some extent at least, the perceived problems are linked with the inadequacies of the health care system in the USA but the objections raised by the Task Force against legalization clearly go beyond this. The Task Force proceeds from a fairly paternalistic stance, with little recognition of the interests of those individuals seeking assistance in dying from their doctors.[99] Further, the Task Force's Report is open to the criticism that insufficient attention has been given to the fact that many doctors are already involved in assisting the suicide of their patients and performing euthanasia. As a result, the report fails to address the existing problems associated with a covert and unregulated practice which must be taken into account in any assessment of the appropriateness of legalization and weighing up of risks. It is, nevertheless, significant that this inquiry had been undertaken, demonstrating a recognition that the issue of active voluntary euthanasia and doctor-assisted suicide need to be addressed. Moreover, the Task Force's Report contains a detailed and scholarly analysis of the issues and has thereby made a significant contribution to the debate.

A more permissive approach to the legalization of active voluntary eu-

---

[99] See also Ogden, R., 'The Power of Negative Thinking' (1994) 13 *Last Rights* 69.

thanasia and physician-assisted suicide was taken by the Michigan Commission on Death and Dying which was established in 1992 and released its report in 1994.[100] The commission's membership was interdisciplinary, comprising representatives from 22 organizations, including medical and nursing associations, hospice, hospital, and nursing home associations, 'right to life', social workers, pro-euthanasia organizations, and legal representatives from the State Bar of Michigan and the Prosecuting Attorneys' Association. In addition to a Consensus Report which made recommendations about a number of matters including improved access to palliative care and greater focus on pain and symptom management, the report of the commission contains three Position Reports which seek to reflect the principal law reform options: 1) a report which recommends that the legislature decriminalize and regulate 'aid in dying' (encompassing both physician-assisted suicide and active voluntary euthanasia); 2) a report which recommends that a series of procedural safeguards be put in place if the legislature decides to legalize physician-assisted suicide; and 3) a report which recommends to the legislature that the ban on physician-assisted suicide be maintained and made permanent. There was support amongst the members of the commission for reform of the law to allow some form of physician 'aid in dying'. With regard to the most far-reaching recommendation contained in the first report, to the effect that support be given for the decriminalization and regulation of 'aid in dying', 9 of the 22 members of the commission voted in favour, 7 against, 4 abstained and 2 were not present. The outcome of the vote in respect of the second report (safeguards for legalized physician-assisted suicide) was similar, with somewhat less opposition recorded (9 in favour, 5 against, 6 abstaining and 2 not present). Only 5 members of the commission voted in favour of the recommendation in the third report that the prohibition on physician-assisted suicide be maintained. In view of the diversity of opinion reflected in these Michigan reports, the unanimous rejection of any form of 'aid in dying' by the New York State Task Force which also was of a similar size and diverse composition is all the more surprising.

IV. CANADA

There have also been significant reform developments in Canada. At the federal level, the issues of active voluntary euthanasia and assisted suicide have been addressed by the Canadian Law Reform Commission and, more recently, by a Special Senate Committee, although recommendations were made against a change to the law. However, at the provincial level, the

---

[100] Michigan Commission on Death and Dying, *Final Report of the Michigan Commission on Death and Dying* (Michigan, 1994).

British Columbia Royal Commission on Health Care has supported an amendment to the Canadian Criminal Code which would permit health care workers to assist the suicide of terminally ill patients. Also noteworthy are the bills that have been introduced over the past few years, seeking the legalization of active voluntary euthanasia and physician-assisted suicide.

The Law Reform Commission of Canada has undertaken extensive work in the area of medical law and ethics, in connection with its Protection of Life Project.[101] In 1982, the commission published a working paper *Euthanasia, Aiding Suicide and the Cessation of Treatment* to address what it saw as a real interest and need in this area.[102] Aside from the commission's consideration of cessation or refusal of treatment which comprized the bulk of its report, the commission identified the following key questions for consideration: (1) should active euthanasia be legalized, or at least decriminalized?; and (2) should aiding suicide be decriminalized? The formulation of the questions in these terms is in itself significant, in that the issue of active voluntary euthanasia[103] was directly considered by the commission. This is in contrast to a number of the government and law reform commission inquiries into the criminal law undertaken in Australia and the United Kingdom which have focused attention on the more general question of mercy killing.[104] The working paper released by the commission set out some preliminary proposals with regard to the matters under consideration, which were largely incorporated in the commission's 1983 report.[105]

The commission recommended against legalizing or decriminalizing active voluntary euthanasia in any form and was in favour of continuing to treat it as culpable homicide. The reasons for this view were stated in the report:

The legalization of euthanasia is unacceptable to the Commission because it would indirectly condone murder, because it would be open to serious abuses, and because it appears to be morally unacceptable to the majority of the Canadian people. The Commission believes that there are better answers to the problems posed by the suffering of the terminally ill. The development of palliative care and the search for

[101] In 1976, a special study group was established under the Protection of Life Project, which has, over the years, examined various topics including abortion, sterilization, criteria for determining death, and consent to medical treatment.

[102] Law Reform Commission of Canada, Working Paper No. 28, *Euthanasia, Aiding Suicide and the Cessation of Treatment* (Ottawa, 1982) (Foreword).

[103] The definition used by the commission was 'the act of ending the life of a person from compassionate motives, when he is already terminally ill or when his suffering has become unbearable'; Law Reform Commission of Canada, Report No. 20, *Euthanasia, Aiding Suicide and the Cessation of Treatment* (Ottawa, 1983) 17.

[104] The issue of mercy killing has also been the subject of earlier consideration by the Canadian Law Reform Commission; see Law Reform Commission of Canada, Working Paper No. 33, *Homicide* (Ottawa, 1984) where it was proposed that mercy killing should be taken out of the category of first-degree murder.

[105] Law Reform Commission of Canada, *Euthanasia, Aiding Suicide and the Cessation of Treatment*, above n. 102.

effective pain control methods constitutes a far more positive response to the problem than euthanasia on demand. To allow euthanasia to be legalized, directly or indirectly, would be to open the door to abuses and hence indirectly weaken respect for human life.[106]

With regard to the more general question of mercy killing, the commission recommended that mercy killings should not be made an offence separate from homicide and that there be no formal provision for special modes of sentencing for this type of killing other than what is already provided for homicide. The commission further recommended against decriminalizing aiding suicide for much the same reasons for which they did not favour the legalization of active voluntary euthanasia.

The commission's report has been subject to criticism for its treatment of the euthanasia issue.[107] It is certainly true that the report merely recites the well established arguments for and against active voluntary euthanasia, including concerns about the risk of abuse, without really advancing the debate or providing any evidence to substantiate such claims. More fundamentally, however, in its forthright rejection of any change to the law with regard to active voluntary euthanasia, and in particular, in the assertion that legalization of active voluntary euthanasia 'appears to be morally unacceptable to the majority of the Canadian people,' the report ignores important evidence of growing public opinion in Canada in favour of legalization of medically administered active voluntary euthanasia.[108] Furthermore, it could be argued that the commission, in rejecting any change, has underestimated the significance of the existing discrepancy between law and practice in this area, and the problems resulting from this discrepancy.[109]

Since the release of the commission's report, growing interest has focused in Canada on physician-assisted suicide and active voluntary euthanasia.[110] In 1991, the British Columbia Royal Commission on Health Care released a report which proposed an amendment to the Canadian Criminal Code that would exempt health care workers from criminal liability for assisting the suicide of a terminally ill patients.[111] The issue of active voluntary euthanasia was also considered, and although a number of the commissioners believed that health care workers should be protected from criminal

[106] Law Reform Commission of Canada, above n. 102, at 18.
[107] e.g. Samek, R., 'Euthanasia and Law Reform' (1984) 17 *Ottawa LRev.* 86; Schiffer, L., 'Euthanasia and the Criminal Law' (1985) 42 *UToronto Fac.LRev.* 91.
[108] See pp. 261–2 above.
[109] For example, the commission relies upon the internal regulating mechanisms to offset the apparent harshness of the law as an argument in favour of retaining the existing prohibition when this is, in fact, one of the strongest arguments for change.
[110] Note also Law Reform Commission of Canada, Report No. 31, *Revised and Enlarged Edition of Report 30, Recodifying Criminal Law* (Ottawa, 1987) which included a recommendation that mercy killing be treated as second-degree rather than as first-degree murder.
[111] British Columbia Royal Commission on Health Care and Costs, *Closer To Home* C-183 (British Columbia, 1991).

charges if they assisted terminally ill patients in ending their lives, a consensus could not be reached on this issue and no recommendations were made. This report is significant, being the first Canadian report where physician-assisted suicide is unequivocally endorsed and where there is some qualified support, from at least some commissioners, for the legalization of active voluntary euthanasia. The issues of euthanasia and assisted suicide were considered further in the province of British Columbia by a Special Advisory Committee on Ethical Issues in Health Care.[112] This committee was unable to reach consensus on the issues of whether it is ever ethically appropriate for a physician to assist a patient to commit suicide or to perform active voluntary euthanasia. There was, however, minority support for both practices amongst committee members.

In other developments, steps have been taken for the legalization of active voluntary euthanasia. In June 1991, a Private Member's Bill for the legalization of active voluntary euthanasia was introduced into the Canadian House of Commons by Mr Chris Axworthy.[113] Under the terms of the proposed legislation, a person suffering from an irremediable condition could make application for euthanasia on a specific form, witnessed by two people who are not related to the applicant, and accompanied by a medical certificate signed by the attending physician. This document would then be presented to a 'referee' appointed by the Attorney-General, and a decision would have to be made within 5 days of receipt. If the application were to be approved, a euthanasia certificate would be issued with a copy to the patient's doctor. Only qualified medical practitioners would be authorized to administer active euthanasia under the legislation, and they would be protected from criminal liability, provided the administration of active euthanasia was performed with reasonable skill and care. The Bill also sought to clarify the law with regard to the administration of pain-killing treatment which may have the effect of hastening death, and the issue of withholding or withdrawing of treatment at the patient's request or in circumstances where the treatment is therapeutically useless. Although Mr Axworthy's efforts in putting forward a bill for the legalization of active voluntary euthanasia were generally welcomed by euthanasia proponents, the terms of the Bill, and in particular the proposal for a euthanasia referee, did not attract much support. On 24 October 1991, the Bill was debated at second reading and dropped from the Order paper. There have also been a number of Private Member's Bills introduced in the Canadian House of Commons by Mr Svend Robinson seeking the legalization of physician-

---

[112] Special Advisory Committee on Ethical Issues in Health Care, *Euthanasia and Physician-Assisted Suicide* (British Columbia, 1994).

[113] Bill C-261: An Act to legalize the administration of euthanasia under certain conditions for persons who request it and who are suffering from a irremediable condition and respecting the withholding and cessation of treatment and to amend the Criminal Code.

assisted suicide upon the request of a terminally ill person. The first of these Bills[114] was introduced in December 1992 but was never debated in Parliament and died on the Order Paper when an election was called. A new bill was then introduced by Mr Robinson in February 1994.[115] This Bill was debated at second reading and then dropped from the Order Paper in September 1994 because the Bill was not deemed votable. In addition to these Bills, there have also been a number of unsuccessful motions put forward in the House of Commons seeking support for legalization of active voluntary euthanasia and physician-assisted suicide.[116]

To a large extent, the growing attention in Canada to the issue of active voluntary euthanasia and physician-assisted suicide can be attributed to the *Rodriguez* case[117] and the enormous publicity and public sympathy that Sue Rodriguez's cause attracted as it proceeded through the courts during the early 1990s. As was outlined in an earlier chapter, the Canadian Supreme Court ultimately decided against her (albeit only by a narrow margin) in her attempt to have the prohibition on assisted suicide in the Canadian Criminal Code declared invalid at least in so far as it applies to mentally competent, terminally ill patients who are unable to commit suicide unaided.[118] Her failure in the courts was highlighted by the fact that she was later reported to have committed suicide with the assistance of a doctor friend, but this was, by necessity, done outside the law. In the wake of these developments which had captured public attention, there was increased pressure on Parliament to address the question of medical assistance in dying. The opportunity was certainly seized by the Canadian voluntary euthanasia organizations[119] which undertook an intensive campaign to lobby politicians to support change to the law.

It was against this background that the Special Senate Committee on Euthanasia and Assisted Suicide was established. On 23 February 1994, the Senate adopted a motion moved by Senator Joan Neiman QC that a special committee of the Senate be established to examine and report upon the legal, social, and ethical issues relating to euthanasia and assisted suicide. The committee was initially to present its final report to the Senate by 15 December 1994, but this was subsequently extended on a number of occasions and the final report was not released until 7 June 1995.[120] The commit-

---

[114] Bill C-385 An Act to amend the Criminal Code (aiding suicide).
[115] Bill C-215 An Act to amend the Criminal Code (aiding suicide).
[116] Mr Ian Waddell's motion presented in February 1993 (active voluntary euthanasia) and Mr Raymond Skelly's motion proposed in June 1993 (physician-assisted suicide).
[117] [1993] 3 SCR 519.
[118] See pp. 86–94 above.
[119] See further pp. 280–3 above.
[120] Special Senate Committee on Euthanasia and Assisted Suicide, *Of Life and Death: Report of the Special Senate Committee on Euthanasia and Assisted Suicide* (Ottawa, 1995).

tee heard testimony for 14 months from witnesses all across Canada as well as from overseas and received hundreds of additional letters and briefs.

Although the motion adopted by the Senate had referred only to euthanasia and assisted suicide, it soon became apparent to the committee that a range of other matters would need to be considered in order to ensure that these issues are examined in the broader health care context. Thus, it was felt that a broad spectrum of 'end of life' decisions which are made by or on behalf of patients needed to be addressed as well as some specific matters such as the availability and quality of palliative care, pain control and sedation practices, and advance directives.

The report acknowledged the lack of consensus regarding the use of terminology in this area and sought to avoid any misunderstanding in defining the terms used in the report, opting for a literal meaning that appears to be undisputed and widely accepted. For the purposes of the report, euthanasia was defined as a deliberate act undertaken by one person with the intention of ending the life of another person to relieve that person's suffering where that act is the cause of death (what has been described in this work as active euthanasia). Assisted suicide was defined as the act of intentionally killing oneself with the assistance of another who provides the knowledge, means or both. It is evident from these definitions and also the examples given in the specific chapters dealing with these issues, that euthanasia and assisted suicide were defined in very general terms, not limited to the health care context of a doctor providing suicide assistance or performing euthanasia at the request of the patient.

Although the committee was able to agree on many of the issues regarding medical and health care practices which were canvassed in its report, it was divided on the more difficult questions of assisted suicide and euthanasia. A majority of the committee (comprized of four of the seven committee members) recommended that no amendment be made to section 241 of the Canadian Criminal Code which contains the prohibition on assisted suicide. Those members opposed to changing the existing law were primarily concerned with maintaining the fundamental social value of respect for life. These members were also concerned about the risks associated with changes to the present law. In their view, legalization could result in abuses, especially with respect to the most vulnerable members of society. There was also some concern that changes in the law with respect to competent persons could lead the way to possible changes in the law for incompetent persons. Of those committee members opposed to change, several thought that if assisted suicide were decriminalized but euthanasia remained illegal, there might be a basis to argue an inequality under section 15 of the Charter in respect of those who are physically incapable of committing assisted suicide. These members thought it preferable to uphold the prohibition on assisted suicide rather than risk opening the door to euthanasia. There was also concern amongst these members about the ability adequately to control, monitor, and enforce the most stringent safeguards on assisted suicide. Among those opposed to change, some felt that more research in the area of assisted suicide is required. Whilst they felt that the lack of available information would make it difficult for them to support a change to the law at this time, it would not preclude a consideration of it at a later date. It was, accordingly, recommended by a majority of the committee that research be undertaken into how many persons are requesting assisted suicide, why it is being requested, and whether there are any alternatives that might be acceptable to those who are making the requests.

The remaining three committee members gave a minority recommendation that an exemption be created to section 241 of the Criminal Code, under clearly defined safeguards to protect individuals who assist in another person's suicide. The principal justifications put forward in support of such a change was the need to protect individual autonomy, and that there is more potential for abuse with the presently unregulated practice of assisted suicide than if legislative changes were made, accompanied by appropriate safeguards. These members of the committee were of the view that the safeguards should at a minimum include the following:

(i)   the individual must be competent and must be suffering from an irreversible illness that has reached an intolerable stage, as certified by a medical practitioner;

(ii) the individual must make a free and informed request for assistance without coercive pressures;

(iii) the individual must have been informed of and fully understand his or her condition, prognosis and the alternative comfort arrangements, such as palliative care, which are available;

(iv) the individual must have been informed of and must fully understand that he or she has a continuing right to change his or her mind about committing assisted suicide;

(v)   a health care professional must assess and certify that all of the above conditions have been met;

(vi) no person should be obliged to provide assistance with suicide.[121]

The minority further recommended that in order to avoid abuse, procedural safeguards must provide for review both prior to and after the act of assisted suicide. They felt that regulations were required to deal with the monitoring and enforcement of the safeguards and that records must be maintained for all cases of assisted suicide.

With regard to euthanasia, the committee made separate recommen-

---

[121] Special Senate Committee on Euthanasia and Assisted Suicide, at 73.

dations with respect to non-voluntary euthanasia, voluntary euthanasia, and involuntary euthanasia.[122] The Committee recommended that non-voluntary euthanasia remain a criminal offence but that the Criminal Code be amended to provide for a less severe penalty where there is the essential element of compassion or mercy. Such a change was thought appropriate because of the difference between a killing motivated by compassion or mercy and other forms of murder, and because the actual practice of the law does not coincide with the letter of the law. Similarly, a majority of the committee (five of the seven members) recommended that voluntary euthanasia remain a criminal offence, but that the Criminal Code should be amended to allow for a less severe penalty in cases where there is the essential element of compassion or mercy. Most of the committee members who recommended against legalization opposed voluntary euthanasia for the same reasons that they were opposed to assisted suicide. They did, however, also have an additional objection based upon the difference between assisting suicide, where the dying person is the principal agent of death, and performing euthanasia where the agent is another person. Because a second person is directly involved in the case of voluntary euthanasia, they did not believe that adequate safeguards could ever be established to ensure the consent of the patient was given freely and voluntarily. There was one member of the committee who, whilst favouring a change in the law with respect to assisted suicide, did not believe that a change of law was appropriate at this point in time with respect to euthanasia because it would be more difficult to design and put in place sufficient controls to prevent abuse.

A minority of two of the seven committee members supported the legalization of voluntary euthanasia for competent individuals who are physically incapable of committing suicide. For these members, the equality argument under section 15 of the Charter was persuasive: if there is to be legalization of assisted suicide as they had recommended, voluntary euthanasia must also be accepted in order to avoid the unequal treatment of those who are physically incapable of committing assisted suicide. The minority was of the view that the fact that the dying person has requested death significantly distinguishes voluntary euthanasia from other forms of euthanasia, and justifies permitting some form of legalization in such cases. They recommended that the Canadian Criminal Code be amended accordingly, subject to the same or similar minimum safeguards as had been recommended in respect of assisted suicide. There was a further recommendation that if voluntary euthanasia were to remain a criminal offence, the Criminal Code be amended to provide for a less severe penalty similar to the penalty recommended by the committee in respect of non-voluntary euthanasia.

---

[122] See the Report at 14 for the Special Senate Committee's definition of these terms.

It was the recommendation of the committee as a whole that research be undertaken into who is requesting euthanasia, why it is being requested, and whether there are any alternatives that might be acceptable to those who are making the requests.

With respect to involuntary euthanasia, the committee recommended that the prohibition under the present murder provision in the Criminal Code should continue.

The report of the Special Senate Committee on Euthanasia and Assisted Suicide and the whole process of examination of these issues have been very significant. The committee conducted a wide-ranging inquiry, including quite detailed consideration of the Netherlands position before reaching its decision. Clearly, proponents of voluntary euthanasia and doctor-assisted suicide would be disappointed with the outcome. Whilst on the whole, the committee's report reflects a well reasoned and balanced approach, there are aspects of the report which are open to question. With regard to the committee's recommendations in respect of euthanasia, it seems odd, to say the least, that non-voluntary and voluntary euthanasia were treated similarly in the recommendations of the majority of the committee—with respect to both forms of euthanasia, it had been recommended that the Criminal Code be amended to allow for a less severe penalty, provided the element of compassion or mercy was established. Even the minority who supported a change to the law agreed with this recommendation in the event that voluntary euthanasia were to remain a criminal offence. Given the fundamental distinction between an act of euthanasia which is performed at a person's request, and one which is performed in the absence of such a request (albeit for reasons of compassion), this conclusion is difficult to justify and has not been adequately explained by the committee. The answer may at least in part lie in the fact that the committee interpreted its terms of reference broadly, as encompassing all forms of assistance in dying and did not specially focus on the issue of active voluntary euthanasia in the health care context where arguably, special considerations apply.

Although the report of the committee recommended against the legalization of either euthanasia or assisted suicide, it is of significance that there has been substantial minority support for these practices: three of the seven committee members were in favour of the legalization of physician-assisted suicide, and two out of the seven recommended that voluntary euthanasia also be permitted. It should be noted, however, that the minority's support for voluntary euthanasia was considerably qualified by the recommendation that it should be limited to individuals who are physically incapable of committing suicide.[123]

---

[123] For comment see pp. 476–8 below.

Also of significance is that the committee has recognized the need for further research in respect of both assisted suicide and euthanasia. By recommending such research be undertaken to ascertain who is requesting such assistance, why it is being requested, and whether there are any alternatives that might be acceptable to those who are making such requests, the way is left open for a review of the situation when more is known about these practices. It is fair to say that the committee's findings, although disappointing for many, were not unexpected. To a large extent, the committee's inability to reach a consensus regarding these issues reflects the divisions of opinion in the wider community and comes after a number of other reports as well as decisions in the Canadian courts where there has been a similar lack of consensus.

Since the release of the Special Committee's Report, attention has once again focused on the Canadian Parliament. Earlier, in 1994, the Prime Minister, Jean Chretien, had given an undertaking that a free vote would be allowed in the Parliament on the issues of euthanasia and assisted suicide. Indeed, the committee's report had referred to this and had welcomed the opportunity to assist all members of Parliament who would be ultimately deciding the issues. However, there have since been indications that the Prime Minister may be unwilling to bring the matters of euthanasia and assisted suicide before the Parliament. Thus the situation in Canada remains uncertain. It is possible that the matter will come before the House by means of a further Private Member's Bill, although a bill is probably more likely to succeed if it is initiated by the Government with the assurance of a free vote in the House.

V. INTERNATIONAL DEVELOPMENTS

Until recently, the issue of euthanasia, and in particular the issue of active voluntary euthanasia, had received little attention at the international level.[124] However, in more recent years, there have been a number of developments of some significance, including preliminary consideration of the issue of active voluntary euthanasia by a committee of the Council of Europe, and attempts to introduce legislation in support of active voluntary euthanasia in the European Parliament.

---

[124] In 1976, the Parliamentary Assembly of the Council of Europe recommended the establishment of national commissions of inquiry to lay down ethical rules for the treatment of persons approaching the end of life which would consider, *inter alia*, the situation which may confront members of the medical profession, such as legal sanctions, whether civil or penal, when they have refrained from effecting artificial measures to prolong the death process in the case of terminal patients whose lives cannot be saved by present day medicine, or have taken positive measures whose primary intention was to relieve suffering in patients and which could have a subsidiary effect on the process of dying. Recommendation 779 (1976).

A. Council of Europe

In 1987, the issue of active voluntary euthanasia was raised before the Council of Europe by the Netherlands Government. The Netherlands Government was at the time considering the introduction of legislation dealing with active voluntary euthanasia and had sought advice on the subject from the Council of Europe.[125] The matter was referred to a working party of the Ad Hoc Committee of Experts on Progress in Biomedical Science of the Council of Europe (CAHBI). Questionnaires on euthanasia, prepared by the secretariat in collaboration with experts from the Netherlands, were sent to all Member States as well as those non-member States that have observer status with the CAHBI. Under its terms of reference, the working party was instructed to examine the replies received to this questionnaire and to prepare a draft opinion on euthanasia. In particular, the working party was requested to give an opinion on the feasibility and the desirability of undertaking a study of the legal, human rights, ethical, and medical problems relating to euthanasia.

On the basis of the opinion provided by the working party, the CAHBI reached the conclusion that whilst it would be possible to undertake a study on problems relating to active euthanasia (which it defined as a deliberate act to end the life of a severely suffering patient at his or her request), such a study was not appropriate or timely.[126] A report was subsequently submitted by the Secretary General of the Council of Europe to the 16th Conference of European Ministers of Justice in respect of the work of the CAHBI. With regard to active voluntary euthanasia, it was reported that in December 1987, the CAHBI adopted an opinion for the Committee of Ministers on the feasibility and the desirability of undertaking a study on the legal, human rights, ethical, and medical problems relating to euthanasia (in particular 'giving death on request') and that, in this very detailed opinion, the conclusion was reached that such a study, even if it is feasible, is not desirable.[127]

B. European Parliament

In 1989, a Dutch member of the European Parliament, Mrs Van Hemeldonck, proposed a resolution on the care of the terminally ill. The matter was referred to committee, and a report ensued dealing with the treatment of terminally ill patients. The report, authored by Leon

---

[125] For further discussion see p. 422 below.

[126] Council of Europe, Ad Hoc Committee of Experts on Progress in Biomedical Science (CAHBI), *Draft Opinion on the Legal, Human Rights, Ethical and Medical Problems Relating to Euthanasia*, Oct. (Strasbourg, 1987).

[127] Report submitted by the Secretary General of the Council of Europe to the 16th Conference of European Ministers of Justice relating to the work of the CAHBI.

Schwartzenberg, Professor of Medicine and world renowned cancer specialist, contained a clause supporting active voluntary euthanasia. That clause provided:

In the absence of any curative treatment, and following the failure of palliative care correctly provided at both a psychological and medical level, each time a fully conscious patient insistently and repeatedly requests an end to an existence which has for him been robbed of all dignity and each time a team of doctors created for that purpose establishes the impossibility of providing further specific care, the request should be satisfied without thereby involving any breach of respect for human life.[128]

The Schwartzenberg report, as it has become known, was narrowly adopted by the European Parliament's Environment, Public Health and Consumers' Committee in June 1991. Debate on the report in the plenary sitting of the European Parliament was originally scheduled to take place later in 1991 but was postponed on a number occasions and is now unlikely to be reactivated in the foreseeable future. Even if the European Parliament were to adopt the resolution, the resolution would have no legal effect unless members of the European Parliament can persuade the European Commission to draft legislation which, if approved by the Council of Ministers, would be binding on Member States.

CONCLUSION

The foregoing analysis of reform developments with regard to active voluntary euthanasia in the common law jurisdictions under consideration reveals considerable progress in recent years. Undoubtedly the most significant development has been the passage in May 1995 of legislation in the Northern Territory of Australia, permitting doctors to perform active voluntary euthanasia and doctor-assisted suicide in carefully controlled circumstances. In addition, a voter-initiated referendum in support of the legalization of physician-assisted suicide was passed in November 1994 in the US State of Oregon. These developments mark a turning point in the history of the movement for voluntary euthanasia and assisted suicide in the common law world.

Apart from these most significant developments, there has been a groundswell of reform activity in all of the jurisdictions under consideration, including the work of the House of Lords Select Committee on Medical Ethics in the United Kingdom, the Special Senate Committee on Euthanasia and Assisted Suicide in Canada, and inquiries established in a

---

[128] Extract from the motion for a resolution on care of the terminally ill. See Note, 'European Support for Euthanasia?' (1991) 69 *Bull.Med. Ethics* 25, 26.

number of states in the USA and Australia. Whilst most have recommended against any form of legalization, it has been shown that in many cases, important considerations in the assessment of whether legalization is appropriate have been overlooked or inadequately addressed. In particular, a number of the recent reports which have rejected legalization have failed adequately to address the problems stemming from the present legal position where, although unlawful, active voluntary euthanasia and physician-assisted suicide do already occur on a significant scale in practice but in a totally hidden and unregulated manner. Although most of these inquiries have ultimately recommended against a change to the law, the very fact that these inquiries have been undertaken and the issues openly debated and addressed, represents a significant development in the reform process.

However, what has been lacking in most considerations of the issue of active voluntary euthanasia has been a detailed analysis of the position in the Netherlands, where, for some time now, active voluntary euthanasia has been practised relatively openly by the medical profession. This omission has tended to undermine the categorical rejection of active voluntary euthanasia by a number of law reform commission bodies and agencies on the grounds that they have based their conclusions on supposition, for example, about feared consequences of legalization, and have failed to take into account the available evidence. In the chapter which follows, the position in the Netherlands will be examined with a view to learning from the Netherlands' experience.

7

The Netherlands

INTRODUCTION

Apart from the Northern Territory of Australia, where legislation has recently been enacted, the country which has come closest to the legalization of active voluntary euthanasia is the Netherlands. Although active voluntary euthanasia is still illegal in that country, it is now practised quite openly by the medical profession and there are very few prosecutions of doctors involved in the practice. Developments in the Netherlands have naturally attracted interest in other jurisdictions, including the United Kingdom, the USA, Canada, and Australia where there is growing pressure for the legalization of active voluntary euthanasia. The Dutch position is often cited by euthanasia proponents as a model of social reform which demonstrates the benefits of sanctioned active voluntary euthanasia and which ought to be followed in other countries. The object of this chapter is to examine the law and practice with regard to active voluntary euthanasia in the Netherlands.

There is no doubt at all that the Netherlands offers a unique opportunity to those interested in the legalization of active voluntary euthanasia to assess the effects of State-sanctioned active voluntary euthanasia upon the law, medicine, health care, and social policy.[1] In essence, the practice of active voluntary euthanasia in the Netherlands constitutes a social experiment which is open to analysis and may provide important lessons for other countries in any future attempts to legalize active voluntary euthanasia.

There has, for some time, been some difficulty in obtaining reliable information about the practice of euthanasia in the Netherlands, not the least of which has been the language barrier, and the lack of scholarly literature on the Dutch position available in English. In more recent years, however, as interest in the Netherlands has heightened, the available literature has increased and many items written by Dutch scholars have subsequently been translated into English. There has also recently been a major government-commissioned inquiry into medical decisions affecting the end of life which has produced the most comprehensive information to date about the practice of euthanasia in the Netherlands.[2]

---

[1] Bostrom, B., 'Euthanasia in the Netherlands: A Model for the United States?' (1989) 4 *Issues Law&Med.* 467, 470.

[2] The Remmelink Committee Inquiry, see pp. 423–35 below.

I. THE LEGAL POSITION IN THE NETHERLANDS

From the outset, it must be made clear that the system of law that exists in the Netherlands is a civil law system derived from Roman law which is quite different from the law in common law jurisdictions. The present legal position in the Netherlands with regard to active voluntary euthanasia is very complex. Contrary to popular belief, active voluntary euthanasia has *not* actually been legalized and doctors engaging in the practice do so in violation of the Dutch Penal Code 1886.[3] In practice, however, they are not prosecuted, provided that they can show that their actions in performing voluntary euthanasia were in accordance with certain guidelines which have been developed by the courts and which have since indirectly been given some recognition under regulations. Thus, through a combination of jurisprudential developments, prosecution policy, and minimal legislative activity, a situation has been reached where there is *de facto* conditional legal tolerance of active voluntary euthanasia in the Netherlands.

The official definition of euthanasia in the Netherlands is the deliberate termination of an individual's life by another, at that individual's request,[4] and this definition is now widely accepted in that country. It is not only linked with the concept of self-determination but also with the legal definition of euthanasia in the Dutch Penal Code 1886.[5] Specifically excluded from the definition of euthanasia are: the withholding or withdrawing of treatment which is medically pointless; the administration of necessary pain-relieving drugs which may shorten life; and the withholding or withdrawing of treatment at the patient's request.[6] It follows from the Dutch definition of euthanasia that it necessarily refers to *voluntary* euthanasia (indeed the Dutch regard the notion of non-voluntary or involuntary euthanasia a contradiction in terms), and it involves *active* steps in the termination of life. However, in the interest of consistency with other chapters of this work, the phrase 'active voluntary euthanasia' will continue to be used for the purposes of discussing the Netherlands position.

A. The Dutch Penal Code

The starting point for an analysis of the legal position in the Netherlands with regard to active voluntary euthanasia is Article 293 of the Dutch Penal

---

[3] See Article 293.

[4] State Commission on Euthanasia (The Hague, 1985). See also Royal Dutch Medical Association (RDMA), *Vision on Euthanasia* (Utrecht, 1986).

[5] Leenen, H., 'Legal Aspects of Euthanasia, Assistance to Suicide and Terminating the Medical Treatment of Incompetent Patients' in RDMA, *Euthanasia in the Netherlands* (Utrecht, 1991) 2.

[6] RDMA, *Vision on Euthanasia*, above n. 4, at 4–5. In so defining euthanasia, the RDMA has rejected the notion of 'passive' euthanasia.

Code 1886. It provides that: 'A person who takes the life of another at that other person's express and serious request is punishable by imprisonment for a maximum of 12 years or by a fine'. Article 293 of the Dutch Penal Code is the Article most frequently applicable in cases of active voluntary euthanasia. It was introduced in 1886 to leave no doubt that the killing of a person is unlawful, even if that person requests death.[7] The inclusion of Article 293 also serves to decrease the maximum term of imprisonment from life as provided for murder[8] to 12 years by virtue of the request of the victim. The rationale behind this diminished punishment is the fact that murder violates the life of a particular person, whereas killing on request is a violation of the respect which is due to human life in general, even though the personal right to life is not violated.[9]

Note should also be made of Article 294 dealing with assisted suicide which is to the effect that: a person who intentionally incites another to commit suicide, assists in the suicide of another, or procures the means to commit suicide is punishable, where death ensues, by imprisonment for up to 3 years or by a fine.

Another relevant provision of the Penal Code is Article 40 which contains a defence of *force majeure* or 'necessity'. It provides that a person committing an offence under *force majeure* is not criminally liable. In the medical context, Article 40 has given rise to a particular defence known as *noodtoestand* or 'emergency' in which the defendant faces an irreconcilable conflict of duties. The recognition of the *noodtoestand* defence has played a central role in the development of Dutch jurisprudence and has ultimately provided a means by which doctors in the Netherlands can perform active voluntary euthanasia without incurring criminal sanction despite the prohibition in Article 293.

B. *Jurisprudential Developments*

Although active voluntary euthanasia is a punishable offence under Article 293 of the Penal Code, the Dutch courts,[10] through a series of decisions, have developed certain exceptions to this prohibition by defining guidelines for its practice.[11] These guidelines have been accepted as also applying to

---

[7] Sluyters, B., 'Euthanasia in the Netherlands' (1989) 57 *Medico-Legal J* 34, 35.

[8] See Article 289.

[9] See Driesse, M. et al., 'Euthanasia and the Law in the Netherlands' (1988) 4 *Issues Law&Med.* 385, 387, referring to the Explanatory Memorandum for the Dutch Penal Code and Schmidt, H. J., *Geschiedenis van het Wetboek van Stafrecht* (History of the Penal Code of 1881), Vol II, 440.

[10] Comprising the District Courts, the Court of Appeal and the Supreme Court.

[11] Note should be made in this context of developments that have occurred in Japan where the courts in a number of cases have outlined guidelines under which euthanasia would be legally permissible, although these have not been developed to the same extent as in the Netherlands. In 1962 a decision was handed down by the Nagoya Court of Appeals (High

the practice of doctor-assisted suicide. If these guidelines are observed, doctors will not incur liability. Essentially, the position is that a doctor can be acquitted, or, if found guilty, released with minimal punishment, and generally will not even be prosecuted, if the act of voluntary euthanasia took place in circumstances creating a conflict of duties for the doctor which constituted a higher necessity. The guidelines, initially developed by the courts, have subsequently been sanctioned by the Dutch medical profession, prosecution guidelines, government commission statements, and hospital protocols, and have recently been given some statutory recognition.

The first reported case of a Dutch doctor being prosecuted for having administered active voluntary euthanasia came before the Leeuwarden District Court in 1973.[12] This case involved a doctor, Dr Geertruida Postma, who was prosecuted for ending the life of her mother. Dr Postma's mother had suffered a cerebral haemorrhage, was partially paralysed, had trouble speaking, and was deaf. She had unsuccessfully tried to commit suicide and had repeatedly expressed the wish to die. In response to her mother's request, Dr Postma killed her mother by injecting her with a fatal dose of morphine. Dr Postma readily admitted what she had done and said that her only regret was that she had not acted earlier. At the time of the trial, quite a number of doctors had signed an open letter to the Dutch Minister of Justice stating that they had committed the same offence at least once. Dr Postma was convicted for contravention of Article 293 of the Penal Code but, because of the purity of her motives, was only sentenced to a symbolic

Court Criminal Reports, Vol. 15, No. 9, 674 (Dec. 22, 1962)) that euthanasia would only be permitted under the following strict conditions: (1) a patient should be suffering from a fatal disease recognized as incurable in the light of modern medical knowledge and techniques and his death should be imminent; (2) he should be suffering from such an excruciating pain that nobody could bear to watch it; (3) it should be performed only for the purpose of relieving the patient's agony of death; (4) there should be a patient's own sincere request or consent when he has a clear consciousness and an ability to express his own will; (5) as a rule it should be performed by a doctor, otherwise there should be special circumstances justifying that it could not be performed by a doctor; (6) appropriate means acceptable from the ethical point of view should be taken. For discussion see Fukada, M., 'A Survey of Research of Doctors' Attitudes Toward Euthanasia in Boston and Japan' (1975) 22 *Osaka ULReview* 19, 19–22. Note also the more recent decision of Presiding Judge Shigeru Matsuura of the District Court in Yokahama (April 1995) where it was held that a doctor would be allowed to conduct a mercy killing if four conditions were met: (1) that the patient is suffering in unbearable physical pain; (2) death is inevitable and imminent; (3) all possible measures have been taken to eliminate the pain with no other treatment left open; and (4) the patient has clearly expressed his or her will to approve the shortening of his or her life.

[12] The *Postma Case, Nederlands Jurisprudentie*, 1973, No. 183, District Court of Leeuwarden, 21 Feb. 1973. See Note, 'Euthanasia Case Leeuwarden—1973' (1988) 3 *Issues Law & Med.* 439. It should be noted that in 1952 the Utrecht Court convicted a doctor who had killed his severely suffering brother. However, the Leeuwarden case is generally cited as the first euthanasia case in the Netherlands, because the court in the earlier Utrecht decision did not consider issues relevant to the acceptability of euthanasia; Leenen, 'Euthanasia, Assistance to Suicide and the Law: Developments in the Netherlands' (1987) 8 *Health Pol'y* 197, 200 n. 7.

and conditional punishment.[13] The Leeuwarden Court did, however, indicate that active voluntary euthanasia would have been acceptable if it was performed in circumstances where the patient is incurably ill, experiencing unbearable suffering, and requests the termination of his or her life, and provided that the termination is performed by the doctor treating the patient or in consultation with him or her.[14]

Whilst there have been some differences in the interpretation of this case,[15] the decision attracted widespread interest and public debate on the subject and was soon hailed as a legal precedent for the performance of active voluntary euthanasia as an exception to Article 293 of the Penal Code.[16] During Dr Postma's trial, the people in her village had banded together in a show of support, and shortly after the passing of sentence, the first Dutch Voluntary Euthanasia Society was formed (the Nederlandse Vereniging Voor Vrijwillige Euthanasie). The aim of this society was to bring about changes to Article 293 of the Penal Code so as to expressly permit active voluntary euthanasia performed by a doctor. At the same time, another organization, the Foundation for Voluntary Euthanasia (Stichting Vrijwillige Euthanasie) was formed under the leadership of lawyer Dr van Till. Unlike the pressure group tactics of the Voluntary Euthanasia Society, the foundation was a 'think tank' of academics who tried to find a way to make a 'good death' accessible for those who really needed it, but without endangering those who were undecided or unwilling to die. This group was not convinced that the Penal Code should be changed, and believed that jurisprudence could adequately deal with the problem. The foundation sought to promote public discussion on the subject and released a number of publications which were later used by the courts in the development of guidelines for the practice of active voluntary euthanasia. During this time opinion polls conducted in the Netherlands showed growing support for the practice.

[13] She was given a suspended sentence of 1 week in gaol and 1 year probation. See Note, 'Euthanasia Case Leeuwarden—1973', above n. 12, at 442.

[14] See Leenen, 'Euthanasia, Assistance to Suicide and the Law: Developments in the Netherlands', above n. 12, at 200; Note, 'Euthanasia Case Leeuwarden—1973', above n. 12, at 439–40.

[15] There was some discussion in this case regarding the medical practice of manipulating medication in order to alleviate the unbearable suffering of an incurably ill patient, even if that course of action would shorten the patient's life. Whilst accepting the prevailing medical standard as a guide, the court held that Dr Postma had deviated from that standard by bypassing the course of alleviation and opting instead for immediate termination of her mother's life; Note, 'Euthanasia Case Leeuwarden—1973', above n. 12. Against this background, some commentators have raised doubts as to the scope of the decision; whether it merely permitted the hastening of death as a side effect of relieving pain or whether it was in fact intended to provide guidelines under which a doctor could avoid punishment under Article 293. For discussion see Driesse et al., 'Euthanasia and the Law in the Netherlands', above n. 9, at 654–6.

[16] van der Sluis, I., 'The Practice of Euthanasia in the Netherlands' (1989) 4 *Issues Law & Med.* 455, 458.

Another important development which took place in 1973 in the wake of the Leeuwarden Court decision was the release of a provisional statement on active voluntary euthanasia by the Royal Dutch Medical Association (RDMA).[17] In this statement, the association softened its earlier opposition to the practice[18] and expressed the somewhat tentative view that:

Legally euthanasia should remain a crime, but that if a physician, after having considered all the aspects of the case, shortens the life of a patient who is incurably ill and in the process of dying, the court will have to judge whether there was a conflict of duties which could justify the act of the physician.[19]

This statement contributed to the opening of wide public debate on active voluntary euthanasia in the Netherlands, and was the beginning of significant interaction on the subject between the courts and the RDMA.[20] The notion of 'conflict of duties' referred to in the association's statement came to be the basis for the defence accepted by the courts for the performance of active voluntary euthanasia.

Following the Leeuwarden Court decision, several other cases were brought before the lower courts in the Netherlands, including a case of assisted suicide which came before the Rotterdam Criminal Court in 1981.[21] Although this case involved a lay person[22] and was therefore distinguishable from the earlier Leeuwarden Court decision, the Rotterdam Criminal Court took the opportunity to lay down specific guidelines under which the practices of active voluntary euthanasia and doctor-assisted suicide would not be punishable. These guidelines represented a synthesis of earlier legal developments, as well as reflecting developments within the medical profession and contributions made by the voluntary euthanasia organizations. In order for a doctor to escape liability:

(i)   The patient must repeatedly and explicitly express the desire to die.

(ii)   The patient's decision must be well informed, free, and enduring.

(iii)   The patient must be suffering from severe physical or mental pain with no prospect of relief.

(iv)   All other options for care must have been exhausted, or refused by the patient.

(v)   Euthanasia must be carried out by a qualified physician.

[17] Koninklijke Nederlandsche Maatschappij tot bevordering der Geneeskunst (KNMG).

[18] See, for example, the RDMA booklet on medical ethics *Medische Ethiek En Gedragsleer*, 3rd edn. (1959) in which active euthanasia and assisted suicide are strongly rejected and strong emphasis is placed on the doctor's duty to preserve life as long as possible.

[19] RDMA, *Provisional Statement on Euthanasia* (1973).

[20] de Wachter, M., 'Active Euthanasia in the Netherlands' (1989) 262 JAMA 3316, 3317.

[21] 1 Dec. 1981. See Leenen, 'Euthanasia, Assistance to Suicide and the Law: Developments in the Netherlands', above n. 12, at 200.

[22] In this case, a woman was convicted and sentenced to 6 months' conditional confinement for having provided the means for, and assisted in the suicide of an old lady who believed she had cancer.

(vi)   The physician must consult at least one other physician.

(vii)   The physician must inform the local coroner that euthanasia has occurred.[23]

These conditions, sometimes referred to as the Leeuwarden and Rotterdam criteria, also became the basis upon which decisions whether to prosecute were made.[24] The Public Prosecutor's Office in the Netherlands has the discretion not to proceed with a criminal case if it is considered to be in the public interest not to do so.[25] Following the decision of the Rotterdam Criminal Court, the Public Prosecutor's Office, in consultation with the Ministry of Justice, decided upon central co-ordination of cases of active voluntary euthanasia and doctor-assisted suicide. Prosecution policy was adopted in conformity with the guidelines established in the cases. A committee consisting of the country's five Chief Prosecutors (each of whom is attached to one of the five regional Courts of Appeal), was formed to review centrally all cases brought to the attention of the public prosecutor, and guidelines were issued by the government stipulating that no cases of medically administered active voluntary euthanasia or doctor-assisted suicide were to be prosecuted before they had been examined by the committee and approved for prosecution.[26]

However, even after the development of these guidelines by the courts and the decision of the prosecution to bring their policy into conformity with those guidelines, considerable uncertainty remained. There was no guarantee that a doctor who performed active voluntary euthanasia or assisted suicide in accordance with the guidelines would not be prosecuted. Moreover, doubt lingered whether decisions taken by the lower courts to accept these practices under certain conditions, notwithstanding the prohibition in Article 293, would be upheld in the higher courts.[27]

The Alkmaar *case 1984*[28]

The *Alkmaar* case was the first case to be brought before the Dutch Supreme Court and thus became a test-case for the permissibility of active voluntary euthanasia performed in accordance with the criteria laid down in the earlier decisions. It also presented the opportunity for the Court of Appeal and the Supreme Court to consider and authoritatively pronounce

---

[23] de Wachter, 'Active Euthanasia in the Netherlands', above n. 20, at 3317.

[24] Leenen, 'Euthanasia, Assistance to Suicide and the Law: Developments in the Netherlands', above n. 12, at 200.

[25] Sutorius, E., 'How Euthanasia was Legalised in Holland', paper delivered in Arnhem (1985) 10.

[26] Sluyters, 'Euthanasia in the Netherlands', above n. 7, at 41.

[27] See, for example, the concern expressed by the RDMA; de Wachter, 'Active Euthanasia in the Netherlands', above n. 20, at 3318. See also Leenen, 'Supreme Court's Decisions on Euthanasia in the Netherlands' (1986) 5 *Med.&Law* 349.

[28] *Alkmaar Case, Nederlands Jurisprudentie* 1985, No.106, Supreme Court, 27 Nov. 1984.

upon various defences which had been advanced in the lower courts since the 1970s on behalf of doctors who had been prosecuted for the perform-ance of active voluntary euthanasia.[29]

A number of different defences had been put forward. One such defence is the 'medical exception', to the effect that a doctor who acts with due care and within generally accepted medical standards should not be convicted under the Penal Code. According to a number of jurists who have vigor-ously argued this viewpoint, active voluntary euthanasia and assisted sui-cide should be considered a normal part of the services which doctors provide to their patients. Another defence, based on the interpretation of Article 293, is that the prohibition contained in this Article was not in-tended by the framers of the Code to cover the act of a physician in ending life.[30]

A further defence which has been advanced is based on the argument that although the *terms* of a certain legal provision may prohibit a certain act, that act may not violate the *spirit* of the legal provision.[31] This defence is also sometimes expressed in terms of 'absence of material illegality'. The origins of this defence date back to a 1933 case in which it was held that a clear legal prohibition against subjecting healthy cattle to infectious disease did not apply to a veterinary surgeon because the infection caused was aimed at improving and not injuring the health of the animals.

Another defence which has been invoked by defence attorneys and is dealt with in Dutch legal literature is the defence of *force majeure* or necessity which derives from Article 40 of the Penal Code. In the context of medically administered active voluntary euthanasia or doctor-assisted sui-cide, this has taken the form of the *noodtoestand* defence which is essen-tially based upon an irreconcilable conflict of duties. According to this defence, the duty of a doctor to abide by the law and to respect the life of the patient may be outweighed by the doctor's other duty to help a patient who is suffering unbearably and for whom, to end this suffering, there is no alternative but death.

The facts of the *Alkmaar* case were that the defendant, Dr Schoonheim, had given a series of lethal injections to his patient, a 95-year-old woman, Maria Barendregt, who was seriously ill and who had no prospect of im-provement. Some years earlier, the patient had discussed her deteriorating condition with her doctor and had signed an advance declaration, stating that she requested active euthanasia if she were to be in such a condition that no recovery to a reasonable and dignified state of life was to be

[29] Sluyters, 'Euthanasia in the Netherlands', above n. 7, at 36–8.

[30] This proposition is based upon field notes recorded by the author in conversations with Professor Henk Leenen, 27 Nov. 1991 (leading Dutch legal commentator on the subject of euthanasia) and Dr Eugene Sutorius, 30 Nov. 1991 (well known barrister who has frequently represented defendants in euthanasia cases before the courts).

[31] Sluyters, 'Euthanasia in the Netherlands', above n. 7, at 37.

expected. At age 94 she fractured her hip, suffered hearing and vision loss, and at times was unable to speak or articulate. The weekend before her death, her condition deteriorated considerably. She was unable to drink or eat and became unconscious. She regained consciousness some days later and declared that she did not want to live through a similar experience. The defendant subsequently discussed the matter with his assistant doctor and with the woman's son, both of whom approved of performing active voluntary euthanasia upon the patient. After a final conversation with the patient later that week, in which she again declared her wish to die, the doctor decided to meet her request because, according to his judgement, every day that she lived would be a heavy burden for her with unbearable suffering.[32] Dr Schoonheim then wrote on the death certificate 'unnatural death', and informed the police of his actions.

At first instance, before the Alkmaar District Court, the doctor was acquitted on the grounds of absence of material illegality.[33] The court found that although he had contravened the terms of Article 293 of the Penal Code, his conduct, judged from a legal point of view, could not be termed undesirable. The court's acceptance of this defence was, to a large extent, based upon its willingness to recognize the principle of self-determination. The court stated that this principle has been so generally accepted that it should prevail in an active voluntary euthanasia situation where the aid of a doctor is necessary to terminate life in a way worthy of a human being, and without violence. The court found that Dr Schoonheim had acted with the greatest possible care, giving serious consideration to the persistent suffering of his patient before taking the decision to perform active voluntary euthanasia. It was held that since he had satisfied the highest standards of conscientiousness, his actions were not legally undesirable and therefore not materially illegal under Article 293. This was the first time that a lower court had actually acquitted a doctor who had performed active voluntary euthanasia.

The prosecution appealed to the Amsterdam Court of Appeal. The Amsterdam Court of Appeal overturned the decision, rejecting outright the doctrine of absence of material illegality.[34] The court held that while the doctor's actions might have been desirable, especially in terms of the patient's right to self-determination, such actions were still illegal, and the doctor was therefore still accountable under Article 293. The defence coun-

---

[32] Gevers, J., 'Legal Developments Concerning Active Euthanasia on Request in the Netherlands' (1987) 1 *Bioethics* 156, 159.

[33] Scholten, H., 'Justification of Active Euthanasia' (1986) 5 *Med. & Law* 169.

[34] Feber, H., 'De Wederwaardigheden van Artikel 293 van het Wetboek van Strafrecht Vanaf 1981 Tot Heden' ('The Vicissitudes of Article 293 of the Penal Code from 1981 to the Present') in van der Wal, G. et al. (ed.), *Euthanasie: Knelpunten in een Discussie* (*Euthanasia: Bottlenecks in a Discussion*) (Baarn, 1987) 54–81, reviewed in 'Abstracts' (1988) 3 *Issues Law & Med.* 455, at 456–7.

sel had, *inter alia*, relied on the notion of *noodtoestand* or emergency. This was presented on the grounds that the doctor had been faced with conflicting duties, and that, after carefully weighing the conflicting duties and interests, in conformity with the standards of medical ethics and expertise, he had made a decision which was objectively justified.[35] However, the Court of Appeal rejected this argument.[36] The court was also critical of the fact that the doctor had relied solely on approval from the patient's son and the assistant doctor. In the opinion of the Court of Appeal, these two people were not sufficiently objective and independent. Thus, the Amsterdam Court of Appeal found the doctor guilty. However, no punishment was imposed on the grounds that, although it was doubtful that Dr Schoonheim had acted out of necessity, it was nonetheless evident that he had acted with integrity and due caution.

The doctor appealed to the Dutch Supreme Court, the highest court in the Netherlands. The Supreme Court affirmed the Court of Appeal's analysis as to the absence of material illegality, but held that the court had wrongly rejected the defence counsel's plea that a conflict of duties caused the doctor to act under *force majeure* in an emergency situation (the *noodtoestand* defence).[37] The Supreme Court ruled that the a doctor's duty to abide by the law and to respect the life of the patient may be outweighed by his other duty to help a patient who is suffering unbearably, who depends upon him, and for whom, to end his suffering, there is no alternative but death. The Supreme Court found that the Court of Appeal had failed adequately to investigate whether, according to responsible medical judgement, tested by norms of medical ethics, *force majeure* existed in this case as the doctor had claimed.[38] According to the Supreme Court, the Court of Appeal could for instance have attached importance to:

(i)   whether, and if so to what extent, according to professional medical judgement, increasing disfigurement of the patient's personality and/ or increasing deterioration of her already unbearable suffering were to be expected;

(ii)   whether, also taking into account the possibility of new serious relapses, it was to be expected that soon she would no longer be in a position to die with dignity;

(iii)   whether, and if so to what extent, there had been ways to alleviate her suffering.[39]

[35] Sutorius, 'How Euthanasia was Legalised in Holland', above n. 25, at 6.

[36] Scholten, 'Justification of Active Euthanasia', above n. 33, at 170.

[37] Sutorius, E., 'A Mild Death for Paragraph 293 of the Netherlands Criminal Code?', paper delivered in Arnhem, (1985).

[38] Leenen, 'Supreme Court's Decisions on Euthanasia in the Netherlands', above n. 27, at 350.

[39] Leenen, 'Euthanasia, Assistance to Suicide and the Law: Developments in the Netherlands', above n. 12, at 200.

Because the Amsterdam Court of Appeal had not adequately investigated the conflict of duties for the doctor, its decision was reversed and the
case was referred to the Court of Appeal of the Hague for final determination, with instructions to review the questions which had not been addressed in the lower court.[40] The Hague Court of Appeal upheld the
reasoning of the Supreme Court and acquitted the doctor. The court found
that although there was no medical consensus as to the permissibility of
active voluntary euthanasia, the doctor's actions were 'justified according to
reasonable medical insight'.[41] In reaching this decision, the court had relied
heavily on the opinion of the RDMA with regard to active voluntary
euthanasia which had been specifically sought for the purposes of this case.

The decision of the Supreme Court in the *Alkmaar* case, and its endorsement by the Hague Court of Appeal, were important developments in
securing the legal acceptability of active voluntary euthanasia and assisted
suicide in the Netherlands. They effectively upheld the *noodtoestand* defence which recognizes that a doctor may be faced with conflicting duties:
the duty to uphold the law of the land which prohibits the taking of life, and
the duty to act in the best interests of the patient. Since doctors cannot
always simultaneously satisfy both duties, they cannot be held criminally
responsible when they do what their professional duty demands, namely
putting the patient's interests first. Although decisions of the Supreme
Court only relate to the particular case before the court, in practice, its
rulings have a strong influence on the lower courts. By accepting the appeal
to *force majeure* in the sense of conflicting duties, the Supreme Court
created an opening for acquittal (or other lenient treatment) in individual
cases of doctors administering active voluntary euthanasia or assisting suicide under certain conditions.[42]

A significant aspect of the Supreme Court's decision was its reliance upon
medical standards in determining the validity of a plea based upon a conflict
of duties. According to the Supreme Court, the primary judgement as to the
permissibility of active voluntary euthanasia rests with the medical profession.[43] The court specifically ruled that in deciding whether, on the basis of
the facts of the case, the doctor should not be held liable because of the

[40] The Supreme Court only has jurisdiction on matters of law. Where it finds that the lower
court has not remained within the law, it refers the decision to one of the Courts of Appeal to
review the case, having regard to all the facts and circumstances; Sutorius, 'How Euthanasia
was Legalised in Holland', above n. 25, at 7.

[41] Feber, 'The Vicissitudes of Article 293 of the Penal Code to the Present', above n. 34, at
462. The only point of departure from the decision of the Supreme Court was the change from
'responsible medical insight' to 'reasonable medical insight'.

[42] Leenen, 'Legal Aspects of Euthanasia, Assistance to Suicide and Terminating the Medical Treatment of Incompetent Patients', above n. 5, at 5. It is, however, possible that the court
finds that the defendant had committed some other offence; e.g. falsification of the death
certificate.

[43] Sutorius, 'How Euthanasia was Legalised in Holland', above n. 25, at 12.

'emergency' he or she faced, the court should take into consideration 'scientific medical views and medical ethical norms'.[44] It could therefore be argued that, to a limited extent at least, the Supreme Court has accepted the medical exception defence outlined above. This is not to say, however, that the question of the permissibility of active voluntary euthanasia or doctor-assisted suicide is solely a medical concern: whilst the view of the medical profession is, in the judgment of the Supreme Court, clearly relevant, where there is any doubt, a plea based upon conflicting duties must ultimately be determined by reference to legal standards, as assessed by the courts.

Although the decision of the Supreme Court has been widely welcomed, having paved the way for the legal acceptability of active euthanasia performed at the patient's request, it has been criticized for its reference to medical ethics.[45] It has been argued that active voluntary euthanasia is not purely a medical act, subject only to medical ethics, and that in any event, no norms exist within the medical profession as to the permissibility of the practice. A better view of the decision is that the Supreme Court has not entirely delegated the decision as to the permissibility of active voluntary euthanasia or doctor-assisted suicide to the medical profession, but rather will refer to medical standards, in so far as they exist, in determining the validity of a defence plea based upon a conflict of duties.

Some consideration should also be given to the role of the principle of self-determination in the *Alkmaar* case. In this, as in earlier cases, the principal focus of the court has been on the position of the defendant doctor, and the issue of patient autonomy has only been dealt with indirectly. Although the principle of self-determination was not a specific basis of the Supreme Court's decision in the *Alkmaar* case, it did clearly play an important role in that one of the preconditions for the performance of active voluntary euthanasia is that it is at the express and earnest request of the patient.[46] The importance of patient self-determination is also evident from the Supreme Court's interpretation of the criterion of 'dying with dignity'[47] as being dependent on the patient's own life perspective. The principle of self-determination is, however, tempered by other considerations and certainly does not entitle a patient to demand the performance of

---

[44] The relevance of medical considerations is also apparent from the Supreme Court's finding that the Court of Appeal had erred in not investigating 'whether, according to responsible medical judgement, tested by norms of medical ethics, *force majeure* existed in this case' and from the specific matters which the Supreme Court identified as being relevant for consideration and which it directed the Hague Court of Appeal to take into account.

[45] Leenen, 'Euthanasia, Assistance to Suicide and the Law: Developments in the Netherlands', above n. 12, at 201; Feber, 'The Vicissitudes of Article 293 of the Penal Code to the Present', above n. 34, at 458.

[46] Gevers, J., 'Euthanasia or Assisted Suicide and the Non-Terminally Ill', in Aycke, O. and Smook, M. (eds.), *Right to Self-Determination* (Amsterdam, 1990) 65, 66.

[47] This was amongst the relevant considerations which could have been considered by the Court of Appeal; see above.

active voluntary euthanasia or doctor-assisted suicide in all circumstances. In the light of the *Alkmaar* case, the permissibility of the doctor's act depends on the existence of a true 'emergency' situation and is, therefore, limited to exceptional circumstances.[48]

It should also be noted that whilst upholding the existence of the *noodtoestand* defence in cases of active voluntary euthanasia, the Supreme Court did not specify the necessary criteria for the performance of lawful euthanasia. This can, to a large extent, be explained by the fact that the role of the Supreme Court is to adjudicate on the law, and any consideration of factual issues must be referred back to another court.[49] One can, however, interpret the Supreme Court's decision as giving at least tacit recognition to the guidelines for the performance of active voluntary euthanasia and doctor-assisted suicide developed by the lower courts in earlier cases.

Since the landmark *Alkmaar* case, and its unequivocal acceptance of the *noodtoestand* or emergency defence, a number of further cases involving doctors performing active voluntary euthanasia have come before the Dutch courts.[50] These cases have confirmed the existence of the *noodtoestand* defence and have examined the application of this defence in different factual circumstances.[51] In a number of cases, the doctors were convicted because it had not been established beyond reasonable doubt that the patient had requested active euthanasia.[52] There have also been a number of cases involving nurses and nursing assistants who have termi-

---

[48] Gevers, 'Euthanasia or Assisted Suicide and the Non-Terminally Ill', above n. 46, at 67.

[49] This proposition is based upon field notes recorded by the author in conversation with Professor Henk Leenen, 27 Nov. 1991.

[50] For a discussion of these cases, see Leenen, 'Euthanasia, Assistance to Suicide and the Law: Developments in the Netherlands', above n. 12, at 202; Leenen, 'Dying with Dignity: Developments in the Field of Euthanasia in the Netherlands' (1989) 8 *Med. &Law* 517, at 521–3. There have also been a number of cases brought before the Medical Disciplinary Courts, sometimes in respect of the same matter that has already come before the courts. The medical disciplinary tribunals have the characteristics and discretion of a court but a different focus, namely, to determine whether the doctor has complied with the requirements of good medical practice. Doctors who fail to comply with the necessary requirements may be subjected to sanctions ranging from a reprimand to suspension of the licence to practise medicine: Griffiths, J., 'The Regulation of Euthanasia and Related Medical Procedures That Shorten Life in the Netherlands' (1994) 1 *Med.Law International* 137, 144.

[51] For example, in 1985, the Hague District Court, following the guidelines in the *Alkmaar* case, acquitted Dr Admiraal in respect of the death of a 34-year-old multiple sclerosis patient who, although totally paralysed and experiencing physical and mental suffering, was not in danger of imminent death.

[52] Gevers, 'Legal Developments Concerning Active Euthanasia on Request in the Netherlands', above n. 32, at 160; Leenen, 'Euthanasia, Assistance to Suicide and the Law: Developments in the Netherlands', above n. 12, at 202. A case has recently come before the courts involving the prosecution of a doctor for the murder of a severely handicapped baby under Article 289 of the Penal Code (article 293 of the Code which is usually relied on in cases of euthanasia was not applicable as the taking of life was not performed at the person's request as required under that provision). The doctor was found guilty of murder by the Alkmaar District Court but no punishment was imposed. At the time of writing, the decision was being appealed.

nated the lives of patients.[53] The courts have held that nurses and nursing assistants cannot invoke the defence of *noodtoestand* or emergency because they are not entitled to undertake acts which may endanger the life of a patient. Arguments based upon pressures of psychic stress have been rejected on the grounds that nurses should be able to cope with stressful conditions. Even where euthanasia is administered by a nurse under a doctor's supervision, liability will be established: it has been held that euthanasia is a medical act which a doctor may not delegate to others.[54] In other cases, doctors have been found guilty of completing a false death certificate which is in itself an offence.[55]

Psychiatric or mental suffering and the Chabot case

One of the most controversial aspects of Dutch euthanasia policy concerns the availability of active voluntary euthanasia (or doctor-assisted suicide) for psychiatric patients or other patients who are suffering mentally. Over recent years, there have been a number of cases in the Netherlands involving doctors who have assisted the suicide of their patients, in circumstances where the patient's suffering has been principally of a psychiatric or mental kind.[56] The earlier cases, whilst not entirely conclusive, did appear to support the view that active voluntary euthanasia and doctor-assisted suicide should not be limited to patients with somatic-based suffering or physical illness, and that in appropriate circumstances, where patient competence could be established, and the other guidelines for careful practice had been adhered to, a doctor could lawfully assist such a patient. This position was essentially endorsed by the Dutch Association of Psychiatry in a 1992 Report, and by the RDMA.[57] Moreover, in 1993 the Inspector for Mental Health released a report which acknowledged that exceptional situations are possible in which assistance with suicide at the request of a psychiatric patient could be legitimate.[58] It was against this background that the courts

[53] Leenen, 'Dying with Dignity: Developments in the Field of Euthanasia in the Netherlands', above n. 50, at 522.

[54] 13 March 1995, Reuters report regarding a case which came before a District Court in Groningen in the Netherlands.

[55] The courts have held that where a patient dies following the administration of active voluntary euthanasia, one cannot say that death occurred as a result of natural causes. The doctor is therefore required to enter a declaration of non-natural death. A doctor cannot rely on the plea of necessity or professional secrecy to escape liability for falsification of a death certificate: Bostrom, B. and Lagerway, W., 'Court of the Hague (Penal Chamber) April 2 1987' (1988) 3 *Issues Law&Med.* 51.

[56] Griffiths, J., 'Recent Development in the Netherlands Concerning Euthanasia and Other Medical Behaviour that Shortens Life' (1995) 1 *Med.Law International* 347, 364.

[57] Commission on the Acceptability of Termination of Life of the RDMA, Discussion Paper, *Assistance with Suicide in the Case of Psychiatric Patients* (1993).

[58] In the light of this report, the National Inspectors for Public Health and for Mental Health withdrew an earlier statement released in 1991 to the effect that the 1990 protocol for reporting of cases (discussed below see pp. 425–6) was not applicable to psychiatric patients because a psychiatric condition could never afford a basis for assistance with suicide.

in the Netherlands, ultimately the Dutch Supreme Court, were called upon to rule authoritatively on the legitimacy of active voluntary euthanasia or doctor-assisted suicide for psychiatric patients in the *Chabot* case.

The *Chabot* case involved the prosecution of a psychiatrist, Dr Boudewijn Chabot, for having assisted in the suicide of one of his patients. The patient in this case was Hilly Boscher, a 50-year-old social worker. Mrs Boscher had married at the age of 22 and had two sons, Patrick and Rodney to whom she was utterly devoted. In 1986, the elder of the two sons, Patrick, committed suicide. Following his death and in the face of growing marital difficulties, she made her remaining son Rodney the sole focus of her attention. In 1990 Rodney was diagnosed as suffering from cancer, and he died in May 1991. On the same day Mrs Boscher unsuccessfully attempted to commit suicide. She subsequently contacted the Dutch Voluntary Euthanasia Society who had put her in touch with Dr Chabot as he had previously indicated his willingness to give psychiatric support to persons who might approach the Association for assistance.[59] Although Mrs Boscher had agreed to enter into an ongoing therapeutic relationship with Dr Chabot, she refused anti-depressants and bereavement therapy. She repeatedly told Dr Chabot that her life no longer held any meaning for her and that she wanted to die. Following a series of consultations between 2 August and 7 September 1992, totalling some 24 hours, Dr Chabot had come to the conclusion that his patient's condition was hopeless and that she would inevitably attempt to commit suicide again. His diagnosis was that there was no question of a psychiatric illness or a major depressive disorder; rather, she was suffering from an adjustment disorder consisting of a depressed mood, without psychotic signs, in the context of a complicated bereavement process. During this period, Dr Chabot had approached seven consultants, and provided them with the transcripts of the therapy sessions. The majority of the experts consulted agreed with his assessment. On this basis, Dr Chabot decided that he would help Mrs Boscher to end her life. He went to her home and supplied her with a lethal dose of medication which she consumed in his presence. Mrs Boscher's own doctor and a friend were also in attendance. She died shortly after, and Dr Chabot reported her death to the local coroner as a suicide which he had assisted.

The case initially came before the District Court of Assen which found the *noodtoestand* or 'emergency' defence to be established. The court accepted that Dr Chabot had been faced with an irreconcilable conflict of duties, and that his decision to assist Mrs Boscher to commit suicide was reasonable in all the circumstances. In reaching this decision, the Court of Appeal placed considerable reliance on the 1993 discussion paper of the RDMA, Commission on the Acceptability of Termination of Life regarding assistance with suicide in respect of psychiatric patients. The court declared

---

[59] Griffiths, J., 'Assisted Suicide in the Netherlands: The *Chabot* Case' (1995) 58 *Mod.L Rev.* 232. 234.

that although the indictment against Dr Chabot was correct, in view of the facts of the case, he was not punishable. An appeal was taken from this decision to the Leeuwarden Court of Appeal which affirmed the initial decision. The Solicitor General of the Court of Appeals subsequently brought an appeal to the Supreme Court.

The Supreme Court accepted that the *noodtoestand* defence can, in appropriate circumstances, also apply where the patient's suffering is mental and in the absence of a physical disorder or a terminal condition. The court said that in deciding whether a person's suffering must be regarded as so unbearable and lacking in any prospect of improvement so as to justify a doctor acting in violation of the Penal Code, the suffering must be distinguished from its cause. The Supreme Court did, however, state that where the suffering does not have a somatic origin, it is more difficult to assess its seriousness and lack of prospect of improvement, and the courts must therefore approach the question of whether the defence of *noodtoestand* has been established with exceptional care.

In upholding, in principle, the availability of doctor-assisted suicide and active voluntary euthanasia for patients with psychiatric or mental suffering, the court specifically rejected the argument advanced by the prosecution that a person suffering from a psychiatric sickness or disorder is legally unable voluntarily to request assistance to die. The Supreme Court affirmed the decision of the Court of Appeal which had, in reliance upon the discussion paper of the RDMA Commission on the Acceptability of Termination of Life, held that a person suffering from a psychiatric disorder can express a wish to die that is legally the result of a competent and voluntary judgement.

One significant aspect of the decision concerns the issue of available treatment. According to the guidelines which have been developed, before active voluntary euthanasia or doctor-assisted suicide can be performed, all of the treatment options have to have been exhausted or, alternatively, declined by the patient. On the basis of established authority, patients whose suffering has a physical cause have the right to refuse all treatment. However, in the case of psychiatric patients and patients who are suffering mentally, a refusal of realistic alternative treatment is likely to disqualify that patient from receiving assistance in committing suicide or active voluntary euthanasia.[60] The Supreme Court had stated that a doctor would only be justified in assisting a patient whose suffering is of a non-somatic origin in circumstances where the suffering lacks any prospect of improvement, that is, where their condition is incurable. This aspect of the decision was also consistent with the position taken by the RDMA Commission Discus-

---

[60] Special Senate Committee on Euthanasia and Assisted Suicide, *Of Life and Death: Report of the Special Senate Committee on Euthanasia and Assisted Suicide* (Ottawa, 1995) A-133 referring to the evidence of Professor H. Leenen.

sion Paper which had stressed the absence of a treatment perspective as the principal justification for a doctor's intervention. It follows from the *Chabot* decision that if a patient, whose suffering is mental, has refused a realistic therapeutic alternative, their suffering cannot be considered incurable or lacking any prospect of improvement. In effect, this obliges such individuals at least to attempt alternative treatments if they wish to be eligible for active voluntary euthanasia or doctor-assisted suicide. As one Dutch commentator points out,[61] this represents an important deviation from the normal rule of consent and the proposition that treatment which has been refused by a patient does not constitute reasonably available treatment.

The actual decision of the Court of Appeal to acquit Dr Chabot was reversed on the grounds that none of the psychiatrists who had been consulted had personally examined the patient, and there was, therefore, no independent evidence available to the court that an emergency situation existed. Dr Chabot was accordingly convicted;[62] however, the court declined to impose any punishment after taking into account the personality of the accused, as well as the surrounding circumstances of the case.[63] It is clear from this decision that in circumstances where non-somatic or mental suffering is involved, the guidelines for the practice of active voluntary euthanasia and assisted suicide must be strictly complied with, including the consultation requirement. Whilst in cases where the patient's suffering is physical, failure to consult a colleague would not necessarily preclude a doctor from bringing a successful plea of *noodtoestand*, where the patient's suffering is non-somatic, consultation is essential and must take the form of an actual examination of the patient by an independent colleague.[64] It was held that the examination must cover not only the seriousness of the suffering and the incurability of the disease, but also other possibilities of providing help. In addition, the specialist will also have to determine whether the patient is in a position to form a free and deliberate opinion, without his or her decision being influenced by the disease or the disorder.

The Supreme Court decision in the *Chabot* case has undoubtedly been of great importance in shaping Dutch euthanasia policy with regard to psychiatric patients and other patients whose suffering is of a mental nature. For the first time, the Supreme Court has accepted that a doctor may be justified in assisting the suicide or performing active voluntary euthanasia in respect

---

[61] Ibid.

[62] He was also subsequently reprimanded by the Amsterdam Medical Disciplinary College for failing to act as cautiously as could have been expected professionally: Spanjer, M., 'Dutch Psychiatrist Reprimanded for Assisting Suicide' (1995) 345 *Lancet* 914.

[63] It should be noted that the Supreme Court took quite an unusual course in imposing a sentence that differed from the decision of the Court of Appeal. As was noted above, the usual practice in cases where the Supreme Court has come to the conclusion that a law has not been correctly applied is to refer the matter to another court for retrial.

[64] For criticism of the court's reasoning regarding this aspect of the decision see Griffiths, 'Assisted Suicide in the Netherlands: The *Chabot* Case', above n. 59, at 241–2.

of a patient whose suffering is of a non-somatic origin. However, the court has stressed the need for exceptional care in such cases, and was clearly concerned to maintain appropriate limits on the practice by specifying the requirements that have to be complied with. These requirements are much more stringent than for other cases of active voluntary euthanasia and doctor-assisted suicide.

The significance of the *Chabot* decision extends beyond the issue of psychiatric or mental suffering, and has more general implications for Dutch jurisprudence on the subject of active voluntary euthanasia and doctor-assisted suicide. One important consequence of the decision is that it has confirmed that the patient need not be in the terminal phase of their disease in order for active voluntary euthanasia or doctor-assisted suicide to be justifiable. There had been earlier cases involving non-terminal patients where the courts had accepted active voluntary euthanasia was permissible. However, the matter had been thrown into doubt in 1993 when the Minister for Justice expressed the view that active voluntary euthanasia was only permissible for patients in the terminal phase, and there was, as a result, a significant increase in the number of prosecutions.[65] On the facts of the *Chabot* case itself, Mrs Boscher was physically healthy, yet the court accepted the decision of the Court of Appeal that this did not categorically exclude the legitimacy of active voluntary euthanasia or assistance with suicide. The case is also of importance for having clarified the status of the consultation requirement. By insisting that in cases where a patient's request for active voluntary euthanasia or assistance in suicide does not have a somatic origin, consultation with an independent doctor who has personally examined the patient is essential, the Supreme Court has acknowledged that this requirement is not applied with the same vigour in other cases. In the course of its judgment the Supreme Court expressly acknowledged that compliance with the consultation requirement does not necessarily entail an examination in person by the doctor consulted and a doctor's failure to consult does not preclude the *noodtoestand* defence from being invoked.[66] It would appear from this decision that the legal requirements with regard to consultation are less strict than the procedures for consultation recommended by the RDMA which has stressed the importance of full consultation in all cases.[67]

The Dutch response to the decision in the *Chabot* case has been de-

---

[65] This is discussed further below: see p. 445.

[66] It should be noted, however, that failure to comply with the consultation requirement may expose the doctor to medical disciplinary proceedings: Griffiths, 'Recent Development in the Netherlands Concerning Euthanasia and Other Medical Behaviour that Shortens Life', above n. 56, at 383.

[67] RDMA, *Vision on Euthanasia* (Utrecht, 1995) in RDMA, *Euthanasia in the Netherlands*, 4th edn. (Utrecht, 1995) 34–6. For further discussion, see below.

scribed generally as being positive,[68] although a degree of disquiet has been expressed.[69] Some Dutch psychiatrists are not at ease with the creation of the possibility of active voluntary euthanasia or assisted suicide for psychiatric patients.[70] Many of them saw the former position where this was prohibited as some kind of support in dealing with this category of patients. The RDMA General Board in its 1995 revision of the earlier Vision on Euthanasia has fully accepted that no distinction can be drawn between physical and mental suffering.[71] The association has also accepted that in cases where the suffering is not evidently of a somatic origin it will be more difficult to assess objectively the suffering and especially the gravity and hopelessness thereof and it has endorsed the position of the Dutch Supreme Court that the utmost caution is required in such cases. The decision in the *Chabot* case has already had practical ramifications. In response to the decision, the prosecutorial guidelines were revised to reflect the holdings of the Supreme Court.[72] In addition, a number of prosecutions were dropped which involved patients whose suffering was of a non-somatic origin, as well as those prosecutions taken in respect of patients who were not in the terminal phase.

C. Evaluation of Dutch Case Law Developments

It is clear from the foregoing analysis that quite an extraordinary situation exists in the Netherlands: despite the seemingly absolute prohibition of active voluntary euthanasia and assisted suicide in Articles 293 and 294 of the Penal Code, in certain circumstances of unbearable suffering of a patient, these practices may be performed by a doctor with the acquiescence of the law. A major step in this development was the acceptance by the Supreme Court in the *Alkmaar* case that *noodtoestand* (or emergency) could be a defence in a prosecution for active voluntary euthanasia or doctor-assisted suicide. Apart from this landmark decision, other cases have also contributed in setting criteria to be followed by doctors when administering active voluntary euthanasia or assisted suicide. In addition to the need for a true emergency situation certain minimum requirements have emerged from the cases: the voluntariness of the patient's request; the

[68] Griffiths, 'Assisted Suicide in the Netherlands: The *Chabot* Case', above, n. 59, at 247.

[69] For criticism also from abroad, see Keown, J., 'Physician-Assisted Suicide and the Dutch Supreme Court' (1995) 111 *Law QRev.* 394.

[70] This proposition is based upon private communication with Dr Rob Dillmann, Secretary of Medical Affairs, RDMA 9 Dec. 1994.

[71] RDMA, *Vision on Euthanasia* (1995), above n. 67, at 34.

[72] In fact, the revised guidelines went beyond the requirements of the court by stipulating that in the case of a patient with a psychic disorder, two independent doctors (one of whom is a psychiatrist) must be consulted: Griffiths, 'Recent Development in the Netherlands Concerning Euthanasia and Other Medical Behaviour that Shortens Life', above n. 56, at 383.

requirement that the patient must suffer unbearably (physically or mentally); that there must be no other way to relieve the patient's suffering; that
only a doctor may perform active voluntary euthanasia; and that in doing
so, he or she must consult with another doctor.

Significantly, the guidelines which have been developed by the Dutch
courts regarding the circumstances under which the performance of active
voluntary euthanasia or doctor-assisted suicide is tolerated (sometimes also
referred to as the 'carefulness requirements'), have subsequently been affirmed and extended by the RDMA, the State Commission on Euthanasia,
and the prosecution authorities, and have recently been given *de facto*
statutory recognition.

II. POSITION OF THE ROYAL DUTCH
MEDICAL ASSOCIATION

In 1984, the General Board[73] of the RDMA issued a report outlining its
official standpoint on active euthanasia, revising the association's provisional view formulated in 1973 (outlined above). The need for publishing a
statement of its views at this time had in part been precipitated by a request
from the State Commission on Euthanasia, so that the commission could
incorporate the association's views in its own work.[74] The association's 1984
statement reflected the significant social and legal developments which had
taken place in the Netherlands since the release of its provisional statement
in 1973. The object of the 1984 report was not to argue the permissibility of
active voluntary euthanasia, but rather, on the assumption that it was already being performed, to provide guidance as to the appropriate conditions under which it is performed, and to draw attention to the legal
uncertainty which existed at that time with regard to the practice of active
voluntary euthanasia, both for doctors and patients.

The conditions for the performance of active voluntary euthanasia
recommended by the RDMA General Board followed quite closely the
guidelines laid down in the court decisions. A strong recommendation
made by the association was that the practice of active voluntary euthanasia
must be confined exclusively to the doctor/patient relationship. This was
not only because the practice requires medical and pharmacological expertise, but also because only doctors were in a position to give a diagnosis and
prognosis of the patient's condition. Moreover, doctors are accountable
for their conduct under the medical code of ethics and can be brought

---

[73] At the time, this body was known as the Central Committee, but in the interests of clarity
and consistency, the term General Board will be used throughout.
[74] For discussion of the State Committee on Euthanasia see below.

before a disciplinary court in the event that they breach the rules. It was accordingly recommended that the medical profession has an obligation to come up with a socially acceptable approach to the practice of active voluntary euthanasia. It was further recommended that the practice of active euthanasia at the patient's request by a doctor must be completely voluntary. A doctor who is opposed to the practice is, however, required to enable the patient to come into contact with another doctor who is willing to assist, but without necessarily breaking off his or her own relationship with the patient. In view of the irrevocable and exceptional character of active voluntary euthanasia, doctors who are willing to perform the practice will have to meet a number of conditions, and active voluntary euthanasia should only be performed as a last resort. Taking into account jurisprudential developments in the Netherlands with regard to the administration of active voluntary euthanasia, it was recommended that doctors will have to meet the following requirements with regard to the exercise of due care:

(i)   that the request for euthanasia is entirely voluntary;
(ii)   that it is a well-considered request;
(iii)   that the request for euthanasia is a durable wish;
(iv)   that the patient is experiencing unacceptable suffering, be it suffering due to pain, whether or not based on a perceivable physical condition, or suffering due to a physical condition, or physical disintegration without pain; and
(v)   that there is consultation with a colleague with experience in the field.

The General Board was of the view that one should not ascribe an overriding importance to whether or not the patient is in the dying phase. This represented a change from the associations' provisional view formulated in 1973, reflecting case law developments in which the courts have not insisted on this being a requirement. According to the General Board, the key question is whether a situation has been reached in which the patient voluntarily expresses a wish for death in a well-founded way and the doctor acknowledges the patient's unacceptable suffering, and that the patient's situation may be considered prospectless. It was, however, recommended that there should be a stipulation to the effect that active voluntary euthanasia be performed in a manner that is medically and pharmacologically justified.

In the interests of a balanced decision-making process, the General Board was of the view that consultation within professional medical circles is indispensable. It recommended that, in addition to informal consultation within the doctor's own team, there should be a more formal evaluation procedure to judge the merits of the request for active euthanasia by way of a committee of medical examiners consisting, for example, of a number of doctors to be appointed regionally by the RDMA.[75]

With regard to the reporting procedure after active voluntary euthanasia has been performed, the General Board acknowledged that it is not unusual for doctors to record cases of active voluntary euthanasia as 'natural deaths' in order to protect the next of kin and/or to protect themselves from the unpleasant consequences attached to legal proceedings, even if no punishment is ultimately imposed. The committee was of the view that this falsification of death certificates was inappropriate, simply obscuring the tension which exists between the strict legal position as reflected in Article 293 of the Penal Code and the practice of active voluntary euthanasia. Moreover, the committee pointed out that such falsification of death certificates has the consequence that the actual practice with regard to active voluntary euthanasia is unverifiable. It was accordingly recommended that doctors exercise due openness in reporting the cause of death. By the same token, however, it was thought that a doctor who complies with the conditions for the exercise of due care in the performance of active voluntary euthanasia may reasonably expect not to be prosecuted. In order to achieve this end unequivocally, the committee called for greater clarity to be instilled into the law. The committee recommended that the necessary change could be introduced by amendment of the legislation dealing with the disposal of the dead. It was further recommended, that until such time that legislation is introduced, clear arrangements be made between the Ministry of Justice and the RDMA with regard to prosecution policy as it applies to doctors performing active voluntary euthanasia or assisted suicide.

Whilst the General Board had expressed its concern about the legal uncertainty concerning active voluntary euthanasia both for doctors and patients, and had strongly urged that this uncertainty be eliminated as soon as possible, the association had refrained from saying whether the introduction of legislation was the appropriate solution. What was important was that there should be legal security for doctors and patients, whether this was achieved through explicit guidelines for prosecution developed by jurisprudence or by legislation.[76]

Since the release of the 1984 revised statement on active voluntary euthanasia by the RDMA, the association has been involved in a number of other initiatives. In 1987, the RDMA and the Dutch Nurses' Union issued a joint paper which laid down practical guidelines for health care professionals participating in the decision to perform active voluntary euthanasia.[77] As

---

[75] The specifics of this recommendation were not in the English translation of the General Board's vision, but appear in various other summaries and accounts, see, for example, Sutorius, 'How Euthanasia was Legalised in Holland', above n. 25, at 15.

[76] van Berkestijn, M. G., 'The Royal Dutch Medical Association and the Practice of Euthanasia and Assisted Suicide' in RDMA, *Euthanasia in the Netherlands* (1991) above n. 5, at 6.

[77] For an English translation of the guidelines, see Note, 'Guidelines for Euthanasia' (1988) 3 *Issues Law & Med.* 429.

with the association's 1984 statement on active voluntary euthanasia, this joint paper does not attempt to evaluate the permissibility of the practice, but rather, to provide practical guidelines with regard to the respective tasks, competences and responsibilities of both doctors and nurses involved in the performance of active voluntary euthanasia. These guidelines, which were revised in 1991, and which are currently again under revision, are intended not only to protect the legal position of doctors and nurses, but also to protect the legal rights and interests of patients by sanctioning only voluntary euthanasia and requiring documentation of the decision-making process.

It is made clear under the guidelines that the decision-making process for active voluntary euthanasia occurs under the final responsibility of a doctor. The doctor must satisfy him or herself that the patient's request is voluntary, that it is a well considered and persistent request, and that the patient is experiencing unacceptable suffering. Furthermore, the doctor must consult with at least one colleague about the request of the patient. The guidelines also recognize the central role of nurses in the care of patients and that, in some cases, the request for active euthanasia may initially be made to the nursing staff. The guidelines emphasize the need for open dialogue between doctors and nurses and for joint participation in the decision-making process. However, they recommend that the ultimate decision of whether or not to proceed with active voluntary euthanasia must be taken by the doctor. With regard to the performance of active voluntary euthanasia, the guidelines recognize that only doctors have the protection of the law, and that a nurse who independently engages in active voluntary euthanasia, even if she observes the standards for appropriate medical care, would almost certainly be prosecuted. It was accordingly recommended that the act of euthanasia be performed by the doctor alone. However, where this is not possible (where, for example, a method is chosen at the request of the patient, involving a number of activities which the doctor cannot carry out alone), the doctor can ask a nursing or caring attendant who was involved in the decision-making process to co-operate in the procedure. If the nursing or caring attendant is convinced that all the criteria of appropriate medical care have been met and, in accordance with his or her conscience, agrees to co-operate, a written agreement must be entered into between the doctor and nurse/caring attendant with regard to the carrying out of the procedure, specifying who performs which action and when. The joint guidelines also stress the desirability of developing procedural agreements for each work organization for the carrying out of active voluntary euthanasia.

In other developments, the RDMA has established a Commission on the Acceptability of Termination of Life. The role of the commission has been to examine certain practices involving the shortening of life of non-competent patients. By definition, this is seen as being distinct from euthanasia in the sense now accepted in the Netherlands, namely killing a person at his or her request. In addition to the paper dealing with assisted suicide for psychiatric patients referred to above, a series of discussion papers have been released dealing with severely defective newborns, comatose patients, and patients suffering from severe dementia.[78] The focus of these papers is principally to question the legitimacy of artificial prolongation of life with a view to abstaining from intervention unless this is of benefit to the patient.[79] Whilst the reports do give some consideration to the issue of active life-terminating treatment, this is seen as only applicable where life-prolonging treatment has been discontinued and the patient does not die in a quick and humane way. The papers contemplate that in these circumstances, adminis-tration of drugs in a fatal dosage may be indicated as a form of 'assistance in the dying process'.[80]

In 1995 the General Board of the RDMA sought to update its policy on euthanasia; the association's Vision on Euthanasia having been developed some 11 years earlier. The object of this move was to incorporate recent developments in the association's standpoint and make necessary modifica-tions and adaptations. The revised standpoint was restricted to active vol-untary euthanasia and doctor-assisted suicide, with a further report foreshadowed in 1996, summarising the Reports of the RDMA Commis-sion on the Acceptability of Termination of Life dealing principally with patients who were not capable of expressing a request for euthanasia.

One significant shift in the association's policy on euthanasia is that an 'in principle' preference is now given to assistance in suicide rather the admin-istration of active voluntary euthanasia in circumstances where the patient is capable of ingesting the medicine in an acceptable way.[81] In the opinion of the General Board, self administration by the patient optimally expresses the patient's autonomy and places ultimate responsibility for the act with the patient. If the patient should have prohibitive objections to taking his or her own life, this should induce the doctor to explore the patient's request once again with respect to the deliberateness of the request. Recommenda-tions were also made with respect to making proper arrangements for the

---

[78] Part 1 (Severely defective newborn babies) (1990); Part 2 (Long-term comatose patients) (1991); Part 3 (Seriously demented patients) (1993); Part 4 (Assistance with suicide in the case of psychiatric patients) (1993).

[79] For detailed discussion see Griffiths, 'Recent Development in the Netherlands Concern-ing Euthanasia and Other Medical Behaviour that Shortens Life', above n. 56, at 352.

[80] Described in Dutch as 'stervensbegeleiding' which the Commission on the Acceptability of Termination of Life considered to constitute 'normal medical practice'.

[81] RDMA, *Vision on Euthanasia* (1995), above n. 67, at 15–16. This represented a definite firming-up of the tentative comments which had been put forward in support of assisted suicide in the 1986 *Vision on Euthanasia* and where the committee had sought to explain the reasons behind the opposition to this practice within the medical profession, namely that assisted suicide has tended to involve non-terminal patients, whose suffering is of a mental rather than a physical nature.

doctor to be present when the patient commits suicide, or, in special circumstances, where for good reason different arrangements are made,[82] the doctor is at least available when the suicide is carried out in order to intervene should that become necessary. According to a spokesperson for the association, the new policy is not aimed at either restricting or expanding euthanasia, rather it is aimed at alleviating the psychological distress doctors experience in performing the practice.[83] The rationale is that doctors' involvement should be kept to a minimum, and a doctor should only be called on to administer active voluntary euthanasia where this is necessary, due to the patient's inability to commit suicide.

With respect to other aspects of the revised policy, the association has again stressed the importance of independent consultation. It was noted by the General Board that in practice, this requirement was not always met and the Board stressed that consultation with an independent colleague with relevant expertise is essential to a meticulous application of euthanasia. As was noted previously, in this respect, it appears that the position taken by the association is more exacting than the interpretation of this requirement by the Dutch Supreme Court.

As with the earlier statement of the association's vision, the revised vision explicitly stresses that active voluntary euthanasia and assisted suicide are to be seen as a last resort in circumstances where the patient's suffering cannot be remedied or alleviated in any other acceptable way. The 1995 Vision on Euthanasia has also again emphasized the importance of openness in the practice of active voluntary euthanasia or assisting in suicide, with full documentation and reporting of cases.

Consideration has so far focused on the position of the RDMA. In order to present a complete picture, it should also be noted that there is some opposition to the practice from within the Dutch medical profession. There are a number of medical organizations including the Nederlands Artsenverbond (Dutch League of Physicians) and the Pro Life Doctors which are officially opposed to active voluntary euthanasia. Some Dutch doctors are also members of the World Federation of Doctors who Respect Human Life, an international organization which is actively campaigning against the legalization of the practice in the Netherlands.[84] There are also many doctors who, although they are not in principle opposed to active voluntary euthanasia, refuse to practise it while it is still illegal. Significantly though, the endorsement of active voluntary euthanasia by the RDMA in its 1984 statement resulted in very few cancellations of membership. On the basis of current membership figures, of a total of some 40,000 Dutch doctors, 25,000 are members of the RDMA. This provides some grounds for

---

[82] e.g. where it is the wish of a patient and/or his family.   [83] Roelof Mulder, RDMA.
[84] 'Euthanasia in Holland' *News Exchange of the World Federation of Doctors who Respect Human Life* Part I No. 97, October 1987 and Part II No. 99, April 1988.

suggesting that the vast majority of Dutch doctors are not opposed to active voluntary euthanasia, provided it is confined to the strict conditions that have been advocated by the General Board of their association. There is also now evidence available from the Remmelink Committee inquiry[85] which clearly establishes that a majority of Dutch doctors support active voluntary euthanasia and doctor-assisted suicide and regard them as actions in which doctors can under certain circumstances collaborate within the framework of their professional actions.[86] Moreover, the great majority of Dutch doctors (66 per cent) believe that legislation should be enacted under which euthanasia is not punishable provided that the doctor has complied with the requirements of due care.[87]

III. INSTITUTIONAL POLICIES AND PROCEDURES

As the practice of active voluntary euthanasia remains potentially punishable, individual doctors, hospitals and health care institutions have attempted to protect themselves by following policies that will prevent a prosecution from being initiated. To this end, many hospitals and nursing homes have developed their own institutional guidelines and prescribed their own procedures for the practice of active voluntary euthanasia.[88] The great majority of all institutions of the health services have a euthanasia protocol or directive.[89] Almost all of the institutional protocols and directives leave some room for the practice, usually under very strict conditions and review, and they also require the doctor to report all cases. Information is readily available to doctors in the Netherlands regarding how to perform active euthanasia.[90]

IV. THE GOVERNMENTAL RESPONSE TO ACTIVE VOLUNTARY EUTHANASIA IN THE NETHERLANDS

The Netherlands State Commission on Euthanasia

In response to calls for reform, a State Commission on Euthanasia was established in 1982 by Royal Decree. The role of this commission was to

[85] For discussion see below.

[86] van der Maas, P. et al., *Euthanasia and Other Medical Decisions Concerning the End of Life: An Investigation Performed Upon Request of the Commission of Inquiry into the Medical Practice Concerning Euthanasia* Health Policy Monographs, Volume 2 (Amsterdam, 1992) 42. See also ibid. at 101.

[87] Ibid. at 103.

[88] de Wachter, 'Active Euthanasia in the Netherlands', above n. 20, at 3318–19.

[89] van Berkestijn, 'The Royal Dutch Medical Association and the Practice of Euthanasia and Assisted Suicide', above n. 76, at 9.

[90] See, for example, the publication by Admiraal, P., *Justifiable Euthanasia* (Amsterdam, 1980). Dr Pieter Admiraal, an anaesthesiologist practising for many years at the Delft General

advise the government concerning its future policy on active voluntary euthanasia and on rendering assistance in self-killing, in particular with respect to legislation and the application of the law. The commission comprized 15 members: 7 lawyers, 3 doctors, 2 psychiatrists, 1 nurse and 2 theologians.[91] The report of the commission was released in August 1985,[92] and its recommendations were set out in the form of a proposal for the amendment of the Penal Code. By a majority of 13 to 2, the commission recommended that the present prohibition in the Penal Code 1886 should be revised to allow doctors to practise active voluntary euthanasia under conditions similar to those developed by the courts. The commission was of the view that the intentional killing of another person at the latter's explicit and earnest request should remain punishable under Article 293 of the Penal Code, but that an exception should be incorporated into the law for a doctor who does so with regard to a patient who is in an untenable situation, without any acceptable prospects for change, and provided the act is carried out within the framework of careful medical practice.[93] It was recommended that assistance to suicide should be regarded within the same circumstances and on the same conditions as active voluntary euthanasia. The commission went on to elaborate the minimum requirements for careful medical practice, including that:

(i)   the patient has been informed of his or her particular circumstances;
(ii)   the doctor has satisfied him or herself that the patient has made his or her request for life to be terminated after careful consideration, and voluntarily abides by that decision;
(iii) the doctor has decided that terminating life on the basis of his or her findings would be justified, because he or she has reached the conclusion together with the patient that there is no other acceptable solution to the patient's untenable situation; and
(iv)   that there has been consultation with another medical practitioner nominated by the Minister of Welfare, Public Health and Culture.[94]

In order to stress the importance of the request of the patient, the commission recommended the introduction of a new provision to the effect

Hospital, was the first Dutch doctor to speak openly about his involvement with active voluntary euthanasia. Dr Admiraal has been a high profile campaigner for the acceptance of active voluntary euthanasia both within his own country and abroad. He has written numerous articles, presented many papers, and has, for a number of years, been involved with the Dutch Voluntary Euthanasia Society (NVVE).

[91] de Wachter, 'Active Euthanasia in the Netherlands', above n. 20, at 3317.

[92] Note, 'Final Report of the Netherlands State Commission on Euthanasia: An English Summary' (1987) 1 *Bioethics* 163 (hereafter referred to as the Report of the Netherlands State Commission on Euthanasia).

[93] Four members of the commission wanted to include the additional requirement that the patient's death be 'impending and inevitable'; Report of the Netherlands State Commission on Euthanasia, above n. 92, at 166.

[94] Ibid. at 173.

that a person who intentionally terminates the life of another person on account of serious physical or mental illnesses or disorders suffered by that person, if the latter is incapable of expressing his or her will, will be guilty of an offence.

The commission was of the opinion that a decision to terminate life should be implemented by a doctor and cannot be delegated to a third party, for example, a member of the family or to nursing staff. In order to demonstrate the importance of the requirement that a doctor must consult another doctor before terminating the life of a patient (included amongst the commission's criteria for careful medical practice), the commission recommended the introduction of a separate punitive sanction to cover any case where the doctor omits to take this step. The commission also recommended the inclusion in any new legislation of a 'conscience clause' to the effect that no medical worker should be obliged to participate in the active termination of life of a patient. In addition, the commission set out procedures with regard to body disposal and for the notification of the prosecution by a doctor following the termination of the life of a patient. It was recommended that body disposal procedures should be designed in such a way as to permit retrospective verification of the way in which the decision to terminate life was taken. The commission recommended that the doctor in charge personally notify the public prosecutor that he or she had terminated the patient's life or assisted the patient to take his or her own life. Such notification should be accompanied by a statement of the way in which the criteria proposed for the Penal Code had been taken into account. The public prosecutor should also be sent a declaration setting out the findings of the doctor consulted by the doctor in charge. It was also recommended that the doctor in charge must notify the occurrence of active voluntary euthanasia on the cause of death form. Further, it was recommended that the deliberate failure to fulfil the statutory requirement to furnish particulars with regard to death, or the provision of incorrect particulars in cases where life has been terminated, should be made a separate offence.

The commission also considered the status of written requests for the termination of life. It considered that a written request of this kind must be treated as an indication of the patient's wishes but should only carry authority when the patient is no longer able to make his or her will known. As long as a patient is still competent, only his or her verbal expression of intent is relevant, and the written instructions can be revoked or amended at any time.

In its report, the commission deemed it essential for Parliament to make plain its position on active voluntary euthanasia. The commission was particularly concerned that the issue could become politicized, and, to this end, urged that Members of Parliament be allowed to vote according to their conscience. The commission was also concerned about the widespread uncertainty regarding the scope of Article 293 of the Penal Code in relation to active voluntary euthanasia. In the commission's view, the development of relevant case law would take so long that it would be many years before the exact definition emerges of what is and what is not an offence. Nor, in the commission's view, does the modification of prosecution policy, in accordance with case law developments, provide the necessary clarity and certainty.

Two members of the commission could not agree to the regulation of active voluntary euthanasia in the law and presented their objections in a minority report, rejecting any change or modification to the present prohibition on killing on request. The objections raised by the dissenters included the fear that if the Netherlands proceeded with the legalization of active voluntary euthanasia, it could result in the isolation of the Netherlands from the international community, particularly through the possible contravention of Article 2 of the European Convention on Human Rights dealing with the 'right to life'.[95] The other main objections were based on the concept of human dignity and on 'slippery slope' arguments.[96]

The report of the State Commission gave rise to an extensive, and often emotional debate in medical and legal journals and in the mass media.[97] It also precipitated critical discussion as to the need for legislation with regard to active voluntary euthanasia and doctor-assisted suicide, and as to what form that legislation should take.

V. MOVES TOWARDS REFORM

Even prior to the release of the State Commission's report, a draft bill for the legalization of active voluntary euthanasia was introduced into the lower house of parliament by one of the smaller non-denominational political parties—D66. The Wessel-Tuinstra Bill (named after the Member of Parliament who introduced it) proposed the amendment of Article 293 of the Penal Code so as to legalize active voluntary euthanasia administered by a doctor in accordance with specified carefulness requirements.[98] It also made provision for the legal recognition of a prior written request (in effect, an advance directive) as evidence of a patient's request for active euthanasia in circumstances where the patient is no longer competent. This Bill

---

[95] Vervoorn, A., 'Voluntary Euthanasia in the Netherlands: Recent Developments' (1987) 6 *Bioethics News* 19, at 20–1.

[96] Roscam Abbing, H., 'Dying with Dignity, and Euthanasia: A View from the Netherlands' (1988) 4 *JPalliative Care* 70, 72.

[97] Gevers, 'Legal Developments Concerning Active Euthanasia on Request in the Netherlands', above n. 32, at 160; de Wachter, 'Active Euthanasia in the Netherlands', above n. 20, at 3318.

[98] Second Chamber of the States-General, Session 1985–86, 18 331, No. 38.

became the focal point for debate on the subject of active voluntary euthanasia both within and outside the government, but no action was taken on the Bill pending the report of the State Commission on Euthanasia. After the commission's report was published, the Bill was revised in accordance with the commission's recommendations.[99] Although the revised Bill had the support of a small majority in the parliament, it was opposed by the Christian Democrats who were in office together with the Conservative Party which supported the proposed legislation.[100] This presented a political problem for the coalition government which the Government attempted to solve by introducing its own, more restrictive, draft bill in January 1986. In addition to the usual carefulness requirements, the government Bill contained an additional requirement that 'according to accepted medical understanding there is concrete expectation of death as a consequence of the illness or affliction, and further medical treatment would serve no reasonable purpose'.[101] However, in a rather unusual step by the Government, the draft Bill was introduced without being given the formal status of a proposed law. In a covering letter accompanying the Bill, the Minister of Justice and the Minister of Welfare, Health, and Cultural Affairs, said that the Government would prefer not to amend the law at this stage and would rather allow case law to develop in this area. In the event that the Lower House was to take the view that it was desirable to enact legislation, the Ministers indicated that the specimen Bill would be revised and put to the State Council for its opinion.[102] At this point the RDMA, which was opposed to the Government's 'draft bill' on the grounds that it would create more uncertainties,[103] came down firmly in favour of legislative reform in accordance with jurisprudential developments and the association's own viewpoint.[104] Parliamentary debate on both Bills took place in March 1986 during which the Conservative Party, as a result of pressure from the

[99] For an English translation of the revised Bill, see Vervoorn, 'Voluntary Euthanasia in the Netherlands: Recent Developments', above n. 95, at 1–23.

[100] Leenen, 'Dying with Dignity: Development in the Field of Euthanasia in the Netherlands', above n. 50, at 524.

[101] Vervoorn, 'Voluntary Euthanasia in the Netherlands: Recent Developments', above n. 95, at 23. This is even more restrictive than case law developments in the Netherlands which have upheld the practice of active voluntary euthanasia in appropriate circumstances notwithstanding that the patient was not terminally ill. It did, however, make provision for the legal recognition of an advance directive as evidence of a patient's request for active euthanasia.

[102] Driesse et al., 'Euthanasia and the Law in the Netherlands', above n. 9, at 395.

[103] For a detailed critique of the government's draft bill from the perspective of the medical profession see van Berkestijn, M. G., 'The Royal Dutch Medical Association Attitude Towards Euthanasia: With the Criterion "Terminal Phase" Things Are Getting Out of Hand' in RDMA, *Euthanasia in the Netherlands* (1991) above n. 5, (translation of an article 'Met het Criterium 'Stervens Fase' is het Hek Van de Dam' (1986) 41 *Medisch Contact* 291–3).

[104] van Berkestijn, 'The Royal Dutch Medical Association and the Practice of Euthanasia and Assisted Suicide', above n. 76, at 7.

Christian Democrats, withdrew its support for the proposed legislation.[105] Following the parliamentary debate, both proposals were submitted to the State Council for its opinion. In the meantime, an election was held and the Conservative Party and the Christian Democrats coalition was restored to government. During the formation of the Cabinet, both parties agreed that the issue of active voluntary euthanasia should not lead to a breakdown of the coalition, and that they would abide by the future advice of the State Council.[106]

In July 1986, the State Council released its advice to the Government. It recommended against the immediate introduction of legislation and suggested that the body of case law be allowed to develop further before any legislative action was taken. However, in view of the ongoing public debate on the subject and the earlier legislative proposal which was still pending in Parliament, this recommendation was unacceptable to the Government. The Government sought advice from the General Health Council,[107] and a compromise position was subsequently reached which differed from the recommendations of both the State Commission on Euthanasia and the State Council. The Government's position, published in January 1987, recommended retention of the existing prohibition on active voluntary euthanasia, but stipulated that doctors could invoke *force majeure* (necessity) when certain requirements for careful medical practice and administrative rules were met, which would be set out in the Act regulating the practice of medicine (Medical Practice Act 1865). These carefulness requirements were essentially to follow the proposal of the State Committee on Euthanasia. This compromise reflected the position of the Christian Democrats that active voluntary euthanasia remain punishable, and at the same time, at the behest of the Conservatives, incorporated in the law the criteria for careful medical practice to be followed by a doctor performing active voluntary euthanasia. This proposal was, however, subject to criticism on the grounds that it was a half-way measure, lacking legal coherence, and disregarding the opinion of the majority of the population which is in favour of immunity for a doctor who administers active voluntary euthanasia in accordance with the rules.[108] One prominent Dutch legal commentator, Professor

---

[105] Leenen, 'Dying with Dignity: Developments in the Field of Euthanasia in the Netherlands', above n. 50, at 524.

[106] Gevers, 'Legal Developments Concerning Active Euthanasia on Request in the Netherlands', above n. 32, at 161.

[107] See Bostrom, 'Euthanasia in the Netherlands: A Model for the United States?', above n. 1, at 472–3 for details of the General Health Council's *Proposal of Advice Concerning Carefulness Requirements in the Performance of Euthanasia* (The Hague, 1987).

[108] e.g. Leenen, 'Dying with Dignity: Developments in the Field of Euthanasia in the Netherlands', above n. 50, at 524; Sluyters, 'Euthanasia in the Netherlands', above n. 7, at 40; Roscam Abbing, 'Dying with Dignity, and Euthanasia: A View from the Netherlands', above n. 96, at 73.

Leenen, has suggested that the main problem with this compromise was that there was no connection between the proposed section of the Medical Practice Act and the Penal Code which prohibits killing on request; as a consequence, doctors who have performed active voluntary euthanasia and have followed the rules of careful medical practice remain punishable, and can only invoke *force majeure*, to be assessed on a case by case basis by the prosecution and the courts.[109]

During the course of 1987, the Dutch Government commenced consultation within the framework of the Council of Europe in order to test the attitudes of other countries to the issue of active voluntary euthanasia.[110] In particular, it sought an opinion of the feasibility and desirability of the Council of Europe undertaking a study of the legal, human rights, ethical, and medical problems relating to euthanasia. This was done in order to avoid the possibility that the Netherlands might find itself in an internationally isolated position as a result of its stance on active voluntary euthanasia. However, the Council of Europe Working Party[111] reached the conclusion that such a study, even if feasible, was not desirable.

Notwithstanding this negative response from the Council of Europe, the government's compromise proposal led to the introduction of draft legislation in December 1987. Under this legislative proposal, Article 293 of the Penal Code was to remain unchanged, except for a decrease of the maximum term of imprisonment from 12 years to 4 years and 6 months. An amendment was proposed to the Medical Practice Act to the effect that 'without prejudice to his or her responsibility under the Penal Code, a medical doctor who wishes to follow the explicit serious wish of a patient to terminate the life of that patient should abide by a number of requirements of careful medical behaviour'. Those requirements, largely based on the recommendations of the State Commission, were also set out in the proposed amendments to the Medical Practice Act.[112]

The critical feature of this proposal was that doctors would remain punishable for performing active voluntary euthanasia. In any particular case, it would be left to the prosecution, and ultimately the courts, to decide whether the doctor had complied with the statutory requirements and if so, whether this would lead to the successful invocation of the *force majeure*

---

[109] Leenen, 'Dying with Dignity: Developments in the Field of Euthanasia in the Netherlands', above n. 50, at 524.

[110] See further pp. 387–9 above.

[111] Working Party of the Ad Hoc Committee of Experts on Progress in Biomedical Science of the Council of Europe.

[112] See Roscam Abbing, 'Dying with Dignity, and Euthanasia: A View from the Netherlands', above n. 96, at 73 for details. The proposed legislation also sought to clarify the meaning of euthanasia by specifying certain medical practices which would not fall within its scope; e.g. withdrawal of useless treatment, refusal of further treatment by the patient, and the administration of pain-relieving drugs which hasten death.

defence. Thus, it would simply give statutory effect to the current position in the Netherlands where *de facto* recognition of active voluntary euthanasia has been achieved through jurisprudential developments and prosecution policy. Debate on both this legislative proposal, and the earlier Wessel-Tuinstra Bill proposing the legalization of active voluntary euthanasia, was due to proceed in April 1989 but did not take place, because in the spring of 1989 the coalition government fell.

The new coalition government of Christian Democrats and Socialists was unable to reach agreement with regard to active voluntary euthanasia legislation. It was decided to postpone a decision until more reliable information was available about the practice of active voluntary euthanasia in the Netherlands. In order to obtain this information, a committee was set up in February 1990 under the Chairmanship of Professor Remmelink, Procurator-General of the Dutch Supreme Court, to conduct a nationwide survey amongst doctors. In the meantime, both draft Bills remained pending in Parliament.

VI. THE REMMELINK REPORT

A. Background to the Report

Prior to the release of the results of the Remmelink Committee inquiry,[113] which for the first time involved a comprehensive nationwide survey, no precise figures have been available regarding the extent to which active voluntary euthanasia is being performed in the Netherlands.[114] This lack of accurate information has largely been attributable to the fact that many doctors have been reluctant to report cases of active voluntary euthanasia to the police as a result of fear of investigation and prosecution, and/

---

[113] For the Report (in Dutch) see van der Maas, P. et al., *Medische Beslissingen Rond het Levenseinde. Het Onderzoek Voor de Commissie Onderzoek Medische Praktijk Inzake Euthanasie* ('s-Gravenhage, 1991). For an English translation of this report see van der Maas *et al.*, *Euthanasia and Other Medical Decisions Concerning the End of Life*, above n. 86. For a report of the first results of this nationwide survey, see van der Maas, *et al.*, 'Euthanasia and Other Medical Decisions Concerning the End of Life' (1991) 338 *Lancet* 669.

[114] There have been a number of smaller surveys conducted in the 1980s which indicated that there were approximately 2,000–3,000 cases of active euthanasia each year by general practitioners, comprising about 2 per cent of all deaths occurring in general practice in the Netherlands; Oliemans A. and Nijhuis, H., 'Euthanasie in de Huisartspraktijk' (1986) 41 *Medisch Contact* 691, cited by Gevers, 'Legal Developments Concerning Active Euthanasia on Request in the Netherlands', above n. 32, at 161–2; de Wachter, 'Active Euthanasia in the Netherlands', above n. 20, at 3316 referring to van Wijmen, F., *Artsen en het Zelfgekozen Levenseinde* (Maastricht, 1989); Borst-Eilers, E., 'Facts About the Actual Euthanasia Practice in the Netherlands' in RDMA, *Euthanasia in the Netherlands* (1991), above n. 5, at 3–5, where she refers to a number of surveys (the 1986 Hague survey conducted by Oliemans and Nijhuis, the 1988 Amsterdam survey conducted by the Municipal Public Service, and the 1989 Continuous Morbidity Registration survey, published by Bartelds et al.).

or the desire to protect the family of the deceased from this type of investigation.[115]

After the death of a patient, the treating doctor may only issue a death certificate in cases of natural death.[116] Active voluntary euthanasia and doctor-assisted suicide are not considered to be a natural death, and therefore a doctor cannot by law issue a death certificate.[117] Indications were, however, that in the majority of cases, doctors were falsifying the death certificate and entering the death as one by natural causes.

As the practice of active voluntary euthanasia and doctor-assisted suicide were gaining acceptance by the courts, a reporting procedure was established whereby a doctor who had performed either of these practices was required to telephone the police to advise that he or she had done so.[118] Before a burial or cremation could proceed, permission had to be obtained from the prosecuting authorities. Upon the reporting of a case, the municipal coroner would come to view the body, and a police detective would come to interview the doctor. Both the municipal coroner and the police detective would then report to the public prosecutor. If it appeared that everything had been done in accordance with the guidelines, the prosecution would give permission to hand over the body to the relatives for burial. In circumstances where the doctor had acted properly and fully recorded in writing all the details of the case, this whole procedure would usually not take more than a couple of hours from the time of the reported death and the release of the body to the family. If, however, there was some reason to believe that all the criteria had not been complied with, a further investigation would be ordered by the public prosecutor, and the doctor would have to wait for some months before he or she would know whether a prosecution would result. Whilst this procedure was widely used, there was still no uniformity amongst the country's prosecutors, with the practice in some Dutch provinces at variance with others. Of particular concern to the medical profession were instances of intrusive police investigation, and the inappropriate questioning of relatives of the deceased.

The courts have, on a number of occasions, confirmed the importance of accurate reporting of non-natural deaths by active voluntary euthanasia or assisted suicide and have punished doctors for the falsification of death certificates.[119] Following the RDMA's direction to members to comply with

---

[115] Note, however, the work of Ciesielski-Carlucci, C. and Kimsma, G., 'The Impact of Reporting Cases of Euthanasia in Holland: A Patient and Family Perspective' (1994) 8 *Bioethics* 151 where it is argued that families in fact benefit from reporting and the open discussion which it fosters.

[116] Sluyters, Euthanasia in the Netherlands', above n. 7, at 40.

[117] For further discussion see above, n. 55.

[118] Borst-Eilers, 'The Status of Physician-Administered Active Euthanasia in the Netherlands' paper presented at the Second International Conference on Health Law and Ethics, London 16–21 July (1989) 5.

[119] See above, n. 55.

the legal reporting requirements, many more cases of active voluntary euthanasia were reported.[120] Nevertheless, it was evident that many cases still went undetected, with doctors continuing to falsify death certificates in order to conceal active voluntary euthanasia or doctor-assisted suicide as the cause of death. As a result of this widespread underreporting, it has been impossible to gauge accurately the extent of these practices in the Netherlands by reference to the official figures held by the police and prosecuting authorities. Estimates in respect of active voluntary euthanasia have varied from 2,000 to 10,000 cases per year out of a total population of 14 million and an annual total of approximately 130,000 deaths.[121] Some estimates have even been higher (mostly put forward by opponents of active voluntary euthanasia), and it has been suggested that the figure may be as high as 20,000.[122]

As noted above, the Remmelink Committee was established by the Government in order to obtain more precise information on the occurrence of active voluntary euthanasia in the Netherlands. In framing the committee's terms of reference, it was decided to take the opportunity to investigate more widely the medical decisions concerning the end of life. The committee's brief was to report on the state of affairs regarding the practice of commission or omission by a doctor leading to a patient's death, whether or not at the latter's explicit or serious request. The aims of the study were: to produce reliable estimates of the incidence of active voluntary euthanasia and other medical decisions concerning the end of life; to describe the characteristics of patients, doctors, and situations involved; to assess how far doctors are acquainted with the criteria for acceptable euthanasia; and to determine under which conditions doctors would be willing to report a death by euthanasia as such. Under the terms of reference, the role of the committee was simply to provide empirical data and not to give an opinion on the moral or legal permissibility of active voluntary euthanasia.

After some negotiation, this study was conducted with the full support and co-operation of the RDMA.[123] One of the conditions laid down by the

---

[120] In 1987 there were 126 reported cases of active voluntary euthanasia; in 1988 there were 184; in 1989 there were 338; in 1990 there were 454; in 1991, 591 cases were reported (information obtained from Josephus Jitta, Chief Public Prosecutor setting out the euthanasia and assisted suicide reports counted by the Board of Prosecutors-General). See below, n. 194 for more recent figures of the number of cases reported.

[121] de Wachter, 'Active Euthanasia in the Netherlands', above n. 20, at 3316; Gevers, 'Legal Developments Concerning Active Euthanasia on Request in the Netherlands', above n. 32, at 161 referring to estimates that there are 5,000–8,000 cases each year.

[122] For example, Fenigsen, R., 'A Case Against Dutch Euthanasia' (1989) 19 *Hastings Center R* 22 where he notes that figures as high as 18,000 or 20,000 have been mentioned.

[123] See van Berkestijn, 'The Royal Dutch Medical Association and the Practice of Euthanasia and Assisted Suicide', above n. 76, at 4 where he notes that initially the General Board of the RDMA refused to participate in the inquiry because it feared that it would be used to push a political decision. However, since the association has always promoted openness in the practice of active voluntary euthanasia, the General Board agreed to an inquiry under

association for its support for members' participation in the survey was for the formal adoption by the prosecuting authorities of guidelines for the reporting and investigation of cases of active voluntary euthanasia and doctor-assisted suicide. Following negotiations between the RDMA and the coalition government, agreement was reached that the revised procedures would be formally adopted and form the basis for the reporting and investigation of all cases of active voluntary euthanasia and doctor-assisted suicide. The new protocol was introduced in November 1990 under the direction of the Minister of Justice. Under that protocol, doctors performing active voluntary euthanasia or assisted suicide are required to notify the coroner of all cases.[124] This aspect of the 1990 protocol, involving notification to the coroner, represented a significant change from the former procedures whereby the doctor would advise the police or the public prosecutor. The new procedure is apparently much preferred by the Dutch medical profession, since it involves reporting to a medical colleague rather than to the legal authorities.[125] Once notified, the coroner then investigates the matter and is required to prepare a report to the public prosecutor, which is to include the coroner's assessment of whether the guidelines for the performance of active voluntary euthanasia have been adhered to. The matter is then referred to the public prosecutor. By virtue of the direction from the Minister of Justice, prosecutors are no longer to ask the police to investigate euthanasia cases, unless there is some reason to suspect that there has not been compliance with the criteria. The new protocol also contains an agreement that in circumstances where police investigation is necessary, the police are to exercise discretion in conducting their investigations.[126] If, on the basis of the doctor's report and the advice from the coroner (and where appropriate, consultation with the Inspector of Health), the prosecutor is satisfied that all requirements have been met, permission is given for the patient's body to be released to the family for burial. The doctor is then advised by the prosecutor that the case will be referred to the committee of Chief Prosecutors for final determination. Almost invariably, the decision taken by the prosecutor is endorsed by the committee of Chief Prosecutors, and no charges are laid against the doctor.[127]

stringent conditions, pertaining mainly to the confidentiality of the data and the dependability of the inquiry.

[124] The information required is gathered by the completion of a standard form check-list.

[125] Most coroners in the Netherlands are medically trained with a background in forensic medicine.

[126] For example, by using non-marked police cars, avoiding police uniforms, and refraining from interviewing the relatives of the deceased unless absolutely necessary.

[127] For example, in 1990, 454 cases were reported and officially investigated but no prosecutions were commenced. In 1991, 590 cases were reported and only one case was prosecuted: this information is based upon field notes recorded by the author in conversations with Chief Prosecutor Jitta, 29 Nov. 1991. Note, however, the increase in prosecutions in 1993, see below.

B. Report Findings and Recommendations

The Remmelink inquiry is, to date, the most comprehensive study of the extent and nature of the practice of active voluntary euthanasia in the Netherlands.[128] Under the auspices of the Remmelink Committee, the study was conducted by a team of researchers from the Department of Public Health and Social Medicine, at Erasmus University, Rotterdam, headed by Professor van der Maas, with the co-operation of the Dutch Central Statistical Office. Three separate studies were undertaken as part of this survey: (i) detailed interviews with a sample of 405 doctors (comprised of general practitioners, nursing home doctors, and clinical specialists); (ii) mailing of questionnaires to the doctors of a sample of 7,000 deceased persons; and (iii) a prospective study in which doctors interviewed in study (i) (referred to above) gave information concerning deaths in their practice in the 6-month period following the interview. An important feature of this survey was the confidentiality of the inquiry, so that participating doctors could be expected to provide full information without fear of repercussions.[129] In addition, the Minister of Justice guaranteed legal immunity in respect of all information collected in the three studies.

Significantly, the three studies yielded similar estimates of incidence. According to these studies, there were 2,300 cases of active voluntary euthanasia in the Netherlands in 1990 amounting to 1.8 per cent of all deaths. Assisted suicide (where a doctor intentionally prescribes or supplies lethal drugs but the patient administers them) occurred in almost 400 cases (0.3 per cent of all deaths). At interview, doctors were asked if they had ever practised active voluntary euthanasia or assisted a suicide at the request of a patient. Fifty-four per cent confirmed that they had, and 24 per cent had done so at least once during the previous 24 months. Doctors working in general practice performed active voluntary euthanasia most frequently (62 per cent had performed it, and 28 per cent had done so during the previous 24 months). Forty-four per cent of clinical specialists had previously performed active voluntary euthanasia, and 20 per cent had done so in the previous 24 months. There was a relatively low incidence of the practice amongst nursing home doctors (only 12 per cent had previously performed active voluntary euthanasia, and 6 per cent had done so in the previous 24 months).

A sizeable proportion of the doctors interviewed (34 per cent) said that they had never practised active voluntary euthanasia or assisted suicide, but could conceive of situations in which they would be prepared to do so. The remaining 12 per cent said that they could not conceive of any such situa-

---

[128] Included in the data are figures regarding the withholding or withdrawing of treatment, but analysis of these results is beyond the scope of this work.

[129] As was noted above, this was a precondition for the co-operation of the RDMA.

tions,[130] but more than half of those (8 per cent) indicated that they would be prepared to refer patients requesting active euthanasia or assistance in suicide to another doctor with a more permissive attitude. From this data, the researchers concluded that a large majority of doctors in the Netherlands see active voluntary euthanasia and doctor-assisted suicide as accepted elements of medical practice under certain circumstances.

The study also found that, in the Netherlands, over 25,000 patients per year seek an assurance from their doctors that they will be given assistance in the form of active voluntary euthanasia if their suffering becomes unbearable. Each year, there are approximately 9,000 explicit requests for active euthanasia or doctor-assisted suicide of which less than one-third are agreed to. The fact that many requests are not acted upon can, at least in part, be explained on the basis that, in many cases, doctors can offer alternatives which render active voluntary euthanasia or assistance in suicide unnecessary.[131]

The study has also shed light on the reasons behind patient requests for active voluntary euthanasia or doctor-assisted suicide.[132] In the course of interviews with respondent doctors, doctors were asked to identify the most frequent reason for the request of the patient.[133] 'Loss of dignity' was mentioned most frequently (57 per cent). Other reasons given included pain (mentioned in 46 per cent of cases, although only in a small proportion of cases was it given as the only reason for the request), 'not dying in a dignified way' (46 per cent), 'dependence' (33 per cent) and 'tiredness of life' (23 per cent).

Of particular note was the fact that many of the doctors who had practised active voluntary euthanasia indicated that they would be reluctant to do so again, other than in exceptional circumstances; that is, in cases of unbearable suffering where there are no alternatives. Many of the respondents indicated that an emotional bond between doctor and patient is required for the administration of active voluntary euthanasia. The researchers conclude that this may be one reason why active voluntary euthanasia was more common in general practice, where doctor and patient have

---

[130] Other findings from the Remmelink inquiry suggests that this may at least in part be due to religious belief. Over 40% of the respondent doctors indicated that they belonged to a religious group or were linked to a specific philosophy of life, and 18% of all doctors regarded this as very important in determining their point of view regarding euthanasia: see van der Maas, et al., *Euthanasia and Other Medical Decisions Concerning the End of Life*, above n. 86, at 104.

[131] Other possible explanations include a change of mind by the patient, cases where the patient died before the request could be implemented, and cases where the doctor is not satisfied that the criteria for active voluntary euthanasia (e.g. voluntariness or unbearable suffering) have been met.

[132] van der Maas, *et al.*, *Euthanasia and Other Medical Decisions Concerning the End of Life*, above n. 86, at 43–4 and see Table 5.8 at 45.

[133] More than one answer could be given to this question.

often known each other for many years and the doctor has shared part of the patient's suffering.

Whilst the study found that there was a high degree of knowledge of the guidelines for the practice of active voluntary euthanasia on the part of doctors, doctors' compliance with these guidelines was varied. Requests for active voluntary euthanasia and doctor-assisted suicide, in cases where this request was fulfilled, were explicit and persistent requests and, in the view of the attending doctor, were hardly ever made under pressure from others. On the basis of data obtained from interviews with doctors, in 96 per cent of instances of active voluntary euthanasia and doctor-assisted suicide, the doctor stated that the patient's request was explicit and persistent. In 94 per cent of cases, the request had been made repeatedly, and in 99 per cent of cases, the doctor felt sure that the request had not been made under pressure from others. In all cases, the doctors were convinced that the patient had sufficient insight and knowledge of the course of the disease to make an informed decision. In most cases (84 per cent), there had been consultation with a colleague before the decision to perform active voluntary euthanasia had been acted upon, and in nearly all cases the decision had been discussed with relatives. In the great majority of cases (79 per cent), there was no alternative treatment available, or if available, the patient had refused that treatment (17 per cent). Doctors were less compliant with the requirement of documenting cases of active voluntary euthanasia by the preparation of a written report (60 per cent). Even fewer (28 per cent) were prepared to notify the authorities of their actions.[134] However, even during the course of the prospective study in which doctors were required to give information concerning every death in their practice over a 6-month period, there was a notable increase in the incidence of reporting.[135]

Pursuant to the Remmelink Committee's terms of reference, the study also sought to ascertain the incidence of cases where a doctor assists in the termination of life other than at the explicit and persistent request of the patient. The study found that in 0.8 per cent[136] of cases (accounting for approximately 1,000 deaths per year), drugs were administered with the explicit intention to shorten the patient's life without an explicit and persistent request from the patient. However, in more than half of these cases, this

---

[134] For example, in 1990 only 454 of the estimated 2,300 deaths by active euthanasia were reported.

[135] An increase in the range of 30–35% was recorded in the study by van der Maas et al.

[136] This was the figure arrived at in relation to the death certificate study—in the prospective study the figure was 1.6% but this was thought to reflect a grey area between the category of termination of life without explicit request and the alleviation of pain with opiodes at dosages that might have shortened life and therefore assumed not to be as accurate: Pijnenborg, L. et al., 'Life Terminating Acts Without Explicit Request of Patient' (1993) 341 *The Lancet* 1196.

possibility had already been discussed with the patient, or the patient had expressed, in a previous phase of the disease, a wish for active voluntary euthanasia, if his or her suffering became unbearable.[137] In other cases, possibly with a few exceptions, the patients were near to death and clearly suffering grievously, yet verbal contact had become impossible. The decision to hasten death was then nearly always taken after consultation with the family, nurses, or one or more colleagues. In most cases, according to the doctors, the amount of time by which life had been shortened was a few hours or days only. In the report of the Remmelink Committee accompanying the research findings these cases were described as 'providing assistance to the dying'. According to the committee, the justification of such acts was that the suffering of the patient had become unbearable, and that according to strict medical norms, the life of the patient must be considered to be over, with death soon likely to occur, regardless of medical intervention. This study also sought to ascertain the doctors' reasons for arriving at a decision to end the life of a patient without a specific request. Almost a third of those respondents referred to the patient's pain, suffering or low quality of life. In almost two-thirds of cases the doctor stated that there was no prospect for improvement of the situation; in 39 per cent of cases the respondent felt that any further medical therapy was futile, and in 33 per cent, that suffering should not be prolonged unnecessarily.

The study also examined cases where dosages of pain-relieving drugs were administered with the potential effect of shortening the patient's life. This category accounted for 17.5 per cent of all deaths. The study found that in 6 per cent of cases where pain medication was administered with possible lethal effect (2 per cent of total deaths), the drugs were administered with the express purpose of accelerating the death of the patient.[138] In about 40 per cent of such cases, the decision to increase dosages and the possibility that this might hasten the end of life had been discussed with the patient. In more than half of the cases where discussion had not taken place, the reason was the inability of the patient to assess the situation and take a decision adequately. Whilst there are clearly strong similarities between this category and cases of active euthanasia, the doctors involved felt there was a material difference. Certainly in terms of methods used[139] and of the certainty and proximity of death following the administration of those drugs, the two categories can be differentiated.

On the basis of these research findings, the Remmelink Committee drew

---

[137] In a small proportion of cases, (approximately 1%) patients had previously made a written declaration indicating their desire for active voluntary euthanasia in the event that their suffering became unbearable.

[138] In 15.5% of the total deaths, pain-relieving drugs were administered partly with the purpose of accelerating the end of life.

[139] The administration of active voluntary euthanasia usually involves curare or insulin whereas morphine and opiodes are administered for pain relief.

certain conclusions and made a number of recommendations. The commit-tee expressed the view that the extent of euthanasia in the Netherlands as shown by the data from this inquiry does not warrant the assumption that euthanasia occurs on an excessive scale or that it is used increasingly as an alternative to good palliative or terminal care. Further it was stated that there is no proof whatsoever in the research results for the suggestion made from time to time that lack of funds in the health sector were (or will become) a cause for the administration of euthanasia. With respect to the consultation requirement the Remmelink Committee report recommended that in order to ensure an independent medical judgement, the general practitioner who is considering the administration of active voluntary euthanasia or doctor-assisted suicide, should consult a specialist (preferably one who is already in attendance) and vice versa. This was thought to be an important element in ensuring the quality of the decision-making process. The committee also recommended that all doctors must strictly observe the requirements for scrupulous care in cases of active voluntary euthanasia and doctor-assisted suicide, with particular emphasis being placed on the requirement of a written report. It was felt that this would enhance the decision-making process and would enable doctors to demonstrate their willingness to justify their conduct. It was also recommended that the 1990 protocol for reporting cases of active voluntary euthanasia and doctor-assisted suicide should also apply to cases of active termination of life by a doctor without an explicit request from the patient except in those situa-tions in which the vital functions have already and irreversibly begun to fail, because in those cases a natural death would have followed in any event. The committee was of the opinion that there is no real justification for retaining a situation in which cases of euthanasia or assistance in suicide are covered by the procedure for reporting, while the cases of active interfer-ence by a doctor in order to shorten the life of a patient whose vital functions are still intact, without an explicit request for the latter, are not.

C. Evaluation of the Remmelink Committee's Inquiry

The study conducted by van der Maas *et al.*, under the auspices of the Remmelink Committee, is widely regarded as being a reliable and credible investigation. It was the first nationwide study to be undertaken on the subject and involved a large number of respondents. Due to the support of the RDMA, there was a high participation rate amongst members of the medical profession. Moreover, because of the anonymity and legal immu-nity assured to doctors participating in the study, there is good reason to believe that the respondent doctors were answering truthfully. As a result, there is widespread acceptance of the research findings as accurately reflect-ing medical practice in the Netherlands. Whilst the release of the

Remmelink Report has eliminated much of the speculation with regard to the extent of active voluntary euthanasia in the Netherlands, some Dutch commentators believe that it has also raised many new questions.[140] Although the findings of the research group are not in dispute, differences exist in the interpretation of the results.[141] The report has generally been received in the Netherlands as demonstrating that active voluntary euthanasia is a well controlled and workable medical practice and that its incidence is not as extensive as had frequently been alleged. Opponents of active voluntary euthanasia, on the other hand, have cited the findings to demonstrate the alarming extent of the practice.[142] Criticism has also been levelled at some aspects of the Remmelink Committee's interpretation of the research findings, particularly with regard to the category of patients whose lives were terminated in the absence of an explicit and persistent request.[143] Some commentators are of the view that the committee has deliberately glossed over these findings in an attempt to make the outcomes of the study politically acceptable.

The results of the study by van der Maas *et al.* tend to confirm the results obtained from a number of smaller surveys, and in particular, surveys of general practitioners and nursing home doctors undertaken by Dr van de Wal, Public Health Inspector of the Province of North Holland, and others under the auspices of the Department of Family Medicine and Nursing Home Medicine at the Free University of Amsterdam. The first of these studies by Dr van de Wal *et al.*[144] was confined to family doctors in the Netherlands and was conducted by means of an anonymous questionnaire sent to 1,042 family doctors. The study found that Dutch family doctors practise active voluntary euthanasia/assisted suicide about 2,000 times per annum. It was estimated that Dutch family doctors receive an average of 5,000 requests for active voluntary euthanasia/assisted suicide, and that an average of 40 per cent of all requests lead to actual administration. Further, the study found that 48 per cent of family doctors in the Netherlands have never engaged in these practices.

---

[140] This proposition is based upon field notes recorded by the author in conversations with Dr Maurice de Wachter, Institute of Bioethics, Maastricht, 28 Nov. 1991.

[141] There has been particular conflict with regard to the 1,000 cases of termination without an explicit and persistent request and the cases where pain-relieving drugs were administered with the express purpose of hastening death: e.g. Fenigsen, R., 'The Report of the Dutch Governmental Committee on Euthanasia' (1991) 7 *Issues Law & Med.* 339.

[142] e.g. Gunning, K., 'Euthanasia' (letter) (1991) 338 *Lancet* 1010; Fergusson, A. et al., 'Euthanasia' (letter) (1991) 338 *Lancet* 1010; Keown, J., 'Euthanasia in the Netherlands: Sliding Down the Slippery Slope?' in Keown, J. (ed.), *Euthanasia Examined: Ethical, Clinical and Legal Perspectives* (Cambridge, 1995), at 261.

[143] e.g. ten Have, H. and Welie, J., 'Euthanasia: Normal Medical Practice?' (1992) 22 *Hastings Center R* 34, 35.

[144] van der Wal, G. et al., 'Euthanasia and Assisted Suicide: I. How Often Practised by Family Doctors in the Netherlands?' (1992) 9 *Fam. Practice* 130; 'Euthanasia and Assisted Suicide: II. Do Dutch Family Doctors Act Prudently?' (1992) 9 *Fam. Practice* 135.

The study also sought to gauge the extent to which family doctors in the Netherlands comply with the guidelines for the practice of active voluntary euthanasia. The study found that most family doctors satisfy the requirements for prudent practice with regard to voluntariness of the patient's request;[145] that it is a well considered and durable request;[146] and the unbearable and pointless nature of the patient's suffering. Moreover, in the majority of cases, there were no further treatment options available. In those cases where treatment options remained, they offered no prospect of cure, and in most cases the patient had refused this further treatment. The study found that there was less compliance with the requirements of consultation, documentation, and reporting of cases of active voluntary euthanasia: 25 per cent of family doctors had not consulted another doctor prior to performing active voluntary euthanasia or assisted suicide; almost half (48 per cent) of all family doctors had kept no written record of their last case of active voluntary euthanasia or doctor-assisted suicide; and 74 per cent had falsely issued a certificate testifying to death from natural causes. A positive correlation was found to exist between obtaining a second opinion, preparing a written report, and not falsifying the death certificate.

The study by van de Wal *et al.* of the practices of family doctors also examined the incidence of active euthanasia other than at the request of the patient. According to the findings of this study, there are approximately 100 cases per year of active euthanasia performed by family doctors in the Netherlands without the explicit and persistent request of the patient, and these cases almost invariably involved exceptional circumstances.[147] Although this survey was confined to family doctors in the Netherlands, the results obtained by van der Wal *et al.* with regard to active terminations without request appear to be significantly lower than this aspect of the findings of the Remmelink inquiry.[148]

Van der Wal *et al.* also conducted a study of voluntary active euthanasia and assisted suicide in Dutch nursing homes.[149] All of the nursing home

---

[145] This was ascertained by questions as to who had taken the initiative in arranging a discussion with the family doctor about active voluntary euthanasia and the reasons for the patient's request.

[146] Whether the request was well considered was ascertained by questions regarding the reasons given for the patient's request and the existence or non-existence of other forms of treatment. The durability of the request was gauged by reference to the time lapse between the first discussion, the first and last explicit request, and the actual implementation.

[147] van der Wal, G. et al., 'Actieve Levensbeëindiging Door Huisartsen Zonder Verzoek van der Patiënt' (1991) 34 *Huisarts en Wetenschap* 523.

[148] See above, where it was estimated that there were approximately 1,000 cases of active terminations of life other than at the explicit and persistent request of the patient.

[149] van der Wal, G. et al., 'Voluntary Active Euthanasia and Physician-Assisted Suicide in Dutch Nursing Homes: Requests and Administration' (1994) 42 *J Am. Geriatric Society* 620; Muller, M. et al., 'Voluntary Active Euthanasia and Physician-Assisted Suicide in Dutch Nursing Homes: Are the Requirements for Prudent Practice Properly Met?' (1994) 42 *J Am. Geriatric Society* 624.

physicians who were members of the Dutch Association of Nursing Home Physicians were sent a questionnaire which had been adapted from the earlier study (a total of 713 physicians representing virtually all of the nursing home physicians in the Netherlands). This study found that the incidence of requests for voluntary active euthanasia and physician-assisted suicide and their administration was much lower in nursing homes than in the home situation and in hospitals.[150] Only 12 per cent of the respondent nursing home physicians had administered voluntary active euthanasia and/or physician-assisted suicide. For the period 1986 to mid-1990, these physicians reported a total of 77 cases which represents only 0.1 per cent of the total number of deaths in nursing homes during this period. Although there were a greater number of requests than cases actually administered (requests on average were 15 times higher than actual cases) the overall number of requests was very limited, averaging approximately 300 a year. In the period 1986 to mid-1990 an average of 7 per cent of the requests for active euthanasia were granted, and 22 per cent of the requests for physician-assisted suicide.

With regard to the question of compliance by nursing home physicians with the guidelines for the practice of active voluntary euthanasia and assisted suicide, the results of this study indicated that all of the requirements are complied with in 41 per cent of cases. In the remaining cases, some shortcomings were found. Some nursing home physicians allowed too little time between the first discussion and the actual administration. In 7 per cent of cases, active voluntary euthanasia or physician-assisted suicide took place within one day of the first request. In half of the cases, the time period between the first request and the compliance with the request was between one day and 2 weeks. The study also found that nursing home physicians did not always keep written records. In three-quarters of the cases, the nursing home physicians had kept notes—in almost half of these cases they had made a note on the patient's medical records, in 28 per cent of the cases a separate report had been prepared, and in 26 per cent of cases, both courses had been followed. It was also found that more than half of the nursing home physicians who had complied with a request for active voluntary euthanasia or assisted suicide, falsified the death certificate, testifying that the patient had died of natural causes, although it was noted that the number of falsified death certificates fell after 1988.

In other areas, there was greater compliance with the requirements. In 88 per cent of the cases the condition of the patient was considered utterly hopeless, and in 64 per cent of the cases, utterly unbearable. Ninety-one per cent of the nursing home physicians stated that there were no alternative

---

[150] For possible explanations see van der Wal et al., 'Voluntary Active Euthanasia and Physician-Assisted Suicide in Dutch Nursing Homes: Requests and Administration', above n. 149, at 622.

treatments left at the time the last request was made. There was a high degree of compliance by nursing home physicians with respect to the consultation requirement. The great majority of the nursing home physicians (85 per cent) arranged a consultation with a colleague, in many cases (46 per cent) involving more than one consultant physician. In the majority of cases where consultation took place, it was amongst other nursing home physicians (63 per cent). Most of the consultations that were held were of a formal character. Nurses were also involved in the consultation process.

On the basis of the Remmelink inquiry and the van der Wal et al. studies which have yielded similar results, thereby mutually confirming the accuracy of these respective surveys, certain conclusions can be drawn with regard to the practice of active voluntary euthanasia in the Netherlands. As the Remmelink Committee itself pointed out in its accompanying Report, the results refute the assertion that active voluntary euthanasia occurs on an excessive scale in the Netherlands, and that it is used increasingly as an alternative to good palliative or terminal care. The extent of the practice appears to be in the range of 2,300 a year, and is most frequently performed by general practitioners. The studies also indicate that doctors are generally reluctant to become involved in its administration and that a significant proportion of requests for active voluntary euthanasia are refused. The research findings do, however, confirm that not all doctors are complying with the stipulated guidelines with regard to the performance of active voluntary euthanasia, particularly with regard to the need for consultation, documentation, and reporting of the practice.

D. *Expanding Boundaries?*

The unique developments in the Netherlands have naturally been the focus of interest in other jurisdictions where there is increasing pressure for the legalization of active voluntary euthanasia. As we have seen, one of the major obstacles for change is concern regarding the operation in practice of a law which permits active voluntary euthanasia, and fear of the 'slippery slope'.[151] There have been claims from some quarters that there is already evidence in the Netherlands of the adverse consequences of any loosening of the legal prohibition on the practice.[152] Assertions have been made about the growing incidence of active euthanasia in the Netherlands and the extension of the practice to non-voluntary and even involuntary euthanasia,

---

[151] See pp. 219–27 above.

[152] e.g. Fenigsen, 'A Case Against Dutch Euthanasia', above n. 122, at 22; Bostrom, 'Euthanasia in the Netherlands: A Model for the United States?', above n. 1, at 467; Segers, J., 'Elderly Persons on the Subject of Euthanasia' (1988) 3 *Issues Law&Med.* 407; Gomez, C., *Regulating Death: Euthanasia and the Case of the Netherlands* (New York, 1991) 127–39, Keown, 'Euthanasia in the Netherlands: Sliding Down the Slippery Slope?', above n. 142; Pollard, B., 'Medical Aspects of Euthanasia' (1991) 154 MJA 613.

overstepping ethical bounds and administrative controls. From this premise, it is inevitably argued by opponents of active voluntary euthanasia that the Netherlands would be a very dangerous model for other countries to follow. In support of these claims, Dutch cases are cited where patients were killed without their consent by nurses and/or doctors, but negligible punishment was imposed on the offender.[153] It is also alleged that there is growing support for non-voluntary euthanasia amongst prominent advocates of voluntary euthanasia,[154] and the Dutch community generally.

As a result of the 'uncontrollable nature' of euthanasia, especially when it is performed by doctors who work alone (for example, family doctors or nursing home doctors), it is claimed that many people, particularly elderly nursing home residents, are fearful that they will be subject to non-voluntary euthanasia.[155] It has further been suggested that the acceptance of active voluntary euthanasia has resulted in a change of attitude of doctors towards patients who are disabled by illness or accident, but who do not meet the guidelines for active voluntary euthanasia.[156] This change, it is claimed, is reflected in decisions regarding withdrawal of treatment from these patients without their knowledge or consent, as well as in pressure being placed on patients by doctors 'voluntarily' to request active euthanasia. Claims have also been made that the availability of active voluntary euthanasia has hindered the development of hospice and palliative care in the Netherlands, with the result that inferior care is available to the terminally ill. In turn, it is argued that patients who are not given appropriate pain relief and other care are more likely to be driven to request active voluntary euthanasia.[157]

These assertions have, however, been sharply rejected, particularly by members of the Dutch medical profession, as being completely unfounded and portraying a totally misleading picture of the practice of active volun-

---

[153] For example, the much publicized case in the De Terp nursing home where a number of patients had allegedly been killed without their knowledge or consent by the head nurse on the doctor's orders. The doctor subsequently pleaded guilty and was convicted of three killings. He was sentenced to 1 year imprisonment. On appeal, the Court of Appeal of the Hague reversed the sentence on the grounds that the criminal investigators had transgressed their competence by seizing documents which were legally privileged. Because the evidence had been wrongfully obtained, it was inadmissible in court. The doctor was however disciplined by the Medical Disciplinary Court of the Hague; Bostrom, 'Euthanasia in the Netherlands: A Model for the United States?', above n. 1, at 476.

[154] Keown, J., 'The Law and Practice of Euthanasia in the Netherlands' (1992) 108 *Law QRev.* 51, 75–6.

[155] Bostrom, 'Euthanasia in the Netherlands: A Model for the United States?', above n. 1, at 477; Segers, 'Elderly Persons on the Subject of Euthanasia', above n. 152, at 407; Fenigsen, 'A Case Against Dutch Euthanasia', above n. 122, at 26.

[156] Bostrom, 'Euthanasia in the Netherlands: A Model for the United States?', above n. 1, at 479–80.

[157] This proposition is based upon field notes recorded by the author in conversations with Dr. J. Willebois, former president of the Nederlands Artsenverbond (Dutch League of Physicians), 19 Nov. 1991.

tary euthanasia in the Netherlands.[158] A number of distinguished Dutch commentators have pointed out that the foreign press (including specialist journals) has tended to seize upon the allegations being made by a hard core minority opposed to the practice of active voluntary euthanasia and give them disproportionate attention.[159] This has resulted in a very inaccurate and unreliable impression being conveyed outside of the Netherlands about the extent and nature of the practice of active voluntary euthanasia in that country. For some time, the absence of reliable data (at least until the recent Remmelink survey) tended to fuel speculative claims, as there was no firm basis upon which these claims could be refuted.

The data obtained by the Remmelink survey has, to a large extent, dispelled allegations about the growing and uncontrollable nature of the practice of active voluntary euthanasia in the Netherlands. Results from that survey, and from a number of other inquiries, have shown that active voluntary euthanasia is in fact performed much less frequently than had earlier been thought. Indeed, some commentators in the Netherlands contend that there is no indication that active euthanasia on request is practised more often in the Netherlands than elsewhere.[160] Rather, they suggest that in the Netherlands, a practice which was formerly kept behind closed doors, as is the case in many other countries, has now been brought into the open. Contrary to claims that once doctors become 'killers', there is the danger that killing comes all too easily, data from the Remmelink survey found that doctors who have performed active voluntary euthanasia indicated that they would be most reluctant to do so again, and would only do so in the face of unbearable suffering where there were no other alternatives.

However, there is by no means agreement regarding the interpretation of the survey findings and some commentators have argued that the results provide cause for alarm. Critics of the Dutch position contend that the guidelines which supposedly regulate the practice of active voluntary euthanasia in the Netherlands are hopelessly vague and imprecise.[161] It is argued that the failure of doctors to comply with the guidelines, and in particular,

[158] See, for example, the reaction to the publication of the article by Fenigsen in the *Hastings Centre Report*, 'A Case Against Dutch Euthanasia' above n. 122. This led to the adoption of a motion by the General Assembly of the Dutch Society of Health Law and its publication in the *Hastings Center Report* claiming that Fenigsen's account was incorrect and misleading, as well as a letter of complaint signed by numerous prominent Dutch doctors: Aartsen, G. et al., (letter) (1989) 19 *Hastings Center R* 47, 48.

[159] e.g. van Berkestijn, 'The Royal Dutch Medical Association and the Practice of Euthanasia and Assisted Suicide', above n. 76, at 8–9; Leenen, 'Legal Aspects of Euthanasia, Assistance to Suicide and Terminating the Medical Treatment of Incompetent Patients', above n. 5, at 1.

[160] e.g. Leenen, 'Dying with Dignity: Developments in the Field of Euthanasia in the Netherlands', above n. 50, at 525.

[161] Keown, 'The Law and Practice of Euthanasia in the Netherlands', above n. 154, at 61–6; (see also Keown, 'Euthanasia in the Netherlands: Sliding Down the Slippery Slope?' above n. 142, at 265–6); Gomez, *Regulating Death*, above n. 152, at 95–125.

the requirement to report cases of active voluntary euthanasia, means that the practice remains unverifiable and uncontrollable. In support of such assertions, critics draw upon the findings of the Remmelink study that in a significant proportion of cases (approximately 1,000 or 0.8 per cent of all deaths), doctors performed acts of termination without an explicit and persistent request from the patient. This, they argue, demonstrates the occurrence of non-voluntary euthanasia. Some commentators have included in their figures regarding unrequested killings, cases where treatment was withdrawn or withheld and where high dosages of palliative drugs were administered without request with the intention, at least in part, to hasten death, arguing that this demonstrates the widespread incidence of intentional life-shortening without explicit request.[162]

To begin with, there is some basis for suggesting that the incidence of active termination of life without the patient's request reported in the Remmelink survey may be disproportionately high. According to the study by van der Wal *et al.*, of more than 1,000 family doctors in the Netherlands, it was found that such cases occur approximately 100 times a year in general practice. If one extrapolates from this figure to the medical profession as a whole (bearing in mind the finding of the Remmelink study that active voluntary euthanasia is most frequently practiced by general practitioners), it would still be substantially less than the findings of the Remmelink survey. In view of the close correlation between the two surveys with respect to most other matters, this discrepancy does perhaps raise some doubt as to the correctness of this aspect of the Remmelink findings: indeed in the report of the results of the Remmelink study, caution was expressed about the estimates given due to some limitations of the data.[163] But, even if one accepts the results of the Remmelink survey as accurately reflecting the incidence of active terminations without the patient's explicit and persistent request, there are a number of grounds on which the critics' claims can, to a large extent, be countered. One point which can be made is that whilst these cases clearly did not strictly comply with the guidelines for the performance of active voluntary euthanasia, closer analysis of this category reveals that 'non-voluntary euthanasia' is not an appropriate label for the majority of these cases; in more than half of these cases the decision was discussed with the patient, or the patient had previously expressed a wish

---

[162] e.g. Keown, 'Euthanasia in the Netherlands: Sliding Down the Slippery Slope?', above n. 142, at 268–79; Fenigsen, 'The Report of the Dutch Governmental Committee on Euthanasia', above n. 141.

[163] This was principally due to different interpretation of relevant questions by respondents, many having interpreted the question relating to life-terminating acts without the patient's explicit request as relating to the alleviation of pain and symptoms: van der Maas et al., *Euthanasia and Other Medical Decisions Concerning the End of Life*: above n. 86, at 65–9, 181–3. The point has also been made that due to the relatively small number of cases of termination of life without explicit request where the patient had made no prior indication, extrapolation from these figures is difficult.

for active euthanasia in the event that his or her suffering became unbearable. In most of the remaining cases where there was no consultation with the patient (that is, where the conduct did constitute non-voluntary euthanasia), the patients were near to death, suffering grievously, and no longer competent. Further, on the basis of the research findings, there is every indication that the doctors' motivation in arriving at the decision to end the life of the patient were based on the best interests of the patient. Moreover, there is no evidence to suggest that the incidence of these cases where life is terminated in the absence of an explicit and persistent request is the product of the *de facto* acceptance of active voluntary euthanasia in the Netherlands. In contrast to cases of active euthanasia, where in the great majority of cases, life is shortened by at least 1 week and in many cases by a period of some months, in most of these cases, life had been shortened by a few hours or days at the most, and the patient had been in a state of extreme suffering. It is, therefore, arguable that these cases, which undoubtedly also occur in other jurisdictions, are unconnected with developments in the Netherlands with regard to active voluntary euthanasia.

There is also another major basis for the rejection of the critics' reasoning that the figures regarding active terminations without the patients' explicit and persistent request is evidence of a 'slippery slope'. In order to substantiate a 'slippery slope' argument, it would need to be shown that cases of non-voluntary euthanasia occur more frequently now than they did prior to the quasi-legalization of active voluntary euthanasia in the Netherlands.[164] There is, however, no evidence to suggest that the incidence of such cases is increasing. The Remmelink report is the first extensive study of its kind so no such figures are available.[165] In countering unsubstantiated claims of a 'slippery slope', it has, in fact, been suggested that, on the basis of the Remmelink figures, the open practice of voluntary euthanasia may have reduced the incidence of doctors acting without the consent of the patient in ways that the doctor foresees will result in the patient's death.[166] In support of this argument, a comparison has been made of deaths involving active euthanasia and doctor-assisted suicide where in the great majority of cases, consent was given or the matter was at least discussed with the patient, and instances of death being hastened by the withholding or withdrawing of life-sustaining treatment and the administration of potentially life-shortening pain and symptom relief where consent was obtained in less than half of the cases. Further, Dutch commentators have suggested that

---

[164] van Delden, J. et al., 'Dances with Data' (1993) 7 *Bioethics* 323.

[165] At the time of writing it had just been reported that funding had been given by the National Medical Research Council in Australia for a major study to be carried out in Australia by Dr Helga Kuhse and Professor Peter Singer of the Monash Centre for Bioethics seeking to replicate the Dutch study and provide some comparative data: see Note, 'Government Funds Big VE Study' (1996) No. 76 *VESNSW Newsletter* 3.

[166] Kuhse, H. and Singer, P., (editorial) (1992) 4 *Bioethics* iii.

there are good reasons to believe that if anything, the incidence of active euthanasia performed other than at the patient's explicit request is likely to decrease in the future.[167] It is thought that due to the increased awareness of the requirements in cases of euthanasia and the awareness of the existence of cases of ending of life without an explicit request, it is likely that doctors will respond by seeking information about patients' views at an earlier time, for example, by the use of living wills.[168]

As was noted, some commentators have referred to the high incidence of cases where a decision was made to either withhold or withdraw treatment or to administer high doses of palliative drugs without an explicit request from the patient, with the intention, at least in part, to hasten death, and have argued that this provides proof of a slippery slope in the Netherlands. However, these are practices which are also known to occur frequently in other jurisdictions and there is no compelling evidence to substantiate the claim that the occurrence of such cases in the Netherlands is evidence of a slippery slope as a result of that country's permissive approach to active voluntary euthanasia.[169] What does appear clear, however, is that the continuing illegality of active voluntary euthanasia under the Penal Code encourages some doctors to conceal their actions:[170] in at least some of the cases where high dosages of pain-relieving drugs were administered the doctors' intention was indistinguishable from that of a doctor performing active voluntary euthanasia,[171] yet the doctors were clearly not willing openly to take active steps to assist the patient to die.

One aspect of the 'slippery slope' argument which has been raised in opposition to active voluntary euthanasia generally[172] and has surfaced in the debate over the practice of active voluntary euthanasia in the Netherlands[173] is that its acceptance will lead to a loss of respect for human life. It has, however, been vigorously denied by doctors and commentators in the

---

[167] Pijnenborg, L. et al., 'Life Terminating Acts Without Explicit Request of Patient', above n. 136, at 1198–9.

[168] e.g. van der Wal, G. and Dillmann, R., 'Euthanasia in the Netherlands' (1994) 308 BMJ 1346, 1349. It should be noted that whilst there is support for the view that a doctor could perform euthanasia on the basis of an advance directive or living will, this issue has not yet come before the courts.

[169] See also van Delden et al., 'Dances with Data', above n. 164 where the researchers who conducted the study are critical of those commentators who seek to group together different categories of medical decisions at the end of life. They argue that this is a flawed approach based on unacceptable simplifications.

[170] Dr Pieter Admiraal (field notes recorded by the author in conversations with Dr Admiraal 26 Nov. 1991).

[171] The research findings indicated that in 6% of cases where pain medication was administered with possible lethal effect, and 2% of total deaths, pain-relieving drugs were administered with the express purpose of accelerating the death of the patient. Consultation had taken place with the patient in nearly half these cases.

[172] See pp. 227–8 above.

[173] e.g. Bostrom, 'Euthanasia in the Netherlands: A Model for the United States?', above n. 1, at 467.

Netherlands that the open practice of active voluntary euthanasia in the Netherlands has led to a lesser respect for human life in that country.[174] Indeed, many doctors have defended the Dutch position and argue that to perform active voluntary euthanasia, as limited by the guidelines, is in fact an act of respect for that patient as a person.[175]

Contrary to the claims of their critics, many of those who are involved in the administration of active voluntary euthanasia in the Netherlands assert that there have been a number of beneficial outcomes of the liberalization of the law and practice. In addition to providing relief to many patients from an existence of subjectively intolerable suffering, it has been suggested that the contemporary debate on the subject of active voluntary euthanasia has had positive consequences for patients generally, in that it has led to a re-evaluation of the patient's role as an actor in the decision-making process.[176] Others see advantages from the practice of active voluntary euthanasia in the Netherlands in that the subjects of death, illness, and ageing have lost much of their terror.[177] This is, to some extent, borne out by the results of the Remmelink survey outlined above, which found that a large number of patients seek assurance from their doctors that active voluntary euthanasia will be available if their suffering becomes unbearable. The very fact that these assurances are sought and given, even though active voluntary euthanasia is only performed in a small proportion of these cases, highlights the importance of its availability for the peace of mind of patients. For many patients facing terminal illness, it is the prospect of uncontrollable suffering and loss of dignity which they fear most, and if they can be given an assurance by their doctor that assistance will be available in the event that it becomes necessary, it appears that much of this anxiety can be avoided.

VII. GOVERNMENT'S RESPONSE TO THE REMMELINK REPORT

The release of the Remmelink survey has made it possible for the Dutch Government to decide on the desirability of legislation from a reasonably

[174] Borst-Eilers, 'Facts About the Actual Euthanasia Practice in the Netherlands', above n. 114, at 12.

[175] Admiraal, P., 'Active Voluntary Euthanasia' (1985) *New Humanist* 23, 24. This view was also expressed by Dr Admiraal and other Dutch doctors in interviews with the writer, Nov./ Dec. 1991.

[176] Bakker-Winnubst, H., 'The Right to Euthanasia During the Terminal Stage of Life' in Aycke and Smook, *Right to Self-Determination*, above n. 46, at 39, 43. See also Admiraal, P., 'Is There a Place for Euthanasia?' (1991) 10 *Bioethics News* 10, 11 where he notes the importance now attached to patient self-determination.

[177] Cohen, H., 'Euthanasia As a Way of Life' in Aycke and Smook, *Right to Self-Determination*, above n. 46, at 61.

informed basis. In April 1992, the Government withdrew its draft law of 1987 and submitted a new bill (Bill 22572).[178] This Bill, which has since been enacted into law, leaves Article 293 of the Penal Code unchanged[179] and merely gives legal effect to the protocol introduced in November 1990 regarding reporting procedures for doctors performing active voluntary euthanasia. This has been achieved by an amendment to the Act dealing with the disposal of the dead (Burial Act 1991). The changes which have been made under Bill 22572 which came into force on 1 June 1994, are predominantly procedural in character, changing the methods by which the forms on which euthanasia is reported are to be promulgated.[180] The object of the changes is to increase accountability and improve conditions of review.[181] The guidelines for the practice of active voluntary euthanasia and doctor-assisted suicide are not specifically referred to in the amended legislation. They are, however, indirectly acknowledged in the list of questions to be answered by a doctor when reporting cases of active voluntary euthanasia or doctor-assisted suicide, which appears as an Appendix to the regulations under the Burial Act.[182]

Thus, the changes which have been made simply involve the regulation of the reporting procedure and make no change at all to the substantive law. This represents a significant retreat from the earlier proposal of the Christian Democrats-Conservatives coalition under which the carefulness requirements to be followed by a doctor performing active voluntary euthanasia or assisted suicide were actually to be specified in the Medical Practice Act 1865. Moreover, the form of this change is also less expansive, involving secondary legislation (promulgation of regulations) which will be more readily open to amendment than if the change were embodied in an Act of Parliament.

In accordance with the recommendations of the Remmelink Committee, the changes introduced by the coalition government also require that cases of termination of life without the express and explicit request of the patient be reported in the same way as cases of active voluntary euthanasia. From the outset, the Government made clear its expectation that such cases should be investigated and, where appropriate, prosecuted. It should be noted that such cases would come within the murder provisions of the Penal

---

[178] Gevers, J., 'Legislation on Euthanasia: Recent Developments in the Netherlands' (1992) 18 *J Med. Ethics* 138, 140.

[179] The earlier proposal for the reduction of penalty is not included in this amendment.

[180] Griffiths, J., 'Recent Development in the Netherlands Concerning Euthanasia and Other Medical Behaviour that Shortens Life', above n. 56, at 349.

[181] Olde Scheper, T. and Duursma, S., 'Euthanasia: The Dutch Experience' (1994) 23 *Age & Ageing* 3.

[182] It would appear that the effect of the questionnaire and accompanying Explanatory Memorandum is to impose a number of stricter requirements, for example, in relation to consultation: see RDMA, *Vision on Euthanasia* (1995) above n. 67, at 40.

Code rather than Article 293 (dealing with killing on request). Even in the absence of a request for active euthanasia, it is possible that the defence of necessity in Article 40 of the Code would apply.

These amendments have been criticized on a number of grounds.[183] Many regard the changes as an inept political compromise. One of the principal criticisms is that it is illogical and contradictory to have under one Act a law which unequivocally prohibits active voluntary euthanasia (Article 293 of the Penal Code), and at the same time, to amend other legislation in a way which appears to condone the practice. As one Dutch commentator has aptly put it, 'maintaining euthanasia as a crime while at the same time pointing out to the physician the way to perform this crime in such a manner that he will not be found guilty creates a confusing paradox'.[184] It has also been argued that these changes will, in any event, not achieve the desired object of securing full reporting by doctors of cases of active voluntary euthanasia, since the practice remains a criminal offence under the Penal Code, and there will always be a proportion of doctors who are not willing to report in these circumstances.[185] One aspect of the reforms which has attracted particular criticism from a number of quarters, including the RDMA,[186] has been the decision to treat cases of termination of life without the express and explicit request of the patient in the same way as cases of active voluntary euthanasia.[187] From a practical point of view, it is unlikely that doctors will report cases of this kind, given the inevitable investigation of the doctor's conduct and the strong possibility of a prosecution resulting. Quite apart from these practical limitations, many people are concerned that extension of the reporting procedure to cases of termination of life without the patient's explicit request blurs the crucial distinction between voluntary and non-voluntary euthanasia, and tends to imply that termination of life other than at the express and explicit request of the patient may, in some circumstances, be acceptable.[188] The views of a number of leading legal commentators in the Netherlands is that cases of this kind are excep-

[183] For critical analysis of the legislation see Gevers, 'Legislation on Euthanasia: Recent Developments in the Netherlands', above n. 178.

[184] Legemaate, J., 'Legal Aspects of Euthanasia and Assisted Suicide in the Netherlands 1973–1994' (1995) 4 *Cambridge QHealthcare Ethics* 112, 118.

[185] Twenty-five per cent of doctors say that they will not report cases of active voluntary euthanasia whilst it remains illegal: this proposition is based upon field notes recorded by the author in conversation with Dr Rob Dillmann, Secretary of Medical Affairs, RDMA, 26 Nov. 1991.

[186] RDMA, *Vision on Euthanasia* (1995) above n. 67, at 38.

[187] This proposition is based upon field notes recorded by the author in conversation with Professor Henk Leenen, 27 Nov. 1991. See also van Delden, J. et al., 'The Remmelink Study: Two Years Later' (1993) 23 *Hastings Center R* 24.

[188] Professor Leenen suggests that this legislative proposal may even be in contravention of Article 2 of the European Convention of Human Rights which protects the right to life (field notes recorded by the author in conversation with Professor Henk Leenen on 27 Nov. 1991).

tional and cannot be legislated for.[189] The obligation to report cases of termination of life without the explicit request of the patient has also been criticized, on the basis that it requires doctors to provide evidence in respect of a criminal matter that would incriminate him or her, which is contrary to the normal legal rules protecting against self-incrimination.[190]

VIII. ARGUMENTS FOR THE LEGALIZATION OF ACTIVE VOLUNTARY EUTHANASIA IN THE NETHERLANDS

Despite the significant jurisprudential developments and the general compliance of prosecuting authorities in bringing prosecution policy in line with the case law developments, a number of problems have been identified with the current position in the Netherlands.[191] Foremost amongst these problems is the continuing legal uncertainty faced by doctors as a result of the inconsistency between law and practice with regard to active voluntary euthanasia. At present, it is still prohibited under Article 293 of the Penal Code, and doctors who engage in the practice are committing a criminal offence. Similarly, a doctor who assists the suicide of a patient commits a criminal offence under Article 293. As was noted earlier, the amendments which have been made to the Burial Act are purely of a procedural nature and do not affect the substantive law. Whilst the courts can, to some extent, bridge the gap between legislation and practice, there are inherent limitations in the capacity for case law to provide certainty in this area. Apart from certain minimum standards which have been more or less uniformly applied, there is no absolute certainty that all courts would abide by the same criteria which have been developed in the mainstream jurisprudence.[192] Thus, the possibility always exists that a doctor, who has performed active voluntary euthanasia or assisted suicide in accordance with established guidelines, could face conviction and substantial punishment under Article 293.[193] The co-ordination of prosecution policy in conformity with the case law developments and more recently, the introduction of a uniform protocol for the

[189] This proposition is based upon field notes recorded by the author in conversations with Professor Leenen, 27 Nov. 1991 and Dr Gevers, 2 Dec. 1991 (Professor of Public Health Legislation, University of Amsterdam).

[190] See the views of Dr Eugene Sutorious, a lawyer specializing in cases of euthanasia, referred to in Note, 'Euthanasia Law Does Not End Debate in the Netherlands' (1993) 307 BMJ 1511.

[191] For detailed consideration of some of these problems, see Leenen, 'Legal Aspects of Euthanasia, Assistance to Suicide and Terminating the Medical Treatment of Incompetent Patients', above n. 5, at 5–6, 11–14.

[192] Leenen, 'Euthanasia, Assistance to Suicide and the Law: Developments in the Netherlands', above n. 12, at 202.

[193] Leenen, 'Legal Aspects of Euthanasia, Assistance to Suicide and Terminating the Medical Treatment of Incompetent Patients', above n. 5, at 5–6, 11–14.

reporting and investigation of cases of active voluntary euthanasia and assisted suicide, which has now recently been given statutory force, has clarified the situation and removed some of the uncertainty. There is now some degree of confidence amongst the medical profession that doctors will not be prosecuted if they perform active voluntary euthanasia or assisted suicide in accordance with the guidelines laid down by the courts and then report their actions as required under the 1990 protocol. This is borne out by the notable increase in the number of reported cases since the introduction of this protocol in November 1990.[194] Despite these developments, doctors who participate in these practices are still acting contrary to law, and must carefully justify their actions in order to escape criminal liability. Their conduct can not be excused in advance, but only after reporting and investigation of the matter. Thus, some uncertainty inevitably remains, and there is clear evidence that some doctors simply will not report cases whilst the practice remains illegal.[195] Concerns about legal liability had recently been fuelled, following a dramatic increase in the number of prosecutions taken against doctors in recent years. In 1993 the number of prosecution jumped to 14—a marked increase on the handful of cases which had been prosecuted in the preceding years.[196] Most of these prosecutions had been initiated in cases in which the patient was not terminally ill.[197] This was in direct response to a statement released by the then Minister for Justice, Ernst Hirsch Ballin, based on his interpretation of a 1988 case, that euthanasia was only legally permissible in cases in which the patient is terminally ill.[198] This viewpoint was widely criticized by Dutch legal commentators and strongly objected to by the RDMA. The matter was later clarified by the Dutch Supreme Court in the *Chabot* case where, as explained above, it was held that assisted suicide and active voluntary euthanasia can, in appropriate circumstances, be acceptable, even where the patient is not in the terminal phase. As a result of this decision, most of these prosecutions were dropped. These events did, however, highlight the vulnerable legal status of doctors and the implications of a shift in prosecution policy.[199]

Because of the ambiguous legal status of the practice, a significant proportion of cases of active voluntary euthanasia and doctor-assisted suicide

[194] In 1990, 454 cases were reported. In 1991 the figure increased to 591 and in the two following years there was a substantial increase—1318 reported cases in 1992 and 1323 in 1993: information obtained from Josephus Jitta, Chief Public Prosecutor setting out the euthanasia and assisted suicide reports counted by the Board of Prosecutors-General.

[195] See above, n. 185.

[196] In 1990 there were in fact no prosecutions; in 1991 there was 1, in 1992 there were 3.

[197] Legemaate, 'Legal Aspects of Euthanasia and Assisted Suicide in the Netherlands 1973–94', above n. 184, at 119.

[198] In the Netherlands, the Minister for Justice has ultimate political responsibility for euthanasia and has to decide whether or not to prosecute a case.

[199] See the RDMA, *Vision on Euthanasia* (1995) above n. 67, at 41 which reflects the concern of the medical profession.

in the Netherlands are still performed behind closed doors, and there is little possibility of fully controlling the practice. In the absence of adequate controlling mechanisms for the administration of active voluntary euthanasia and doctor-assisted suicide, the interests of the patient are at risk. The recent survey results have shown that active euthanasia is performed quite frequently, and although in the majority of cases, it is performed at the explicit and persistent request of the patient, in some cases, lethal drugs are administered without such a request.[200] There is, therefore, some justification for calls for the introduction of legislation to establish effective control mechanisms and to protect against the possibility of patients' lives being terminated without their explicit request.[201] Neither case law nor prosecution policy can provide the necessary clarity, legal uniformity, and certainty, and it is only through legislation that the patient's right of self-determination can be specifically protected.[202] On the basis of the foregoing arguments, there is a strong case for introducing legislation which goes beyond the procedural changes which have been made and actually legalizes active voluntary euthanasia and doctor-assisted suicide performed in accordance with strict safeguards (for example, along the lines of the Wessel-Tuinstra Bill, discussed above). If these practices were legalized, with the criteria for their performance clearly spelt out in the legislation, doctors would have the protection of the law and would be immune from liability unless the prosecution could show that the doctor had acted outside the criteria. Whilst it would be unrealistic to suppose that the introduction of legislation legalizing the practice of active voluntary euthanasia and doctor-assisted suicide would result in full reporting or completely eliminate the risk of inappropriate practices, it would certainly be an improvement on the present situation. There is good reason to believe that many more doctors would, in these circumstances, be willing to report cases and subject themselves to legal scrutiny, and the practice would generally be more open.[203] Further, it would be a strong inducement for doctors to comply strictly with the stipulated safeguards in order to come within the protection of the immunity.

[200] See above for discussion of the 0.8% of cases in which doctors terminated life without an explicit and persistent request, in approximately half of which there was no consultation with the patient. Note also the category of cases where drugs for the relief of pain and symptoms were administered with the express purpose of hastening the death of the patient. Although this possibility was discussed with the patient in 40% of cases, in many cases this was not possible because the patient was incompetent.

[201] e.g. Leenen, 'Legal Aspects of Euthanasia, Assistance to Suicide and Terminating the Medical Treatment of Incompetent Patients', above n. 5, at 11; Roscam Abbing, 'Dying with Dignity, and Euthanasia: A View from the Netherlands', above n. 96, at 73.

[202] By virtue of the terms of Article 293 of the Penal Code 1886, case law has very much focused on the position of the doctor, only indirectly referring to the autonomy of the patient.

[203] Support for this view can be found in the fact that 25% of doctors refuse to report cases of active voluntary euthanasia whilst the practice remains illegal; see above, n. 185. Moreover, in relation to the prospective study in the Remmelink survey (where doctors were guaranteed legal immunity) there was a notable increase in reporting. See above.

There certainly appears to be considerable support for the legalization of active voluntary euthanasia amongst the Dutch medical profession and the community generally. According to figures obtained in the Remmelink survey, 66 per cent of doctors are in favour of the introduction of a statutory immunity excluding doctors from the liability of Article 293 of the Penal Code, provided the specified criteria are satisfied.[204] For some time now, the RDMA has indicated its preference for legislation which allows an immunity to doctors.[205] So far as community attitudes are concerned, opinion poll evidence suggests that a large majority of the Dutch population favours the introduction of legislation permitting active voluntary euthanasia.[206]

However, some commentators have argued there are potential difficulties associated with the introduction of legislation which legalizes active voluntary euthanasia. Gevers, for example, points out that there are inevitably limitations with legislation, in that it is impossible to delineate precisely the situations in which active voluntary euthanasia should be allowed.[207] Consequently, it is argued, a new law cannot add very much to what has already been developed by the courts and will only partially reduce legal uncertainty. Some opponents of legalization have further argued that there is no evidence to suggest that there is less risk of abuse if the criteria are statutory.[208] Others point out that in a democracy, law on any issue is a compromise solution and therefore likely to be unsatisfactory.[209] Related to this is the possibility of difficulties being encountered in the interpretation of any new legislation. This concern has led some notable advocates for active voluntary euthanasia, such as Dr Pieter Admiraal and Dr Herbert Cohen, to express reservations about the introduction of legislation as the means for solving present difficulties.[210]

It remains to be seen whether any further changes are made to the law in the Netherlands. Significantly, in August 1994 a new government was

[204] van der Maas et al., *Euthanasia and Other Medical Decisions Concerning the End of Life*, above n. 86, at 103.

[205] For a recent statement of this position see the RDMA, *Vision on Euthanasia* (1995) above n. 67, at 41, 43–4.

[206] In a 1985 survey, 70% of respondents indicated their support for legislation; Waller, S., 'Trends in Public Acceptance of Euthanasia Worldwide' (1986) 1 *Euthanasia Rev.* 33, 41. For detailed analysis of public opinion in the Netherlands on the subject of active voluntary euthanasia, see Hilhorst, H., 'Religion and Euthanasia in the Netherlands: Exploring a Diffuse Relationship' (1983) 30 *Social Compass* 491 and van der Maas, P. et al., 'Changes in Dutch Opinions on Active Euthanasia, 1966 Through 1991' (1995) 273 JAMA 1411. According to more recent public opinion polls (1993), support for active voluntary euthanasia is in the range of 80%.

[207] Gevers, 'Legal Developments Concerning Active Euthanasia on Request in the Netherlands', above n. 32, at 162.

[208] Keown, 'The Law and Practice of Euthanasia in the Netherlands', above n. 154, at 77.

[209] Dr Adrienne van Till; field notes recorded by the author in conversation with Dr van Till (well known lawyer who had been instrumental in the formation of the Foundation for Voluntary Euthanasia in the wake of the Postma case), 24 Nov. 1991.

[210] Kennedy, L., *Euthanasia: The Good Death* (London, 1990) 39–45.

elected without the Christian Democrats who, as we have seen, had strongly opposed legalization and had blocked earlier reform efforts during their time in coalition government. In 1994 when the amendments came into force, the new Government announced that the reporting procedures would be evaluated over the next 2 years, to examine the extent to which doctors are complying with the reporting requirements and, where relevant, to ascertain reasons for non-reporting. The overall approach taken in the current evaluation is similar to the earlier Remmelink inquiry, although this investigation is more wide-ranging, encompassing also coroners and public prosecutors.[211] Depending on the outcomes of this survey, which is scheduled to be completed later in 1996, there may be new pressure for more substantive reforms. In view of the change in government in the Netherlands, in particular the absence of the Christian Democrats, it is quite possible that the government will decide to take positive steps towards legalization of active voluntary euthanasia and doctor-assisted suicide. In the meantime, the Dutch Voluntary Euthanasia Society has launched its own Bill for the legalization of active voluntary euthanasia.

IX. WHY THE NETHERLANDS?

A question which has often been raised is why the Netherlands appears to be at the forefront in the practice of active voluntary euthanasia. Many explanations have been advanced, some of which relate to the unique characteristics of the Netherlands and its people.

The Netherlands is a small, densely populated country. It has a pluriform society with a tradition of religious and moral tolerance,[212] which is very democratic and permissive. It values freedom of thinking and expressing one's views. A variety of opinions exist in Dutch society from strict Calvinism and Catholicism to liberal Christianity and Humanism. In a population of 14 million, there are more than 380 churches or denominations.[213] Whilst the Netherlands is nominally Catholic, Dutch Catholicism is very democratic, and aggressively anti-Vatican. A sizeable proportion of the Dutch population claim no religious affiliation. Dutch society as a whole is interested in moral issues such as active voluntary euthanasia, and the Dutch enjoy open and free discussion on such subjects. It is also a society where the views of others are respected. This community tolerance is reflected in the opinion poll results with regard to active voluntary euthanasia which

---

[211] This proposition is based upon private communication with Dr Rob Dillmann, Secretary of Medical Affairs, 21 Dec. 1995.

[212] This is, for example, illustrated in the liberal approach taken by the Dutch to prostitution and drug use.

[213] Terborgh-Dupuis, H., 'The Netherlands: Tolerance and Teaching' (1984) 14 *Hastings Center R* 23, 23.

show that a great majority (87 per cent) of the Dutch population is quite tolerant of others who hold opposite attitudes on the subject.[214]

Dutch people are also known for their fierce independence, moral integrity, and defence of civil liberties. The independence of Dutch doctors was demonstrated during the war-time occupation when, despite threats and the withdrawal of their licences, they refused to play any part in the Nazi programme of sterilization of, and medical experiments upon Jews, gypsies, and mental defectives.[215] As in other countries, there has been growing recognition in the Netherlands of the importance of individual autonomy and respect for the individual's right of self-determination, and this has directly contributed to the contemporary acceptance and practice of active voluntary euthanasia.[216]

There are also special features of the Dutch health care system which have played a role in the development of active voluntary euthanasia. In the Netherlands, at the centre of the health care system is the family doctor, or 'huisarts', who has typically looked after the family for a number of years[217]—in many cases, for 10 or more years. Although Dutch doctors are esteemed as professionals, to many people they are like a family friend. In the context of provision of terminal care, much of the care is provided in the patient's home, with the family doctor making frequent house-calls to assure the patient of adequate pain control and symptom relief, supported by nurses and other health care providers. Unlike many other Westernized countries where the majority of people die in hospitals, many patients in the Netherlands die at home, in their natural surroundings.[218] The nature of the family doctor's relationship with his or her patients has important consequences with regard to the performance of active voluntary euthanasia. It is a relationship characterized by close personal contact in which the doctor has a good knowledge of the patient and his or her family circumstances, including any family support or pressures that might be relevant to a request for active euthanasia.[219] A patient's family doctor would therefore be in a very good position to assess the voluntariness of the patient's request and other pertinent factors in the euthanasia determination. Significantly,

---

[214] Hilhorst, 'Religion and Euthanasia in the Netherlands: Exploring a Diffuse Relationship', above n. 206, at 496.

[215] Alexander, L., 'Medical Science Under Dictatorship' (1949) 241 *New Eng.J Med.* 39.

[216] See Dillmann, R., 'Euthanasia in a Dutch Perspective' in RDMA, *Euthanasia in the Netherlands* (1991) above n. 5, at 6–7; Borst-Eilers, 'The Status of Physician-Administered Active Euthanasia in the Netherlands', above n. 118, at 7.

[217] Dupuis, H., 'The Right to a Gentle Death' in Aycke and Smook, *Right to Self-Determination*, above n. 46, at 53, 56.

[218] This is to be compared with the USA for example, where 80% of deaths occur in hospitals; see President's Commission for the Study of Ethical Problems in Medicine and Biomedical and Behavioural Research, *Deciding to Forgo Life-Sustaining Treatment: A Report on the Ethical, Medical and Legal Issues in Treatment Decisions* (Washington, 1983) 17–18.

[219] Battin, M., 'Seven Caveats Concerning the Discussion of Euthanasia in Holland' (1990) 34 *Perspectives in Biology&Med.* 73.

the Remmelink survey has confirmed that active voluntary euthanasia is most frequently practised by general practitioners.[220]

In addition to the key role performed by the family doctor, it has also been suggested that the situation in the Netherlands has come about because of the openness of Dutch doctors; because some doctors were prepared to act openly in what they judged to be their patients' best interests and to defend their actions in the law courts. The approach taken by these doctors contrasts markedly with the position in other countries such as the United Kingdom, the USA, Canada, and Australia, where the practice of active euthanasia is largely hidden. In those few cases where a doctor is exposed and faces prosecution, technical defences are usually invoked, and the case is generally not defended as a case of active voluntary euthanasia.[221]

So far as jurisprudential developments are concerned, coincidence has arguably also had an important role to play.[222] When the first case came before the court in Leeuwarden in 1973, the Foundation of Voluntary Euthanasia heard of it and provided the President of the court with a number of publications by lawyers, doctors, philosophers, and theologians who did not condemn active voluntary euthanasia, but found it acceptable if necessary as a last resort. Copies of these publications, which had appeared in medical journals (and therefore were probably unknown to the legal profession), went to the prosecutor and defence in this case. This meant that the first case to consider the issue of active voluntary euthanasia was based on academic data, which may help to explain the willingness of the court to take an accommodating view on the subject.

Another factor which has played some role in shaping legal outcomes concerns the Dutch legal system and the absence of a minimum level of punishment.[223] This has left the courts free to impose very lenient sentences in cases where doctors have been brought before the courts for performing active voluntary euthanasia.

X. EVALUATION OF THE NETHERLANDS' MODEL: SUITABLE FOR EXPORT?

It was suggested from the outset of this chapter that the Netherlands presents itself as a living model for other countries to assess the effects of

---

[220] 62% of the general practitioners surveyed had performed active euthanasia compared with 44% of the clinicians and 12% of the nursing home physicians. 28% of the general practitioners had performed active euthanasia within the previous 24 months compared with 20% of the clinicians and 6% of the nursing home physicians. For further discussion see above.

[221] See pp. 141–5 above.

[222] Written communication with Dr. Adrienne van Till, Jan. 1992.

[223] This proposition is based upon field notes recorded by the author in conversation with Chief Prosecutor Jitta, 29 Nov. 1991.

State-sanctioned active voluntary euthanasia upon the law, medicine, health care, and social policy. It is therefore necessary to come to some conclusion about the position in the Netherlands and to ask whether it is a model suitable for other countries to follow.

It is evident from the foregoing discussion that there are some problems with the present situation in the Netherlands. However, these problems appear to stem mainly from the fact that the administration of active voluntary euthanasia is still a criminal offence under the Penal Code, and consequently there is still a reluctance on the part of many doctors to perform the practice openly and to report such cases. It cannot, therefore, be extrapolated from the situation in the Netherlands that other countries contemplating the legalization of active voluntary euthanasia through legislation would necessarily face the same difficulties.

In assessing the current situation in the Netherlands with regard to the practice of active voluntary euthanasia, we are greatly assisted by the recent surveys which have been conducted, in particular, the nationwide survey of doctors conducted under the auspices of the Remmelink Committee. This survey indicated that the practice of active euthanasia in the Netherlands is, in fact, significantly *less* than had been previously estimated. Whilst there may be some scope for concern in view of the 0.8 per cent of cases in which active steps were taken to terminate life without an explicit and persistent request from the patient, claims about the uncontrollable nature of euthanasia and the widespread practice of non-voluntary and even involuntary euthanasia have been shown to be unfounded. What the Netherlands experience has shown is that active voluntary euthanasia can be practised in accordance with the wishes of patients in a caring and humane way which, at the same time, respects the sensitivities of doctors.[224] By and large, it appears that the contemporary practice of active voluntary euthanasia in the Netherlands is serving the interests of patients, and there is no evidence of large scale abuses or extensions of the practice. Thus, it makes the option of an earlier death a reality for the small minority of patients that seek it, without causing any apparent harm or damage to society.

Even if the conclusion is reached that the contemporary practice of active voluntary euthanasia in the Netherlands is working satisfactorily, consideration must be given to the implications of the Netherlands situation for other countries, and the 'exportability of Dutch euthanasia practices'.[225] In particular, care must be taken that a practice, operating satisfactorily in one country, is not unthinkingly adopted in another, where, for a variety of reasons, it may operate quite differently.

Some attention has already been given to special features of Dutch society which may have contributed to the development of active voluntary

---

[224] Pabst Battin, M., 'Holland and Home: On the Exportability of Dutch Euthanasia Practices' in Aycke and Smook, *Right to Self-Determination*, above n. 46, at 124.
[225] Ibid.

euthanasia in that country. For the purposes of the present inquiry, consideration needs to be given to those aspects of the contemporary practice of active voluntary euthanasia in the Netherlands and Dutch society in general which may limit the applicability of the Dutch experience.

First, consideration must be given to a number of features of the Dutch health care system which appear to facilitate the performance of active voluntary euthanasia free from coercion or abuse. A central feature of Dutch health care is the comprehensive scheme of national health insurance.[226] The coverage of this insurance is in all cases substantial, including basic care, as well costly high technology care. This is to be contrasted with the situation in some countries, such as the USA, where there is, at present, no national health care system or scheme of national health care insurance, and where a large number of people have no insurance at all, or are substantially underinsured. Since the Netherlands has a health care system available to every citizen, there are not the same financial pressures on patients, as there may be in some countries, for the performance of active voluntary euthanasia.

Another observation which has been made by commentators, from both within and outside the Netherlands, is that the medical establishment in the Netherlands as a rule is not commercially inclined,[227] and there are certainly no financial or other incentives for hospitals or doctors to terminate the lives of their patients.[228] Moreover, many have spoken of the integrity of the Dutch medical profession.[229]

Yet another special feature of the position in the Netherlands is that, as noted above, that country has a strongly developed system of general practice, with additional nursing care, and other forms of care provided to the patient at home. Many patients (approximately 40 per cent) die at home under the care of their family doctor. For those who are admitted to hospital or nursing homes, the Dutch pride themselves on uniformly high quality care. There is a very well developed system of nursing home care, and nursing home medicine is a distinct speciality.

In evaluating the suitability of the Netherlands model, attention is often drawn to the absence of hospices or separate palliative care facilities, and the suggestion is sometimes made that the demand for euthanasia in the Netherlands results from deficiencies in palliative care.[230] Whilst it is true

[226] Almost all patients (99.4%) have health insurance and the remainder of the population are covered under legislation for the cost of protracted illness.

[227] e.g. Cohen, 'Euthanasia As a Way of Life', above n. 177, at 62.

[228] Dillmann, 'Euthanasia in a Dutch Perspective', above n. 216, at 8. This has been borne out in the findings of the Remmelink study: health case expenses were never a reason for either requesting or performing euthanasia.

[229] See, for example, the discussion in Aycke and Smook, *Right to Self-Determination*, above n. 46, at 70–1.

[230] See, for discussion, the Canadian Special Senate Committee on Euthanasia and Assisted Suicide, *Of Life and Death*, above Ch. 3 n. 10, at A-120.

that there are relatively few hospices in the Netherlands,[231] this is the result of a deliberate policy rather than a sign of neglect—the Dutch philosophy being to bring the palliative care to where it is needed.[232] As a consequence, palliative care is in the main integrated into other aspects of the health care infrastructure, including the practice of general practitioners, hospitals, and nursing homes.[233] Every hospital is required to have a special pain team which functions within the hospital as well as for outpatients, and can also be consulted by general practitioners. There are also regional pain teams available for consultation. In addition, there are regional cancer centres where advice or consultation is available from cancer specialists, including palliative care specialists. Thus, palliative care is widely available, and a request for active euthanasia cannot be seen as an indication that inadequate care has been provided.[234]

It has been suggested that these elements of Dutch health care are important in that they constitute the social background for the practice of active voluntary euthanasia which is free from restraint and coercion.[235] There are obviously difficulties in attempting to draw conclusions from the Dutch experience which may be applicable in other countries. Attention has been drawn to some of the differences in health care and culture between the Netherlands and other jurisdictions. For example, social and economic disparities in health care, particularly in the USA, which may create inappropriate demand or pressure for the use of euthanasia.[236] Further, it has been pointed out that in the jurisdictions under consideration, most physician care is provided in a professional or institutional setting, and the system of general family practice is not developed to the same degree as in the Netherlands, where most primary care is provided by family physicians in the patient's home, or in an office in the physician's home. However, consideration of the Dutch position suggests that some of the elements which comprise the Dutch situation may not be completely unique; for example, a number of jurisdictions under consideration also have a national scheme of health insurance, claim good

---

[231] In a recent overview the Dutch Government indicated that some 10 to 15 hospices are in operation now, aside from new facilities for palliative care offered by Cancer Centres: this proposition is based upon private communication with Dr Rob Dillmann, Secretary of Medical Affairs, 23 April 1996.

[232] van Delden, J., 'Euthanasia in the Netherlands: The Medical Scene' in Sneiderman, B. and Kaufert, J. (eds.), *Euthanasia in the Netherlands: A Model For Canada?* (Manitoba, 1994) 20, 24.

[233] This policy of bringing palliative care to where it is needed as an integral part of health care has recently been confirmed in a letter by the Minister of Health to the Second Chamber of Parliament. (This proposition is based upon private communication with Dr Rob Dillmann, Secretary of Medical Affairs, 23 April 1996.)

[234] Admiraal, 'Is there a Place for Euthanasia?', above n. 176, at 15–16.

[235] Dillmann, 'Euthanasia in a Dutch Perspective', above n. 216, at 8.

[236] But see arguments why doctor-assisted suicide may in fact work better in the USA: Cipriani, T., 'Give Me Liberty and Give me Death' (1995) 3 *JLaw&Med.* 177, 191.

quality health care, and a high degree of integrity amongst the medical profession.

It should be noted that there are a number of distinguishing features between the legal systems in the Netherlands and the common law jurisdictions under consideration. As was earlier observed, the legal system in the Netherlands has its roots in Roman law and is a civil law orientated system.[237] This contrasts with the situation in common law jurisdictions which are derived from Anglo-Saxon law. However, as in most common law jurisdictions, judges in the Netherlands are appointed for life,[238] and their independence is constitutionally guaranteed. There also appear to be some differences with regard to the role of the prosecuting authorities. In the Netherlands, there is considerable prosecutorial discretion, more so than in common law jurisdictions. Moreover, the prosecution in the Netherlands appears to occupy more of a policy-making role than is evident in other countries, and this is illustrated by the development of prosecution policy with regard to active voluntary euthanasia and doctor-assisted suicide.[239] Indeed, it would be very difficult for other countries to emulate the current position in the Netherlands, where cases of active voluntary euthanasia and doctor-assisted suicide coming to the attention of the authorities are not prosecuted, even though they are in breach of the criminal law.

CONCLUSION

The object of this chapter has been to examine the legal position and practice of active voluntary euthanasia in the Netherlands, with a view to assessing the suitability of this model for adoption in the common law jurisdictions under consideration. The position which has been reached in the Netherlands with regard to active voluntary euthanasia is the product of a complex interplay which has taken place over the past two decades between the courts, prosecution policy, and medical practice. Now, more recently, the parliament has also become involved, acknowledging these developments at least indirectly, by giving legal effect to the procedure for the notification of cases of active voluntary euthanasia and doctor-assisted suicide. What is clear from the Netherlands experience is that, notwithstanding the ambiguous legal framework which remains, there are certainly benefits to be gained from a policy of greater transparency and openness in

[237] Sutorius, 'How Euthanasia was Legalised in Holland', above n. 25, at 9.

[238] Compare this, for example, with the situation in the USA where the judges are typically subject to public re-election; Pabst Battin, 'Holland and Home: On the Exportability of Dutch Euthanasia Practices', above n. 46, at 127.

[239] Pabst Battin, 'Holland and Home: On the Exportability of Dutch Euthanasia Practices', above n. 46, at 127.

the practice of euthanasia, particularly with regard to regulation and safe-guarding the interests of patients.

Whilst it would be impossible to replicate this particular development elsewhere, valuable insight can be gained from examining the Dutch prac-tice of active voluntary euthanasia which has at least been given *de facto* legal recognition. This, in turn, may be influential in other countries which are reassessing the criminal law prohibition on active voluntary euthanasia and doctor-assisted suicide and examining options for reform. Indeed, as was pointed out in the preceding chapter,[240] the influence of the Nether-lands guidelines for the practice of active voluntary euthanasia and doctor-assisted suicide can already be seen in the formulation of statutory guidelines for legalized active voluntary euthanasia and doctor-assisted suicide in the Northern Territory of Australia. In the remaining chapter, specific attention will be given to the various options for reform in this area.

[240] See p. 357 above.

8

Options For Reform

INTRODUCTION

Whilst there is strong support for reform of the law as borne out by recent public opinion polls[1] and polls conducted amongst the medical profession,[2] there is less certainty or agreement about the exact direction any reform of the law should take. In earlier chapters, it has been suggested that there are various problems with the present law which call for a reassessment of the present legal prohibition of active voluntary euthanasia and doctor-assisted suicide.[3] Consideration must now be given to possible legal responses to these difficulties to determine whether legislative reform is called for, and if so, what form it should take. Quite a number of reform options have been advanced over the years, and, as we have seen, legislation has been passed in the Northern Territory of Australia legalizing both active voluntary euthanasia and doctor-assisted suicide. In addition, in the US State of Oregon an Act permitting doctor-assisted suicide has been passed, although this has subsequently been challenged on constitutional grounds.[4] The object of this chapter is to examine the various possible models for change and their respective merits and shortcomings, with a view to ascertaining the most appropriate model for reform.

Before embarking on consideration of possible reforms, consideration needs to be given to one suggestion which has been made, but which does not in fact represent an option for change, namely that the most appropriate solution is to do nothing at all. This was, for example, the approach favoured by the Canadian Law Reform Commission in its review of the law with regard to active voluntary euthanasia.[5] The commission was of the view that the present criminal law prohibition of active voluntary euthanasia should be retained, but that the strictness of the law should continue to be ameliorated in individual cases through the internal mechanisms of the criminal justice system. This approach is said to have the advantage of recognizing the appropriateness of active voluntary euthanasia in individual cases, yet avoiding the dangers and difficulties in drafting legislation to

---

[1] See pp. 257–68 above.   [2] See pp. 292–332 above.   [3] See, in particular, Ch. 3.
[4] For discussion of these developments see pp. 345–57, 369–73 above.
[5] Law Reform Commission of Canada, Working Paper No. 28, *Euthanasia, Aiding Suicide and the Cessation of Treatment* (Ottawa, 1982) 51–2; Law Reform Commission of Canada, Report No. 20, *Euthanasia, Aiding Suicide and the Cessation of Treatment* (Ottawa, 1983) 19–20.

more formally accommodate the practice.[6] However, as outlined in the earlier chapter dealing with the position in practice, this approach entails enormous problems.[7] It inevitably produces uncertainty and does not adequately protect the position of either doctors or their patients. Moreover, toleration of the discrepancies which presently exist between the law on the books and the law in practice tends to lead to disrespect for the law. Some change to the current criminal law prohibition of active voluntary euthanasia is therefore required.

Looking at the situation realistically, if there is going to be any change to the present law dealing with active voluntary euthanasia, it will have to be achieved through legislative action. Possibilities certainly exist for non-legislative solutions,[8] and the situation in the Netherlands demonstrates that change can be effected through the courts.[9] Indeed, one leading commentator in the United Kingdom, Professor Ian Kennedy, has recently argued that the courts are under a duty as they deal with cases coming before them to reshape and develop the law relating to euthanasia.[10] Practically speaking, however, there is little prospect of the courts in the United Kingdom and other common law jurisdictions under consideration taking the initiative to secure reform[11] and there are, in any event, arguments to suggest that the legislature is the more appropriate forum to bring about change in this area.[12] Indeed, on a number of occasions, members of the judiciary have highlighted some of the anomalies of the present law and have called on the legislature to deal with the issue.[13]

---

[6] Browne, A., 'Assisted Suicide and Active Voluntary Euthanasia' (1989) 11 *Can.JLJuris.* 35, 50.

[7] See pp. 148–52 above.

[8] For example, the suggestion of Professor Glanville Williams in his text *The Sanctity of Life and the Criminal Law* (London, 1958) 284 that active voluntary euthanasia may, in extreme circumstances, be justified under the general doctrine of necessity. See also Lanham, D., 'Euthanasia, Painkilling, Murder and Manslaughter' (1994) *JLaw &Med.* 146 where he suggests that the offence of manslaughter has a role to play as an alternative charge to that of murder where the intention of the accused in killing the deceased was to relieve pain and that in exceptional circumstances, killing could be lawful homicide.

[9] See pp. 393–409 above.

[10] 'The Quality of Mercy: Patients, Doctors and Dying' (1994) The Upjohn Lecture.

[11] The opportunity for modification of the criminal law by the courts is even more circumscribed in those jurisdictions where the criminal law is dealt with under a Criminal Code, for example in Canada and some Australian jurisdictions: see p. 13, n. 2 above.

[12] Richards, D., 'Constitutional Privacy, the Right to Die and the Meaning of Life: A Moral Analysis' (1981) 22 *Wm.& Mary LRev.* 327, 418; Miller, F. et al., 'Regulating Physician-Assisted Death' (1994) 331 *New Eng.JMed.* 119, 120. See also *In re Farrel* 529 A2d 404, 407–8 (1987) per Garibaldi J for arguments regarding the advantages of legislative, as distinct from judicial, guidelines in matters of this nature.

[13] See for example, Lord Mustill in *Airedale NHS Trust* v. *Bland* [1993] 1 All ER 82 and in the course of the *Rodriguez* litigation, Proudfoot J of the British Columbia Court of Appeal (*Rodriguez* v. *Attorney General of British Columbia, Attorney General of Canada* (1993) 79 CCC (3d) 1, 30) and McLachlin J of the Supreme Court: *Rodriguez* v. *British Columbia (Attorney General)* [1993] 3 SCR 519, 628.

Special note should be made here of the quite extraordinary developments which have recently taken place in the USA with two federal courts (the Ninth and Second Circuit Courts of Appeals) declaring the statutory prohibition of assisted suicide to be unconstitutional in the States of Washington and New York respectively, in so far as they apply to competent, terminally ill patients who seek physician-assisted suicide.[14] As was outlined in an earlier chapter,[15] by virtue of the federal court structure in the USA, these decisions apply in those states within the relevant Circuit Court's jurisdiction. Unless the United States Supreme Court reverses these holdings, physician-assisted suicide is lawful in these jurisdictions and the responsibility will lie with the legislatures in the affected states to introduce legislation to regulate the practice of physician-assisted suicide. Thus, whilst these developments in the USA illustrate that some opportunity exists for judicial reform, at least within the US constitutional framework,[16] they also demonstrate the constraints on the courts in these circumstances. For example, in the *Compassion in Dying* case,[17] although the majority of the court was clearly of the view that the practice of physician-assisted suicide must be regulated, the court was not in a position to formulate authoritative guidelines safeguarding the practice. Instead, it was recommended that this task be taken up by the legislature and some suggestions were made regarding the possible terms of such legislation.

To suggest that a legislative option is the most suitable method for reform with regard to active voluntary euthanasia is by no means to suggest that legislation should be seen as the inevitable response to a legal problem, particularly in the field of law and medicine where a myriad of complex ethical and professional issues are involved. Clearly, legislation is not a universal panacea and there are, in fact, many difficulties and limitations associated with legislative solutions. To begin with, the legislative process is subject to many pressures and constraints,[18] and the outcome of this process is often the product of political compromise. This may, in many instances, jeopardize or even undermine the integrity of the legislation. Moreover, legislation can never hope to be exhaustive, and the potential always exists for difficulties in interpretation. There are also problems with the inflexibility of legislative solutions. Once enacted, statute law is in force until such time as it is amended or repealed and it is far less amenable to change than judge-made law which can be more directly responsive to the fluctuating

---

[14] *Compassion in Dying* v. *State of Washington* No. 94-35534 (9th Cir. March 6 1996) (*en banc*); *Quill* v. *Vacco* No. 60 (2nd Cir. April 2 1996). See further pp. 101–21 above.

[15] See pp. 115, 116 above.

[16] Note also the Canadian position, in the light of the Canadian Charter of Rights and Freedoms which was relied upon in *Rodriguez* v. *British Columbia (Attorney General)* (see above n. 13): for discussion see pp. 86–94 above.

[17] See above n. 14.

[18] Twining, W. and Meyers, D., *How to Do Things With Rules* 2nd edn. (London, 1982) 293.

demands of society.[19] A further limitation on the operation of legislation is that it is often, on its own, not a complete answer to the difficulties raised. In many instances, legislation will only be successful in achieving its aims if it is accompanied by an educational campaign and the allocation of appropriate resources. In view of these various limitations, there is every reason to reflect carefully before proceeding to a legislative solution and to give due consideration to alternative remedies such as changes in institutional practices or the introduction of voluntary codes of self-regulation.[20] However, notwithstanding its shortcomings, in some instances legislation is a necessary and, indeed, an appropriate response. In view of the unequivocal prohibition of active voluntary euthanasia under existing criminal law, and the fact that any change to the law is likely to require carefully formulated safeguards, this is an area where a legislative approach is particularly appropriate.

Before going on to consider specific options for legislative reform, brief consideration must be given to the claims of some commentators that legalization of active voluntary euthanasia would be contrary to international law on human rights.[21] Essentially the argument takes the form that the introduction of legislation would be contrary to those human rights instruments which make provision for the right to life.[22] However, as was argued in an earlier chapter,[23] the right to life must be capable of being waived,[24] and legislation permitting a doctor to administer active voluntary euthanasia would therefore not be an infringement of the individual's right to life. Thus, there is nothing in international human rights instruments which would prevent the introduction of legislation permitting active voluntary euthanasia.

REFORM OPTIONS

It should be noted from the outset that the various reform options which have been advanced fall into two distinct categories: those which deal

---

[19] For a critique of the inflexibility of statute law and suggestions for change see Calabresi, G., *A Common Law for the Age of Statutes* (Cambridge, Massachusetts, 1982).

[20] Twining and Meyers, *How to Do Things With Rules*, above n. 18, at 303.

[21] See, for example, the view of the European Association of Centres of Medical Ethics regarding the resolution in favour of active voluntary euthanasia before the European Parliament; see Note, 'Euthanasia Vote Deferred' (1991) 70 *Bull.Med.Ethics* 6. Note also the minority view of the Dutch State Commission on Euthanasia; see p. 419 above.

[22] e.g. Article 6 (para. 1) of the International Covenant on Civil and Political Rights 1976 which provides that: 'every human being has the inherent right to life. This right shall be protected by law. No one shall be arbitrarily deprived of his life'. See also Article 2 of the European Convention on Human Rights.

[23] See pp. 216–17 above.   [24] See p. 217 above.

generally with 'mercy killings';[25] and those which are specifically confined to active voluntary euthanasia (or doctor-assisted suicide) in the medical context. Recognition of this distinction is important, because it has implications with regard to the content and potential application of the respective proposals. Consideration will initially be given to options for reform falling within the first category, dealing generally with mercy killing.

A. Mercy Killing

One possible direction for change would be to establish lesser penalties for mercy killing. This could be achieved in a number of ways. One possibility is for the creation of a separate offence for compassionate murder with a lower penalty than for murder. This would enable the courts to take account of the motive of the defendant in determining liability. A proposal along these lines has been supported by a number of commentators and agencies,[26] and has the advantage that the offender is charged with a specific offence other than murder and is liable to a lesser punishment.[27] An alternative possibility is for the introduction of a sentencing discretion allowing for the reduction, or even setting aside, of penalties in cases of homicide prompted by compassionate motives.[28] These two proposals are similar to the position in a number of European countries, where the actor's motive is a critical factor in determining culpability.[29] For example, in both Switzerland and Germany, compassionate killing does not come within the classification of murder but rather manslaughter.[30] Moreover, in determining the appropriate punishment, the courts are required to take into account the defendant's motive which may justify a reduction in sentence.[31] In circum-

---

[25] For a definition of mercy killing, see p. 5 above.

[26] e.g. Meyers, D., *The Human Body and the Law* (Chicago, 1970) 155; Castel, J., 'Nature and Effects of Consent with Respect to the Right to Life and the Right to Physical and Mental Integrity in the Medical Field: Criminal and Private Law Aspects' (1978) 16 *Alta.LRev.* 293, 323. A proposal for the creation of a separate offence was put forward by the English Criminal Law Revision Committee in its working paper on Offences Against the Person (Criminal Law Revision Committee, *Working Paper on Offences Against the Person* (London, 1976) paras 79–87), but the committee resiled from this position in its final report (Criminal Law Revision Committee, Fourteenth Report, *Offences Against the Person* (London, 1980) Cmnd. 7844, para. 115). A similar proposal was considered by the *Royal Commission on Capital Punishment* (London, 1953) Cmnd. 8932; see p. 336, n. 14 above.

[27] Law Reform Commissioner Victoria, Working Paper No. 8, *Murder: Mental Element and Punishment* (1984) 27.

[28] At present, a mandatory sentence of life imprisonment applies in respect of murder in most jurisdictions.

[29] For an excellent discussion of the position under the German and Swiss Penal Codes, see Silving, H., 'Euthanasia: A Study in Comparative Criminal Law' (1954) 103 *UPa.LRev.* 350, 360–8.

[30] See Articles 211 and 212 of the German Penal Code and Article 63 of the Swiss Penal Code.

[31] See Article 213 of the German Penal Code and Article 64 of the Swiss Penal Code.

stances where the killing took place at the victim's request, it falls within a separate category of 'homicide upon request' which attracts a lesser penalty than murder.[32] These factors, either singly or in combination, operate to provide considerable leniency in the treatment of mercy killers in these jurisdictions.

A further possibility is for the creation of a new defence which would reduce the offence from murder to manslaughter.[33] The onus would rest upon the defendant to adduce evidence in support of the defence, and if established, the defendant would be convicted of manslaughter rather than murder. Some commentators have favoured one or more of the foregoing solutions on the grounds that they represent an appropriate compromise. They acknowledge that cases of euthanasia are generally considered less reprehensible than ordinary acts of homicide and therefore deserving of special treatment, yet do not go so far as to formally endorse euthanasia by legalization.[34]

Whilst the implementation of any of these reforms would arguably be an improvement on the present unsatisfactory situation, these proposals are not the appropriate solution to the particular difficulties in the area of medically administered active voluntary euthanasia. The main objection to all of the foregoing proposals in this context is that doctors remain at risk of criminal liability if they engage in the practice.[35] It may, admittedly, be a liability for some lesser offence than murder, or the penalty may be nominal, depending on which proposal is implemented and the form in which it is introduced. The fact remains, however, that doctors who perform active euthanasia at the patient's request would still potentially be exposed to criminal prosecution. One must bear in mind that these particular proposals were not intended to deal specifically with the issue of active voluntary euthanasia in the medical context, but rather were directed generally at compassionate or mercy killings which may arise in a whole range of circumstances. This accounts for the limited nature of these proposals, seeking simply to diminish the liability of the defendant, rather than providing complete immunity.

[32] See Article 216 of the German Penal Code and Article 114 of the Swiss Penal Code respectively.

[33] For consideration of this option see the Law Reform Commissioner Victoria, Working Paper, *Murder: Mental Element and Punishment*, above Ch. 6 n. 22, at 27–8.

[34] Silving, 'Euthanasia: A Study in Comparative Criminal Law', above n. 29, at 388; Meyers, *The Human Body and the Law*, above n. 26, at 155; Sneiderman, B., 'Why not a Limited Defence? A Comment on the Proposals of the Law Reform Commission of Canada on Mercy Killing' (1985) 15 *Man.LJ* 85, at 95–6.

[35] See also Wilson, J., *Death by Decision: The Medical, Moral, and Legal Dilemmas of Euthanasia* (Philadelphia, 1975) 165 where he notes that a legal system that only reduces the penalty for active voluntary euthanasia is not sufficient to meet the problems of contemporary medical practice in terminal cases because it fails to provide adequate guidelines for the difficult life and death decisions that must be made in this context.

An alternative, and more far-reaching reform, would be to create a complete defence to murder in circumstances where the defendant has acted out of compassionate motives. Rachels, for example, has suggested that a plea of mercy killing be acceptable as a defence against a charge of homicide in much the same way that a plea of self-defence is acceptable.[36] Accordingly, someone charged with homicide could plead mercy killing; if it could be shown that the victim while competent requested death, and that the victim was suffering from a painful and terminal illness, the defendant would be acquitted. The onus would be on the mercy killer to present clear and convincing evidence that the patient was competent, terminally ill, and voluntarily chose to die.

Although this proposal has the advantage of offering a doctor (and any other mercy killer) the possibility of a complete acquittal, it still falls short of legalization. Active voluntary euthanasia performed by a doctor would still *prima facie* be unlawful as murder. It would be up to the doctor to raise the defence and a matter for the court to determine whether the defence should be accepted in a particular case. This proposal for a mercy killing defence does not, therefore, provide sufficient protection either to doctors or their patients with regard to medically-administered active voluntary euthanasia. This shortcoming stems from the general nature of the proposal aimed at all mercy killings which is arguably too broad, thereby disregarding the special considerations that arise in cases of medically-assisted death.

Another proposal, which goes somewhat further has been put forward by Williams. In contrast to the other solutions considered above, this particular one is specifically confined to active voluntary euthanasia administered by a medical practitioner.[37] On the basis of this proposal:

No medical practitioner should be guilty of an offence in respect of an act done intentionally to accelerate the death of a patient who is seriously ill, unless it is proved that the act was not done in good faith with the consent of the patient and for the purpose of saving him from severe pain in an illness believed to be of an incurable and fatal character. Under this formula it would be for the physician, if charged, to show that the patient was seriously ill, but for the prosecution to prove that the physician acted from some motive other than the humanitarian one allowed to him by law.[38]

This suggested formulation differs from that of Rachels in that it proceeds on the basis that it is lawful for a medical practitioner to terminate the life of a seriously ill patient and that the onus would be on the prosecution to prove that the act was not done in good faith and with the consent of the

---

[36] Rachels, J., *The End of Life: The Morality of Euthanasia* (Oxford, 1986) 185.

[37] See also Brody, H., 'Assisted Death—A Compassionate Response to Medical Failure' (1992) 327 *New Eng.JMed.* 1384 where he puts forward a proposal for the creation of a defence to a charge of murder or assisted suicide in a genuine case of medically-assisted death.

[38] Williams, *The Sanctity of Life and the Criminal Law,* above Ch. 3 n. 63, at 303.

patient. It therefore represents a form of legalization of active voluntary euthanasia.[39] This proposal also has the advantage that it is specifically confined to medically administered active voluntary euthanasia and can consequently address the special needs in that area. Williams' proposal is nevertheless open to criticism on the grounds that it contains inadequate safeguards for the practice of active voluntary euthanasia. It affords doctors too much discretion in the matter and, as a result, does not provide sufficient protection for patients.[40]

The foregoing analysis has shown that reforms which are directed generally at mercy killings are not the appropriate solution for the particular difficulties raised by the issue of active voluntary euthanasia in the medical context. This is because mercy killing performed by family or friends on the one hand, and medically-administered active voluntary euthanasia on the other, are quite different in nature and involve quite distinct issues. Whilst there is a widespread desire to show leniency to mercy killers few would contend that such offenders should completely escape liability. In the medical context, however, where a doctor acts *bona fide* at the request of a patient and performs active euthanasia, there is a case for saying that a doctor should be protected from incurring criminal liability, provided he or she has acted in accordance with acceptable criteria. The present problems which confront the law with regard to active voluntary euthanasia, therefore, require specialized attention, and the discussion which follows will be confined to this area.

Significantly, many of the objections which have been advanced against the various proposals for change with regard to compassionate or mercy killing do not apply with the same force to medically-administered active voluntary euthanasia. For example, concerns have been raised about the difficulties in establishing the real motives behind a killing in circumstances where the killer may have acted out of mixed motive; partly motivated by compassion for the patient, but also, in part, driven by a desire to put an end to a difficult family situation or to gain some material benefit from the patient's death.[41] More general concerns have also been expressed about

[39] See below pp. 467–93 for further discussion of possible legislative models.

[40] See also Browne, 'Assisted Suicide and Active Voluntary Euthanasia', above Ch. 4 n. 163, at 53. Indeed, Williams himself recognized that this proposal confers on the medical practitioner a wide discretion; Williams, *The Sanctity of Life and the Criminal Law*, above Ch. 3 n. 63, at 302. In fairness to Williams, however, it must be pointed out that this proposal was developed in response to the criticisms of some of the opponents of earlier measures for the legalization of active voluntary euthanasia which had contained rigorous safeguards and procedures. See the Voluntary Euthanasia (Legalisation) Bill 1936 (UK); see p. 334 above.

[41] e.g. Law Reform Commission of Canada, Working Paper, *Euthanasia, Aiding Suicide and the Cessation of Treatment*, above Ch. 6 n. 101, at 50–1. It should be noted, however, that the Canadian Law Reform Commission also raised specific concerns in connection with the legalization of active voluntary euthanasia; see the Law Reform Commission of Canada, Working Paper, above Ch. 6 n. 101, *Euthanasia, Aiding Suicide and the Cessation of Treatment*, 44–8.

the possibility of abuse of any liberalization of the law, with for example, *mala fide* murders being committed and disguised as compassionate murders.[42] However, compared with the more general mercy killing situation, it is reasonable to assume that doctors, operating under their professional codes of practice, are less likely to have some ulterior motive in hastening the death of the patient.

B. *Legalization of Doctor-Assisted Suicide*

One possibility for reform with specific reference to the medical context is for the legalization of doctor-assisted suicide.[43] Such a measure would provide legal protection to a doctor who, at the patient's request, provides the patient with the necessary assistance to commit suicide by, for example, providing the patient with the means for taking his or her life. There is, undeniably, a strong similarity between medically-administered active voluntary euthanasia and doctor-assisted suicide, though under the law as it presently stands, the legal outcomes are markedly different.[44] Obviously, if active voluntary euthanasia is legalized, it would be logical also to legalize doctor-assisted suicide.[45] Indeed, it would be strange if it were lawful if a doctor were to take active steps to end a patient's life, but could not, in the same circumstances, provide the patient with the means of taking his or her own life. The option being considered here, however, presupposes retention of the existing prohibition on medically-administered active voluntary euthanasia and envisages doctor-assisted suicide as the *only* legislative measure.

The possibility of legalization of doctor-assisted suicide has been advanced by a number of commentators and organizations[46] and is seen by many as a preferable alternative to any change with regard to active volun-

[42] Law Reform Commission of Canada, Working Paper, *Euthanasia, Aiding Suicide and the Cessation of Treatment,* above Ch. 6 n. 102, at 51.

[43] This particular option is distinct from proposals for review of the law with regard to assisting suicide generally; see, for example, Law Reform Commission of Canada, Working Paper, *Euthanasia, Aiding Suicide and the Cessation of Treatment,* above Ch. 6 n. 102, at 52–5, and the proposed amendment to the Suicide Act 1961 (Eng.) in England, pursuant to the Suicide Act (Amendment) Bill 1985.

[44] See Chs. 1 and 2.

[45] A law could be framed in such a way that both options would be available to a patient. Alternatively, legislation permitting active voluntary euthanasia could be based on the requirement that the patient is incapable of committing suicide unaided and requires assistance to end his or her life.

[46] For an example of such a proposal, see the bill proposed for the legalization of physician-assisted suicide in New Hampshire, USA; see p. 373, n. 87 above. A number of the voluntary euthanasia societies have put forward legislative proposals for the decriminalization of physician-assisted suicide as an initial reform measure: see, for example, the Death with Dignity Act (better known as 'Measure 16') sponsored by Oregon Right to Die, and in Australia, the Medical Treatment (Assistance to the Dying) Bill 1993 put forward by the Voluntary Euthanasia Society of Victoria. See further, pp. 279, 285–6, 369–73 above. The concept of doctor-assisted suicide has also received support from quite a number of commen-

tary euthanasia. Indeed, as noted earlier, the citizen-initiated referendum in the State of Oregon for legislation permitting physician-assisted suicide was passed by a majority of voters, whereas similar efforts in other states for more far-reaching change have failed.[47] A number of arguments have been put forward in support of this method of reform. An obvious advantage is that patients genuinely wishing to commit suicide would have the benefit of appropriate medical information and assistance in achieving that result. This would reduce many of the risks associated with patient suicide; for example, that the patient's diagnosis and prognosis are inadequately confirmed, and that the means chosen for suicide will be unreliable or inappropriately used. From a practical point of view, the implementation of this proposal of doctor-assisted suicide would require minimal change to existing law. Most jurisdictions have legislation dealing with assisted suicide[48] which could easily be amended to allow for doctor-assisted suicide and regulation of the practice. Achieving legalization of medically-administered active voluntary euthanasia would, by comparison, inevitably be more complicated. Another advantage which is claimed in respect of this particular option is that acceptance of doctor-assisted suicide would at least provide some guarantee of the voluntariness of the patient's decision. One of the concerns often raised with regard to the legalization of active voluntary euthanasia is the difficulty in ascertaining truly voluntary consent.[49] Where, however, the patient's death is precipitated by the patient's own act, there is some assurance that the patient genuinely desired death. It is argued that if a patient who has requested assistance in suicide becomes ambivalent about the idea, they can simply put off the final step.[50] The situation is quite different, it is claimed, if death is brought about by the hand of the doctor: some patients would be too embarrassed or intimidated to express uncertainty to a doctor on the verge of giving a lethal injection, or would be concerned that the doctor might be hesitant to administer the injection at a later time.[51] Another consideration which is advanced in support of doctor-assisted suicide in preference to active voluntary euthanasia is that it minimizes third party involvement. It is reasoned that where

tators: e.g. Crisp, R., 'A Good Death: Who Best to Bring It?' (1987) 1 *Bioethics* 74, 74–5; Gostin, L., 'Drawing a Line Between Killing and Letting Die: The Law, and Law Reform of Medically Assisted Dying' (1993) 21 *JLaw, Med.&Ethics* 94; Syme, R. 'A Patient's Right to a Good Death' (1991) 154 MJA 203.

[47] See pp. 364–8 above.

[48] See pp. 56–7 above.

[49] See pp. 228–34 above.

[50] New York State Task Force on Life and the Law, *When Death Is Sought: Assisted Suicide and Euthanasia in the Medical Context* (New York, 1994) 84.

[51] Note, in this regard, the distinction that is sometimes made between the situation where a doctor provides information or a prescription and instances where the doctor is present at the time of the suicide and directly aids or supervises the act which is argued to pose the same sort of risk of pressure arising from the doctor's presence as active voluntary euthanasia: New York State Task Force on Life and the Law, *When Death Is Sought*, above n. 50, at 84.

the patient is capable of performing the death-inducing act, there is no justification for others to do what that patient can do for him or herself. Further, it is argued, by minimizing the involvement of doctors, one avoids placing the responsibility of killing on others, and avoids the possible risk of emotional trauma to the person who brings death.[52] Finally, proponents of doctor-assisted suicide point out that since this is a far less drastic proposal than the legalization of active voluntary euthanasia, it is likely to enjoy wider acceptability amongst doctors and the community generally.

Although the option of doctor-assisted suicide may be seen as preferable in some respects over the option of active voluntary euthanasia, it is not, on its own, a satisfactory legal response to the present problems with regard to medically-assisted dying. Whilst the possibility of doctor-assisted suicide may be appropriate and adequate in many cases, it does not represent a complete solution to the difficulties in this area. There will always be a proportion of patients who are physically unable to commit suicide. For others, the concept of suicide may for some reason be objectionable, yet they may willingly seek active voluntary euthanasia.[53] If the legal response was limited to doctor-assisted suicide, these categories of individuals would not be provided for.[54] Moreover, in cases of doctor-assisted suicide, there is also the possibility that the patient does not die as quickly as anticipated and further medical intervention is required in order to prevent a lingering death. Such intervention would not be possible if only doctor-assisted suicide were permitted.[55]

In the event that reform of the law were to take this particular course of allowing doctor-assisted suicide, careful consideration would have to be given to the appropriate legislative model for securing such reform. In particular, it would be necessary to define the circumstances in which a doctor could lawfully assist the suicide of a patient;[56] whether, for example, a doctor should be able to assist a person to commit suicide if that person is suffering from a terminal or incurable disease or whether a doctor should be able to assist any sane person who has determined to take his or her own life.[57] Similar problems of definition would of course also arise with at-

[52] See pp. 414–15 above for discussion of the basis of the revised policy of the Royal Dutch Medical Association in the Netherlands where doctor-assisted suicide is now put forward as the preferred option.

[53] See also the argument in Ch. 4.

[54] See also Schiffer, L., 'Euthanasia and the Criminal Law' (1985) 42 *UToronto Fac.LRev.* 93, 107, where she argues that this could even be construed as a form of discrimination against incapacitated people.

[55] The appropriate interrelationship between active voluntary euthanasia and doctor-assisted suicide is dealt with in more detail below.

[56] Note the possible safeguards suggested by the Ninth Circuit Court in *Compassion in Dying* v. *State of Washington* (see above n. 14) (for discussion see pp. 108–9 above).

[57] Trowell, H., 'Suicide and Euthanasia' (1971) BMJ 275.

tempts to legalize active voluntary euthanasia (and will be considered in more detail in that context), but in the area of suicide, special care would need to be taken to ensure that irrational suicide was not encouraged.[58]

C. *Legalization of Active Voluntary Euthanasia*

The most far-reaching legislative option for reform would be the legalization of active voluntary euthanasia so as to enable doctors who choose to do so to respond to a patient's request. It is acknowledged that this would not necessarily be the only way to ensure that doctors are protected from criminal liability. Active voluntary euthanasia could be decriminalized (but still potentially attracting non-criminal penalties), or alternatively, an attempt could be made to emulate the Dutch model through legislation: that is, retaining the criminal sanction for murder in respect of active voluntary euthanasia, but legislating for immunity from prosecution in specified circumstances. Some commentators have stressed the symbolic significance of an approach which reinforces the importance of maintaining a strict prohibition against the deliberate taking of life and emphasizes the exceptional nature of genuine cases of active voluntary euthanasia.[59] However, providing an immunity from prosecution arguably does not go far enough—whilst doctors are provided protection under the law, their conduct would still be characterized as criminal with all the negative implications that would entail. Thus, it is submitted, outright legalization of active voluntary euthanasia would be the most appropriate approach to reform and practically speaking, is the most likely means by which substantive reform is to be achieved. And, as was suggested earlier, this would also logically entail the legalization of doctor-assisted suicide as is the case under the Northern Territory legislation.[60]

Some commentators have argued that even if active voluntary euthanasia is in principle appropriate, it is simply not possible to frame adequate safeguards for its legalization.[61] It is certainly true that concerns about abuse have figured prominently in the debate as to whether or not active voluntary euthanasia should be legalized.[62] Although the task of drawing up suitable legislation is undoubtedly a very difficult one, it would not be impossible, and the difficulty of the task is not a justifiable reason to avoid addressing the problems inherent in the present law and practice. Furthermore, concern regarding the adequacy of safeguards must be interpreted in

---

[58] See further, p. 74 above.

[59] Somerville, M., 'The Song of Death: The Lyrics of Euthanasia' (1993) 9 *JContemp. Health L&Pol'y* 1, 38. See also the New York State Task Force on Life and the Law, *When Death Is Sought*, above Ch. 4 n. 97, at 140–1.

[60] For discussion of the position in the Northern Territory, see pp. 345–57 above.

[61] Kamisar, Y., 'Some Non-Religious Views Against Proposed Mercy-Killing Legislation' (1958) 42 *Minn.LRev.* 969, 978–85.

[62] See pp. 231–4 above.

the light of current practice. As was noted in an earlier chapter, there is incontrovertible evidence to suggest that active voluntary euthanasia is to some extent already being performed, but in a totally unregulated fashion.[63] Thus, the current situation inevitably involves some risk of abuse, and there is good reason to believe that the legalization of the practice, with appropriate regulatory procedures, would in fact reduce the possibility of covert and improper practices. It would, however, be naive to suggest that a proposal for the legalization of active voluntary euthanasia would be completely free of risk. All existing laws are potentially open to abuse, and a law permitting the practice of active voluntary euthanasia would be no exception. Looking at the situation realistically, the aim of legislation legalizing active voluntary euthanasia would be to minimize the risk of abuse by the imposition of stringent safeguards regulating the practice.

An initial matter which must be addressed is the approach which legislative reform should take. There are obviously a whole host of possibilities, ranging from very formal procedures, requiring judicial review of all euthanasia decisions[64] at one extreme, to a very simple legislative model with a minimum of safeguards and formality which vests an enormous discretion in the doctor.[65] As we have seen, over the years, quite a number of proposals have been put forward for the legalization of active voluntary euthanasia.[66] Some have actually taken the form of legislative initiatives (including the Rights of the Terminally Ill Act 1995 which has been passed in the Northern Territory),[67] others have been proposed by commentators in the campaign for legalization.[68] The Netherlands' model for the practice of active voluntary euthanasia is also an option upon which legislation could

[63] See pp. 134–8 above.

[64] See, for example, the early legislative proposals in the USA, in particular, the 1937 Nebraska Bill and the 1938 New York Bill for the legalization of voluntary active euthanasia. The English Voluntary Euthanasia (Legalisation) Bill of 1936, upon which these US bills were largely based, proposed the use of a euthanasia referee, appointed by the Minister of Health; see p. 334 above. A number of commentators have also proposed a system of judicial review; e.g. Fletcher, J., 'Morals Medicine and the Law—Symposium: The Issues' (1956) 31 *NYULRev.* 1157, 1159–60; Alschuler, A., 'The Right to Die' (1991) 141 *New LJ* 1637.

[65] e.g. Williams' proposal in *The Sanctity of Life and the Criminal Law*, above Ch. 3 n. 63, at 302–9.

[66] See pp. 334–6, 363–8 above.

[67] Other examples include the English Voluntary Euthanasia (Legalisation) Bill 1936 and the Voluntary Euthanasia Bill 1969, and more recently, the proposed physician 'aid in dying' legislation in the USA. For fuller coverage of these legislative developments, see pp. 334–6, 364–8 above.

[68] e.g. Williams' proposal in *The Sanctity of Life and the Criminal Law*, above Ch. 3 n. 63, at 302–9. Note also the model acts which have been suggested by commentators in the USA: e.g. Cole, S. and Shea, M., 'Voluntary Euthanasia: A Proposed Remedy' (1975) 39 *Alb.LRev.* 826; Steele, W. and Hill, B., 'A Plea for a Legal Right to Die' (1976) 29 *Okla.LRev.* 328. Note should also be made of the conditions which were set out in the course of the *Rodriguez* litigation by McEachern CJ of the British Columbia Court of Appeal (*Rodriguez* v. *Attorney General of British Columbia, Attorney General of Canada* see above n. 13, at 24–5) and Lamer CJ of the Supreme Court of Canada *Rodriguez* v. *British Columbia (Attorney General)* (see above n. 13) (both dissenting). For discussion, see p. 92, n. 116 above.

be based.[69] Although the guidelines for the practice of active voluntary euthanasia in the Netherlands have been developed by the courts, as distinct from the legislature, the experience which has been gained in that country provides a valuable insight into the appropriate criteria and safeguards that legislation permitting active voluntary euthanasia might contain.

The dilemma inevitably faced in framing legislation for the legalization of active voluntary euthanasia is to strike the appropriate balance between the inclusion of adequate safeguards and procedures for the protection of both doctors and patients and, at the same time, to avoid excessive formality and bureaucratization of the procedures for active voluntary euthanasia.[70] Proposals for legalization which involve judicial review of the patient's request for active euthanasia, or the involvement of a 'euthanasia referee' or other official or body,[71] seek to provide for a formalized application procedure; the patient seeking active euthanasia brings an application or petition, together with supporting medical evidence, before the court or euthanasia official, and following an investigation of the case, and having regard to the criteria for active voluntary euthanasia under the enabling legislation,[72] a determination would be made as to whether the patient's request should be granted. Proponents of this model for reform contend that the advantage of such a procedure is that there is an independent investigation of the circumstances and an objective determination as to the permissibility of active voluntary euthanasia. This, they claim, provides an important opportunity to ascertain the patient's decision-making capacity, the voluntariness of the patient's request, and other specified preconditions for the fulfilment of the euthanasia request. However, legislative reform based upon a model of judicial review is subject to the criticism that it is a cumbersome procedure which unnecessarily bureaucratizes the handling of euthanasia requests. There is also the argument that the courts (or similar bodies) are, in any event, not a suitable decision-making forum for euthanasia determinations. The legiti-

---

[69] For discussion of the Netherlands' position see Ch. 7.

[70] Note Williams, *The Sanctity of Life and the Criminal Law*, above Ch. 3 n. 63, at 298–302 where he comments on the irony that legislation which provided for the legalization of active voluntary euthanasia and contained stringent safeguards (the 1936 Voluntary Euthanasia (Legalisation) Bill) (UK) was criticized on the grounds that it would bring too much formality into the sickroom.

[71] For example, Helme, T. and Padfield, N., 'Setting Euthanasia on the Level' (1993) 15 *Liverpool LRev.* 75, where it is suggested that a system of euthanasia tribunals be introduced in addition to an alternative procedure of formal euthanasia notification. Note also the early suggestion made by the Australian Voluntary Euthanasia Society (as it then was) for the use of a euthanasia commissioner. See Note, 'Euthanasia Commissioner' (1974) Vol. 1 No. 3 *AVES Newsletter* 5. Note also Miller *et al.*, 'Regulating Physician-Assisted Death', above n. 12, at 121–2 where the authors suggest the creation of a palliative care committee for prospective review in difficult or disputed cases. A number of commentators have also suggested the use of ethics committees to review patients' requests and authorize the performance of active voluntary euthanasia; e.g. Zaremba, J., 'Death with Dignity: Implementing One's Right to Die' (1987) 64 *UDet.LRev.* 557, 572.

[72] See below.

mate need to provide safeguards and to protect against abuse can be met without requiring judicial or quasi-judicial participation in the euthanasia procedure. There is obviously a need for certain formal procedural requirements if active voluntary euthanasia is to be legalized, but these must be kept to a minimum if we are to avoid their becoming a barrier to relief.

Consideration must now be given to the appropriate safeguards and criteria for the legalization of active voluntary euthanasia. Whilst the following discussion is focused on active voluntary euthanasia, it should be understood that most of the issues raised apply equally to the legalization of doctor-assisted suicide.

Possible safeguards for the legalization of active voluntary euthanasia

Condition of the patient

An initial question which arises is whether it is appropriate to have any reference to the condition of the patient as a precondition for eligibility for active voluntary euthanasia. Taking a very liberal view of self-determination, it could be argued that all patients who have decision-making capacity should be free to seek active euthanasia, regardless of their medical condition. However, if there were no requirements at all as to the condition of the person seeking active euthanasia, the spectre would be raised of euthanasia upon request, for whatever reason. The focus of this work is on the contemporary understanding of euthanasia, that is, euthanasia in the medical context in circumstances where the patient is suffering from some illness or disability,[73] and it is in this area that there are particular problems with law and practice which need to be addressed. The arguments which have been developed in this work have proceeded on the basis that only in rare and unusual circumstances is there justification for creating an exception to the normal criminal prohibition on the taking of life.[74] Applying this principle in the present context, the justification for permitting active voluntary euthanasia is therefore only established in cases where the person requesting it is suffering from a terminal or other serious incurable condition which he or she finds intolerable. Aside from these considerations, there is an additional argument in support of confining the category of candidates for active euthanasia in the interests of minimizing the potential for abuse and mistake. Thus, on the assumption that it is both necessary and appropriate to include some reference to the patient's condition in the eligibility criteria for active voluntary euthanasia,[75] attention will now be given to possible preconditions which could be imposed.

---

[73] See p. 4 above.　　[74] See pp. 14–21 above.

[75] For an example of a proposal for voluntary euthanasia legislation which deliberately does not contain any limitation as to the condition of the patient, see Steele and Hill, 'A Plea for a Legal Right to Die', above n. 68, at 343.

A number of the legislative proposals, including the legislation which has been enacted in the Northern Territory, have proceeded on the basis that the patient must be in a 'terminal' state before he or she is eligible for active voluntary euthanasia. This would certainly be one way of confining the category of candidates for whom active voluntary euthanasia would be available and it could be argued that the case for legalization is at its strongest in respect of patients whose condition is terminal.[76] However, proposals of this kind are arguably too limited in their operation, and would not permit active voluntary euthanasia in respect of an incurable and suffering patient who is not expected to die from his or her condition.[77] There are also problems in the application of this requirement (particularly where terminal illness is defined by reference to a specified period of time[78]), because of the notorious difficulties in accurately predicting a terminal patient's life expectancy. In the Northern Territory, at the recommendation of the Northern Territory Select Committee on Euthanasia, the specific reference in the original bill to the likelihood of death within 12 months was removed and replaced with the more general requirement that the patient's condition be terminal: the Act limits requests for assistance to patients who, in the course of a terminal illness, are experiencing pain, suffering and/or distress to an extent unacceptable to the patient.[79] As we have seen, because of the fairly broad definition of 'terminal illness',[80] the legislation provides the option of assistance in dying to patients whose condition will result in death regardless of available treatment, as well as patients whose condition may not strictly be terminal, but who reject certain life-saving treatment as

[76] Note, for example, the reasoning in *Compassion in Dying* v. *State of Washington* (see above n. 147 p. 219) (for discussion see pp. 103, 108–9 above) where it was held that the State's interest in the preservation of life and the prevention of suicide was at its lowest, and the individual's interest in controlling the manner and time of death, at its highest, in circumstances where the patient's condition was terminal.

[77] Indeed, it could be argued that provided pain is adequately controlled, the terminally ill patient is less likely to need active voluntary euthanasia than someone whose equally distressing illness or disability is not terminal, since the latter could face many years of suffering; see Smoker, B., 'Remember the Non-Terminally Ill and Disabled' (1991) 43 *VES Newsletter* 10. In the Netherlands, the requirement of a terminal illness was rejected at quite an early stage by the Dutch courts and attempts by the Dutch Minister for Justice to argue for a more restrictive interpretation have been unsuccessful: for discussion see pp. 408, 445 above.

[78] e.g. under the Californian Humane and Dignified Death Act proposed in 1988: see pp. 365–6 above. Note also the Oregon Death with Dignity Act 1994 (providing for doctor-assisted suicide) which contains a requirement that the patient is suffering from a terminal disease defined as an incurable and irreversible disease that has been medically confirmed and will, within reasonable medical judgement, produce death within 6 months.

[79] Note also s. 7(1)(b)(i) which stipulates that before a doctor may assist a patient to die, the patient must be suffering from an illness that will, in the normal course and without the application of extraordinary measures, result in the death of the patient. For detailed discussion of the Northern Territory legislation see pp. 345–57 above.

[80] Defined in s. 3 as an illness which, in reasonable medical judgement, will in the normal course, without the application of extraordinary measures or of treatment unacceptable to the patient, result in the death of the patient.

being unacceptable to them, provided there is some degree of imminence of death in the absence of that treatment. Whilst the amendments made are an improvement on the original bill, in particular, the removal of a rigid time-frame for the interpretation of 'terminal illness', the provision made under the Northern Territory Rights of the Terminally Ill Act 1995 is arguably still too limiting.

One possibility is to include incurability as a criterion for active voluntary euthanasia as has been suggested in some legislative proposals.[81] A require-ment that the patient's condition be either terminal or incurable is less restrictive, since, by definition, the patient need not actually be dying, but simply have a condition which cannot be cured. If this approach were adopted the field of potential candidates for active voluntary euthanasia would be significantly expanded. For example, a quadriplegic or a person suffering from some degenerative disorder such as multiple sclerosis, would potentially be eligible for active voluntary euthanasia. The advantage of including incurability as a criterion as an alternative to 'terminal illness' is that it is less arbitrary and uncertain in its application and leaves greater scope to the patient to determine whether active voluntary euthanasia is an appropriate option.[82] However, in view of the wide variety of possible incurable conditions ranging from the trivial to the life-threatening, it would be necessary to stipulate that the condition of which the patient complains must be objectively serious.[83]

It is instructive in this context to have regard to the Netherland' criteria for active voluntary euthanasia which simply require that there must be 'physical or mental suffering which the sufferer finds unbearable'.[84] This clearly implies that the patient's suffering stems from a physical or mental condition, but there is no stipulation as to the nature or seriousness of that condition. This formulation has the advantage of conceptual simplicity and avoids the need to determine the state of the patient's condition (whether it be 'terminal' or 'incurable'.) It does, however, represent an expansion of

[81] See, for example, the Voluntary Euthanasia Bill 1969 (UK) which had substituted the requirement of an 'irremediable' condition for the requirement of a 'fatal' condition contained in the 1936 Voluntary Euthanasia (Legalisation) Bill (UK). 'Irremediable' condition was defined under the legislation as a serious physical illness or impairment reasonably thought in the patient's case to be incurable and expected to cause him severe distress or render him incapable of rational existence; see p. 334 above.

[82] Carl, L., 'The Right to Voluntary Euthanasia' (1988) 10 *Whittier LRev.* 489, 548. This was also the view taken by the Institute of Medical Ethics, Working Party on the Ethics of Prolonging Life and Assisting Death, 'Assisted Death' (1990) 336 *Lancet* 610.

[83] For example, O'Brien, S., 'Facilitating Euthanatic, Rational Suicide: Help Me Go Gentle Into That Good Night' (1987) 31 *St.LouisULJ* 599, 665 where she refers, with approval, to the suggested requirement that the 'health of the suicide beneficiary is permanently, implacably and seriously impaired'.

[84] See p. 400 above. There is an additional requirement that the suffering and the desire to die must be lasting but this relates more to the durability of the request (discussed below) and is not tantamount to requiring that the patient's condition be incurable.

the range of potentially eligible candidates for active voluntary euthanasia; theoretically, *any* physical or mental condition would suffice, provided that it causes unbearable suffering to the patient. Although there is no evidence from the Dutch case law that this criterion causes difficulties in practice, there is a case for suggesting that in framing legislation, a somewhat stricter and more objective requirement be imposed with regard to establishing the condition of the patient. The Netherlands' guidelines do, however, provide a useful model in their approach to the issue of a patient's suffering. The existence of unbearable suffering caused by the patient's condition is a critical consideration under any proposal for legalization as it constitutes an important justification for a doctor to take steps at the patient's request to end the life of the patient. Under the Netherlands' criterion, the measure of suffering is to be determined subjectively, by reference to what the *patient* finds unbearable. Because of the impossibility of objectively quantifying suffering that a patient experiences as a result of a particular condition, the assessment of this criterion must inevitably be subjective.

Some proposals for legalization also refer to the presence of pain as an additional requirement alongside other preconditions.[85] It would be impossible to gauge objectively the extent of pain that a patient is experiencing, so as with the notion of 'suffering', a patient's pain would have to be subjectively assessed. However, it could be argued that the reference to pain is, in any event, inappropriate. With the development of palliative care, the situation has now been reached where most pain can be relieved.[86] Moreover, experience has shown that the presence of pain is rarely of itself a reason for a patient to request active euthanasia.[87] It is therefore recommended that pain not be included as an additional criterion. The notion of suffering in the criterion considered above is, in any event, sufficiently broad to encompass circumstances where a patient is experiencing pain.

A difficult question which arises with regard to eligibility for active voluntary euthanasia concerns the status of mental disorders. The more expansive proposals for legalization have extended eligibility to persons suffering

[85] See, for example, the Bill introduced into the New York State legislature in 1938 which referred to a person suffering from 'severe physical pain caused by a disease for which no remedy affording relief or recovery is at the time known to medical science'.

[86] See p. 238 above.

[87] The Remmelink study in the Netherlands found that the most frequent reason for patient requests for euthanasia was 'loss of dignity': pain was mentioned in a significant number of cases but was only rarely put forward as the sole reason behind the request: van der Maas, P. *et al.*, *Euthanasia and Other Medical Decisions Concerning the End of Life: An Investigation Performed Upon Request of the Commission of Inquiry into the Medical Practice Concerning Euthanasia* Health Policy Monographs, Volume 2 (1992) 45. See further p. 239 above. Note also Back, A. et al., 'Physician-Assisted Suicide and Euthanasia in Washington State: Patient Requests and Physician Responses' (1996) 275 JAMA 919, 924 where the concerns of the patients requesting physician-assisted death were analysed from the perspective of their physicians: most patients were worried about losing control, being a burden, being dependent, and losing dignity—severe pain was not a common patient concern.

from certain organically based mental disorders,[88] and it could be argued that this category should be broadened even further to include all mental illnesses which cause the person severe distress.[89] Under the Netherlands' criteria for example, active voluntary euthanasia is potentially available to all patients who are experiencing 'physical *or mental* suffering which the sufferer finds unbearable'[90] and the recent decision of the Dutch Supreme Court in the *Chabot* case clearly establishes that the mental suffering of a patient can be the basis for the defence of *noodtoestand*.[91]

An obvious difficulty when considering mentally impaired patients is their capacity to request active euthanasia voluntarily. Whilst some forms of mental impairment are permanent and would render a patient permanently incompetent, there are other mental conditions, such as certain forms of depression and anxiety, which do not affect the patient's decision-making capacity. The question then arises as to whether a patient who suffers from some form of irremediable mental impairment, but has decision-making capacity, should be eligible for active voluntary euthanasia. As was acknowledged by the Dutch Supreme Court, there is no reason in principle why such persons should be excluded, simply because they suffer from a mental, rather than a physical condition. Indeed, it has been officially recognized that there is no necessary correspondence between mental illness and the presence or absence of decision-making capacity either in fact or in law.[92] However, extra care would obviously need to be taken in such cases in ascertaining the patient's capacity to make this decision and the voluntariness of the patient's request.

On the basis of the foregoing analysis it is submitted that the eligibility criteria for the legalization of active voluntary euthanasia should comprise a twofold test: first, that the person requesting active euthanasia has a terminal or serious incurable physical or mental condition (to be objectively assessed and documented by medically qualified persons[93]); secondly, that the patient's condition causes suffering intolerable to the patient.

One issue which needs to be addressed is the status of alternative treatments which may be available to the patient. It might, for example be argued that there should be an additional requirement that the patient's

[88] See, for example, the HB 137 (1973) and HB 256 (1975) of the Montana Legislature and HB 143 of the Idaho Legislature (1969) which include reference to mental impairment provided that it is founded in a condition of 'brain damage or deterioration'.

[89] e.g. Browne, 'Assisted Suicide and Active Voluntary Euthanasia', above Ch. 4 n. 163, at 54.

[90] Author's emphasis.

[91] See pp. 404–9 above.

[92] President's Commission for the Study of Ethical Problems in Medicine and Biomedical and Behavioural Research, *Deciding to Forgo Life-Sustaining Treatment: A Report on the Ethical, Medical and Legal Issues in Treatment Decisions* (Washington, 1983) 123.

[93] The role of medical practitioners with regard to active voluntary euthanasia including the need for independent verification of certain key matters, is dealt with in more detail below.

suffering cannot be relieved or mitigated by other means. This would have the advantage of ensuring that all other options have been explored, including the provision of palliative care, thus reinforcing that active voluntary euthanasia should only be available as a last resort. However, if we are to avoid undermining the patient's autonomy, this additional requirement is only acceptable if it is determined by reference to the patient's wishes; that is, framed in terms that there are no alternatives *acceptable to the patient*. This is the approach which has been taken under the Netherlands' criteria: in the Netherlands, patients (with the exception of psychiatric patients) are free to reject any medical interventions even though that may rule out reasonable alternative treatments.[94] Under the Northern Territory legislation, the requirements are somewhat more stringent in that palliative care options must be considered and tried where there is a reasonable prospect of their providing relief. The Rights of the Terminally Ill Act 1995 (NT) stipulates that the doctor must advise the patient about his or her palliative care options, and the doctor is precluded from assisting a patient if he or she is of the view that there are palliative care options reasonably available to the patient to alleviate the patient's pain and suffering to levels acceptable to the patient.[95] As we saw from the earlier analysis of this legislation, this provision in effect precludes a patient from rejecting reasonable palliative care options. If available, reasonable palliative care options must at least be tried. It is only in circumstances where such palliative care has been provided, but does not alleviate the patient's pain and suffering to levels acceptable to the patient (that is, subjectively assessed) that a medical practitioner can proceed to provide a patient with assistance to terminate his or her life.[96] The approach taken under the Rights of the Terminally Ill Act 1995 (NT) strongly promotes the use of palliative care but it does mean that patients are required to try reasonable palliative care options that are available before being at liberty to reject them. Clearly one must strike a balance between individual autonomy and freedom of choice on the one hand and on the other, the need to promote the use of palliative care and ensure that active voluntary euthanasia is a measure of last resort. In all the circumstances, the approach taken under the Northern Territory legislation does not appear unreasonable as the effect of palliative care options for a particular patient cannot be known until they are tried. Significantly though, the decision rests with the patient as to whether the available palliative care can alleviate the patient's pain and suffering to levels acceptable to the patient.

One particular issue warranting consideration is whether pregnant

---

[94] See pp. 406–7 above.   [95] See p. 353 above.

[96] Note the requirement in s. 8(2) of the Rights of the Terminally Ill Act 1995 (NT) that the patient must first indicate to the medical practitioner the patient's wish to proceed in pursuance of the request.

women should be eligible for active voluntary euthanasia.[97] In a number of the proposals for the legalization of active voluntary euthanasia, pregnant women are expressly excluded from eligibility,[98] and this has raised opposition from supporters of the rights of women.[99] Significantly, these proposals have emanated from the USA where the State is recognized as having a compelling interest in preserving the life of the foetus, once the foetus becomes 'viable'.[100] In common law jurisdictions such as the United Kingdom and Australia, however, an unborn child has no legal rights separate from its mother,[101] so if active voluntary euthanasia were legalized, there would be no legal impediment to permitting a pregnant woman, who in all other respects meets the eligibility criteria, from seeking and being given active euthanasia.[102] Whether, as a matter of policy, it is appropriate to exclude pregnant women from eligibility is of course a separate matter. In the interests of protecting the autonomy of the patient, as well as avoiding undue complexity in the legislation, it is recommended that no such limitation be included in any legislative reform. There would, in any event, be significant difficulties in the application of any such requirement.[103]

Reference was made earlier to some of the claimed advantages of allowing medically-assisted suicide over active voluntary euthanasia. Because

[97] For discussion, see, for example, Cole and Shea, 'Voluntary Euthanasia: A Proposed Remedy', above n. 68, at 845–7. This issue has already arisen with regard to living will legislation; Gelfand, G., 'Living Will Statutes: The First Decade' (1987) *Wis.L.Rev.* 737, 778–80.

[98] e.g. under the Humane and Dignified Death Act proposed in California (discussed by Risley, R., 'What the Humane and Dignified Death Initiative Does' (1986) 1 *Euthanasia Rev.* 221, 224), and the proposal of Cole and Shea, 'Voluntary Euthanasia: A Proposed Remedy', above n. 68, at 845–7 where a female who is 20 or more weeks pregnant, and who, with reasonable certainty could survive to deliver a child, is excluded from the definition of a 'qualified person'.

[99] For a critical discussion of the issues see Carl, 'The Right to Voluntary Euthanasia', above n. 82, at 549–50.

[100] *Roe* v. *Wade* 410 US 113 (1973).

[101] *Re F (in utero)* [1988] Fam. 123 (C.A.); *C* v. *S* [1988] QB 135 (C.A.); *Paton* v. *BPAS* [1979] QB 276 (C.A.); *F and F* [1989] FLC 92-031; *Attorney-General for the State of Queensland (ex rel. Kerr) and Anor* v. *T* (1983) 57 ALJR 285, 286.

[102] Note, however, the English case of *Re S (Adult: Refusal of Treatment)* [1992] 3 WLR 806 in which a pregnant woman, carrying a viable foetus was forced to undergo an emergency caesarean against her wishes to save the life of the foetus. For criticism of this decision see Morgan, D., 'Whatever Happened to Consent?' (1992) 142 *New LJ* 1448. This ruling was influenced by comments made by Lord Donaldson MR in *Re T* [1992] 3 WLR 782 where, whilst upholding the right of a competent adult to refuse medical treatment, he left open the question whether it was appropriate for a court to intervene in circumstances where the decision of a pregnant woman to refuse medical treatment would affect the life of a viable foetus. However, the status of this decision must be questioned in the light of subsequent cases, particularly *Airedale NHS Trust* v. *Bland* (see above Ch. 1 n. 41). For further discussion, see p. 42, n. 137 above.

[103] For example, how would the limitation be framed? Would it, as Cole and Shea suggest, ('Voluntary Euthanasia: A Proposed Remedy', above n. 68) be limited to circumstances where the woman could with reasonable certainty survive to deliver a live child or would it also apply in circumstances where the woman is not expected to survive the normal period of gestation?

medically-assisted suicide is seen by some as a preferable option, the suggestion has been made that the option of active voluntary euthanasia should be confined to patients who are physically unable to commit suicide.[104] Whilst there may be some advantages attached to such a proposal, it is submitted that on balance, it would be an unjustifiable restriction on access to medical assistance in dying. As noted earlier, some people may find the concept of suicide objectionable, yet would willingly avail themselves of the option of medically-administered active euthanasia. To impose a rigid requirement that all patients who seek death must be actively involved in the bringing about of that death (assuming they are physically capable of doing so) does not, in all the circumstances, seem warranted or appropriate. A more moderate approach has been advocated by the Royal Dutch Medical Association in its 1995 *Vision on Euthanasia*. As was explained in the preceding chapter,[105] the General Board of the Association has stated its preference for the patient, where possible, to self-administer the drugs; if a patient should have prohibitive objections to doing so, it would be necessary to once again examine the deliberateness of the patient's request. If such an approach were adopted, active voluntary euthanasia would only be administered in cases where the patient was unable to self-administer the necessary drugs, or where the patient had real objections to doing so, yet could establish the genuineness of their request. This approach may have some merit: the involvement of doctors is kept to a minimum (they would supervise the patient's suicide), and active voluntary euthanasia would only be administered where necessary. It would be important, however, to ensure that patients who do not wish to self-administer the drugs are not inappropriately denied assistance. Doctors would have to be sensitive to patient's concerns and the reasons they put forward in seeking the direct assistance of a doctor in the form of active voluntary euthanasia. Doctor-assisted suicide certainly has some role to play under a system which contemplates active voluntary euthanasia as a last resort. As some of the surveys of the medical profession have indicated,[106] there would always be some doctors who would be willing to assist a patient to commit suicide but would not perform active voluntary euthanasia. In circumstances where a patient turns to a doctor for assistance in dying, doctor-assisted suicide should be canvassed as a genuine alternative which may be more acceptable

---

[104] e.g. Wolhandler, S., 'Voluntary Euthanasia for the Terminally Ill and the Constitutional Right to Privacy' (1983–84) 69 *CornellLRev* 363, 382. See also the legislative proposal put forward by Michael Moore MLA in the Australian Capital Territory: Voluntary and Natural Death Bill 1993. Significantly, this limitation was removed from a subsequent proposal he put forward: Medical Treatment (Amendment) Bill 1995. This Bill did, however, contain a clause to the effect that if a person is capable of doing so, they may self-administer or assist in administering the substance to terminate his or her life. For general discussion, see pp. 342–4, 361 above.

[105] See pp. 414–15 above.   [106] For discussion, see pp. 135–7, 307–9, 328–9 above.

to some doctors and some patients. Provided that each of these forms of assistance in dying are potentially available the autonomy of both patients and doctors would be maximized.

Voluntariness of the patient's request

One of the main concerns about the legalization of active voluntary euthanasia is the fear that it may lead to abuse, with patients' lives being terminated without their explicit request, or through more subtle means, such as pressure being brought to bear on a patient to request active voluntary euthanasia.[107] Ascertaining the voluntariness of the patient's request is, therefore, of the utmost importance in the decision to administer euthanasia. It would accordingly be appropriate for any legislation permitting active euthanasia to require clear and convincing evidence that the patient genuinely wants such assistance and that the patient has made that request free from coercion and pressure from others.

There are a number of preconditions which are connected with the voluntariness of the patient's request.[108] First, the patient must have decision-making capacity of a level commensurate with the gravity of the decision. There has been some debate as to whether psychiatric evaluation of the patient should be a mandatory requirement to confirm decision-making capacity.[109] Some commentators have argued for the need for careful psychiatric scrutiny in all cases. Others have suggested that it would be inappropriate for this to be prescribed in legislation; it should be left to the discretion of the treating doctor to seek specialist medical assistance as he or she deems appropriate in the circumstances.[110] As was evident from the earlier discussion regarding the Northern Territory legislation,[111] from the outset, the aim of the Rights of the Terminally Ill Act 1995 (NT) has been to ensure independent evaluation of the patient's mental state in all cases. In its original form, the Rights of the Terminally Ill Act contained a requirement that the consulting medical practitioner holds a diploma of psychological medicine or its equivalent and can confirm that the patient is not

---

[107] See pp. 231–4 above.

[108] One possible precondition which could be imposed is that the request for active euthanasia must originate from the patient and must not be the product of suggestion by any other person. Although such a requirement might provide some assurance that the patient's request is voluntary, it would appear to be somewhat limiting. Circumstances can readily be envisaged where a doctor *bona fide* discusses options with the patient, including the possibility of an early release from suffering by the administration of active euthanasia and once informed of the possibility, the patient genuinely and voluntarily wishes to proceed with this option. This practice occurs in the Netherlands and is accepted as active voluntary euthanasia; see generally Ch. 7.

[109] See Carl, 'The Right to Voluntary Euthanasia', above n. 82, at 544–6.

[110] See also Ashby, M., 'Hard Cases, Causation and Care of the Dying' (1995) 3 *JLaw&Med*. 152, 159. This is, in effect, the approach that has been adopted under the Oregon Death with Dignity Act 1994 in relation to doctor-assisted suicide: see pp. 370–1 above.

[111] See pp. 345–57 above.

suffering from a treatable clinical depression in respect of the illness. However, as was noted earlier, the diploma of psychological medicine is an obsolete qualification. Amendments have since been made by the Northern Territory Parliament for the removal of this requirement and the inclusion of an additional requirement (quite apart from the involvement of a second medical practitioner) that the patient be assessed by a qualified psychiatrist and that the psychiatrist has confirmed that the patient is not suffering from a treatable clinical depression in respect of the illness.[112] This aspect of the Northern Territory legislation has merit and ought to be adopted in future legislative proposals for the legalization of active voluntary euthanasia.[113] Whilst this is, without doubt, an onerous requirement to impose, it would virtually eliminate doubt about a patient's mental state. Problem of undiagnosed clinical depression in terminal patients, particularly the elderly, have recently been highlighted.[114] This would suggest that leaving the decision of whether such assessment is necessary to the judgement of the treating doctor would be insufficient protection for those patients whose request stems from treatable, but undiagnosed, clinical depression.

Secondly, in view of the seriousness and finality of active voluntary euthanasia, it is appropriate to impose an age limitation, such that only an adult (that is, a person over the age of 18 years) is eligible for its administration.[115] Thirdly, the patient's doctor must be satisfied, on reasonable grounds, that the patient's decision to request active euthanasia has been made freely and voluntarily and has not been induced by pressure from others. This should be verified by an independent medical practitioner as well as the psychiatrist who assesses the patient mental state.[116] Fourthly, the patient's decision to request active euthanasia must be an informed one. In order for the patient to make an informed choice the patient must be given full information about his or her condition and prognosis, including any element of uncertainty in diagnosis or prognosis. Full disclosure is essential to the unfettered exercise of the right to self-determination. Fifth,

---

[112] Rights of the Terminally Ill Amendment Act 1996 (NT). For further discussion, see pp. 348–9 above.

[113] It should be noted that this was amongst the conditions laid down by McEachern CJ of the British Columbia Court of Appeal in *Rodriguez* v. *Attorney General of British Columbia, Attorney General of Canada* (above n. 13) and supported by Lamer CJ of the Supreme Court of Canada (*Rodriguez* v. *British Columbia (Attorney General)* (above n. 13)) (both dissenting). For discussion see p. 92, n. 161 above. It was also amongst the list of possible safeguards put forward by the majority in *Compassion in Dying* v. *State of Washington* (above n. 14) (for discussion see p. 92 above).

[114] Chochinov, H. et al., 'Desire for Death in the Terminally Ill' (1995) 152 *Am. JPsychiatry* 1185; Conwell, Y. and Caine, E., 'Rational Suicide and the Right to Die' (1991) 325 *New Eng.JMed.* 1100.

[115] This has in fact been a feature of most proposals. For some notable exceptions, see for example, the euthanasia Bill introduced into the Wisconsin Legislature (HB 1207) which allowed for a person of 7 years of age to request active euthanasia.

[116] This is discussed in more detail below.

the patient's request for active euthanasia must be durable. The durability of the patient's request can be confirmed by requiring that the request be repeated over an extended period of time before it is acted upon. This would ensure that there is ample opportunity for the patient to reflect upon his or her decision. It also provides some guarantee that the patient's request for active euthanasia is made earnestly and is enduring and not the product of a hasty and ill-conceived decision. Various suggestions have been made as to the appropriate duration of a 'cooling off' or 'waiting period' to provide some objective evidence of the durability of the patient's request.[117] What matters is not so much a fixed time-frame, which may in practice be rather arbitrary,[118] but that there is some objective assessment of the patient's request and the circumstances in which it is made to establish that the request is in fact a durable one. It is also important that the patient be given the opportunity to revoke the request at any time, regardless of his or her physical or mental condition and that the patient be informed of their continued right to change their mind. Whilst the patient should, in practice, be encouraged to inform his or her family of the decision to request active euthanasia, this is a matter which must be left to the discretion of the patient.[119]

Finally, certain formalities with regard to evidencing patient consent are essential. The patient's request for active euthanasia should be in writing, and signed by the patient.[120] Further, the request should be witnessed by two independent witnesses, who can testify that to the best of their knowledge, the patient is acting voluntarily and in an informed manner. Although these requirements may attract the criticism of excessive formality, they are important procedural safeguards for the performance of active voluntary euthanasia. If a patient is required to make his or her request in writing, it is more likely to be the product of serious thought and reflection. Moreover, a written request for active euthanasia constitutes evidence of a patient's

---

[117] For example, the Northern Territory Rights of the Terminally Ill Act 1995 specifies a 7-day waiting period from the initial making of the request and the completion of the certificate of request and a further 48 hours must elapse after the signing of the certificate before a doctor can lawfully assist in terminating the life of the patient.

[118] It should be noted that in the Netherlands, the durability of the patient's request is one of the well established requirements for the performance of active voluntary euthanasia, however, no fixed time-frame is specified.

[119] Note the terms of the Oregon Death with Dignity Act 1994 (in relation to doctor-assisted suicide). See further, pp. 370–2 above. There is nothing in the Northern Territory legislation about informing relatives, although there is a requirement that the medical practitioner is satisfied that the patient has considered the possible implications of the patient's decision on his or her family: s. 7(1)(g).

[120] Although a signed request from the patient is not included in the criteria developed by the courts in the Netherlands, it is one of the requirements under euthanasia protocols adopted by some of the hospitals. The Royal Dutch Medical Association has also recommended that requests for euthanasia be in writing: RDMA, *Vision on Euthanasia* (Utrecht, 1995) in RDMA, *Euthanasia in the Netherlands* 4th edn. (Utrecht, 1995) 31.

voluntary request and thereby provides some protection both to patients, and to doctors involved in its administration. The procedural requirements for the legalization of active voluntary euthanasia should include written proof of the patient's medical condition and of the patient's decision-making capacity to request euthanasia from the attending doctor, as well as the consulting medical practitioner and the psychiatrist, so that there can be verification with regard to these key matters.[121]

The foregoing requirements and safeguards are all designed to ensure that the patient has decision-making capacity and that the patient's choice is fully informed and voluntary and, accordingly, represents a true exercise of patient self-determination.

Status of advance directives and other mechanisms for future consent

A difficult question which must be addressed in framing any legislation for the legalization of active voluntary euthanasia concerns the possible role of advance directives or living wills[122] and other mechanisms for future consent such as the enduring power of attorney.

Considering first of all the use of advance directives, an important matter to be determined is whether a patient's request for active euthanasia in such a document, made at a time when the patient had decision-making capacity, should be recognized as a voluntary request, empowering a doctor to perform active euthanasia at some later time when the patient is incompetent, provided the other eligibility criteria are satisfied. Some of the legislative proposals for the legalization of active voluntary euthanasia have made provision for the use of advance directives or living wills. For example, the 1969 Voluntary Euthanasia Bill proposed in the United Kingdom provided for persons to request in advance the administration of active euthanasia in the event of their suffering from an irremediable condition.[123] Under such proposals, the advance declaration only comes into effect if the patient no longer has the decision-making capacity to express his or her wishes.

There are a number of competing considerations which must be carefully weighed in determining whether advance directives should be recognized in this area. Recognition of some form of advance directives would have the

---

[121] In framing the legislation, it would be advisable to avoid imposing on doctors an absolute standard of certainty in determining patient decision-making capacity, diagnosis, prognosis etc.; see Cole and Shea, 'Voluntary Euthanasia: A Proposed Remedy', above n. 68, at 840–1 for reference to their proposed bill which imposes 'reasonable certainty' as the standard.

[122] See Ch. 1 for reference to developments in the UK and other jurisdictions with regard to advance directives or living wills as a mechanism for refusing medical treatment.

[123] See cls. 2(1) and (2). Under these provisions, a declaration signed by an adult and re-executed within 12 months would remain in force for life unless revoked. Note also the proposals under the Californian initiatives for physician 'aid in dying' (the 1988 Humane and Dignified Death Act and the Death with Dignity Act proposed for the 1992 referendum) which made provision for the appointment of a durable power of attorney, with the power to seek 'aid in dying' on behalf of a formerly competent patient. See pp. 364–6, 368 above.

advantage of maximizing patient autonomy by enabling patients to indicate their wishes in advance in the event that they suffer from a terminal or incurable condition and no longer have the decision-making capacity to request active euthanasia. This would, in turn, provide considerable reassurance to many patients.[124] There are, however, serious problems inherent with advance directives or living wills, particularly where they make provision for active voluntary euthanasia.[125] As noted earlier, the voluntariness of the patient's request is fundamental to any proposal for reform of active voluntary euthanasia. Although a patient's advance request for active euthanasia expressed in a document of this kind does constitute a form of consent, it is undeniably not as certain and reliable as the request of a patient expressed at the time of the patient's terminal or incurable condition, repeated over a period of time and capable of verification prior to the administration of active voluntary euthanasia. It is certainly true that legislation permitting active voluntary euthanasia could impose requirements to establish the voluntariness of the patient's request at the time the directive or living will is executed. There is, however, no guarantee that this request continues to accord with the wishes of the patient, once he or she loses decision-making capacity. Moreover, since advance directives inevitably involve some speculation about future circumstances, it is simply not feasible for a patient to make an informed decision about a hypothetical future condition.[126] As a result, advance directives entail an increased risk that decisions are made which do not in fact accord with the patient's wishes. Further, since there is no practical means of confirming the voluntariness of the patient's decision at the time the decision is to be acted upon, there is also a greater risk of mistake and abuse. To require eligible patients presently to have decision-making capacity does, admittedly, limit the availability of active voluntary euthanasia, but this is necessary in order to ensure that the patient's request is truly voluntary and informed, and to minimize the risk of error and abuse.[127] This is not to say that advance directives are completely irrelevant: as one commentator has pointed out, if euthanasia has been requested in advance for a given set of circumstances and the

---

[124] For general commentary regarding the benefits of advance directives (in the context of refusal of treatment) see the Age Concern Institute of Gerontology and Centre of Medical Law and Ethics, *Living Will, Working Party Report* (London, 1988) 46–7.

[125] See also Francis, L., 'Advance Directives for Voluntary Euthanasia: A Volatile Combination?' (1993) 18 *JMed&Phil.* 297.

[126] This was also the view of the Missouri Supreme Court in *Cruzan* v. *Harmon* 760 SW 2d 408, 417 (1988).

[127] Angell, M., 'Euthanasia' (1988) 319 *New Eng.JMed.* 1348, 1350. Note also the argument considered by Angell that incompetent patients, particularly those in a persistent vegetative state, do not suffer to the same extent as competent patients. Although the issue of advance directives is not specifically addressed in the criteria for active voluntary euthanasia which have been developed by the Dutch courts, in practice, doctors have relied on the advance directives of formerly competent patients; see pp. 429–30 above.

request has been reaffirmed under those circumstances, some of the doubts that may exist about that request (for example that it stems from depression in respect of their illness)[128] may be lessened. In the Netherlands, the Royal Dutch Medical Association has also taken the view that a previously prepared advance directive can have a supportive effect with respect to a patient's verbal request for active voluntary euthanasia and would be of assistance in establishing a durable request.[129]

For much the same reasons, the possibility of empowering a health care power of attorney or other agent to choose active euthanasia on one's behalf in the event of loss of decision-making capacity must also be rejected.[130] The legalization of active voluntary euthanasia is a serious undertaking, and any proposal for reform should, therefore, err on the side of caution. The decision to seek active euthanasia requires a level of self-determination which can only be exercised by individuals acting on their own behalf. Despite the undoubted benefits of advance directives and other mechanisms for having health care decisions made on behalf of patients who lack decision-making capacity in other contexts, legislation providing for active voluntary euthanasia must be limited to patients who *presently* have that capacity and who personally request active euthanasia because of a current condition. In order to be as certain as possible that the administration of active euthanasia does in fact continue to represent the patient's wish, it would be advisable if there was a legislative requirement that the patient is able to confirm their request immediately prior to the doctor providing such assistance. In this context, note should be made of the Northern Territory legislation. As was suggested in the earlier discussion,[131] one aspect of the Rights of the Terminally Ill Act 1995 (NT) which is arguably unsatisfactory is that the patient need not be competent at the time that euthanasia is administered. Under that Act, it is sufficient that the patient had at no time given the doctor any indication that it was no longer his or her intention to go through with the request for the doctor to assist in ending his or her life:[132] it is not necessary for the patient to be in a position to confirm his or her request at the time that assistance is to be given. It is clear from the parliamentary debates that this was intended to enable assistance to be given to those who had requested active euthanasia, but

---

[128] Francis, 'Advance Directives for Voluntary Euthanasia: A Volatile Combination?', above n. 125, at 307–8.

[129] *Vision on Euthanasia* (1995), above Ch. 7 n. 67, at 30.

[130] See, for example, the 1988 Californian proposal under the Humane and Dignified Death Act which provided for a nominated power of attorney to seek 'aid in dying' on behalf of the patient, subject to the review of a three-person ethics committee. Note also the proposals put forward in the Australian Capital Territory (Voluntary and Natural Death Bill 1993 and the Medical Treatment (Amendment) Bill 1995) which sought to make provision for a power of attorney to request active voluntary euthanasia on behalf of the grantor: see pp. 342–3, 361 above.

[131] See p. 353 above.   [132] Section 7(1)(o).

who subsequently lose decision-making capacity; the view being taken that it would be inappropriate to deny a person's request in these circumstances. However, in the interests of minimizing error and abuse, it would be preferable if active voluntary euthanasia were confined to those patients who have full decision-making capacity—both at the time when the request is made and at the time active voluntary euthanasia is to be administered—even though this will inevitably exclude some persons.

The role of the medical profession

An important consideration under any proposal for legalization of active voluntary euthanasia is what role doctors will play and this merits separate and detailed consideration. Doctors will inevitably have some role to play in the event that active voluntary euthanasia is legalized. Verification of a number of the eligibility criteria for the performance of active voluntary euthanasia discussed above necessarily rely on the participation of the medical profession.[133] First, a determination must be made as to the patient's decision-making capacity. Conceivably, the decision-making capacity of the patient could, in many cases, be determined by someone *other* than a doctor. However, doctors are clearly the most suitable persons to make this assessment, and it was suggested earlier that the most appropriate course would be to require a full psychiatric assessment of a patient before active euthanasia can be administered, to confirm that the patient is not suffering from a treatable clinical depression. Secondly, medical knowledge is required to determine that the patient is suffering from a terminal or serious incurable condition and to provide information to the patient about diagnosis, likely prognosis, and available medical options.

One of the major arguments which has been advanced by opponents of active voluntary euthanasia relates to the difficulties in ascertaining the voluntariness of the patient's request.[134] Euthanasia opponents have also focused attention on the risks of mistaken diagnosis or prognosis.[135] An important safeguard to minimize the risks of error or abuse is the involvement of an independent doctor to verify the voluntariness of the patient's request and to confirm the diagnosis of the patient's condition and the patient's prognosis. The involvement of another doctor would go some way to overcome the objection raised by some commentators to permitting private killings, involving a private transaction between a doctor and his or her patient.[136] Significantly, under the guidelines for active voluntary eutha-

---

[133] This is accepted even by those commentators who are opposed to doctors being involved in the administration of active voluntary euthanasia; e.g. Richards, 'Constitutional Privacy, the Right to Die and the Meaning of Life: A Moral Analysis', above Ch. 2 n. 153, at 418.

[134] See pp. 228–34 above.

[135] See pp. 234–5 above.

[136] e.g. Callahan, D., 'Aid-In-Dying: The Social Dimension' (1991) 118 *Commonweal* 476, 477.

nasia applicable in the Netherlands, consultation with another doctor is considered to be an important factor,[137] and this requirement has been given legislative force under the Northern Territory Rights of the Terminally Ill Act 1995.[138] It is accordingly recommended that legislation for the legalization of active voluntary euthanasia should include a requirement of consultation with another doctor to confirm the voluntariness of the patient's request, the diagnosis of the patient's condition, and the patient's prognosis. It would be desirable if there was a requirement that the second medical practitioner have expertise in the area of the patient's terminal illness. Note should be taken, in this regard, of an amendment that was made to the Northern Territory legislation as originally enacted. By virtue of the Right of the Terminally Ill Amendment Act 1996, an additional requirement has been introduced to the effect that the second medical practitioner must hold prescribed professional qualifications, or have prescribed experience, in the treatment of the terminal illness from which the patient is suffering.[139]

As was recommended earlier, the mental state of a patient requesting active voluntary euthanasia should be assessed by a psychiatrist who should also confirm the voluntariness of the patient's request before active voluntary euthanasia can be performed. There should be a further requirement of full documentation of both medical practitioners' findings as well as those of the psychiatrist.

One interesting suggestion which has been made is for a system of palliative care consultants.[140] 'Palliative care consultants' would be physicians with experience in treating dying patients, who are knowledgeable about and committed to comfort care, skilled in the assessment of decision-making capacity of patients suffering from terminal or incurable conditions, and well educated abut the ethics of 'end-of life' decision-making. The stated goal of this proposal is to require a rigorous, independent second opinion by an accountable expert in the light of the objectives of the regulatory policy. The role of the consultant would be to review the patient's diagnosis and prognosis and explore whether the treating physician and patient had considered carefully all reasonable alternatives. It is suggested that through this consultation process, it may be possible for pain management to be improved or for other means of comfort care to be used.

This proposal for creation of 'palliative care consultants' certainly highlights the importance of palliative care options being fully explored before

---

[137] See pp. 397–409 above.   [138] Section 7. For discussion, see pp. 347–351 above.

[139] The necessary qualifications and experience are prescribed in the regulations: see Rights of the Terminally Ill Regulations discussed at Ch. 6 n. 41 above. Also in the Netherlands, the Royal Dutch Medical Association has stressed the importance of ensuring that the consultant has appropriate expertise. See RDMA, *Vision on Euthanasia* (1995), above Ch. 7 n. 67, at 34–5. See also the Oregon Death with Dignity Act, discussed at pp. 370–1 above.

[140] Miller *et al.*, 'Regulating Physician-Assisted Death', above n. 12, at 121.

a decision is made to accede to a patient's request for active euthanasia. It was suggested earlier that one of the preconditions for the administration of euthanasia should be that the patient's suffering cannot be relieved or mitigated by other means which are acceptable to the patient. In order to give this real meaning, it would be necessary to ensure that either the patient's doctor, or the consultant (preferably both) have appropriate palliative care experience. Note should be made, in this context, of the requirements under the Northern Territory legislation. The Act requires that the patient must be informed *inter alia* of the palliative care options and the Act specifies that if a patient's medical practitioner has no special qualifications in the field of palliative care, the information to be provided to the patient on the availability of palliative care must be given by a medical practitioner who has such qualifications as prescribed under the legislation.[141] This would, presumably, in most cases be the consulting medical practitioner but the legislation does contemplate that some other medical practitioner may be involved. And as was explained previously,[142] the Northern Territory legislation precludes a medical practitioner from assisting a patient under the Act, if, after considering the advice of the other medical practitioner, he or she is of the opinion that there are palliative care options reasonably available to the patient to alleviate the patient's pain to levels acceptable to the patient.

Whilst there may be little dispute with medical involvement in ascertaining the eligibility of a patient for active voluntary euthanasia, the more controversial issue is whether doctors should be involved in its actual administration. The essence of the opponents' arguments on this point is that the deliberate taking of life is completely contrary to the whole ethics and training of the medical profession and would seriously undermine the doctor/patient relationship. These arguments have already been considered in an earlier chapter where it was suggested that these concerns are largely unfounded.[143] Indeed, arguments can be advanced that allowing a doctor to assist a patient to die at the patient's request as a measure of last resort, is perfectly consistent with a doctor's professional role and principles of professional integrity. From a practical point of view, the alternatives to doctors administering active voluntary euthanasia are limited. The possibility of friends or relatives performing active euthanasia at the request of a loved one can be readily discounted. As one commentator has pointed out, friends and relatives are likely to be emotionally involved with the patient and are consequently more likely to be traumatized by the experience if

---

[141] The Rights of the Terminally Ill Regulations set out the meaning of 'special qualifications' in palliative care and prescribe the qualifications that must be held by a medical practitioner who provides information to a patient under s. 7(3) on the availability of palliative care. See Ch. 6 n. 44.

[142] See p. 353 above and also the discussion above.   [143] See pp. 242–7 above.

they participate directly in bringing about the patient's death.[144] One may also question the involvement of family members on the grounds that they are perhaps more likely to have a vested interest in the death of the patient. Active euthanasia is a medical procedure requiring medical and pharmacological expertise. The very nature of the act would therefore suggest that it be performed by a registered medical practitioner. It is certainly true that lay persons or para-professionals could be trained to administer a painless death. However, this would entail its own dangers and problems.[145] Another possibility would be for health care professionals other than doctors to perform active voluntary euthanasia, for example nurses. There are good grounds though for suggesting that the responsibility for this practice should be confined to doctors. Prominent amongst these considerations is the fact that doctors possess the most extensive medical and pharmacological expertise, and already have the responsibility of making life and death decisions. Moreover, it is well established that many patients turn to their doctors for assistance to die.[146] Given the inevitable involvement of the medical profession in ascertaining compliance with the eligibility criteria, it would be far preferable for doctors also to be vested with the responsibility of administering active voluntary euthanasia. And, as was suggested in an earlier chapter, there are other valid reasons why doctors are the most appropriate group to administer active voluntary euthanasia.[147] They are in close contact with the patient and have direct knowledge of the patient's medical circumstances. Moreover, they are subject to strict codes of professional conduct and medical ethics and can be assumed to be acting in the best interests of the patient.

A novel suggestion which has been made in order to avoid the involvement of ordinary doctors in the practice of active voluntary euthanasia, is that active voluntary euthanasia be developed as an area of specialization in medicine.[148] According to this proposal, active voluntary euthanasia could become an important part of the care provided to the terminally ill. The feasibility of this proposal would depend on the willingness of sufficient numbers of doctors to pursue this area of specialization. There is also the consideration that if the practice of active voluntary euthanasia was confined to an area of medical specialization, fewer physicians would be involved in the practice, but they would be called upon to administer active voluntary euthanasia more frequently than if the practice were distributed amongst the medical profession. It is, therefore, necessary to weigh up the

[144] Crisp, 'A Good Death: Who Best to Bring It?', above Ch. 4 n. 241, at 75–6.

[145] There is, for example, very real concern about extending this kind of knowledge beyond the medical profession because of the risk that it may be misused.

[146] See pp. 130–4 above for discussion of evidence of patient requests for active voluntary euthanasia.

[147] See p. 243 above.

[148] Crisp, 'A Good Death: Who Best to Bring It?', above Ch. 4 n. 241, at 77.

potential advantages of specialization against the argument that, given the extraordinary nature of active voluntary euthanasia, it would be preferable if the practice by any individual doctor would be kept to a minimum. There are also grounds to suggest that it would be preferable if the practice of euthanasia occurs within the context of the existing doctor/patient relationship as the patient's own doctor is more likely to know and understand the patient and his or her circumstances and is therefore better placed to evaluate properly a patient's request.

On balance, the most preferable and realistic proposal is for doctors to be involved in the administration of active voluntary euthanasia. As noted in a previous chapter, evidence from survey results indicates that some doctors are already involved in the practice and an even greater proportion support its legalization, and would be willing to engage in the practice if it were legal.[149] Strong support has also been shown for the view that if active voluntary euthanasia were to be made legal, it should be medicalized by restricting it to be performed by doctors and taught at medical sites.[150] Thus, the available evidence suggests that many doctors do not regard the practice of active voluntary euthanasia as inconsistent with their professional role.

A number of commentators have stressed the importance of a meaningful doctor/patient relationship before a doctor provides a patient with assistance to die.[151] It is suggested that whilst ideally, the doctor would have been involved throughout the patient's illness and suffering, there may not always be a pre-existing relationship: in these circumstances, the doctor must get to know the patient personally in order to understand fully the reasons behind the request, and to be able to confirm that the preconditions for performing euthanasia have been met.

If it is decided that it is appropriate for doctors to be involved in the practice of active voluntary euthanasia, careful consideration would have to be given to the position of those doctors who do not wish to participate. It was argued in an earlier chapter that any reforms should not confer any rights on patients to demand the administration of active voluntary eutha-

---

[149] See pp. 134–8, 295–332 above.

[150] Kinsella, T. and Verhoef, M., 'Alberta Euthanasia Survey: 2. Physicians' Opinions About the Acceptance of Active Euthanasia as a Medical Act and the Reporting of Such Practice' (1993) 148 CMAJ 1929, reporting on a survey of Alberta doctors which found in excess of 70% support for this view.

[151] e.g. Quill, T. et al., 'Care of the Hopelessly Ill: Proposed Clinical Criteria for Physician-Assisted Suicide' (1992) 327 *New Eng.JMed.* 1380. See also Boyd, K., 'Euthanasia Back to the Future' in Keown, J. (ed.), *Euthanasia Examined: Ethical, Clinical and Legal Perspectives* (Cambridge, 1995) 72, 79 where he suggests that the only way to determine whether active voluntary euthanasia is morally justified in a given case is for the doctor to engage in conversation with the patient: a conversation of the kind once described by Simone Weil as one in which each of them, without ceasing to think in the first person, really understands what the other thinks in the first person.

nasia, and that under no circumstances should doctors be under a legal obligation to provide assistance at the patient's request.[152] This principle could be reflected in the legislation by the inclusion of a conscience clause, making it clear that doctors are free to refuse to participate in the practice of active euthanasia.[153] Alternatively, legislation providing for active voluntary euthanasia could be framed in permissive terms only, enabling a patient to request active euthanasia but making it clear that doctors who administer active euthanasia at the request of a patient in accordance with the legislation will not be criminally liable, without in any way creating an *obligation* to comply with a patient's request for active euthanasia.[154]

A related consideration is whether a doctor who chooses not to be involved in the practice of active voluntary euthanasia should be required to transfer the patient or refer the patient to another doctor. Some of the legislative proposals for the legalization of active voluntary euthanasia specifically provide for the transfer of patients in these circumstances.[155] Although such a requirement would maximize the patient's opportunity to have his or her request for active voluntary euthanasia granted, doctors strongly opposed to the concept of active voluntary euthanasia may find a requirement of this kind to be against their principles.[156] It is therefore probably preferable not to enshrine this in legislation but to leave it to the guidelines for medical practice.

In the light of the current criminal law prohibition on active voluntary euthanasia, an important feature of any proposal for legalization is the introduction of an immunity to protect doctors from liability when acceding to the patient's euthanasia request. Moreover, doctors engaged in the practice of active voluntary euthanasia must also be protected from civil and disciplinary proceedings. Such immunities have been an integral feature of most of the legislative proposals.[157] Alongside such an immunity, there should be a saving provision to the effect that nothing in the legislation shall be construed to authorize or permit the deliberate taking of life other than

---

[152] See pp. 201–2 above.

[153] See, for example, the 1969 Voluntary Euthanasia Bill (UK) cl. 4(3) which provides that 'No person shall be under any duty, whether by contract or by any statutory or other legal requirement, to participate in any treatment authorised by this Act to which he has a conscientious objection'.

[154] e.g. Northern Territory Rights of the Terminally Ill Act 1995, ss. 5 and 20(2). For discussion, see p. 346 above.

[155] See, for example, the Californian Humane and Dignified Death Act proposed in 1988, cl. 7191 of which provides 'A failure by a physician to effectuate the directive of a qualified patient pursuant to this division shall constitute unprofessional conduct if the physician refuses to make arrangements, or fails to take reasonable steps, to effect the transfer of the qualified patient to another physician who will effectuate the directive of the qualified patient'.

[156] Wildes, K., 'Conscience, Referral and Physician Assisted Suicide' (1993) 18 *JMed&Phil.* 323.

[157] e.g. s. 20 of the Rights of the Terminally Ill Act 1995 (NT). For discussion, see p. 355 above.

in accordance with the procedures contained therein.[158] Provided that there is some provision to this effect making it abundantly clear that the current criminal law prohibitions continue to apply to cases falling outside the legislation, it is probably unnecessary to introduce new penalties.

The preceding analysis has principally concentrated on an appropriate legislative framework for permitting active voluntary euthanasia. However, as discussed earlier, there is a close interrelationship between active voluntary euthanasia and doctor-assisted suicide, and legalization of active voluntary euthanasia would also logically entail the legalization of doctor-assisted suicide. The same criteria and standards should apply for both practices, as is presently the case in the Netherlands and under the Northern Territory legislation. The point has been made previously that the only difference between these two forms of assistance is the extent of the doctor's involvement in the patient's death. Because the patient is ultimately responsible, in a case of doctor-assisted suicide, for bringing about his or her own death, it is necessary to consider what the role of the doctor should be in these circumstances. Although not directly bringing about the patient's death, the doctor plays an important supervisory role. Not only should the doctor ensure the suitability of the drugs to be taken, he or she should be present at the time that the patient takes the drugs to end his or her life and should supervise the death of the patient.[159] At the very least, this would require that the doctor is available and can be contacted in the event that there are any unforeseen complications. There may, for example, be circumstances where the patient's death becomes prolonged and further assistance is needed. In accepting a patient as suitable for doctor-assisted suicide, it is then the doctor's responsibility to ensure that this is properly effected in a manner which secures a dignified and peaceful death that is not protracted. It follows that doctors who are willing to assist the suicide of a patient, should, at least in these exceptional circumstances, also be willing to participate more directly in bringing about the patient's death should that become necessary.

As other commentators have pointed out, if the law is changed to permit doctors to provide their patients with assistance in dying, it is important that there be open sharing of information within the medical profession regarding appropriate methods for bringing about death by the administration of

---

[158] See cl. 2443 of the Humane and Dignified Death Act proposed in California in 1988.

[159] The Royal Dutch Medical Association has taken the view that whilst it is preferable in most cases for the doctor to be in attendance, there may be circumstances where this is not the case, for example, where it is the wish of the patient and/or the family that the doctor not be present. The Northern Territory Rights of the Terminally Ill Act 1995 which provides for both active voluntary euthanasia and doctor-assisted suicide, requires that the medical practitioner him or herself provides the assistance and/or is and remains present while the assistance is given and until the death of the patient: see s. 7(1)(p). Note, however, the differing views as to the merit of having doctors present in cases of doctor-assisted suicide: see New York State Task Force on Life and the Law, *When Death Is Sought,* above Ch. 4 n. 97, at 84.

active voluntary euthanasia or doctor-assisted suicide.[160] As noted previously, in the Netherlands, information is freely available to doctors regarding how to perform active euthanasia or provide assistance in suicide.[161] Above all, the methods should be reliable and should not contribute to the patient's suffering. In terms of appropriate legislative models, the provision made under the Northern Territory Rights of the Terminally Ill Act 1995 is instructive. As was outlined in an earlier chapter,[162] that Act requires that in assisting a patient under the Act, a medical practitioner must be guided by appropriate medical standards and such guidelines as are prescribed in the regulations, and shall consider the appropriate pharmaceutical information about any substances reasonably available for use in the circumstances.

Witnessing requirements for the administration of active voluntary euthanasia

A procedural safeguard included in a number of the proposals for legislative reform (although not included in the Northern Territory legislation) is that the administration of active voluntary euthanasia must be performed in the presence of witnesses.[163] This requirement has considerable merit. One of the principal arguments for the legalization of active voluntary euthanasia is that the practice can be brought into the open and appropriately regulated.[164] A requirement that active voluntary euthanasia be performed in the presence of suitable witnesses would provide an important check on the procedure and provide some protection against the possibility of error and abuse. It is also important that the doctor administering active voluntary euthanasia remains present until the death of the patient.[165]

Reporting requirements

A final matter that needs to be addressed is whether legislation should specify any formal reporting requirements which must be complied with by a doctor who has performed active voluntary euthanasia. Consistent with the objective of ensuring that the practice is performed openly and subject to public scrutiny, doctors should be required to keep proper records with regard to the administration of active voluntary euthanasia. However, in developing an appropriate reporting procedure, caution must be exercised in avoiding a procedure that is unnecessarily intrusive and bureaucratic. A

---

[160] Quill et al., 'Care of the Hopelessly Ill: Proposed Clinical Criteria for Physician-Assisted Suicide', above Ch. 4 n. 88, at 1382–3.

[161] See p. 416 above.

[162] See pp. 347–8 above.

[163] See, for example, the Voluntary Euthanasia (Legalisation) Bill 1936 (UK) which required that active euthanasia must be administered in the presence of an 'official witness'. The latter must be a justice of the peace, or a barrister, solicitor, medical practitioner, clergyman or other minister of religion, or a State registered nurse.

[164] See pp. 150–2 and 207–8 above.

[165] This is a requirement under the Rights of the Terminally Ill Act 1995 (NT).

fundamental requirement would be that the cause of death recorded on the patient's death certificate is medically-administered active voluntary euthanasia as distinct from death from natural causes. It also follows from the foregoing recommendations that there would be documentation of the patient's request for active voluntary euthanasia as well as documentation from the patient's doctor, the consultant doctor, and the psychiatrist.

In order to ensure that doctors do in fact comply with the legislative requirements, it may be desirable to introduce a procedure for the routine investigation of all cases of medically-administered active voluntary euthanasia. For example, the Netherlands practice could be adopted which requires the doctor to notify the coroner that active voluntary euthanasia has been performed.[166] The coroner would then investigate the death, having regard to the doctor's written report and supporting documentation, and if active voluntary euthanasia was justified in the circumstances and the various conditions and procedural safeguards were complied with, the doctor would be protected from legal action.[167]

CONCLUSION

The object of this chapter has been to evaluate critically the various possible models for change to the law with regard to active voluntary euthanasia. In addition to the useful guidance and direction available from the many proposals which have been advanced over the years, particular assistance has been derived from a consideration of the legislation which has recently been introduced in the Northern Territory, and from the Netherlands' model for the practice of active voluntary euthanasia.

In view of the unequivocal prohibition on the practice of active voluntary euthanasia under the present criminal law in the common law jurisdictions

---

[166] For discussion, see p. 335 above. It was suggested earlier (p. 357 above) that the provision made under the Rights of the Terminally Ill Act 1995 (NT) whereby the coroner is merely given the responsibility of gathering the documentation and reporting the number of deaths annually to the Attorney-General falls short of what is required for a full investigation.

[167] One commentator, Dr David Ranson, the Deputy Director of the Victorian Institute of Forensic Medicine, has gone considerably further, suggesting that a coronial investigation involving a full autopsy would be the best way of ensuring that medically-assisted deaths only occur in appropriate circumstances: 'The Coroner and the Rights of the Terminally Ill Act 1995 (NT)' (1995) 3 *JLaw&Med.* 169. Note also the preconditions for doctor-assisted suicide laid down by McEachern CJ of the British Columbia Court of Appeal (*Rodriguez* v. *Attorney General of British Columbia, Attorney General of Canada*, above n. 13, at 24–5) and approved by Lamer CJ of the Supreme Court of Canada in *Rodriguez* v. *British Columbia (Attorney General)* (above n. 13) (both dissenting) which included a requirement that the regional coroner be notified 3 days before the psychiatric examination of the patient, and that the coroner or his nominee may be present at the examination of the patient in order to confirm that the patient has the mental competence to decide and does in fact decide to terminate his or her life. For discussion of the *Rodriguez* case see pp. 86–94 above.

under consideration, it has been argued that any substantive change in this area can only be achieved through legislation. After considering a number of possible legislative solutions, it is suggested that, in principle, outright legalization of active voluntary euthanasia would be the most appropriate course, subject to strict safeguards. This would involve introducing a very limited exception to the homicide laws, conferring on doctors an immunity from liability, provided active voluntary euthanasia is performed in accordance with the specified safeguards. The criteria and safeguards for the performance of active voluntary euthanasia recommended in this chapter mirror, to a large extent, those presently in use in the Netherlands for the practice of active voluntary euthanasia, which have also been adopted under the Northern Territory legislation.[168] That these criteria are both practicable and workable is borne out by the experience in the Netherlands.

It is readily acknowledged that a number of the criteria and safeguards which have been recommended considerably limit the scope of any reform, by, for example, stipulating that the availability of active voluntary euthanasia be confined to patients who presently have decision-making capacity, and who have a terminal or serious incurable condition which the patient finds unbearable. However, safeguards of this kind are necessary for the protection of both doctors and their patients. Given the significance of any change in this area, it is appropriate to proceed cautiously and to set clear parameters which confine the practice. Further, it must be emphasized the introduction of legislation in accordance with the foregoing recommendations would not create a 'right' to active voluntary euthanasia, but would simply empower doctors to comply with patients' requests in appropriate cases. Moreover, apart from the limited exception created for doctors to perform active voluntary euthanasia in certain circumstances, the existing prohibition on taking of life remains, to protect individuals from being killed without their consent.

With regard to implementation of the proposed legislative reforms, there is much to be said for keeping the legislation as simple as possible. It should consist of a concise legislative statement containing the key elements of the foregoing recommendations, leaving the finer details to regulations and guidelines for medical practice. By its very nature, euthanasia reform is an area where an interdisciplinary approach is essential and the medical profession has an important role to play in providing input into this process.

---

[168] As explained at pp. 441–2 above, in the Netherlands these criteria are not presently in statutory form.

Conclusion

As was acknowledged from the outset, active voluntary euthanasia is a notoriously complex and controversial issue. This work is by no means the last word on the subject, but simply a contribution in a vast debate which is developing at an accelerating pace and becoming increasingly prominent.

On the basis of the analysis in the foregoing chapters, certain conclusions can be drawn. It is clear from the analysis of the criminal law in Chapter 1 that there is a sharp distinction in the law's approach to passive and active euthanasia. Whilst the law recognizes the patient's right to refuse treatment and permits passive euthanasia in certain circumstances, active voluntary euthanasia is unequivocally prohibited in most jurisdictions as murder regardless of the special mitigating circumstances usually existing in such cases.[1] Further, as was explained in Chapter 2, a doctor who actively assists a patient to commit suicide will be criminally liable for the offence of assisting suicide irrespective of the special circumstances.[2] However, a doctor may lawfully comply with a patient's request for the withholding or withdrawing of life-saving treatment which will result in death: although the patient's conduct may in fact constitute a form of suicide by omission, the courts have rejected this characterization, albeit on spurious grounds, and have thus been able to hold that the issue of assisted suicide is not implicated in these circumstances.

Notwithstanding the present legal prohibition on active voluntary euthanasia and doctor-assisted suicide, substantial evidence has been put forward in Chapter 3 from all common law jurisdictions under consideration which indicates that doctors are already involved in these practices. However, this conduct is largely hidden and doctors are very rarely prosecuted for performing active voluntary euthanasia or assisting the suicide of their patients. From the experience to date, there is every possibility that if a prosecution does arise in a genuine case, the doctor would escape the full rigours of the criminal law. However, as the prosecution of Dr Cox in the

---

[1] Note, however, the position in the Northern Territory of Australia discussed at pp. 345–57 above. Note also the Netherlands position discussed at pp. 391–455 above.

[2] Note, however, the US case law developments recognizing a constitutionally-protected interest in physician-assisted suicide for competent, terminally ill patients: *Compassion in Dying* v. *State of Washington* No. 94-35534 (9th Cir. March 6 1996) (*en banc*) and *Quill* v. *Vacco* No. 60 (2nd Cir. April 2 1996) discussed at pp. 101–121 above. Note also the legislative developments in the US State of Oregon: see pp. 369–73 above.

United Kingdom has shown,[3] this cannot be relied upon as a certainty, and doctors who compassionately assist their patients to die run the risk of incurring serious criminal liability. It has been argued that there are a number of fundamental problems with the present legal position which tolerates inconsistencies between legal principles and the law in practice. Although in most of the cases where doctors have been prosecuted for assisting their patients to die they have been treated extremely leniently by the criminal justice system, as the *Cox* case has shown, there is no guaranteed consistency in the application of the law, thus raising serious questions regarding justice and equality before the law. There is also the risk that allowing such major discrepancies between law in theory and practice threatens to undermine public confidence in the law and bring it into disrepute. In addition there are concerns that the present position provides inadequate medical guidance for doctors in the practice of active voluntary euthanasia and that patients' rights are likely to be jeopardized if the practice is allowed to occur in an unregulated fashion.

Attention was also drawn in Chapter 3 to a number of legal anomalies in other areas of medical practice, in particular, the court's characterization of turning off life-support and the administration of palliative drugs which are known to be likely to cause death. It has been acknowledged that the aim of the courts in perpetuating certain characterizations has been to avoid the conclusion that such conduct is criminal. It has, however, been argued that the prevailing analysis has produced highly artificial and unsustainable distinctions and that a more honest and consistent approach to difficult issues associated with assistance in dying is required.

In Chapter 4 of this work, a detailed analysis of the euthanasia debate has been undertaken. On the strength of the arguments of the case for legalization it has been concluded that a *prima facie* case exists for changing our laws to permit active voluntary euthanasia in carefully defined circumstances. Further, it was found that those opposing legalization have failed to demonstrate why individuals who voluntarily request such assistance should be prevented from receiving it from a doctor who wishes to comply. Consideration has also been given to philosophical issues regarding the proper role of the criminal law, and it has been argued that there are no pressing social interests which demand retention of the criminal law prohibition: indeed, it is arguable that harm is more likely to be caused to individuals by the retention of the blanket prohibition. In this chapter the human rights dimension of the euthanasia debate has also been examined and it was suggested that although there are a number of possible grounds for the recognition of active voluntary euthanasia or doctor-assisted suicide as a human right, it is unlikely that such recognition will be given on the

---

[3] See pp. 143–5 above.

basis of current human rights instruments and the interpretation they have received to date.

Factors which have contributed to the changing climate for reform have been analysed in Chapter 5. Significantly, the conclusions from this chapter indicate substantial support for active voluntary euthanasia amongst the medical profession and in the community generally. The evidence presented in this chapter of substantial support amongst doctors for legalization of active voluntary euthanasia and the degree of willingness to participate in the practice if it were legalized largely debunks claims that the performance of active voluntary euthanasia is inconsistent with a doctor's professional role. And, judging from the evidence of public opinion polls, nor does the overwhelming majority of the public appear to have any difficulty with the concept that doctors may, in exceptional circumstances, be involved in the termination of life. On the basis of the findings of these chapters, it can be concluded that there is now a definite body of evidence which suggests that the present law does not meet social needs and that change is in the interests of the community. There is, therefore, a strong case for the reappraisal of the present legal prohibition on active voluntary euthanasia.

In Chapter 6 attention has been given to reform developments which have occurred in recent years. It is significant that in all jurisdictions, major inquiries have been undertaken to examine the issue of active voluntary euthanasia and whether legalization is appropriate. Whilst most have recommended against any form of legalization (although, in some instances, with significant dissents), it has been argued that important considerations in the assessment of whether legalization is appropriate have been overlooked or inadequately addressed. In particular, a number of the recent reports which have rejected legalization have failed adequately to address the problems stemming from the present legal position where, although unlawful, active voluntary euthanasia already occurs on a significant scale in practice, but in a totally hidden and unregulated manner.

Consideration has also been given to the reform initiatives aimed at securing legalization of active voluntary euthanasia. Particular attention has been devoted to an examination of the Rights of the Terminally Ill Act 1995 enacted in the Northern Territory of Australia, which marks a major watershed in the history of the euthanasia movement. In addition, reform initiatives in the USA for the legalization of physician-assisted suicide have been examined, including the Death with Dignity Act which was passed by a citizen-initiated referendum in the State of Oregon in 1994 but has since been challenged on constitutional grounds. Attention has also been given to the major case-law developments which have recently taken place in the USA with the recognition by two separate federal courts of a constitutionally protected interest in physician-assisted suicide for competent, terminally ill patients. With growing likelihood of review by the United States

Supreme Court, the status of these decisions and their ramifications also for the issue of active voluntary euthanasia remains to be seen. Clearly, however, these cases, particularly the decision of the Ninth Circuit Court of the US Court of Appeals in *Compassion in Dying* v. *State of Washington*,[4] have already played a significant role in advancing the debate regarding medical assistance in dying.

In assessing the appropriateness of reform in this area, valuable assistance has been gained from the experience in the Netherlands which was the subject of detailed consideration in Chapter 7. As we have seen, although not actually legal, active voluntary euthanasia has been openly practised in the Netherlands for some years, and has been officially sanctioned by the courts and the prosecuting authorities. More recently, the guidelines for the practice of active voluntary euthanasia have indirectly been given recognition through regulations dealing with the procedure for notifying cases of euthanasia to the authorities. This is clearly not equivalent to legalization, but the Netherlands experience does, nevertheless, provide some opportunity for empirically testing claims about the harmful effects of State-sanctioned active voluntary euthanasia. It has been suggested that a careful examination of the Netherlands experience does not support the assertions made by opponents of euthanasia, and in fact demonstrates that active voluntary euthanasia can be safely incorporated into medical practice, subject to certain well defined criteria. It must be recognized however, that regardless of its intrinsic merit, the model which has been developed in the Netherlands is not necessarily the appropriate solution for other countries contemplating reform in this area. It is, therefore, vital to view the Netherlands' situation in its wider context and to be culturally sensitive in developing solutions to the problem of active voluntary euthanasia. It was suggested earlier that although the Netherlands' position is in some respects unique, particularly in relation to the manner in which change to the law has been brought about, there are certain features in common between the Netherlands and a number of common law jurisdictions, in particular, the United Kingdom, Canada, and Australia, which suggest that the Netherlands' model for active voluntary euthanasia may be of potential relevance in shaping legislative reform in these jurisdictions. However, commentators in the USA have drawn attention to some important differences between their country and the Netherlands, particularly in relation to the system of health care, and have cautioned against the uncritical adoption of the Netherlands' model.[5]

Examination of options for reform in Chapter 8 has required evaluation

---

[4] See above Ch. 2 n. 54.
[5] Pabst Battin, M., 'Holland and Home: On the Exportability of Dutch Euthanasia Practices' in Aycke, O. and Smook, M. (eds.), *Right to Self-Determination*, Proceedings of the 8th World Conference of the Right to Die Societies (Amsterdam, 1990) 124; Battin, M., 'Seven Caveats Concerning the Discussion of Euthanasia in Holland' (1990) 34 *Perspectives in Biology & Med.* 73.

of the suitability of a legislative solution. Whilst some of the difficulties with legislation have been acknowledged, it has been argued that this is an area where legislative reform is both necessary and appropriate: in view of the unequivocal prohibition of active voluntary euthanasia under the present criminal law a legislative solution is required to provide doctors with the necessary protection from criminal liability and is the most appropriate means of establishing safeguards for the regulation of the practice. This is the approach which has been taken in the Northern Territory of Australia. On the whole, the Rights of the Terminally Ill Act 1995 represents a cautious and balanced approach to legalization and taken together with the Netherlands' guidelines on which it is largely based, provides useful guidance in the formulation of legislative reform. It is accordingly recommended that a very limited exception to the criminal laws be introduced, with respect to active voluntary euthanasia and doctor-assisted suicide, provided assistance in dying is performed in accordance with strict criteria and safeguards. It must be emphasized that this would not create a 'right' to active voluntary euthanasia in the sense of entitling a person to demand such assistance be given; rather, it would simply empower doctors who are willing to comply with patients' requests to do so in appropriate cases. Moreover, the existing criminal law prohibition on the wrongful taking of life would obviously remain in place to protect individuals from being killed without their consent.

The legalization of active voluntary euthanasia through legislative reform is unquestionably a significant step for a society to take, and concerns have understandably been raised about the implications of incorporating into law and public policy a practice which allows doctors to kill their patients. Indeed, we have seen that many people who are, in principle, prepared to accept the legitimacy of active voluntary euthanasia in some circumstances, are opposed to the prospect of introducing legislation which would legalize and thereby institutionalize the practice. They are, instead, prepared to tolerate the existing discrepancies between law and practice and the subterfuge which occurs with regard to active voluntary euthanasia. The conclusion of this work is that the present problems which have been identified must be more honestly and directly addressed, and we need to overcome what is an understandable resistance to contemplate the deliberate taking of life by means of active voluntary euthanasia. It is certainly true that legalization of active voluntary euthanasia implies ethical approval of such conduct,[6] but the performance of active voluntary euthanasia in appropriate circumstances already enjoys widespread acceptance and support, so legalization would be a decisive step towards formalizing the present situation.

Moreover, it has been argued that there are significant advantages to be

[6] Silving, H., 'Euthanasia: A Study in Comparative Criminal Law' (1954) 103 *UPaLRev.* 350. 388.

gained from legalization of active voluntary euthanasia. It will promote the autonomy and self-determination of patients by giving eligible patients the freedom to choose active voluntary euthanasia. Although only a small minority of patients are likely to exercise this option, it is important that the option is made available and that patient choice is maximized. Another advantage to be gained from legalization of active voluntary euthanasia is that it will instil some equilibrium into the law; a suffering patient will not only have the choice of refusing treatment which may bring about his or her death, but may seek more active assistance in dying. Legislative reform will thereby address the present inconsistency in the law which gives a patient the legal authority to direct that no further treatment be administered, even in circumstances where this will clearly result in the patient's death, but holds that a patient cannot give a legally effective consent to having his or her life terminated by more direct means. There will also be greater certainty of outcome for those patients seeking active euthanasia: whilst there can be no guarantee that assistance will be available in a particular case, as the proposal is for permitting rather than requiring doctors to perform active voluntary euthanasia, patients could have some confidence that, provided they come within the legislative conditions, a doctor is likely to be found who will accede to the patient's request. This would largely avoid the inequities of the present situation under which active voluntary euthanasia is not openly available and, therefore, not equally accessible to all. Making the option of medicalized active voluntary euthanasia openly available is also likely to reduce the incidence of mercy killings outside the medical context where individuals often feel compelled to respond to the request of a loved one for assistance to die.

If active voluntary euthanasia is legalized, there will also be significant benefits for the medical profession which are ultimately in the interests of good medical practice. Doctors who already perform active voluntary euthanasia would no longer need to fear the possibility of criminal prosecution, provided they comply with the statutory criteria. Other doctors, who presently refrain from the practice for fear of prosecution, would be free to respond to patients' requests for active euthanasia in appropriate circumstances. Indeed, as we have seen, there is strong evidence to suggest that a significant proportion of doctors would be willing to administer active voluntary euthanasia if it were legalized. One of the important advantages of legalization is that it would encourage greater visibility and more open scrutiny of the practice. Doctors wishing to benefit from the protection of the legislation will be fully accountable for their conduct. So long as active voluntary euthanasia remains illegal, it is likely to be performed in secrecy, without the benefit of professional discussion and guidance, essential for good medical practice. By specifying criteria and procedures for the lawful performance of active voluntary euthanasia, legislative reform would reduce the risk of unacceptable conduct. This would ensure that patients would have a greater measure of protection than they presently have and there would generally be greater certainty and predicability in the law. It would, however, be naive to assume that the introduction of legislation would remove all difficulties. Obviously, one cannot completely eliminate the possibility of unacceptable conduct, and cases will undoubtedly arise which fall outside the statutory exception. Such cases should be dealt with according to the existing criminal law prohibition, and the full force of the law should be brought to bear. There is no evidence to suggest that the legalization of active voluntary euthanasia would increase the incidence of such cases; on the contrary, it has been argued there are good grounds for the belief that the risk of unacceptable practices would be reduced. Evidence obtained from surveys of the medical profession on the issue of legalization of active voluntary euthanasia suggest that doctors would prefer to operate within the law and would be willing to comply with the terms of a statutory scheme if active voluntary euthanasia were legalized.

In conclusion, it is submitted that the time has come for the issue of medically-administered active voluntary euthanasia to be squarely confronted and for suitable legislative reform to be developed. A decisive step has already been taken with the passage of the Northern Territory Rights of the Terminally Ill Act 1995, and this will, no doubt, be influential in securing reforms in other jurisdictions. In time we will have the opportunity to evaluate the operation of this legislation and begin to gather hard data on the practice and regulation of legalized active voluntary euthanasia and doctor-assisted suicide and their impact on society. This will in turn inform future debate on the most appropriate legislative solutions.

It must, however, be acknowledged that, irrespective of how well or carefully a legislative solution is formulated, it can at best be a partial response to the difficulties which are encountered by many patients, and the importance of non-legal solutions must not be underestimated. Active voluntary euthanasia should not be a substitute for alternative forms of care such as palliative and hospice care, but rather should be seen as a last resort available to patients in circumstances where all other available options have been carefully canvassed. It is, therefore, of the utmost importance that the developments in palliative and hospice care be continued so that patients are assured of adequate pain relief, control of symptoms, and treatment of psychological distress.[7] There should also be continuing attention given to the needs of the sick and dying generally, with emphasis on better training of health care professionals in this area, and on improved communication with patients. The development of optimal palliative and hospice care obviously requires appropriate government expenditure in these areas, but

---

[7] Foley, K., 'The Relationship of Pain and Symptom Management to Patient Requests for Physician-Assisted Suicide' (1991) 6 *Journal of Pain & Symptom Management* 289.

society has an obligation to do all that is reasonably possible to improve the situation of dying and suffering patients and to ensure that they are shown kindness and compassion. The provision of comprehensive care would certainly go some way towards minimizing the need for active voluntary euthanasia and ensuring that lives are not unnecessarily terminated. It cannot, however, provide a solution in all cases, and active voluntary euthanasia should be a legally available option in carefully defined circumstances. In this way individuals are given the opportunity to decide for themselves on the basis of their own values and beliefs, without undermining respect for opposing viewpoints.

Appendix

Northern Territory of Australia

Rights of the Terminally Ill Act 1995

(As amended by the Rights of the Terminally Ill Amendment Act 1996)

TABLE OF PROVISIONS

20. Immunities
21. Regulations

SCHEDULE

to confirm the right of a terminally ill person to request assistance from a medically qualified person to voluntarily terminate his or her life in a humane manner; to allow for such assistance to be given in certain circumstances without legal impediment to the person rendering the assistance; to provide procedural protection against the possibility of abuse of the rights recognised by this Act; and for related purposes

BE it enacted by the Legislative Assembly of the Northern Territory of Australia, with the assent as provided by the Northern Territory (Self Government) Act 1978 of the Commonwealth, as follows:

Part 1—Preliminary

1. Short title

This Act may be cited as the Rights of the Terminally Ill Act 1995.

2. Commencement

This Act shall come into operation on a date to be fixed by the Administrator by notice in the Gazette.

3. Interpretation

In this Act, unless the contrary intention appears—

'assist', in relation to the death or proposed death of a patient, includes the prescribing of a substance, the preparation of a substance and the giving of a substance to the patient for self administration, and the administration of a substance to the patient;

'certificate of request' means a certificate in or to the effect of the form in the Schedule that has been completed, signed and witnessed in accordance with this Act;

'health care provider', in relation to a patient, includes a hospital, nursing home or other institution (including those responsible for its management) in which the patient is located for care or attention and any nurse or other person whose duties include or directly or indirectly relate to the care or medical treatment of the patient;

'illness' includes injury or degeneration of mental or physical faculties;

'medical practitioner' means a medical practitioner who has been entitled to practise as a medical practitioner (however described) in a State or a Territory of the Commonwealth for a continuous period of not less than 5 years and who is resident in, and entitled under the Medical Act to practise medicine in, the Territory;

'qualified psychiatrist' means—

  (a) a person entitled under a law of a State or Territory of the Commonwealth to practise as a specialist in the medical specialty of psychiatry;

  (b) a specialist whose qualifications are recognised by the Royal Australian and New Zealand College of Psychiatrists as entitling the person to fellowship of that College; or

  (c) a person employed by the Commonwealth or a State or Territory of the Commonwealth, or an Agency or authority of the Commonwealth or a State or Territory, as a specialist or consultant in the medical specialty of psychiatry;

'terminal illness', in relation to a patient, means an illness which, in reasonable medical judgment will, in the normal course, without the application of extraordinary measures or of treatment unacceptable to the patient, result in the death of the patient.

Part 2—Request for and Giving of Assistance

4. Request for assistance to voluntarily terminate life

A patient who, in the course of a terminal illness, is experiencing pain, suffering and/or distress to an extent unacceptable to the patient, may request the patient's medical practitioner to assist the patient to terminate the patient's life.

5. Response of medical practitioner

A medical practitioner who receives a request referred to in section 4, if satisfied that the conditions of section 7 have been met, but subject to section 8, may assist the patient to terminate the patient's life in accordance with this Act or, for any reason and at any time, refuse to give that assistance.

6. Response of medical practitioner, &c., not to be influenced by extraneous considerations

(1) A person shall not give or promise any reward or advantage (other than a reasonable payment for medical services), or by any means cause or threaten to cause any disadvantage, to a medical practitioner or other person for refusing to assist, or for the purpose of compelling or persuading the medical practitioner or other person to assist or refuse to assist, in the termination of a patient's life under this Act.

Penalty: $10,000.

(2) A person to whom a reward or advantage is promised or given, as referred to in subsection (1), does not have the legal right or capacity to receive or retain the reward or accept or exercise the advantage, whether or not, at the relevant time, he or she was aware of the promise or the intention to give the reward or advantage.

7. Conditions under which medical practitioner may assist

(1) A medical practitioner may assist a patient to end his or her life only if all of the following conditions are met:

(a) the patient has attained the age of 18 years;

(b) the medical practitioner is satisfied, on reasonable grounds, that—

    (i) the patient is suffering from an illness that will, in the normal course and without the application of extraordinary measures, result in the death of the patient;

    (ii) in reasonable medical judgment, there is no medical measure acceptable to the patient that can reasonably be undertaken in the hope of effecting a cure; and

    (iii) any medical treatment reasonably available to the patient is confined to the relief of pain, suffering and/or distress with the object of allowing the patient to die a comfortable death;

(c) two other persons, neither of whom is a relative or employee of, or a member of the same medical practice as, the first medical practitioner or each other—

    (i) one of whom is a medical practitioner who holds prescribed professional qualifications, or has prescribed experience, in the treatment of the terminal illness from which the patient is suffering; and

    (ii) the other who is a qualified psychiatrist,

have examined the patient and have confirmed—

    (iii) in the case of the medical practitioner referred to in subparagraph (i)—

        (A) the first medical practitioner's opinion as to the existence and seriousness of the illness;

        (B) that the patient is likely to die as a result of the illness; and

        (C) the first medical practitioner's prognosis; and

    (iv) in the case of the qualified psychiatrist referred to in subparagraph (ii)—that the patient is not suffering from a treatable clinical depression in respect of the illness;

(d) the illness is causing the patient severe pain or suffering;

(e) the medical practitioner has informed the patient of the nature of the illness and its likely course, and the medical treatment, including palliative care, counselling and psychiatric support and extraordinary measures for keeping the patient alive, that might be available to the patient;

(f) after being informed as referred to in paragraph (e), the patient indicates to the medical practitioner that the patient has decided to end his or her life;

(g) the medical practitioner is satisfied that the patient has considered the possible implications of the patient's decision to his or her family;

(h) the medical practitioner is satisfied, on reasonable grounds, that the patient is of sound mind and that the patient's decision to end his or her life has been made freely, voluntarily and after due consideration;

(i) the patient, or a person acting on the patient's behalf in accordance with section 9, has, not earlier than 7 days after the patient has indicated to his or her medical practitioner as referred to in paragraph (f), signed that part of the certificate of request required to be completed by or on behalf of the patient;

(j) the medical practitioner has witnessed the patient's signature on the certificate of request or that of the person who signed on behalf of the patient, and has completed and signed the relevant declaration on the certificate;

(k) the certificate of request has been signed in the presence of the patient and the first medical practitioner by another medical practitioner (who may be the medical practitioner referred to in paragraph (c)(i) or any other medical practitioner) after that medical practitioner has discussed the case with the first medical practitioner and the patient and is satisfied, on reasonable grounds, that the certificate is in order, that the patient is of sound mind and the patient's decision to end his or her life has been made freely, voluntarily and after due consideration, and that the above conditions have been complied with;

(l) where, in accordance with subsection (4), an interpreter is required to be present at the signing of the certificate of request, the certificate of request has been signed by the interpreter confirming the patient's understanding of the request for assistance;

(m) the medical practitioner has no reason to believe that he or she, the countersigning medical practitioner or a close relative or associate of either of them, will gain a financial or other advantage (other than a reasonable payment for medical services) directly or indirectly as a result of the death of the patient;

(n) not less than 48 hours has elapsed since the signing of the completed certificate of request;

(o) at no time before assisting the patient to end his or her life had the patient given to the medical practitioner an indication that it was no longer the patient's wish to end his or her life;

(p) the medical practitioner himself or herself provides the assistance and/ or is and remains present while the assistance is given and until the death of the patient.

(2)   In assisting a patient under this Act a medical practitioner shall be guided by appropriate medical standards and such guidelines, if any, as are prescribed, and shall consider the appropriate pharmaceutical information about any substance reasonably available for use in the circumstances.

(3)   Where a patient's medical practitioner has no special qualifications in the field of palliative care, the information to be provided to the patient on the availability of palliative care shall be given by a medical practitioner (who may be the medical practitioner referred to in subsection (1)(c)(i) or any other medical practitioner) who has such special qualifications in the field of palliative care as are prescribed.

(4)   A medical practitioner shall not assist a patient under this Act where the medical practitioner or any other medical practitioner or qualified psychiatrist who is required under subsection (1) or (3) to communicate with the patient does not

share the same first language as the patient, unless there is present at the time of that communication and at the time the certificate of request is signed by or on behalf of the patient, an interpreter who holds a prescribed professional qualification for interpreters in the first language of the patient.

8. Palliative care

(1)   A medical practitioner shall not assist a patient under this Act if, in his or her opinion and after considering the advice of the medical practitioner referred to in section 7(1)(c)(i), there are palliative care options reasonably available to the patient to alleviate the patient's pain and suffering to levels acceptable to the patient.

(2)   Where a patient has requested assistance under this Act and has subsequently been provided with palliative care that brings about the remission of the patient's pain or suffering, the medical practitioner shall not, in pursuance of the patient's original request for assistance, assist the patient under this Act. If subsequently the palliative care ceases to alleviate the patient's pain and suffering to levels acceptable to the patient, the medical practitioner may continue to assist the patient under this Act only if the patient indicates to the medical practitioner the patient's wish to proceed in pursuance of the request.

9. Patient who is unable to sign certificate of request

(1)   If a patient who has requested his or her medical practitioner to assist the patient to end the patient's life is physically unable to sign the certificate of request, any person who has attained the age of 18 years, other than the medical practitioner or a medical practitioner or qualified psychiatrist referred to in section 7(1)(c), or a person who is likely to receive a financial benefit directly or indirectly as a result of the death of the patient, may, at the patient's request and in the presence of the patient and both the medical practitioner witnesses (and where, in accordance with section 7(4) an interpreter has been used, also in the presence of the interpreter), sign the certificate on behalf of the patient.

(2)   A person who signs a certificate of request on behalf of a patient forfeits any financial or other benefit the person would otherwise obtain, directly or indirectly, as a result of the death of the patient.

10. Right to rescind request

(1)   Notwithstanding anything in this Act, a patient may rescind a request for assistance under this Act at any time and in any manner.

(2)   Where a patient rescinds a request, the patient's medical practitioner shall, as soon as practicable, destroy the certificate of request and note that fact on the patient's medical record.

11. Improper conduct

(1)   A person shall not, by deception or improper influence, procure the signing or witnessing of a certificate of request.

Penalty: $20,000 or imprisonment for 4 years.

(2) A person found guilty of an offence against subsection (1) forfeits any financial or other benefit the person would otherwise obtain, directly or indirectly, as a result of the death of the patient, whether or not the death results from assistance given under this Act.

Part 3—Records and Reporting of Death

12. Medical records to be kept

A medical practitioner who, under this Act, assists a patient to terminate the patient's life shall file and, subject to this Act, keep the following as part of the medical record of the patient:

(a) a note of any oral request of the patient for such assistance;
(b) the certificate of request;
(c) a record of the opinion of the patient's medical practitioner as to the patient's state of mind at the time of signing the certificate of request and certification of the medical practitioner's opinion that the patient's decision to end his or her life was made freely, voluntarily and after due consideration;
(d) the reports of the medical practitioner and qualified psychiatrist referred to in section 7(1)(c);
(e) a note by the patient's medical practitioner—
  (i) certifying as to the independence of the medical practitioner and qualified psychiatrist referred to in section 7(1)(c) and the residential and period of practice qualifications of the patient's medical practitioner;
  (ii) indicating that all requirements under this Act have been met;
  (iii) indicating the steps taken to carry out the request for assistance; and
  (iv) including a notation of the substance prescribed,
and such other information, if any, as is prescribed.

Penalty: $10,000 or imprisonment for 2 years.

13. Certification as to death

(1) A medical practitioner who, under this Act, assists a patient to end the patient's life shall be taken to have attended the patient during the patient's last illness for the purposes of Part IV of the Registration of Births, Deaths and Marriages Act or any provision in substitution for that Part.

(2) A death as the result of assistance given under this Act shall not, for that reason only, be taken to be unexpected, unnatural or violent for the purposes of the definition of 'reportable death' in the application of Part 4 of the Coroner's Act, or be a reportable death by reason only of having occurred during an anaesthetic.

14. Medical record to be sent to Coroner

(1) As soon as practicable after the death of a patient as the result of assistance given under this Act, the medical practitioner who gave the assistance shall report

the death to a Coroner by sending to the Coroner a copy of the death certificate under the Registration of Births, Deaths and Marriages Act and so much of the medical record of the patient (including that required by section 12 to be kept) as relates to the terminal illness and death of the patient.

(2)   As soon as practicable after the end of each financial year the Coroner shall advise the Attorney-General of the number of patients who died as a result of assistance given under this Act and the Attorney-General, in such manner or report as he or she thinks appropriate, shall report the number to the Legislative Assembly.

15.   Coroner may report on operation of Act

The Coroner may, at any time and in his or her absolute discretion, report to the Attorney-General on the operation, or any matter affecting the operation, of this Act and the Attorney-General shall, within 3 sitting days of the Legislative Assembly after receiving the report, table a copy of the report in the Assembly.

Part 4—Miscellaneous

16.   Construction of Act

(1)   Notwithstanding section 26(3) of the Criminal Code, an action taken in accordance with this Act by a medical practitioner or by a health care provider on the instructions of a medical practitioner does not constitute an offence against Part VI of the Criminal Code or an attempt to commit such an offence, a conspiracy to commit such an offence, or an offence of aiding, abetting, counselling or procuring the commission of such an offence.

(2)   Assistance given in accordance with this Act by a medical practitioner or by a health care provider on the instructions of a medical practitioner is taken to be medical treatment for the purposes of the law.

17.   Certificate of request is evidence

A document purporting to be a certificate of request is, in any proceedings before a court, admissible in evidence and is prima facie evidence of the request by the person who purported to sign it or on whose behalf it is purported to have been signed, for assistance under this Act.

18.   Effect on construction of wills, contracts and statutes

(1)   Any will, contract or other agreement, whether or not in writing or executed or made before or after the commencement of this Act, to the extent that it affects whether a person may make or rescind a request for assistance under this Act, or the giving of such assistance, is not valid.

(2)   An obligation owing under a contract, whether made before or after the commencement of this Act, shall not be conditioned or affected by the making or rescinding of a request for assistance under this Act or the giving of that assistance.

19. Insurance or annuity policies

The sale, procurement or issuing of any life, health or accident insurance or annuity policy or the rate charged for such a policy shall not be conditioned on or affected by the making or rescinding of a request for assistance under this Act or the giving of that assistance.

20. Immunities

(1) A person shall not be subject to civil or criminal action or professional disciplinary action for anything done in good faith and without negligence in compliance with this Act, including being present when a patient takes a substance prescribed for or supplied to the patient as the result of assistance under this Act to end the patient's life.

(2) A professional organisation or association or health care provider shall not subject a person to censure, discipline, suspension, loss of licence, certificate or other authority to practise, loss of privilege, loss of membership or other penalty for anything that, in good faith and without negligence, was done or refused to be done by the person and which may under this Act lawfully be done or refused to be done.

(3) A request by a patient for assistance under this Act, or giving of such assistance in good faith by a medical practitioner in compliance with this Act, shall not constitute neglect for any purpose of law or alone constitute or indicate a disability for the purposes of an application under section 8 of the Adult Guardianship Act.

(4) A health care provider is not under any duty, whether by contract, statute or other legal requirement, to participate in the provision to a patient of assistance under this Act, and if a health care provider is unable or unwilling to carry out a direction of a medical practitioner for the purpose of the medical practitioner assisting a patient under this Act and the patient transfers his or her care to another health care provider, the former health care provider shall, on request, transfer a copy of the patient's relevant medical records to the new health care provider.

21. Regulations

The Administrator may make regulations, not inconsistent with this Act, prescribing all matters—
(a) required or permitted by this Act to be prescribed; or
(b) necessary or convenient to be prescribed for carrying out or giving effect to this Act.

SCHEDULE
Section 7

Request for assistance to end my life in a humane and dignified manner

I have been advised by my medical practitioner that I am suffering from an illness which will ultimately result in my death and this has been confirmed by a second medical practitioner.

I have been fully informed of the nature of my illness and its likely course and the medical treatment, including palliative care, counselling and psychiatric support and extraordinary measures that may keep me alive, that is available to me and I am satisfied that there is no medical treatment reasonably available that is acceptable to me in my circumstances.

I request my medical practitioner to assist me to terminate my life in a humane and dignified manner.

I understand that I have the right to rescind this request at any time.

Signed:

Dated:

Declaration of witnesses

I declare that—
(a)   the person signing this request is personally known to me;
(b)   he/she is a patient under my care;
(c)   he /she signed the request in my presence and in the presence of the second witness to this request;
(d)   I am satisfied that he/she is of sound mind and that his/her decision to end his/her life has been made freely, voluntarily and after due consideration.

Signed: Patient's Medical Practitioner

I declare that—
(a)   the person signing this request is known to me;
(b)   I have discussed his/her case with him/her and his/her medical practitioner;
(c)   he/she signed the request in my presence and in the presence of his/her medical practitioner;
(d)   I am satisfied that he/she is of sound mind and that his/her decision to end his/her life has been made freely, voluntarily and after due consideration;
(e)   I am satisfied that the conditions of section 7 of the Act have been or will be complied with.

Signed: Second Medical Practitioner

[Where under section 7(4) an interpreter is required to be present]

Declaration of interpreter

I declare that—
(a)   the person signing this request or on whose behalf it is signed is known to me;

(b) I am an interpreter qualified to interpret in the first language of the patient as required by section 7(4);

(c) I have interpreted for the patient in connection with the completion and signing of this certificate;

(d) in my opinion, the patient understands the meaning and nature of this certificate.

Signed: Qualified Interpreter.

Northern Territory of Australia

Rights of the Terminally Ill Regulations 1996

TABLE OF PROVISIONS

Rights of the Terminally Ill Regulations

CITATION

These Regulations may be cited as the Rights of the Terminally Ill Regulations.

COMMENCEMENT

These Regulations shall come into operation on the commencement of the Rights of the Terminally Ill Act 1995.

PRESCRIBED QUALIFICATIONS IN TREATING TERMINAL ILLNESS

For the purposes of section 7(1)(c)(i) of the Act, the medical practitioner shall hold a qualification in a medical specialty related to the terminal illness of the patient recognised by a medical specialist college in Australia and which entitles the medical practitioner to fellowship of that college.

GUIDELINES

For the purposes of section 7(2) of the Act, a medical practitioner assisting a patient shall be guided by the guidelines set out in Schedule 1.

SPECIAL QUALIFICATIONS IN PALLIATIVE CARE

(1)   For the purposes of section 7(3) of the Act, 'special qualification' is taken to include competence by reason of ability, knowledge and skills acquired through experience.

(2)   The medical practitioner who, under section 7(3) of the Act, provides information to the patient on the availability of palliative care shall have one of the special qualifications described in Schedule 2.

QUALIFICATIONS FOR INTERPRETERS

For the purposes of section 7(4) of the Act, the interpreter shall hold one of the following professional qualifications in the first language of the patient:

(a)   accreditation as a Conference Interpreter from the National Accreditation Authority for Translators and Interpreters;

(b)   accreditation as an Interpreter from the National Accreditation Authority for Translators and Interpreters.

MEDICAL RECORDS

For the purpose of keeping the medical record of the patient referred to in section 12 of the Act, a medical practitioner may use the checklist set out in Schedule 3.

MEDICAL PRACTITIONER TO NOTIFY HEALTH CARE PROVIDER OF REQUEST FOR ASSISTANCE

For the purpose of enabling a health care provider to decide whether or not he, she or it is able or willing to carry out a direction of a medical practitioner for the purpose of the medical practitioner assisting a patient under the Act, the medical practitioner shall, as soon as practicable after agreeing to assist the patient, inform the health care provider of his or her intention to do so.

SCHEDULE 1
Section 7(2)
Regulation 4

Guidelines

1.   The medical practitioner is to assist the patient to end his or her life by administering to the patient, or giving to the patient for self-administration, a drug or a combination of drugs which the medical practitioner determines is the most appropriate to assist the patient.

2.   The medical practitioner should advise the members of the patient's family and the patient's friends who wish to be present at the time of the death of the patient—

(a) of the effects of the drug or drugs to be administered to the patient; and

(b) when the drug is, or drugs are, to be administered to the patient so that those members of the family or friends who do not wish to be in attendance for the administration of the drug or drugs may be absent at that time.

3. The medical practitioner should remain for a reasonable time after the death of the patient with the family and friends of the patient who are in attendance to answer any questions they may have relating to the death of the patient.

SCHEDULE 2
Section 7(3)
Regulation 5

Special Qualifications in Palliative Care

1. A qualification which is recognised by the National Specialist Qualification Advisory Committee as a specialist qualification together with one year full time employment (whether or not for a continuous period) by a palliative care service as a consultant in the field of palliative care.

2. Two years full time practice (whether or not for a continuous period) in palliative medicine together with employment (whether or not for a continuous period) by a palliative care service.

3. A graduate certificate in palliative care together with one year full time employment (whether or not for a continuous period) by a palliative care service.

4. Successful completion of a course in palliative care recognised by a tertiary institution or a medical professional body together with one year full time employment (whether or not for a continuous period) by a palliative care service as a consultant, a specialist or a health care provider.

5. Current registration (having been so registered for a period of not less than 5 years), but not including registration which is subject to conditions or limitations, on the Vocational Register established and maintained by the Royal Australian College of General Practitioners and the Health Insurance Commission.

6. Fellowship of the Royal Australian College of General Practitioners.

SCHEDULE 3
Section 12
Regulation 7

Checklist for Medical Practitioner Assisting Patient

Name and address of medical practitioner:

Name and address of patient:

The following conditions enabling a medical practitioner to assist a patient to end his or her life under the Rights of the Terminally Ill Act have been met:

1. The patient has requested that I assist him/her to end his/her life and I have agreed to do so.
2. The patient has attained the age of 18 years.
3. I am satisfied, on reasonable grounds, that—
    - the patient is suffering from an illness that will, in the normal course and without the application of extraordinary measures, result in his/her death; and
    - in reasonable medical judgement, there is no medical measure acceptable to the patient that can reasonably be undertaken in the hope of effecting a cure; and
    - any medical treatment reasonably available to the patient is confined to the relief of pain, suffering and/or distress with the object of allowing the patient to die a comfortable death.
4. A second medical practitioner who—
    (a) is neither a relative or employee, nor a member of the same medical practice, of mine or the qualified psychiatrist referred to in clause 5; and
    (b) is qualified in the treatment of the terminal illness from which the patient is suffering as prescribed by the Rights of the Terminally Ill Regulations, and has examined the patient and confirms my opinion as to the existence and seriousness of the illness, that the patient is likely to die as a result of the illness and my prognosis.

(Attach report of second medical practitioner)

5. A qualified psychiatrist (within the meaning of the Rights of the Terminally Ill Act), who is neither a relative or employee, nor a member of the same medical practice, of mine or the medical practitioner referred to in clause 4, has examined the patient and confirms that the patient is not suffering from a treatable clinical depression in respect of the illness.

(Attach report of qualified psychiatrist)

6. In my opinion the illness is causing the patient severe pain or suffering.
7. I have special qualifications in the field of palliative care and therefore provided the information on the availability of palliative care to the patient.

OR I do not have special qualifications in the field of palliative care and therefore the information on the availability of palliative care was provided to the patient by—

(Insert name of medical practitioner holding special qualifications in the field of palliative care as prescribed)

8. The patient has been informed of the nature of the illness and its likely course, and the medical treatment, including palliative care, counselling and psychiatric support and extraordinary measures for keeping the patient alive, that might be available of the patient.

9. It is my opinion that, after considering the advice and opinion of the medical practitioner referred to in clause 4, there are no palliative care options reasonably available to the patient to alleviate the patient's pain and suffering to levels acceptable to the patient.

OR It is my opinion that, despite an earlier request from the patient for assistance to end his/her life, palliative care was provided to the patient that brought about the remission of the patient's pain and suffering, that palliative care now ceases to alleviate the patient's pain and suffering to levels acceptable to the patient.

10. After the patient had been informed of the matters specified in clause 8, the patient indicated to me that he/she has decided to end his/her life.

OR The patient requested assistance under the Rights of the Terminally Ill Act but was subsequently provided with palliative care and after the palliative care ceased to alleviate his/her pain and suffering the patient indicated to me that he/she has decided to proceed in pursuance of his/her earlier decision to end his/her life.

Date patient indicated his/her decision:

11. I am satisfied that the patient has considered the possible implications of the patient's decision to his/her family.
12. I am satisfied on reasonable grounds that the patient—
     • at the time of indicating to me his/her decision to end his/her life and of signing the certificate of request, is of sound mind; and
     • made the decision to end his/her life freely, voluntarily and after due consideration.
13. The patient or, if the patient is physically unable to do so, a person acting on the patient's behalf in accordance with section 9 of the Rights of the Terminally Ill Act signed the part of the certificate of request required to be completed by or on behalf of the patient not earlier than 7 days after the patient indicated his/her decision to end his/her life to me.

Name and address of person signing on behalf of patient:

Data signed the certificate:
14 I have witnessed the patient, or the person signing on behalf of the patient, signing the certificate of request and have completed and signed the relevant declaration on the certificate.

Data signed the certificate:

15. After I signed the certificate of request another medical practitioner signed the certificate. That medical practitioner had discussed the case with me and the patient before signing the certificate.
Name and address of that other medical practitioner:

Data signed the certificate:

(Attach certificate of request)

16. An interpreter was required to be present at the signing of the certificate of request in accordance with section 7(4) of the Rights of the Terminally Ill Act, and has signed the certificate confirming the patient's understanding of his/her request for assistance.

Name and address of interpreter:

Data signed the certificate:

17. I have read and been guided by appropriate medical standards and by the guidelines prescribed by the Rights of the Terminally Ill Regulations, and have considered the appropriate pharmaceutical information about any drug reasonably available for use in the patient's circumstances.
18. I share the same first language as the patient.

OR As I do not share the same first language as the patient, when assisting the patient under the Rights of the Terminally Ill Act, I communicated with the patient in the presence of an interpreter qualified as required by section 7(4) of that Act.

19. I have no reason to believe that I, the countersigning medical practitioner or a close relative or associate of either of us, will gain a financial or other advantage (other than a reasonable payment for medical services) directly or indirectly as a result of the death of the patient. I have not caused the patient to be influenced in his/her decision to end his/her life by way of any duress or undue influence.
20. I did not commence to assist the patient to end his/her life until after 48 hours had elapsed since the signing of the completed certificate of request.
21. At no time before assisting the patient to end his/her life had the patient—
    • given to me an indication that it was no longer his/her wish to end his/her life; and/or
    • rescinded his/her request for assistance
22. I provided the patient with the assistance to end his/her life by—
    • administering the drug or drugs to end his/her life to the patient; and/or
    • providing the drug or drugs and remaining present while the drug was or drugs were administered to the patient and until his/her death.

(Attach note indicating the drug or drugs administered to the patient, the steps taken to administer the drug or drugs and generally carry out the request for assistance, and the date and time of death of the patient)

23. I am satisfied that the conditions of section 7, and the other requirements, of the Rights of the Terminally Ill Act have been met.

24. I confirm that—
*   I have been entitled to practise as a medical practitioner in a State or a Territory of the Commonwealth of Australia for a continuous period of not less that 5 years; and
*   I am entitled under the Medical Act to practise medicine in the Northern Territory; and
*   I am resident in the Northern Territory.

Signed:

Dated:

(To be completed as applicable)

Select Bibliography

BOOKS

ADMIRAAL, P., *Justifiable Euthanasia: A Manual for the Medical Profession* (Amsterdam, 1980)

AUSTIN, J., *Lectures on Jurisprudence or the Philosophy of Positive Law* (London, 1920)

AYCKE, O. and SMOOK, M. (eds.), *Right to Self-Determination*, Proceedings of the 8th World Conference of the Right to Die Societies (Amsterdam, 1990)

BAER, L. S., *Let the Patient Decide* (Philadelphia, 1978)

BAKKER-WINNUBST, M., 'The Right to Euthanasia During the Terminal Stage of Life' in Aycke, O. and Smook, M. (eds.), *Right to Self-Determination*, Proceedings of the 8th World Conference of the Right to Die Societies (Amsterdam, 1990) 39

BARNARD, C., *Good Life, Good Death* (Englewood Cliffs, New Jersey, 1980)

BATTIN, M., 'Suicide: A Fundamental Human Right?' in Battin M. and Mayo, D. (eds.), *Suicide: The Philosophical Issues* (New York, 1980) 267

—— and MAYO, D. (eds.), *Suicide: The Philosophical Issues* (New York, 1980)

BEAUCHAMP, T., 'A Reply to Rachels on Active and Passive Euthanasia' in Beauchamp, T. and Perlin, S. (eds.), *Ethical Issues in Death and Dying* (Englewood Cliffs, New Jersey, 1978) 246

—— and PERLIN, S. (eds.), *Ethical Issues in Death and Dying* (Englewood Cliffs, New Jersey, 1978)

BEHNKE, J. and BOK, S., *Dilemmas of Euthanasia* (Garden City, New York, 1975)

BORST-EILERS, E., 'Facts About the Actual Euthanasia Practice in the Netherlands' in Royal Dutch Medical Association, *Euthanasia in the Netherlands* (Utrecht, 1991)

BOYD, K., 'Euthanasia Back to the Future' in Keown, J. (ed.), *Euthanasia Examined: Ethical, Clinical and Legal Perspectives* (Cambridge, 1995) 72

BRANDT, R., 'The Rationality of Suicide' in Battin, M. and Mayo, D. (eds.), *Suicide: The Philosophical Issues* (New York, 1980) 117

BRIM, O. *et al.* (eds.), *The Dying Patient* (New York, 1970)

BRITISH MEDICAL ASSOCIATION, *Handbook of Medical Ethics* (London, 1984)

——, *Medical Ethics Today* (London, 1993)

BRODY, B., 'A Non Consequentialist Argument for Active Euthanasia' in Brody, B. and Engelhardt, T., *Bioethics: Readings and Cases* (Englewood Cliffs, New Jersey, 1987) 161

——, *Life and Death Decision Making* (New York, 1988)

—— and Engelhardt, T., *Bioethics: Readings and Cases* (Englewood Cliffs, New Jersey, 1987)

BYRNE, P. (ed.), *Medicine, Medical Ethics and the Value of Life* (Chichester, England, 1990)

CALABRESI, G., *A Common Law for the Age of Statutes* (Cambridge, Massachusetts, 1982)

CAMERON, N., *Death Without Dignity: Euthanasia in Perspective* (Edinburgh, 1990)

CAMPBELL, R. and COLLINSON, D., *Ending Lives* (Oxford, 1988)

CANTOR, N., *Legal Frontiers of Death and Dying* (Bloomington, 1987)

CARRICK, P., *Medical Ethics in Antiquity: Philosophical Perspectives on Abortion and Euthanasia* (Dordecht, 1985)

CHARLESWORTH, M., *Life, Death, Genes and Ethics* (Crows Nest, New South Wales, 1989)

CHURCH OF ENGLAND, National Assembly Board for Social Responsibility, *Decisions About Life and Death: A Problem of Modern Medicine* (London, 1965)

——, *On Dying Well: An Anglican Contribution to the Debate on Euthanasia* (London, 1975)

COHEN, H., 'Euthanasia As a Way of Life' in Aycke, O. and Smook, M. (eds.), *Right to Self-Determination*, Proceedings of the 8th World Conference of the Right to Die Societies (Amsterdam, 1990) 61

COKE, E., *Institutes of the Laws of England* 3rd Part (London, 1641)

CONCERN FOR DYING, *The Living Will and Other Advance Directives: A Legal Guide to Medical Treatment Decisions* (New York, 1986)

——, *A Twenty Year History 1967–1987* (1987)

DEVLIN, P., *Samples of Law Making* (London, 1962)

——, *The Enforcement of Morals* (London, 1965)

——, *Easing the Passing* (London, 1985)

DOUDERA, A. and PETERS, J. (eds.), *Legal and Ethical Aspects of Treating Critically and Terminally Ill Patients* (Ann Arbor, Michigan, 1982)

DOWNING, A. and SMOKER, B., *Voluntary Euthanasia: Experts Debate the Right to Die* (London, 1986)

DU BOULAY, S., *Cicely Saunders: The Founder of the Modern Hospice Movement* (London, 1984)

DUPUIS, H., 'The Right to a Gentle Death' in Aycke, O. and Smook, M. (eds.), *Right to Self-Determination*, Proceedings of the 8th World Conference of the Right to Die Societies (Amsterdam, 1990) 53

DURKHEIM, E., Translated by Spaulding, J. and Simpson, G., *Suicide: A Study in Sociology* (London, 1970)

DWORKIN, R., *Life's Dominion: An Argument About Abortion and Euthanasia* (London, 1993)

DYCK, A., 'An Alternative to the Ethics of Euthanasia' in Weir (ed.), *Ethical Issues in Death and Dying* (New York, 1977) 281

EDELSTEIN, L., *The Hippocratic Oath: Text Translation and Interpretation* (Baltimore, 1943)

ENGELHARDT, T., *The Foundations of Bioethics* (New York, 1986)

EUTHANASIA SOCIETY, *A Plan for Voluntary Euthanasia*, revised edn. (London, 1962)

FEBER, H., 'De Wederwaardigheden van Artikel 293 van het Wetboek van Strafrecht Vanaf 1981 Tot Heden' ('The Vicissitudes of Article 293 of the *Penal Code* to the Present') in van der Wal, G. (ed.), *Euthanasie Knelpunten in ein*

Discussie (*Euthanasia: Bottlenecks in a Discussion*) (Baarn, 1987) 54–81, reviewed in 'Abstracts' (1988) 3 *Issues Law & Med.* 455, 456–7

FEINBERG, J., 'Voluntary Euthanasia and the Inalienable Right to Life' in Feinberg, J., *Rights, Justice, and the Bounds of Liberty: Essays in Social Philosophy* (Princeton, New Jersey, 1980) 220

——, *The Moral Limits of the Criminal Law:* Vol. I, *Harm to Others* (New York, 1984) and Vol. III, *Harm to Self* (New York, 1986)

FELDMAN, D., *Human Rights and Civil Liberties in England and Wales* (Oxford, 1993)

FISSE, B., *Howard's Criminal Law*, 5th edn. (Sydney, 1990)

FLETCHER, G., *Rethinking Criminal Law* (Boston, 1978)

FLETCHER, J., *Humanhood: Essays in Biomedical Ethics* (Buffalo, New York, 1979)

——, *Morals and Medicine* (Princeton, New Jersey, 1979)

FLETCHER, J. C., 'Is Euthanasia Ever Justifiable?' in Wiernik, P. (ed.), *Controversies in Oncology* (New York, 1982) 297

FLEW, A., 'The Principle of Euthanasia' in Downing, A. and Smoker, B., *Voluntary Euthanasia: Experts Debate the Right to Die* (London, 1986) 40

GEVERS, J., 'Euthanasia or Assisted Suicide and the Non-Terminally Ill' in Aycke, O., and Smook, M. (eds.), *Right to Self-Determination*, Proceedings of the 8th World Conference of the Right to Die Societies, (Amsterdam, 1990) 65

GLOVER, J., *Causing Death, Saving Lives* (Harmondsworth, 1977)

GOMEZ, C., *Regulating Death: Euthanasia and the Case of the Netherlands* (New York, 1991)

GORDON, G., *The Criminal Law of Scotland*, 2nd edn. (Edinburgh, 1978)

GORMALLY, L., 'A Non-Utilitarian Case Against Voluntary Euthanasia' in Downing, A. and Smoker, B., *Voluntary Euthanasia: Experts Debate the Right to Die* (London, 1986) 72

GOULD, J. and LORD CRAIGMYLE (eds.), *Your Death Warrant? Implications of Euthanasia: A Medical, Legal and Ethical Study* (New Rochelle, New York, 1971)

GRISEZ, G., 'Suicide and Euthanasia' in Horan, D. and Mall, D. (eds.), *Death, Dying and Euthanasia* (Frederick, Maryland, 1980) 742

—— and BOYLE, J. M., *Life and Death with Liberty and Justice: A Contribution to the Euthanasia Debate* (Notre Dame, Indiana, 1979)

HALE, J., *Pleas of the Crown* (London, 1736)

HAMEL, R. (ed.), *Active Euthanasia, Religion and the Public Debate* (Chicago, 1991)

HARRIS, J., 'Euthanasia and the Value of Life' in Keown, J. (ed.), *Euthanasia Examined: Ethical, Clinical and Legal Perspectives* (Cambridge, 1995) 6

HART, H., *Law, Liberty and Morality* (London, 1962)

HEIFETZ, M. with MANGEL, C., *The Right to Die: A Neurosurgeon of Death with Candour* (New York, 1975)

HINTON, J., *Dying* (Harmondsworth, 1967)

HOGAN, B., 'Omissions and the Duty Myth' in Smith, P. (ed.), *Criminal Law: Essays in Honour of J.C. Smith* (London, 1987) 85

HOHFELD, W. in Cook, W. (ed.), *Fundamental Legal Conceptions* (New Haven, 1919)

HOLMES, O. W., *The Common Law* (Boston, 1881)

Horan D. and Mall, D. (eds.), *Death, Dying and Euthanasia* (Frederick, Maryland, 1980)

Hospers, J., *An Introduction to Philosophical Analysis*, 2nd edn. (London, 1967)

Humphry, D. (ed.), *Compassionate Crimes, Broken Taboos* (Los Angeles, 1986)

——, *Let Me Die Before I Wake: Hemlock's Book of Self-Deliverance for the Dying*, 5th edn. (Eugene, Oregon, 1987)

——, *Final Exit: The Practicalities of Self-Deliverance and Assisted Suicide for the Dying* (Eugene, Oregon, 1991)

——, *Lawful Exit: The Limits of Freedom for Help in Dying* (Oregon, 1993)

—— and Wickett, A., *Jean's Way* (New York, 1978)

—— and ——, *The Right to Die: Understanding Euthanasia* (Sydney, 1986)

Hunt, R., 'Palliative Care: The Rhetoric-Reality Gap' in Kuhse, H. (ed.), *Willing to Listen: Wanting to Die* (Victoria, 1994)

Johnson, G., *The Right to Die, Voluntary Euthanasia: A Comprehensive Bibliography* (Los Angeles, 1987)

Johnstone, M., *Bioethics—A Nursing Perspective* (Sydney, 1989)

Kant, I., Introduction, translation and notes by Gregor, M., in *The Metaphysics of Morals* (Cambridge, 1991)

Keown, J., 'Euthanasia in the Netherlands: Sliding Down the Slippery Slope?' in Keown, J. (ed.), *Euthanasia Examined: Ethical, Clinical and Legal Perspectives* (Cambridge, 1995) 261

——, *Euthanasia Examined: Ethical, Clinical and Legal Perspectives* (Cambridge, 1995)

Kelly, G., *Medico-Moral Problems* (St. Louis, 1958)

Kennedy, I., *Treat Me Right: Essays in Medical Law and Ethics* (Oxford, 1988)

—— and Grubb, A., *Medical Law: Text and Materials*, 2nd edn. (London, 1994)

Kennedy, L., *Euthanasia: The Good Death* (London, 1990)

Keyserlingk, E., *Sanctity of Life or Quality of Life in the Context of Ethics, Medicine and Law* (Ottawa, 1979)

Kohl, M., *The Morality of Killing* (London, 1974)

—— (ed.), *Beneficent Euthanasia* (Buffalo, 1975)

——, 'Euthanasia and the Right to Life' in Spicker, S. and Engelhardt, H. (eds.), *Philosophical Medical Ethics: Its Nature and Significance* (Holland, 1975) 73

——, 'Voluntary Beneficent Euthanasia' in Kohl, M., *Beneficent Euthanasia* (Buffalo, New York, 1975) 130

Kluge, E., *The Ethics of Deliberate Death* (New York, 1981)

——, *The Practice of Death* (New Haven, 1975)

Kubler-Ross, E., *On Death and Dying* (New York, 1969)

Kuhse, H., *The Sanctity of Life Doctrine in Medicine: A Critique* (Oxford, 1987)

—— (ed.), *Willing to Listen: Wanting to Die* (Melbourne, 1994)

Ladd, J. (ed.), *Ethical Issues Relating to Life and Death* (New York, 1979)

LaFave W. and Scott, A., *Criminal Law*, 2nd edn. (Minnesota, 1986)

Lanham, D., *Taming Death by Law* (South Melbourne, 1993)

Larue, G., *Euthanasia and Religion: A Survey of the Attitudes of World Religions to the Right to Die* (Los Angeles, 1985)

Lebacqz, K. and Engelhardt, H. T., 'Suicide' in Horan, D. and Mall, D. (eds.), *Death, Dying and Euthanasia* (Frederick, Maryland, 1980) 669

LEENEN, H., 'Euthanasia in the Netherlands' in Byrne, P. (ed.), *Medicine, Medical Ethics and the Value of Life* (Chichester, England, 1990) 1

——, 'Legal Aspects of Euthanasia, Assistance to Suicide and Terminating the Medical Treatment of Incompetent Patients' in Royal Dutch Medical Association, *Euthanasia in the Netherlands* (Utrecht, 1991)

LOCKE, J., *Second Treatise*, in Laslett, P. (ed.), *Two Treatises of Government*, revised edn. (New York, 1965)

MAGUIRE, D., *Death by Choice* (Garden City, New York, 1984)

MAIR, G., *Confessions of a Surgeon* (London, 1974)

——, *How to Die with Dignity* (Glasgow, 1980)

MANNES, M., *Last Rights* (London, 1973)

MARSHALL, T., *The Physician and Canadian Law* (Toronto, 1979)

MEYERS, D., *The Human Body and the Law: A Medico-Legal Study* (Chicago, 1970)

——, *Medico Legal Implications of Death and Dying* (Rochester, New York, 1981)

MILL, J., *On Liberty*, 2nd edn. (London, 1859)

MOORE, G., 'The Common Law Doctrine of Necessity' in Church of England, National Assembly Board for Social Responsibility, *Decisions About Life and Death* (London, 1965) 49

OGDEN, R., *Euthanasia and Assisted Suicide and AIDS* (New Westminster, British Columbia, 1994)

OKI, T. (ed.), *The Living Will in the World*, Proceedings of the 9th International Conference of the World Federation of the Right to Die Societies, Kyoto, Japan (Tokyo, 1992) 147

PABST BATTIN, M., 'Holland and Home: On the Exportability of Dutch Euthanasia Practices' in Aycke O. and Smook, M. (eds.), *Right to Self-Determination*, Proceedings of the 8th World Conference of the Right to Die Societies (Amsterdam, 1990) 124

PICARD, E., *Legal Liability of Doctors and Hospitals in Canada*, 2nd edn. (Toronto, 1984)

POLLARD, B., *Euthanasia: Should we Kill the Dying?* (Crows Nest, New South Wales, 1989)

PORTWOOD, D., *Commonsense Suicide: The Final Right* (Los Angeles, 1983)

QUILL, T., *Death and Dignity: Making Choices and Taking Charge* (New York, 1993)

RACHELS, J., *The End of Life: The Morality of Euthanasia* (Oxford, 1986)

RAMSEY, P., *Ethics at the Edges of Life: Medical and Legal Intersections* (New Haven, 1978)

RICE, C., *The Vanishing Right to Life* (Garden City, New York, 1969)

RISLEY, R., *Death with Dignity: A New Law Permitting Physician Aid-In-Dying* (Eugene, Oregon, 1989)

ROBERTS, H., *Euthanasia and Other Aspects of Life and Death* (London, 1936)

ROSSEAU, J., *The Social Contract and Discourses* (London, 1913)

ROYAL DUTCH MEDICAL ASSOCIATION, *Euthanasia in the Netherlands* (Utrecht, 1991)

——, *Euthanasia in the Netherlands*, 4th edn. (Utrecht, 1995)

RUSSELL, R., *Freedom to Die: The Legal Aspects of Euthanasia*, revised edn. (New York, 1977)

SEGUIN, M., 'Freedom to Choose' in Oki, T. (ed.), *The Living Will in the World*,

Proceedings of the 9th International Conference of the World Federation of the Right to Die Societies, Kyoto, Japan (Tokyo, 1992), 147, 152

——, *A Gentle Death* (Ontario, Toronto, 1994)

SHARPE, G., *The Law and Medicine in Canada*, 2nd edn. (Toronto, 1987)

SINGER, P., *Practical Ethics* (Cambridge, 1979)

SKEGG, P., *Law Ethics and Medicine* (Oxford, 1984)

——, *Law Ethics and Medicine*, revised edn. (Oxford, 1988)

SMITH, C. *et al.*, *Beyond Final Exit: New Research in Self-Deliverance for the Terminally Ill* (Victoria, British Columbia, 1995)

SMITH J. C. and HOGAN, B., *Criminal Law*, 5th edn. (London, 1983)

——, *Criminal Law*, 6th edn. (London, 1988)

SMITH, P. (ed.), *Criminal Law: Essays in Honour of J.C. Smith* (London, 1987)

SNEIDERMAN, B. and KAUFERT, J. (eds.), *Euthanasia in the Netherlands: A Model for Canada?* (Manitoba, 1994)

SOCIETY FOR THE RIGHT TO DIE, *Handbook of Living Will Laws* (New York, 1984)

——, *The Handbook of 1985 Living Will Laws* (New York, 1985)

——, *The Physician and the Hopelessly Ill Patient: Legal, Medical and Ethical Guidelines* (New York, 1985)

——, *Handbook of Living Will Laws* (New York, 1987)

——, *The First Fifty Years 1938–1988* (New York, 1988)

SOUTH AUSTRALIAN VOLUNTARY EUTHANASIA SOCIETY, *The Right to Choose: The Case for Legalising Voluntary Euthanasia*, 2nd edn. (Kent Town Centre, South Australia, 1990)

——, *Voluntary Euthanasia and the Medical Profession: An Invitation to Dialogue* (Kent Town Centre, South Australia, 1990)

SPICKER, S. and ENGELHARDT, H. (eds.), *Philosophical Medical Ethics: Its Nature and Significance* (Holland, 1975)

ST. JOHN STEVAS, N., *Life, Death and the Law: Law and Christian Morals in England and the United States* (Bloomington, 1961)

——, *The Right to Life* (London, 1963)

STEDEFORD, A., 'Confusional States' in Twycross, R. and Ventafridda, V. (eds.), *The Continuing Care of Terminal Cancer Patients* (New Haven, 1980) 179

STEINBOCK, B. (ed.), *Killing and Letting Die* (Englewood Cliffs, New Jersey, 1980)

STEINFELS, P. and VEATCH, R. (eds.), *Death Inside Out: The Hastings Center Report* (New York, 1974)

Stephen's Digest of the Criminal Law, 4th edn. (London, 1887)

STODDARD, S., *The Hospice Movement: A Better Way of Caring for the Dying* (New York, 1978)

SULLIVAN, J., *Catholic Teaching on the Morality of Euthanasia* (Washington, 1949)

——, *The Morality of Mercy Killing* (Westminster, 1950)

THORNTON J. and WINKLER, E., *Ethics and Aging: The Right to Live and the Right to Die* (Vancouver, 1988) 155

TRICHE, C. and TRICHE, D., *The Euthanasia Controversy 1812–1974: A Bibliography with Select Annotations* (New York, 1975)

TROWELL, H., *The Unfinished Debate On Euthanasia* (London, 1973)

TWINING W. and MEYERS, D., *How to Do Things with Rules*, 2nd edn. (London, 1982)

TWYCROSS, R., 'Where There is Hope There is Life: A View from the Hospice' in Keown, J. (ed.), *Euthanasia Examined: Ethical, Clinical and Legal Perspectives* (Cambridge, 1995) 141

—— and VENTAFRIDDA, V. (eds.), *The Continuing Care of Terminal Cancer Patients* (New Haven, 1980)

VAN BERKESTIJN, M. G., 'The Royal Dutch Medical Association Attitude Towards Euthanasia: With the Criterion "Terminal Phase" Things Are Getting Out of Hand' in Royal Dutch Medical Association, *Euthanasia in the Netherlands* (Utrecht, 1991)

——, 'The Royal Dutch Medical Association and the Practice of Euthanasia and Assisted Suicide' in RDMA, *Euthanasia in the Netherlands* (Utrecht, 1991)

VAN DELDEN, J., 'Euthanasia in the Netherlands: The Medical Scene' in Sneiderman, B. and Kaufert, J. (eds.), *Euthanasia in the Netherlands: A Model For Canada?* (Manitoba, 1994) 20

VAN DER WAL, G. *et al.* (ed.), *Euthanasie: Knelpunten in een Discussie (Euthanasia: Bottlenecks in a Discussion)* (Baarn, 1987)

VEATCH, R., *Death, Dying and the Biological Revolution: Our Last Quest for Responsibility* (New Haven, 1976)

VERE, D., *Voluntary Euthanasia: Is There an Alternative?* (London, 1971)

VOLUNTARY EUTHANASIA SOCIETY, *A Guide to Self-Deliverance* (London, 1981)

VOLUNTARY EUTHANASIA SOCIETY OF NEW SOUTH WALES, *Voluntary Euthanasia—A Choice* (Sydney, 1991)

VOLUNTARY EUTHANASIA SOCIETY OF VICTORIA, *Voluntary Euthanasia: The Right to Choose*, revised edn. (Mooroolbark, Victoria, 1982)

WALLACE, S. and ESER, A. (eds.), *Suicide and Euthanasia: The Rights of Personhood* (Knoxville, 1981)

WEIR, R. (ed.), *Ethical Issues in Death and Dying* (New York, 1977)

——, *Abating Treatment with Critically Ill Patients* (New York, 1989)

WENNBERG, R., *Terminal Choices: Euthanasia, Suicide, and the Right to Die* (Grand Rapids, Michigan, 1989)

WILLIAMS, G., *The Sanctity of Life and the Criminal Law* (London, 1956)

'Euthanasia and the Physician' in M. Kohl, *Beneficent Euthanasia* (Buffalo, New York, 1975) 145

——, *Textbook of Criminal Law*, 2nd edn. (London, 1983)

——, 'Euthanasia Legislation: A Rejoinder to the Non-Religious Objections' in Downing, A. and Smoker, B. (eds.), *Voluntary Euthanasia: Experts Debate the Right to Die* (London, 1986) 156

WILNER, D. *et al.*, *Who Believes in Voluntary Euthanasia?* (Los Angeles, 1983)

WILSHAW, C., *The Right to Die: A Rational Approach to Voluntary Euthanasia* (London, 1974)

WILSON, J., *Death by Decision: The Medical, Moral, and Legal Dilemmas of Euthanasia* (Philadelphia, 1975)

WINKLER, E., 'Forgoing Treatment: Killing vs. Letting Die and the Issue of Non-Feeding' in Thornton J. and Winkler, E., *Ethics and Aging: The Right to Live and the Right to Die* (Vancouver, 1988) 155

ZWART, H., 'Psychology, Self-Determination and the Veil' in Aycke, O. and Smook, M. (eds.), *Right to Self-Determination*, Proceedings of the 8th World Conference of the Right to Die Societies (Amsterdam, 1990) 33

ARTICLES AND PAPERS

AARTSEN, G. *et al.*, (letter) (1989) 19 *Hastings Center R* 47

ADMIRAAL, P., 'Active Voluntary Euthanasia' (1985) *New Humanist* 23

——, 'Euthanasia in the Netherlands' (1988) 3 *Euthanasia Rev.* 107

——, 'Justifiable Euthanasia' (1988) 3 *Issues Law & Med.* 361

——, 'Is There a Place for Euthanasia?' (1991) 10 *Bioethics News* 10

ALBERT, L., '*Cruzan* v *Director, Missouri Department of Health*' (1991) 12 *J Legal Med.* 331

ALEXANDER, L., 'Medical Science Under Dictatorship' (1949) 241 *New Eng.JMed.* 39

ALLSOPP, M., 'Active Euthanasia in America' (1987) 3 *Humane Med.* 133

——, 'Active Euthanasia in America: The Domino Falls' (1987) 54 *Linacre Q* 20

ALSCHULER, A., 'The Right to Die' (1991) 141 *New LJ* 1637

ANDERSON, J. and CADDELL, D., 'Attitudes of Medical Professionals Toward Euthanasia' (1993) 37 *Soc. Sci. Med.* 105

ANDREWS, J., 'Euthanasia Dilemma Splits the Profession' (1995) *Doctor* 9 Feb. 43

ANGELL, M., 'Euthanasia' (1988) 319 *New Eng.JMed.* 1348

ANNAS, G., 'Elizabeth Bouvia: Whose Space is This Anyway?' (1986) 16 *Hastings Center R* 24

——, 'Nancy Cruzan and the Right to Die' (1990) 323 *New Eng.JMed.* 670

——, 'Killing Machines' (1991) 21 *Hastings Center R* 33

——, 'The Long Dying of Nancy Cruzan' (1991) 19 *Law, Med. & Health Care* 52

——, 'Physician-Assisted Suicide—Michigan's Temporary Solution' (1993) 328 *New Eng.JMed.* 1573

ARKES, H., 'Once More Unto the Breach: The Right to Die—Again' (1992) 8 *Issues Law & Med.* 317

ARRAS, J., 'The Right to Die on the Slippery Slope' (1982) 8 *Social Theory & Practice* 285

ASHBY, M., 'Hard Cases, Causation and Care of the Dying' (1995) 3 *JLaw & Med.* 152

ASHWORTH, A., 'The Scope of Criminal Liability for Omissions' (1989) 105 *Law QRev.* 424

AYD, F., 'Voluntary Euthanasia: The Right to be Killed' (1970) 2 *Medical Counterpoint* 12

BACHMAN, J. *et al.*, 'Attitudes of Michigan Physicians and the Public Toward Legalizing Physician-Assisted Suicide and Voluntary Euthanasia' (1996) 334 *New Eng.JMed.* 303

BACK, A. *et al.*, 'Physician-Assisted Suicide and Euthanasia in Washington State: Patient Requests and Physician Responses' (1996) 275 JAMA 919

BARRY, R., 'Aid in Dying: Problems and Paradoxes' (1987) 54 *Linacre Q.* 22

——, 'Death Induction, Active Euthanasia by Omission and Protecting the Vulnerable' (1989) 13 *International Review* 205

—— and MAHER, J., 'Indirectly Intended Life-Shortening Analgesia: Clarifying the Principles' (1990) 6 *Issues Law & Med.* 117

BATTIN, M., 'The Least Worst Death' (1983) 13 *Hastings Center R* 13

——, 'Age Rationing and the Just Distribution of Health Care: Is There a Duty to Die?' (1987) 97 *Ethics* 317

——, 'Seven Caveats Concerning the Discussion of Euthanasia in Holland' (1990) 34 *Perspectives in Biology & Med.* 73

——, 'Euthanasia: The Way We Do It, The Way They Do It' (1991) 6 *JPain & Symptom Management* 298

——, 'Voluntary Euthanasia and the Risks of Abuse: Can We Learn Anything from the Netherlands?' (1992) 20 *Law Med. & Health Care* 133

BAUDOUIN, J., 'Cessation of Treatment and Suicide: A Proposal for Reform' (1982) 3 *Health Law in Canada* 72

BAUGHAM, W. *et al.*, 'Euthanasia: Criminal, Tort, Constitutional and Legislative Considerations' (1973) 48 *Notre Dame Law.* 1202

BAUME, P. and O'MALLEY, E., 'Euthanasia: Attitudes and Practices of Medical Practitioners' (1994) 161 MJA 137

BAUME, P. *et al.*, 'Professed Religious Affiliation and the Practice of Euthanasia' (1995) 21 *JMed.Ethics* 49

BEAUCHAMP, T. and DAVIDSON, A., 'The Definition of Euthanasia' (1979) 4 *JMed.& Phil.* 294

BELOFF, J., 'Why the BMA is Wrong' (1989) Jan. *VESS Newsletter* 1

BENRUBI, G., 'Euthanasia: The Need for Procedural Safeguards' (1992) 326 *New Eng.JMed.* 197

BERNHOFT, R., 'The Human Costs of Euthanasia: A Risk/Benefit Analysis of Physician Assisted Suicide' (1993) 15 *Clinical Therapeutics* 1185

BEYNON, H., 'Doctors as Murderers' (1982) *Crim.LRev.* 17

BIX, B., 'Physician Assisted Suicide and the United States Constitution' (1995) 58 *Mod.LR* 404

BLEICH, J., 'Life as an Intrinsic Rather than Instrumental Good: The Spiritual Case Against Euthanasia' (1993) 9 *Issues Law & Med.* 139

BLENDON, R. *et al.*, 'Should Physicians Aid Their Patients in Dying?' (1992) 267 JAMA 2658

BLIJHAM, G., 'The Person from Porlock, Ethical Issues in Terminal Care: The Dutch Perspective' (1995) 3 *Support Care Cancer* 61

BLISS, M., 'Resources, the Family and Voluntary Euthanasia' (1990) 40 *Brit.JGeneral Med. Practice* 117

BLOCK, S. and BILLINGS, A., 'Patient Requests to Hasten Death: Evaluation and Management in Terminal Care' (1994) 154 *Arch. Intern. Med.* 2039

BLOOM, M., 'Article Embroils *JAMA* in Ethical Controversy' (1988) 239 *Science* 1235

BOORMAN, J., 'To Live or Not to Live: The Moral and Practical Case Against Active Euthanasia' (1979) 121 CMAJ 484

BOPP, J., 'Nutrition and Hydration for Patients: The Constitutional Aspects' (1988) 4 *Issues Law & Med.* 3

—— and MARZEN, T., '*Cruzan*: Facing the Inevitable' (1991) 19 *Law, Med. & Health Care* 37

BORST-EILERS, E., 'The Status of Physician-Administered Active Euthanasia in the Netherlands', paper presented at the Second International Conference on Health Law and Ethics, London, 16–21 July 1989

BOSTROM, B., 'Euthanasia in the Netherlands: A Model for the United States?' (1989) 4 *Issues Law & Med.* 467

—— and LAGERWEY, W., 'Court of the Hague (Penal Chamber) April 2 1987' (1988) 3 *Issues Law & Med.* 451

BOYD, K., 'The Price of Euthanasia' (1995) Jan. *VESS Newsletter* 1

BRAHAMS, D., 'Euthanasia in the Netherlands' (1990) 58 *Medico-Legal J* 98

——, 'Euthanasia: Doctor Convicted of Attempted Murder' (1992) 340 *Lancet* 783

BRANDT, C. *et al.*, 'Model Aid-In-Dying Act' (1989) 75 *Iowa LRev.* 125

BREWER, C., 'Voluntary Euthanasia or Assisted Suicide? A Question of Freedom' (1993) 44 *Catholic Med Q* 22

BROCK, D., 'Euthanasia' (1992) 65 *Yale Journal of Biology and Medicine* 121

——, 'Voluntary Active Euthanasia' (1992) 22 *Hastings Center R* 10

BRODY, H., 'Assisted Death—A Compassionate Response to Medical Failure' (1992) 327 *New Eng.JMed.* 1384

——, 'Causing, Intending and Assisting Death' (1993) 4 *J Clinical Ethics* 112

BROWN, H. *et al.*, 'Is it Normal for Terminally Ill Patients to Desire Death?' (1986) 143 *Am.J Psychiatry* 208

BROWN, N. *et al.*, 'The Preservation of Life' (1970) 211 JAMA 76

BROWNE, A., 'Assisted Suicide and Active Voluntary Euthanasia' (1989) 2 *Can.JLJuris.* 35

BRUERA, E. *et al.*, 'Cognitive Failure in Patients with Terminal Cancer: A Prospective Study' (1992) 7 *JPain &Symptom Management* 192

BUCHANAN, J., 'Euthanasia: The Medical and Psychological Issues' (1995) 3 *JLaw & Med.* 161

BURGESS, J., 'The Great Slippery-Slope Argument' (1993) 19 *JMed. Ethics* 169

BURGESS, M., 'The Medicalization of Dying' (1993) 18 *JMed.&Phil.* 269

BUTLER, R., 'Physician-Assisted Suicide: The Wrong Way to Go' (1990) 45 *Geriatrics* 13

BYOCK, I., 'The Euthanasia/Assisted Suicide Debate Matures' (1993) 10 *Am. J Hospice and Palliative Care* 8

——, 'Consciously Walking the Fine Line: Thoughts on a Hospice Response to Assisted Suicide and Euthanasia' (1993) 9 *J Palliative Care* 25

CALLAHAN, D., 'On Feeding the Dying' (1983) 13 *Hastings Center R* 22

——, 'Can We Return Death to Disease?' (1989) 19 *Hastings Center R* 4

——, 'Aid-In-Dying: The Social Dimension' (1991) 118 *Commonweal* 476

——, 'When Self-Determination Runs Amok' (1992) 22 *Hastings Center R* 52

CAMPBELL, C., 'Aid-in-Dying and the Taking of Human Life' (1992) 18 *JMed. Ethics* 128

——, 'Religious Ethics and Active Euthanasia in a Pluralist Society' (1992) 2 *Kennedy Institute of Ethics J* 253

CAMPBELL, T., 'Euthanasia and the Law' (1979) 17 *Alta LRev.* 188

CANNON, W., 'The Right to Die' (1970) 7 *Hous.LRev.* 654

CANTOR, N., 'A Patient's Decision to Decline Life-Saving Medical Treatment: Bodily Integrity Versus the Preservation of Life' (1973) 26 *Rutgers LRev.* 228

——, 'The Permanently Unconscious Patient, Non-Feeding and Euthanasia' (1989) 15 *Am.JLaw & Med.* 381

CAPLAN, H. *et al.*, 'When A Doctor Gives a Deadly Dose' (1987) 17 *Hastings Center R* 20

CAPRON, A., 'Legal and Ethical Problems in Decisions for Death' (1986) 14 *Law, Med. & Health Care* 141

——, 'The Right to Die: Progress and Peril' (1987) 2 *Euthanasia Rev.* 42

——, 'Medical Decisionmaking and the Right to Die After *Cruzan*' (1991) 19 *Law, Med. & Health Care* 5

——, 'Euthanasia in the Netherlands: American Observations' (1992) 22 *Hastings Center R* 30

——, 'Sledding in Oregon' (1995) 25 *Hastings Centre R* 34

CARL, L., 'The Right to Voluntary Euthanasia' (1988) 10 *Whittier LRev.* 489

CARNERIE, F., 'Euthanasia and Self-Determinism: Is there a Charter Right to Die in Canada' (1987) 32 *McGill LJ* 299

CARSON, R., 'Washington's I-119' (1992) 22 *Hastings Center R* 7

CASSEL, C. and MEIER, D., 'Morals and Moralism in the Debate Over Euthanasia and Assisted Suicide' (1990) 323 *New Eng.JMed.* 750

CASSEL, E., 'The Nature of Suffering and the Goals of Medicine' (1982) 306 *New Eng.JMed.* 639

CASTEL, J. G., 'Nature and Effects of Consent with Respect to the Right to Life and the Right to Physical and Mental Integrity in the Medical Field: Criminal and Private Law Aspects' (1978) 16 *Alta.LRev.* 293

CASWELL, D., 'Rejecting Criminal Liability for Life-Shortening Palliative Care' (1990) 6 *JContemp. Health Law & Pol'y* 127

CAVANAUGH, J. and. GUNZ, F., 'Palliative Hospice Care in Australia' (1988) 2 *Palliative Med.* 51

CELOCRUZ, M., 'Aid-in-Dying: Should We Decriminalize Physician-Assisted Suicide and Physician Committed Euthanasia?' (1992) 18 *Am.J Law & Med.* 369

CHAMBERS, D., 'Ethics or Medical Ethics' (1984) 24 *Med. Science & Law* 17

CHILDRESS, J., 'Civil Disobedience, Conscientious Objection, and Evasive Noncompliance: A Framework for the Analysis of Illegal Actions in Health Care' (1985) 10 *JMed. & Phil.* 63

CHOCHINOV, H. *et al.*, 'Desire for Death in the Terminally Ill' (1995) 12 *Am.JPsychiatry* 1185

CHURCHILL, L., 'Examining the Ethics of Active Euthanasia' (1990) 5 *Med. Ethics for the Physician* 16

CIESIELSKI-CARLUCCI, C., 'Physician Attitudes and Experiences with Assisted Suicide: Results of a Small Opinion Survey' (1993) 2 *Cambridge Q Healthcare Ethics* 39

—— and KIMSMA, G., 'The Impact of Reporting Cases of Euthanasia in Holland: A Patient and Family Perspective' (1994) 8 *Bioethics* 151

CIPRIANI, T., 'Give Me Liberty and Give Me Death' (1995) 3 *JLaw&Med.* 177

CLARKE, D., 'Physician Assisted Aid in Dying: A Californian Proposal' (1988) 2 *Euthanasia Rev.* 207

CLOUSER, K. 'The Challenge for Future Debate on Euthanasia' (1991) 6 *JPain & Symptom Management* 306

COHEN, H., 'Euthanasia as a Way of Life' (1991) 43 *Hemlock Q* 7

COHEN, J. *et al.*, 'Attitudes Toward Assisted Suicide and Euthanasia Among Physicians in Washington State' (1994) 331 *New Eng.JMed.* 89

COLE, S. and SHEA, M., 'Voluntary Euthanasia: A Proposed Remedy' (1975) 39 *Alb. LRev.* 826

CONNOLLY, M., 'Alternatives to Euthanasia: Pain Management' (1989) 4 *Issues Law & Med.* 497

CONWELL, Y. and CAINE, E., 'Rational Suicide and the Right to Die: Reality and Myth' (1991) 325 *New Eng.JMed.* 1100

CRANE, D., 'Physicians' Attitudes Toward the Treatment of Critically Ill Patients' (1973) 23 *Bio. Science* 471

CRISP, R., 'A Good Death: Who Best to Bring It?' (1987) 1 *Bioethics* 74

CURRAN, W., 'Quality of Life and Treatment Decisions: The Canadian Law Reform Commission Report' (1984) 310 *New Eng.JMed.* 297

DAVIES, J., 'Euthanasia' (1988) 297 BMJ 131

——, 'Raping and Making Love are Different Concepts: So are Killing and Voluntary Euthanasia' (1988) 14 *JMed. Ethics* 148

DAWSON, J., 'Last Rights and Wrongs—Euthanasia: Autonomy and Responsibility' (1992) 1 *Cambridge Q of Healthcare Ethics* 81

DE WACHTER, M., 'Active Euthanasia in the Netherlands' (1989) 262 JAMA 3316

DELGADO, R., 'Euthanasia Reconsidered: The Choice of Death as an Aspect of the Right of Privacy' (1975) 17 *Ariz.LRev.* 474

DESSAUR, C. and RUTENFRANS, C., 'The Present Day Practice of Euthanasia' (1988) 3 *Issues Law & Med.* 399

DEVETTERE, R., 'Reconceptualising the Euthanasia Debate' (1989) 17 *Law, Med. & Health Care* 145

——, 'The Imprecise Language of Euthanasia and Causing Death' (1990) 1 *JClin. Ethics* 268

DICKENS, B., 'The Right to Natural Death' (1981) 26 *McGill LJ* 847

——, 'The Final Freedom: Deciding to Forgo Life-Sustaining Treatment' (1984) *Public Law* 34

——, 'Terminal Care, Incompetent Persons and Donation' (1986) 3 *Transplantation Today* 54

——, 'Medically Assisted Death: *Nancy B* v. *Hotel-Dieu de Quebec* (1993) 38 *McGill LJ* 1053

——, 'When Terminally Ill Patients Request Death: Assisted Suicide Before Canadian Courts' (1994) 10 *JPalliative Care* 52

DICKEY, N., 'Euthanasia: A Concept Whose Time Has Come?' (1993) 8 *Issues Law & Med.* 521

DIEKSTRA, R., 'Assisted Suicide and Euthanasia: Experiences from the Netherlands' (1993) 25 *Annals Med.* 5

DILLMANN, R. 'Euthanasia in a Dutch Perspective' paper, Royal Dutch Medical Association (1991)

—— and LEGEMAATE, J., 'Euthanasia in the Netherlands: The State of the Legal Debate' (1994) 1 *European J Health Law* 81

DOERFLINGER, R., 'Assisted Suicide: Pro Choice or Anti Life?' (1989) 19 *Hastings Center R* 16

DOUGHERTY, C., 'The Common Good, Terminal Illness and Euthanasia' (1993) 9 *Issues Law & Med* 151

DOUKAS, D. *et al.*, 'Attitudes and Behaviours on Physician-Assisted Death: A Study of Michigan Oncologists' (1995) 13 *JClin.Oncology* 1055

DRIESSE, M. *et al.*, 'Euthanasia and the Law in the Netherlands' (1988) 4 *Issues Law & Med.* 385

DUBERSTEIN, P. *et al.*, 'Attitudes Toward Self-Determined Death: A Survey of Primary Care Physicians' (1995) 43 *JAm.Geriatric Society* 395

DYCK, A., 'The Good Samaritan Ideal and Beneficent Euthanasia: Conflicting Views of Mercy' (1975) 42 *Linacre Q* 176

——, 'Physician-Assisted Suicide: Is It Ethical?' (1992) 7 *Trends in Health Care, Law & Ethics* 19

DWIGHT, E. *et al.*, 'Statement on Euthanasia and Physician-Assisted Suicide' (1994) 10 *JPalliative Care* 80

EDMUND DAVIES, Lord, 'On Dying and Dying Well: Legal Aspects' (1977) 70 *Proc. Royal Soc.Med.* 71

ENGELHARDT, T. and MALLOY, M., 'Suicide and Assisting Suicide: A Critique of Legal Sanctions' (1982) 36 Sw.LJ 1003

ERGO!, 'What's in a Word?: The Results of a Roper Poll of Americans on How They View the Importance of Language in The Debate Over The Right to Choose to Die' (1993)

EVERHART, M. and PEARLMAN, R., 'Stability of Patient Preferences Regarding Life-Sustaining Treatments' (1990) 97 *Chest* 159

FAIRBAIRN, G., 'Kuhse, Singer and Slippery Slopes' (1988) 14 *JMed. Ethics* 132

FEINBERG, J., 'Overlooking the Merits of the Individual Case: An Unpromising Approach to the Right to Die' (1991) 4 *Ratio Juris.* 131

FENIGSEN, R., 'A Case Against Dutch Euthanasia' (1989) 19 *Hastings Center R* 22

——, 'The Report of the Dutch Governmental Committee on Euthanasia' (1991) 7 *Issues Law & Med.* 339

——, 'The Netherlands: New Regulations Concerning Euthanasia' (1993) 9 *Issue Law and Med.* 167

FINDLAY, M., 'Hunger Strikes and the State's Right to Force Feed—Recent Australian Experience' (1984) 19 *Ir. Jurist* 304

FINKEL, N. *et al.*, 'Right to Die, Euthanasia, and Community Sentiment: Crossing the Public/Private Boundary' (1993) 17 *Law & Human Behaviour* 487

FINNIS, J., '*Bland*: Crossing the Rubicon?' (1993) 109 Law QRev. 329

FISHER, L., 'The Suicide Trap: *Bouvia* v. *Superior Court* and the Right to Refuse Medical Treatment' (1987) 21 *Loy.LALRev.* 219

FLETCHER, G., 'Prolonging Life' (1967) 42 *Wash.LRev.* 999

——, 'Legal Aspects of the Decision Not to Prolong Life' (1968) 203 JAMA 65

FLETCHER, J., 'Morals Medicine and the Law—Symposium: The Issues' (1956) 31 *NYULRev.* 1157

——, 'The Patient's Right to Die' (1960) 221 *Harper's Magazine* 139

——, 'Voluntary Euthanasia: The New Shape of Death' (1970) 2 *Medical Counterpoint* 13

——, 'Ethics and Euthanasia' (1973) 73 *Am.JNursing* 670

——, 'The "Right" to Live and the "Right" to Die' (1974) 34 *Humanist* 12

——, 'Medical Resistance to the Right to Die' (1987) 35 *JAm. Geriatrics Society* 679

——, 'The Courts and Euthanasia' (1987–88) 15 *Law, Med. & Health Care* 223

FLEW, A., 'Dying Decently' (1981) *Quadrant* 45

FOLEY, K., 'The Relationship of Pain and Symptom Management to Patient Requests for Physician-Assisted Suicide' (1991) 6 *J Pain & Symptom Management* 289

FOOT, P., 'Euthanasia' (1977) 6 *Phil. & Public Affairs* 85

FOREMAN, P., 'The Physician's Criminal Liability for the Practice of Euthanasia' (1975) 27 *Baylor LRev.* 54

FOWLER, M., 'Legislation to Legalise Active Euthanasia' (1988) 17 *Heart & Lung* 458

FERGUSSON, A. *et al.*, 'Euthanasia' (letter) (1991) 338 *Lancet* 1010

FRANCIS, L., 'Advance Directives for Voluntary Euthanasia: A Volatile Combination?' (1993) 18 *JMed&Phil.* 297

FRIED, T. *et al.*, 'Limits of Patient Autonomy: Physician Attitudes and Practices Regarding Life-Sustaining Treatments and Euthanasia' (1993) 153 *Arch. Intern.Med.* 722

FUKADA, M., 'A Survey of Research of Doctors' Attitudes Toward Euthanasia in Boston and Japan' (1975) 22 *Osaka ULReview* 19

FYE, B., 'Active Euthanasia: An Historical Survey of its Conceptual Origins and Introduction into Medical Thought' (1978) 52 *Bull. of the History of Med.* 492

GAYLIN, W. *et al.*, 'Doctors Must Not Kill' (1988) 259 JAMA 2139

GELFAND, G., 'Euthanasia and the Terminally Ill Patient' (1984) 63 *Neb. LRev.* 741

——, 'Living Will Statutes: The First Decade' (1987) *Wis.LRev.* 737

GEVERS, J., 'Legal Developments Concerning Active Euthanasia on Request in the Netherlands' (1987) 1 *Bioethics* 156

——, 'Legislation on Euthanasia: Recent Developments in the Netherlands' (1992) 18 *JMed. Ethics* 138

GILBREATH, V., 'The Right of the Terminally Ill to Die with Assistance if Necessary' (1986) 8 *Crim.Just.J* 403

GILLETT, G., 'Euthanasia, Letting Die and the Pause' (1988) 14 *JMed. Ethics* 61

——, 'Learning to Do No Harm' (1993) 18 *JMed.&Phil.* 253

——, 'Ethical Aspects of the Northern Territory Legislation' (1995) 3 *JLaw & Med.* 145

GILLON, R., 'Acts and Omission, Killing and Letting Die' (1986) 292 BMJ 126

——, 'Ordinary and Extraordinary Means' (1986) 292 BMJ 259

——, 'Euthanasia, Withholding Life-Prolonging Treatment, and Moral Differences Between Killing and Letting Die' (1988) 14 *JMed. Ethics* 115

GLANTZ, L., 'Withholding and Withdrawing Treatment: The Role of the Criminal Law' (1987/88) 15 *Law, Med. & Health Care* 231

GOFF, R., 'A Matter of Life and Death' (1995) 3 *Med LRev.* 1

GOLDSMITH, L., 'Physician Acquitted of Charges of Murdering Patient' (1974) 2 *J Legal Med.* 47

GOMEZ, C., 'Euthanasia: Consider the Dutch' (1991) 118 *Commonweal* 469

GOSTIN, L., 'A Right to Choose Death: The Judicial Trilogy of *Brophy*, *Bouvia* and *Conroy*' (1986) 14 *Law, Med. & Health Care* 198

——, 'Drawing a Line Between Killing and Letting Die: The Law, and Law Reform, on Medically Assisted Dying' (1993) 21 *J Law Med. & Ethics* 94

GRABER, G., 'Assisted Suicide is Not Voluntary Active Euthanasia, but It's Awfully Close' (1993) 41 *J Am. Geriatric Society* 88

GRIFFITHS, J., 'Assisted Suicide in the Netherlands: The *Chabot* Case' (1995) 58 *Mod. L Rev.* 232

——, 'Recent Development in the Netherlands Concerning Euthanasia and Other Medical Behaviour that Shortens Life' (1995) 1 *Med. Law International* 347

——, 'The Regulation of Euthanasia and Related Medical Procedures That Shorten Life in the Netherlands' (1994) 1 *Med. Law International* 137

GRUBB, A., 'Refusal of Medical Treatment: I—The Competent Adult' (1992) Vol. 3 No. 1 *Dispatches* 1

——, '*Sue Rodriguez* v. *Attorney General of Canada and Others*' [1994] 2 *Med. L Rev.* 119

——, 'Treatment Without Consent: Adult: *Re C (Refusal of Medical Treatment)*' [1994] 2 *Med. LR* 92

GRUMAN, G., 'An Historical Introduction to Ideas About Voluntary Euthanasia' (1973) 4 *Omega* 87

GULA, R., 'Euthanasia: A Catholic Perspective' (1987) 68 *Health Progress* 28

——, 'Moral Principles Shaping Public Policy on Euthanasia' (1990) 14 *Second Opinion* 73

GUNDERSON, M. and MAYO, D., 'Altruisim and Physician Assisted Death' (1993) 18 *J Med. & Phil.* 281

GUNN, M. and SMITH, J. C., 'Arthur's Case and the Right to Life of a Down's Syndrome Child' (1985) *Crim. L Rev.* 705

GUNNING, K., 'Euthanasia in the Netherlands' (1987) 96 *News Exchange of the World Federation of Doctors Who Respect Human Life* 8

——, 'Euthanasia' (letter) (1991) 338 *Lancet* 1010

——, 'Terminal Patients in Holland' (1991) 58 *Linacre Q* 57

GURNEY, E., 'Is there a Right to Die?—A Study of the Law of Euthanasia' (1972) 3 *Cumberland-Samford L Rev.* 235

HABGOOD, J., 'Euthanasia—A Christian View' (1974) 94 *Royal Society of Health J* 124

HADDING, C., 'Right to Die—A Corollary to the Right to Live and the Right to Leave' (1989) 7 *Med. & Law* 511

HAILSHAM, Lord, 'The Law, Politics and Morality' (1988) *Denning LJ* 59

HARE, R., 'Euthanasia: A Christian View' (1975) 6 *Philosophic Exchange* 43

HARRIS, C., 'Can Doctors Decide if Euthanasia is "The Good Death"?' (1983) 26 *Mod. Med. Aust.* 9

HARVARD, L., 'The Influence of the Law on Clinical Decisions Affecting Life and Death' (1983) 23 *Med. Science & Law* 157

HASL, J., 'Patient Autonomy and the Right to Refuse Treatment: Available Remedies' (1989) 33 *St. Louis ULJ* 711

HAYRY, H. and HAYRY, M., 'Euthanasia, Ethics and Economics' (1990) 4 *Bioethics* 154

HEGLAND, K., 'Unauthorised Rendition of Lifesaving Medical Treatment' (1965) 53 *Calif. L. Rev.* 860

HEILIG, S., 'The S.F.M.S. Euthanasia Survey: Results and Analyses' (1988) *San Francisco Med.* (May) 24

HELME, T., ' "A Special Defence": A Psychiatric Approach to Formalising Euthanasia' (1993) 163 *British JPsychiatry* 456

——, 'The Voluntary Euthanasia (Legalisation) Bill (1936) Revisited' (1991) 17 *JMed. Ethics* 25

—— and PADFIELD, N., 'Setting Euthanasia on the Level' (1993) 15 *Liverpool LRev.* 75

HENDIN, H., 'Seduced by Death: Doctors, Patients, and the Dutch Cure' (1994) 10 *Issues Law & Med.* 123

HICKIE, J., 'Euthanasia 1984' (1984) 141 MJA 140

HIGGS, R., 'Cutting the Thread and Pulling the Wool—A Request for Euthanasia in General Practice' (1983) 9 *JMed. Ethics* 45

——, 'Not the Last Word on Euthanasia' (1988) 296 BMJ 1348

HILHORST, H., 'Religion and Euthanasia in the Netherlands: Exploring a Diffuse Relationship' (1983) 30 *Social Compass* 491

HIRSCH, D., 'Euthanasia: Is it Murder or Mercy Killing? A Comparison of the Criminal Law in the United States, the Netherlands and Switzerland' (1990) 12 *Loy.LAInt'l. & Comp.LJ* 821

HOCKLEY, J. *et al.*, 'Survey of Distressing Symptoms in Dying Patients and their Families in Hospital and the Response to a Symptom Control Team' (1988) 296 BMJ 1715

HOWE, E., 'Clinical Dilemmas When Patients Want Assistance in Dying' (1994) 5 *J Clinical Ethics* 3

HUGHES, G., 'Criminal Omissions' (1957–8) 67 *Yale LJ* 590

HUI, E. and GIBBARD, W., ' "Thou Shalt Not Kill": A Case Against Active Euthanasia' (1993) 9 *Humane Med.* 207

HUMPHRY, D., 'Euthanasia for the Elite' (1986) 1 *Euthanasia Rev.* 203

——, 'Legislating for Active Voluntary Euthanasia' (1988) 48 *Humanist* 10

——, 'Physicians and Euthanasia' (1988) 3 *Euthanasia Rev.* 79

HUNT, R. *et al.*, 'The Incidence of Requests for Quicker Terminal Course' (1995) 9 *Palliative Med.* 167

HUSAK, D., 'Killing, Letting Die and Euthanasia' (1979) 5 *JMed. Ethics* 200

HUSEB, S., 'Is Euthanasia a Caring Thing to Do?' (1988) 4 *JPalliative Care* 111

HUYSE, F. and VAN TILBURG, W., 'Euthanasia Policy in the Netherlands: The Role of Consultation-Liaison Psychiatrists' (1993) 44 *Hospital and Community Psychiatry* 733

JARRET, C., 'Moral Reasoning and Legal Change: Observations on the Termination of Medical Treatment and the Development of the Law' (1988) 19 *Rutgers LJ* 1017

JECKER, N., 'Giving Death a Hand: When the Dying and the Doctor Stand in a Special Relationship' (1991) 39 *JAm.Geriatrics Society* 831

JENKINS, D., 'Why Not Choose Death in the End' (1991) 7 *Care of the Critically Ill* 6

JENNETT, B., 'Euthanasia 1990—Attitudes in Britain, USA and the Netherlands' (1991) 49 *Health Bulletin* 176

JENNINGS, B., 'Active Euthanasia and Forgoing Life-Sustaining treatment: Can We Hold the Line?' (1991) 6 *J Pain & Symptom Management* 312

JOCHEMSEN, H., 'Euthanasia in Holland: An Ethical Critique of the New Law' (1994) 20 *J Med Ethics* 212

JONSEN, A., 'To Help the Dying Die—A New Duty for Anesthesiologists?' (1993) 78 *Anesthesiology* 225

JOHNSON, M., 'Voluntary Active Euthanasia: The Next Frontier?' (1992) 8 *Issues Law & Med.* 343

JOHNSON, S., 'From Medicalization to Legalization to Politicization: *O'Connor, Cruzan* and the Refusal of Treatment in the 1990s' (1989) 21 *Conn. L Rev.* 685

JORGENSON, D. and NEUBECKER, R., 'Euthanasia: A National Survey of Attitudes Towards Voluntary Termination of Life' (1980–81) 11 *Omega* 281

KAMISAR, Y., 'Some 'Non-Religious Views Against Proposed Mercy-Killing Legislation' (1958) 42 *Minn. L Rev.* 969

——, 'The Right to Die' (1988) 33 *Mich. L Quadrangle News* 7

——, 'Active v. Passive Euthanasia: Why Keep the Distinction?' (1993) 29 *Trial* 32

——, 'Are Laws Against Assisted Suicide Unconstitutional?' (1993) 23 *Hastings Center R* 32

KAPLAN, R., 'Euthanasia Legislation: A Survey and a Model Act' (1976) 2 *Am. J Law & Med.* 41

KASS, L., 'Neither for Love Nor Money: Why Doctors Must Not Kill' (1989) 94 *Public Interest* 25

——, 'Is There a Right to Die?' (1993) 23 *Hastings Center R* 34

KELLY, G., 'Survey on Euthanasia' (1950) 17 *Linacre Q* 3

——, 'The Duty of Using Artificial Means of Preserving Life' (1950) 11 *Theological Studies* 203

——, 'The Duty to Preserve Life' (1951) 12 *Theological Studies* 550

KENNEDY, I., 'The Legal Effect of Requests by the Terminally Ill and Aged Not to Receive Further Treatment from Doctors' (1976) *Crim. L Rev.* 217

——, 'Switching Off Life Support Machines: the Legal Implications' (1977) *Crim. L Rev.* 443

——, 'The Quality of Mercy: Patients, Doctors and Dying' (1994) The Upjohn Lecture

—— and GRUBB, A., 'Withdrawal of Artificial Hydration and Nutrition: Incompetent Adult: *Airedale NHS Trust* v. *Bland*' [1993] 1 *Med. LR* 359

KEOWN, J., 'On Regulating Death' (1992) 22 *Hastings Center R* 39

——, 'The Law and Practice of Euthanasia in the Netherlands' (1992) 108 *Law QRev.* 51

——, 'Physician-Assisted Suicide and the Dutch Supreme Court' (1995) 111 *Law QRev.* 394

KEY, P., 'Euthanasia: Law and Morality' (1989) 6 *Auckland ULRev.* 225

KEYSERLINGK, E., 'Euthanasia' (1979) 45 *Can. Doctor* 18

——, 'Public Opinion on Legalizing Active Euthanasia' (1987) 3 *Humane Med.* 139

KIMSMA, G., 'Clinical Ethics in Assisting Euthanasia: Avoiding Malpractice in Drug Application' (1992) 17 *J Med. & Phil.* 439

—— and VAN LEEUWEN, E., 'Dutch Euthanasia: Background, Practice, and Present Justifications' (1993) 2 *Cambridge Q Healthcare Ethics* 19

KINSELLA, T. and VERHOEF, M., 'Alberta Euthanasia Survey: 1. Physicians' Opinions About the Morality and Legalization of Active Euthanasia' (1993) 148 CMAJ 1921

——, 'Alberta Euthanasia Survey: 2. Physicians' Opinions About the Acceptance of Active Euthanasia as a Medical Act and the Reporting of Such Practice' (1993) 148 CMAJ 1929

KIRBY, M., 'Euthanasia—Old Issue: New Debate' (1984) 14 *Aust & NZJMed.* 691

KLAGSBRUN, S., 'Physician-Assisted Suicide: A Double Dilemma' (1991) 6 *JPain & Symptom Management* 325

KLOSS, D., 'Consent to Medical Treatment' (1965) 5 *Med., Science & Law* 89

KOMESAROFF, P. *et al.*, 'The Euthanasia Controversy: Decision-making in Extreme Cases' (1995) 162 MJA 594

KOHL, M., 'Altruistic Humanism and Voluntary Beneficent Euthanasia' (1992) 8 *Issues Law & Med.* 331

KOOP C. and GRANT, E., 'The Small Beginnings of Euthanasia: Examining the Erosion in Legal Prohibitions Against Mercy-Killing' (1986) 2 *JLaw, Ethics and Public Pol'y*

KORGAONKAR, G. and TRIBE, D., 'Medical Manslaughter' (1992) 136 *Sol.J* 105

KUHSE, H., 'Extraordinary Means and the Intentional Termination of Life' (1981) 15 *Social Sciences & Med.* 117

——, 'Debate: Extraordinary Means and the Sanctity of Life' (1981) 7 *JMed. Ethics* 74

——, 'Euthanasia—Again' (1985) 142 MJA 610

——, 'Active and Passive Euthanasia—Ten Years into the Debate' (1986) 1 *Euthanasia Rev.* 108

——, 'The Case for Active Voluntary Euthanasia' (1986) 14 *Law, Med. & Health Care* 145

——, 'The Alleged Peril of Active Voluntary Euthanasia: A Reply to Alexander Morgan Capron' (1987) 2 *Euthanasia Rev.* 60

——, 'Voluntary Euthanasia in the Netherlands' (1987) 147 MJA 394

——, 'Voluntary Euthanasia in the Netherlands and Slippery Slopes' (1992) Vol. 11 No. 4 *Bioethics News* 1

—— and SINGER, P., 'For Sometimes Letting and Helping Die' (1986) 14 *Law, Med. & Health Care* 149

——, 'Age and the Allocation of Medical Resources' (1988) 13 *JMed. & Phil.* 101

——, 'Doctors' Practices and Attitudes Regarding Voluntary Euthanasia' (1988) 148 MJA 623

——, 'Euthanasia: A Survey of Nurses' Attitudes and Practices' (1992) 21 *Aust. Nurses J* 21

——, 'Active Voluntary Euthanasia, Morality and the Law' (1995) 3 *JLaw & Med* 129

KURTZ, P., 'The Case for Euthanasia: A Humanistic Perspective' (1992) 8 *Issues Law & Med.* 309

KUTNER, L., 'Due Process of Euthanasia: The Living Will, A Proposal' (1969) 44 *Ind.LJ* 539

LACEWELL, L., 'A Comparative View of the Roles of Motive and Consent in the

Response of the Criminal Justice System to Active Euthanasia' (1987) 6 *Med. Law* 449

LACHS, J., 'Active Euthanasia' (1990) 1 *JClinical Ethics* 11

LAING, J. A., 'Assisting Suicide' (1990) 54 *JCrim. Law* 106

LANDER, H., 'Some Medical Aspects of Euthanasia' (1984) MJA 173

LANHAM, D., 'Murder by Instigating Suicide' (1980) *Crim.LRev.* 215

——, 'The Right to Choose to Die with Dignity' (1990) 14 *Crim.LJ* 401

——, 'Withdrawal of Artificial Feeding from Patients in a Persistent Vegetative State' (1994) 6 *Current Issues in Criminal Justice* 135

——, 'Euthanasia, Painkilling, Murder and Manslaughter' (1994) *JLaw & Med.* 146

LAPPE, M., 'Dying While Living: A Critique of Allowing-to-Die Legislation' (1978) 4 *JMed. Ethics* 195

LATIMER, E., 'Euthanasia, Physician-Assisted Suicide and the Ethical Care of Dying Patients' (1994) 151 CMAJ 1133

LEE, M. *et al.*, 'Legalizing Assisted Suicide—Views of Physicians in Oregon' (1996) 334 *New Eng. JMed.* 310

LEENEN, H., 'The Right to Health Care and the Right of Self-Determination' (1982) 7 *Jus. Medicum* 7

——, 'The Definition of Euthanasia' (1984) 3 Med. & Law 333

——, 'Supreme Court's Decisions on Euthanasia in the Netherlands' (1986) 5 *Med. & Law* 349

——, 'Euthanasia, Assistance to Suicide and the Law: Developments in the Netherlands' (1987) 8 *Health Pol'y.* 197

——, 'Dying with Dignity: Developments in the Field of Euthanasia in the Netherlands' (1989) 8 *Med. & Law* 517

LEGEMAATE, J., 'Legal Aspects of Euthanasia and Assisted Suicide in the Netherlands 1973–1994' (1995) 4 *Cambridge QHealthcare Ethics* 112

LENG, R., 'Mercy Killing and the C.L.R.C.' (1982) 132 *New LJ* 76

LERNER, M., 'State Natural Death Acts: Illusory Protection of Individuals' Life-Sustaining Treatment Decisions' (1992) 29 *Harv.J on Legis.* 175

LESCHENSKY, W., 'Constitutional Protection of the "Refusal-of-Treatment": *Cruzan v. Director, Missouri Department of Health*, 110 S.Ct. 2841 (1990)' (1991) 14 *Harv.JL&Pub. Pol'y* 248

LEVISOHN, A., 'Voluntary Mercy Deaths' (1961) 8 *J Forensic Med.* 57

LO, B., 'Euthanasia—The Continuing Debate' (1988) 149 *Western JMed.* 211

—— *et al.*, 'Ethical Decisions in the Care of a Patient Terminally Ill with Metastatic Cancer' (1980) 92 *Annals Intern.Med.* 107

LOUISELL, D., 'Euthanasia and Biathanasia: On Dying and Killing' (1973) 22 *Catholic ULRev.* 723

LOWY, F. *et al.*, 'Canadian Physicians and Euthanasia: 4. Lessons from Experience' (1993) 148 CMAJ 1895

LUNDBERG, G., 'Debate Over the Ethics of Euthanasia' (1988) 259 JAMA 2143

LYNN, J., 'The Health Care Professional's Role When Active Euthanasia is Sought' (1988) 4 *J Palliative Care* 100

—— and CHILDRESS, J., 'Must Patients Always be Given Food and Water?' (1983) 13 *Hastings Center R* 17

MACKINNON, K., 'Active Euthanasia: A "Cop-Out"?' (1989) 4 *JPalliative Care* 110

MacKinnon, P., 'Euthanasia and Homicide' (1983–4) 26 *Crim.LQ* 483

MacMoran, J., 'On Killing and Allowing to Die' (1985) 52 *Linacre Q* 170

McCormick, R., 'The Quality of Life, the Sanctity of Life' (1978) 8 *Hastings Center R* 30

McIntyre, R., 'Physician-Assisted Dying: Contemporary Twists to an Ancient Dilemma' (1992) 7 *Trends in Health Care, Law and Ethics* 7

McSherry, B., 'Death by the Withholding of Medical Treatment and Death by Lethal Injection: Is There a Difference?' (1993) 1 *J Law & Med.* 71

Maddocks, I., 'Changing Concepts in Palliative Care' (1990) 152 MJA 535

Maguire, D., 'Death by Chance, Death by Choice' (1974) 233 *Atlantic Monthly* 57

——, 'Death, Legal and Illegal' (1974) 233 *Atlantic Monthly* 72

——, 'The Freedom to Die' (1972) 96 *Commonweal* 423

Marker, R., 'Euthanasia, the Ultimate Abandonment' (1990) 6 *Ethics & Med.* 21

Martin, T., 'Euthanasia and Modern Morality' (1949–52) 9 *Jurist* 437

Marzen, T., 'Euthanasia: The Handwriting on the Wall' (1988) 3 *Euthanasia Rev.* 44

—— et al., 'Suicide: A Constitutional Right?' (1985) 24 *Duq.LRev.* 1

Matthews, M., 'Suicidal Competence and the Patient's Right to Refuse Life-Saving Treatment' (1987) 74 *Calif.LRev.* 707

May, W., 'Is There A "Right" to Die?' (1993) 60 *Linacre Q* 35

Mayo, D., 'The Concept of Rational Suicide' (1986) 11 *JMed. & Phil.* 143

—— and Gunderson, M., 'Physician Assisted Death and Hard Choices' (1993) 18 *JMed. & Phil.* 329

Meier, D., 'Physician-Assisted Dying—Theory and Reality' (1992) 3 *JClinical Ethics* 35

Mendelson, D., 'The Northern Territory's Euthanasia Legislation in Historical Perspective' (1995) 3 *JLaw & Med.* 136

Menzel, P., 'Are Killing and Letting Die Morally Different in Medical Contexts?' (1979) 4 *JMed. & Phil.* 269

Messinger, T., 'A Gentle and Easy Death: From Ancient Greece to Beyond *Cruzan* Toward a Reasoned Legal Response to the Societal Dilemma of Euthanasia' (1993) 71 *Denv. ULRev.* 175

Mettyear, B., 'Video Recording as a Safeguard in V.E.' (1991) Vol. 8, *No. 4 SAVESBull.* 5

Meyers, D., 'The Legal Aspects of Medical Euthanasia' (1973) 23 *Bio. Science* 467

——, 'Legal Aspects of Withdrawing Nourishment from an Incurably Ill Patient' (1985) 145 *Archives Internal Med.* 125

Miles, S., 'Informed Demand for Non-Beneficial Treatment' (1991) 325 *New Eng.JMed.* 512

Millard, C., 'The Case for Euthanasia' (1931) 130 *Fortnightly Rev.* 701

Miller, F., 'Is Active Killing of Patients Always Wrong?' (1991) 2 *J Clinical Ethics* 130

—— and Brody, H., 'Professional Integrity and Physician-Assisted Death' (1995) 25 *Hastings Center R* 8

Miller, F. and Fletcher, J., 'The Case for Legalized Euthanasia' (1993) 36 *Perspectives in Biology and Medicine* 159

Miller, F. et al., 'Regulating Physician-Assisted Death' (1994) 331 *New Eng.JMed.* 119

MILLER, R., 'Hospice Care as an Alternative to Euthanasia' (1992) 20 *Law, Med& Health Care* 127

MILLS, M. *et al.*, 'Care of Dying Patients in Hospital' (1994) 309 BMJ 583

MISBIN, R., 'Physicians' Aid-in-Dying' (1991) 325 *New Eng.JMed.* 1307

MOLENDA, F., 'Active Euthanasia: Can it Ever be Justified?' (1988) 24 *Tulsa LJ* 165

MOMEYER, R., 'Does Physician Assisted Suicide Violate the Integrity of Medicine?' (1995) 20 *JMed.&Phil.* 13

MOORE, M., 'The Case for Voluntary Euthanasia' (1974) 42 *UMKCLRev.* 327

MORGAN, D., 'Whatever Happened to Consent?' (1992) 142 *New LJ* 1448

MORRIS, A., 'Voluntary Euthanasia' (1970) 45 *Wash.LRev.* 239

MULLEN, P., 'Euthanasia: An Impoverished Construction of Life and Death' (1995) 3 *JLaw & Med.* 121

MULLER, M. *et al.*, 'Voluntary Active Euthanasia and Physician-Assisted Suicide in Dutch Nursing Homes: Are the Requirements for Prudent Practice Properly Met?' (1994) 42 *JAm.Geriatric Society* 624

MULLOOLY, J., 'Ordinary/Extraordinary Means and Euthanasia' (1987) 54 *Linacre Q* 50

NEELEY, G., 'The Constitutional Right to Suicide, The Quality of Life, and the "Slippery-Slope": An Explicit Reply to Lingering Concerns' (1994) 29 *Akron LRev.* 53

NERLAND, L., 'A Cry for Help: A Comparison of Voluntary, Active Euthanasia Law' (1989) 13 *Hastings Int'l. & Comp.LRev.* 115

NEWMAN, N., 'Euthanasia: Orchestrating "The Last Syllable of. . . . Time" ' (1991) 53 *UPitt.LRev.* 153

NOWELL-SMITH, P., 'A Plea for Active Euthanasia' (1987) 7 *Geriatric Nursing & Home Care* 23

——, 'Death by Request as a Right' (1987) 2 *Euthanasia Rev.* 80

——, 'Euthanasia and the Doctors—A Rejection of the B.M.A.'s Report' (1989) 15 *JMed. Ethics* 124

O'BRIEN, S., 'Facilitating Euthanatic, Rational Suicide: Help Me Go Gentle into That Good Night' (1987) 31 *St. Louis ULJ* 651

O'DONNELL, T., 'Review of "The Physician's Responsibility Toward Hopelessly Ill Patients" ' (1984) 51 *Linacre Q* 351

OGDEN, R., 'Palliative Care and Euthanasia: A Continuum of Care' (1994) 10 *J Palliative Care* 82

——, 'The Power of Negative Thinking' (1994) 13 *Last Rights* 69

——, 'The Right to Die: A Policy Proposal for Euthanasia and Aid in Dying' (1994) 20 *Canadian Public Policy* 1

OGNALL, H., 'A Right to Die? Some Medico-Legal Reflection' (1994) 62 *Medico-Legal J* 165

OLDE SCHEPER, T. and DUURSMA, S., 'Euthanasia: The Dutch Experience' (1994) 23 *Age &Ageing* 3

ORENTLICHER, D., 'Physician Participation in Assisted Suicide' (1989) 262 JAMA 1844

——, 'The Right to Die After *Cruzan*' (1990) 264 JAMA 2444

O'ROURKE, K., 'Value Conflicts Raised by Physician Assisted Suicide' (1990) 57 *Linacre Q* 38

OSGOOD, N., 'Assisted Suicide and Older People—A Deadly Combination: Ethical Problems in Permitting Assisted Suicide' (1995) 10 *Issues Law& Med.* 415

OSTHEIMER, J., 'The Polls: Changing Attitudes Towards Euthanasia' (1980) 44 *Public Opinion Q* 123

OTLOWSKI, M., 'Mercy Killing Cases in the Australian Criminal Justice System' (1993) 17 *Crim.LJ* 10

PALMER, H., 'Dr Adams' Trial for Murder' (1957) *Crim.LRev.* 365

PARACHINI, A., 'The California Humane and Dignified Death Initiative' (1989) 19 *Hastings Center R* 10

PARKER, G., 'You Are a Child of the Universe: You Have a Right to be Here' (1977) 7 *Manitoba LRev.* 151

PARKER, M., 'Moral Intuition, Good Deaths and Ordinary Medical Practitioners' (1990) 16 *JMed. Ethics* 28

PENCE, G., 'Do Not Go Slowly into That Dark Night: Mercy Killing in Holland' (1988) 84 *Am.J Med.* 139

PENROSE, M., 'Assisted Suicide: A Tough Pill to Swallow' (1993) 20 *Pepperdine LRev.* 689

PERSELS, J., 'Forcing the Issue of Physician-Assisted Suicide: Impact of the Kevorkian Case on the Euthanasia Debate' (1993) 14 *JLegal Med.* 93

PETERS, P., 'The State's Interest in the Preservation of Life: From *Quinlan* to *Cruzan*' (1989) 50 *Ohio St.LJ* 891

PIJNENBORG, L. *et al.*, 'Life Terminating Acts Without Explicit Request of Patient' (1993) 341 *Lancet* 1196

POHLMAN, K., 'Pain Control: Euthanasia or Criminal Act?' (1990) 17 *Focus on Critical Care* 260

POHLMEIER, H., 'Suicide and Euthanasia—Special Types of Partner Relationships' (1985) 15 *Suicide & Life Threatening Behaviour* 117

POLLARD, B., 'Killing the Dying—Not the Easy Way Out' (1988) 149 MJA 312

——, 'Medical Aspects of Euthanasia' (1991) 154 MJA 613

POPE PIOUS XII, 'Religious and Moral Aspects of Pain Prevention in Medical Practice' (1957) 88 *Ir. Ecclesiastical Rec.* 193

POTAS, I., '*Schneidas* v. *Corrective Services Commission and Ors*' (1983) 7 *Crim.LJ* 353

POTTS, S., 'Looking for the Exit Door: Killing and Caring in Modern Medicine' (1988) 25 *Hous.LRev.* 493

PRESTON, T., 'Professional Norms and Physician Attitudes Toward Euthanasia' (1994) 22 *JLaw&Med.*36

QUILL, T., 'Death and Dignity: A Case of Individualised Decision Making' (1991) 324 *New Eng.JMed.* 691

——, 'The Ambiguity of Clinical Intentions' (1993) 329 *New Eng.JMed.* 1039

——, 'Doctor, I Want to Die. Will You Help Me?' (1993) 270 JAMA 870

——, 'Physician-Assisted Death: Progress or Peril?' (1994) 24 *Suicide & Life Threatening Behaviour* 315

——, 'Risk Taking by Physicians in Legally Gray Areas' (1994) 57 *Alb.Law Rev.* 693

—— *et al.*, 'Care of the Hopelessly Ill: Proposed Clinical Criteria for Physician-Assisted Suicide' (1992) 327 *New Eng.JMed.* 1380

RACHELS, J., 'Active and Passive Euthanasia' (1975) 292 *New Eng.JMed.* 78

——, 'Barney Clark's Key' (1983) 13 *Hastings Center R* 17

RAFUSE, J., 'CMA Rejects Neutral Stand, Comes Out Firmly Against MD Participation in Euthanasia' (1994) 151 CMAJ 853

RAMSEY, P., ' "Euthanasia" and Dying Well Enough' (1977) 44 *Linacre Q* 37

RANSON, D., 'The Coroner and the Rights of the Terminally Ill Act 1995 (NT)' (1995) 3 *JLaw&Med.* 169

RAWLS, J., 'Rational and Full Autonomy' (1980) 77 *JPhil.* 524

RAYNER, K., 'Euthanasia—A Church Perspective' proceedings from the 5th Biennial National Aged Care Conference of the Uniting Church of Australia, Aug. (1986) 43

REED, N., 'Mercy Killing: Exit's Evidence to the Royal Commission on Criminal Procedure' (1982) 7 *Polytechnic LRev.* 17

——, 'Recent Thinking About Voluntary Euthanasia' (1977) 92 *New Humanist* 173

REEVES, R., 'When is it Time to Die? Prolegomenon to Voluntary Euthanasia' (1972–3) 8 *New Eng.LRev.* 183

REICHEL, W. and DYCK, A., 'Euthanasia: A Contemporary Moral Quandry' (1989) *Lancet* 1321

REICHENBACH, B., 'Euthanasia and the Active—Passive Distinction' (1987) 1 *Bioethics* 51

RICHARDS, D., 'Constitutional Privacy, the Right to Die and the Meaning of Life' (1981) 22 *Wm. & Mary LRev.* 327

RICHARDSON, J., 'The Accountant as Triage Master: An Economist's Perspective on Voluntary Euthanasia and the Value of Life Debate' (1987) 1 *Bioethics* 226

RICHTER, R., 'The Hastings Center and Euthanasia' (1988) 3 *Euthanasia Rev.* 56

RIGTER, H., 'Euthanasia in the Netherlands: Distinguishing Facts from Fiction' (1989) 19 *Hastings Centre R* 31

—— et al., 'Euthanasia Across the North Sea' (1988) 297 BMJ 1593

RISLEY, R., 'What the Humane and Dignified Death Initiative Does' (1986) 1 *Euthanasia Rev.* 221

——, 'In Defense of the Humane and Dignified Death Act' (1988–89) *Free Inquiry* 10

—— and WHITE, M., 'Humane and Dignified Death Initiative for 1988' (1986) 1 *Euthanasia Rev.* 226

ROSCAM ABBING, H., 'Dying with Dignity and Euthanasia: A View from the Netherlands' (1988) 4 *J Palliative Care* 70

ROY, D. and RAPIN, C., 'Regarding Euthanasia' (1994) 1 *European J Palliative Care* 57

SACHS, T., 'Criminal Law: Humanitarian Motive as a Defense to Homicide' (1950) 48 *Mich.LRev.* 1199

SACLIER, A., 'Good Death: A Responsible Choice in a Changing Society' (1976) 10 *Aust. & NZJPsychiatry* 3

SAMEK, R., 'Euthanasia and Law Reform' (1985) 17 *Ottawa LRev.* 86

SANDAK, L., 'Suicide and the Compulsion of Lifesaving Medical Procedures: An Analysis of the Refusal of Treatment Cases' (1977–78) 44 *Brooklyn LRev.* 285

SANDER, J., 'Euthanasia: None Dare Call it Murder' (1969) 60 *JCrim.L, Criminology & Police Science* 351

SAWYER, D., 'What do Canadian MDs Think About Euthanasia? An Update Following the CMA Annual Meeting' (1994) 150 CMAJ 395

—— *et al.*, 'Canadian Physicians and Euthanasia: 2. Definitions and Distinctions' (1993) 148 CMAJ 1463

——, 'Canadian Physicians and Euthanasia: 5. Policy Options' (1993) 148 CMAJ 2129

SAYID, M., 'Euthanasia: A Comparison of the Criminal Laws of Germany, Switzerland and the United States' (1983) 6 *BCInt'l. & Comp.LRev.* 533

SCHEPENS, P., 'Euthanasia, Our Own Future?' (1987) 97 *News Exchange of the World Federation of Doctors Who Respect Human Life* 5

SCHER, E., 'Legal Aspects of Euthanasia' (1972) 36 *Alb.LRev.* 674

SCHIFFER, L., 'Euthanasia and the Criminal Law' (1985) 42 *U Toronto Fac.LRev.* 93

SCHNEIDERMAN, L., 'Euthanasia: Can We Keep it a Special Case?' (1990) 50 *Humanist* 15

—— and SPRAGG, R., 'Ethical Decisions in Discontinuing Mechanical Ventilation' (1988) 318 *New Eng.JMed.* 984

SCHOLTEN, H., 'Justification of Active Euthanasia' (1986) 5 *Med. & Law* 169

SCHWARTZ, R., 'Euthanasia and Assisted Suicide in the Netherlands' (1995) 4 *Cambridge Q Healthcare Ethics* 111

SCOTT, J., 'Lies and Lamentation—A Solid No to Euthanasia' (1988) 4 *J Palliative Care* 119

SEGERS, J., 'Elderly Persons on the Subject of Euthanasia' (1988) 3 *Issues Law & Med.* 407

SHAFFER, C., 'Criminal Liability for Assisting Suicide' (1986) 86 *Colum.LRev.* 348

SHAPIRO, R. *et al.*, 'Willingness to Perform Euthanasia: A Survey of Physicians Attitudes' (1994) 154 *Arch.Intern.Med.* 575

SHARMA, K., 'Euthanasia in Australasia' (1986) 2 *JContemp. Health Law & Pol'y.* 131

SHERLOCK, R., 'Public Policy and the Life Not Worth Living: The Case Against Euthanasia' (1980) 47 *Linacre Q* 121

——, 'Liberalism, Public Policy and the Life Not Worth Living: Abraham Lincoln on Beneficent Euthanasia' (1981) 26 *Am.JJuris.* 47

——, 'For Everything there is a Season: The Right to Die in the United States' (1982) *BYULRev.* 545

SHEWMON, D., 'Active Voluntary Euthanasia: A Needless Pandora's Box' (1987) 3 *Issues Law & Med.* 219

SILVING, H., 'Euthanasia: A Study in Comparative Criminal Law' (1954) 103 *U.Pa.LRev.* 350

SINGER, P. A. and SIEGLER, M., 'Euthanasia—A Critique' (1990) 322 *New Eng. JMed.* 83

SKEGG, P., 'A Justification for Medical Procedures Performed Without Consent' (1974) 90 *Law QRev.* 512

——, 'Medical Procedures and the Crime of Battery' (1974) *Crim.LRev.* 693

——, 'The Termination of Life-Support Measures and the Law of Murder' (1978) 41 *Mod.LRev.* 423

——, 'Living Wills and New Zealand Law' (1993) 2 *Bioethics Research Centre Newsletter* 2

——, 'Omissions to Provide Life-Prolonging Treatment' (1994) 8 *Otago LRev.* 205

SKENE, L., 'The Fullagar Judgment' (1989) 14 *Legal Service Bulletin* 42

SLACK, A., 'Killing and Allowing to Die in Medical Practice' (1984) 10 *JMed. Ethics* 82

SLATER, E., 'The Case for Voluntary Euthanasia' (1971) 219 *Contemp.Rev.* 84

SLOME, L. *et al.*, 'Physicians' Attitudes Toward Assisted Suicide in AIDS' (1992) 5 *J Acquired Immune Deficiency Syndromes* 712

SLOVENKO, R., 'Doctor-Assisted Suicide' (1990) 9 *Med. & Law* 1006

SLUYTERS, B., 'Euthanasia in the Netherlands' (1989) 57 *Medico-Legal J* 34

SMALL, P., 'Euthanasia—the Individual's Right to Freedom of Choice' (1970) 5 *Suffolk ULRev.* 190

SMITH, C., 'What About Legalized Assisted Suicide?' (1993) 8 *Issues Law & Med.* 503

SMITH, G. P., 'All's Well That Ends Well: Toward a Policy of Assisted Rational Suicide or Merely Enlightened Self-Determination?' (1989) 22 *UCalif., Davis* 275

——, 'Re-thinking Euthanasia and Death with Dignity: A Transnational Challenge' (1990) 12 *Adel.LRev.* 480

——, 'Reviving the Swan, Extending the Curse of Methuselah, or Adhering to the Kevorkian Ethic?' (1993) 2 *Cambridge Q HealthCare Ethics* 49

——, 'Futility and the Principle of Medical Futility: Safeguarding Autonomy and the Prohibition Against Cruel and Unusual Punishment' (1995) 12 *JContemp. Health Law& Pol'y.* 1

SMITH, H., 'Termination of Life' (1971) BMJ 111

SMITH, J. C., 'Liability for Omissions in the Criminal Law' (1984) 4 *Legal Stud.* 88

SMITH, K., 'Assisting Suicide—The Attorney-General and the Voluntary Euthanasia Society' (1983) *Crim.LRev.* 579

SMITH, R., 'Euthanasia: Time For A Royal Commission' (1992) 305 BMJ 728

SMITH, W., 'Judeo-Christian Teaching on Euthanasia: Definitions, Distinctions and Decisions' (1987) 54 *Linacre Q* 27

SMOKER, B., 'Remember the Non-Terminally Ill and Disabled' (1991) 43 *VES Newsletter* 10

SNEIDERMAN, B., 'Why Not a Limited Defence? A Comment on the Proposals of the Law Reform Commission of Canada on Mercy Killing' (1985) 15 *Man.LJ* 85

——, 'Euthanasia in the Netherlands: A Model for Canada?' (1992) 8 *Humane Med.* 104

SNYDER, L., 'Artificial Feeding and the Right to Die' (1988) 9 *JLegal Med.* 349

SOLNICK, P., 'Withdrawal and Withholding of Life-Support in Terminally Ill Patients' (Part I) (1984) 3 *Med. & Law* 309

——, 'Withdrawal and Withholding of Life-Support in Terminally Ill Patients' (Part II) (1984) 4 *Med. & Law* 1

SOMERVILLE, M., 'Pain and Suffering at the Interfaces of Law and Medicine' (1986) 36 *U Toronto LJ* 286

——, 'The Song of Death: The Lyrics of Euthanasia' (1993) 9 *JContemp.Health Law&Pol'y* 1

——, ' "Death Talk" in Canada: The *Rodriguez* Case' (1994) 39 *McGill LJ* 602

SOUTH AUSTRALIAN VOLUNTARY EUTHANASIA SOCIETY, 'Discussion Paper on Decriminalising Voluntary Euthanasia in South Australia', Dec. 1989

SPANJER, M., 'Dutch Psychiatrist Reprimanded for Assisting Suicide' (1995) 345 *Lancet* 914

ST. JOHN-STEVAS, N., 'Euthanasia: A Pleasant Sounding Word' (1975) 131 *America* 421

STANLEY, J., 'The Appleton International Conference: Developing Guidelines for Decisions to Forgo Life-Prolonging Medical Treatment' (1992) 18 *JMed. Ethics* 3

STEELE, W. and HILL, B., 'A Legislative Proposal for a Legal Right to Die' (1976) 12 *Crim.LBull.* 140

——, 'A Plea for a Legal Right to Die' (1976) 29 *Okla.LRev.* 328

STERN, K., 'Advance Directives [1994] 2 *Med LRev.* 57

STEVENS, C. and HASSAN, R., 'Management of Death, Dying and Euthanasia: Attitudes and Practices of Medical Practitioners in South Australia' (1994) 20 *JMed.Ethics* 41

SULLIVAN, P., 'Take a Stand on Euthanasia, Assisted Suicide, MDs tell CMA in Survey Released During Annual Meeting' (1993) 149 CMAJ 858

SUTORIUS, E., 'A Mild Death for Paragraph 293 of the Netherlands Criminal Code?', paper delivered in Arnhem, the Netherlands (1985)

——, 'How Euthanasia was Legalised in Holland', paper delivered in Arnhem, the Netherlands (1985)

SYME, R., 'A Patient's Right to a Good Death' (1991) 154 MJA 203

TEMBY, I., 'Euthanasia—Is It Murder?' (1988) 21 *Aust.JForensic Science* 2

TEN HAVE, H. and WELIE, J., 'Euthanasia: Normal Medical Practice?' (1992) 22 *Hastings Center R* 34

TENO, J. and LYNN, J., 'Voluntary Active Euthanasia: The Individual Case and Public Policy' (1991) 39 *JAm. Geriatrics Society* 827

TERBORGH-DUPUIS, H., 'The Netherlands: Tolerance and Teaching' (1984) 14 *Hastings Center R* 2

THOMPSON, M., 'Doctors Divided Over Helping Patients Die' (1995) *NZ Doctor* 28 April, 3

THURMAN, V., 'Euthanasia: The Physician's Liability' (1976–77) 10 *John Marshall J* 148

TINDALL, B. *et al.*, 'Attitudes to Euthanasia and Assisted Suicide in a Group of Homosexual Men with Advanced HIV Disease' (1993) 6 *J Acquired Immune Deficiency Syndrome* 1069

TROLLOPE, S., 'Legislating a Right to Die: The Rights of the Terminally Ill Act 1995 (NT)' (1995) 3 *JLaw&Med.* 19

TROWELL, H., 'Suicide and Euthanasia' (1971) BMJ 275

——, 'The Legal Threat to Medicine' (letter) (1982) 284 BMJ 1562

TRUOG, R. and BERDE, C., 'Pain, Euthanasia, and Anesthesiologists' (1993) 78 *Anesthesiology* 353

TUOHEY, J., 'Euthanasia and Assisted Suicide: Is Mercy Sufficient?' (1993) 60 *Linacre Q* 45

TWYCROSS, R., 'Debate: Euthanasia—A Physician's Viewpoint' (1982) 8 *JMed. Ethics* 86

——, 'Assisted Death: A Reply' (1990) 336 *Lancet* 796

UBEL, P., 'Assisted Suicide and the Case of Dr Quill and Diane' (1993) 8 *Issues Law&Med.* 487

UNIACKE, S., 'The Doctrine of Double Effect' (1984) 48 *The Thomist* 188

VAN DELDEN, J. *et al.*, 'Dances with Data' (1993) 7 *Bioethics* 323

——, 'The Remmelink Study: Two Years Later' (1993) 23 *Hastings Center R* 24

VAN DER BURG, W., 'The Slippery Slope Argument' (1991) 102 *Ethics* 42

VAN DER MAAS, P. and LOOMAN, C., 'Euthanasia and Other Medical Decisions Concerning the End of Life' (1991) 338 *Lancet* 669

VAN DER MAAS, P. *et al.*, 'Euthanasie en Andere Medische Beslissingen Rond Het Leenseinde in Nederland. II. Zorgvuldigheid en Melding' (1991) 135 *Ned Tijdschr Geneeskd* 2082

——, 'Changes in Dutch Opinions on Active Euthanasia, 1966 Through 1991' (1995) 273 JAMA 1411

VAN DER MEER, C., 'Euthanasia: A Definition and Ethical Conditions' (1988) 4 *J Palliative Care* 103

VAN DER SLUIS, I., 'The Movement for Euthanasia 1875–1975' (1979) 66 *Janus* 131

——, 'How Voluntary is Voluntary Euthanasia?' (1988) 4 *J Palliative Care* 107

——, 'The Practice of Euthanasia in the Netherlands' (1989) 4 *Issues Law & Med.* 455

VAN DER WAL, G. and DILLMANN, R., 'Euthanasia in the Netherlands' (1994) 308 BMJ 1346

VAN DER WAL, G. *et al.*, 'Actieve Levensbeëindiging Door Huisartsen Zonder Verzoek van der Patiënt' (1991) 34 *Huisarts en Wetenschap* 523

——, 'Euthanasia and Assisted Suicide: I. How Often Practiced by Family Doctors in the Netherlands?' (1992) 9 *Fam. Practice* 130

——, 'Euthanasia and Assisted Suicide: II. Do Dutch Family Doctors Act Prudently?' (1992) 9 *Fam. Practice* 135

——, 'Voluntary Active Euthanasia and Physician-Assisted Suicide in Dutch Nursing Homes: Requests and Administration' (1994) 42 *J Am. Geriatric Society* 620

VAN DER WEYDEN, M., 'Medicine and the Community—the Euthanasia Debate' (1995) 162 MJA 566

VAUGHAN, N., 'The Right To Die' (1973–4) 10 *Cal.WL Rev.* 613

VEATCH, R., 'Death and Dying: The Legislative Options' (1977) 7 *Hastings Center R* 5

VELLEMAN, J., 'Against the Right to Die' (1992) 17 *J Med. & Phil.* 665

VERVOORN, A., 'Voluntary Euthanasia in the Netherlands: Recent Developments' (1987) 6 *Bioethics News* 19

VOLUNTARY EUTHANASIA SOCIETY, 'Doctors and Euthanasia: A Rejoinder to the British Medical Association's Report "The Problem of Euthanasia"' (1971)

WALLER, S., 'Trends in Public Acceptance of Euthanasia Worldwide' (1986) 1 *Euthanasia Rev.* 33

WAINEY, D., 'Active Voluntary Euthanasia: The Ultimate Act of Care for the Dying' (1989) 37 *Clev. St. L Rev.* 645

WANZER, S., 'Maintaining Control in Terminal Illness: Assisted Suicide and Euthanasia' (1990) 6 *Humane Med.* 86

—— *et al.*, 'The Physician's Responsibility to the Hopelessly Ill Patient' (1984) 310 *New Eng.J Med.* 955

——, 'The Physician's Responsibility Toward Hopelessly Ill Patients: A Second Look' (1989) 320 *New Eng.J Med.* 844

WARD, B. and TATE, P., 'Attitudes Among NHS Doctors to Requests for Euthanasia' (1994) 308 BMJ 1332

WATTS, D, and HOWELL, T., 'Assisted Suicide is Not Voluntary Active Euthanasia' (1992) 40 *JAm.Geriatric Society* 1043

WEDDINGTON, W., 'Euthanasia: Clinical Issues Behind the Request' (1981) 246 JAMA 1949

WEAR, A. and BRAHAMS, D., 'To Treat or Not to Treat: The Legal, Ethical and Therapeutic Implications of Treatment Refusal' (1991) 17 *JMed. Ethics* 131

WEINFELD, J., 'Active Voluntary Euthanasia—Should it be Legalized?' (1985) 4 *Med. & Law* 101

WEINRIB, L., 'The Body and the Body Politic: Assisted Suicide Under the Canadian Charter of Rights and Freedoms' (1994) 39 *McGill LJ* 618

WEIR, R., 'The Morality of Physician-Assisted Suicide' (1992) 20 *Law, Med. & Health Care* 116

WELIE, J., 'The Medical Exception: Physicians, Euthanasia and Dutch Criminal Law' (1992) 17 *JMed &Phil.* 419

WERTH, J. and COBIA, D., 'Criteria for Rational Suicide' (1995) 25 *Suicide and Life-Threatening Behaviour* 231

WILDES, K., 'Conscience, Referral, and Physician Assisted Suicide' (1993) 18 *J Med. & Phil* 323

WILLIAMS, G., 'The Defence of Necessity' (1953) 6 CLP 216

——, 'Consent and Public Policy' (1962) *Crim. LRev.* 74 (Part 1), 154 (Part 2)

——, 'Euthanasia and Abortion' (1966) 38 *UColo.LRev.* 178

——, 'Euthanasia' (1970) 63 *Proceedings for the Royal Society of Medicine* 663

——, 'Euthanasia' (1973) 41 *Medico-Legal J* 14

——, 'What Should the Code do About Omissions?' (1987) 7 *Legal Stud.* 92

WILLIAMS, J., 'When Suffering is Unbearable: Physicians, Assisted Suicide, and Euthanasia' (1991) 7 *JPalliative Care* 47

—— et al., 'Canadian Physicians and Euthanasia: 1. An Approach to the Issues' (1993) 148 CMAJ 1293

——, 'Canadian Physicians and Euthanasia: 3. Arguments and Beliefs' (1993) 148 CMAJ 1699

WILLIAMS, P., 'Rights and the Alleged Rights of Innocents to be Killed' (1976–77) 87 *Ethics* 383

WILLIAMS, R., 'Our Role in the Generation, Modification and Termination of Life' (1969) 124 *Arch. Internal Med.* 215

WINKLER, E., 'Reflections on the States of Current Debate Over Physician-Assisted Suicide and Euthanasia' (1995) 9 *Bioethics* 313

WINSLADE, W., 'Guarding the Exit Door: A Plea for Limited Toleration of Euthanasia' (1988) *Hous.LRev.* 517

WOLBARST, A., 'Legalize Euthanasia' (1935) 94 *Forum* 330

WOLF, S., 'Holding the Line on Euthanasia' (1989) 19 *Hastings Center R* 13

WOLHANDLER, S., 'Voluntary Euthanasia for the Terminally Ill and the Constitutional Right to Privacy' (1984) 69 *Cornell LRev.* 363

WOOTEN, B., 'The Right to Die' (1976) 46 *New Society* 202

YOUNG, K., 'A Cross-Cultural Historical Case Against Planned Self-Willed Death and Assisted Suicide' (1994) 39 *McGill LJ* 657

YOUNG, R., 'Voluntary and Non-Voluntary Euthanasia' (1976) 59 *The Monist* 264

——, 'What is So Wrong with Killing People' (1979) 54 *Phil.* 515

ZAREMBA, J., 'Death with Dignity: Implementing One's Right to Die' (1987) 64 *UDet.LRev.* 557

ZELLICK, G., 'The Forcible Feeding of Prisoners: An Examination of the Legality of Enforced Therapy' (1976) *Pub. Law* 153

ZISSER, P., 'Euthanasia and the Right to Die: Holland and the United States Face the Dilemma' (1988) 9 *NYLSch.JInt'l. & Contemp. Law* 361

NOTES

'All Party Parliamentary Group' (1991) 43 *VES Newsletter* 9

'Attempted Murder Conviction of Euthanasia Doctor in England' (1992) 62 *VESNSW Newsletter* 2

'Attempted Murder of Terminally Ill Patient' [1993] 1 *Med.LR* 232

'BC Physicians Wary of Discussing Experiences Concerning Dying Patients' (1993) 148 CMAJ 1366

'Doctors' Reform Society Policy Statement' (1988) 49 *New Doctor* para. 3.1.12 and 3.3

Editor's note, (1994) 11 *Last Rights* 17

'European Support for Euthanasia?' (1991) 69 *Bull.Med. Ethics* 25

'Euthanasia Case Leeuwarden—1973' (1988) 3 *Issues Law & Med.* 439

'Euthanasia Commissioner' (1974) Vol. 1 No. 3 *AVES Newsletter* 5

'Euthanasia in Holland' Part I (1987) No. 97 *News Exchange of the World Federation of Doctors who Respect Human Life*

'Euthanasia in Holland' Part II (1987) No. 99 *News Exchange of the World Federation of Doctors who Respect Human Life*

'Euthanasia Law Does Not End Debate in the Netherlands' (1993) 307 BMJ 1511

'Euthanasia: New Issue for Conscience' (1991) 303 BMJ 1422

'Euthanasia Vote Deferred' (1991) 70 *Bull.Med. Ethics* 6

'Final Report of the Netherlands State Commission on Euthanasia: An English Summary' (1987) 1 *Bioethics* 163

'Government Funds Big VE Study' (1996) No. 76 *VESNSW Newsletter* 3

'Guidelines for Euthanasia' (1988) 3 *Issues Law & Med.* 429

'It's Over, Debbie' (1988) 259 JAMA 272

'"It's Over, Debbie" and the Euthanasia Debate' (1988) 259 JAMA 2142

'Manitoba Doctor Not Charged in the ALS Death' (1994) Vol. 11 No. 2 *Dying with Dignity Newsletter* 8

'Most California Doctors Favour New Euthanasia Law' (1988) 31 *Hemlock Q* 1

'Now is the Time' (1990) Vol. 7 No. 1 *Dying with Dignity Newsletter* 7

'Ontario Physicians Respond' (1987) Vol. 4 No. 4 *Dying with Dignity Newsletter* 1

'Profiles of World Federation of Right to Die Societies Members' (1989) 15 *World Right-to-Die Newsletter* 2

'Report of the Executive Director' (1990) Vol. 7 No. 3 *Dying with Dignity Newsletter* 3

'The Final Autonomy' (1995) 346 *Lancet* 259

'The "Marta Alfonso-Bowes Memorial Award"' (1996) 2 *NTVES Newsletter* 5

'Voluntary Euthanasia is "an Idea Whose Time Has Come" Says Derek Humphry' (1992) 78 *VESV Report* 3

'World Federation Submission to United Nations' (1988) Vol. 5 No. 2 *Dying with Dignity Newsletter* 1

'Wrong to do Right' (1990) 38 *VES Newsletter* 1

REPORTS AND STATEMENTS

Age Concern Institute of Gerontology and Centre of Medical Law and Ethics, Working Party Report, *Living Will* (London, 1988)

Alberta Medical Association, Committee on Ethics, 'Alberta Medical Association: Statement Reflecting the Range of Ethical Opinions on Abortion and Euthanasia' (1991) *Alberta Doctors Digest* Aug/Oct 11

American Medical Association, *Code of Medical Ethics and Current Opinions of the Council of Ethical and Judicial Affairs*

——, House of Delegates, 1969–1978 *Digest of Official Action* (1973)

——, House of Delegates, *Proceedings*, 140th Annual Meeting (1991)

——, Council of Judicial and Ethical Affairs, Statement, *Withholding or Withdrawing Life-Prolonging Medical Treatment*, March 1986

——, Council on Ethical and Judicial Affairs, Report, *Euthanasia* (Chicago, 1988)

——, Council on Ethical and Judicial Affairs, Council Report, *Decisions Near the End of Life* (1992) 267 JAMA 2229

——, Council on Ethical and Judicial Affairs, Report 59, *Physician-Assisted Suicide* (1993)

Australian Association for Hospice and Palliative Care Inc., *Ethics: Voluntary Euthanasia, Issues Involved in the Case For and Against* (Sydney, 1995)

Australian Medical Association, *Position Statement: Care of Severely Ill and Terminally Ill Patients* (1996)

British Columbia Royal Commission on Health Care and Costs, Report, *Closer To Home* (British Columbia, 1991)

British Medical Association, *The Problem of Euthanasia: A Report by a Special Panel Appointed by the Board of Science and Education of the British Medical Association* (London, 1971)

——, *Euthanasia: Report of the Working Party to Review the British Medical Association's Guidance on Euthanasia* (London, 1988)

Canadian Medical Association, *Statement on Terminal Illness* (1982)

——, *Joint Statement on Terminal Illness* (1984)

——, CMA Policy Summary: Physician Assisted Death' (1995) 152 CMAJ 248A

Center for Health Ethics and Policy, Graduate School of Public Affairs, University of Colorado at Denver, Report, *Withholding and Withdrawing Life-Sustaining Treatment: A Survey of Opinions and Experiences of Colorado Physicians* (Colorado, 1988)

Council of Europe, Ad Hoc Committee of Experts on Progress in Biomedical Science (CAHBI), *Draft Opinion on the Legal, Human Rights, Ethical and Medical Problems Relating to Euthanasia* (Strasbourg, 1987)

Criminal Law Revision Committee, *Working Paper on Offences Against the Person* (London, 1976)

——, Fourteenth Report, *Offences Against the Person*, Cmnd. 7844 (London, 1980)

General Health Council, *Proposal of Advice Concerning Carefulness Requirements in the Performance of Euthanasia* (The Hague, 1987)

Government Response to the Report of the Select Committee on Medical Ethics, Cmnd. 2553 (London, 1994)

Hastings Center Report, *Guidelines on the Termination of Life-Sustaining Treatment and Care for the Dying* (Bloomington, 1987)

House of Lords, *Report of the Select Committee on Medical Ethics*, HL Paper 21, Vol 1 (London, 1994)

——, Report of the Select Committee, *Murder and Life Imprisonment*, HL Paper (London, 1988–89)

Institute of Medical Ethics, Working Party on the Ethics of Prolonging Life and Assisting Death, Discussion Paper, *Assisted Death* (1990) 336 *Lancet* 610

Law Commission of England and Wales, *Mental Incapacity* (London, 1995)

Law Reform Commission of Canada, Study Paper, *Consent to Medical Care* (Ottawa, 1979)

——, Working Paper No. 26, *Medical Treatment and the Criminal Law* (Ottawa, 1980)

——, Report No. 20, *Euthanasia, Aiding Suicide and the Cessation of Treatment* (Ottawa, 1983)

——, Working Paper No. 33, *Homicide* (Ottawa, 1984)

——, Report No. 30, *Recodifying Criminal Law* (Ottawa, 1986)

——, Report No. 31, *Revised and Enlarged Edition of Report 30, Recodifying Criminal Law* (Ottawa, 1987)

Law Reform Commission of Victoria, Report No. 1, *Law of Murder* (Melbourne, 1974)

——, Working Paper No. 8, *Murder: Mental Element and Punishment* (Melbourne, 1984)

Law Reform Commission of Western Australia, Project No. 84, Report, *Medical Treatment for the Dying* (Perth, 1991)

Legislative Assembly for the Australian Capital Territory, Select Committee on Euthanasia, *Voluntary and Natural Death Bill 1993* (Canberra, 1994)

Linacre Centre, Working Party Report, *Euthanasia and Clinical Practice: Trends, Principles and Alternatives* (London, 1982)

Medical Council of New Zealand, *Persistent Vegetative State and the Withdrawal of Food and Fluids* (1993)

Medical Practitioners Concerned with Assisted Dying, Media Release, 'South Australian Doctors Help Incurable Patients to Die', 28 July 1992

Michigan Commission on Death and Dying, *Final Report of the Michigan Commission on Death and Dying* (Michigan, 1994)

National Council for Hospice and Specialist Palliative Care Services, *Key Ethical Issues in Palliative Care*, Occasional Paper 3 (London, 1993)

New York State Task Force on Life and the Law, *When Death is Sought: Assisted Suicide and Euthanasia in the Medical Context* (New York, 1994)

Northern Territory Select Committee on Euthanasia, *The Right of the Individual or the Common Good?: Report of the Inquiry by the Select Committee on Euthanasia* (Darwin, 1995)

Parliament of Victoria Social Development Committee, Second and Final Report, *Inquiry into Options for Dying with Dignity* (Melbourne, 1987)

President's Commission for the Study of Ethical Problems in Medicine and Biomedical and Behavioural Research, *Making Health Care Decisions* (Washington, 1982)

——, *Deciding to Forgo Life-Sustaining Treatment: a Report on the Ethical, Medical and Legal Issues in Treatment Decisions* (Washington, 1983)

Report of a Working Party on the Teaching of Medical Ethics (The Pond Report) (London, 1987)

Report of the Committee on Homosexual Offences and Prostitution (The Wolfenden Report) Cmnd. 247 (London, 1957)

Royal Commission on Capital Punishment, Cmnd. 8932 (London, 1953)

Royal Australasian College of Physicians, *Ethics: Voluntary Euthanasia, Issues Involved in the Case For and Against* (Sydney, 1995)

Royal Dutch Medical Association, *Provisional Statement on Euthanasia* (1973)

——, *Vision on Euthanasia* (Utrecht, 1986)

——, *Vision on Euthanasia* (Utrecht, 1995)

——, Commission on the Acceptability of Termination of Life, Discussion Paper, *Assistance with Suicide in the Case of Psychiatric Patients* (1993)

Sacred Congregation for the Doctrine of the Faith, *Declaration on Euthanasia* (Vatican City, 1980)

South Australian Criminal Law and Penal Methods Reform Committee, Fourth Report, *The Substantive Criminal Law* (Adelaide, 1977)

South Australian Select Committee of the House of Assembly on the Law and Practice Relating to Death and Dying, *Interim Report of the Select Committee of the House of Assembly on the Law and Practice Relating to Death and Dying* (Adelaide, 1991)

——, *Second Interim Report of the Select Committee of the House of Assembly on the Law and Practice Relating to Death and Dying* (Adelaide, 1992)

——, *Final Report of the Select Committee of the House of Assembly on the Law and Practice Relating to Death and Dying* (Adelaide, 1992)

Special Advisory Committee on Ethical Issues in Health Care, *Euthanasia and Physician-Assisted Suicide* (British Columbia, 1994)

Special Senate Committee on Euthanasia and Assisted Suicide, *Of Life and Death: Report of the Special Senate Committee on Euthanasia and Assisted Suicide* (Ottawa, 1995)

van der Maas, P. *et al., Medische Beslissingen Rond het Levenseinde. Het Onderzoek Voor de Commissie Onderzoek Medische Praktijk Inzake Euthanasie* (Den Haag, 1991)

van der Maas, P. *et al., Euthanasia and Other Medical Decisions Concerning the End of Life: An Investigation Performed Upon Request of the Commission of Inquiry into the Medical Practice Concerning Euthanasia*, Health Policy Monographs, Volume 2 (Amsterdam, 1992)

World Medical Association, *Declaration of Venice on Terminal Illness* (1983)

——, *Declaration on Euthanasia* (1987)

——, *Declaration of Geneva* (1948)

——, Policy Statement *Care of Patients with Severe Chronic Pain in Terminal Illness* (1990)

——, *Statement on Therapeutic Abortion* (1983)

Working Party on the Implementation of the Rights of the Terminally Ill Act, *Report on the Implementation of the Rights of the Terminally Ill Act* (Darwin, 1996).

Index

act
  causing death, liability of doctor for *see* doctor
  definition 15
advance directives
  life-support, withdrawal of 168
  power of attorney 483
  status of 481–4
  refusal of treatment, as to 42–4
AIDS
  euthanasia, drawing attention to 1–2
American Medical Association (AMA)
  active voluntary euthanasia, rejection of 305, 313
  Council on Ethical and Judicial Affairs, report of 313–14
  journal, publication of euthanasia article in 311–12
Americans for Death with Dignity
  activities of 279
  legislation, campaign for 362
Appleton International Conference
  activities of 325–6
assault
  administration of treatment without consent as 44
  unauthorized touching as 35
  victims, withdrawal of treatment from 31
assisting suicide
  abetting 78–9
  abuse, considerations relevant to 92
  active involvement by doctor 60–1
  adequate definition of suicide 62
  affirmative action as 77–8
  aiding, abetting, counselling or procuring 56–9
  booklet, methods detailed in 58
  causal connection 58–9
  common law, at 56
  criminal liability for 56
  doctors, by
    admissions of 137–8
    Canada, prosecutions in 145–7
    consistency in application of law, lack of 149
    criminal law principles and law in practice, discrepancies 148–52
    criminal liability 125
    doctors' practices 134–8
    drugs, administration of 139–10
    extent of practices 134
    lack of evidence 148

law, bringing into disrepute 149–50
legal precedent, lack of 150–1
legalization 464–7, 490
life-support, withdrawal of *see* life-support
medical guidance, lack of 150–1
patients' requests for 130–4
patients' rights, undermining 151
practices, survey of 135–7
prosecutions 135, 140–8
punishment of offenders 150
sparsity of cases on 147
UK, prosecutions in 143–5
US, prosecutions in 140–3
encouragement, by mere presence and acquiescence 79
EXIT manual, prosecution of 270
human rights instruments, under 196–7
legal requirements for criminal liability 57–60
legislation, constitutional challenges to
  autonomy, protection of 89
  blanket prohibition, fairness of 89
  Canada, in 86–94
  coercion, and 96
  complete ban, impact of 108
  constitutional remand, principle of 120
  cruel and unusual punishment, protection from 90
  death-inducing medication, right to administer 103
  Due Process Clause, violation of 96, 101, 119, 122–4
  equal treatment provisions 90–1, 113, 121–4
  exploitation, protecting from 105
  fundamental and non-fundamental liberty interests 111–13
  fundamental justice, principles of 88
  historical analysis 102
  human dignity, right to respect for 88
  innocent third parties, protection of 111–12
liberty interests
  recognition of 98–102, 109–10
  violation of 118
life-support, persons on 99
local laws 113
medical profession, integrity of 105–7
mentally competent terminally ill adults, interest of 111
Michigan, in 95

Index